Victory on Earth or in Heaven

Victory on Earth or in Heaven

MEXICO'S RELIGIONERO REBELLION

Brian A. Stauffer

University of New Mexico Press | Albuquerque

© 2019 by the University of New Mexico Press
All rights reserved. Published 2020
Printed in the United States of America

First Paperback Edition, 2021
Paperback ISBN: 978-0-8263-6336-7

Library of Congress Cataloging-in-Publication Data
Names: Stauffer, Brian A., author.
Title: Victory on earth or in heaven: Mexico's Religionero rebellion / Brian A. Stauffer.
Description: Albuquerque: University of New Mexico Press, 2020. | Revision of author's thesis
    (doctoral)—University of Texas at Austin, 2015, titled Victory on earth or in heaven: religion,
    reform, and rebellion in Michoacán, Mexico, 1869–1877. |
    Includes bibliographical references and index.
Identifiers: LCCN 2019032057 (print) | LCCN 2019032058 (e-book) |
    ISBN 9780826361271 (cloth) | ISBN 9780826361288 (e-book)
Subjects: LCSH: Catholic Church—Mexico—Michoacán de Ocampo—History—
    19th century. | Government, Resistance to—Religious aspects—Catholic Church. |
    Government, Resistance to—Mexico—Michoacán de Ocampo—History—
    19th century. | Revolutions—Mexico—Michoacán de Ocampo—Religious aspects—
    Catholic Church. | Church and state—Mexico—Michoacán de Ocampo—History—
    19th century. | Church and state—Catholic Church—History—19th century.
Classification: LCC BX1429.M53 S73 2020 (print) | LCC BX1429.M53 (e-book) |
    DDC 972.08/12—dc23
LC record available at https://lccn.loc.gov/2019032057
LC e-book record available at https://lccn.loc.gov/2019032058

Cover illustration: *El Padre Cobos*, February 24, 1876. Reprinted in *El Padre Cobos y La
Carabina de Ambrosio* (Mexico City: Cámara de Senadores de la LVII Legislatura, 2000).
Photo courtesy of Daniel Alonzo.
Designed by Felicia Cedillos
Composed in Adobe Caslon Pro 10.15/13.5

To the memory of Adrian Bantjes.

Contents

List of Illustrations IX

Acknowledgments XI

INTRODUCTION 1

CHAPTER 1
Death to the Protestants! Long Live Religion!
The Religionero Rebellion in Michoacán, 1873–1876 23

CHAPTER 2
The Other Reforma
Clerical Accommodation and Catholic Restoration in Central-Western Mexico 61

CHAPTER 3
A Levitical City Divided
Religious Culture and Religionero Violence in Northwestern Michoacán 97

CHAPTER 4
Martyrs for Our Lord
Baroque Catholicism, Religionero Mobilization, and the Taming of the Reforma in Central Michoacán 133

CHAPTER 5
"Spiritual Orphans"
Religioneros and the Modernization of Southwest Michoacán 173

CHAPTER 6
Lerdismo Derailed
The Religioneros, Porfirio Díaz, and the Twilight of the Reforma in Michoacán, 1876–1878 209

CONCLUSIONS   239

Appendix A. The Plan of Nuevo Urecho   251

Appendix B. The Manifesto of Tzitzio   255

Appendix C. Proclamation of Colonel Juan de Dios Rodríguez   257

Notes   259

Bibliography   343

Index   367

Illustrations

Maps
1. Map of Michoacán in 1863 — 29
2. The Bishopric of Michoacán before the diocesan restructuring of 1862 — 64
3. The new Bishopric of Zamora in 1862 — 76
4. The district of Jiquilpan in Michoacán's northwest — 100
5. Central Michoacán in the mid-nineteenth century — 138
6. The district of Coalcomán in the late nineteenth century — 177
7. Crescencio García's map of western Michoacán, 1865 — 183

Figures
1. Cartoon. Religioneros in the Minister of War's Mustache — 53
2. Cartoon. General Mariano Escobedo and the campaign against the Religioneros — 55
3. Padre Plancarte, acme of the Ultramontane reform — 78
4. José Ignacio Árciga y Ruiz de Chávez, second archbishop of Michoacán — 83
5. The Chapala region — 108
6. Father Plancarte's tram project — 121
7. Cartoon. The latest scene from the war in Michoacán — 150
8. Cartoon. He doesn't want any more cheese! — 213

Acknowledgments

This book would not have been possible without the extensive support and guidance that I have received over its ten-year gestation. My doctoral advisor, Matthew Butler, deserves special recognition. During my time at the University of Texas at Austin, Matthew was the model of generosity, freely sharing his time, his energy, and the gifts of his keen intellect to refine my research. He has been an ideal mentor and a great friend. Any value the reader finds in this study owes much to Matthew's guidance (the flaws, of course, are my own). I am also grateful to my dissertation committee members, Virginia Garrard, Susan Deans-Smith, Erika Pani, and Margaret Chowning, who put their time, energy, and extensive expertise at my service. Throughout my graduate career, I have benefited from faculty members who shaped my ideas and pushed me out of my comfort zone. Among them, I would like to specifically acknowledge Linda Hall, Frank Guridy, Elizabeth Hutchison, Kim Gauderman, and Jorge Cañizares-Esguerra.

At UT I was fortunate to partake in the vibrant culture of intellectual exchange and inquiry fostered by fellow students Claudia Carreta, José Adrián Barragán Álvarez, Maria José Afanador-Llach, Karín Sánchez, Chris Heaney, and Felipe Cruz. Pablo Mijangos has helped me decode nineteenth-century Mexicanisms, provided crucial feedback on my work, and been a model colleague and friend. Elizabeth O'Brien helped me get my hands on an elusive book and shared with me the joys and frustrations of parenting in academia. My Latin Americanist cohort, Blake Scott, Franz Dieter Hensel Riveros, and Manuel Salas offered solidarity and inspiration, and I am deeply grateful for their friendship. On the conference circuit, I have been fortunate to exchange ideas with Ulises Iñiguez Mendoza, Ben Smith, Aaron Van Oosterhout, Will Fowler, Brian Connaughton, Zachary Brittsan, Eduardo Camacho, Sergio Rosas Salas, David Carbajal, Terry Rugeley, Marco Savarino, Andrea Mutolo, Berenise Bravo Rubio, and Moisés Ornelas.

My work has benefitted from significant financial and institutional support. The UT History Department funded exploratory trips to Mexico. The

Fulbright-García Robles Commission underwrote my primary research year, and the American Council of Learned Societies/Mellon Foundation generously funded the writing phase of the dissertation upon which this book is based. A postdoctoral stint at UT-Austin's Institute for Historical Studies gave me the breathing room necessary to revise the manuscript and surrounded me with brilliant scholars who helped me to refine its key arguments. Seth Garfield, Bianca Premo, Isabel Huacuja, Paul Hirsch, Brian McNeil, Peter Hamilton, and Julia Gossard deserve special mention. Marilyn Lehman and Courtney Meador, who both epitomize professionalism and generosity, helped me navigate my graduate and postgraduate career at UT. Clark Whitehorn has been an ideal editor—flexible, encouraging, and insightful. I am also grateful for the excellent suggestions for revision from the two anonymous reviewers contracted by the University of New Mexico Press.

In Mexico, I benefitted from the support of an extensive network of academics, archivists, and friends. Antonio Escobar Ohmstede, Marta Eugenia García Ugarte, Manuel Ceballos Ramírez, Martín Sánchez Rodríguez, Antonia Pi-Suñer Llorens, Luis Arrioja, Graciela Bernal, and Robert Curley offered me invaluable advice and pointed me toward crucial resources. Marco Antonio Pérez Iturbe bent over backward to provide access to the riches of the archdiocesan archive of Mexico. I am especially indebted to Cecilia Adriana Bautista García, whose exceptional work has greatly influenced my own, for her insights and friendship. In Morelia's archives, I wish to acknowledge María Fernández Ramos, Hugo Sandino Bautista Mercado, and María de los Angeles García Santoyo. At the Archivo Diocesano de Zamora, I benefitted especially from the guidance of Jorge Moreno, a passionate preserver of Church records and a gifted historian in his own right.

I have been extremely fortunate to count on the love, encouragement, and aid of my extended family and friends throughout the long journey of this book. My parents, Jill and Alan Stauffer, have offered unwavering support and encouragement, for which I am ever grateful. My nine siblings have lent their many and diverse talents to my cause and continually inspired me. My late, beloved grandparents, Joseph and Beverly Northrop, generously purchased my textbooks throughout my college career and encouraged me at every step. My wonderful in-laws, members of the Winebarger, Prause, and Romero families, have helped my family move across the country multiple times in the pursuit of this goal. In Austin, Irma Rosas, Eduardo Villarreal, Martha Reyna Villanueva, Verónica Tijerina, Elisama Alemán, and Lincoln

Ward have been our second family and a crucial support network. I would also like to acknowledge my friends and colleagues at the Texas General Land Office, where I have worked as a translator since 2016. Daniel Alonzo, James Harkins, and Mark Lambert deserve special mention. I am especially grateful to Daniel for helping me obtain quality images for the book.

Above all, I would like to acknowledge Ronda Romero-Stauffer and our amazing children, Abigail and Diego Romero-Stauffer, without whom I would be lost. Ronda is the best human being I have ever known. Her sharp intellect, unfaltering kindness, contagious laugh, and courage in the face of adversity have been a constant source of inspiration, and her support has made this book possible. She and the children have stuck by me even when graduate study destabilized their lives, repeatedly took them away from friends and family, and plunged them into new, unfamiliar territory. For that, and for the love and inspiration they offer me every day, I am eternally grateful.

Introduction

This book tells the story of ordinary Catholic men and women who stymied Mexico's most radical nineteenth-century secularization project while simultaneously challenging a vigorous program of Catholic modernization. Specifically, it reconstructs the history of the forgotten Religionero rebellion of 1873–1877 and analyzes its origins, impact, and internal religious logics. An eminently popular movement, the Religionero rebellion erupted in response to a series of anticlerical measures raised to constitutional status by the government of Sebastián Lerdo de Tejada in 1873. An outgrowth of Mexico's polarizing liberal-conservative civil wars (1855–1861) and the French Intervention of 1862–1867, these Laws of Reform decreed the full independence of Church and state, secularized marriage and burial practices, prohibited acts of public worship, and severely curtailed the Church's ability to own and administer property. They also overturned the Catholic Church's long spiritual monopoly by declaring the freedom of religion and clearing the way for the arrival of Protestant missionaries from the United States. The straw that broke the camel's back, though, was the institution of a mandatory oath of fidelity to the liberal Constitution of 1857 and the new reform laws, to be taken by all public employees.

To many Catholics, those who cooperated with the anticlerical mandates were more than simple political antagonists; they were heretics. The Mexican hierarchy flatly forbade the faithful from taking the oath of allegiance, adjudicating nationalized Church property, or using the civil registry. Catholic editorialists condemned the measures as an attack on the faith of the majority, and hundreds of (mostly female) lay Catholics petitioned the government for the repeal of the reform laws. Other Catholics took the path of violence. To the cry of "Death to the Protestants! Long live religion!" the rebels sacked municipal buildings, burned archives, kidnapped and assassinated local officials, and attacked government troops and the National Guard battalions called up in the central-western states of Michoacán, Guanajuato, Mexico, and Jalisco. Over the course of 1874, rebel numbers climbed to ten thousand, and the disparate, locally oriented *gavillas* (rebel bands) moved toward greater coordination and military sophistication. Subsequently, they began carrying out large-scale attacks on fortified plazas, burning and sacking the Michoacán towns of Tancítaro, Taretan, Los Reyes, Paracho, and Zacapu. By mid-1875, Religionero attacks paralyzed local governments and regional commerce, and the Lerdo administration deployed the federal army in Michoacán—the state at the center of the Religionero storm—in an attempt to impose order. Though the increasingly centralist Lerdo government instituted a kind of martial law in the state, the Religionero movement did not subside until a more moderate liberal coalition under Porfirio Díaz toppled the president in the 1876 Revolution of Tuxtepec.

Nonetheless, Religionero rebels did not simply wait for Díaz to overthrow the federal government. Rather, the movement's chieftains negotiated informal pacts with Díaz's agents and adopted the banner of Tuxtepec, transforming Michoacán into a crucial stepping-stone in don Porfirio's rise to power. Though the Oaxacan caudillo quickly turned his back on his Religionero allies, purging many rebel leaders in mid-1877, his shrewd engagement with the Catholic movement had already won him other, more powerful conservative allies in Michoacán and elsewhere. During his revolution, furthermore, Díaz had signaled his intention to relax enforcement of the Laws of Reform, and he nurtured the hopes of conservative *michoacanos* that their post–French Intervention exile from politics was coming to an end. For their part, Mexican clerics responded by moderating their stance on the hated oath of fidelity. Such Church-state détente would deepen significantly over the course of the Porfiriato (1876–1911), providing a measure of political stability unknown in Mexico since independence and allowing for both the consolidation of the Porfirian state and the institutional renaissance of the Catholic Church. The Religionero rebellion was thus crucial to the rise of Porfirio Díaz, and it helped to shape the decidedly lopsided state secularism of the Porfiriato.

This book offers a comprehensive reconstruction of the revolt and a critical reappraisal of its significance, but it also unearths the religious history of the

Religionero movement and explores its links to Catholic modernity. Such a task necessitates a nuanced analysis of the Church's internal conflicts and a careful attention to local religious dynamics. In a country where Catholicism's pull remained nearly universal, we cannot assume that Religioneros were simply antimodern fanatics or dupes of the clergy.[1] By the time of the rebellion, the Mexican Church was in the midst of an ambitious internal reform, the product of both the global Church's struggle against liberalism and the national clergy's attempt to break free from a colonial legacy of state tutelage. The clearest manifestation of what I call "Catholic restorationism" in Mexico was the reorganization of the episcopate in 1862, which resulted in the creation of new dioceses in the historically devout center-west. As this book shows, however, restorationism in practice also meant the reform of popular religious customs, the promotion of European-influenced practices, the diffusion of modern lay associations, and an attack on the religious prerogatives of indigenous communities. The most significant Catholic revitalization since the Bourbon Reforms, the nineteenth-century restoration shifted the Church's center of gravity toward Rome and introduced new strategies for opposing liberalism.[2] Ultramontane in its religious style yet often accommodationist in its approach to the state, Catholic restorationism proved deeply disruptive to many rural parishioners, who were already facing liberal legislative attacks on their religious traditions. Indeed, a key finding here is that religious conflict stemming from Catholic restorationism shaped patterns of Religionero mobilization in Michoacán, sometimes uniting parishioners against the government but more often dividing them over the nature of the faith and the best strategies for its defense. As such, the Religionero revolt was as much a battle for the soul of Catholicism as it was a traditional Church-state conflict.

Church and State in Nineteenth-Century Mexico

The conflict around the Lerdo reforms of 1873 grew out of longer-range debates initiated by Mexico's rupture with Spain. The Mexican clergy generally supported independence, content to sacralize the Catholic republic of 1824 through providentialist sermons. Yet it was deeply divided over the question of whether the new state had inherited the powers of the Patronato, the colonial pact that had given the Crown the authority to staff vacant bishoprics and generally shape the Church to its tastes. While liberal clerics and their civilian allies pressed for Patronato powers in order to sculpt a more "enlightened" national clergy, clerical hardliners made a bid for Church independence by insisting that any such arrangement would have to be negotiated directly with the Holy See in Rome. Crisis beset the Church by 1830, as bishops dwindled and political positions hardened. Indeed, an ad hoc arrangement naming a new cohort of bishops in 1831 failed to defuse the underlying struggle between liberals and increasingly intransigent and Ultramontane conservatives, who by the 1850s had begun to resist state dictates by arguing that the Church was a sovereign, supranational entity.[3]

For their part, a new generation of liberals under Benito Juárez, convinced of the need to sweep away colonial holdovers, took aim at Church wealth and privilege when they came to power in the 1855 Revolution of Ayutla. In a flurry of legislative initiatives and executive actions dubbed the "Reforma," state-makers hacked away at the Church's colonial legal immunity (Juárez Law, 1855), mandated the privatization of entailed ecclesiastical property (Lerdo Law, 1856), and widened the state's jurisdiction over marriage and burials (Civil Registry Law, 1857). Notwithstanding its laicizing bent, though, the early Reforma declined to fully separate Church from state and even furnished the latter with new regalist powers over the former. The Iglesias Law prohibited priests from collecting obventions (clerical fees for baptism, marriage, and burial services) from poor parishioners, and the Constituent Congress of 1857 enshrined the state's right to intervene in religious worship and "external discipline" in the new constitution. Clerical defiance followed on the heels of the constitution's promulgation and especially the institution of a mandatory oath of fidelity (*juramento*) for public employees. Under the leadership of Michoacán's Bishop Clemente de Jesús Munguía and Puebla's Bishop Pelagio Antonio de Labastida y Dávalos, the Mexican Church threw in its lot with conservative strongmen, and the country descended into a series of destructive civil wars.[4]

Under such polarizing conditions, the embattled Juárez government brought the hammer down on the Church, decreeing the series of anticlerical measures between July 1859 and December 1861. Sweeping away the more moderate tendencies of the Constituent Congress, these Laws of Reform aimed to strip the Church of the resources used to fund conservative movements and definitively subjugate the clergy to state power. To such ends, Juárez decreed the nationalization of ecclesiastical property and the separation of Church and state, defined marriage as a purely civil contract, and secularized all cemeteries.[5] Subsequent decrees mixed this laicizing tendency with an unambiguous regalism. In accordance with Church-state separation, for instance, priests were to be taxed as ordinary citizens and prohibited from wearing clerical garb in public; but the state assumed the right to regulate Church finances by decreeing that the institution could sustain itself only through voluntary, cash donations. In December 1860, Juárez then declared freedom of worship, a measure that not only cleared the way for the arrival of Protestant missionaries but also introduced a ban on the celebration of religious acts outside church walls, thus prohibiting the ancient Catholic customs of the public procession and the viaticum (the carrying of the Eucharist in procession to be administered to a dying person). Other decrees suppressed Mexico's religious communities (with the exception of the Hermanas de la Caridad, the congregation that ran most of the country's hospitals) and expelled several influential bishops.[6]

Conservative backlash and foreign intervention soon forced the Juárez government into internal exile and placed the radical measures on hold, yet for Catholics, the wounds of the Laws of Reform would not quickly heal. In fact, Maximilian of Habsburg's failure to fully repeal Reforma legislation during the ill-fated Second Empire (1862–1867) alienated his clerical backers and helped bring about his own downfall.[7] Returning to power, the Juárez government extended an olive branch, inviting exiled bishops to return and allowing only ad hoc enforcement of the reform laws in many places. Catholics used verbalized "reservations" when taking the juramento to avoid jeopardizing their souls, for example, and many communities obtained exemptions to the ban on public processions from pliant local authorities.[8] Yet such conciliation was to end abruptly after Juárez's death in 1872, when the Veracruz lawyer Sebastián Lerdo de Tejada came to power and signaled his attention to consolidate the gains of the Reforma.

Lerdo's first act was to expel a number of foreign Jesuits, whom many liberals considered agents of papalist subversion and authors of the Roman Church's increasingly revanchist antiliberalism.[9] Undeterred by the ensuing Catholic backlash, the president then turned to the matter of the reform laws, which would be transformed from temporary wartime measures into constitutional writ. In October 1873, congress formally enshrined the principles of Church-state separation, religious liberty, and civil jurisdiction over marriage and codified the prohibition of public worship, monastic life, and the acquisition of property by the Church. The implementation of more precise federal legislation codifying the Laws of Reform would take another year, with the passage of the Ley Orgánica de las Adiciones y Reformas a la Constitución

(December 1874). In the meantime, however, the congress mandated that every public employee take an oath (now known as the *protesta* or promise) to uphold and enforce the additions to the Constitution "without any reservations."[10] Shortly after, the health care–focused congregation Las Hermanas de la Caridad was dissolved.

Here, then, was proof that the partial enforcement and informal arrangements that had characterized Church-state relations under Juárez were a thing of the past. Catholics could no longer dilute the constitutional oath with reservations, and the Hermanas would no longer be allowed to skirt the prohibition on communal religious life and the wearing of clerical garb in public.[11] Henceforth, the lerdista state would constitute itself as a bulwark against the threat of jesuitical "equivocation" concerning federal law. The state would also reserve the right to intervene in Church matters, since the provisions of the Ley Orgánica provided for the surveillance over religious services by the police, prohibited tithe collection outside church walls, and criminalized "subversive" sermons.[12] Freedom of worship, too, would become the law of the land. The president even met with a group of US missionaries as part of a diplomatic reunion in August 1873, signaling that Protestant proselytizers would have a friend in the executive office.[13] In short, Lerdo would insist on a full enforcement of the Laws of Reform in order to consolidate the Reforma and protect the nation against a revanchist global Church, even if that brought down the ire of the national Church and its supporters. The ire of Mexican Catholics, it turned out, was not long in coming.

Locating the Religioneros in Mexican History

Unlike the Cristero rebellions of the 1920s and 1930s, the Religionero revolt has largely evaded the interest of historians, despite its impact on the rise of Porfirio Díaz. The few historical treatments of the movement that do exist, meanwhile, alternately obscure the Religioneros' significance to Díaz, downplay the movement's power, or fail to interrogate the religious complexity of the revolt.[14] Porfirian writers tended to dismiss the rebellion as both ineffective and anachronistic, and they declined to interrogate the links between the Religioneros and Díaz's Tuxtepec rebels for obvious political reasons. For Francisco Cosmes in 1902, the rebellion constituted a kind of modern Jacquerie—a violent and knee-jerk revolt of "ignorant peasants" who lacked ideas and the internal coordination necessary for a real political movement.

A contemporary, Ciro Ceballos, considered the revolt of little importance, since the Religioneros' vision for a Catholic republic condemned their movement to the dustbin of history.[15]

Such a teleological view of liberalism triumphant was subtly reworked into a critique of Porfirio Díaz by Daniel Cosío Villegas, the distinguished historian of the Restored Republic during the heyday of the Partido Revolucionario Institucional (PRI).[16] In fact, though he did allow for some genuine Catholic outrage at the Laws of Reform, Cosío Villegas ultimately considered the rebellion little more than a *porfirista* ploy. In his retelling, the porfirista conspirators Vicente Riva Palacio and Sóstenes Rocha take center stage, cynically stirring up Catholic rage in order to hasten Lerdo's fall from power. Here, then, both Religionero rebels and the Church appear as bit players in a larger drama of liberal state-making, the rebels simply pawns in the hands of the omnipotent Porfirio Díaz.[17]

Subsequent treatments of the revolt have challenged facile notions about rebel impotence and elite manipulation. Jean Meyer, for example, paints the revolt as both a serious threat to the liberal order and an essentially popular rising.[18] However, Meyer's national-level perspective and insistence on the absolute autonomy of Catholic rebels flattens the complexity of the Religionero movement and the religious and sociopolitical milieu from which it arose. Widespread and popular in nature but heterogeneous in makeup, the revolt responded to distinct local constellations of religious, political, and agrarian factors. Yet even the vast local historiography of Michoacán does not take us far toward an understanding of the rebellion's causes, since the extant studies tend to adopt Cosío Villegas's view of the movement as anachronistic, insignificant, or motivated by simple opportunism.[19] With the exception of Álvaro Ochoa Serrano's crucial work on the Religionero chief Eulogio Cárdenas and Religionero corridos, local histories have largely declined to investigate the cultural or material underpinnings of Religionero violence.[20] Instead, Religionero agitation appears as the last in a long line of conservative conspiracies against the inevitably triumphant liberal order.

At the other extreme, José Carmen Soto Correa's chapter on the revolt in eastern Michoacán mostly discards political and religious motivations in favor of a near-totalizing material determinism.[21] In 1869, Michoacán's state government had implemented laws privatizing indigenous communal lands, a long-sought goal of liberal state-makers who saw the colonial commons as an obstacle to modernization.[22] For Soto Correa, the *reparto* (land division process) was chiefly responsible for rural unrest, even if such unrest cloaked itself in religious garb. Disentailment brought a brutal dislocation of indigenous communities from their land base and—in neat succession—it turned the ex-*comuneros* first into Hobsbawm's "social bandits" and then into Religioneros.[23] Seductive in its simplicity, such an interpretation also requires a significant leap of faith, since Soto Correa is unable to show that Religioneros were indeed the same people who lost land during the reparto. Neither can such material determinism explain the participation of nonindigenous actors in the revolt, many of whose leaders belonged to a class of rural rancheros (smallholders) more likely to profit from the division of communal lands.[24] Certainly, the 1869 reparto law should be taken seriously as a variable influencing local revolts. However, as this book's case studies demonstrate, agrarian pressure alone lacks sufficient explanatory power, since local revolts resulted from distinct constellations of religious, agrarian, and political factors.

Ulises Iñiguez Mendoza's recent dissertation, the first systematic study of the Religionero revolt, represents a significant step forward in elucidating the political and institutional context of the movement. The author rightly situates the Religioneros in a long trajectory of conservative militancy in Michoacán, and he painstakingly reconstructs the discursive tactics employed by high clerics, Catholic editorialists, and middle-class laypeople in their respective campaigns against *lerdismo*. Nonetheless, Iñiguez Mendoza tends to paint Catholic conservatism in Michoacán in monolithic tones, and he overstates the power of clerical elites in controlling Catholic responses to anticlericalism. Indeed, though he acknowledges that priestly involvement in the rebellion was negligible and that the hierarchy even condemned it, Iñiguez Mendoza also characterizes the Church as a "preeminent" and "dominant" force in rural Michoacán, largely able to control the behavior of the faithful through spiritual censures.[25] Yet if the Church's social dominion allowed it to negate much of the liberal program, as he avers, why did the Religioneros need to rebel at all?

Perhaps because he sees the Church as a conservative bulwark and the Religioneros as an inevitable reaction to attacks on the faith, Iñiguez Mendoza largely ignores the religious cultures of the belligerents and the local particularities of the revolt across Michoacán's fragmented terrain. By contrast, a principal contribution of the present study is its sensitivity to the internal dynamics of Catholicism in Michoacán and its attention to local variation within the Religionero movement. Despite attempts to organize the scores of gavillas in Michoacán into a unitary Religionero army over the course of 1875, the rebellion remained a generally localocentric affair. Rebel chiefs led their flexible gavillas through relatively well-defined zones of operation, and most were caught or killed near their hometowns. Some indigenous villages aided the government even while their ethnic kin in neighboring communities threw in with the rebels. Meanwhile, plebeian groups from surrounding ranchos and pueblos joined Religionero attacks on their municipal seats but broke ranks later to tend to the harvest. Such military localism ultimately reflected local idiosyncrasies of other sorts. Religious reform projects led by the ecclesiastical hierarchies of Morelia and Zamora significantly affected local religious cultures and community responses to anticlerical legislation. However, those impacts were far from uniform. Further, in the context of Catholic modernization and globalization, Religionero militancy became a way for nonelite Catholics to engage in larger debates about the place of the Church in society and, ultimately, the nature of Catholicism itself. Local Religionero revolts thus followed distinct local logics, reflecting the interplay of various religious and extrareligious factors, including diocesan reform projects, priest-parishioner relations, experiences of land privatization, and local political divisions. In its three subregional case studies, this book untangles these factors to provide a nuanced and differentiated view of Religionero mobilization that contrasts sharply with the monolithic, Church-based protest that appears in the existing literature.

Conceptual Considerations

This book's contention that Religionero rebels shaped Mexican history builds on the insights of scholars of popular politics and state formation, whose studies of peasant engagement with national processes have revolutionized Mexican historiography. Correcting earlier treatments that made popular actors passive witnesses (or, more often, victims) of elite state-making projects, historians such as Guy Thomson, Florencia Mallon, and Peter Guardino have demonstrated widespread engagement with the ideologies of nationalism, republicanism, federalism, and liberalism among subaltern people in various Mexican regions.[26] Such "popular liberalism" studies have unearthed the contributions of nonelites to the formation of the Mexican nation-state and highlighted the importance of negotiation and contestation to hegemonic rule. Since historians considered liberalism the dominant ideology of the nineteenth century, the study of popular liberalism seemed the clearest way to write peasants back into the story of Mexican state formation.[27]

Yet if peasants mediated state formation from within, other nonelite actors just as clearly helped to mediate it from without—through conservative militancy and resistance. Thousands of rural Mexicans fought for conservative leaders such as Antonio López de Santa Anna, Tomás Mejía, and Manuel Lozada, rallying to cries of "Long live religion!" and "Religion and *fueros*!" In so doing, they contested the secularizing and anticorporate bent of liberal state formation, and they demanded respect for traditionalist values such as village corporatism, order and central authority, and Catholic exclusivity. Scholars have often assumed peasant conservatism in Mexico was timeless and automatic—a natural traditionalism that made peasant liberalism all the more noteworthy.[28] Yet recent work demonstrates that popular conservatism was historically contingent and internally diverse. Channeling E. P. Thompson and James C. Scott, Ben Smith argues that a "moral [and spiritual] economy" organized relations among the Mixtec peasants, Catholic priests, and conservative elites of northwestern Oaxaca, who endeavored to control and moderate changes related to modernity.[29] Aaron Van Oosterhout, meanwhile, demonstrates that Cora villagers in Nayarit adopted conservatism as a way to broker new religious arrangements with the Archdiocese of Guadalajara and ensure a measure of autonomous control over land.[30] Taken together, these studies offer a nuanced picture of popular conservatism in nineteenth-century Mexico and elucidate the contingent and historical nature of its relationship with Catholicism.

Crucially, the new work on popular conservatism helps to explain the endurance of Catholic-inspired conservatism in Mexico despite several waves of radical state anticlericalism in the nineteenth and twentieth centuries. Even if, as is commonly asserted, the execution of Maximilian sounded the death knell for the conservatism of Lucas Alamán's generation, Catholic politics clearly did not die with the archduke.[31] The militant social Catholicism of the late Porfiriato, the Cristero movements of the 1920s and 1930s, the rise of the Partido de Acción Nacional (PAN), and even the religious undertones that color the ongoing *narco* and vigilante wars in Michoacán all contradict classical views of secularization.[32] Indeed, Mexican secularization attempts in the modern era have proven highly uneven, even reversible. If we take seriously the task of examining how marginalized actors shaped national processes, we must also understand how mobilized conservatives and Catholics blunted the laicizing edge of Mexican state formation.

The broad outlines of the secular capitalist state emerged during the nineteenth-century Reforma and were consolidated by Porfirio Díaz during his three-decade regime of "order and progress." However, as is widely acknowledged, Díaz's conciliatory stance toward the Catholic Church undermined aspects of Reforma secularization and allowed the Church to recoup some of its social and material losses. In fact, the Mexican Church enjoyed a veritable institutional renaissance during the Porfiriato, which saw the centralization of clerical authority and the tightening of relations with Rome, a far-reaching seminary reform that produced a powerful clique of intransigent prelates, and the social empowerment of the laity through Catholic associationalism.[33] Despite renewed interest in the Catholic resurgence of the Porfiriato, however, little attention has been paid to the contributions of ordinary Catholic conservatives to the ascent of Díaz himself. Instead, historians have tended to make don Porfirio and his more plutocratic clerical allies solely responsible for the Church-state modus vivendi of the late nineteenth century.[34] Certainly, Díaz's personal relationships with powerful clerics and papal envoys played an important role in Church-state rapprochement. Yet popular inputs should not be discounted, especially given that Díaz rose to power on a wave of popular aspiration that included overtly conservative elements. In fact, I argue that Díaz's successful diplomacy with the Catholic Church in the late nineteenth century owed much to his experience brokering alliances with Religioneros and Catholic laypeople in Michoacán. As Patrick McNamara's work shows, Díaz's ascendancy rested on negotiations with subaltern actors such as the indigenous veterans of Ixtlán.[35] But it also relied on an even more contentious set of negotiations with a resurgent Catholic conservatism at both the elite and popular levels.

As we shall see, the Religionero rebellion played a crucial role in the rise of Porfirio Díaz. Though far from omnipotent, Díaz proved capable of harnessing popular discontent with the Lerdo regime in its many forms and regional manifestations. Opposition to lerdismo was widespread in 1875 and particularly acute in Michoacán, which found itself engulfed in Religionero violence. Despite the weakness and isolation of the liberal porfirista faction in the state, Michoacán nonetheless represented key strategic terrain for Díaz, given its historic importance as a Reforma battleground, its crucial role in destabilizing the Lerdo government, and its standing as the vanguard Catholic state par excellence. Under such circumstances, don Porfirio's heterogeneous Tuxtepec coalition brokered informal alliances with the principal Religionero chiefs, and Michoacán became a major battleground of the revolution. Meanwhile, the Lerdo regime's attempts to quash the Religionero movement via scorched-earth military campaigns and the suppression of constitutional rights in Michoacán proved highly controversial even among liberals and moderates, further eroding support for the government.

As Lerdo's federal regime disintegrated in the fall of 1876, the Religioneros moved to assume formal roles as porfirista generals with autonomous control over their respective zones of operation, and more well-heeled Michoacán conservatives emerged from the political exile to which support of Maximilian's empire had condemned them in order to engage in a flurry of electoral organizing. The conservative resurgence did not go unnoticed by Díaz's liberal supporters, who complained loudly and warned of an impending civil war within the victorious Tuxtepec camp. Beset by competing visions for a post-Lerdo Mexico, Díaz embarked on a precarious balancing act in his policies toward Michoacán after November 1876—here signaling his intention to halt the persecution of the Church, there restating his commitment to the Laws of Reform. With the help of key intermediaries, he ultimately settled on a style of politics that offered conservative Catholics reasons for hope without formally turning his back on Reforma liberalism. Such a balancing act was not without its setbacks and pitfalls. However, the disordered and complex milieu of Religionero-infested Michoacán ultimately taught the Oaxacan caudillo important lessons about the exercise of power in Mexico, and it helped set the stage for the thawing of relations between the government and the Catholic clergy and faithful on the national level. Michoacán Catholics, then, mediated liberal state formation both from without (through resistance to lerdismo) and from within (through alliances with Díaz), and they helped to moderate the terms of Mexico's secular state.

Even so, Catholic opposition to anticlericalism was neither inevitable nor uniform, and we cannot conflate Church missives against the Laws of Reform or journalistic broadsides against Lerdo with armed uprising. Rather, we must situate the Religionero revolt in its proper religious context. Such a task requires a more nuanced understanding of the history of the Catholic Church in Mexico, a field currently undergoing a welcome renaissance. In recent works, historians have done much to disaggregate and historicize the nineteenth- and twentieth-century Church, rescuing the institution from the neglect of earlier generations, which tended to treat it as monolithic, backward-looking, or inert.[36] For the purposes of understanding Religionero mobilization in Michoacán, the most important developments in this new historiography are the insights that Mexican Catholicism contained a plurality of voices, perspectives, and projects and that the Church changed over time, both in response to the era's sociopolitical transformations and as a result of periodic bouts of internal reformism.[37] As this book demonstrates, the Michoacán Church was no monolith. Its diverse parish clergy included ambitious Ultramontane reformists, old-fashioned mendicants, and liberals who flirted with schism. Further, the Reforma period witnessed significant (though geographically uneven) institutional change and internal reform within state boundaries. Such changes were intimately linked to the global Church's increasingly transnational response to liberalism. In 1862, Mexican prelates exiled in Rome sought Pius IX's aid to plan a restoration of the Church in Mexico. Together, they redrew the country's ecclesiastical map, carving the new diocese of Zamora from the ancient, expansive bishopric of Michoacán, which was then raised to the status of ecclesiastical province (archbishopric). Though they shared a set of basic goals such as seminary reform, increased pastoral supervision, and the promotion of lay devotional societies, the hierarchies of Zamora and Morelia in fact diverged sharply in their methods and styles of internal reform.[38] Relishing their newfound independence from the control of Morelia and its tight-knit circle of clerics, Zamora's reformers aligned themselves with Mexico's Archbishop Labastida and his project for the restoration of the faith through new links with European Catholicism and Ultramontane Rome. Meanwhile, the Morelia Church mostly rejected the European-oriented reformism of Zamora and instead endeavored to cut its own, inward-looking path to restoration, guided principally by a rediscovery of its heritage as an evangelizer of Michoacán's indigenous communities. Such divergences ensured that ordinary Catholics in Michoacán would experience the mid-nineteenth century's political and religious crises in very different ways. As we will see, the Zamora Church's Europeanizing reformism set it on a collision course with more traditional Catholic communities of the countryside, while archdiocesan authorities in Morelia proved move flexible in their reformism and more tolerant of popular religious practices.

Catholic restorationism, then, was an internally divided project, and it encountered equally fragmented religious terrain as it spread from Rome to the episcopal capitals of Zamora and Morelia to the far-flung parishes of rural Michoacán. Although nineteenth-century michoacanos almost universally identified as Catholics, the faith was nevertheless fragmented into myriad local varieties. To borrow Matthew Butler's apt metaphor, the state had a complex "religious topography" in which clericalized ranchero communities nestled up against Purépecha villages with strong traditions of religious autonomy, and Afro-mestizo religious guilds performed mock battles of "Moors and

Christians" in towns a few scant miles from cities where liberal Catholics endeavored to streamline and de-Romanize the faith.[39] Indeed, Ben Smith's argument that in Mexico "there were probably as many religious cultures as there were distinct parishes," faithfully describes nineteenth-century Michoacán.[40] Local religious cultures pivoted around unique patron saints and festive traditions, and they conceded different roles to clerical figures. They were structured according to distinct patterns of land tenure, and they were organized by a variety of local confraternities, indigenous councils, and lay associations. Far from static constructs, however, local religions were dynamic and porous, continually remade through dialogue with outside forces.[41] Much like William Christian's sixteenth-century Spanish communities, in many Michoacán parishes such religious cultures were broadly shared among priests, elites, and plebeians and therefore cannot be described as strictly "popular." However, in its tendency to minimize conflicts within the local flock, Christian's conception of "local religion" has its limits when applied to Reforma-era Mexico, which saw the appearance of various rifts within parishes.[42] The most important of such rifts for our purposes was the widening gulf between the Ultramontane piety of Catholic reformers and the baroque Catholicism practiced by more traditional and ethnicized sectors of the faithful. Since I use "Ultramontane" and "baroque" as conceptual tools for analyzing conflict within local Catholicism throughout the book, it is worth briefly examining the philosophical and stylistic underpinnings of each.

In a nutshell, Ultramontanes looked to Rome and Catholic Europe for devotional inspiration, and they privileged individual and interiorized piety over communal public worship. Their religion shared some of the puritanical and heavily sacramentalized qualities of the eighteenth-century "enlightened piety" described by Pamela Voekel, a foundational component of Mexican republicanism and liberalism.[43] Yet in almost every other aspect, nineteenth-century Ultramontane religion went against the "enlightened" grain. The liberal heirs of the enlightened piety increasingly privileged reason in matters of conscience, sought to restore the Church to its more "democratic" and primitive glory, and cast a jaundiced eye on Rome and its jesuitical allies. Ultramontanes, meanwhile, reaffirmed the supremacy of the Catholic hierarchy and especially the papacy, rejected rationalism through a renewed emphasis on miracle and apparition (as at Lourdes), and celebrated new dogmas and devotions of an intransigent hue—the Immaculate Conception of Mary, the Sacred Heart of Jesus, papal infallibility. Increasingly transnational in orientation, Ultramontane Catholicism ultimately sought to create a universal, militant Catholic order to combat liberalism. However, it would do so primarily on the spiritual plane, through acts of prayer, penitence, and expiation for modern sins.⁴⁴ While it did not reject communal forms of worship such as pilgrimage and procession, it reconceived them as mass, democratic acts and privileged a more modern, voluntary style of "collective action" over the corporate and entailed structure that had ordered colonial worship.⁴⁵ In the Ultramontane model, voluntary lay associations would supplant colonial *cofradías* (confraternities) and councils of indigenous elders in the realm of local religious leadership, and interiorized spiritual exercises and regimented pilgrimage movements would substitute for the raucous festive piety of the popular classes.

By contrast, baroque Catholicism was distinguished by its collective and performative nature and preference for lavish external worship, by its corporate material base (often organized around indigenous sodalities), and by a strong belief in the presence of the sacred in the physical world.⁴⁶ Though its practitioners were moved by a diverse array of local saints and devotions, they nonetheless shared a reverence for sacred objects and images, a desire to find communion with the divine through ritual performances, and a preference for splendorous display during frequent religious feasts. Above all, perhaps, Michoacán's various baroque catholicisms were vehicles for performing local identity. Corporate solidarities, such as those attached to indigenous communities and religious brotherhoods, had ordered colonial life during the long period of Habsburg rule, and such identities often persisted (albeit in altered form) despite vigorous reforms in the Bourbon and early republican periods aimed at weakening or erasing religious and ethnic corporations.⁴⁷

It is important to note that the use of the term *baroque* here is not meant to freeze village religious cultures in an idealized past. Rather, following the late cultural theorist Bolívar Echeverría, I see the baroque not simply as an ossified aesthetic tradition but as a durable and specifically modern "cultural totalization," an "ethos" by which people organize their lives in order to assimilate the disjunctures of modernity.⁴⁸ Originally an outgrowth of Tridentine theological responses to the Reformation, the baroque ethos illuminated the threads connecting heaven and earth and thoroughly aestheticized and ritualized everyday life, reaching for divinity in a world increasingly dominated by the market.⁴⁹ Particularly at home in an Iberian society built upon the ruins of an indigenous one—its rich array of signifiers favoring cultural *mestizaje* and the hierarchical ordering of corporate identities under the Church's universal banner—the baroque ethos dominated Spanish America during the "long seventeenth century." If it was driven to the margins of society by other *ethe* between the mid-eighteenth and late twentieth centuries, it never was completely vanquished. Rather, baroque ways of seeing and being—and ways of approaching the divine—have persisted into the present, albeit often in muted forms and in dynamic admixture with other ethe.[50]

That baroque religious forms did not suddenly disappear in 1767 or 1821 should not surprise us. Neither, though, should we assume they remained frozen in stone. Just as movement, complexity, and multiplicity of form are all traits of the baroque in art, so too did baroque religion "move"—evolving, fragmenting, and reinventing itself in tandem with broader social changes related to the unfolding of (Northern Atlantic, Protestant) modernity. Certainly, the material and social relations undergirding local religious cultures were changing in the nineteenth century, as the logic of liberalism threw the validity of corporate identity and land tenure into question. Nevertheless, certain features of the colonial past persisted in nineteenth-century baroque religion. Corporate actors such as the Purépecha cabildo (council of elders) and the baroque confraternity still played primary roles in shaping parish religious life, and new religious actors and institutions such as the mayordomo (individual fiesta sponsor) and the civil-religious hierarchy (or *cargo* system) emerged to buttress the troubled colonial model without supplanting it completely. Indeed, as Matthew O'Hara argues, indigenous people remade their ethnic and parish identities in response to Bourbon and republican reformism, and they used religious understandings of corporate privilege and belonging in order to defend their collective interests in the face of liberal challenges.[51]

In Michoacán, corporate identities and baroque ways of accessing the sacred remained at the heart of many local religious cultures. Though its influence was felt most strongly among popular groups (indigenous peasants, rural laborers, Afro-mestizo artisans), baroque religiosity sometimes cut across class lines, uniting more traditionalist priests and male religious with plebeian and even elite believers who held a stake in the local religious status quo. Ultramontane piety, meanwhile, tended to attract members of the provincial elite and rural middle classes. Outside the elite clerical circles of the provincial cities, Ultramontane religiosity was most often promoted by secular priests who had trained during the tumultuous Reforma years, when ecclesiastical leaders and seminary rectors had begun to devise new strategies for confronting liberalism.[52] These clerics often found eager allies among mestizo merchants and rancheros (small property holders) and middle-class

Catholic women, who were finding new leadership roles in devotional, educational, and charitable associations such as the Vela Perpetua, the Sociedad Católica, and the Conferences of Saint Vincent de Paul.[53] Thus, although we cannot divide the religious cultures of Michoacán neatly into "popular" and "elite" versions, the mid-nineteenth century did witness increasing polarization along religious lines, and spiritual rifts often did have significant class, ethnic, and gendered dimensions. To be sure, Catholic restorationism sometimes unified the local faithful around new devotions and religious projects, such as the refurbishing of neglected church buildings or the promotion of Catholic schooling. More often, however, restorationism divided parishes internally, as the Ultramontane styles of piety promoted by Catholic reformers collided with baroque sensibilities and threatened to eclipse older modes of religious organization. Further, local restorationists undermined the power of traditional religious leaders such as indigenous *principales* and cofradía members and their priestly allies, and they often adopted different strategies for confronting lerdista anticlericalism than those advocated by their more baroque-minded counterparts.

A central finding here is that religious change and conflict stemming from the advance of Catholic restorationism shaped Religionero violence. Simply put, in many places Ultramontane reformism marginalized baroque Catholics, a group already under pressure from liberal legislation mandating the subdivision of communal property (issued in Michoacán in 1869) and whose external, collective religiosity was most threatened by the prohibition of public worship. In such circumstances, armed rebellion became an attractive option for Catholics seeking to both overturn the Laws of Reform and reassert their religious preferences in the face of Ultramontanism. This is not to suggest that the two conservative Catholic factions went to war in 1873, since the conflict most often pitted Catholic gavillas against civil and military authorities. However, baroque and Ultramontane Catholics adopted different strategies in the defense of the Church and promoted different visions of Catholicism; and such divergences sometimes did bring the two sides to blows. By the time of the revolt, the hierarchies of Zamora and Morelia had shifted their strategy away from violent confrontation with the state toward internal reform and the accommodation of liberal legal tenets in order to foster a Catholic counterculture. Following such dictates, which were explicitly articulated in an 1875 joint pastoral letter by the three archbishops of the Mexican episcopate, Ultramontane priests and their followers at the local level tended to favor a less bellicose approach to confronting lerdista anticlericalism, including informal agreements with local civil authorities, political abstention, and the use of petitions in order to demonstrate that the Laws of Reform contravened the "will of the people." Such an accommodationist approach was rejected by the Religionero rebels, who sought more direct methods of confronting the state and sometimes even punished their Ultramontane counterparts for collaborating with civil authorities. These were not only differences in strategy, however; they also took the form of local conflicts over religious culture. Crowded out of their leadership roles by the Ultramontane upstarts and subjected to increasing spiritual scrutiny by the reformist clergy and its local allies, many baroque Catholics took to the rebellion as an avenue for asserting their religious prerogatives and contesting both liberal anticlericalism and Catholic restorationism.[54]

This is not to suggest a monocausal religious motivation for the Religionero revolt or to insist on a crude cultural determinism. Rather, like recent works on conservative revolts of the 1850s and 1860s and the Cristero Wars, this book hews to a middle path between the "culturalist" approach to peasant revolt pioneered by Eric Van Young and the materialist/structuralist analyses that have dominated the literature until recent years.[55] Van Young's view of peasant mobilization as eminently localocentric and shaped by cultural factors, while it may well describe the Independence era, has less explanatory power for Mexico's midcentury tumults, in which national ideologies were invoked by actors at all levels and republican legislative programs were actively remaking rural life. Michoacán's tumultuous post-independence history left a legacy of deep partisan cleavages that evolved with each electoral cycle, each new coup, and each new episcopal regime. Partisan conflict reached into the rural countryside, where rural caciques, parish priests, or indigenous principales adapted national political categories—liberal/conservative, *juarista*/lerdista—to local circumstances. Such local cleavages, often built upon an older foundation of village rivalries or family hatreds, proved integral to the logic of Religionero mobilization.

Changes in material relations, owing in large part to liberal legislation that mandated the disentailment of ecclesiastical and communal properties, held even more significant consequences for the conflict of the 1870s. However, the relationship between Religionero violence and the 1869 reparto law are far from straightforward, and material concerns were often deeply intertwined with spiritual ones at the local level. Land privatization proceeded slowly and unevenly across the Michoacán countryside after 1869, often provoking complex and protracted debates among community members, hacendados, ranchero tenants, and state authorities. Far from heralding a uniform dispossession of indigenous communities at the hands of non-Indian outsiders, the reparto law's outcomes were complicated and multiple—here dividing the community internally over the validity of the procedures, there stimulating communal retrenchment or legal challenges that dragged on for decades. In many places, the reparto did not in fact take place until many years after the Religioneros had come and gone. In others, the reparto targeted religious properties such as cofradía lands, church atriums, and the Indian hospitals founded by Franciscan missionaries. In such cases, disentailment could and did contribute significantly to partisan polarization and Religionero mobilization, especially when the community preserved most of its holdings but lost properties with which it funded and organized local religious life.

Thus, if we cannot characterize the Religionero revolt as a knee-jerk reaction to peasant dislocation, we need not conjure equally reductionist caricatures of cultural defense. Rather, different constellations of religious, material, and political factors produced distinct patterns of mobilization across Michoacán's variegated terrain. This book's case studies demonstrate such patterns at close range. In northwestern Michoacán, where Religionero leaders Eulogio Cárdenas and Ignacio Ochoa amassed some of the state's largest gavillas, the Ultramontane reformism of the Zamora hierarchy created deep spiritual rifts within a conservative bastion, marginalizing indigenous and Afro-mestizo Catholics and suppressing their baroque traditions even while it provided more well-heeled Ultramontanes with new social and political outlets. If the region's conservative heritage and proximity to the diocesan seat at Zamora ensured that Religioneros would enjoy strong support and even attract some orthodox rancheros to their cause, the movement's leaders—and most of its rank and file—were nevertheless subaltern Catholics whose religious leadership had been undermined by Catholic restorationism. In central Michoacán, territory of the celebrated Religionero chief Socorro Reyes, the Purépecha Catholics of Coeneo successfully mitigated lerdista anticlericalism by negotiating with local liberals and the more tolerant Archdiocese of Michoacán and then mostly declined to join the revolt. Even so, Coeneo provided a passive transit point for gavillas of mixed-race Catholics from the nearby hamlets of Huaniqueo and Huango, whose own baroque religious cultures had been imperiled by the reparto's attack on their religious properties. In the southwestern coastal sierra, meanwhile, Zamora-style Catholic restorationism came as part and parcel of a mestizo second conquest of an indigenous hinterland, since it sacralized a new ranchero economy based on subdivided communal lands and helped enshrine a new spiritual economy of voluntary, individual tithes. The Religionero revolt there, led by indigenous communal leaders and a family of juarista caciques that had seen its power eroded by the ranchero transformation, subsequently took on distinctly anti-Ultramontane hues. In sum, if similar religious, political, and material factors prevailed across Michoacán, they combined in different balances to produce unique patterns of revolt.

Sources, Methods, and Organization

This book relies on a large and diverse corpus of documentation. Its military narrative is based primarily on state-level correspondence between Michoacán's Interior Ministry and the various military and political authorities charged with suppressing the Religionero revolt. National military reports resulting from the federal army's involvement in the state in 1875–1876, as well as newspaper accounts from Morelia, Zamora, and Mexico City, round out this military documentation.[56] My analysis of the Religioneros' relationship with the Revolution of Tuxtepec, meanwhile, relies principally on Díaz's personal correspondence with allies in Michoacán.

A diffuse and informally organized movement led by characters largely unknown in the annals of Mexican history, the Religionero rebellion presents some daunting analytical obstacles. Military and periodical accounts paint a two-dimensional picture of the rebels themselves and offer only occasional clues as to their identities, motivations, and beliefs.[57] Further, the Religionero movement was far from uniform. *Cabecillas* (rebel chieftains) hailing from a middling stratum of rural society generally figured as leaders, and they carved out more or less defined zones of operation centered on their respective *patrias chicas*. However, Religionero constituencies within such zones varied with Michoacán's complex socioethnic topography. I have therefore used two sets of locally generated archival documentation in order to illuminate local patterns of revolt and understand which kinds of Catholics would have joined the rebellion. The most important of these are Church records, and especially the correspondence between rural parishes and diocesan authorities in Morelia and Zamora. Though it may tend to exaggerate episodes of intraparish conflict or fail to capture some of the nuances of quotidian religious practice, parish correspondence nevertheless offers a ground-level view of local religious life and an appreciation for its historical movement.[58] Letters from priests and parishioners to their diocesan superiors reveal much about the spiritual preferences of the populace. Further, the realm of "parish politics"—broadly defined as the ever-evolving dispute among priests and parishioners for control of local religious life—offers a window into the contentious process of religious change. Certainly, as William Taylor's classic study demonstrates, parishioners have long endeavored to remove their priests for perceived deficiencies or fought among themselves over spiritual and earthly matters.[59] But the larger context in which such conflicts took place had changed by the mid-nineteenth century, and the nature of the conflicts changed with it. Priests and parishioners reacted to liberal legislation and attempted to mitigate its effects; cofradía structures broke down and new religious associations appeared; parishioners rallied around their priests to rebuild their churches or fell into rancorous debate about the attempts to suppress their customs. If parish politics was an arena for defining the shape of the local faith, then, it was nested within larger political and religious dialogues related to the rise of liberalism and Ultramontanism. Parish correspondence is thus key to both reconstructing local religious cultures and understanding the conflict that animated Religionero mobilization.

The second set of more grounded sources are the documents related to the division of indigenous communal lands, a project initiated in Michoacán in the 1820s with little success until after 1869, when the restored liberal government issued its reparto law. Consisting principally of correspondence between the governor's office and district prefects and other local actors, the so-called *hijuelas* collection provides a close-range view of the disentailment process and illuminates the local stakes of Reforma liberalism in the indigenous countryside. As this book will make clear, the pre-Porfirian reparto process had complex and sometimes contradictory effects on local patterns of Religionero mobilization.

The book is organized into six chapters. Chapter 1 reconstructs the military and political history of the Religionero conflict from the first risings of 1873 to the conversion of the Religionero bands to the cause of Tuxtepec in late 1875. Chapter 2 analyzes the Church's evolving responses to anticlericalism. It demonstrates that the hierarchy largely abandoned the sphere of partisan politics after 1867, instead reconfiguring itself as a countercultural silo within Mexico's civil society and undertaking a vigorous Ultramontane revival that spread unevenly throughout the center-west. Chapters 3 to 5 offer three subregional case studies, which together demonstrate how various religious, material, and political factors combined to produce different kinds of local revolts. Chapter 3 analyzes the spiritual and political rifts that developed among the devout Catholics of northwestern Michoacán, where baroque and Ultramontane religion prescribed widely different strategies for confronting lerdista anticlericalism. Chapter 4 examines the role of baroque religious culture, land division, and liberal politics in shaping the unique topography of Socorro Reyes's revolt in central Michoacán, whose parishes belonged to the Archdiocese of Michoacán. Returning to the diocesan jurisdiction of Zamora, chapter 5 demonstrates how Ultramontane reformism, agrarian conflict, and strongman politics combined to produce the explosive Religionero milieu of the southwestern coastal sierra, where rebels directly attacked Ultramontane religious leaders. Chapter 6 traces the rise and fall of the fragile yet decisive alliance between Porfirio Díaz's Tuxtepec Revolution and the Religionero movement in Michoacán between 1876 and 1878.

CHAPTER 1

Death to the Protestants! Long Live Religion!

The Religionero Rebellion in Michoacán, 1873–1876

In its May 1875 sessions, the Federal Congress of Mexico played host to a vigorous debate about whether to grant President Lerdo emergency powers in order to deal with the spiraling Religionero crisis in Michoacán and other nearby states. Michoacán's state congress had authorized the use of such powers there in April, in the wake of a shocking series of Religionero assaults on Michoacán towns, and Lerdo had brought the matter before the national congress shortly afterward. Emergency powers would give the president broad control over the Ministries of War and Treasury in order to raise revenues for the war effort, organize and recruit soldiers, and dispense with constitutional guarantees for presumed rebels in the course of the government's campaigns. But in the lower chamber of the Mexican congress, a number of deputies opposed the measure. They demanded to know more about the nature of the Religionero crisis, the extent of its threat to the nation, and the measures taken to quash it. Who were the rebels? What "political plan" did they proclaim? Did they control a specific territory in Michoacán from which they could launch attacks on larger cities? Was this, properly speaking, a political "revolution" or simply a widespread "rebellion" perpetrated by opportunistic highwaymen and a few holdouts from Maximilian's imperialist army? In sum, did the Religioneros really constitute a mortal threat to the Mexican nation?[1]

In response, Lerdo's emissary from the Ministry of Interior read a detailed report on the situation in Michoacán, indicating the names of various rebel chiefs, the number of rebels they commanded, the locations of their bases of operation, and the various strategies employed by state and federal troops against the Religioneros. The report enumerated some 3,800 rebels under the orders of principal *cabecillas* (rebel chiefs), primarily in the state of Michoacán, but with several hundred operating in Guanajuato and Jalisco, and it declared the existence of "innumerable" smaller rebel bands and bandit gangs commanded by unknown leaders. Although rebel *cabecillas* had shown considerable valor in skirmishes with government troops, the report described them as primarily men "without clear military antecedents" who eschewed formal military tactics for hit-and-run guerrilla warfare. The rebels' mobility, local knowledge of Michoacán's fragmented terrain, and predilection for dispersing in the face of government persecution only to regroup quickly afterward made the rebellion very difficult to extinguish, even with the aid of substantial federal forces. Some two thousand federal troops had been sent to fight the Religioneros since January 1875, concentrating their activities on the Jalisco/Michoacán and Guanajuato/Michoacán borderlands, and the celebrated liberal *michoacano* General Nicolás de Régules was leading expeditionary troops through central and southern portions of his state in persecution of the larger Religionero armies.[2] Such efforts had failed to bring the conflict under control, however, and President Lerdo believed that the situation called for the formation of more "irregular" forces (conscripted National Guard and counterguerrilla units) to pursue the rebels into the hinterlands while federal and state forces protected vulnerable plazas and patrolled major highways between problematic towns.[3] But the congressional dissenters, with Deputies Briseño and Silva at the head, objected further, decrying the "highly inexact" nature of the Interior Minister's report and suggesting that, even if the Religioneros had paralyzed Michoacán, it was not true that Jalisco and Guanajuato were in a state of "revolution." Michoacán's problems did not warrant the unconstitutional expansion of executive powers nationwide, and Lerdo's attempt to assume emergency powers portended deeper, despotic desires. In fact, Briseño sensed in the measure a conspiracy by Lerdo and his supporters to ensure their control over the upcoming presidential elections of 1876, perhaps even a ploy to dissolve congress and re-enshrine dictatorship in the style of Santa Anna.[4] For him, the government's request for extraordinary powers was "not about eradicating the rebellion, but rather about dragging out a secure [lerdista] vote from the Mexican people; it is about ensuring that this body, which is now formed by enlightened people, is instead filled with adepts of the Executive. . . . It is about removing any kind of obstacle for the Eighth Congress, which is the one that will be involved in the presidential election, in order to ensure the reelection of our actual First Chief of the Nation."[5]

At this point, Michoacán's congressional deputy (and former governor) Justo Mendoza rose to defend Lerdo and then-current Michoacán Governor Rafael Carrillo's efforts to extinguish the reactionary candle. Michoacán faced conditions unimaginable to politicians whose own constituents did not live with constant threats of violence, pillage, and the "rape of honorable women." Further, the religious character of the rebellion made it an existential threat to the restored liberal republic, even if it often served only as a pretext for plunder by rebels of no political conviction. Raising the specter of the defeated Conservative Party, Mendoza saw in the Religionero rebellion the beginnings of a broad counterrevolution that would eventually win the support of Catholic intellectuals, intransigent clerics, and former conservative caudillos. To preserve the liberal republic, the Mexican government would need emergency powers, not only in the military repression of the Religionero gavillas but also in the suffocation of the social bases of reaction—traitorous newspapers, seditious priests, even Catholic ladies brandishing letters of protest against the Laws of Reform. Mendoza had personally fought French imperialists and Mexican "traitors" in Michoacán in the 1860s in order to safeguard Juárez's republic; he would not see those gains reversed now in the name of constitutional purity. The majority of his colleagues agreed, and the measure passed with a vote of 115 to 26.[6] The Lerdo government and its congressional supporters had decided that the Religionero crisis was one of national importance, and they would employ increasingly repressive measures to strangle it.

The congressional debates of 1875 highlight both the elusive nature of the Religionero conflict and the divisive political context that it helped to create at the national level. Most contemporary observers outside of Michoacán lacked conclusive information about the rebellion—its leaders, its extent, its goals, and its potential for power—and so confusion reigned while a host of contrary interpretations proliferated.[7] The Religionero rebellion evaded easy categorization, residing somewhere between an amorphous banditry and a strategically sophisticated movement to roll back the liberal Reforma of 1855–1861. Its grassroots character and the paucity of high-profile caudillos in its ranks set it apart from the conservative movements of the 1850s and 1860s, yet its political plans, manifestos, and war cries suggested a reactionary core. Moreover, the participation of various liberal dissidents and known highwaymen further muddied public conceptions of the revolt. Imperiled officials in

Michoacán viewed the rebellion as the rebirth of the traitorous Conservative Party, which had thrown in its lot with petty bandits in an attempt to take power. For their part, Catholic newspapermen, many of them sympathetic to the movement, saw in the Religioneros a surge of genuine popular political discontent, the natural outgrowth of the liberals' attack on the faith of the nation. Others perceived only avarice and opportunism in the uprisings. For antilerdista politicians like Briseño and Silva, the Religioneros were simply a malleable front for a power grab by lerdistas.

This chapter untangles the web of rumors, contradictory reports, and hidden political agendas that characterize the historical record in order to reconstruct the military and political history of the revolt from the first risings of late 1873 until the advent of Porfirio Díaz's Tuxtepec Revolution in early 1876. It should be stated from the outset that much about the Religioneros remains unknowable: The historical records are often opaque or incomplete, and the military and periodical sources upon which we primarily rely sometimes prove problematic.[8] If contemporary observers (and, indeed, twentieth-century historians) had difficulty drawing firm conclusions about the revolt, this owed much to the diffuse, disjointed, and often unreliable character of available information. Yet it also owed to the fragmented nature of the rebellion itself—particularly in its early iterations—and to the diverse political motivations of those who invoked it. Nevertheless, we can arrive at a clearer understanding of the rebellion, its origins, development, and trajectory, through the careful triangulation of sources and by paying attention to the regional and local manifestations of the conflict. As we will see, the banner of "Religion" provided space for a variety of often-contradictory political projects, and the rebellion took on distinct subregional and local flavors. Although the movement found greater strategic cohesion over time, its ultimate failure to take power resulted in large part from such fluidity and stubborn internal diversity.

Despite such a failure, however, the Religionero movement exerted a powerful influence on the course of Michoacán's—and Mexico's—history. The rebels ground local government to a halt, slowed efforts to reactivate the state's mining industry, and debilitated rural commerce in Michoacán over the course of three years. Their rebellion exhausted the state's military and economic resources. It also exacted political costs, becoming an increasingly damaging thorn in Lerdo's side as the conflict wore on. Not only did it distract the administration from the business of consolidating the restored liberal republic and promoting the nation's nascent agrarian and extractive capitalism, it also exposed Lerdo to vigorous criticism and widened rifts within the liberal governing coalition. Pilloried both for his inability to stamp out the revolt and his reliance on extraconstitutional measures in the persecution of the rebels, Lerdo lost political capital, made new enemies, and ultimately became vulnerable to a challenge by a more moderate strongman.

Since little is known about even the basic events of the rebellion, this chapter largely takes the form of a narrative reconstruction. It begins by considering the various historical precedents for conservative political mobilization in Michoacán in the nineteenth century, before detailing the advent of a widespread antigovernment and anti-Protestant movement after 1873. This second section balances narrative and analysis in order to offer a sociologically grounded understanding of the revolt—its social origins, military characteristics, ideology, and culture. It highlights the decentralized, grassroots nature of the rebellion and examines the attempts by its nascent leadership to develop a military structure and ideological framework for the movement over time. However, it also points to the centrifugal forces that undermined the Religioneros' coherence, such as localism, inconsistencies in motivation, ideology, and strategy, and the vasciliating support of conservative elites. Given such fragmentation, the revolt is best understood from a subregional and local perspective, a task taken up in the book's case studies. The final section of this chapter, meanwhile, chronicles the rebellion's increasingly destabilizing effects on state and national politics after the proclamation of the Plan of Nuevo Urecho in mid-1875 and the forging of ties with porfirista emissaries shortly after. A full examination of the Religionero-porfirista alliance is undertaken in chapter 6.

Religionero Precedents:
Conservative Rebellion in Michoacán before 1873

Michoacán served as a preeminent battleground in the liberal-conservative wars of the nineteenth century.[9] Home to myriad grassroots political movements and caudillos, the state developed a fractured partisan geography in which liberal and conservative towns often nestled close together. Larger regional patterns are evident, however, with Pátzcuaro and northern Michoacán distinguishing themselves for their political conservatism and the southern *tierra caliente* (hot country) and pockets of the center and east tending toward liberalism. Most of Michoacán's early republican and federalist movements originated or gestated in the tierra caliente, but the central-Michoacán hamlet of Coeneo also produced several of the state's most celebrated liberal warriors of the period (Epitacio Huerta, Rafael Arias, Rafael Rangel, and Rafael Garnica). Meanwhile, northwestern Michoacán's homegrown centralist and conservative caudillos included Anastasio Bustamante, the three-term centralist president (1830–1832, 1837–1839, 1839–1841) who helped to bring Mexico's first federalist republic to an end with the assassination of Vicente Guerrero, as well as Diego Moreno Jaso, noted royalist and owner of the extensive Guaracha estate near Lake Chapala.[10] Moreno Jaso and his heirs funded and fomented armed movements in support of Antonio López de Santa Anna throughout the 1840s and 1850s, providing a conservative counterweight to the liberal caudillos Gordiano and Francisco Guzmán, who operated from nearby Tamazula (Jalisco). Conservative leaders in Zamora, La Piedad, and Morelia seconded the 1852 "Revolution of Guadalajara" that led to Santa Anna's last dictatorship, meanwhile, as a direct reaction to the anticlerical reforms of Governor Melchor Ocampo.[11] José de Ugarte, scion of a wealthy Morelia family who had consistently supported centralist and conservative causes in the 1830s and 1840s, played an important role here, and he served briefly as governor of Michoacán under the last Santa Anna government. The French invasion of 1862 also fostered conservative political mobilization, particularly in northwestern towns like Zamora and La Piedad, where the imperialists could count on strong support.[12] The eastern town of Zitácuaro and several towns in the Bajío district of Puruándiro, meanwhile, supplied homegrown liberal chieftains and patriotic National Guard battalions that resisted the imperialist advance in Michoacán. For Zitácuaro in particular, participation in the War of the Intervention solidified a nascent liberal, anticlerical identity—one further strengthened by the advent of Presbyterian congregations in 1877.[13] Yet the Reform Wars also helped to cement local conservative identities in many places, producing small-scale conservative leaders and cementing local memories of liberal impiety that would provide Religioneros with a potent discursive weapon later. Small-scale imperialist leaders arose all across the state, many of whom became major regional chiefs of the Religionero rebellion a decade later. The latter category included Taximaroa's Jesús "El Ranchero" González, the Bajío bandit/caudillo Casimiro Alonso, the Pátzcuaro captain Abraham Castañeda, Coalcomán's indigenous communal leader, Antonio Cándido, and Jiquilpan's Francisco Gutiérrez and Eulogio Cárdenas. Cárdenas, an Afro-mestizo *rebocero* (artisan shawl maker) and the uncle of "Tata" Lázaro Cárdenas, even

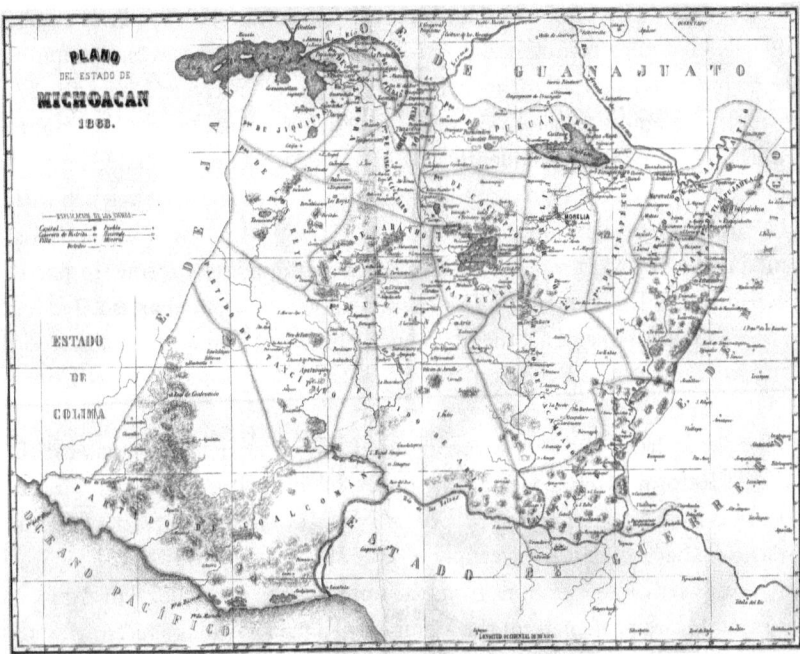

Map 1. Plano del Estado de Michoacán (1863). Courtesy of the Mapoteca "Manuel Orozco y Berra," del Servicio de Información Agroalimentaria y Pesquera, SAGARPA, Classification No. 1719-OYB-7234-A.

earned the rank of colonel in Maximilian's army.[14] The high-profile Religionero generals Socorro Reyes, of Huaniqueo, and Antonio Reza, of Taretan, had also fought in Maximilian's army.[15]

After the fall of Maximilian's empire in 1867 (and notwithstanding the general amnesty proclaimed by President Benito Juárez), Michoacán's homegrown imperialist chiefs largely turned to banditry. Some maintained a constant, low-level guerrilla war against the state government until the outbreak of Religionero rebellion offered the chance for a more organized movement against liberalism. Eulogio Cárdenas survived between 1867 and 1873 by robbing mule trains on the road between Cotija and Mazamitla (Jalisco).[16] "El Ranchero" González and a number of his former imperialist comrades-in-arms, meanwhile, remained organized in a rebel gavilla after 1867, apparently relying on petty banditry and the aid of indigenous communities in the

Zinapécuaro district for material support.[17] A chieftan with solid ties to local villages, González commanded a strong organic following, which he put to use in 1874 after adopting the Religionero mantle. Between 1868 and 1873, however, he seems to have operated purely as a "social bandit," without a political plan and while frequently getting mixed up with the dissident liberal movement against the Juárez government, which was organized in Michoacán by Epitacio Huerta and Juan Cervín de la Mora.[18] Abraham Castañeda also joined the anti-Juárez movement of 1868–1869, though few former imperialists and future Religioneros followed suit. Socorro Reyes led an isolated and short-lived uprising against the liberal government at Tendeparacua in 1870.[19] Porfirio Díaz's Noria Rebellion of 1871, meanwhile, garnered few adherents in Michoacán, either liberal or conservative.[20]

The first stirrings of a more broad-based conservative reaction against the Laws of Reform in Michoacán came in early August 1871, when a significant Catholic riot shook the capital city of Morelia after the arrest of Father Hilario Cabero. According to liberal observers, Cabero was in the habit of delivering "seditious" sermons from the pulpit of the church of San Agustín, directing his ire principally at the members of a masonic lodge recently established in a section of the city's Franciscan convent, nationalized under the provisions of the Lerdo Law in 1859.[21] The sprawling San Francisco, for centuries an immutable feature of Morelia's catholicized landscape, had been divided into lots and auctioned off to the highest bidder. When it fell into the hands of liberal anticlericals, the ire of Catholics was not long in coming.[22] Concerned that Cabero's sermons might provoke violence against the masons, Morelia's prefect, José Dolores Vargas, called the priest to his personal residence to deliver a warning. Cabero's parishioners, seeing their pastor escorted by the police, amassed outside the prefect's house, and when he appeared on the balcony to explain the matter, they showered him with rocks and insults.[23] In the midst of the resulting chaos, Cabero slipped out of the prefect's house and joined the "multitude," which directed itself back to San Agustín, where Cabero was to lead the Mass.

Seeing his authority undermined, Prefect Vargas took a public security battalion and surrounded the Augustinian church. Police captain José María Alvarado was sent in to ask Cabero to suspend the service, but the latter refused, saying he would finish the liturgy first. The priest finally acceded under threat of state violence, but on the street a crowd gathered in defense of Cabero.[24] A swarm of Catholics, "armed and committing disorders," hurled *mueras* at the "Protestants," the masons, Prefect Vargas, and the "impious government."[25] Prefect Vargas then ordered troops to open fire on the mob, an action that precipitated a violent confrontation. The mob broke up into smaller groups, which roamed the city looting the houses of presumed Protestants. The conflict only began to subside with the intervention of Governor Mendoza, who, upon arriving at the scene, freed the wounded Cabero—sending him to a nearby hospital for treatment—and instead arrested Prefect Vargas. In the process, however, Mendoza was threatened by a "fanatic" wielding a rifle.[26] Even after Vargas's arrest, the mob remained unsatisfied: It attempted to extract Father Cabero from the ex-Capuchin hospital, and bands of armed Catholics roamed the streets through the next day, in open defiance of the state army patrols.

When the smoke cleared, a couple of soldiers had lost their lives, as had at least seven of the rioters (including one young woman).[27] The fallen rioters came largely from the city's middling classes, with artisans and tradespeople dominating. Government forces confiscated a motley assortment of weapons—from rifles to clubs—and made a few arrests.[28] The quelling of the riot required the intervention of state army troops, and authorities considered the matter serious enough to send news to President Juárez himself.[29] Local political turmoil followed, too, since Governor Mendoza's attempt to diffuse the situation by arresting the prefect drew sharp criticism from fellow liberals. In response, Mendoza remanded Cabero to the judicial authorities, and he ordered an investigation of the riot in order to bring to justice the "fanatics" responsible for the violence.[30] In the end, though, Cabero and Vargas were both exonerated for their roles in the bloodshed.[31]

Riot, Rebellion, and Pronunciamiento

The Morelia riot portended more serious and widespread religious conflict across rural Michoacán. The state government's eagerness to adopt and enforce anticlerical measures—sometimes even preempting its federal counterpart—played no small part in such tensions. A long-running feud between Father Felipe Castañón and the police chief of Chucándiro, for example, ended in the arrest of the former for seditious behavior in early 1872.[32] Among Castañón's crimes were the willful disregard for the prohibition of public religious acts, the delivering of sermons against the Laws of Reform, and disrespect for the civil authority.[33] Anticlerical measures adopted by the government of Rafael Carrillo (1872–1876) prior to the formal codification of the

Laws of Reform provoked further discontent. An early 1873 circular ordering district prefects to ferret out foreign Jesuits in Michoacán created conflict in Zitácuaro district, whose prefect accused the priest of Tuzantla of conspiring to hide a clandestine Jesuit convent.[34] In May 1873, meanwhile, the state government issued a decree formally and permanently prohibiting the celebration of religious acts outside church walls (a measure that was soon codified nationally by the Ley Orgánica). Even in places famed for their liberalism, such as Zitácuaro, the preemptive decree provoked opposition and "continuous entreaties" from indigenous communities, whose highly public, festive religious cultures mandated regular processions and fireworks.[35] The Carrillo administration flatly refused to allow local officials to contravene the Laws of Reform in this regard, however, thus signaling its intention to close down the juarista loophole that had allowed local officials to grant licenses for religious processions at their discretion.[36] In the eastern mining town of Angangueo, meanwhile, the municipal president failed even to publish the decree on public worship, for fear of the ire of the local populace, "all of [which] ha[d] expressed their disgust at the law, as it very directly attack[ed] their religious beliefs."[37] The prefect of Zitácuaro, Juan Saucedo, obtained permission from the governor to organize a battalion of one hundred National Guard troops to march to Angangueo, but by the time they arrived the situation had been defused. Nevertheless, Saucedo and his patriotic National Guardsmen would soon have another chance to serve the liberal cause, distinguishing themselves in the fight against the Religioneros in eastern Michoacán.

A conflictual election cycle in the fall of 1873 proved to be the breaking point for Michoacán's Catholics. This was largely because the federal government, as part of its constitutional reforms, had reintroduced the requirement for newly elected officials to take an oath of fidelity to the Constitution of 1857. The protesta now covered not only the charter of 1857 but also the Laws of Reform, and it now had to be taken "without any reservations." The scene was thus being set for another ritual showdown like that of 1857, when oath-swearing ceremonies set off numerous, sometimes bloody, conflicts across Mexico's devout center-west.[38] This time, Michoacán's José de Jesús Cuevas fired the first salvo, refusing to swear the protesta in September 1873 after being elected to represent the district of Maravatío in the federal congress the past July.[39] Even liberal editorialists found Cuevas's courage of conviction admirable, and his high-profile removal from congress sparked widespread outrage from Catholics all over Mexico.[40] In Michoacán, a host of lesser government officials followed Cuevas's lead after the state congress adopted the federal mandate on the protesta in October.[41] District and municipal governments were paralyzed as the state government scrambled to replace officials who refused to take the protesta or engaged in other forms of civil disobedience.[42] In Pátzcuaro, district authorities declined to publish the decree on the new requirements. Officials in Acuitzio, Puruándiro, Tacámbaro, and Pátzcuaro flatly refused to take the protesta, and the government had to name new authorities in late October.[43] Maravatío's local government remained acephalous for several weeks, meanwhile, in the absence of a qualified candidate willing to take the protesta. The prefecture of Zamora had to take over the functions of the city's municipal government when the ayuntamiento (municipal council) resigned en masse.[44] Priests sometimes involved themselves directly in the conflict. In La Piedad, the parish priest refused to ring the church bells as prescribed by the civil ceremony that accompanied the publication of the Laws of Reform, and so received a fifty-peso fine.[45] News that the *cura* of Charapan had delivered a sermon encouraging his parishioners to disobey local authorities who had taken the protesta reached all the way to the federal government in Mexico City.[46]

By mid-October, rumors of armed rebellion in eastern Michoacán were circulating. "El Ranchero" González, a smallholder from Taximaroa (today, Ciudad Hidalgo) seemed a likely suspect, as the eastern districts' most noteworthy conservative warrior. However, El Ranchero initially denied any interest in rebelling against the government, penning a letter to the prefect of Zinapécuaro in which he "appealed to the testimony of the townspeople of Huajúmbaro and Anangueo, where [he] had lived for some time."[47] Given such an appeal to local legitimacy, we might speculate that González's Catholic constituency pressed him to lead the charge against lerdismo and he eventually acceded. At any rate, González did join the revolt in January 1875.

Nevertheless, "El Ranchero" was not the first to rally to the defense of religion. Instead, indigenous villagers—whose names no one in the press had ever heard—would protagonize the initial violent struggles against the Lerdo government. Like the 1871 riot in Morelia, many of the early Religionero uprisings were sparked by the suppression of public religious acts or the perceived persecution of priests by local officials carrying out the Laws of Reform. Many others took the form of anti-Protestant revolts, though actual Protestant missionaries or converts were present in only one of these events— in Ahualulco, Jalisco. In the other cases, the anti-Protestant fervor of the movement resulted from popular confusion between religious dissidence and cooperation with the Laws of Reform—specifically the swearing of the protesta. Protestant congregations remained virtually unknown in Michoacán until after 1876, and Religionero rebels largely directed their attacks not at Protestant missionaries but at local government authorities.[48] Religionero ire against "protestants"—a defining feature of the movement—thus confused "heretical" Protestantism with the act of swearing the protesta in order to retain a government post, conflating legal with theological protest. Given that the Church had promised to excommunicate those who took the protesta, it is not hard to see how such a semantic confusion could have arisen, notwithstanding attempts by prelates such as Ramón Camacho of Querétaro to clarify the difference between Protestants and "protestados."[49] Under such circumstances, local officials who remained in their posts after the October decree of the protesta requirement became the first Religionero targets.

In its early forms, the Religionero rebellion developed most significantly in rural zones rather than provincial cities; its adherents were more often rural plebeians than urban artisans. Indeed, indigenous communities in Mexico State, Michoacán, and Jalisco registered the first serious sparks of the conflict. Zinacantepec, in western Mexico State, played host to a bloody and widely discussed revolt in November 1873, when popularly elected officials were removed from office and replaced by outsiders willing to swear the protesta.[50] A multitude of poorly armed indigenous rioters, shouting "vivas" to religion and "mueras" to the "protestants," killed all but one of the municipal interlopers and sacked government offices before district troops under the *jefe político* of Temascaltepec, Colonel Telésforo Tuñón Cañedo, violently put down the revolt, summarily executing perhaps dozens of Indians in the process. Tuñón Cañedo's actions became the subject of a heated debate in the regional press over the use of summary executions in the repression of local riots.[51]

Days later, indigenous rebels from nearby Tejupilco staged another rebellion in the name of religion, killing two government officials and amassing a larger attack on the liberal head town of Temascaltepec. Routed by Tuñón Cañedo, the Tejupilco rebels returned home, but the region saw sporadic protests and low-level violence for several months.[52] The scandal surrounding the events of November deepened when an indigenous rebel taken prisoner by district troops implicated both the priest and vicar of Tejupilco as the instigators of the uprising—a confession an anonymous local correspondent for *La Voz de México* insisted was extracted under threat of violence.[53] Initially condemned to death, both men were eventually pardoned by local judicial authorities, provoking accusations of reactionary complicity by the editors of Mexico City's *El Monitor Republicano*.[54] Catholic observers, for their part, claimed that the federal battalion sent to aid Tuñon Cañedo was full of "defenders of Protestantism" who used the opportunity to spread their religious ideas, "especially against the public worship of the Cross and images, the efficacy of the Mass and the sacrament of confirmation."[55] In short, the conflict in Mexico State was beginning to look like a war of religion. For the editor of *El Monitor Republicano*, the violence exposed the insidious designs of the "clerical party," which sought "to plunge [Mexico] into religious war and caste war."[56] Interestingly, such dire warnings did not keep conservative and rumored ex-imperialist candidates from sweeping local elections in Tejupilco in April, delivering a symbolic rebuke of Tuñón Cañedo's heavy-handed suffocation of the uprising.[57]

Anti-protestant ferment and sporadic outbreaks of violence soon spread into Michoacán, which by mid-1874 would establish itself as the center of the Religionero uprising. Indigenous communities in the remote and sparsely populated Coalcomán district were the first to take up arms in the state in November 1873, when rebel chief Bonifacio Vaca organized Nahua villagers in Huizontla and Ostula against the new district officials, whom he painted as "protestant" usurpers. District military forces quickly quelled this initial rebellion, but over the next two years, Coalcomán district would develop into a hotbed of Religionero mobilization.[58] Further Religionero uprisings in Michoacán in late 1873 and early 1874 followed a similar pattern, with rural populations rebelling against local officials, attacking and looting municipal offices and the houses of presumed "protestants," and often attempting to destroy municipal archives. In December 1873, some thirty Purépecha villagers in Patamban, in the district of Zamora, rose up against local officials who had taken the protesta, attempting to break down the doors of the municipal offices to the cry of "Death to the Protestants! Long live religion!"[59] National Guard troops from Zamora suppressed the revolt, but within a few weeks similar uprisings were underway in other parts of the state. The northwestern district of Jiquilpan proved particularly troublesome, establishing itself as early as January 1874 as a focal point of Religionero rebellion with the pronunciamiento of Florencio Gálvez in Sahuayo and that of Eulogio Cárdenas and Ignacio Ochoa in the district head town.[60] Both of these January uprisings, involving a few dozen rebels, were directed at local authorities imposed by the district prefect after elected officials refused to swear the protesta. The first official pronouncements registered by the state and national press, they seemed to mark a transition in the conflict away from short-lived village riots to something approaching a revolutionary movement.[61] The pronunciamiento of Socorro Reyes in Huaniqueo followed in late January, and although reportedly his gavilla comprised only five rebels, it would soon become one of the most powerful in the state, commanding the loyalty of various Indian and ranchero communities in the Puruándiro district.[62] Spring brought a rash of small-scale pronunciamientos by heretofore unknown rebel leaders in the districts of Uruapan, Morelia, and Zamora.[63] Though local rioting would continue across the Michoacán countryside, by spring of 1874 the indigenous riots in the style of Zinacantepec, Tejupilco, and Patamban were transitioning into a rebellion with broader political implications.

Signs of spiraling unrest did not compel the Carrillo administration and its local allies to change course in their rigid enforcement of the Laws of Reform. In Zirizícuaro, for example, local authorities fined Father Aurelio López de Nava twenty-five pesos for leading a procession of Our Lord of Zirizícuaro around the public square in January 1874, despite the "immemorial" status of the tradition and the fact that local police had always given their permission for the *romería* in the past. The priest petitioned the state government for a reprieve, and although Carrillo's office lowered the fine to fifteen pesos, it also reminded López de Nava that "ignorance of the law [was] not a legitimate excuse."[64] In April, Angangueo became the scene of a violent confrontation between the prefect of Zitácuaro and a group of pilgrims on their way to the shrine of Atotonilco (near San Miguel de Allende, Guanajuato), when the official tried to break up the pilgrimage.[65] Indigenous civil and religious leaders in San Felipe los Alzati (Zitácuaro municipality) also saw their petition for Holy Week processions shot down in early 1874, notwithstanding their invocation of a local liberal heritage. Explaining that their "idea" for the procession was not motivated by fanaticism, the pueblo's judicial authority and mayordomo further assured the government that such an act of religion "would not affect in any way the political ideas that reign in all of the pueblos that form the municipality of Heroic Zitácuaro."[66] Governor Carrillo's office replied that it could not allow the contravention of the laws against public worship.[67] In June, the state government ordered the prefect of Uruapan to prosecute the indigenous leader of the village of Nurio for granting a license for Holy Week processions.[68] The days of local autonomy in handling requests for public religious acts—a feature of the Juárez years—were over.

Despite increasing conflict over public worship and the rapid spread of Catholic protest and violence, Michoacán officials attempted to remain upbeat. Through its official mouthpiece, *El Progresista*, the Carrillo government assured the public that the uprisings represented no real threat to public security, and it regularly reported the "destruction" of small gavillas. However, a series of measures taken by state officials to stabilize local government and quash rebel gavillas suggests a more serious problem. In early March, the state congress authorized Carrillo to name municipal officers directly, bypassing the prefectures—some of which, like Pátzcuaro and Zamora, inspired little confidence in state officials—in an attempt to restaff municipal offices.[69] In the same month, Carrillo called up the state's First Company of Lancers to lead the persecution of the three gavillas operating in the northwest.[70] In July, another decree reduced the number of officials needed to form a municipal quorum from five to three.[71] Meanwhile, the government instructed the prefects of Zamora and Jiquilpan to collaborate in the persecution of the northwestern rebels, and it charged those of Pátzcuaro and Puruándiro with extinguishing the Socorro Reyes revolt, which grew larger by the day.[72]

Military victories remained elusive, though, since Religionero gavillas preferred hit-and-run style guerrilla warfare and often dispersed in the face of government repression only to regroup in the folds of the sierra later. If such Religionero restlessness allowed the government to claim daily victories in the "destruction of gavillas," it also obscured the extent and gravity of the rebellion. Despite continual routing by government troops through the summer and fall of 1874, in fact, the number of reported Religioneros climbed ever upward.

As the conflict simmered across Michoacán, an explosion of genuine anti-Protestant violence shook the small village of Ahualulco (Jalisco) when a Catholic mob murdered a Protestant missionary from the United States and a Mexican convert. The "martyrs" were Minister John Stephens, part of a small Congregationalist mission established in Guadalajara in 1872, and Jesús Islas, a Mexican convert who lived in Stephens's rented property in Ahualulco. On the night of March 2, a mob of some two hundred mostly indigenous Catholics stormed Stephens's house, to the cry of "Death to the Protestants! Long live our priest!" When Islas attempted to prevent the mob from entering the house, he was stabbed to death. Stephens's acolytes would later aver that the minister offered no resistance when confronted by the rioters, instead helping two other Mexican converts to escape before the Catholics fell upon him with machetes, daggers, hatchets, and clubs. Order was quickly restored, and Ahualulco's parish priest, Victorio Reynoso, was arrested as an instigator.[73] Though the priest was later exonerated, the Ahualulco riot reverberated far beyond the borders of Jalisco, becoming a minor diplomatic scandal and inflaming liberal news editors across the country. Indeed, Mexican diplomats and federal officials scrambled to demonstrate their commitment to protecting US citizens in Mexico, and Mexico City editorialists called for more strident measures against Catholic "bandits."[74] Michoacán and Ahualulco suggested that a more serious conservative upheaval was underway.

By the summer of 1874, the Religionero uprising had begun to pose a larger political problem for the Carrillo administration, too, as several of Michoacán's provincial cities fell into acrimonious partisan conflict. Specifically, liberal circles detected collusion between their municipal authorities and the forces of "reaction." In contrast, conservative periodicals decried the heavy-handed tactics of liberal prefects who attempted to suppress the revolt. In May, a treasury official in La Piedad came under fire from local liberals for his supposed harassment of municipal officers who had taken the protesta.[75] In Jiquilpan, civil judge José Dolores del Río was accused of failing to prosecute the authors of the January tumult that led to the Florencio Gálvez uprising because of his sympathies for the "mochos" that dominated the population.[76] Conservatives in Jiquilpan and Zamora, meanwhile, complained loudly via newspaper editorials and petitions to Governor Carrillo about the abuses of liberal authorities in their districts. Such abuses included the imprisonment of the editors of Zamora's Catholic newspaper, *La Causa del Pueblo*, in the wake of an altercation with the prefect.[77] The Catholic press in Morelia became even more enraged by the news that the government planned to execute Manuel Rangel, a close companion of Socorro Reyes who was captured by district authorities in Puruándiro in September. Morelia's *El Pensamiento Católico* argued that Rangel was not a "bandit" subject to the 1868 *ley de salteadores y plagiarios* (which provided for the summary execution of bandits and kidnappers) but a political revolutionary with a constitutional guarantee to a fair trial.[78]

Such a repositioning represented a larger discursive shift among Catholic newspapermen in Morelia and Mexico City. If initially they invoked Religionero violence as a way to criticize Carrillo's incompetency in establishing order, they now characterized the rebellion as a legitimate political revolution, brought on by the liberal government's betrayal of the popular will through the codification of the Laws of Reform.[79] In order to underline popular discontent with the Ley Orgánica and the imminent expulsion of the Hermanas de la Caridad (to take place in January 1875), the Catholic press published dozens of *cartas de protesta* signed by Catholic *vecinos* (townspeople) from all over Mexico in late 1874 and early 1875. Michoacán towns and villages played an important role in the letter campaign, and the documents showcase the variety of Catholic discursive tactics against anticlericalism. The January 1875 petition of the indigenous villagers of Maravatío perhaps captured Catholic sentiment in the state most clearly:

> We want the Honorable Congress, acceding to our desires, to revoke not only the tyrannical [Ley Orgánica], but also all of those articles of our political Constitution that undermine the independence and liberties of the Catholic Church, whose doctrines the entire country professes, leaving us in absolute liberty to follow those doctrines, because such is the national will.[80]

The bold women of Maravatío, too, reminded the congress that it could never take away their religion, but they also dared the government to "use violence if you want; we, far from resisting force with force, will follow the example of the seven-times martyr Saint Felicitas, teaching our children to prefer to lose their lives rather than betray God or their consciences."[81] The vecinos of Zamora, meanwhile, made thinly veiled threats of violence, declaring that they were "ready to spill all of [their] blood, with God's aid," in the defense of their religion.[82] The Catholic backlash in Michoacán had reached threatening proportions, crossing ethnic, gender, and class lines.

Perhaps equally distressing to Carrillo, liberal journalists outside of Michoacán had begun to murmur about the governor's inability to stamp out the Religionero threat.[83] In his annual speech to congress in September, Carrillo finally acknowledged the gravity of the situation, admitting that government actions in the Religionero hotspots of Jiquilpan and Puruándiro had proven ineffective and warning that, although the rebellion did not represent an existential threat to the state government, Religionero "terror" in local communities was effectively dissuading good candidates from serving the government. Carrillo wanted to organize more rurales (mounted rural security forces) but the state lacked resources. He ended the speech by asking the congress to consider a general suspension of constitutional guarantees, since the ley de salteadores y plagiarios did not provide the state with enough power to attack the social bases of the rebellion.[84] Under pressure, the Carrillo regime was increasingly revealing its authoritarian impulses.

The president of the state congress assured Carrillo that the legislature would consider his recommendations. In the meantime, however, the government procured new weapons in the fight against the Religioneros. In October, the Carrillo administration received a cache of new Remington (repeating) rifles from the federal government with which to improve Michoacán's state forces.[85] District officials in several head towns, including Puruándiro and Zamora, also inaugurated new telegraph offices between September and November, allowing for rapid communication among district officials, military leaders, and the state government.[86] Such measures would ultimately prove insufficient, however, and the Carrillo administration began soliciting the aid of the federal army in late 1874.

The Lerdo government quickly complied. The arrival of federal troops—the first two hundred in mid-January 1875 and three hundred more in early February—coincided with increasingly threatening rumors of a mass Catholic uprising to occur at the start of 1875, when the Ley Orgánica would take effect and the Hermanas de la Caridad would leave for exile.[87] The Hermanas left Morelia and Jiquilpan without bloodshed, but other signs pointed to a major Religionero groundswell, with existing gavillas growing in number and audacity and new leaders appearing. New uprisings occurred in Cotija, Tzitzio, Huaniqueo, and Taretan (the last led by future Religionero general Antonio Reza) between November 1874 and March 1875, and local officials reported swelling numbers among the gavillas of Puruándiro and Jiquilpan districts. If most Religionero gavillas had initially consisted of five to thirty rebels, by early 1875 military officials reported well-armed rebel bands hundreds strong in the districts of Apatzingán, Puruándiro, Zamora, and Jiquilpan.[88] The northwestern rebels, in particular, had begun to execute more brazen attacks on civilian officials, such as Florencio Gálvez's assassination of the Sahuayo municipal president in January and the kidnapping and murder of municipal authorities in Panindícuaro in February and Paracho in March.[89]

The spring of 1875 marked a turning point in the conflict, as Religionero gavillas grew significantly in strength and number and carried out a series of dramatic attacks on town plazas. In part, the uptick in violent conflict reflected heightened tensions in the religious sphere, as communities faced the prospect of passing through the high point of the liturgical year without public worship and civil officials interpreted public devotion as a threat of insurrection. In Zinapécuaro district, for example, Prefect Jesús Corral arrested thirty-two men from a local "brotherhood" (almost certainly the cofradía of the Lord of Araró) who were carrying three images in procession from Queréndaro to Araró. He explained that he had taken such measures in response to rumors he would be assaulted by Religioneros that night and because the "fanaticism" of the local residents required preemptive action.⁹⁰ "El Ranchero" González also staged his first major Religionero actions at the climax of the religious year, fomenting rebellions among the miners and hacienda workers of Angangueo and Ocampo in late February (the first week of Lent) and late March (Holy Week).⁹¹ But spring also saw the advent of new kinds of Religionero attacks. In late February, the Religionero chief Francisco Ortíz assaulted the tierra caliente town of Tancítaro, looting and burning the buildings in the plaza after the small National Guard force exhausted its ammunition and fled the town.⁹² Attacks on Paracho, Taretan, Los Reyes, and Zacapu followed soon after.⁹³ Paradoxically, during many such Religionero attacks municipal and district authorities mounted a defense of their plazas from the church tower, leaving Religioneros with the unseemly option of attacking and perhaps burning the fortified church building or abandoning the offensive.⁹⁴ The Taretan attack, led by Antonio Reza and Abraham Castañeda, reportedly attracted several hundred poorly armed "plebeians" from nearby haciendas, who looted and set fire to the house of the municipal president and the municipal school building before being driven out by local National Guard troops.⁹⁵ Eulogio Cárdenas and Ignacio Ochoa's attack on Los Reyes proved even more destructive. On March 7, a reported three hundred rebels and three hundred rural "plebeians" from the surrounding haciendas and pueblos attacked the fortified plaza for several hours. The National Guard force, composed of only twenty men and already low on ammunition, was forced to retreat to the church tower while the rebels took the town, looting several stores, burning eleven houses and buildings, and reportedly raping and kidnapping several young women. The Religioneros, unwilling to defile the church in order to get to the government troops, finally left the town early next morning, but the municipal president reported that they had left behind such misery and desolation that many of Los Reyes's vecinos were emigrating to other towns.⁹⁶

The Revolt Becomes a Movement

Perhaps inevitably, liberals blamed the high clergy for the Religionero crisis. *El Siglo Diez y Nueve* charged the bishop of Zamora with "taking advantage of the deplorable ignorance of the weaker sex" in order to promote cartas de protesta, and it proclaimed that Michoacán's worsening situation "indicate[d] that the clericals think the time has come for a new crusade."⁹⁷ The same paper singled out Archbishop Árciga (Michoacán), Bishop de la Peña y Navarro (Zamora), and Archbishop Labastida (Mexico) as the "principal instigators" of the rebellion, and *El Correo del Comercio* claimed that the "directorate" of the revolt could be found in the episcopal palaces of Morelia, Zamora, and León (Guanajuato).[98] Hard evidence for clerical authorship was not forthcoming, however. The hierarchy of Michoacán had not addressed the Religionero rebellion directly in its writings or pronouncements; yet, as we will see in chapter 2, the prelates of the center-west rejected violent confrontation as a strategy for recouping the Church's losses, even penning a collective pastoral letter to that effect at the height of the crisis in March 1875.[99] Liberal commentators almost uniformly applauded the collective pastoral, which they hoped would discourage further mobilization.[100] And yet, the Catholic backlash in Michoacán continued to grow, and Catholic newspapers grew more celebratory in their treatment of the Religioneros. If the bishops were powerless to stop it, who could? And what could explain the increasing strength of the "bandit-Catholic" gavillas?

The increased Religionero bellicosity of the spring reflected greater sophistication and organization within the movement. March 1875 saw the publication of the first true Religionero political plan, the famed "Plan of Nuevo Urecho," and the first attempts to organize the disparate subregional rebellions would follow soon after. Authored by Abraham Castañeda and Antonio Reza after taking the plaza of the remote, tierra caliente hamlet of Nuevo Urecho from government troops, the plan decried the Lerdo administration's "violation" of popular sovereignty and its "persecution of Catholicism, religion of the majority of Mexicans." It called for the abolition of the Constitution of 1857 and the Laws of Reform, the removal of Lerdo from office, and the repeal of the 1875 Stamp Duty (a federal tax collected for the stamped paper required for official documents). The National Guard Act and the personal contributions collected in Michoacán and other states for the government campaign against rebel gavillas would also be repealed.[101] The plan's authors envisioned a representative, popular republic, but they would impose upon the government a "strict respect" for the Catholic religion, which would henceforth regain its status as official faith of the nation. Indeed, the first task of the interim president (to be elected by popular vote after a majority of the country had adopted the plan) would be to name an ambassador to the Holy See, "invested with the necessary powers to negotiate a Concordat, which, in order to soothe the consciences [of the people], will repair the effects of the acquisitions of ecclesiastical property carried out under the Laws of Reform."¹⁰² The Religioneros would thus commit the future government to making a deal with Rome to protect the Mexican Church's property rights. Such a concordat certainly ran counter to the Lerdo government's refusal to recognize the papacy as a diplomatic partner, which was based on the Laws of Reform's injunction against recognizing the juridical personality of religious corporations.¹⁰³ Interestingly, though, it would also presumably supersede the will of the Mexican Church, since it would employ a state emissary in direct negotiations with the Holy See. As such, the Plan of Nuevo Urecho would resolve the most contentious issues raised by the Reforma while effectively subjecting the Mexican Church to state patronage.

Anticipating the plan's adoption in other states, the authors specified that the "principal leader" of the revolution in each state should organize municipal councils tasked with electing a governor. Members of the Mexican military who joined the revolution would retain their rank in the rebel army, but those who opposed the plan would be treated as "enemies of the people and of national independence."¹⁰⁴ This crude and martial Catholic nationalism would find echo in future Religionero documents.

The Plan of Nuevo Urecho gave the Religionero movement further shape and inspired a number of internal changes. In its wake, government observers noticed that Religionero chieftains had adopted military titles and zones of operation and begun to coordinate their movements. By this time, a new class of more well-to-do Religionero leaders had also joined the fray. In December 1874, the ex-imperialist general Ignacio Buenrostro had issued a pronunciamiento in Tulillo (Mexico State).¹⁰⁵ Félix Venegas and Juan de Dios Rodríguez, known supporters of Maximilian, followed suit in early summer of 1875, pronouncing in Zamora and Patámbaro, respectively.¹⁰⁶ These new leaders worked to refine the movement's nascent ideology. Venegas, explicitly aligning his pronunciamiento with the Plan of Nuevo Urecho, declared that the rebellion would enjoy the protection of God and the Virgin of Guadalupe, the fount of all civilization in Mexico.¹⁰⁷ Meanwhile, Rodríguez, who had served as the "right hand" of General Ramón Méndez in Michoacán during the Intervention, met with eastern Religionero leaders in the spring and united them under his own command.¹⁰⁸ In June, he issued a proclamation calling for mass defections from the state and federal armed forces, institutions he considered illegitimate because of the government's contravention of the popular will.¹⁰⁹ "You are not the servants of the oppressor of the Nation," Rodríguez reminded the soldiers, "but rather [the servants of] the oppressed

Nation. The Nation, and only the Nation, is the owner of your obedience." Echoing the nationalism of the Plan of Nuevo Urecho, Rodríguez aligned the Religionero movement with the glorious struggles of Hidalgo and Iturbide, and he assured his military audience that the sympathies of the majority were with the Religioneros.[110] This, then, was an eclectic ideology, incorporating the Catholic nationalism of the early republic, conservative arguments for Catholic exclusivity and the restoration of Church rights, and a liberal discourse of "popular will" in nearly equal measure.

Yet not all Religioneros were ideologues. In addition to old conservatives and imperialists, the rebellion attracted a number of known highwaymen during this gestational period between late 1874 and mid-1875. Liberals seized upon the participation of "bandits" as a primary way to discredit the movement, often referring to Religionero bands as "gavillas latro-católicas" (bandit-Catholic gangs).[111] The widespread use of aliases among Religionero chieftains—who assumed nicknames such as "el coyote," "el mono" (the monkey), "busca-vida" (life-seeker), and "el grillo" (the cricket)—reinforced popular associations between highwaymen and Religioneros.[112] High profile bandits-turned-Religioneros included Victoriano Ortíz, Silvestre Llamas, Casimiro Alonso, and Macario Romero, leaders of the "Potreros gavilla," a gang with a long history of highway robbery and mercenary activity in the Bajío borderlands between Pénjamo (Guanajuato) and Puruándiro (Michoacán).[113] However, even Religionero leaders described as bandits demonstrated significant consistency in their political sympathies over the course of their careers. The rebels of the Potreros gavilla, for example, fought for Maximilian before joining the Religioneros.[114] Religionero leaders also demonstrated a concern to separate their rebellion from petty banditry in the public mind. Socorro Reyes and Eulogio Cárdenas, especially, cultivated a reputation as "honorable" rebel chiefs who took steps to stamp out looting among their forces and repaid their debts to local property owners.[115] Despite such attempts at moralization, the political instability brought by the Religionero rebellion certainly did provide plenty of scope for petty banditry, agrarian revolt, political opportunism, pillage, and the settling of personal scores.

Ultimately, though, the presence of "bandits" in the rebellion stimulated attempts by more ideological and well-connected leaders to take the reins of the movement. Near Cotija, the "general" Benito Meza appeared on the scene in April 1875 and assumed command of all of the northwestern Religionero bands, totaling some five hundred rebels.[116] The surviving records offer few clues as to the provenance or political trajectory of this important Religionero.

Liberal sources held that Meza was the nephew of a Zamora canon who had fought for the French in Michoacán and that he had been sent by a circle of wealthy Zamora conservatives to take the helm of the movement.[117] That rebel chiefs such as Cárdenas, Ochoa, and Gálvez accepted his command of the northwestern rebellion—the largest of all of Michoacán's subregional Religionero movements—suggests that he was a known and trusted leader.[118] Clearly, though, Meza's presence was considered to be of some importance, especially since it corresponded with the arrival of other high-profile conservatives on the Religionero scene. In May, for example, Morelia was abuzz with rumors that Domingo Olaciregui, brother of "a favorite priest of Archbishop Árciga," and Francisco Ugarte, son of the noted conservative and ex-imperialist general José de Ugarte, had ridden out of Morelia on a mission to "moralize" the rebellion.[119] *La Bandera de Ocampo* accused the Ibarrola family, two of whose members were priests, of sheltering Olaciregui and Ugarte at their hacienda at Tirio.[120] Their political connections did not translate to success on the battlefield, however: Olaciregui was cut down by government troops in August 1875 near Santa Ana Maya, and Ugarte was captured and pardoned soon after.[121] Higher profile newcomers such as these obtained leadership roles on the strength of their family name or reputation as conservative militants, but they generally did not overshadow the homegrown Religionero captains who had forged the movement. Indeed, Cárdenas, Reza, Reyes, and "El Ranchero" all adopted the title of general in early 1875, and many other local chiefs were named to the rank of colonel or captain.

Religionero Culture

Judging by intercepted rebel communications, the nascent Religionero leadership established "zones of operation" in the eastern, central, northern, and southern sections of Michoacán by the summer of 1875, though rebel chiefs used the terms inconsistently. Rebel documents are also inconsistent on the matter of the title given to the Religionero army itself. Jiquilpan's Eulogio Cárdenas referred to his own band of one hundred fighters as the "first company" of the "Ejército Restaurador" (Restorationist Army). Socorro Reyes headed up the "central operations" of the "Ejército Salvador de México" (Army of Salvation of Mexico).[122] Pátzcuaro's Domingo Juárez, meanwhile, used a more unwieldy title: the "Ejército Salvador de la Religión y Buen Orden" (Army of the Salvation of Religion and Good Order).[123] Government reports confirm the existence of several distinctive Religionero flags, too. Antonio Reza carried a red flag with a white cross in the center, and Bonifacio Vaca used a tricolor.[124] According to the historian Álvaro Ochoa Serrano, Benito Meza carried a tricolor with a red cross in the center emblazoned with the phrase "with this you will be victorious."[125] Rebels in Tancítaro used the pass-code "God and the Virgin" to distinguish enemies from friends, and Religionero chiefs signed their letters with various phrases, including "God and Order," "God and Law," or "God and Liberty."[126] Such inconsistencies reflect the inchoate, ad hoc character of the movement as well as a stubborn tendency for localism. Despite the existence of a national political plan and gestures toward an overarching organization, Religionero chiefs tended to stick close to home and carry out their operations with a high level of autonomy, especially in the early stages of the movement.[127] In large part, Religionero chieftains came by such localism organically, since they relied on local constituencies whose socioethnic, political, and religious characteristics varied from place to place. Indigenous communities in the municipalities of Zinapécuaro and Maravatío formed the popular base of "El Ranchero" González's rebellion, for example, and other important indigenous constituencies could be found among the rebels of Coalcomán, those of the Zamora district, and in Socorro Reyes's stronghold in the district of Puruándiro.[128] The crucial role of Cárdenas and several of his cousins in the Jiquilpan revolt suggests that the Religioneros could also expect some support from the local Afro-mestizo population.[129] The March 1875 Religionero uprising in Angangueo, meanwhile, attracted rural plebeians and mineworkers in equal measure.[130] The famous attacks on Los Reyes (March 1875) and Taretan (April 1875) involved hundreds of "plebeians" from each town and from nearby "ranchos and haciendas," perhaps suggesting an agrarian component to the local movement. Hacienda peons likely formed much of the rank and file of the northwestern Religionero movement, too, since the vast Guaracha Hacienda served as a headquarters and stronghold for Benito Meza and Eulogio Cárdenas.[131] In short, though the Religionero movement was an eminently popular rebellion, its precise social makeup and even its religious signifiers varied across Michoacán's broken terrain.

Furthermore, the fragmentary evidence of rebel culture—extracted from government military reports—suggests that the Religioneros were also religiously diverse. While Félix Venegas's Religionero pronunciamiento was inspired by the Virgin of Guadalupe, for example, the northwestern rebels who attacked Purépero in December 1874 invoked the Virgin of Remedies (likely that of Totolan, near Jiquilpan); and Socorro Reyes later revealed himself to be a devotee of Huaniqueo's Señor de la Salud.[132] Rebels in Tlazazalca reportedly received "relics" to wear around their necks as a gift from their parish priest.[133] Some Religioneros wore "amulets" or scapulars emblazoned with that most characteristic emblem of intransigent nineteenth-century Catholicism, the Sacred Heart of Jesus.[134] In at least one case, this scapular was accompanied by the words "Stop! The Sacred Heart of Jesus is with me!"—a slogan used by opponents of liberalism in France throughout the nineteenth century.[135] Religioneros operating near Zipiajo, in Socorro Reyes's central zone of operations, carried "printed prayer books that they call[ed] relics [that would] prevent them from dying without confession."[136] Here, then, was a motley assortment of religious devotions, symbols, and accoutrements that—as subsequent chapters will demonstrate—ultimately reflected different styles of local devotion.

Religionero leaders also represented distinct local constituencies. The most successful Religionero chiefs maintained cordial or at least tolerable relations with local *pacíficos* and sometimes with the local elite. Military reports indicate that the rebels often received voluntary support and supplies from rural communities in their operational zones.[137] As organized gavillas became larger and required more resources, however, they began assessing loans upon merchants and hacendados in their zones of operation. Certainly, such exactions—when coming at the point of a rifle—could increase tensions between Religioneros and civilians, but most rebel chieftains sought more harmonious civil-military relationships.[138] Socorro Reyes, though not alone in the matter, prioritized the issuing of IOU's (*boletas de préstamo*) for such loans, to be paid back upon the triumph of the revolution.[139] Agreeable relations with local hacendados sometimes paid off handsomely, too. In May, Reyes asked that a forced loan on the principal vecinos of Paracho be delivered to the administrator of the Bellas Fuentes Hacienda, who would hold the funds for him.[140] No doubt the heirs of Diego Moreno Jaso used the resources of the Guaracha Hacienda to fund the activities of Meza, Cárdenas, and Ochoa, and at the very least they allowed the rebels to use estate lands as a headquarters, as chapter 3 will demonstrate.

In lieu of nationally recognized leaders, a more tightly controlled ideology, and more sophisticated military structures, then, the Religionero movement at its mid-1875 apogee relied on cumulative local protest and organization in order to destabilize the government. This is not to suggest that Religionero leaders did not communicate or collaborate. But collaboration or movement outside of local zones of operation remained infrequent and was often limited to geographically contiguous zones. As we shall see, Benito Meza's northwestern movement established its firmest links to the rebellion of the southwestern sierra. Socorro Reyes's central Michoacán movement collaborated most often with the Potreros gavilla in the nearby Guanajuato Bajío. "El Ranchero" González, meanwhile, maintained connections to the tierra caliente general Antonio Reza and to rebel operations to the west of Toluca (Mexico State). Further gestures toward centralization and organization would not come until late 1875, as a response to new government strategies against the rebellion, as we will see below.

From the Plan of Nuevo Urecho to the Plan of Tuxtepec

Despite the persistent internal diversity of the rebel movement, the Religioneros' efforts to professionalize in the spring and summer of 1875 constituted a serious threat to the state government. From Guadalajara, Jalisco governor Jesús Camarena warned the federal Minister of War in early May that the gavillas in the Jalisco/Michoacán borderlands grew stronger every day and were "commanded by more intelligent and capable chiefs than before."[141] Clearly, Camarena feared contagion, as did Guanajuato governor Florencio Antillón, who in his annual report to the state legislature in 1875 admitted that although Michoacán remained the "principal focus" of the rebellion, gavillas of fanatics and criminals did pass frequently into his state, with "fatal consequences" for public security.[142] Meanwhile, coverage of the conflict in the liberal newspapers of Morelia and Mexico City registered a notable discursive shift away from jeering mockery of the "soldiers of Pius IX" to shrill denunciations of Religionero barbarity and dark warnings about the future if the government did not quash the rebellion. Liberal correspondents in Zamora lamented to the editors of *La Bandera de Ocampo* that the landowners and merchants of the region remained at the mercy of Religionero bands, which frequently extracted forced loans and made rural highways impassable.[143] In a May 5 speech to his membership, the president of Morelia's *junta patriótica* (patriotic club) declared that the revolution had paralyzed provincial commerce. Meanwhile, conservative papers such as *El Pájaro Verde* and *El Pensamiento Católico* undermined the moral authority of the government campaign by decrying the military's scorched earth policy—such as the army's burning of suspected Religionero homes near Cotija and

Patámbaro—and describing harmonious relationships between rural michoacanos and Religionero chieftains.¹⁴⁴

For his part, Governor Carrillo admitted to the state congress in February that the Religioneros had succeeded in "perturbing public order," and he asked for expanded powers in order to deal with the crisis. In March, *El Progresista* informed its readers that, since the government did not have enough troops at its disposal, some defenseless pueblos would unfortunately continue suffering the "depredations" of the rebels. Towns without military protection were thus ordered to organize their own defense—vecinos should not flee or allow rebel troops to occupy their plazas.¹⁴⁵ The governor called an emergency legislative session in April, in the wake of the dramatic Religionero assaults of the previous month, and by May the congress handed him the suspension of guarantees he sought, along with a new constitutional mandate for citizens to defend their own towns and a new emergency personal tax to help fund the anti-Religionero campaign.¹⁴⁶ The federal legislature quickly followed suit in late May by granting Lerdo emergency powers over the fiscal and military branches of government (which would allow him to unilaterally decree new taxes and raise new military forces) and suspending individual guarantees in order to deal with what had now become a multistate, regional revolution.¹⁴⁷ In Michoacán, Carrillo used his new powers to suppress the partisan press of all political stripes, though the true target of such a measure was likely Morelia's *El Pensamiento Católico*, whose editors had grown more and more supportive of the Religioneros since the publication of the Plan of Nuevo Urecho.¹⁴⁸ Carrillo also told district prefects that failure to warn the military about gavilla activity in their jurisdictions would be interpreted as collusion with the rebellion and punished harshly.¹⁴⁹

The federal military—refreshed with six hundred additional troops in May—set up its general headquarters in La Piedad, from which General Prisciliano Flores would coordinate the campaign against the northwestern and Bajío rebels. Ultimately, federal authorities hoped to contain the rebellion in Michoacán. Federal military authorities thus created a line of defense from Cotija in the west to Pénjamo (Guanajuato) in the northeast, hoping that state forces based in Toluca would hem in the "Ranchero" rebellion from the east and that the vast, inhospitable tierra caliente would discourage the rebels from moving south into the state of Guerrero.¹⁵⁰ From La Piedad, Flores sent federal cavalry columns against the Religioneros in the northwest and set up infantry garrisons in the plazas most susceptible to attack, particularly in the districts of Zamora and Jiquilpan. The entire federal operation was placed in the hands of General Régules, who formed two expeditionary columns to move in persecution of rebel gavillas throughout the state.[151] In May, Régules personally toured the state to reorganize infantry garrisons and help district officials establish volunteer defense forces. According to new state mandates, as Régules warned the prefect of Jiquilpan, local officials and vecinos now had the obligation to arm themselves and aid in the defense of their own plazas. The government simply did not have enough troops to cover every population in the state, and the mobile and diffuse nature of the rebellion gave the rebels a significant advantage in the open terrain outside of provincial cities.[152]

These military measures, if they resulted in increased belligerence between government and Religionero forces, did not immediately tilt the scales in the government's favor. In fact, the Religioneros made major gains in the summer and fall of 1875, sacking and burning Apatzingán and Zacapu and defeating federal troops in battles at Rancho Caurio and Guaracha, in late May and early June, respectively. Benito Meza's five hundred–strong rebel army killed a federal commander, Captain Camilo Moreno, in the former battle, and in mid-June Pedro González's Religionero gavilla struck a blow against the liberal circle of Coeneo, cutting down the celebrated liberal warrior Rafael Arias in a skirmish near Rancho Cortijo.[153] Religionero assaults on Pátzcuaro (May), Apatzingán (May), Zinapécuaro (August), and Uruapan (November) demonstrated that larger towns and cities would no longer be immune from the conflict.[154]

However, Carrillo could point to some significant victories by late fall of 1875. Government forces killed the high-profile Morelia rebel Domingo Olaciregui in August, followed by Generals Juan de Dios Rodríguez in September and Abraham Castañeda in October, thus cutting several heads off of the Religionero hydra.[155] Further, federal military pressure in northern Michoacán led General Meza to break up the biggest Religionero army in the state into smaller divisions, the largest of which he led south along the sierra into the districts of Apatzingán and Coalcomán. Government sources took such a development as proof of the effectiveness of the federal intervention in Michoacán, though it later became apparent that Meza's sojourn into the south was part of a strategy to unify his movement with those of the tierra caliente.[156] The government also took measures to ensure the loyalty of its district officials. After his reelection in September, Carrillo moved to purge insufficiently loyal district officials and replace them with trusted subordinates—often military men. He replaced Zamora's Andrés Villegas Rendón with Prudencio Casillas, a member of Zamora's "liberal circle," and arrested Puruándiro's Albino Fuentes Acosta on suspicions of collusion with the rebels who broke out of jail in the head town in November.[157] He also promoted Colonel Jesús Ocampo to prefect of Maravatío and Colonel Manuel Treviño to prefect of Apatzingán.[158] Through such a militarization of the prefectures, Carrillo hoped to replicate the successes of Zitácuaro's Juan Saucedo, whose own military leadership of the Zitácuaro National Guard had provided a strong counterweight to "El Ranchero" González's actions in eastern Michoacán.[159] In the field, military detachments also employed increasingly severe tactics in attempting to suffocate the revolt and dissuade pacífico populations from aiding the rebels. Most famously, federal troops sacked and burned San Juanico and Patámbaro in May and June, respectively, scorched-earth tactics that occasioned bitter protests from Catholic editorialists.[160] According to the editors of *La Voz de México*, General Rafael Garnica set fire to Patámbaro, an indigenous village of some three hundred souls near the Guanajuato border, in retaliation for a defeat his troops suffered there to Juan de Dios Rodríguez and "El Ranchero" González. "Which article of the emergency powers law," wondered the Catholic journalist, "authorizes the incineration of villages?"[161]

In the end, such severe government measures proved not only unpopular but also insufficient. A correspondent for *La Voz de México* assured the paper's readers that the burning of San Juanico had driven three hundred rancheros into the arms of the rebels.[162] Religionero chiefs adapted to government pressure by turning increasingly to collaboration with other rebel forces and moving into the tierra caliente when pursued. After a major battle with federal troops at their stronghold of San Juanico in October, during which Benito Meza and Eulogio Cárdenas's Religioneros allegedly threw "a multitude of copies of the newspaper *El Pájaro Verde*" down at government troops from their hilltop fortress and unfurled a large tricolor upon the summit, the northwestern rebels moved south to join forces with Antonio Reza for attacks on Apatzingán and Uruapan in early November.[163] Repulsed by the garrison at Apatzingán, the reported 1,400 rebels took Taretan unopposed and began planning for an attack on Uruapan.[164] Meanwhile, correspondents for the state's official newspaper reported that the central Michoacán rebels under Socorro Reyes and Domingo Juárez had met with "El Ranchero" González near Zinapécuaro, their combined number climbing toward five hundred. Smaller sections of González's eastern army sacked Taximaroa in late November and took Indaparapeo without resistance on the first of December.¹⁶⁵ In all, Michoacán offered a depressing panorama for liberals. Morelia correspondents took to the pages of Mexico City newspapers to lament economic paralysis, the dwindling of state resources, and the failure of government troops to protect many of the state's municipalities. Worse still, michoacanos in many places remained subject to two separate kinds of unjust exactions—forced loans demanded by Religionero chiefs and the state government's emergency war tax.¹⁶⁶ Surveying the situation from Mexico City, an editorialist at *El Eco de Ambos Mundos* assured his readers that Michoacán's reactionary revolution now constituted a threat to the entire republic. "That black dot that appeared on the political horizon of Michoacán has grown little by little," he warned in late November, "and today it is a tempestuous cloud that threatens to fall and destroy everything: the gavillas grow in number, in audacity, in discipline; that war, which was once worthy only of disdain, has taken on vast proportions, and if it is not held back by a powerful dam, it will flood everything with ruins and blood."¹⁶⁷ The editorialist concluded by suggesting that the time had come for Lerdo to declare a state of emergency, removing the existing government and imposing martial law. Such drastic measures were likely discussed when Lerdo summoned Governor Carrillo to Mexico City in late November, though the details of the meeting remain unknown.¹⁶⁸ Carrillo's delegation to the federal congress in May had explicitly stopped short of requesting a state-of-emergency declaration, considering it "unnecessary in light of the frank and efficient cooperation of the authorities of the state [with the federal government]."¹⁶⁹ Observers outside of Michoacán, however, were clearly not convinced that the Carrillo government was up to the task.

Lerdo also found himself increasingly under attack from within the liberal fold, pilloried by Mexico City editorialists for his authoritarian streak and the costly and ineffective campaign in Michoacán. The high-profile porfiristas Vicente Riva Palacio and Ireneo Paz, the latter the editor of *El Padre Cobos* (and grandfather of the noted revolutionary intellectual Octavio Paz), led the attack on Lerdo in Mexico City's satirical press, but even former supporters like the editors of *El Siglo Diez y Nueve* were losing their lerdista faith.¹⁷⁰ Like its conservative counterparts, Riva Palacio's *El Ahuizote* was fond of pointing out the inconsistencies between the government's continual trumpeting of its successes against the Religioneros, on the one hand, and its demand for authoritarian powers, on the other, often referring to Lerdo as a modern "Caesar" or comparing his government to Maximilian's.¹⁷¹ But while Riva Palacio tended to see the government's anti-Religionero campaign in

Figure 1. A satirical take on the failure of the federal government's Michoacán campaign, under Minister of War Ignacio Mejía. *El Padre Cobos*, 9 April 1876. Reprinted in *El Padre Cobos y La Carabina de Ambrosio* (Mexico City: Cámara de Senadores de la LVII Legislatura, 2000). Photo courtesy of Daniel Alonzo. The caption reads: "The *pronunciados* stroll through the mustache of the minister of war after being completely defeated."

Michoacán as a simple ploy for dictatorial powers, Paz's *El Padre Cobos* perceived an administration in the midst of a true crisis of legitimacy:

> [The government] says that all of the states where recently the revolutionary spark was burning are now completely at peace, that the gavillas that still exist do not represent a revolution because they lack a political plan and prestigious leaders, etc., and in a more general vein it adds that it is not the nation [writ-large] that harries the government, but only the malcontents, vagabonds, and criminals; that Mexico will not see the return of an oppressive minority to power; and that the government has

the support of the majority. This is very language that Maximilian used . . . during his period of agony!¹⁷²

Deeply critical of the Lerdo government's war efforts, Paz saw the people of Michoacán as trapped between bloodthirsty *bandoleros* and heavy-handed *federales* who "killed whoever they found, leaving towns as deserted as a bout of cholera."¹⁷³ Meanwhile, the House of Deputies played host to rancorous debates over the president's request for extraordinary powers, with a vocal minority characterizing the Lerdo government's request as a duplicitous power-grab on par with the intrigues of the Society of Jesus. As Jalisco deputy José López Portillo declared, to great applause, "there are in the world two central houses of Jesuitism; one is in Rome and is called the Convent of Jesus; the other is in Mexico and is called the National Palace. The only difference between them is that the one in Rome proclaims papal infallibility and the one in Mexico proclaims presidential infallibility!"¹⁷⁴ Even the (newly resurrected) Senate—a body widely thought to be Lerdo's personal fiefdom—witnessed testy exchanges between senators critical of the emergency powers and military officials such as Lerdo's secretary of war, Ignacio Mejía, and Senator (and General) Mariano Escobedo, who interpreted critiques of Lerdo's military policy as disrespect for the "chiefs and officials who are spilling their blood in Michoacán."¹⁷⁵ Antilerdista ferment had reached new heights earlier that spring, when War Ministry officials uncovered an apparent plot by Riva Palacio and the veteran liberal General Sóstenes Rocha to lead a rebellion against the president. Rocha quickly repented his error, and Lerdo later received written affirmations of loyalty from various high-profile Reforma liberals, but Rocha's flirtation with the porfirista opposition boded ill for the liberal coalition and derailed the president's plans for the Michoacán campaign.¹⁷⁶

Perhaps the most distressing news from Michoacán in late 1875 was the rumor—originally appearing in *El Progresista* but quickly thereafter making its rounds in the Mexico City press—that Porfirio Díaz had sent agents into the state to confer with the Religionero leaders.¹⁷⁷ According to local correspondents, these early talks broke down quickly because Díaz and Benito Meza could not agree whether the Constitution of 1824 or 1857 should form the basis for their joint political movement. Nevertheless, Díaz's interest in the Religionero movement was troubling. The intervention of a seasoned national military leader with a strong organic following could turn the tide definitively against Lerdo and Carrillo. Díaz would lend a familiar name and

Figure 2. Porfirista satirists take aim at General Mariano Escobedo and the campaign against the Religioneros. *El Padre Cobos*, 30 March 1876. Reprinted in *El Padre Cobos y La Carabina de Ambrosio* (Mexico City: Cámara de Senadores de la LVII Legislatura, 2000). Photo courtesy of Daniel Alonzo. The caption reads: "3,000 soldiers are on their way; I'll go with the other 3,000 if my sword is needed!"

face to the movement to depose a president who had become increasingly unpopular even in liberal circles. Seeking a way to tip the scale back in his direction, Lerdo announced that he would send General Mariano Escobedo to Michoacán to take the helm of the five thousand federal troops in the state.[178]

Escobedo, a seasoned general celebrated for his capture of Maximilian in Querétaro in 1867, inspired respect and confidence among Mexicans of all political stripes. Liberals celebrated his arrival in Michoacán in November 1875 with jubilation, despite some whisperings that the general would take a more conciliatory stance with the Religioneros. Escobedo toured the state the following January to reorganize federal and state forces and impart the government's new strategy to local officials. Michoacán's congress had extended the suspension of individual guarantees in December, but Escobedo would rely less on the scorched-earth tactics that characterized the federal campaign in San Juanico and Patámbaro in the summer. Instead, he would maintain military pressure on the large Religionero gavillas while making generous use of the indulto, or battlefield pardon. Upon entering a population, Escobedo would announce that rebel combatants who voluntarily laid down their arms would not face further state persecution and could return peacefully to their lives.[179] By early February, *El Progresista* began printing lists of Religioneros who had taken advantage of the pardon, starting with Huango, in the heart of Socorro Reyes's territory.[180] The pardons would pick up considerably over the next few months, but the Religionero leadership countered Escobedo's gambit with one of their own.

In late December, the major rebel leaders of the northwest, south, center, and east published a manifesto in the pages of Mexico City's *El Pájaro Verde* calling for their soldiers and supporters to remain firm in the face of the new government campaign and reasserting the political and religious motivations of the movement. Signed by "El Ranchero" González, Benito Meza, Domingo Juárez, Socorro Reyes, and Antonio Reza, the manifesto represented a clear attempt to shape public narratives about the rebellion. It answered the charge that the Religioneros were simply opportunist bandits, maintaining that the leadership could not take responsibility for the actions of a few ignorant and "perverse" opportunists. The true "bandits," they averred, were liberal soldiers who looted churches during the 1854–1855 Revolution of Ayutla and liberal politicians who exacted new taxes from the people. The authors also decried government atrocities in northwestern Michoacán and in Taretan, which Religioneros and Catholic newspapers had maintained was burned by government troops. Finally, they justified armed insurrection against the government as the only means left for the people to halt the "destruction" of Mexican society heralded by the attack on the Catholic Church. Here, the rebels made recourse to classic conservative arguments about the central role of Catholicism in holding together the "heterogeneity of races, contradictory interests, partisan divisions, and factional rivalries" that characterized the nation. Indeed, employing a nationalist flourish, they asserted, "the day that Mexico loses its religion . . . it will either become a state in the Yankee empire or perish dispersed in the forests, a collection of savage, warring tribes."[181]

The manifesto concluded by inviting all of the pueblos of Michoacán, Guanajuato, Jalisco, and Guerrero to join the revolution. Claiming that the movement already had the support of Michoacán's landholders and "the rich," the Religionero generals offered to provide armaments, horses, and leadership to those who joined the fight. They themselves had "left their workshops and their fields" in order to lead the revolution, and now they asked ordinary Mexicans to do the same, led by the conviction that justice and public opinion were on their side. They should expect and even welcome death, though, since "if to triumph with this cause is glorious, it is even more glorious to die for it."[182] Even if the rebels did not find victory on earth, then, they would find it in heaven.

Though well received by Catholic editorialists in Mexico City, the manifesto did not stem the tide of indultos, which *El Progresista* continued publishing every week. Government reports indicated a dwindling of Religionero forces in most parts of the state except the northwest and southwest, where the bulk of the rebels had amassed under Meza, Cárdenas, and Reza. Socorro Reyes's central operation was hardest hit by the indultos, which the prefect of Puruándiro reported by the dozens each week. In late January, for example, the Religionero captain Francisco Martínez Salazar requested an indulto for himself and twenty of his subordinates in Huango.[183] Other reports of skirmishes in Zipiajo (Michoacán) and Abasolo (Guanajuato) suggested that Reyes's army of Indians, poor rancheros, and hacienda peons now lacked adequate weaponry and war material and were reduced to fighting with poorly made lances, clubs, and machetes.[184] In February, the northeastern rebellion also suffered a major setback when government forces captured Benito Meza.[185] Government sources claimed Meza was apprehended south of Los Reyes after federal troops dealt a terrible blow to his gavilla. The Religionero general allegedly tried to hide among the bodies of fallen compatriots, but when government troops began to inspect the dead for signs of their rank or identity, Meza was discovered alive and identified by local vecinos. Government forces then escorted Meza to Los Reyes, where he was quickly tried and executed.[186] However, a Los Reyes–based correspondent for *La Voz de México* disputed the official version of the events, claiming that Meza had voluntarily laid down his arms and asked for an indulto, only to suffer an unceremonious execution.[187] Whatever the case, the northwestern Religionero was dead, and Eulogio Cárdenas had assumed command of his weakened gavilla and fled back toward Cotija.

If the tide had begun to turn against the Religioneros by early spring, however, the news of the Revolution of Tuxtepec would soon breathe new life into the movement. Rumors of Díaz's flirtation with the northwestern Religionero rebellion had preceded the publication of the Plan of Tuxtepec by several months, and doubt swirled around the issue of Díaz's own connection to the Tuxtepec rebellion for weeks after the plan's initial publication in January.[188] Consequently, discussions of the Hero of Puebla in Michoacán's *El Progresista* during this time centered squarely on the question of whether Díaz might adopt the Catholic mantle. Would the liberal hero of May 5th cynically proclaim the Plan of Nuevo Urecho and carry Michoacán's conservative rebellion to other states? Would he turn his back on his liberal principles in the name of a base power grab?[189] Such questions suggest that, for liberal observers in Michoacán, understandings of Díaz's movement were inextricably tied up with discussions of the Religionero threat. Catholic editors were even more forceful about the connection between the two "revolutions." *La Voz de México* took the antilerdista liberal press to task for ignoring the Religioneros and focusing solely on Díaz, arguing that the Religionero movement was the first organized opposition to Lerdo and that its political plan showed greater ideological sophistication than the Plan of Tuxtepec. The editorial encouraged liberal dissidents to take some lessons from the Catholic rebels: "If the revolution of Oaxaca is to triumph, it would do well to approach the political arena in which the revolution of Michoacán fights."[190] For their part, the editors of *La Idea Católica* chastised the porfiristas for ignoring the grievances that had "obligated the people of Michoacán to make use of their right to insurrection."[191]

Initially, many liberal observers did not believe that Díaz would really pursue an alliance with the Religioneros, since, according to Eduardo Ruiz at *El Progresista*, such a move would tarnish his reputation and program. "Sr. Díaz would either have to bargain with the neo-Catholic party, offering it dangerous and cowardly concessions, or, faithful to the liberal flag, he would have to present himself to [the conservatives of Michoacán] with the Constitution and the Laws of Reform in his hand, and if he did so the Conservative Party, if it is not outwardly hostile [to him], would want no part of his struggle."[192] Mexico City's *El Monitor Republicano* agreed, declaring that "the revolution headed by General Porfirio Díaz does not, and could not, have any contact with that promoted by the throng of callous Religioneros."[193] Yet such confidence in Díaz's liberal convictions soon proved to be misplaced, as rumors of the Tuxtepec movement's complicity with the "reaction" piled up. In February 1876, *The Two Republics* circulated the rumor that Díaz's revolutionary motto would be "Constitution, without the additions" (that is, the Laws of Reform), a political promise that would represent a significant concession to the Catholic opposition.[194] Liberal papers noted the appearance of ex-imperialists in porfirista ranks by early 1876.[195] *El Siglo Diez y Nueve*, by this time an increasingly fierce opponent of lerdista authoritarianism, charged that Díaz's rebels were so opportunistic that they would see no problem making common cause with those who proclaimed "Religion and fueros!"[196]

As it happened, however, Díaz would not have to adopt the Religionero plan. Instead, he issued a revised liberal plan in Palo Blanco, Tamaulipas, in March 1876. The plan duplicated all of Tuxtepec's points—the validity of the Constitution of 1857 and the Laws of Reform, no reelection, municipal autonomy—but added a clause providing for Díaz's own succession to the presidency.[197] This, perhaps, was the kind of assurance that the Religioneros needed, since it would allow them to negotiate the terms of post-Lerdo rule with a trusted partner. Indeed, if the Religioneros had balked at the overtures of Díaz's agents in late 1875, by early 1876 their position had shifted markedly, perhaps as much in response to the fluid national political context as to the impact of Escobedo's indultos on their armies. Whatever the cause, the Religioneros had begun to proclaim for Tuxtepec. By late March, the change in banners was nearly universal, and rumors even circulated that Díaz would appoint "El Ranchero" González governor of Michoacán after toppling Lerdo and Carrillo.[198] The Religioneros had become Porfiristas.

Conclusions

As the foregoing narrative has demonstrated, the Religionero movement threw Michoacán's lerdista government into crisis and—as it elicited an increasingly authoritarian response from civil and military officials—destabilized the liberal coalition in Mexico City. Indeed, the Lerdo government ultimately had to impose a kind of martial law in Michoacán in mid-1875 in order to enforce the Laws of Reform and keep the Religionero rebellion from infecting other states. In so doing, however, Lerdo squandered the political capital he had inherited as the successor of Juárez and fueled the flames of Porfirista opposition. In the end, the Religionero movement proved so damaging to Lerdo that it attracted Díaz himself, who would over the course of 1876–1877 attempt to use Michoacán as a springboard to national power.

The humble origins and popular character of the Religionero movement makes such a trajectory all the more striking. Originating in indigenous village riots in late 1873 and early 1874, the rebellion moved only tentatively toward internal organization, professionalization, and cross-class collaboration over the course of 1875. As it attracted a cadre of ex-imperialist notables to its ranks, the rebellion developed an eclectic ideology that combined traditional conservative ideas (Catholicism as Mexico's social glue, state protection of the Church), Ultramontanism (the insistence on a concordat), and liberal discourse on popular sovereignty and individual rights. However, the localist orientation of rebel chiefs and their popular bases throughout the conflict, the inconsistencies in practice and self-identification among Religionero armies, and the diversity of rebel motivations (religious, political, material) kept the revolt rooted to a specific central-western geography and prevented it from cohering into a larger national movement. In short, if the Religionero rebellion captured the widespread popular discontent with liberal anticlericalism in Michoacán and nearby states, the movement was ultimately still diffuse, locally based, and internally diverse when it insinuated itself within the Revolution of Tuxtepec in early 1876. If we are to know more about the meaning of the revolt, therefore, we will need to analyze the complex interplay of religious, political, and material factors driving Religionero mobilization in the regions and localities that proved most susceptible to rebellion—a task undertaken in the book's three case studies. Before that, however, we will need to address the question of the Religioneros' relationship to the Church hierarchy and to Catholic restorationism, more specifically.

CHAPTER 2

The Other Reforma

Clerical Accommodation and Catholic Restoration in Central-Western Mexico

In the fall of 1874, as the Religionero crisis spiraled out of control in Michoacán, Archbishop Labastida introduced a novel weapon in the Church's struggle against liberal anticlericalism. He had obtained a special dispensation from Pope Pius IX for all Mexican dioceses to take part in a "spiritual pilgrimage," a pious practice inaugurated by lay Catholics in Bologna as a response to the prohibition of mass pilgrimages in the flesh in the former Papal States.[1] Since the Laws of Reform had likewise outlawed public worship in Mexico, Labastida hoped that Mexican participation in the new devotional exercise would stimulate the faith and foment lay solidarity with the embattled Church. For thirty days, "spiritual pilgrims" would transport themselves mentally to renowned temples and shrines in Europe, Mexico, and the Holy Land, reliving the emotion of the saints, mystics, and martyrs who had sanctified each place and praying for "peace among Christian princes, the conversion of sinners, the extirpation of heresies, and the exaltation of the Holy Mother Church." Pilgrims undertaking the spiritual journey would earn indulgences for the souls of loved ones in purgatory. The Archdiocese of Mexico distributed a special pamphlet prescribing the virtual itineraries of each of the three *decades* (ten-day periods) of the pilgrimage and offering pilgrims a rudimentary primer for undertaking such an imaginary journey.[2] The first decade would take Mexican Catholics to Italian, Spanish, and French holy places such as Loreto, Padua, Assisi, Santiago de Compostela, and Lourdes; the second to Mexico's great shrines, including that of the Virgin of Guadalupe, the Virgen de la Salud in Pátzcuaro, the

Señor de la Salud in Zamora, and the Virgen de San Juan de los Lagos in Jalisco; the final decade would transport them to Bethlehem, Nazareth, the hill of Calvary, and other sites associated with Jesus's life and death. Those Catholics who lived in Mexico City were enjoined to go to particular churches in small groups in order to carry out the mental exercise, thereby approximating the collective nature of a bodily pilgrimage.

Although the archbishop intended for all Mexican dioceses to join the pilgrimage, he found particularly enthusiastic collaborators in central-western dioceses such as Zamora, a bastion of Ultramontanism headquartered in Labastida's own patria chica. There, Bishop José Antonio de la Peña promoted the pilgrimage to his priests as an effective means to counteract "liberalism's crude attack," and he provided for a particularly modern form of lay participation. "In the spirit of common prayer," the bishop announced, priests would gather their flocks in the parish church in order to perform the rituals on each day of the three decades. In places where priests could not supervise, however, lay Catholics could organize the practice themselves, electing a "head of the chorus" to lead the spiritual journey.[3]

A ritual of guided, collective contemplation, the spiritual pilgrimage dodged the Laws of Reform's prohibition of public worship, and it aligned the plight of the Mexican Church imaginatively with that of Pius IX's besieged Rome, by quite literally asking Mexicans to imagine themselves as part of a larger sacred geography imperiled by the march of liberalism. As such, Labastida considered the exercise a perfect remedy to the challenge of anticlericalism in Mexico. Not only would it show the "enemies of the Church" that laws could not extinguish religion, it would also expose the hypocrisy of the liberal program itself, since the latter proclaimed freedom of association yet restricted the rights of Catholics to carry out collective acts of devotion in public. Indeed, Labastida closed his pilgrimage instructions by offering thanks that God had not allowed the civil power to restrict the "liberty of conscience, the liberty of thought, the liberty, in sum, of the spirit."[4]

In its interiorized, spiritual character, its affinity for European models of religiosity, and its calls to the laity to make use of modern "liberties" in the service of a Catholic restoration, the spiritual pilgrimage offers a vivid example of the direction Mexican Catholicism was heading in the mid-1870s. The fall of the Second Empire in 1867 had led Mexican clerics to abandon plans for a throne/altar alliance and instead focus on institutional renovation and the promotion of a Catholic counterculture within a secular regime. In fact, the Church entered a sustained period of revival during the Restored Republic

(1867–1877), mostly turning its energies inward to focus on clerical reform, the re-Catholicization of a demoralized flock, and the creation of a new Catholic civil society based on lay collective action of a devotional and charitable nature. The institutional foundations of such a restoration had been laid in 1862, with the ecclesiastical restructuring that raised Michoacán and Guadalajara to the status of ecclesiastical provinces (archdioceses) and created the new suffragan dioceses of León, Zamora, Querétaro, Veracruz, Chilapa, Tulancingo, and Zacatecas. Such a restructuring reflected a highly regionalized strategy: it prioritized the states of the central-western Bajío, a historic Catholic stronghold and more recently the home of strong local liberal movements. At the helm of the new dioceses, a new cohort of bishops and archbishops who had cut their teeth during the Reforma crisis sought to combat "religious indifference" and devotional error as well as the new threat of Protestant infiltration among the flock. Such regional reform projects drew direct inspiration from the Ultramontane Catholicism of Europe, especially in its Roman and French varieties.[5] As the Mexican hierarchy deepened its ties to the embattled Roman papacy and imbibed the devotional and educational trends of French and Italian Catholic reformers, however, it cast an increasingly jaundiced eye upon the syncretic, often-raucous religiosity of the rural popular classes in Mexico. The Church's restoration thus attempted a kind of "spiritual reconquest" of Mexico's rural hinterlands, affected through Catholic educational initiatives, frequent pastoral visits and missions, and close supervision of the rural clergy and their flocks.[6]

Crucially, the hierarchy in this period tended to cede the public sphere to the restored liberal government, adopting a more conciliatory tone in its pronouncements and counseling its clergy to avoid open conflict with civil authorities. Instead, when the Lerdo administration took a radical turn in 1873, the institutional Church increasingly made use of a liberal discourse of individual rights, popular will, and freedom of association in order to defend its prerogatives and advance its project of restoration. One particularly important product of such an engagement with liberal tenets was the explosion of pious associations—especially charitable and educational organizations but also a variety of purely devotional groups—that proliferated rapidly across the Mexican center-west after 1869.[7] As a complementary strategy to the creation of new sees and seminaries, the Church depended on pious lay associations to help the reformed clergy propagate a new model of Ultramontane religiosity and to meet the challenges of the Laws of Reform, which had severely restricted its social and economic power and its ability to minister publicly.

Map 2. The Bishopric of Michoacán before the diocesan restructuring of 1862. José María Arizaga, *Carta geográfica del obispado de Michoacán en 1863* (1863). Courtesy of the Mapoteca "Manuel Orozco y Berra," del Servicio de Información Agroalimentaria y Pesquera, SAGARPA, Classification No. 115-OYB-7234-A.

The aim was to create a robust Catholic civil society, led by sectors of the provincial middle class, whose actions would fortify the Church and moralize Mexican society while remaining immune to anticlerical legislation.[8] If pious laymen and -women, in collaboration with the hierarchy, could indeed re-Catholicize the Mexican populace through such social and religious means, then political and legislative victories would soon follow, since the popular will would demand a reversal of the most damaging anticlerical laws.

Thus, the Church moved to spiritualize its activities as part of its larger war with the state, though this was not its sole strategy. Rather, in the face of state anticlericalism, prelates in Mexico's central-western Catholic heartland combined this new focus on religious revival and Catholic civil society with older tactics, especially the condemnation of liberal legislation via pastoral writings and the leveling of spiritual censures against the authors of anticlerical policy and those who participated in civil administration.[9] The combination of such old and new tactics greatly influenced the religious conflict of 1873–1877, though the relationship between Catholic restorationism and Religionero mobilization is complex and often contradictory, as subsequent chapters will make clear.

Meanwhile, this chapter analyzes the Church's turn away from partisan politics and toward Catholic restorationism in Michoacán and the greater center-west[10] in the years between the ecclesiastical restructuring of 1862 and the end of the Religionero conflict in 1877. It traces the evolution of the larger ecclesiastical project for clerical reform, the spread of Europeanized devotions, and the creation of a Catholic civil society, while identifying the particular variants of the project at the diocesan level. Focusing on the Archdiocese of Michoacán and the new diocese of Zamora, the chapter then identifies the various drivers of Catholic restoration at the diocesan and parish levels, including the pastoral missions of the regional hierarchy, clerical and seminary reform, and the proliferation of charitable and educational projects led by (mainly female) religious congregations and lay associations. A key finding is that the restorationist projects of Morelia and Zamora were far from identical. While the Zamora hierarchy looked to Ultramontane Europe as a model for institutional and devotional renovation, Morelia's no-less-reformist clerics devised a more locally sensitive and inward-looking revitalization. Catholic restorationism thus cut an uneven path through Michoacán. Further, as subsequent chapters show, the reform projects of Zamora and Morelia were not received in an uncritical or uniform manner. Local communities often contested, assimilated, or reshaped reformist strains of

Catholicism, and a complex and often acrimonious dialogue ensued between the Ultramontane and myriad popular religious cultures of rural Michoacán. Such a variegated landscape of religious change and conflict would affect Religionero mobilization in unexpected ways.

A Clerical Retreat from Politics?

The Restored Republic marked a notable shift in the political posture of Mexico's high clerics. After directly funding and solemnizing conservative rebellion in the 1850s and actively collaborating in the construction of the Second Empire, Mexican churchmen in the 1870s retreated from the political sphere.[11] Though Mexican bishops remained vocal critics of anticlericalism, especially after Lerdo's 1873 codification of the Laws of Reform, they generally counseled their flocks to avoid open confrontation with civil authorities. Parish priests were enjoined to prevent "scandals" when confronted by secular authorities wielding the reform laws, and lay Catholics were to abstain from confessional politics and public administration altogether. Instead, they should commit themselves to acts of collective prayer and expiation and contribute to the re-Catholicization of society through charitable and educational projects. They could, however, raise their voice publicly in support of the "rights and liberties" of the Church, notably by penning "letters of protest" written to President Lerdo and the congress.[12] Peaceful dissent in the form of political abstention and written protests would serve to demonstrate that the "will of the people" resided with the Church. Thus did the Mexican clergy steer the flock to engage with liberal legal and political discourse—especially popular sovereignty and individual guarantees—in order to establish the foundations for a projected Catholic civil society. Henceforth, the Church would embrace liberal tenets and endeavor to turn them against the liberals.

One clerical strategy rested on depriving government of personnel by prohibiting Catholics from serving in public administration, a notable shift from earlier precedents. During Juárez's last term (1867–1872) Catholics and state officials found ways to work around many aspects of liberal laws, tolerating the deployment of mental or verbal "reservations" in the taking of the protest, merely ad hoc enforcement of the prohibition of public worship, and the use of "arrangements of conscience" for adjudicators of clerical property.[13] With Lerdo's anticlerical turn, however, the state would no longer countenance half measures in the implementation of the reform legislation, and, as it hardened its stance, Mexican prelates resurrected their Reforma-era threats of excommunication in cases of collaboration with the state.[14] Such threats extended to the protesta, which the lerdista government now demanded be taken "without reservation." Responding to a flurry of queries from parish priests and lay Catholics who sought political office in local elections in 1873 and 1874, ecclesiastical authorities declared definitively that the taking of the protesta—even with "mental restrictions" prioritizing the liberties of the Church—was illicit and heretical. Those who had done so would be denied the sacraments until they "repaired their heresy" by way of a public, official retraction of the oath.[15]

Some clerics held that good Catholics should abstain completely from serving in public administration. In his 1873 pastoral, Bishop José María de Jesús Diez de Sollano y Dávalos of León declared that he would rather that all public posts be staffed with heretics than see God offended by the collaboration of the faithful with the impious. Further, he prohibited the use of "mental restrictions," since such a practice "is repudiated by all of the Moralists of sound doctrine." Denying that his flock could be ignorant of the Church's stance, the bishop then raised the pious example of José de Jesús Cuevas, who was elected to the federal congress by the district of Maravatío (Michoacán) in September 1873 but removed by federal officials after refusing to take the protesta. True Catholics must do as Cuevas did, the bishop averred, and those who collaborated with the liberal regime would find themselves cast out of the Catholic communion. In imitation of the early Christian martyrs of Abitinae, the faithful should answer the protesta query ("Do you promise to uphold and enforce the Constitution of 1857 and its additions and reforms?") with the simple yet powerful phrase "Non possumus"—we cannot. Christians must obey God before man, Diez de Sollano reminded them, and they should accept persecution without physical resistance.[16]

Obeying God before man also meant repudiating the civil registry and the suggestion that civil contracts trumped sacraments. Indeed, Diez de Sollano told his flock in 1874 that Catholics who bypassed sacramental marriage in favor of the civil registry would be subject to "grave penalties and censures of the Church." If couples refused to marry canonically after priestly warnings, they would be denied subsequent sacraments until they "repaired their heresy." The bishop further enjoined magistrates and judges who served the civil registry and the government to "meditate seriously before God" about how they should adjust their procedures to avoid trespassing against the Church, "warning them that it does no good to say that in their private lives they are Catholics but as magistrates or judges they are not, since this distinction does not exist before God."[17] As for priests, the bishop instructed them to continue to preach the word of God, even if the police "lay siege to your pulpits."[18]

Diez de Sollano's fiery rhetoric set him apart from other Mexican bishops, whose more moderate pastoral letters tended only to refer to contemporary Mexican politics obliquely. In fact, prelates such as Labastida and Michoacán's newly minted archbishop, José Ignacio Árciga (appointed 1868), limited their pastoral commentary during this time to general statements on the calamitous effects of global liberalism, the importance of bearing persecution stoically, and the promotion of expiation, prayer, and sacramental piety as remedies for the ills of the day.[19] Such statements and prescriptions were framed in global terms, since the drama of the Ley Orgánica was unfolding against a backdrop of global Catholic crisis and retrenchment related to the Italian Risorgimento and the First Vatican Council. In response to the invasion of the Papal States and the advance of liberal nationalism across the Catholic world, Pius IX had convened the First Vatican Council in 1869, during which the Church reiterated the *Syllabus of Errors*'s condemnation of liberalism, rationalism, and materialism and proclaimed the pope to be infallible when defining Church doctrine. Ten Mexican prelates, including the archbishops of Mexico, Michoacán, and Guadalajara, attended Vatican I, and the Mexican clergy uniformly supported the controversial dogma of papal infallibility.[20] Yet Victor Emmanuel's invasion of Rome interrupted the Council, which was suspended indefinitely.

Clerical leaders in Mexico could not but be affected by the battle raging in Europe between Catholicism and liberalism, and their responses to the Ley Orgánica reflected the fierce Ultramontanism of Vatican I. Archbishop Árciga, in an 1871 pastoral describing the work of the council, lauded Pius IX's refusal to capitulate to Emmanuel's terms after the fall of Rome and underlined the duty of the clergy to defend the "sacred rights and immunities of the Church" in the face of persecution. Nonetheless, Árciga declined to comment specifically on the political situation of Mexico, and he counseled only prayer, penitence, and participation in a special papal blessing ceremony—authorized by Pius IX and carried out by the bishops of Mexico. Such acts, Árciga insisted, were the best weapon against the "indifferentism" of the age.[21] Crucially, spiritual struggle with liberalism did not rule out clerical clemency toward liberals themselves. In his 1873 pastoral to mark the occasion of Pius IX's allocution condemning the legislative attacks on Church property and monastic life in Italy, Labastida ruminated on the theme of reconciliation:

> Observe well, children, in the matter of principles, the Church is inexorable, it employs all of its resources in order to preserve its rights uninjured, it makes use of exhortations and threats, and if this is not enough, it employs the appropriate weapon against the offenders of its laws, even, when it judges it to be prudent, up to its most severe penalties and censures. However, when the crisis passes, when the usurpations are consummated, when the plunder is perfected . . . the [Church, as a] tender mother, cries inconsolably for the loss not only of her properties but of her children.[22]

By late 1874, as the federal congress published the Ley Orgánica, even the firebrand Diez de Sollano had begun to adopt new tools in his rhetorical assault on lerdismo. Now he not only condemned the Laws of Reform on Ultramontane grounds but also underlined inconsistencies between liberal individual guarantees and the punitive and regalist provisions of the laws. In his 1874 "exposition," for example, the bishop condemned the protesta requirement for "shackling [Mexican] consciences by force" to the state, thus violating the freedom of conscience.[23] Likewise, the Ley Orgánica's regalist provision for civil intervention in public worship, the suppression of monastic orders, and the prohibition of the clergy to acquire property violated the principle of religious freedom. If the suppression of the Hermanas de la Caridad was an act of "capriciousness and arbitrariness, nurtured by a hatred of Catholicism," it also contravened the liberal tenets of freedom of association and of education.[24] Diez de Sollano was thus turning liberal tenets against liberalism.

However much they denounced the reform laws, the diocesan authorities of the center-west rejected violence and rebellion as a strategy to confront the Lerdo government. Rather, Catholics should seek recourse primarily in the spiritual realm and offer only passive resistance when confronted by government agents. Pastoral letters encouraged the faithful to emulate Pius IX's stoic suffering in the face of the Risorgimento and recommended spiritual solidarity with the pope through collective prayer and expiation.[25] Zamora's bishop, José Antonio de la Peña, ordered his priests in 1873 to cooperate with the civil power "in all of those places where the local authorities demand the punctual compliance with the Laws of Reform," and he further counseled local priests to avoid open conflict with civil officials.[26] Even Diez de Sollano struck a more conciliatory tone in his December 1874 circular, directing the clergy to use "prudence" when discussing controversial topics from the pulpit. The faithful should obey God's laws before man's laws, but parish priests should also condemn rebellion explicitly.[27] In an 1872 pastoral combatting the "errors" of Protestantism, Bishop de la Peña likewise prohibited the faithful from entering into open conflict with religious "dissidents." Only humility, patience, charity, and a "spirit of evangelism," and not violence, could resolve the fundamental doctrinal dispute between Catholicism and Protestantism.[28] In a special "warning" to his flock in November 1873, Bishop Camacho of Querétaro even acknowledged the problems occasioned by the popular use of the epithet "protestant" to describe those who had taken Lerdo's protesta. He clarified the Church's position on the matter, distinguishing the religious heresy of Protestantism from the civil heresy of the protesta and emphasizing the ability of good, repentant Catholics to rejoin the Catholic fold through a public retraction.[29] The faithful should obey the law when it did not conflict with God's laws, and if their consciences mandated civil disobedience, they should accept punishment resignedly "rather than provoking scandals and disorder which religion condemns."[30]

The definitive statement regulating Catholic responses to the Ley Orgánica and signaling a new approach to Church-state affairs, however, was the 1875 collective pastoral of Mexico's three archbishops. Published in the heat of the Religionero rebellion, and only months after the suppression of the Hermanas de la Caridad, the collective pastoral was designed to provide the laity with concrete instructions on how to weather the lerdista storm. Although they offered a brief refutation of the Ley Orgánica, the authors maintained a strikingly conciliatory tone throughout the text. As the visible leadership of the Mexican Church, the prelates knew that the "anti-Catholic" press would interpret any "prudent silence in the presence of profound and general disgust" as collusion with the rebellion. In the preamble, therefore, the prelates explained that they were raising their voices in order to "corroborate the faith of [Mexico's] pueblos" but also to "impede them from being dragged and impelled by their religious susceptibility into hostile demonstrations and threats of violence, which we are far from desiring and positively condemn as contrary to the peace and public order, and, as such, contrary to the doctrine of the Church and religion."[31] They even inveighed against the use of "injurious" and "sarcastic" language by the Catholic press, which they considered undignified for Christians.[32]

But clerical injunctions against rebellion did not necessarily mean that Catholics had to suffer the calamities of the Ley Orgánica in silence. Although the prelates of Mexico emphasized spiritual remedies and penitence, they also allowed for acts of passive resistance and the use of "peaceful manifestations" directed at the government. Just as, in 1873, Bishop Diez de Sollano had encouraged Catholics to "be counted" publically among those citizens who rejected liberal anticlericalism, the archbishops framed their 1875 collective pastoral as a respectful example of how the laity should manifest their dissent to the congress and government.[33] In the document's conclusion, indeed, they further averred that "the legitimate right of petition can and should be exercised by all Mexicans in the current circumstances."[34] Such pronouncements, which evinced a clear clerical embrace of the notion of popular sovereignty, effectively sanctioned the widespread campaign of written protest that was already underway in the form of the so-called cartas de protesta (letters of protest).

The letter-writing campaign had begun in the provincial capitals of central Mexico—notably Morelia, Puebla, and Guanajuato—before spreading both to larger cities such as Guadalajara and Mexico City and small towns and villages throughout the country. By early 1875, cartas de protesta—most of them written by women—occupied the front pages of Catholic newspapers in Mexico City, Morelia, and Zamora on a nearly daily basis.[35] Often invoking the "right to petition," the cartas uniformly condemned the Ley Orgánica as injurious to Catholicism, the faith of the "immense majority." Though they varied widely in tone—from incendiary condemnation to injured supplication—the cartas nevertheless tended to share a self-conscious appropriation of the discourse of liberal rights. Typical was the petition of the men of Chalchicomula (Puebla), who declared that the Ley Orgánica's persecution of Catholicism violated of principle of religious liberty. As for the Hermanas de la Caridad, they asked "that they be allowed to stay among us, since they have a right of association [as] enshrined in the general Constitution of the republic."[36] The suppression of the Hermanas proved a central theme throughout the petitions, and it motivated particularly bitter commentary. A group of women from Guadalajara, for example, denounced government action against the Hermanas as "a crude, inept, reckless, and *antiliberal* attack," and they vowed to defend the "religion that [they] inherited from [their] fathers" by boycotting secular schools and converting themselves into "Apostles of Christian education."[37] The women of Guanajuato declared that since the "weaker sex" constituted half of the population and was united in opposition to the Ley Orgánica, and since many Catholic men also opposed the law, the will of the majority was clearly with the Church. Yet they would not depend on men to defeat lerdismo, either:

> And now that fear has turned many men who still call themselves Catholics into Quakers, we the women swear to disobey in whatever manner possible, the edicts of the modern Julianos, we swear to obey our ecclesiastical superiors until we die . . . we swear not to recognize as brothers, husbands, or sons those who have participated in the iniquitous expatriation of the Hermanas, and we swear finally to suffer with pleasure and valor the persecutions that this frank manifestation may bring us.[38]

Such strident threats of civil disobedience are relatively rare in the corpus of the cartas de protesta. Nonetheless, the Guanajuato women's invocation of popular sovereignty underlines a wider trend: the use of liberal discourse by lay as well as ecclesiastical Catholics opposed to the Ley Orgánica. Further, though bishops cautioned against disrespectful language, they approved of the cartas de protesta as a strategy for demonstrating the will of the people.

Written protests were only the beginning of the Church's appropriation of liberal discourse. Indeed, the bulk of the prelates' 1875 collective pastoral consisted of instructions for reviving the faith within the bounds of lerdismo and using the protections offered by constitutional guarantees. Thus, in response to the prohibition of religious education in public schools, priests and lay Catholics should work to create parochial and (preferably free) private Catholic schools, availing themselves of constitutional guarantees for the liberty of instruction. Faced with the prohibition of tithe collection outside of church walls, the prelates exhorted Catholics to assume individual financial responsibility for the Church. Instead of "waiting in the streets and plazas" for requests from tithe collectors, Catholics should "come to the aid of your temples, threatened with ruin, and your ministers embittered by hunger" and make direct donations.[39] To stimulate such individual remittances, the bishops offered eighty days of indulgence for each pious donation. In response to the expulsion of the Hermanas de la Caridad, finally, the prelates enjoined Catholics to revitalize the charitable work of the lay Conferences of Saint Vincent de Paul, reminding the faithful that such work would be protected under the principle of freedom of association. The archbishops proclaimed that such "collective action" had proved to be a highly successful response to liberal legislation in France, and they recommended that Catholic laywomen, especially, take up and expand upon the work of the Hermanas through the formation of pious associations.[40]

The 1875 collective pastoral letter thus provided the clerical blueprint for Mexico's Catholic restoration under the adverse conditions of lerdismo, a project that entailed an unprecedented call for lay mobilization.[41] Indeed, in closing, the prelates exhorted Catholics to "fortify [themselves] and work; work within this circle that we have drawn."[42] Such a "circle" clearly embraced the right to petition and to engage in "collective action" in the educational and charitable spheres, activities protected by the individual guarantees enshrined in the constitution. As such, it represented not only an adjustment to the constraints of liberalism but an embrace of liberal tenets—individual rights, voluntary association, popular sovereignty—in the pursuit of Catholic revival.[43] Within such a framework, armed rebellion was no longer a credible option. In fact, despite the bishops' condemnation of the Ley Orgánica, the hierarchy of Mexico now adopted a conciliatory tone and denounced violence and even disrespect to liberal authorities. Such conciliatory gestures were not lost on liberal commentators. The editors of Michoacán's official newspaper, *El Progresista*, approvingly republished an extract of Bishop Camacho's 1873 circular on the confusion between Protestants and those who had taken the protesta.[44] They also lauded the 1875 collective pastoral, informing their readers that the document "frequently repeats that Catholics should not give themselves over to the proscribed course of revolution, and it even reproaches the women who have used a disrespectful style in their petitions for the repeal of the law."[45] That the lerdistas of Morelia assumed that the collective pastoral's injunctions against "disrespect" were meant specifically for women reveals much about liberal views of female political action, but *El Progresista*'s larger approval of the collective pastoral demonstrates that the episcopate's changing stance on politics did not go unnoticed. In the face of the spiraling Religionero crisis in their state, Morelia's liberal literati clearly hoped that clerical injunctions against rebellion could help calm the populace. And, despite a notable failure in this regard, the high clergy did condemn armed rebellion as a strategy for confronting lerdismo. Instead, it counseled a withdrawal from partisan politics in order to focus on the institutional reconstruction of the Church and the reconquest of civil society through social, educational, and charitable projects. It also promoted a new kind of Catholicism aligned with European Ultramontanism.

Europeanizing the Mexican Center-West

The second half of the nineteenth century saw the deepening of connections between the Mexican Church and Pope Pius IX's Rome and the wider Catholic world of Europe. Such "Europeanizing" trends encompassed personal relations between Mexican churchmen and Pius IX himself, symbolic gestures of affinity between Mexican and European devotions, and institutional ties meant to shore up Mexico's seminary system and augment its ability to counter Reforma-style liberalism.[46] European devotional culture, especially in its Italian and French varieties, also began to exert a strong pull on the imagination of Mexican Catholic reformers, as they steeped themselves in a more modern, cosmopolitan piety.[47] In a general sense, Mexican churchmen hoped that this new relationship with Europe would fortify Mexican institutions and lay associations and revitalize local religious devotions and practices, imbuing them with more Ultramontane and fashionable European traits. As we will see, these Europeanizing trends developed a regional flavor in Mexico, exerting their strongest pull on Zamora and other central-western dioceses.[48] Such a regionalism owed as much to the influence of several high-profile Michoacán churchmen exiled in Rome in the 1850s and 1860s as to the particular attraction of Ultramontanism among certain central-western Catholics.

The 1862 ecclesiastical reorganization, a project of the influential Michoacán prelates Labastida and Munguía, represented a direct response to the threat of liberal anticlericalism in Mexico. In Roman exile, the Mexican bishops cultivated an unprecedentedly close relationship with Pope Pius IX before pitching the idea of a significant diocesan restructuring in their home country, one that would redistribute priests, create new seminaries, bring bishops closer to their flocks, and tighten clerical control over a historically important region. The center-west, where the Church had retained a strong presence since at least the seventeenth century, would receive both of the new archdiocesan provinces and four of the seven new dioceses. Pius IX approved the scheme and sent Labastida and Munguía back to Mexico in 1865 at the helm of the reformed episcopate, as archbishops of Mexico and Michoacán, respectively.

The see of Michoacán, second only to that of Mexico in terms of historical depth and importance, received priority attention in this restructuring and special favors from the pope. As an ecclesiastical province, Morelia would preside over three of the seven new dioceses created by Pius IX (Querétaro,

León, and Zamora).[49] Crucially, thanks to Labastida's influence, the prelate's patria chica of Zamora was chosen as the site of one of these new suffragan bishoprics, edging out the more liberal Uruapan.[50] The new diocese, which was carved out of the western half of the state of Michoacán, comprised thirty-five parishes extending from the Zamora Bajío in the north through the central Purépecha Highlands and southward to the western tierra caliente (hot country) and coastal sierra.[51] The importance of Zamora's promotion to diocesan seat was not lost on José Antonio de la Peña, Zamora's first bishop and a native of nearby Tangamandapio.[52] In his first pastoral letter, of December 1864, de la Peña stressed the providential nature of the diocese's creation, concluding that Zamora had received the honor chiefly because of its long history of piety, charity, and stoic suffering in the face of epidemic diseases and ruinous revolutions. De la Peña considered Zamora a "Levitical city"—a cradle of the clergy, like the cities of the biblical tribe of the Levites—whose elect nature God had signaled in a powerful 1861 earthquake that left the town unscathed. Perhaps to underline the relationship between the intransigent papacy and the Mexican restoration, Pius IX had consecrated the diocese of Zamora to the Immaculate Conception of Mary, a devotion defined as dogma by Pius himself in 1854 as part of the Church's response to the European Revolutions of 1848. De la Peña, for his part, called on *zamoranos* to imitate the purity and perfection of Mary Immaculate, who would serve as Zamora's patroness.[53]

As the first bishop of León, Diez de Sollano greeted the news of his city's episcopal promotion in a similar fashion, attributing León's fortune to the divine favor of his favorite saint, La Virgen de la Luz.[54] A notably European avocation of Mary Immaculate, La Virgen de la Luz was an apt selection for a prelate who espoused an orthodox and European-oriented piety.[55] The former rector of the Jesuit Colegio de San Gregorio in Mexico City, Diez de Sollano showed himself throughout his prelature to be an acolyte of the Ultramontane devotions of contemporary Europe, and especially those of Jesuit origin (though he was not personally a member of the Society of Jesus). Indeed, his first act as bishop in 1864 was to order Masses of thanksgiving dedicated to La Virgen de la Luz and the Sacred Heart of Jesus—another Jesuit devotion strongly associated with Ultramontane intransigence.[56] Throughout his episcopacy, moreover, Diez de Sollano proved particularly keen on fostering new, European-derived devotional trends and associations in León, instituting the Italian Association of the Good Death and promoting devotion to the Virgin of Loreto, Lourdes, the Holy Infancy, and the

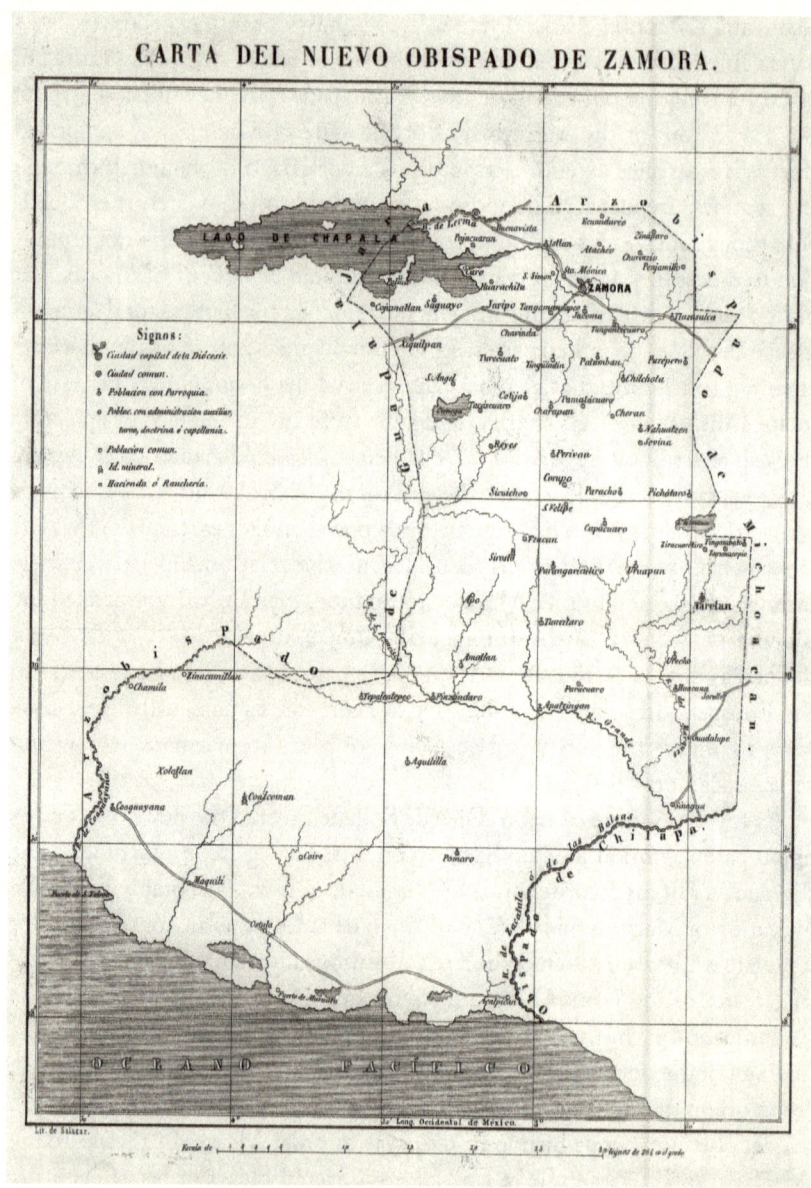

Map 3. The new Bishopric of Zamora in 1862. Anonymous, *Carta del Nuevo Obispado de Zamora* (1862). Courtesy of the Mapoteca "Manuel Orozco y Berra," del Servicio de Información Agroalimentaria y Pesquera, SAGARPA, Classification No. 1161-OYB-7234-A.

Sacred Heart of Mary. Notably, he was among the first of the Mexican bishops to consecrate his diocese to the Sacred Heart, in 1875.[57]

Such symbolic gestures formed part of a larger web of devotional and personal ties connecting the high clergy of Mexico's center-west to the world of European Catholicism. These connections largely dated from the late 1850s, when eight of Mexico's eleven bishops were reunited in exile in the Holy City, where several of them developed a personal rapport with Pius IX. Labastida used his exile not only to plan Mexico's ecclesiastical reform but also to tour the Holy Land in 1861. Along with Michoacán's Bishop Munguía and Guadalajara's Pedro Espinosa, he attended the canonization ceremony of Mexico's first saint, San Felipe de Jesús, in Rome in 1862.[58] Ten Mexican bishops, including Labastida and Árciga, also attended the First Vatican Council of 1869–1870, the meeting that produced the definitive statement of Catholic intransigence—the doctrine of papal infallibility. Although Vatican I became the site of controversy and internal division over the infallibility question, Mexico's prelates all closed ranks around Pius IX and adopted the Ultramontane position.[59] During the Council, Labastida also received a special dispensation from Pius IX, enabling him to grant papal blessings and plenary indulgences to penitent Mexican Catholics who prayed for the triumph of the Church. This precedent-setting privilege—which in effect turned the Mexican prelate into a kind of papal vicar—was later followed by other papal favors to Mexican clerics, including permission to participate in the spiritual pilgrimage of 1874 and the various concessions granted to Labastida's nephew, José Antonio Plancarte y Labastida, in his rechristening and pontifical coronation of the Virgin of the Root in Jacona, Michoacán.[60]

Here, in fact, it is worth pausing to review the early career of José Antonio Plancarte, the influential and polarizing figure at the center of Mexico's late nineteenth-century Catholic revival, since in many ways he served as a primary conduit for Romanizing reform in Michoacán.[61] As a young man in the 1850s, Plancarte accompanied his uncle in his Roman exile and sojourns in Europe and the Holy Land. Making the best of Labastida's expulsion, Plancarte studied at an elite Catholic school in Birmingham, England, before transferring to the Pontifical Academy of Ecclesiastical Nobles in Rome to complete his clerical training.[62] This European training proved a formative experience for Plancarte, who became enamored of European devotions and educational methods.

Upon returning to Mexico in 1867, he was named parish priest of Jacona, Michoacán, a dusty town of some 3,500 souls just a couple of miles south of

Figure 3. Portrait of Father José Antonio Plancarte, the enterprising Ultramontane priest of Jacona. Box 14, folder 1, #33, Genaro García Photograph Collection, Benson Latin American Collection, General Libraries, University of Texas at Austin. Photo courtesy of Daniel Alonzo.

the new cathedral of his native Zamora.[63] Plancarte may have initially lamented this assignment, as an elite, European-trained priest sent to preside over a town so "lacking in culture and civilization," but he soon accepted his fate and set to work recreating Jacona in the image of Ultramontane Europe.[64] He began by attempting to reform the devotional practices of his parishioners and especially those of the surrounding indigenous communities, suppressing the celebration of Carnaval in 1866 and working to curtail drunkenness and the use of profane and unorthodox images during Purépecha celebrations of Corpus Christi.[65] As mentioned, Plancarte's project for the reform of the region's baroque religiosity would eventually culminate in his overhauling of a popular indigenous devotion in direct collaboration with the pope. During an 1877 sojourn to Rome, Plancarte presented Pius IX with a lithographic print of Jacona's Virgin of the Root, a seventeenth-century Marian image in the form of a tree root hauled out of Lake Chapala by a humble Indian. Taken with the image but perhaps nonplussed by its rustic name, the pope redubbed her the "Virgin of Hope."[66] Thus was a baroque icon born of the sixteenth-century spiritual conquest resignified as another kind of conquest—the Ultramontane triumph over liberalism.

Undeterred by a flurry of complaints by indigenous leaders to Bishop de la

Peña against his suppression of their religious customs, Plancarte then set his sights on another pet project: educational reform. As early as 1867 he could be found working to create Catholic educational establishments for Jacona's youth, converting a defunct "casa de ejercicios" into a girls' school, the Colegio de la Purísima Concepción. He later founded a school for boys, and when the Lerdo government announced the expulsion of the Jesuits from Mexico in 1873, Plancarte conspired with his uncle Pelagio to bring two of them to Jacona to serve as professors.[67] Using his influential contacts in Mexico City and Europe, he also began sending groups of young men from his San Luis Gonzaga School to study for the priesthood at the Jesuit-run Colegio Pío Latinoamericano in Rome, the first of whom left Jacona for the Holy City in 1870.[68] This generation of *piolatinos*, which owed its existence to institutional links and personal affinity between Plancarte and his European counterparts, came to wield an outsized influence on the Mexican Church by the early decades of the twentieth century.[69] Even as early as the 1870s, however, Plancarte and his uncle had demonstrated their preference for a kind of "European strategy," one that sought the reconstruction of the Mexican clergy along European lines by sending students abroad and recruiting European Jesuits at home.

Like his Europeanized devotions, Plancarte's educational reformism drew criticism from more traditional sectors of Zamora's society, though for different reasons. In particular, his focus on Catholic education for girls and women ruffled the feathers of Catholics with more traditional understandings of gender roles. Controversy erupted in 1870 over his use of devotional pageants that, in the eyes of more traditional and indigenous Catholics, promoted the unseemly public exposition of young girls and the social mixing of children of both sexes. Plancarte defended himself by pointing to European precedents and suggesting that his detractors were ignorant and out of touch with current Catholic trends.[70] He considered the education of girls of paramount importance given their potential as moralizing agents in a secularizing world.[71] Of course, in such a view women's religious agency remained securely relegated to the domestic sphere, but Plancarte's pious projects nonetheless did expand female religious roles beyond their traditional boundaries. Indeed, he would later go on to found a female "active life" congregation (that is, one focused principally on charitable and educational work "in the world"), which he named Las Hijas de María Inmaculada de Guadalupe.[72]

Plancarte's life and work, then, exemplify one particular strain of the restorationist project in Mexico in the 1860s and 1870s—reformist, European-oriented, focused on pious education and Catholic social engagement, and amenable to the "feminization" of piety as a strategic response to the pull of liberalism on Mexican men.[73] As Cecilia Bautista argues, such a project found especially fertile ground in the new diocese of Zamora, where the ecclesiastical elite saw in the European strategy a chance for autonomy from the circle of Morelia-based clerics that had long decided Zamora's fate.[74] Crucially, the devotional repertoire of European Ultramontanism provided the model for such a project, which privileged devotional renovation while also establishing new institutional and personal links with Catholic Europe and Pius IX himself. More than a purely symbolic and elite concern, however, Ultramontane revivalism motivated concrete reform projects aimed at both the parish clergy and the laity.

Correcting Popular Religious Practices, Reforming the Clergy

As Plancarte's Corpus Christi reforms demonstrate, the reformist clergy's new engagement with European Catholicism also signaled changing attitudes about Mexico's popular religious cultures, which were increasingly viewed with suspicion. The men at the helm of the new dioceses of León and Zamora distinguished themselves in this regard.[75] An 1867 circular of the Diocese of León decried abuses that had crept into public worship and the use of profane music in Church services. It also warned the rural clergy about the spread of unofficial devotions such as "La Mano Poderosa"—an image of Christ's stigmatized hand above whose fingers floated, puppet-like, the holy family of Saints Mary, Joseph, Anne, and Joachim, and the infant Jesus—and "la Cuenta de Mil" (the Count of a Thousand, perhaps a kind of extended rosary prayer).[76] In 1869, Diez de Sollano issued another circular prohibiting the "changing of one [saint's] image into another" through the substitution of clothing or accoutrements.[77] Meanwhile, an 1873 circular from Zamora surveyed a landscape of clerical decadence, Protestant infiltration, and devotional errors. In the latter category, the bishop identified the proliferation of "imperfect" and "immodest" images of the Virgin of Refuge, popularly depicted with the Christ child as a naked toddler. De la Peña considered such a depiction an affront to the purity of the Blessed Virgin. To counter such devotional error and laxity among the rural clergy, the bishop prescribed the propagation of Catholic schooling, the increased vigilance of parish priests over religious functions, and frequent ecclesiastical conferences between priests to improve clerical education and ensure uniformity of parish administration.[78]

In places such as Zamora and León, then, the Church's turn away from the political in favor of the spiritual and social after 1867 also involved a strong impulse toward internal reformism. Paradoxically, the Laws of Reform's restrictions on public worship served to advance such internal reformism, providing bishops with the opportunity to scrutinize popular religious practice and impose new, more puritanical standards of devotion.[79] In 1873, Bishop de la Peña, echoing the Laws of Reform, prohibited priests from leading any procession outside of a church building—even in the adjacent atrium or cemetery—and charged the rural clergy with suppressing the drunken dances that often attended saints' day festivals. He further moved to impose doctrinal orthodoxy on the celebration of Corpus Christi in the indigenous parishes of the diocese by prohibiting the procession of the Holy Sacrament on any other day but that precisely marked by the liturgical calendar, thus suppressing the rotational system of Corpus Christi celebrations traditionally employed in the close-knit communities of the Purépecha Highlands.[80] To be fair, high clerical injunctions against public worship sometimes reflected pragmatic conciliation rather than devotional puritanism. Pedro Loza, the archbishop of Guadalajara, for example, ordered his rural clergy in 1874 to "persuade" the faithful, and especially the indigenous, to refrain from soliciting permission for public processions from the local authorities. Under the current circumstances, he insisted, congressional action—and not informal arrangements with sympathetic officials—was the only way to restore public worship in Mexico. "To attempt to recover [the right to public worship] by other means," he averred, "could cause conflicts and disorders contrary to the spirit of our religion."[81] For clerics such as Diez de Sollano, however, there were powerful theological reasons for obeying the civil law and refraining from public worship. Notably, he used the fact that Eucharistic processions were banned as an excuse to deny ecclesiastical permits for other, emphatically popular religious processions. As he explained:

> In the present circumstances we will not permit any type of processions, since this would mean deceiving the pueblos, making them think that more veneration is owed to [saints'] images than to the Most Holy Sacrament, since the latter is not allowed to be carried in procession during the festival of Corpus Christi, which belongs to the Dogmatic

Liturgy, and since it is only being carried secretly in the *viáticos*. [We] cannot concede any licenses for processions of images until the Church recovers its canonical liberty.[82]

Here, then, was an attempt to put the myriad popular cults of the Mexican countryside "in their place" beneath the universal and clerically controlled mystery of the Eucharist, while blaming the decision on liberal infringements of canon law. The suppression of popular, public cults—if it indeed represented a dire threat to the faith—also provided an opportunity for clerical elites to increase their control over the flock. This was clearly understood by Mexico's three archbishops, who, in their 1875 collective pastoral, urged the faithful to remain calm and patient with regard to the prohibition of public worship. The parish clergy would simply have to increase their pastoral efforts in order to bring the people to church, and they should take advantage of the prohibition of public processions in order to stamp out popular customs such as feast-day dancing, drunkenness, and gambling.[83] In important ways, then, Mexican prelates shared the liberals' concerns about the "disorderly" character of collective religious practice, and they saw in the Laws of Reform a chance to stimulate internal reform. They would not allow the end of public worship to become the end of religion in Mexico, but they would use the law to purify the faith where possible.

The reformist impulses of the central-western hierarchy were aimed as much at the parish clergy as at lay Catholics. Indeed, if rural parishes suffered from rampant devotional error and profane entertainment, the "laxity," decadence, and even willful disobedience of rural priests was largely to blame. As we will see, the clerical elites of Morelia and Zamora diverged sharply in their strategies for clerical reform, with the former favoring a more inward-looking revitalization while the latter pursued even greater Europeanization of the diocesan clergy. Nevertheless, the shared project of seminary and clerical reform found fertile terrain in Michoacán, where postindependence instability and decadence had proven particularly damaging.[84] Left "destitute and desolate" by the chaos of the previous decades, the Archbishopric of Michoacán was plagued with vacant parish administrations, defiled churches, and a far-flung rural clergy that resisted diocesan authority. Upon taking possession of the province in 1868, Archbishop Árciga mandated the reform and regularization of ecclesiastical conferences in order to bring the extant clergy under diocesan control, and he undertook a serious reform of the conciliar seminary. Indeed, Árciga's tenure marked the beginning of a "golden age" for the seminary—a time of

Figure 4. Portrait of José Ignacio Árciga y Ruíz de Chávez, second archbishop of Michoacán. Box 14, folder 1, #13, Genaro García Photograph Collection, Benson Latin American Collection, General Libraries, University of Texas at Austin. Photo courtesy of Daniel Alonzo.

material expansion and revitalization born of increasingly efficient collection of the *pensión conciliar* (a small tax paid by parish priests for the support of the seminary) and corresponding with a larger trend of urban renewal in Michoacán's capital city. Árciga expanded the seminary's footprint through the recuperation of the building belonging to the extinguished Hermanas de la Caridad, and he overhauled the seminary's curriculum, implanting an educational model that balanced neo-Thomist thought with contemporary scientific reasoning.[85] Such reforms would ideally produce a class of priests better versed in the fundamentals of the faith and well prepared to do battle with modern rationalism and Protestantism. Current priests, meanwhile, could no longer escape from diocesan oversight. In 1869, Árciga issued a universal revocation of parish tenure, requiring each priest to reapply for his license and ordering a detailed report on the educational profile and career trajectories of each curate.[86] Such measures attest to Árciga's autocratic spirit and his conviction that the Catholic restoration should begin with the renovation of the clergy. Until the reformed Morelia seminary could produce enough high-quality priests to staff each of the forty-nine parishes in his jurisdiction, Árciga would attempt to bring the "decadent" rural clergy of the Reforma generation in line with his reform.

The Zamora hierarchy also prioritized clerical reform, though it understood the problem differently and prescribed different remedies. To de la Peña, clerical laxity and resistance to diocesan authority were apiece with Protestant heresy. In 1866, he had issued an edict condemning a group of dissident priests in the tierra caliente of Michoacán who had continued to exercise their ministry despite excommunication for swearing the oath of allegiance to the Constitution of 1857.[87] These dissidents, he declared, led innocent Catholics to damnation, and some even flirted with the notion that they did not require ecclesiastical licenses in order to carry out their ministry, since their authorization came directly from Christ. We lack evidence of the extent and trajectory of this schismatical movement in Michoacán, but the specter of clerical dissidence and Protestantism continued to haunt de la Peña's thoughts throughout his life, becoming a central theme for his reform project. In late 1871, fearing the creep of Protestantism in his jurisdiction, de la Peña instructed his rural clergy to combat the dissidents through patient, educational work among the laity, some of whom lacked an understanding of the fundamentals of the Catholic faith and were thus easily deceived.[88] In an 1873 circular, he decried the "decadent" state of the diocese, scolding the clergy for failing to fulfill its duties to preach routinely, provide spiritual leadership, and serve as the last line of defense against the diffusion of Protestant literature. Like Árciga, he prescribed more regular and rigorous ecclesiastical conferences and enjoined priests to take responsibility for each other's spiritual and intellectual progress.[89] Unlike Árciga, however, de la Peña and others in his clerical circle would turn increasingly to the Colegio Pío Latinoamericano in Rome for the long-term goal of forming a more disciplined and Ultramontane clergy. The seeds for such a project, as we have seen, were sown by Father Plancarte, whose Jesuit-run Colegio de San Luis Gonzaga had begun sending young men from Zamora to train in Rome by 1873.[90]

Nonetheless, Europeanizing trends within central-western Catholicism were not universally embraced among Mexican reformers or the vested clerical interests of cathedral chapters and seminaries. As we have seen, Plancarte's project received vigorous criticism from a variety of sectors within the Catholic Church, ranging from indigenous leaders alarmed by his attack on baroque religion to zamoranos who objected to his views on gender. High clerics, too, found fault with Plancarte/Labastida's European-dominated model of Catholic education and clerical formation. Most famously, Bishop Diez de Sollano quarreled with Archbishop Labastida over his plan to staff

Mexico's conciliar seminary with foreign Jesuits, with the former favoring Mexican secular priests.[91] In Morelia, meanwhile, entrenched clerical factions obstructed the path of Europeanization. Archbishop Árciga declined to participate in Plancarte's Pío Latino program, despite his own zeal for reforming Michoacán's clergy. The entrenched power of the Morelia seminary—which since its founding in the 1770s had proclaimed a distinct identity connected to the evangelical heritage of Vasco de Quiroga in the sixteenth century—likely had much to do with such resistance to Romanization. Indeed, Árciga and his cabildo endeavored to keep the reform of clerical education "in-house," focusing particular attention on pedagogical reforms in the diocesan seminary and the imposition of a more stringent disciplinary regime in order to combat the "laxity" and the often defiant autonomy Árciga found among the parish clergy when he took the reins of the archbishopric in 1868.[92] The Roman spirit thus had its limits—often set by established and powerful cabildos—even if the central-western clergy tended to share a desire for a larger Europeanization of the faith.

Bringing the Restoration to the Parishes: Pastoral Projects in Michoacán

The diocesan administrations of Michoacán took their respective reformist projects directly to the rural parishes of their jurisdictions through various kinds of pastoral work, including canonical visitations, Catholic schooling initiatives, and the promotion of pious associations. Pastoral visits became an increasingly important tool of ecclesiastical reformism in the 1860s and 1870s, since they allowed for direct episcopal intervention in parish administration and provided an opportunity for interaction between bishops and their dispersed flocks. During the pastoral visit, the bishop toured his jurisdiction in order to ensure proper parish administration and religious practice, resolve disputes among priests and parishioners, and bestow the sacrament of confirmation upon all of those who had reached the proper age.[93] While the Council of Trent (1545–1563) had charged bishops with carrying out the visits every year or two, institutional instability had made such punctuality impossible. Regular pastoral visits had not taken place in the immense diocese of Michoacán in the decades after independence because the see remained vacant between 1809 and 1831. The slated pastoral visits of Bishops Juan Cayetano Gómez de Portugal (1831–1850) and Clemente de Jesús Munguía (1852–1868), meanwhile, were often interrupted by civil wars or the expulsion of the prelate.⁹⁴ Political instability notwithstanding, the immense size of the ancient bishopric of Michoacán had long prevented its pastors from carrying out a complete survey of the parishes, and the impracticality of regular visits had in large part motivated the campaign for the subdivision of the diocese, begun under Gómez de Portugal.⁹⁵ When Michoacán's two prelates began to carry out regular pastoral visits in their new, more manageable jurisdictions in the late 1860s, most of the rural parishes had not received a visit in over a decade.⁹⁶ Not only did such ecclesiastical neglect deprive thousands of young Catholics of the sacrament of confirmation, it also left priests and parishioners in far-flung rural communities to their own religious devices. As far as Michoacán's prelates were concerned, such spiritual neglect was a recipe for clerical laxity, "devotional error," and even religious dissidence.⁹⁷

Regular pastoral visits provided the most immediate antidote to these problems. Though neither could keep pace with the enterprising Diez de Sollano, who visited each of the parishes in his (much smaller) jurisdiction five times between 1864 and 1873, the frequency and regularity of the visits in Michoacán nonetheless increased considerably in the 1860s and 1870s.⁹⁸ With a few brief interruptions, Archbishop Árciga toured his still-vast jurisdiction three times during the Restored Republic (1867–1869, 1871–1872, and 1873–1874), though he likely did not visit every parish during each tour. Enduring grueling itineraries through the stifling and difficult terrain of the archdiocese's tierra caliente, Árciga soon developed a reputation as a zealous reformer and caring pastor.⁹⁹ In his visits, the archbishop scrutinized parish records for evidence of poor bookkeeping, inspected the material state of church buildings and their inventory of images and ornaments, and observed local religious customs and ritual practices. Where the latter diverged from Roman orthodoxy, as in the informal "races" between saints' images that the Purépecha parishioners of Zacapu staged during their Christmas celebrations, Árciga ordered the parish priests to undertake a thorough "reform of customs."¹⁰⁰ On subsequent visits, the archbishop reviewed the notes from his previous visit to confirm that the prescribed changes had taken place.¹⁰¹ Yet, as a native of Pátzcuaro, Árciga was no stranger to Purépecha Catholicism. Indeed, he was personally devoted to Pátzcuaro's Virgen de la Salud, a sixteenth-century evangelizing image made by Indians under the supervision of Bishop Vasco de Quiroga. In fact, the archbishop's first order of business upon returning from the Vatican Council in 1870 was to travel to her shrine (which doubled as the resting place of Quiroga) in order to fulfill a "sacred vow."¹⁰² Árciga's insistence upon frequent, face-to-face engagement with his flock, it should also be noted, owed much to his desire to follow in the footsteps of Quiroga, the sixteenth-century founder of the Michoacán Church and the evangelizer of the Purépechas, whose legacy Árciga and other Michoacán clerics increasingly claimed as their own. Árciga was an ardent admirer of Quiroga, and in later years he even undertook the revitalization of indigenous artisan industries founded by Tata Vasco in the archdiocese's Purépecha heartland.[103]

Bishop de la Peña, owing to his sickly nature, completed one pastoral visit in the Zamora diocese in a more halting and piecemeal fashion, visiting the northwestern parishes near the Jalisco border and the Purépecha parishes of the highlands between 1867 and 1869 and carrying out separate trips to the southern tierra caliente in 1872 and 1874.[104] The death of the bishop cut short a second pastoral tour in 1877. De la Peña's biographer, the Zamora canon Ignacio Águilar, highlighted the evangelical character of the bishop's pastoral visits, making note of the thousands of Catholics of all ages who received the sacrament of confirmation in each parish and lauding the "missionary" zeal of the bishop in imparting doctrinal lessons and spiritual exercises in order to prepare the faithful for confession and Communion.[105] Beyond the work of scrutinizing parish archives and ornaments and correcting the errors of priests and parishioners, then, de la Peña's visits also served as re-Catholicizing missions, reintroducing the rural laity to the fundamentals of the faith and readmitting the errant to the Catholic fold through the imparting of the sacraments.[106]

Concerns about the "de-Catholicization" of the rural laity weighed particularly upon the conscience of de la Peña, who in his scant pastoral writings demonstrated an overriding preoccupation with religious indifference and the spread of Protestantism.[107] In an 1873 circular, de la Peña's diocesan administration issued a stern warning to priests who had ignored earlier calls for more regular preaching of the Divine Word and more vigorous pastoral work to combat the sins and errors that afflicted many parishes—particularly drunkenness, immoral social mixing, and the diffusion of "impious" publications.[108] For de la Peña, the lack of proper clerical training and discipline were primary causes of such religious "decadence," and—as we have seen—he prescribed seminary reform and the professionalization of the rural clergy as the primary antidotes. But Catholic education, too, represented an important tool for the re-Catholicization of the rural laity. Thus, in response to the civil government's renewed push for secular public education after the restoration of the liberal republic, de la Peña made the case for the revival of parochial schools and the proliferation of new private Catholic schools. In 1873, he ordered his clergy to establish parochial schools in each of the diocese's head towns that lacked one and to promote the creation of private Catholic schools in smaller pueblos. Each parish priest would then head up a commission (of between three and five Catholic parents) tasked with performing a monthly review of each of the schools in his jurisdiction, in order to ensure proper administration. Catholic parents and rural priests were also enjoined to keep vigil over existing private schools, ensuring that they were staffed with good Catholic teachers and maintained uniformity in their instructional content, which should be based primarily on Father Jerónimo de Ripalda's catechism.[109]

The extant sources suggest such Catholic educational initiatives were relatively successful. Certainly, Catholic schooling was a priority of Morelia's Sociedad Católica (a lay educational and charitable association founded in 1868), which had opened a Catholic school in that city by 1874 and promoted other such projects throughout the archbishopric.[110] For the diocese of Zamora, the cases of Plancarte's schools—the girls' Colegio de la Purísima Concepción and the boys' San Luis Gonzaga—remain instructive of the kinds of educational projects pursued by clerical reformers, though the latter proved exceptional in terms of their success, recognition, and measure of external support.[111] Moreover, an 1877 report produced by the prefecture of Zamora identified twenty private primary schools in the district's seven municipalities, including four expressly Catholic institutions.[112] Of the remaining private schools, ten offered religious education.[113] Tangamandapio and Tancítaro also boasted Sociedad Católica–run schools by 1874.[114] Jiquilpan's school for indigent girls went dormant when its directors, the Hermanas de la Caridad, left the town in 1874, but new school projects were already underway in other parishes in the Zamora diocese, including Aguililla and Coalcomán.[115]

Catholic Devotional and Charitable Associations: Lay "Motors" of Restoration

If the clergy prohibited both involvement in politics and armed rebellion, it nevertheless encouraged other kinds of Catholic collective action to moralize society and fortify the Church. Such social engagement included not only lay-based Catholic schooling but also acts of charity, missionary efforts, and the revitalization of devotional practice. In a political climate that had severely restricted the Church's social and economic power, lay associations such as the Sociedad Católica came to play an increasingly important role in defending the faith and carrying out the Church's social mission. Explicitly invoked by the hierarchy in its collective pastoral of 1875, lay "collective action" represented a strategic adaptation to lerdista anticlericalism as well as a crucial link between high clerical projects and local religious change in Michoacán in the 1860s and 1870s.

Catholic associations in the second half of the nineteenth century were of two main types: those with a primarily devotional mission and those focused on social action. Pious or devotional associations, such as the Association of the Good Death, the Association of the Sacred Heart of Jesus, and the Association of the Perpetual Vigil of the Most Holy Sacrament (hereafter, the Vela Perpetua), were lay Catholic groups organized around particular devotions and supervised by parish priests. They utilized spiritual tools—collective prayer, expiation, vigil, and pious contemplation—to achieve primarily spiritual goals, such as preparing members for a "good death," funding Masses for deceased members, and organizing religious functions in their parishes. The associations' simplified and voluntary structure made them an effective alternative to the cofradías that had dominated local religion in Mexico in the colonial period, and they utilized (often Rome-endorsed) statutes that provided for tighter clerical control than the cofradía's more modern cousin, the *mayordomía*. While baroque cofradías depended on colonial corporations and entailed lands to sustain their activities, the new pious associations relied only upon the energies and dues of their individual members.[116] Not only did such a modernized structure find favor among clerical reformers, who had since the era of the Bourbon Reforms striven to replace Mexico's lavish and collective baroque religiosity with a more quiet, reserved, and individually focused piety, it also dodged the problems of liberal legislation, which had outlawed corporate property holding in 1856. Interestingly, though, ecclesiastical authorities sometimes struggled to keep up with lay innovation. The cathedral chapter of Mexico City, for example, fielding a request for a license for a new devotional association called the Vigil-Keepers of the Sacred House of Loreto in Mexico City in 1874, waded into an instructive internal debate about the nature of such new pious associations. Were they the same as confraternities? Did they come under Church jurisdiction? Or did their lay and voluntary character make them autonomous organizations? Would they become the target of anticlerical legislation? Ultimately, Archbishop

Labastida agreed with his provisor (chief canon judge): The new association was good for the faith, it did require hierarchical supervision, and its lay associational character meant it did not violate the Laws of Reform.[117]

The foundation of many of these lay organizations in Mexico predated the Reforma, a direct response to the decline of the colonial confraternities, yet their numbers and importance increased substantially during and immediately after the Church-state conflict of 1855–1877.[118] Parish records point to the increased presence of devotional organizations in both of Michoacán's dioceses in the 1870s. A local chapter of the Association of the Good Death appeared in Zamora in 1873, and the eastern Michoacán villa of Maravatío and the nearby mining town of Angangueo saw the foundation of the Association of the Patriarch Saint Joseph. Catholics from the latter population also created an organization called the Operarios del Santo Niño in 1874.[119] A group of pious Catholics in Sahuayo, meanwhile, founded a novel association devoted to a local image of Our Lady of Sorrows in the early 1870s.[120] The Vela Perpetua, which had enjoyed steady growth in Michoacán since its founding in nearby Guanajuato in the 1840s, also made further gains in the 1860s and 1870s, particularly in the diocese of Zamora. New or revived chapters appeared in Tangancícuaro (1855), Coalcomán (1867), Peribán (1868), Los Reyes (1869), Aguililla (1872), Buenavista (1873), Huango (1873), Pajacuarán (1874), Ixtlán (1874), and Presa de Herrera (1875).[121]

The Vela Perpetua, perhaps the most important devotional organization in Michoacán in the nineteenth century, was dedicated to the keeping of a quiet and constant vigil over the Blessed Sacrament in the parish church. Its simple economic structure and lay-focused recruitment strategy helped it to flourish in the liberal era. Devout laywomen (and some laymen) formed chapters of thirty-one dues-paying *cabezas del día*, each tasked with organizing the vigil over the Blessed Sacrament for one day of the month. Since the vigil was to be kept perpetually from 6 a.m. to 6 p.m., the cabezas del día recruited other parishioners to keep watch in thirty-minute increments. Dues payments were used primarily for purchasing candles for the vigil, subsidizing religious functions, and funding Masses for deceased members. In practice, Vela funds also paid for a host of improvement projects in their parishes, with chapters financing church repairs, purchasing new ornaments, and subsidizing the salaries of parish personnel.[122]

As subsequent chapters will show, the primarily female members of the Vela Perpetua in rural Michoacán often figured as a powerful constituency in their parishes by the 1870s. Not only did they often head up local restorationist projects (church rebuilding, antiprotestant campaigns, educational endeavors, etc.), they also helped to shape local religious tastes, promoting a more modern devotional style of quiet, internal contemplation. Their wide recruitment networks reached a large segment of parishioners, and through their organization of monthly Masses and yearly Corpus Christi festivities they helped to set the tone for local religious culture. Perhaps most importantly, excess Vela funds helped to keep many parishes afloat economically in an era that witnessed a steep decline in parish revenues as a result of liberal legislation that ended state enforcement of the tithe.[123] In large part, then, the restoration of the Catholic Church at the local level depended on pious laywomen organized into devotional associations.

Lay organizations with a social mission represented the other major form of Catholic associationalism in the nineteenth century, and here the Conferences of Saint Vincent de Paul and the short-lived but influential Sociedad Católica (1868–1878) loom large. Like the devotional associations, Catholic collective action in Mexico also predated the Reforma but took on an increasingly important role in the restorationist response to anticlericalism. Religious orders of the "active life" variety arrived in Mexico from France and Spain in the 1840s, organized under the auspices of the Congregation of Saint Vincent de Paul. The congregation comprised two religious orders, the male Missionaries of Saint Vincent de Paul and the female Hermanas de la Caridad (who worked as nurses in hospitals throughout the country), but in Mexico the Vincentians wasted no time in also organizing lay charitable societies like those in Europe. Male and female chapters of the new volunteer Society of Saint Vincent de Paul spread rapidly in Mexico in the 1850s and 1860s, with male foundations peaking in 1875. The female wing of the organization, the Ladies of Charity, proved even more successful, outpacing its male counterpart by the mid-1860s and forging new roles for middle-class laywomen in the public sphere. Vincentian volunteers fed and clothed the poor and sometimes paid their rent, sponsored apprenticeships for young men who wished to enter a trade, and visited inmates in prison and the sick in hospitals. Pious volunteers also accompanied their charitable practices with spiritual work—praying with the sick and imprisoned, offering basic doctrinal lessons to adults, teaching the catechism to the young, and exhorting the poor to reform their domestic habits.[124] This, then, was charity work as well as a means for Catholic restoration.

Historian Silvia Arrom identifies the states of Jalisco and Michoacán, especially, as hotbeds of action by the Ladies of Charity by the final decade of the nineteenth century, though regional data or documentation of Vincentian work on the ground for earlier periods remains scarcer.[125] Nonetheless, an 1869 report from the Central Council of the male Society of Saint Vincent in Mexico City touted the "prodigious growth" of the organization in the Diocese of Zamora, home to a regional council. Chapters had been established in provincial cities such as Uruapan but also rural towns like Tangancícuaro, Sahuayo, Jacona, and Cotija. Their social and spiritual work included burial services, offering "moral and material" aid to poor families, procuring marriages, legitimating children, catechizing children and adults, attending the sick and dying, serving in hospitals, and "sanctifying themselves with spiritual exercises."[126] As chapter 3 will show, moreover, the Vincentian Hermanas de la Caridad maintained a strong presence in several northwestern parishes in the Diocese of Zamora.

Evidence of the activities of the Sociedad Católica in Michoacán is more readily available. Founded in Mexico City in 1868 by a who's-who of the defeated Conservative Party, the Sociedad Católica represented a conspicuous shift in Catholic discourse—away from party politics and toward an accommodation of the rights-based liberal order with an eye toward forging a new Catholic civil society. Short-lived and unstable in its membership, the Sociedad nevertheless came to exert a disproportionate influence in some communities, and it established a powerful precedent for Catholic collective action that lived on in the social Catholicism of the succeeding generation. Availing themselves of liberal discourse on individual guarantees, the founders organized a voluntary association of Catholic citizens whose aim was to "defend and revive" Catholicism in Mexico.[127] The association adopted the centralized structure of the Vincentian Conferences, with regional hubs subject to a central council in Mexico City. Its various specialized commissions diffused Catholic periodicals and other literature, performed volunteer work in parish churches, and offered Sunday doctrinal classes for children. Its periodical wing was especially influential, since it gave birth to the widely diffused and long-lived *La Voz de México* (1870–1908), as well as several other, more ephemeral papers. Following the example of the Vincentian conferences, other commissions dedicated themselves to direct social and charity work, visiting prisons and hospitals, establishing night classes in basic education and Catholic doctrine for artisans and laborers, and working to counter Protestant conversions. A female auxiliary, the Sociedad Católica de Señoras, was created in 1869 to attend to poor and imprisoned women and to take up the education of Catholic girls. Perhaps most important, the Sociedad

Católica played a fundamental role in promoting the Mexican hierarchy's educational project. Under the auspices of its commissions for *colegios* and *instrucción gratuita*, the Sociedad began opening Catholic primary and secondary schools in Mexico City as early as 1870, providing an alternative to the schools run by the civil authorities.[128]

As we have seen, such educational initiatives soon reached into Michoacán, where the Sociedad's Zamora council proved particularly active in promoting Catholic schooling. Indeed, the Sociedad established a strong presence in northwestern Michoacán, thanks to the direct involvement of local clerics. Canon Águilar in Zamora established the association in January 1870, hosted its meetings in his private residence, and acted as its first president. Two other canons, Rafael Ochoa and Juan R. Carranza, served on the Literary Commission, and several Zamora priests served on other commissions. The Sociedad also counted the wealthy landowner Nicolás Dávalos, the lawyer Demetrio Méndez, and the "professors of medicine" José Antonio López de Lara and José Dolores Méndez Garibay among its members. Adapting the organization to the particularities of Zamora's religiosity, Canon Águilar placed the chapter under the spiritual protection of the Immaculate Conception, and he charged the *cultos* commission with planning a new temple dedicated to La Purísima Concepción.[129] This, then, was an organization that reflected the intimate ties between the region's bourgeoisie and the new diocesan hierarchy, and it quickly aligned itself to the Ultramontane, Marian piety that characterized the nascent church of Zamora.[130]

Notwithstanding such auspicious beginnings, however, the male chapter of the Sociedad Católica in Zamora quickly floundered and was overtaken by the female auxiliary.[131] The female auxiliary was elevated to the status of regional council in 1873, and by 1874 it presided over dependent chapters in Cotija, Coalcomán, Chavinda, Jiquilpan, Tangamandapio, and Tancítaro. The more active Zamora hub imparted doctrinal lessons to youth on Sundays, prepared children for their first Communion, visited inmates at the local jail and the sick at the hospital, and propagated the Association of the Good Death. The rural chapters shared Zamora's primary focus on Sunday doctrinal lessons, but two of them (Tangamandapio and Tancítaro) also established primary schools. Interestingly, several chapters also fomented particular devotions in their parishes. Cotija's chapter promoted devotion to the Good Death and arranged an annual religious service for the Month of Mary; Coalcomán's financed a service dedicated to Our Lady of Health; Jiquilpan's active and influential chapter paid for several services dedicated to Saint Joseph.[132]

For the Archdiocese of Michoacán, impressionistic sources suggest an active female auxiliary with a focus on similar charitable, educational, and devotional projects. Archbishop Árciga collaborated with the Ladies of the Sociedad Católica in Morelia on at least one occasion, delivering a special Mass to the Señoras and bestowing the sacrament of confirmation upon seventy children whom the Ladies had prepared for the rite. Morelia's female auxiliary also served as a regional council, presiding over chapters in Maravatío, Puruándiro, Tacámbaro, and Uruapan (which actually belonged to the Diocese of Zamora). Morelia's Sociedad offered Sunday doctrinal lessons, directed a primary school for girls, and imparted spiritual exercises and moralizing lessons to poor women. They prepared three hundred children for their first Communion, helped confirm seventy, and coached six couples in the legitimation of their unions. They also maintained the grounds at the Templo de la Santa Cruz and helped to fund the festivities of the Immaculate Conception. The Maravatío chapter, meanwhile, headed up fundraising activities for the Month of Mary celebrations, and it also promoted the Association of Saint Joseph.[133] Little is known about the work of the other suffragan chapters.

Conclusions

The preceding survey of the activities of Michoacán's lay devotional and social organizations demonstrates the importance of pious laymen and especially laywomen to the restoration of the Catholic Church in Michoacán, which increasingly turned away from the political to the spiritual and social spheres in order to revive the faith and combat "religious indifference" and Protestantism. But the uneven success of lay devotional associations and collective action in Michoacán also reflects larger patterns of religious change related to the spread of Ultramontane Catholicism. The reformist impulses that drove the activities of the Vincentian volunteers and the Sociedad Católica proved strongest in the diocese of Zamora, whose high clergy maintained close relations with both Pius IX's Rome and the provincial bourgeoisie. There, even isolated, rural parishes hosted new restorationist projects and embraced the devotional trends emanating from Ultramontane Europe. Zamora led Morelia in Catholic schooling initiatives, and it saw more new chapters of the Vela Perpetua founded in the 1860s and 1870s. Zamora's first bishop and Jacona's enterprising Father Plancarte also left ample evidence of their zeal for reforming the rural clergy, imposing orthodoxy and uniformity on popular religious practices, and importing foreign ideas and personnel. Meanwhile, the Europeanizing reformism that characterized Zamora made more tentative and partial gains in the ancient Archdiocese of Michoacán. The Sociedad Católica de Señoras stuck to provincial cities such as Maravatío and Puruándiro, and the Vela Perpetua expanded much more slowly in the archbishopric than in the rural parishes of Zamora.

Archbishop Árciga and Morelia's clerical elite certainly shared many of their Zamora counterparts' concerns for reforming the clergy and imposing new standards of devotion, as Árciga's pastoral writings and visits attest. In its fight against religious indifference, however, the archdiocese made more limited use of European devotional and institutional tools. Árciga would not turn over his seminary to foreign Jesuits, and he would not send Morelia's young men to Rome for priestly training. Nor does he appear to have promoted European-derived devotions such as the Sacred Heart of Jesus or the Immaculate Conception as stridently as other prelates in the center-west. Not coincidentally, Catholic restorationism in the Archdiocese of Michoacán retained a more localist, inward-looking character, prioritizing seminary reform in Morelia and Árciga's personal pastoral mission among his dispersed and diverse flock. Such an inward-looking reformism makes sense in light of the Morelia clerical elite's self-conception as the inheritors of the legacy of Vasco de Quiroga, the evangelizer of Michoacán and the spiritual father of the Purépechas. Conscious of their see's history and prerogatives, they saw the reform of religious manners as the work of local institutions, such as the seminary and the cathedral chapter. If Zamora's clerical reformers looked abroad for inspiration, Morelia's rediscovered their past and, like Quiroga, took the faith directly to the far-flung people of Michoacán through the pastoral mission. As the subregional case studies of this book will demonstrate, these distinct but related clerical projects, and their related patterns of religious change and Catholic collective action, affected the Religionero rebellion in complex ways. Ultramontane Catholicism rejected partisan politics and armed revolt in favor of spiritual renewal and the reconquest of civil society within a liberal juridical order. As such, its acolytes often disapproved of Religionero mobilization as a strategy for confronting lerdismo, and their reformist projects often threatened popular religious cultures. Yet the uneven fortunes of Catholic restorationism in Michoacán meant that such intraflock tension would vary greatly from place to place. Without this religious context, Michoacán's Religionero violence cannot be properly understood.

CHAPTER 3

A Levitical City Divided

Religious Culture and Religionero Violence in Northwestern Michoacán

In late March 1873, word of a "disorder" in Jiquilpan's Rancho de la Cofradía circulated through Michoacán's northwest. The commotion began with the abrupt departure of Jiquilpan's parish priest, the Franciscan friar José María Najar, who had resigned his post and was bound for the town of Cojumatlán. Though Rancho de la Cofradía lay only about five miles from the government offices at Jiquilpan, news of a tumult traveled first to the diocesan secretariat at Zamora, which then queried Crescencio García, the prefect of the district, about the conduct of Fray Najar. After investigating, however, García concluded that Najar had committed no crime. As far as he knew, all that had happened at La Cofradía was "the gathering of a multitude of families" from Jiquilpan and its surrounding ranchos to bid the friar farewell.[1] But if the groundswell around Najar—which drew a heavily indigenous and Afro-mestizo following—caused no concern for Jiquilpan's civil authorities, it did worry another group of *jiquilpenses*: a clique of devout but reformist local Catholics who had already petitioned the diocese for Najar's removal.[2] The pro-Najar faction, meanwhile, had lobbied even more fiercely on behalf of their beloved cura over the past two years, even alleging that the opposition only wanted a priest more in line with its "liberal" political affinities.[3]

Ultimately, Najar did leave Jiquilpan, replaced by the younger and more austere secular priest Pascual Bayllac, a French national. Jiquilpan's reformist faction had won this battle; yet the larger conflict between the supporters of Najar and Bayllac remained unresolved, and it would only intensify as the Religionero storm clouds gathered. Crucially, the two sides adopted radically different strategies for confronting lerdista anticlericalism after 1873, with the acolytes of Najar joining the rebellion while more reformist Catholics remained on the sidelines or even supported the government. Indeed, when Jiquilpan's homegrown Religionero chiefs targeted local civil authorities, the latter were more likely to be devout Catholic reformers than anticlerical *puros*. In short, the Religionero conflict in Jiquilpan was also a war within Catholicism, and the distinct Catholic and ecclesiastical cultures in dispute during the Najar/Bayllac affair helped to shape how parishioners responded to the lerdista state.

The story of Najar's removal complicates historiographical understandings of Church-state conflict in the Restored Republic. On the eve of Lerdo's codification of the Laws of Reform, we might expect to find parish priests at the center of local political struggles. Yet the conflict in Jiquilpan did not pit an intransigent priest and his fanatical followers against an anticlerical civil authority. Instead, the uniformly Catholic community suffered powerful divisions within the flock.[4] Moreover, these religious factions linked to political ones. In this case, the diocesan hierarchy at nearby Zamora cooperated with civil officials to investigate allegations of subversion against one of its priests, and Prefect García—a member of the district's small liberal circle—sided with the Franciscan friar against his accusers.

There is yet another reason for stressing such Catholic pluralism. The historical record preserves frustratingly little information about the Religionero leaders and even less about the hundreds of peasants, rancheros, and hacienda laborers that rallied to the cause in any given place.[5] Given such paucity, historians must make creative use of extant qualitative sources that illuminate the rural regions from which the revolt sprang. If we cannot come to know Ignacio Ochoa directly from the historical record, we must attempt to know, in the aggregate, his fellow jiquilpenses and especially his Religionero compatriots. The fragmented quality of nineteenth-century archives makes such a task arduous but not impossible. State- and municipal-level archives acquaint us with the "principal" families and key political actors of the rural townships; newspapers highlight moments of local conflict or controversy; and land division documents paint an intimate portrait of the changing agrarian landscape of rural Michoacán. Church records are perhaps the richest source for details about rural life and culture, and they prove particularly important for our understanding of the various revolts of 1873–1877. Hence, this chapter utilizes parish correspondence, especially, to analyze the religious cultures of northwestern Michoacán during the Reforma and Restored

Republic. It demonstrates that, although the region's conservative, Catholicized political affinities served to buttress the Religionero movement in a general sense, the particular character of the revolt there also had much to do with local religious change and conflict within the Catholic flock.

Northwestern religious cultures were not timeless or internally uniform, but historical and complex.[6] The 1860s and 1870s saw the rapid diffusion through northwestern Michoacán of the Ultramontane reformism of the regional high clergy, though responses to such reformism proved highly uneven. The foundation of the Diocese of Zamora, in particular, made the region a laboratory for Catholic restoration, since the curia actively promoted a European-oriented, Marianist, and feminized style of piety. While some restorationist projects—such as church rebuilding or doctrinal lessons for children—unified the region's diverse flock, others created deep divisions, often along ethnic, class, and gender lines. Indeed, the more internalized, affective, and cosmopolitan style that was favored by Ultramontane priests and laypeople often represented a grave threat to indigenous and Afromestizo Catholics and their more old-fashioned (often mendicant) pastors, whose baroque religiosity now faced pressure from both within and without the Church. Through their involvement in the Religionero movement, then, such baroque Catholics not only resisted state anticlericalism, they also implicitly protested the Romanization of Mexican Catholicism from on high. Hemmed in by liberal legislation that threatened to sever the ties between communities and their divine patrons, on the one hand, and by new forms of officially sanctioned piety that relegated their cultic traditions to the sidelines, on the other, the baroque Catholics of northwestern Michoacán rallied to the Religionero cause.

In geographical terms, this chapter focuses on the political districts of Zamora and Jiquilpan and their rural environs in the Bajío Zamorano.[7] It begins by introducing the zone and its principal towns and considering the region's patterns of political organization and agrarian relations. After a brief recapitulation of the Religionero revolt in the region, the chapter then analyzes the cultural and religious patterns that helped to make the area a Religionero stronghold and assesses the spiritual characteristics of its rebelliousness. It pays special attention to the role of the Catholic restorationist projects pursued by the new diocese of Zamora, which inadvertently opened a spiritual rift between baroque constituencies and more reformist, Ultramontane priests and parishioners. The diocesan assault on baroque religion was particularly ferocious in northwest Michoacán, where a powerful

Map 4. The district of Jiquilpan in Michoacán's northwest. R. Sánchez, *Mapa del distrito de Jiquilpan de Juárez* (1896). Courtesy of the Mapoteca "Manuel Orozco y Berra," del Servicio de Información Agroalimentaria y Pesquera, SAGARPA, Classification No. 197-OYB-7234-A.

clique of clerics subjected Indian festive traditions to a kind of Ultramontane trial by fire. Favoring an internal and private (albeit clerically run) religion, the reformers thus paradoxically joined the liberal critique of the baroque-minded clergy and its Purépecha and Afro-mestizo constituency. In order to demonstrate how religious change and conflict within the flock affected the development of the Religionero revolt, the chapter ends by revisiting the case of Jiquilpan—home of the largest and most tenacious gavillas in the state—where political partisanship reflected distinct pious habits.

An attention to religious dynamics should not obscure other factors affecting the revolt. Agrarian pressure, especially, deserves close attention, given the economic dynamism of the Bajío Zamorano in the nineteenth century and the coincidence of the revolt with the implementation of liberal land-division laws statewide. However, the structuralist reading that has dominated the analysis of the rebellion misses important religious factors, and in northwestern Michoacán in particular, agrarian pressure alone lacks sufficient explanatory power.[8] It can be shown, for instance, that northwestern political revolts corresponded closely to secularization drives throughout the mid-nineteenth century and that the local Religionero revolt in particular coincided with the high point of the ritual year (January to May). Further, where communities were divided over the revolt (such as in Jiquilpan), Religionero partisanship and nonpartisanship followed a specific baroque/Ultramontane axis. In sum, the case study that follows endeavors to demonstrate not only what is lost through strictly materialist interpretations of the revolt but also what is to be gained by adding religious ones to the constellation of factors that drove local conflict.[9]

Northwestern Michoacán to 1873

The ethnic and religious conflicts that characterized the departure of Fray Najar in 1873 had deep historical roots in northwestern Michoacán. A zone of high demographic dynamism and ethnic diversity, northwest Michoacán had been contested terrain for centuries. Prior to the Spanish conquest, for instance, Teco- and Sayulteco-speaking peoples disputed the region with settlers from the Nahua confederation of central Mexico before the expanding Purépecha Empire brought the territory into its orbit in the fifteenth century.[10] By the time Spanish conquerors under Cristóbal de Olid arrived in the 1520s, the region contained a patchwork of ethnolinguistic communities, a pattern that the Spaniards further complicated through the establishment of encomiendas and settlements, intermarriage with the local populace, and the importation of enslaved Africans to work the abundant plains south of the great Lake Chapala.[11]

Embracing the rich plains and valleys of the Bajío Zamorano, the fertile marshlands of Chapala to the northeast, and the mountainous folds of the Trans-Mexican Volcanic Belt to the south and west, northwestern Michoacán was a historically dynamic region, beginning as an outpost of the Chichimeca frontier before developing into an agricultural center and finally a commercial hub tied to the mining zones of Guanajuato and Zacatecas.[12] It fostered a bifurcated plains/highlands pattern of settlement typical of the Spanish project.

Lowland communities such as Jacona, Jiquilpan, Sahuayo, and Guaracha, given in short-lived encomienda to Spanish conquerors, received a steady stream of Spanish and African immigration and were slowly transformed into mestizo-dominated towns and haciendas by the coming of Mexican independence in 1821.[13] In contrast, Zamora and Cotija lacked indigenous antecedents altogether and were founded by small groups of Spanish families in the late sixteenth century.[14] Meanwhile, surrounding indigenous communities such as Quitupan (Jalisco), Tacátzcuaro, and Jaripo, and the Meseta Purépecha communities of Chilchota and Tarecuato, looked down on the burgeoning Spanish agricultural projects from the highlands.[15]

Despite such broken terrain, however, the settlements of northwestern Michoacán were tied together through trade, relations of patronage and compadrazgo (fictive kinship), and, above all, through religious solidarity. Franciscan missionaries evangelized much of the region, and their influence marked religious life for centuries after their arrival. In the 1590s, crown officials congregated many Indian communities into larger religious units administered by Franciscans. The latter, under the guidance of Bishop Vasco de Quiroga, instituted indigenous cofradías, trained the neophytes in the Spanish artisan trades, and directed the construction of Indian hospitals and chapels.[16] The Franciscans' utopian religious project put down deep roots in Michoacán, and the hospitals and their attendant chapels (often dedicated to the Lord or Lady of Health) came in large part to define popular religiosity among the indigenous communities of the northwest. Marian, Christological, and titular saints' devotions with an indigenous cast helped constitute unique local identities, which were reinforced each year through public, communal observances of feast days, often replete with idiosyncratic local dances, masquerades, oversized plaster puppets called *mojigangas*, music, and plenty of alcohol.[17] Patron saints, bestowed upon towns by the Franciscan missionaries or chosen by parishioners for their spiritual efficacy, opened up lines of communication between communities and the divine and became focal points of local identity. To give but one example, it was by such a process that Jacona's Virgin of the Root, a driftwood image hauled out of Lake Chapala and put to use in abating an epidemic of typhus in the seventeenth century, came into being as a symbol of Purépecha Christianity.[18]

Such a hybrid indigenous-Franciscan religiosity could not remain aloof, however, from the religious influences of ordinary Spanish settlers and the enslaved Africans brought to grow sugar cane and raise cattle on the southern shores of Chapala. At Guaracha, for example, the porous borders separating the extensive (96,000 hectare) hacienda of the same name and its sizable African population from the shrinking Indian communities of Jiquilpan and Sahuayo allowed for substantial intermixing and cultural hybridization.[19] Over the course of the eighteenth century, the Afro-mestizo population in and around Guaracha exploded and became enmeshed in the increasingly Hispanized society based in the larger towns surrounding the great estate, though trade networks and the festive calendar made social mixing with Indians inevitable. In the cultural realm, such demographic dynamism and intermixture resulted in a syncretic, baroque religiosity focused on public, collective worship and funded by ethnicized sodalities such as the indigenous cofradía of San Cayetano and the Afro-mestizo/artisan cofradía of the Lord of Esquipulas, both in Jiquilpan.[20]

This mixed society was largely the product of intensive agricultural and livestock development on several estates formed in the sixteenth century, above all Guaracha. Conflict between the masters of Guaracha and other haciendas and the surrounding indigenous communities began early and recurred often throughout the colonial and early national periods. At issue was both the haciendas' expansion at the expense of Indian communal lands and—during the viceregal period—the mixing of African hacienda laborers with members of the indigenous pueblos.[21] Indian communities in the shadows of the estates maintained their communal political autonomy and festive economies more successfully by renting out parcels of their ever-shrinking lands to hacendados and mixed-race rancheros. Such a strategy proved untenable in the long run, however, and when Michoacán's state government implemented liberal land division laws in 1827–1828, steady encroachment and the expenses of continual litigation against usurpers encouraged several communities to sell off their holdings.[22]

Historians have generally understood the liberal agrarian legislation of the Reforma period—which mandated the breakup of corporate properties controlled by indigenous communities and the Catholic Church—to have heralded the end of the long period of "agrarian decompression" that characterized the early decades of Mexican independence, since it opened once-protected Indian lands to unscrupulous hacendados, ambitious rancheros, and foreign investors.[23] For Soto Correa, such renewed agrarian pressure explains both the plague of "social banditry" that gripped Michoacán in the Juárez years and the Religionero uprising itself.[24] If indeed the Religionero conflict followed closely on the heels of Michoacán's 1869 push for disentailment under the auspices of Ley Lerdo, however, it cannot be reduced to an inevitable peasant reaction to agrarian pressure. The relationship between agrarian, religious, and political conflict was complex and sometimes contradictory. Indeed, as the following pages show, land-division documents suggest that the rebellion was emphatically not agrarian in some places, only partially agrarian in others, and differently agrarian (i.e., linked to agrarian decompression, not compression) in a third category of localities.

In many places, the 1869 reparto law did not represent a watershed in agrarian relations and caused only minor conflict. Unlike other parts of Michoacán, where the land division process faltered until after the fall of Maximilian, the northwest underwent significant subdivision in the 1830s. These early repartos mostly affected communities already under pressure from mestizo settlement and hacienda expansion. The indigenous communities of Jiquilpan, Guarachita, and Cojumatlán, for example, had already subdivided and sold most of their communal lands by the time Michoacán's state government issued its 1869 disentailment law.[25] The remaining properties, such as those belonging to defunct Indian hospitals and cofradías, were mostly divided and sold between 1869 and 1872, and though long-standing legal conflicts with Guaracha resurfaced during the division, the communities carried out the process relatively quickly and without significant conflict.[26] A short-lived intracommunal dispute in Jiquilpan in 1869, for example, featured two factions competing over which one could most quickly and effectively complete the reparto, something that the community "unanimously" supported.[27] Here and elsewhere in northwestern Michoacán, Indian communities accepted disentailment, albeit grudgingly, as a way out of their unresolvable disputes with Guaracha, whose encroachments would likely continue while the legal process dragged on. The communal leaders of Totolan, an indigenous barrio of Jiquilpan situated to the east of the municipal seat, explained in 1869 that they could not complete the reparto as they desired, because the majority of their lands were under litigation with Guaracha. The reparto law forbade the division of lands in legal dispute, and Totolan thus carried out a partial reparto and retained its status as an indigenous community.[28] More distant Indian pueblos such as Tacátzcuaro and Tingüindín, meanwhile, largely sidestepped the process in the 1870s, and they did not face serious pressure to subdivide until the mid-1880s.[29] In the Zamora district, the community of Pajacuarán initiated a reparto in 1869 but abandoned it in 1870 in the face of a dispute with the San Simón Hacienda and an intercommunal conflict over control of the process. The land division could not proceed until 1879.[30]

Nevertheless, other indigenous communities in the Zamora district did suffer increased agrarian conflict after 1869, when the reparto resurrected decades-old disputes both within communities and between communities and encroaching haciendas and ranchos. Yet such agrarian conflict did not find outlet in Religionero mobilization. In Jacona, for example, communal leaders expressed their support for liberal land laws as a way to safeguard their properties from neighboring haciendas, including the Tamándaro estate owned by the Plancarte clan (of ecclesiastical fame).[31] The Plancartes had used the 1830s reparto to usurp the majority of the "vast terrain" granted to the community by the King of Spain in 1539.[32] The community sought legal redress in the intervening decades, demanding that the usurpers show their titles, but in response the hacendados colluded with civil officials to harass communal leaders. In 1866, don José María Plancarte (Father Plancarte's older brother) arranged for judicial officials to imprison Indian leaders for planting crops on disputed lands and then took advantage of the community's impotence to extend his holdings further.[33] In their defense, communal leaders in Jacona invoked republican rights in their petitions to the governor, underlining their conviction that the liberal government wanted to "rescue us from ignorance and stupidity, offer us enlightenment, and put us in the category of true citizens."[34] A corrupt oligarchy and its powerful friends in local government, however, stood in the way of such Indian redemption. If anything, therefore, agrarian pressure in Jacona bred popular liberalism rather than the pro-Church conservatism that animated the Religionero revolt.

In other cases, agrarian tensions were often inseparable from religious and political considerations, and the local Religionero revolt can therefore only be considered partially agrarian. In Chilchota, for example, communal leaders also claimed they could not undertake a reparto because of long-standing legal conflicts within the community stemming from a division carried out in 1839. In the decades following the earlier reparto, the community's *apoderado* (legal representative), José María Reyes Constantino, had used the Ley Lerdo to denounce and adjudicate local cofradía lands, which he parceled out to his grandchildren. The Reyes Constantino family then rented these ex-cofradía lands to third parties, charging "exorbitant rents" that they funneled into "fomenting revolutions" of the liberal variety. The apoderado's adversaries even claimed that Reyes Constantino had given six hundred pesos to Juan Cervín de la Mora during his 1871 campaign against Juárez.[35] In Chilchota's case, then, intracommunal religious, political, and agrarian conflicts were intertwined, since Reyes Constantino's use of liberal laws and support for liberal political movements damaged the community's religious economy and estranged him from other community members. In fact, dozens of Chilchota women signed a carta de protesta against the Laws of Reform in 1874, and the town produced a Religionero uprising in June 1875.[36] If the agrarian question was an aggravating factor in the development of the revolt there, it could not be neatly disentangled from religious matters, and it did not revolve around the familiar narrative of hacienda encroachment and peasant resistance.

Although the encroachment of haciendas on pueblo lands constituted an old and widespread problem in northwestern Michoacán, the surviving archival evidence does not suggest that hacienda-pueblo relations had reached a boiling point by the time of the 1869 repartos or that the Ley Lerdo necessarily represented a watershed for indigenous people.[37] Rather, land division served to reinforce processes already under way—increasing mestizaje and the decline of indigenous communal holding in Jiquilpan, Sahuayo, Guarachita, Pajacuarán, and Jacona; intracommunal conflicts over land, politics, and religion in Chilchota; and slow but steady encroachment by haciendas and communal retrenchment in Indian towns such as Tingüindín and the barrio of Totolan. Furthermore, Religionero militancy does not map neatly onto agrarian tension. Jiquilpan district fostered considerably more Religionero ferment than did Zamora district, despite the latter's more conflictual agrarian relations. Even where agrarian conflict ran high, finally, it could often not be separated from religious and political conflict, as the case of Chilchota again demonstrates. Strictly materialist readings of the Religioneros both fail to account for the complexity of local circumstances and overstate the power of hacendados in steamrolling indigenous communities.

It should be noted that a significant portion of the region was undergoing agrarian decompression during the mid-nineteenth century.[38] Even the massive Guaracha Hacienda, for example, had at the time of the rebellion only begun to recover from a period of serious decline in the mid-nineteenth century, and its heights of prosperity (and exploitation) lay decades into the Porfirian future. Facing fiscal insolvency in 1861, its owner had sold off half of its terrain to ambitious mestizo rancheros who would go on to form the townships of San José de Gracia and Cojumatlán.[39] The misfortunes of estates such as Guaracha thus directly benefitted the dynamic ranchero class that would come to characterize much of the "JalMich" (Jalisco/Michoacán borderlands) region. They led to an explosion of ranchero smallholding, spurred mestizo immigration, and encouraged further commercial growth in the market town of Sahuayo and the muleteering hub of Cotija. In such places, indigenous populations fell off sharply over the course of the nineteenth century, a trend that coincided with a dramatic increase in mixed-race but culturally Hispanic artisans, arrieros (muleteers), and rancheros. This group, more than the Zamora-based hacendados of Guaracha, Platanal, and San Simón, represented the most dynamic sector of northwestern Michoacán's population in the Restored Republic.[40] Highly mobile and ambitious, mestizo migrants moved south from the Altos de Jalisco region into Jiquilpan district, and, when opportunities began to run dry, they continued south into Michoacán's tierra caliente and coastal sierra.[41] Such demographic changes soon affected local cultural patterns, too, as values and traits associated with the central-western rancheros—individualism, rigid gender roles, a reverence for private property, and a more orthodox religious outlook—slowly rose to preeminence.[42] When the upper clergy of Mexico City and Zamora—many of whose members originally hailed from Michoacán's northwest—set in motion a movement to restore the faith, they therefore found a receptive audience in this mestizo middle stratum of rancheros, merchants, and muleteers.[43] The triple processes of demographic change, agrarian transformation, and religious revivalism reinforced each other, and a diverse corner of central-western Mexico began moving toward the relative cultural homogeneity and Ultramontane Catholicism associated with Zamora and the JalMich region today.[44] If the transformation of northwestern Michoacán into a bastion of mestizo Ultramontanes accelerated in the second half of the nineteenth century, however, it did not go uncontested. Rather, the social dislocations inherent in such processes caused deep rifts in the region, even among populations widely given to Catholic conservatism. Simply put, conservatism was not homogeneous, and the version that rose to prominence in northwestern Michoacán—Ultramontane in its Catholicism, pragmatic in its engagement with the liberal state—collided with a more ethnicized, communal conservatism inherited from Michoacán's past.

Political history further complicated the cultural milieu. By the time of the revolt, northwestern Michoacán had a long history of involvement in the national partisan turmoil of independent Mexico. A major battleground for the independence struggle—the territory of insurgents Francisco and Gordiano Guzmán—the region subsequently developed deep partisan divisions mirroring those of the larger nation. Unlike the Guzmáns' nearby liberal hamlet of Tamazula (Jalisco), however, the Jiquilpan and Zamora

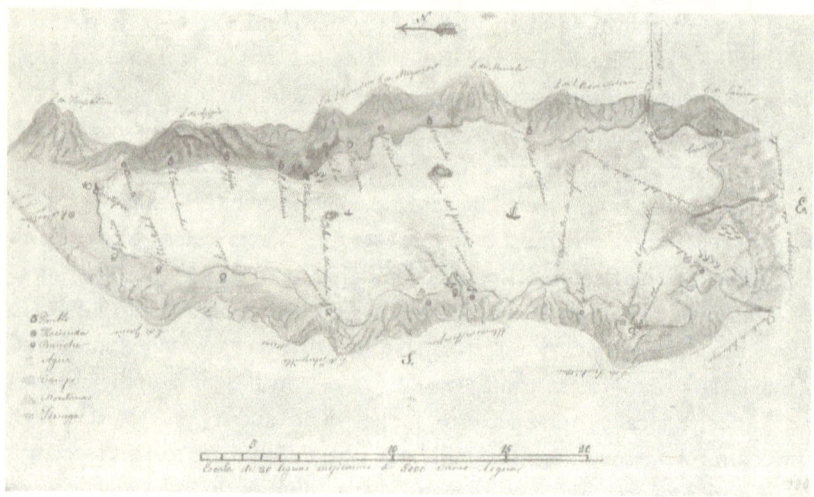

Figure 5. The Chapala region and its dynamic patchwork of haciendas, ranchos, and indigenous pueblos. *Plano de la Laguna de Chapala* (date unknown). Courtesy of the Mapoteca "Manuel Orozco y Berra," del Servicio de Información Agroalimentaria y Pesquera, SAGARPA, Classification No. 380-OYB-7233-A.

districts displayed a marked tendency for political conservatism throughout the nineteenth-century conflicts. Foils to the federalist/liberal Guzmáns, the region's homegrown centralist and conservative caudillos included the royalist Diego Moreno Jaso, owner of Guaracha; Francisco Velarde, owner of the opulent Buenavista Hacienda and supporter of Santa Anna and Maximilian; and Anastasio Bustamante. Moreno Jaso and his allies battled the Guzmáns sporadically throughout the 1830s and 1840s, each side recruiting locals through patronage networks and the dreaded *leva* (draft). Moreno Jaso used the abundant land and capital from the Guaracha estate to stage conservative movements, and he recruited heavily among the hacienda's labor force.[45]

The Reform Wars affected the region more unevenly. The Jiquilpan district largely served as a passive transit point for partisan armies in the 1850s. Indeed, the most important event of 1854 for the residents of Jiquilpan, Sahuayo, Cotija, and Tingüindín was not the publication of the Plan of Ayutla but the tour of Bishop Clemente de Jesús Munguía, who conducted the region's first pastoral visit since 1810.[46] Zamora, in contrast, suffered famously at the hands of liberal intruders and—later—republican troops fighting Maximilian's Intervention. Antonio Rojas's brief occupation of 1861, during which he reportedly kidnapped priests in Zamora and Purépero and forcibly conscripted dozens of pacíficos, left a bad taste in local mouths. In Jacona, Ayutla rebels under Juan García robbed tithing revenues, and Nicolas de Régules's republican troops and their female companions profaned the parish church of Charapan and robbed ornaments from the inventory in 1865.[47] Such outrages surely added to Zamora's historic distaste for liberalism, which they had blamed for the divine punishment of cholera outbreaks in 1833 and 1850.[48]

News of the triumph of the Ayutla Revolution in 1856 and the subsequent constitutional congress were generally received poorly in Michoacán's northwest. Conspirators from Sahuayo, Cotija, and Jiquilpan fomented a small, ephemeral revolt against the Juárez government in 1858. Félix Zuloaga's Tacubaya movement, though it fared poorly throughout Michoacán, briefly held Zamora in the summer of 1858.[49] The French invasion of 1862, meanwhile, fostered more durable conservative political mobilization. The imperialists quickly gained a foothold in Michoacán with the adhesion of Zamora and La Piedad, and although the nearby Jiquilpan district changed hands between liberal and Interventionist forces several times between 1863 and 1866, its towns tended to favor the empire overall.[50] Zamora proved one of the last redoubts of the Intervention (one of whose authors was local son Pelagio Labastida). For conservative Catholics in Michoacán's northwestern parishes, such loyalty to the Intervention was rewarded handsomely in 1862, with the creation of the new diocese of Zamora, a development that would tighten clerical control over key religious constituencies and create new avenues to spiritual power and influence for devout northern michoacanos.[51]

In the absence of more experienced and moneyed local leaders like Moreno Jaso (who had died in 1846), the region's imperialist mobilization took on a more decentralized, ad hoc style. Small-scale imperialist leaders appeared in the zone, including Mazamitla's Rafael Alcázar and Jiquilpan's future Religioneros Francisco "El Nopal" Gutiérrez and Eulogio Cárdenas. Cárdenas earned the rank of colonel in Maximilian's army, under whose auspices he gained fighting experience and access to weapons and recruiting networks.[52] Yet it also made him a persona non grata in his hometown when liberals returned to power in 1867. To make ends meet, he turned to holding up mule trains on the road between Cotija and Mazamitla with a small gang of bandits.[53] Knowledge of the physical and human geography of this particular corner of Michoacán would serve him well later, though, when he would establish a Religionero headquarters at the small lakeside community of San Juanico and direct a series of attacks on nearby government detachments.

Cárdenas's "banditry" aside, popular political mobilization in northwestern Michoacán tended to coincide with strong bouts of state anticlericalism. Unlike the highly mobile but Pátzcuaro-based Religionero Abraham Castañeda, for example, who had joined the uprisings against Benito Juárez, the northwestern Religionero chieftains generally sat out the liberal rebellions of 1869–1870. Díaz's Noria rebellion of 1871, meanwhile, achieved almost no traction in the zone. Further, as we will see below, Religionero violence coincided with the climax of the ritual year. This is not to say that the region's Religioneros were ideologically pure.[54] However, compared with the rebels of Coalcomán (profiled in chapter 5), the northwestern rebellion displayed significantly more ideological cohesion, and its leaders proved less opportunistic.

The Religionero Revolt in the Northwest

Some of the most intense fighting of the Religionero conflict occurred in northwest Michoacán, which state and local officials considered "focal point" of the rebellion.[55] Patamban was the scene of Michoacán's first indigenous Religionero riot; and Jiquilpan district hosted the first formal uprisings in the state with the pronunciamientos of Florencio Gálvez, Eulogio Cárdenas, and Ignacio Ochoa in January 1874. After skirmishes with state troops, the Jiquilpan gavillas expanded their operations west to the Indian communities of Quitupan and Mazamitla (Jalisco) and east into sympathetic Indian communities in the Zamora district (especially Charapan and Chilchota). They recruited hacienda workers, indigenous peasants, and family members—rebel chiefs Narciso "Valeriano" and Teodoro "Quino" Mejía were cousins of Cárdenas and Ochoa—into their rapidly swelling ranks.[56] In June, new gavillas under José María del Río and Cesario Ceja appeared in the mestizo community of Chavinda, where they prevented new authorities from taking the protesta. In fact, the municipalities of Chavinda and Jacona were temporarily subsumed by the municipality of Zamora because district authorities "could not find a single person [in those communities] that wanted to attract the wrath of the fanatics by complying with the law."[57] A few months later, "El

Nopal" Gutiérrez joined the fray, after leading a jailbreak in Jiquilpan and rallying thirty prisoners to the cause of religion.[58] In Zamora, meanwhile, partisan conflict threatened to boil over into outright civil war in September, when municipal president Rafael Valdéz briefly jailed José María Ochoa and Jesús Plancarte, editors of the conservative *La Causa del Pueblo*, for "convening meetings to defame the government." Prefect Andrés Villegas Rendón later exchanged blows with Ochoa.[59] Ironically, *La Causa del Pueblo* had been established earlier that year in order to denounce the authoritarianism of local officials.

By the start of 1875, the Jiquilpan Religioneros had established rebel camps in San Juanico and on the Guaracha estate, and they began coordinating attacks on the plazas of Cotija, Tingüindín, Sahuayo, and Los Reyes, often with the help of scores of "plebeians" from the surrounding ranchos, pueblos, and haciendas.[60] In January, Ignacio Ochoa's gavilla assassinated Sahuayo municipal president Sabas Osio, a committed anticlerical who had violently suppressed Catholic protest, curtailed the local custom of reciting the rosary in public, and fined Franciscan friar Miguel del Castillo for carrying the viaticum in procession.[61] Liberal reports indicated that the "fanatics" of Sahuayo celebrated the assassination with music and festivities outside Osio's house.[62] In response, the federal army dispatched a force to Jiquilpan, but definitive victories eluded it.[63] Worse yet, the Religionero gavillas continued to multiply. The Zamora district witnessed new pronunciamientos by Purépero's Manuel Gutiérrez and the Zamora-based Blas Torres and Atilano Montes, and it suffered frequent incursions by the La Piedad–based bandit/rebel Francisco Vega.[64] In February, the rebels killed three municipal employees in Purépero and burned the municipal archives of Ixtlán and Chavinda.[65]

By Easter, the region was in crisis. Cárdenas and Ochoa sacked and burned Los Reyes in March with some six hundred rebels, half of whom military reports indicated were rural "plebeians" who had joined the movement spontaneously.[66] In Zamora, scores of men and women defied the Laws of Reform by marching through the streets praying on Good Friday, and a small riot attended the prefect's attempts to disperse the participants.[67] Shortly afterward, several hundred Religioneros under Blas Torres, Francisco Vega, and Manuel Ponce attacked the plaza of Zamora, taking the federal military detachment and local government completely by surprise. Political scandal followed: Zamora's municipal president was fired for ineptitude and cowardice, and Prefect Villegas Rendón was replaced with another Zamora liberal, Prudencio Casillas.[68] In Jiquilpan district, meanwhile, Ochoa's hundred-strong gavilla routed government troops at Cojumatlán, killing the treasury official from Tingüindín.[69] In May, Religionero forces cut down federal Captain Camilo Moreno and four other soldiers in a pitched battle at Rancho Caurio, east of Purépero.[70] Civil authorities abandoned their posts at Tingüindín and Sahuayo, and Jiquilpan's prefect threatened to pull the small military garrison out of the latter town completely if he did not receive reinforcements.[71] The revolt was rapidly spiraling out of control.

By May 1875, Religionero ranks had grown to over five hundred in Jiquilpan and three hundred in Zamora, and the appearance of veterans Benito Meza and Félix Venegas in rebel ranks signaled increasing Religionero professionalization in the northwest.[72] In response, civil and military officials turned up the pressure on civilian populations and led increasingly destructive attacks on Religionero strongholds. In April, the governor's office had instructed the prefect of Zamora to apply the ley de salteadores y plagiarios to civilians who aided the Religioneros, and in May the state legislature issued a circular mandating careful vigilance of civilian populations by district officials.[73] For its part, the army initiated a scorched earth campaign in the Jiquilpan district. Troops burned San Juanico and two other ranchos near Cotija in May and June, and Generals Prisciliano Flores and Nicolás de Régules toured the zone in late summer in order to reorganize garrisons in the towns most frequently threatened by gavillas and to take the fight to Meza at Guaracha.[74] During this time, federal troop levels in the northern districts swelled to nine hundred.[75]

The troop surge was partially successful, since it led Meza to split his army into smaller gavillas and move southward along the Sierra Madre del Sur into the district of Coalcomán. Subsequently, the Religionero general traveled frequently between San Juanico/Guaracha and the southern sierra in order to dodge federal persecution, but the threat he represented to Jiquilpan had not abated.[76] Meza and Cárdenas handed a small government expeditionary force what the army admitted was a "complete defeat" near Guaracha on June 11, after the force went to investigate false rumors of a minor gavilla and instead fell into an ambush of three to four hundred rebels.[77] The Religioneros captured several officers, dispersing most of the thirty infantry in the expeditionary force and killing several others. The government's own reports indicated that many of its soldiers joined the rebels.[78] In August, five hundred Religioneros attacked Cotija, burning houses at the edge of town in an attempt to drive out the federal garrison.[79] It took a major military collaboration—involving 150 federal troops and the National Guards of Quitupan,

Jiquilpan, and Cotija—to finally dislodge Meza's army from its principal stronghold atop the steep Cerro Blanco (in San Juanico) in October. The fighting lasted for eight hours. By late afternoon the Religioneros had abandoned their fortress and fled, but their heroic defense of Cerro Blanco was to be enshrined in a popular ballad ("The Laguna of San Juanico / Place of many snails / Where men come together / To fight for religion").[80] Reaching the rebel fortress, Colonel Calixto Mariles encountered four "young girls from Cotija," allegedly kidnapped by the Religioneros, and a multitude of "arms, munitions, equipment, food, papers, beds, etc.," used to supply and organize the rebellion.[81] This was a significant win for the government, though it merely displaced Religionero strength. Meza subsequently moved south and joined Antonio Reza for attacks on Apatzingán and Uruapan in November.[82]

By early 1876, though, the tide began to turn against the Religioneros. Escobedo's arrival in Michoacán heralded another troop surge and a major change of tactic. The general's indulto policy quickly began to thin Religionero ranks, as eighteen rebels laid down their arms in Jiquilpan in late January and dozens more did the same in Zamora in February.[83] Meza's secretary, Adolfo Sandoval, followed suit, reportedly telling the government that Religionero chiefs were facing mass defections as soldiers returned to their homes and fields. By the time government troops captured Meza in Los Reyes in February, the northwestern Religionero army had been severely weakened, and Ochoa could only muster eighty rebels for an attack on Jiquilpan.[84] Nonetheless, as we will see in chapter 6, the northwestern Religioneros proved key strategic allies for Porfirio Díaz, since they helped him both to overthrow the lerdista government and to broker alliances with Michoacán conservatives.

Díaz's alliance with the Religioneros made less sense after the successful reintegration of the region into the national fabric in early 1877, and the remaining bands were quickly neutralized. Still, the northwest had figured as a Religionero bastion throughout the conflict, and it had drawn a tenacious and diverse array of supporters, including Afro-mestizos from Jiquilpan, indigenous comuneros from Charapan and Chilchota, mixed-race hacienda workers from Guaracha, and rancheros from Cotija, Chavinda, and Zamora. Religionero armies could count on substantial civilian support in the northwest, as local officials frequently complained.[85] Eulogio Cárdenas frankly expected civil authorities at Cotija to collaborate with him, declaring in a letter to the local police commissioner in late 1874 that he "[knew] all of the vecinos of Cotija, and they all [had] religion."[86] Messengers carrying military communications between Quitupan and Jiquilpan, when not detained or killed by gavillas, were often harassed by the residents of both towns' outlying ranchos.[87] In the wake of the Religionero assault on Zamora in April 1875, Prefect Villegas Rendón confided that he could not trust many of the prefecture's messengers, much less any local rancheros or peons, since they had a "record of hiding even the most insignificant [rebel] movements" from officials.[88] In August 1875, meanwhile, military authorities discovered that rebel uniforms were being manufactured in the home of a Cotija vecino.[89] In short, the government fought on hostile terrain in the northwest, where Religionero sympathy ran especially high.

Of all probable motives in the northwest, religion loomed largest. Yet an attention to Catholic pluralism is especially important, given that the Catholic elite of northwestern Michoacán—whose interests dovetailed most closely with the official Church and whom we might therefore expect to find in the vanguard of any armed defense—failed to join the rebellion. "Principal vecinos" such as Antonio Mora, Judge José Dolores del Río, Judge Amadeo Betancourt, and Jesús Ordónica, all of Jiquilpan, served the government throughout the crisis, although they all either resisted implementing the Laws of Reform locally or renounced their own protestas subsequently.[90] Francisco Farías, a surgeon from Cotija in good standing with the diocesan Church, served as municipal president of Cotija and later died fighting Eulogio Cárdenas.[91] Meanwhile, dozens of Jacona vecinos—many of them supporters of Father Plancarte—signed a manifesto in January 1876 declaring their intention to defend the town from Religionero depredations.[92] Despite clear religious convictions, then, the region's educated Catholic elite largely declined to take up with the Religioneros, perhaps hoping to defend Catholicism from within local government or content to pursue educational, spiritual, or charitable forms of Catholic restoration within the secular order.

Despite rumors about Zamora elites' ties to the rebels, the Religionero conflict retained an organic, plebeian character. Even if conservative Zamora or Morelia news editors supported Religionero leaders in their editorials, they proved ill-disposed to join a decentralized, popular revolt that often targeted committed Catholics who held government posts. Middle-class, Ultramontane Catholics therefore tended to remain on the sidelines or even actively support the government, while indigenous and Afro-mestizo Catholics took the fight to the "protestants."[93] The crucial distinction, as the following sections argue, was that many of the Catholics who opted for the path of armed rebellion in the Zamora and Jiquilpan districts were precisely those who found themselves marginalized by the Catholic restoration that had taken hold in the region. Catholic reformism divided the region's faithful into popular and Ultramontane camps that struggled for control of the faith. Even if these factions agreed that the liberal regime represented a grave threat to the Mother Church, they nevertheless adopted distinct strategies in rallying to her defense. To be sure, more orthodox rancheros joined the revolt in places such as Cotija, Zamora, and Chavinda, but the larger regional movement was substantially more indigenous and popular. In short, the imbrications of northwestern conservatism and Catholicism dictated multiple—sometimes violently contradictory—responses to lerdismo. This point can be brought home by cross-referencing the public and military half of the historical record with the ecclesiastical half.

"That Repugnant Mix of the Ancient and Modern"

Northwestern Michoacán's religious culture was in a state of flux in the 1850s, with colonial piety already subject to various Ultramontane intrusions. This reformism accelerated significantly after the creation of the new diocese of Zamora in 1862, but before then its inroads were more tentative and isolated. Zamora, for example, experienced a spiritual reawakening in 1850, when it was believed that the intercession of the Virgin of the Immaculate Conception helped to halt a deadly epidemic of cholera morbus. After the epidemic, Zamora's ecclesiastical and civil leaders proclaimed La Purísima Concepción the patroness of the city in celebrations that doubled as a rebuke of liberalism and an affirmation of a newfound Levitical identity.[94] Such events stimulated a project to restore the parish church (later converted to diocesan cathedral), an endeavor that necessitated a thorough reform of the parish's finances, which Father Francisco Enríquez had found in complete disarray when he took over in 1843.[95] Enríquez's fashionably neo-Gothic refurbishment, which according to a clerical contemporary resulted in "one of the few parish churches in this bishopric free of that repugnant mix of the ancient and modern," cost some 100,000 pesos, mostly procured through pious donations. The town also saw the foundation of a Nazarene *beatería* (a community of laywomen who take informal religious vows and wear religious habits) and a religious school in 1851.[96]

The famed Ultramontane cleric Clemente de Jesús Munguía, then bishop of the diocese of Michoacán, also helped to stir Michoacán's northwestern communities to pious action. His 1854 pastoral visit produced important administrative changes, stimulated local renovation projects, and reversed the instability and diocesan neglect that had followed Mexican independence. Notably, the bishop created a new parish in Cotija on the eve of his visit there (separating it from the parish of Tingüindín), prompting the building of a new parish church to replace the small colonial chapel. Not to be outdone, Cotija's neighboring parishes each followed suit with their own improvement projects, which included a new organ for the parishioners of Jiquilpan and a major renovation for the antiquated parish church of Sahuayo.[97] Tlazazalca also replaced its colonial chapel with a completely new parish church, one that Canon José Guadalupe Romero considered the pride of the diocese.[98] In the course of his visit, Munguía also proved keen to correct devotional "errors" and revitalize dormant practices. In Chilchota, for example, he ordered the priest to reposition the baptismal font, repair the temple's deteriorated roof, and rectify the disordered archive. He also instructed the priest to revive the cofradía of Nuestro Señor de la Salud (which financed the town's Indian hospital), name a new mayordomo, and put the account books in order.[99]

An ardent defender of Church sovereignty, Munguía's chief tasks were to straighten out parish finances and shore up the legal status of Church properties that had been thrown into question by Mexican liberalism. In practice, this meant setting the rural clergy to work regularizing Church property records to protect them from litigation or intervention, often by asking their benefactors to sign more clear-cut legal documents.[100] Thus did the "Lawyer of the Church" attempt to prepare local populations to resist the coming onslaught of anticlericalism.[101] In Cotija, for example, it was not dormant indigenous cofradías but a host of improperly documented *obras pías* that caught the bishop's attention, a detail that helps us to understand the particularly Levitical character of local religiosity. Though Cotija did not lack devotions of a more communal appeal, such as the Virgin of San Juan located in the eponymous indigenous and Afro-mestizo barrio to the northeast, the documentation from Munguía's visit reveals a predominance of *capellanías* founded by individuals or families and funded with lands from private estates.[102] These entails provided regular Masses for the souls of deceased family members or funded feast-day celebrations for a preferred family saint. They also provided a way to subsidize the clerical careers of elite local sons: wealthy *cotijenses* from the Oceguera, Valencia, and Carranza families sent younger members into the clergy, who could theoretically be counted on to say the Masses provided for in their families' capellanías.[103] Such an individualized and family-based religiosity was befitting a burgeoning town of mestizo muleteers and rancheros, whose distinctive character must not have evaded diocesan authorities when they decided to separate Cotija from the Purépecha parish of Tingüindín in 1854.[104]

Neither the baroque cofradías nor the capellanias of northwestern Michoacán would survive the coming storm of the Reforma, which mandated their disentailment as part of the nationalization of Church property. To a significant extent, however, the threat to the faith and clergy represented by the liberal attack on Church entailments was blunted by the establishment of the Vela Perpetua and other lay associations, which grew explosively in Michoacán in the second half of the nineteenth century.[105] The Reforma era saw new Vela chapters open in Buenavista, Tangancícuaro, Pajacuarán, Ixtlán, and Tlazazalca.[106] In 1867, Bishop de la Peña explicitly instructed the parish priest of Charapan to establish the Vela after civil unrest precipitated a hasty removal of the Blessed Sacrament from the parish church.[107] Diocesan authorities clearly viewed the Vela as a means to protect the Blessed Sacrament, then, but the association was also a boon for parish coffers. The Vela of Tangancícuaro supplied Father Pedro Arroyo with a thirty-peso personal loan in 1860 and purchased minor accessories for the church in the 1870s.[108] In Sahuayo, the women of the Vela offered excess association funds to cover the expenses of the priest's assistant in 1869.[109] In 1873, Jiquilpan's Vela paid for the monthly services of an organist and cantor, the regular washing of the clerical vestments and fabrics, and a Mass on the last Thursday of each month. In May of the same year, they also purchased a new pallium, several candlesticks, and other ornaments for the parish church.[110] The parish priest of Pajacuarán established the Vela Perpetua in May 1874. By February 1876 the association had a nearly 300-peso surplus, which the priest put to use in the construction of a new church building.[111] In large part, then, the Catholic restoration taking place in the northwest depended on pious laywomen, who were taking up the slack left by the decline of tithing revenue and the colonial cofradías.

Female devotional and political ferment in the northwest did not stop with the Vela Perpetua, however. As chapter 2 demonstrated, the Vincentian Ladies of Charity maintained a strong presence in the diocese of Zamora. Zamora's regional council oversaw chapters in Tangancícuaro, Jacona, Purépero, and Cotija whose charitable and doctrinal efforts complemented those of clerical reformers.[112] In Jiquilpan, the Hermanas de la Caridad played an important role in advancing the Church's social mission, and—despite their brief tenure there—they came to wield significant influence within the parish. The Hermanas arrived in Jiquilpan in 1865 and were invited to take the helm of Casa de la Caridad, a new asylum and hospital founded by the wealthy widow Juana de la Parra in 1850. The Casa de la Caridad supplanted the dilapidated Indian hospital, and the more modern vision of its Vincentian directors contrasted sharply with the baroque character of the original. Attending the sick and sheltering Jiquilpan's orphans, the Hermanas also took an active role in providing Catholic education and diffusing their maternalist style of piety.[113] Female chapters of the Sociedad Católica also took root in Zamora, Cotija, Chavinda, and Jiquilpan, where the association shared various members with the Vela.[114] Indeed, after the Hermanas left Jiquilpan for exile in January 1875, the Sociedad took over many of their educational operations.[115] Jiquilpan's Sociedad even purchased a special carriage for transporting the viaticum, allowing the parish priest to bypass the prohibition of public worship when conferring last rites on believers in their homes.[116]

A Marian devotionalism of a particularly nineteenth-century hue also made an appearance in the zone. Far removed from the popular Marian images from Mexico's spiritual conquest, the new avocations such as the Immaculate Conception tied rural Mexicans into the larger imagined community of the *orbe católico* and mobilized their devotional energies for the purposes of expiation for modern sins and retrenchment against the advance of liberalism. Zamora, in particular, cultivated a burgeoning devotion to Mary Immaculate, who was patroness of both the city and the local Sociedad Católica chapter and, increasingly, a symbol of local resistance to liberalism.[117] Fray Miguel del Castillo built a new altar to the Immaculate Conception in the parish church of Sahuayo in 1868, and he petitioned the diocese for a plenary indulgence to stimulate local devotion.[118] Notably, reformist priests in the northwest also endeavored to introduce and promote the Month of Mary, a cycle of pious acts, rosary praying, and reflection observed each May. A Jesuit innovation of the eighteenth century, Month of Mary devotions spread slowly in Europe before papal indulgences in 1812 and 1822 carried the practice throughout the Catholic world.[119] In northwestern Michoacán, the practices became increasingly common after Bishop de la Peña promoted them in an 1870 circular.[120] Month of Mary devotions were established in Purépero in the late 1860s and in Pajacuarán in 1874.[121] In Charapan, Father Juan Bautista Morales used the Month of Mary to promote devotion to the Immaculate Conception.[122] Jiquilpan's Cosme Santa Anna energetically promoted pious exercises of enclosure, reflection, and atonement as part of the Month of Mary devotions in 1870, which he hoped would replace the raucous indigenous celebrations associated with the feast day of the Virgin of Totolan.[123]

Lay Catholics also introduced new Marian devotions and associations, for which they sometimes received clerical support. As the Religionero conflict raged all around his native Sahuayo, Crisóforo Villaseñor, the son of a prominent local family, petitioned his priest and the diocesan authorities to sanction a new association dedicated to the Virgin of Sorrows. This new association deserves close attention, since it gathers together all of the threads of the Ultramontane devotionalism that was fast overtaking northwestern parishes. As his priest, Macario Saavedra, explained, Villaseñor's association began with just a handful of devotees, who gathered for Friday evening prayers at the parish church, where they "implore[d] the Most Holy Virgin of Sorrows for peace and the conversion of all sinners." The devotion then spread "to all of the barrios of the town," moving to a private home after Municipal President Sabas Osio prohibited public praying at the temple doors in early 1874. Each meeting concluded with "the Holy Rosary, seven *salves* to the seven sorrows of Mary, a Mass to the same Virgin, five *credos* to the five wounds of Christ, and three to the Sacred Heart of Jesus." Diocesan authorities at Zamora approved the new association and granted a plenary indulgence to its practitioners, though they also ordered the parish priest to supervise all exercises.[124]

This, then, was the veritable face of northwestern Michoacán's ascendant devotionalism—clericalist, heavily feminized and Marianist, centered on expiation, quiet reflection, and prayer, and often utilizing a modern associational structure. When not actively stripping away the corporate, entailed structure of baroque Catholicism, local reformers sought new ways to fund their parishes and to avoid open conflict with the civil authorities over public worship, all the while leading a revival of the faith along Ultramontane lines. As we saw with the 1875 collective pastoral, such an approach entailed a tacit concession to liberalism—Catholics ceded the public space to civil society while pursuing their restoration internally and behind closed doors. Yet through their appropriation of the principles of voluntary association, they could also counter the "ills" of modern liberalism through work in civil society, such as the visits of Zamora's Sociedad Católica to the inmates of the local prison or the renowned Catholic schools founded by Father Plancarte in Jacona. Crucially, Catholic modernizing efforts sometimes even dovetailed with state ones. Father Plancarte spearheaded civil improvements such as street paving, garden planting, and rail development alongside his religious and educational reforms in Jacona, earning him praise from liberal journalists.[125] A writer at *El Siglo Diez y Nueve,* for instance, contrasting Plancarte's modernizing ethic with the supposed obscurantism and corruption of Michoacán's rural clergy, even compared the priest of Jacona to Monseigneur Bienvenu, the progressive and compassionate prelate from Victor Hugo's *Les Misérables.* Asking rhetorically why Plancarte, the European-educated son of an elite family, came to Jacona, the editorialist affirmed:

> To rebuild the temple that serves as parish church with a magnificence to which Catholics are accustomed, without any resources except the will of the priest and the work of the vecinos; to pave the plaza and streets of the town, since he is often observed with a crowbar in one hand and a breviary in the other; to plant and cultivate new gardens, acclimatizing flowers unknown among us . . . ; to found and sustain, almost out of his own pocket, a girls' school, with the understanding that the destiny of society depends on the education of the woman; also to establish, as he is currently doing, a boys' school, diverging in its teaching [methodology] from the systems . . . decreed at the Council of Trent.[126]

Here was a priest that liberals could love: politically disinterested, socially enlightened, and privately pious.

Notwithstanding such liberal praise for Catholic modernization, Ultramontane reformism did not find universal favor among the flock, especially as it gained in intensity after the creation of the diocese of Zamora. Certainly, many restorationist projects—efforts to restore dilapidated church buildings or rekindle pious devotion—found broad support among the diverse clergy and laity of northwestern Michoacán. Yet Ultramontane projects aimed at "reforming" popular customs or curtailing popular religious expression caused significant controversy. Not only did the new devotional styles promoted by reformers threaten to eclipse older forms of Catholicism still practiced by thousands of Michoacán Catholics, their ascendance also coincided with a sustained attack from within the Church on indigenous and Afro-mestizo devotions and communal control over religious functions and spiritual property. In Cotija, for instance, indigenous parishioners from the barrio of San Juan complained that the mayordomo of the cult of the local

Figure 6. Ultramontane modernity. Father José Antonio Plancarte y Labastida developed a plan to connect Jacona to Zamora via *tranvía* (mule-drawn tramway) in 1877, drawing praise from liberal editorialists and support from the state government. Ignacio Ochoa Villagómez, *Copia del plano y perfil del proyecto de tranvía de Zamora a Jacona* (1878). Courtesy of the Mapoteca "Manuel Orozco y Berra," del Servicio de Información Agroalimentaria y Pesquera, SAGARPA, Classification No. 2135-OYB-7234-A.

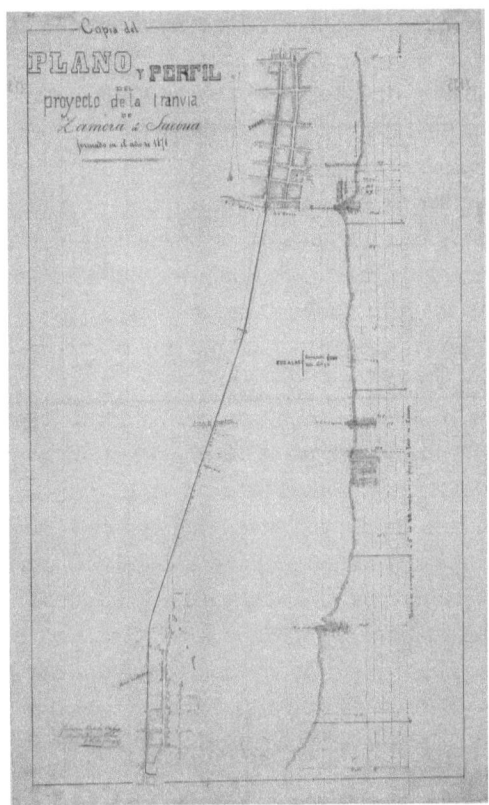

virgin mistreated the image, and they accused the mayordomo and their priest of failing to carry out the Virgin's feast day celebration in 1870.[127] Queried about the matter, Father Benigno Tejeda denied the very existence of an "indigenous community" in San Juan, and he insisted testily that he would never have tolerated abuses of the image in any case. Instead, he characterized the petitioner as a man of "bad faith" who only wanted to gain control of the cult.[128] Bishop de la Peña agreed to disregard the petition.

Jiquilpan's embattled indigenous community also faced increasing threats to its spiritual property from within the faith. In 1871, a non-Indian beneficiary of the 1830s reparto sought to expand his holdings at the expense of the old Indian hospital, one of the few remaining pieces of communal patrimony in the town. Hemmed in on three sides by private plots, the chapel of the hospital retained only one entrance, through the ancient cemetery, and it was this cemetery that don Francisco Torres targeted for purchase. Writing to Bishop de la Peña in February, communal representative Julián Pulido insisted that what don Francisco really coveted was the entire plot of the old hospital, which he could gain after sealing off the chapel's sole entrance and rendering it useless. Meanwhile, Torres argued that the diocese—not the community itself—retained ownership of the property and that it should sell it to him because the Indians committed a host of abuses in the chapel and cemetery, including using them as stables for animals.[129] If the Indians managed to hold on to their chapel temporarily, it was only because the beloved Fray Najar came to their defense.

Indigenous and Afro-mestizo Catholics faced increased scrutiny in the spiritual realm, as well. Catholic reformers appear often to have agreed with the Sahuayo liberal Sabas Osio, who in 1874 critiqued the region's popular religiosity as overly external, wasteful, and given to disordered communal excess.[130] Bishop de la Peña mandated that Corpus Christi processions in Patamban only take place behind church walls in 1866.[131] He issued the same instructions to Chavinda and Tacátzcuaro in 1874, and he forbade the priest of Chavinda from seeking permission for the processions from the civil authority.[132] In July 1874, Sahuayo Catholics discovered that the feast day of their patron saint, Santiago, would no longer include a procession, "public diversions," or traditional mock battles between Moors and Christians (the latter replete with Afro-mestizo cultural influences), since, in the words of the diocesan secretary, such "profane entertainment prejudice[d] the Church service, distracting the faithful with objects not only unrelated to devotion and piety but opposed to them."[133] For his part, Father Plancarte, the most ambitious of the region's Ultramontane reformers, suppressed the custom of Carnaval in Jacona in 1866. In 1869–1870, meanwhile, he took his iconoclastic reformism to the indigenous communities of the Meseta, literally subjecting the unique saints' images used by the community of Cherán in their Corpus Christi processions to a kind of inquisitorial auto de fé. Bishop de la Peña, in Cherán for a pastoral visit, appears to have participated directly in the act. As the priest recorded in his diary:

> The 27th of May a Pontifical Mass and Corpus were celebrated, and I took great pains to correct the thousands of abuses that occur among the Indians during such occasions. To that effect, I made the Indians bring to the sacristy all of the monsters that under the title of saints

[traditionally] adorned the thousand steps of the procession, in order to see if His Holiness [the bishop] would concede them indulgences. When the sacristy was packed with those effigies, I came in with the bishop, and arranged—as did the housekeeper of Don Quijote—an examination not much less severe than that suffered by the library of the Hidalgo of Manchego.[134]

Plancarte admitted that such iconoclasm brought him into conflict with some community members, but he refused to back down. Indeed, he repeated the tactic in the indigenous barrios of Jacona in 1871, "reforming" the "imperfect" saints' images in the town's two colonial chapels and suppressing their feast-day customs.[135] Plancarte's antagonists, led by the community's principales (traditional communal leaders), accused him of removing saints' images from church buildings, overcharging for religious functions, and even excommunicating pueblo leaders for challenging his authority.[136] Meanwhile, Plancarte's defenders—who included mestizo vecinos as well as contingents of indigenous men and women—averred that he had simply "perfected" the images (meaning, perhaps, the replacement of indigenous images with more European ones or the removal of unorthodox clothing or accoutrements) and removed the mojigangas from the church. His reform of customs, meanwhile, aimed only at curtailing the "drunkenness, irreverence, scandal, and disorder" that had traditionally accompanied the titular saint's feasts.[137] Lastly, if the priest had excommunicated the principales, it was because they had availed themselves of cofradía lands, renting them out to third parties and keeping the profit for themselves.[138] Diocesan officials in Zamora sided with Plancarte. Not only did the bishop not take any action against the priest, he ultimately entrusted Plancarte with the task of intervening in religious conflicts in other, nearby parishes on the curia's behalf. In the midst of the scandal in Jacona, for example, diocesan authorities sent Plancarte to Pajacuarán to investigate reports that Father Macario Saavedra unduly intervened in the affairs of the indigenous community and insulted the indigenous sacristan, demanding that he turn over the key to the sacristy entrusted to him by communal leaders. After taking several depositions from "honorable" vecinos of Pajacuarán, Plancarte sided with the priest, and the curia of Zamora declared the matter closed.[139] In disputes over communal religious autonomy and clerical control, then, the diocese of Zamora proved little disposed to find for Indian principales.

An emphasis on uniformity and orthodoxy also motivated diocesan actions against baroque religion and indigenous corporate privileges. In June 1870, the curia of Zamora had prohibited Corpus Christi processions held outside of the eight days marked by the Roman liturgy, thereby suppressing the local custom of holding Corpus Christi feasts on other days, often according to local agricultural cycles. Diocesan Secretary Rafael Ochoa explained the change explicitly in terms of a desire for "uniformity."[140] The decree precipitated aggrieved petitions by parishioners in Ixtlán and Pajacuarán, but the diocese stood firm.[141] On other occasions, de la Peña's administration demonstrated hostility to arguments about indigenous corporate privileges. In 1871, in response to falling parish revenues in the wake of the liberal Reforma, his administration issued a circular emphasizing the duties of Catholics to pay their tithes and obventions. The circular indicated that "the descendants of the first inhabitants or indigenes" who had since colonial times been exempted from the payment of "pensions" for the maintenance of their parish priests would no longer enjoy that privilege, and they would be expected to pay their tithes at the same rate as all other classes.[142] Circular Number 24 of the same year further clarified that indigenous parishes designated as *de tasación*—which had traditionally paid tithes in kind according to a fixed quota recorded in colonial documents called *pindecuarios*—had ceased to exist with the "emancipation of the republic."[143] The decree effectively put the diocese in line with liberal anticorporatism, and it was bitter medicine to some Purépecha communities in the diocese. Indeed, in January 1873, Canon Manuel Bruno Gutiérrez warned de la Peña that indigenous communities of the Meseta Purépecha had met the demand for "integral" tithe payment with a complaint to the prefecture of Uruapan, which had in turn issued a circular ordering municipal authorities to curtail the abuses of priests who demanded payment of what the liberal government considered simple voluntary donations.[144] (The Iglesias Law of 1857 had prohibited the charging of clerical fees to poor parishioners.) In Charapan, Purépecha leaders had long insisted that their priest adhere to the colonial pindecuario.[145] Conflict erupted in the midst of the French Intervention, when priest José María Sandoval and members of the indigenous community reportedly came to blows over the issue of clerical fees. Sandoval had refused to carry out traditional religious functions, and in return community members had filed complaints to both civil and ecclesiastical authorities. Even after the diocesan decree of 1871, the community's critics of "arbitrary" obventions managed to get both Father Morales and his successor, Juan de P. Álvarez, removed from the parish through lobbying efforts with the diocesan curia. Presbyter Rafael Méndez, meanwhile, who had colluded with diocesan authorities to compel the Indians to clean and restore the chapel of San Andrés before they received the necessary license for the patron's Mass, was accused by one of his own parishioners of sedition against the government and arrested by the prefect of Uruapan in March 1875.[146]

Tensions over clerical fees and communal autonomy clearly contributed to unrest in the lead-up to the Religionero revolt, and priests did not always emerge victorious in their imbroglios with parishioners, as the Charapan case makes clear. Yet more subtle changes in religious culture also worked against baroque Catholics. Across the region, the old religious topography wrought by Franciscans, Purépecha neophytes, and African slaves and freedmen was falling into decay. Adjudication of cofradía lands under the Ley Lerdo—as occurred in case of Chilchota—hindered communal traditions and imperiled the communities' relationship to the divine. Indian hospitals and cofradía lands in Jiquilpan and Sahuayo also passed into private hands or were destroyed, and Jiquilpan's ancient chapels of the Holy Spirit, San Cayetano (both serving indigenous barrios), and the Lord of Esquipulas fell into disrepair and disuse.[147] The latter devotion, it should be noted, had exerted a strong pull on local artisans, such as the family of Eulogio Cárdenas.[148] Thus, in the midst of a regional wave of church restorations—often funded by voluntary donations and Vela funds—some chapels and their religious constituencies were forgotten, and these were disproportionately indigenous and Afro-mestizo.

Few parish priests demonstrated the level of reformist zeal of Father Plancarte, whose European training had set him on a collision course with the popular religiosity of rural Mexico. Other clerics embraced the reforming spirit to varying degrees, and some priests clung to older models of devotion or resented the Zamora hierarchy's centralism or the newfound spiritual influence of female religious associations. As Bautista García has noted, Plancarte's Europeanizing reformism rubbed many local priests the wrong way, since it constituted a critique of their own customs and educational models.[149] In Pajacuarán, the priest and native son Juan N. Pérez supported several indigenous men in their bid to remove Father Saavedra for meddling in communal affairs.[150] Jiquilpan's Fray Najar objected to the increasing power of the Hermanas de la Caridad in shaping parish culture, as we will see below. Sahuayo's Fray Castillo, meanwhile, collided dramatically with diocesan authorities over jurisdiction and rank in 1871. Bishop de la Peña had asked him to discipline Fray Manuel Chacón, a member of the

Franciscan Colegio Apostólico de Zapopan (Jalisco), where Castillo served as president. Castillo refused, claiming that the Franciscans of Zapopan were autonomous from the diocese and that if the bishop continued to tread on their sovereignty, Castillo and his fellow Franciscans who served as parish priests would renounce their posts en masse.[151] Further, in order to underline Franciscan autonomy, Castillo invoked his order's connections to Rome. A bold stand against diocesan centralization, Castillo's letter betrays an understanding of the Church better suited to the colonial period, when a host of semiautonomous corporations jockeyed for position under the banner of the distant King. Tellingly, male religious such as Castillo and Najar attracted the same popular constituencies that rallied to the Religionero rebellion. In Sahuayo's case, in particular, Fray Castillo's arrest by civil authorities for his infraction of the Laws of Reform triggered the rebellion of Florencio Gálvez.[152] Jiquilpan's Fray Najar was also a favorite among the Religionero leadership, as we will see below. In short, Religioneros and baroque Catholics more broadly favored certain kinds of priests—old-line mendicants, native curas with strong ties to their communities, and those committed to upholding local traditions. Ultramontane clerics, by contrast, tended to be younger, secular priests, as in the cases of Plancarte, Macario Saavedra, Cosme Santa Anna, and Benigno Tejeda, and they attracted more mestizo constituencies.[153]

Thus, a widening spiritual—as well as class and ethnic—gulf separated Catholics of Ultramontane and baroque stripes in northwestern Michoacán during the Reforma era, and the latter faction found itself in decline as the former rose to prominence. Such intraflock dynamics had important ramifications for the Religionero rebellion in the region. This is not to say that the two sides went to war in 1874. As we have seen, northwestern populations—especially those of Cotija, Sahuayo, and Chavinda—generally supported the rebellion, at least passively, and they almost uniformly rejected the protesta. It does, however, offer clues about what kind of Catholics would have chosen armed rebellion against the Lerdo administration, and—conversely—what kind would have sat out the struggle or instead pursued Catholic revival through the new associational means available to them. Indigenous and other baroque Catholics faced a more existential threat, since the processions they performed to renew a pact with local deities were being banned, and those they might have expected to sympathize with them—their priests and diocesan leaders—did not. Ultramontane Catholics, meanwhile, were engaged in an unpleasant jurisdictional dispute with the state, but since the region's restorationist project provided ample opportunities for them to counter lerdista anticlericalism in the arena of civil society, they saw little need to join the revolt. Though the task is arduous and its results partial, historians can establish patterns of partisanship by comparing names of known Religionero militants—identified by local civil officials or appearing in lists of pardoned rebels—with the signatures that appear on petitions addressed to diocesan authorities in Zamora. For the case of Jiquilpan, which closes this chapter, this methodology shows that baroque Catholics, especially, preferred rebellion to restoration. Already in decline and facing further pressure from both liberal legislation and Catholic reformism, they sought new paths to local political power and religious leadership, including armed revolt.

Religion and Partisanship in Jiquilpan

As we saw above, the Religionero revolt in the northwest attracted a diverse constituency, ranging from mestizo rancheros to Afro-mestizo artisans to indigenous comuneros.[154] However, military correspondence and prisoner rolls suggest that Indians and Afro-mestizos were especially prominent in the rebel ranks. Afro-mestizos from the Cárdenas family served as principal Religionero leaders in the Jiquilpan district, and indigenous communities such as Charapan, Chilchota, Tarecuato, Cherán, and Pajacuarán all provided key support to the rebels or—in the case of Chilchota—led their own rebellions.[155] "Plebeian" populations from the heavily Afro-mestizo Sahuayo and the Indian village of San Pedro Caro joined Ochoa and Cárdenas in early 1875.[156] Meanwhile, indigenous comuneros in Mazamitla frequently sheltered Cárdenas and Ochoa, and they later did the same for the porfirista Donato Guerra.[157] The heavily indigenous villages of Guarachita and Tingüindín produced the middling Religionero leaders Manuel Sandoval and Esteban Farías, respectively.[158] Finally, indulto lists from 1876 suggest that many rank-and-file Religioneros came from Jiquilpan, Mazamitla, Tizapan, Guarachita, and Jaripo.[159] In short, Religionero activity tended to be especially intense in indigenous zones and in towns where baroque religiosity faced an acute challenge from Ultramontane reformers (Pajacuarán, Cherán, Charapan). Further, as the case of Jiquilpan demonstrates, conflict between baroque and Ultramontane factions sometimes served to divide communities internally over the nature of the faith and the proper strategies for its defense.

Jiquilpan merits close scrutiny, since it produced one of the most important and durable movements in the state (that of Cárdenas and Ochoa). Further, divisions between rebels and government loyalists ran especially deep in Jiquilpan's municipal seat during the conflict. Yet as the vignette that opened the chapter demonstrated, such divisions were as much spiritual in nature as they were political. At the center of the local religious conflict stood the ageing Franciscan Fray José María Najar, whose departure from the parish in the fall of 1872 ignited a dispute between two local factions that each sought to influence the bishop's choice about the administration of the parish. Najar, who also belonged to the Colegio Apostólico de Zapopan, had come to administer Jiquilpan in 1867, the first Franciscan to do so since the secularization of the parish in 1775. Beloved by many parishioners, Najar was also reputed to perform miracles, including bilocation and the averting of natural disasters through prayer.[160] In 1871, he had promoted the construction of a new tower on the seventeenth-century parish church, a project for which he raised over 3,000 pesos in pious donations. By this time, however, Najar was beginning to show the deleterious effects of old age. Cosme Santa Anna, who had served as his temporary substitute in 1870, had complained to diocesan authorities that Najar suffered a "perturbation of reason." Further, he tried too hard to please his flock, a trait that led to him to perform "a multitude of religious acts with too much frequency" at the expense of his "principal tasks" of preaching and administering the sacraments.[161] Such defects, according to Santa Anna, owed as much to Najar's monkish character as to his old age and mental illness. "Accustomed [as he is] to the things of the cloister and of propaganda, as a missionary, he seems to be out of his element [here], and therefore lacking the composure necessary to be at the front of a parish in the present circumstances."[162] Perhaps apprised of his substitute's attempt to have him replaced, Najar returned unannounced to Jiquilpan in May 1870 and demanded that Santa Anna turn the parish over to him.[163] The friar reportedly demanded proof of Santa Anna's recent confession before he would allow him to say Mass, and he treated him as a "usurper or a thief" for insisting on collecting obventions for parish services rendered.

Najar successfully regained control of the parish in May 1870, when diocesan authorities honored his request to return, but his enemies soon multiplied. In late 1872, he once again left Jiquilpan on a temporary license to attend to his "broken health," but his acolytes suspected that the diocese would replace him permanently, something a significant number of vecinos desired.[164] Specifically, a contingent of parishioners headed by Sor Magdalena, prioress of the Hermanas de la Caridad, sought Najar's ouster and lent vocal support to his eventual replacement, Pascual Bayllac, a French secular priest who had come to Michoacán during the Intervention.[165] The conflict originated with a daytrip to the wilderness organized by the Hermanas for the children under their care, a project that Najar and his followers opposed because it would expose the children to "every class of danger" and allow the social mixing of boys and girls.[166] Sor Magdalena and her defenders, including the women's chapter of the Sociedad Católica, members of the Vela Perpetua, two former leaders of the Indian community, Julián and Juan Pulido, and the "principal" vecinos Antonio Mora, Amadeo Betancourt, and Jesus Ordónica, decried Najar's "capriciousness and hostility" toward the Hermanas. The women of the Sociedad Católica worried that perhaps Najar's known "sickness of the brain" could be to blame for his hostile and inconstant temperament with the Hermanas.[167] Interestingly, the liberal firebrand Sabas Osio himself even joined the petitioners in their final missive against Najar in December 1872, a document that claimed that the friar's "systematic hostility" to the Hermanas had emboldened their other enemies in the parish, who resorted to verbal insults and the pasting of "immoral broadsides" around the city.[168]

If he had rankled various groups within the community of Jiquilpan—and especially the activist Hermanas and the women of the Sociedad—Najar also aroused great sympathy in others. Members of Jiquilpan's indigenous community were the friar's most steadfast supporters. Communal representatives Herculano Mendoza (Jiquilpan) and Mateo Mariscal (Totolan) had likely not forgotten that the friar had come to their defense when don Francisco Torres attempted to buy their cemetery from the diocese the year before. Further, Najar had respected their "immemorial" custom of celebrating the Virgin of Remedios's feast day with a procession from her chapel in Totolan to the parish church in Jiquilpan, an act whose purpose was to "beseech [the Virgin] for her divine intercession in bringing a good rainy season."[169] Indeed, it was Najar's substitute and enemy, Cosme Santa Anna, who had asked the bishopric for a permanent prohibition of the practice in 1870, favoring more austere Month of Mary exercises. The conflict over the Remedios celebration likely played a role in the drama that unfolded between the two clergymen in late May 1870, when Najar returned suddenly from his sick leave.

Najar's second leave of absence, in August 1872, and the news of his ouster in July 1873, stimulated a flurry of petitions in his favor, and these reveal even more interesting patterns of spiritual and political partisanship. Joining the communal leaders in their petitions in favor of Najar in 1872 and 1873 were a collection of "vecinos" (here, non-Indians), among whose signatures we find the future Religioneros Teodoro Mejía, Francisco Amezcua, M. Macías (perhaps Manuel, a Religionero chieftain from Jiquilpan), and several members of the Cárdenas family, including Eulogio's brother Francisco.[170] Women signatories were notably absent. Together with the pueblo's communal leaders, the petitioners lamented the "scandalous" and "disgraceful" attacks on Fray Najar by his enemies. But the "vecinos of Jiquilpan in association with the Indian community," as they introduced themselves, reserved the harshest words for the acolytes of the new priest, Pascual Bayllac, whom they charged with "indifferentism, or rather, modern enlightenment." Najar's detractors preferred the French curate because of his fame as a "liberal," they insisted. Further, Bayllac himself had humiliated the supporters of Najar from the pulpit, blasting them for failing to contribute sufficient donations to the Month of Mary functions and calling them "idolatrous" for their devotion to Najar.[171]

Perhaps most tellingly, the petitioners pointed to discouraging changes in Jiquilpan's religious culture with the departure of Najar. The latter had ensured that the festivities of Corpus Christi and the Virgin of Remedios "were always splendid and brilliant," a feat the new priest proved either unwilling or unable to replicate.[172] Further, under Bayllac the Vincentian conferences (chapters) of both sexes established by Friar Najar had been extinguished, along with a Catholic school for indigent girls run by the women's conference. The school had served girls whose lack of even basic financial support barred their admission to the Casa de la Caridad. Even the practice of the evening rosary had fallen into decline.

The see of Zamora, which considered the friar too old and sick to continue at the head of such an important parish, ultimately failed to hear the protests of the petitioners. Najar left the town in March 1873, much to the vexation of the "multitudes of families" that came to bid him farewell at the Rancho de la Cofradía. The outpouring of support for Najar concerned unnamed local Catholics, who reported a possible disturbance at la Cofradía to the Diocesan Secretary. Yet if Najar's departure did not signal the beginning of a "disorder" in Jiquilpan, it did reveal the spiritual fault lines that would help define Religionero violence after 1874.

The imposition of the protesta and the expulsion of the Hermanas were experienced as a profound crisis by Catholics on both sides of Jiquilpan's spiritual divide. However, different kinds of local Catholics responded to the crisis differently. As we have seen, several of Najar's supporters, exponents of a more male-run, ethnicized, and corporatist devotional style fast becoming obsolete in Jiquilpan, resorted to armed revolt in the defense of their embattled and changing faith. Not coincidentally, such Catholics looked to Najar for spiritual leadership, a man whose training and devotional style aligned him with baroque constituencies. Prominent acolytes of the French priest Pascual Bayllac and the more Ultramontane devotional style he favored, meanwhile, figured among the defenders of Jiquilpan's plaza and municipal offices. Such men seem to have pined for more harmonious Church-state arrangements predicated on moderate liberalism and a more modern, spiritualized Catholicism less given to intransigence. Don Antonio Mora, Jesús Ordónica, and Pedro Ortíz, all signatories to anti-Najar petitions, were installed as municipal authorities in January 1875, and Amadeo Betancourt retained his post as a judge of the first appeal. Miguel Cárdenas Sánchez, another pro-Bayllac signatory, served as a district tax official until he was assassinated by Religioneros in April 1875.[173] Meanwhile, the former communal leader and Bayllac supporter Juan Pulido served in the Jiquilpan National Guard.[174]

In general, then, Bayllac and his more Ultramontane supporters did not join the Religionero rebellion. Whether we should consider them "liberals" or "lerdistas" is quite another matter. Betancourt had attempted to halt the publication of the protesta decree in October 1873, and he had also met with Bayllac to discuss the possibility of preparing an alternate protesta that good Catholics could take without jeopardizing their souls. Such a scheme had the expressed purpose of keeping true enemies of the Church out of municipal office. When it failed, Bayllac asked the municipal president of Jiquilpan to "absent himself" from the town during the week scheduled for protesta ceremonies, thereby temporarily avoiding the protesta requirement while the priest consulted diocesan authorities about the best course of action.[175] Jesús Ordónica, for his part, renounced the protesta in June 1876.[176] Thus, Ordónica was temporarily willing to incur spiritual censures in order to help steer Jiquilpan's course through the crisis, knowing well that he could return to the fold later. Such were the Ultramontanes' strategies for confronting lerdista anticlericalism, and they kept to them even as their estranged baroque brethren stole out of the town and prepared to take the fight to the "protestants."

Conclusions

Religion had much to do with the partisan divisions in Jiquilpan and the greater northwest during the Religionero rebellion. As we have seen, the region was a laboratory of Catholic restoration in the second half of the nineteenth century. Zamora and other towns in the northwest had experienced a spiritual revival in the 1850s, as a local reaction to liberal reformism and epidemic disease. The creation of the diocese of Zamora complemented and deepened such a revival and harnessed it to the Ultramontane reformism of Labastida and Plancarte. Lay-focused reformism of both a social and spiritual nature and nineteenth-century Marian devotionalism took root in many northwestern communities, where they began to change local religious culture and affect the balance of power within rural parishes. While some reforms achieved wide traction in northwestern Michoacán, uniting priests and parishioners of various stripes, others served alternately to empower or marginalize specific religious constituencies. In places such as Jiquilpan, Sahuayo, Jacona, and Pajacuarán, Catholic reformism was experienced as an attack on religious traditions and communal control over the cult by more popular constituencies.

Such an attack was amplified by lerdista anticlericalism, which threatened to sever the ties between local communities and their divine patrons, undermine traditional spiritual economies, and make civil officials complicit in the attack on the faith by way of the protesta requirement. If Religionero violence was a form of resistance against anticlericalism, it also constituted a rejection of the accommodationist strategies of Catholic vecinos who were willing to serve local government under the terms of lerdismo. Not coincidentally, such vecinos often belonged to the Ultramontane circle, since their desire to shape the public administration without jeopardizing their souls dovetailed with a more modern, Europeanized spiritual outlook and a disdain for the raucous Catholicism of the masses.

CHAPTER 4

Martyrs for Our Lord

Baroque Catholicism, Religionero Mobilization, and the Taming of the Reforma in Central Michoacán

On April 19, 1876, government authorities executed Socorro Reyes, one of Michoacán's most important Religionero chiefs, in the provincial city of Puruándiro. Reyes had been captured two days earlier on Rancho Zirimicua, near Quiroga, when district forces under Commander Antonio Ruiz surprised his small gavilla as they ate.¹ Aware of the national implications of the arrest, Ruiz brought Reyes and five other rebels to Puruándiro, where he turned them over to local liberal strongman Rafael Garnica and the prefect of Puruándiro, Albino Fuentes Acosta. The latter conducted a summary trial of Reyes and condemned him to death by firing squad. According to local sources, Reyes had showed himself "frank and truthful" in his trial, and he asked forgiveness for any wrongs he had committed during the rebellion. Asked why he had taken up arms against the government, he responded simply, "My conscience ordered me to do it." A widely circulated eyewitness report of the execution described the Religionero titan as "well-built, with an abundant beard." He was forty-five years old and had been born in Cañada de San Isidro, a rancho near the town of Huaniqueo. "The man they called general," the correspondent continued, wore the garb of a peasant—"loose-fitting white pants and a shirt made of cotton, a felt sombrero, and a borrowed *serape*."² He had only a few reales to his name, and of those he donated nine and one-half for the purchase of candle wax for Our Lord of Health, an image of the crucified Christ that hung in Huaniqueo's hospital chapel.³

Before he faced the firing squad, Reyes received extreme unction. When he heard of the impending execution, Father Vicente Valdéz, parish priest of

Puruándiro, mobilized his coadjutor and two vicars, and "between the four of [them], [they] imparted the sacraments" to Reyes and the four other condemned rebels, day laborers who ranged in age from fourteen to twenty-five.[4] Valdéz was "anguished" to learn that district authorities would only allow the clerics ninety minutes to carry out the sacraments—including confession, absolution, and the viaticum—but "since [the rebels] were Christians, and such honorable ones, we did not have much work to do. They died as martyrs. We were very satisfied. The entire population made a great show of emotion and directed many prayers to God [for Reyes's soul]."[5]

The faithful of Puruándiro were not alone in their sympathy for Socorro Reyes. He commanded a broad following in his native Huaniqueo, in the towns of Huango (today, Villa Morelos) and Coeneo, as well as in surrounding ranchos and haciendas. Further, the Catholic press of Mexico City and Michoacán considered Reyes a principled leader of a legitimate political revolution who died a "victim of his convictions."[6] Even the editors of *El Siglo Diez y Nueve* lamented the summary execution, which they characterized as unfitting the political nature of Reyes's crimes. In fact, outside of Morelia's lerdista circle, Reyes was almost universally considered a genuine revolutionary—cut from a different cloth than the "bandit-Catholics" of the liberals' imagination.[7] To such observers, Reyes might have been a Catholic fanatic, but at least he was not a bloodthirsty bandolero.

If Reyes's religious conscience had "ordered" him to rebel against the government, however, the content of that conscience nevertheless deserves further exploration, especially in light of the chieftain's candle-buying devotion to Our Lord of Health. As such a baroque flourish suggests, Socorro Reyes and his comrades from the central district of Puruándiro were no avatars of papist intransigence, as liberal editors liked to depict them.[8] In fact, Ultramontane Catholicism fared poorly in the Religionero-prone parishes of Huaniqueo, Huango, and Coeneo, and indeed the Archdiocese of Michoacán itself proved less committed to Catholic modernization than its counterpart in Zamora. Instead, Reyes and his followers professed a religiosity steeped more in the colonial baroque than in the rigid reformism for which the papacy of Pius IX was known, and they followed old-fashioned, avuncular local priests with little of the reforming zeal of Father Plancarte and Bishop de la Peña. This is not to suggest that they did not fight for the universal Church. However, accounts that reduce the Michoacán Religioneros to simple agents of an intransigent Church fail to comprehend the complexity of the region's Catholicism and the connection between particular styles of faith and

Religionero mobilization.[9] Baroque Catholicism, in particular, played a crucial role in shaping the Religionero rebellion in central Michoacán, though its impacts were complex and locally varied. In Huaniqueo and Huango, for example, baroque devotions served as lightning rods for community solidarity against lerdismo, and Religionero bellicosity took the form of a village defense of religious traditions and spiritual properties targeted for adjudication. Coeneo, meanwhile, is the exceptional case that proves the rule. Here, conflict between baroque and Ultramontane strains of Catholicism was more acute, the liberal tradition better entrenched, and patterns of political partisanship more complex. In Coeneo, Purépecha Catholics disgusted with the reformist parish priest instead negotiated with local liberals and the more flexible Archdiocese of Michoacán in order to safeguard their traditions, and they mostly stayed out of the armed conflict. Collectively, the three cases therefore show that baroque Catholicism was both positively and negatively correlated with Religionero violence. Where popular traditions felt the full weight of lerdista anticlericalism, rebellion followed. However, where Ultramontane reformism threatened local religious cultures and the liberal elite was amenable to other forms of negotiation on the religious question, baroque Catholics declined to join the movement.

This chapter examines the links between religious culture, material relations, and Religionero bellicosity in the Bajío of Puruándiro and ciénega (marshland) of Zacapu. The region under survey corresponds roughly to the district of Puruándiro as it existed in the Restored Republic, which represented the primary stronghold of Socorro Reyes, Pedro González, Jesús Ortega, and other Religionero chiefs. Rebels in this zone conceived of themselves as a "central Michoacán" division of the larger movement, and I have thus adopted their terminology for simplicity's sake. In a schematic sense, the district stood at the meeting ground of the Bajío and the Purépecha heartland. It encompassed the fertile Bajío plains south of Puruándiro, the haciendas and Purépecha communities of the Zacapu marshland, and the indigenous hamlets and mestizo rancherías in the foothills of the Sierra Purépecha. As such, the district was internally diverse in both ethnic and material terms, home to ancient Purépecha pueblos, dynamic haciendas, and mixed-race rancherías. However, the towns and ranchos of the region shared a strong baroque Catholic heritage, the result of a long and intense relationship with the missionary friars. Unlike the Levitical northwest, central Michoacán belonged not to the new Diocese of Zamora but to the ancient Archdiocese of Michoacán, headquartered in nearby Morelia. Its communities also enjoyed a wholly different relationship with the institutional Church, which in Morelia prided itself on its evangelistic heritage and at this time mostly rejected the European-oriented reformism of Zamora. This unique institutional context had important ramifications for the Religionero revolt, as we will see.

The chapter begins with a survey of the *longue durée* history of the region, highlighting the pervasive influence of the Franciscan and Augustinian orders and the conquistador/patrician Villaseñor family in shaping local realities. It then reconstructs the region's conflictual nineteenth-century history, a period during which Coeneo became a hotbed of liberalism and republicanism.[10] As we shall see, the protagonists of such movements, and particularly Epitacio Huerta, used liberal patriotic service in order to enrich and empower themselves at the expense of the Church and entailed Indian communities, and consequently the 1869 reparto process became especially conflictive in the region. However, we cannot draw a direct causal link between liberal land reform and Religionero rebellion. Indeed, the marshland Purépecha communities most afflicted by straightforward hacienda encroachment and the destabilizing effects of the reparto turned out to be the region's most tepid Religionero supporters. Coeneo and its sujetos failed to produce Purépecha Religionero leaders. In pro-Religionero Huango and Huaniqueo, meanwhile, the reparto proved more disruptive to local religious cultures than it did to communal subsistence economies, since spiritual property was targeted for disentailment even while communities sidestepped or managed to control the larger land division. Paradoxically, then, although the ciénega saw outright agrarian violence in the 1860s and 1870s, such conflict was tangential to Religionero bellicosity. Rather, as the second section of the chapter shows, Coeneo and its satellites produced a much weaker local mobilization than did Huaniqueo and Huango, where lerdista privatization was comparatively weak but fatally compromised the villages' spiritual well-being.

The third major section of the chapter explores the religious histories of the central communities in order to show how they influenced patterns of political partisanship. Here, special attention is afforded to the popular, Christological devotions introduced by the mendicants and patronized by the powerful landowning families of the region, including Huaniqueo's Lord of Health, Huango's Lord of Mercy, and the Coeneo area's Purépecha feast of Corpus Christi. Each of these devotions, as we will see, exerted a powerful influence on local religious cultures, and they would play important roles in the development of the Religionero rebellion. Far from static relics of the colonial past, local religious cultures were dynamic, enduring both changes in their organizational structures and periodic attempts at reform. Unlike the high clergy of Zamora, however, archdiocesan authorities in Morelia generally tolerated baroque religion, accepting local claims of "immemorial" tradition and eschewing the stringent Catholic reformism of their northwestern counterparts. As a result, central parishes experienced comparatively less of the intraflock conflict that characterized Jiquilpan. As we will see, only in Coeneo did a more reformist Catholic faction find much traction against baroque religion in the period under survey. However, in attacking Purépecha religiosity, the local priest alienated indigenous communities, who in turn failed to come to his defense when local anticlericals got him in their sights. Indeed, Coeneo's Purépecha Catholics found greater success by supporting the local liberal elite, on the one hand, while petitioning archdiocesan authorities for a more amenable priest, on the other. In so doing, they settled the religious question via negotiation before the revolt and subsequently declined to join the comparatively small, mestizo-led Religionero movement in Coeneo. Meanwhile, Huaniqueo and Huango rallied to their baroque devotions in the face of both Ultramontane reformism and lerdista anticlericalism.

Central Michoacán to 1873

The Bajío of Puruándiro had long served as a military and cultural frontier, buffering the Purépecha strongholds on Lake Pátzcuaro and the surrounding highlands of the Meseta Purépecha from the Chichimeca (here, denoting Otomí and Guamare) territories to the north as early as the fifteenth century. Puruándiro itself was established as a contested military outpost, and it was only incorporated into the Purépecha Empire in the mid-fifteenth century, along with the settlements of Huaniqueo, Teremendo, and Chucándiro.[11] Such conquests were likely carried out from the ancient town of Zacapu, at the southern end of the basin, which served as a regional hub of Purépecha power. Despite its importance to the Purépecha state, however, Zacapu's surrounding villages still faced periodic incursions by hostile groups from the Guanajuato Bajío in the early sixteenth century.[12]

The Spanish conquest (1529–1533) reinforced the frontier quality of the zone while carving it up into private fiefs. After the conquest of Tenochtitlán, Hernán Cortés, Nuño Beltrán de Guzmán, and Juan de Villaseñor attempted

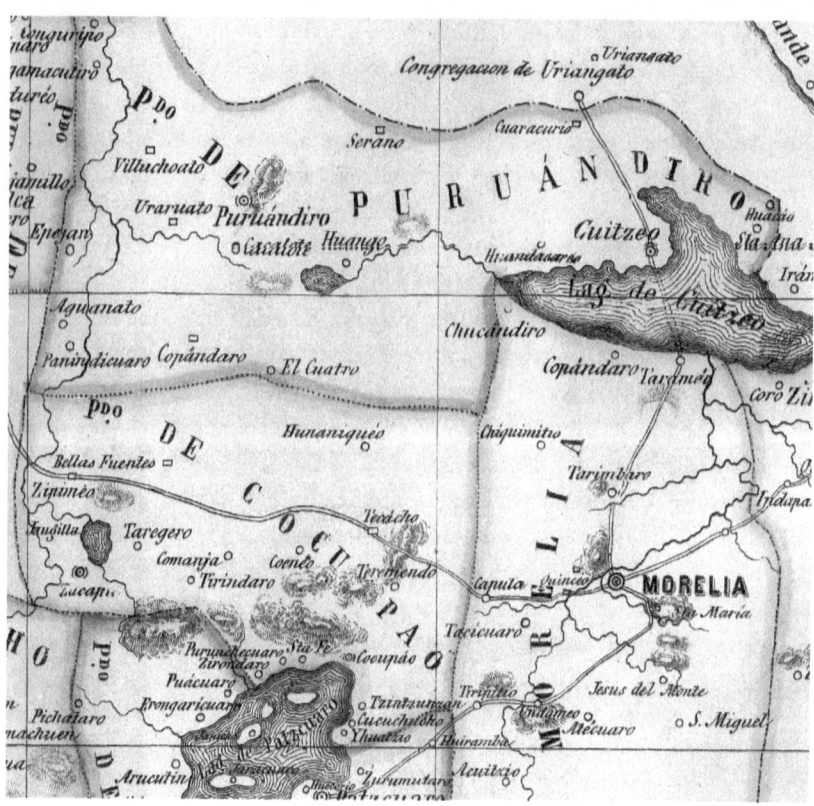

Map 5. Central Michoacán in the mid-nineteenth century. The area under study includes the former *partidos* of Puruándiro and Cocupao. From *Plano del Estado de Michoacán* (1863). Courtesy of the Mapoteca "Manuel Orozco y Berra," del Servicio de Información Agroalimentaria y Pesquera, SAGARPA, Classification No. 1719-OYB-7234-A.

to establish competing encomiendas in the Bajío. The matter ended up before Spanish courts, which awarded Villaseñor's claims in present-day Guanajuato to Nuño de Guzmán. For his part, Villaseñor was granted an expansive terrain encompassing a large swath of the Michoacán Bajío, from Puruándiro to Numarán. Cortés retained the southern tier, including Huaniqueo and Zacapu, which he soon parceled out to various followers.[13] Bucking the instability that characterized his rivals' fiefs, Villaseñor established himself as an entrenched regional power. He built opulent homes in Puruándiro and

Huango, dubbed the "Small Court" for its active social life among the Spanish elite, and his six American-born children would go on to administer much of the rural property of the Michoacán Bajío in the colonial period. In fact, Villaseñor was dubbed the "Abraham of the New World" for his role in populating the Bajío, and many of the "principal families" of Mexican history figure among his progeny.[14] Renowned for both their piety and their wealth, the Villaseñor family built chapels, established local devotions, and served as protectors of the fledgling Augustinian missionary project, which had been established in the region in the 1530s.[15] For their part, the Augustinians built convents at Yuriria (Guanajuato), Cuitzeo, and Huango and established a number of missionary *doctrinas* along the Chichimeca frontier, with the twin goals of protecting the sedentary (Franciscan) missionary project of interior Michoacán and subjugating the mobile Chichimecas to Spanish rule.[16]

Meanwhile, the utopian project of Vasco de Quiroga, headquartered in the heart of the old Purépecha Empire, extended north to Zacapu, where the Franciscans established a convent in the 1530s. The missionaries relocated sierra settlements to the marshlands surrounding Zacapu, built hospitals and chapels, and introduced artisan trades.[17] Three centuries later, the indigenous villages between Zacapu and Coeneo still specialized in reed work and shoemaking, and they held tightly to the hybrid Purépecha-Franciscan religiosity of the Quirogan project, centered as it was on the festival of Corpus Christi.[18] Further north, the Franciscans also incorporated Coeneo, Teremendo, and Huaniqueo, extending their domain to the Augustinians' doorstep at Huango.[19] By contrast, the secular clergy took control of Puruándiro, which remained an ecclesiastical backwater throughout the colonial period.[20] Thus, while central Michoacán served as a military frontier, it was also internally divided in its religious jurisdiction.

With the slow death of the encomienda system in the seventeenth century, the progeny of Juan de Villaseñor and other Spanish families established haciendas such as Villachuato and Janamuato in the Bajío of Puruándiro, and Bellas Fuentes, Zipimeo, and Cortijo in the ciénega of Zacapu. They brought enslaved Africans to grow commercial crops and tend cattle, and by the mid-eighteenth century their estates also hosted significant numbers of employees, tenants, and sharecroppers.[21] Such commercial projects encouraged the mixing of Africans, Spaniards, and indigenous people, especially in the northern settlements of Puruándiro and Huango. Yet the Purépecha communities of the Quirogan project—and particularly those of the ciénega—maintained strict ethnic barriers and insisted on communal autonomy. Here, the Bellas Fuentes Estate represented a long-term adversary of the pueblos of Zacapu, Tiríndaro, Zipiajo, Naranja, Comanja, Azajo, and Tarejero, steadily encroaching on communal lands and provoking continual litigation by pueblo leaders.[22] Nevertheless, Purépecha communities maintained a fierce legal resistance, and by the time of Mexican independence most of the ciénega communities and those of Huaniqueo and Coeneo still retained their communal land bases. In the wake of the 1869 state reparto law, the pueblos of the ciénega faced increasing pressure to subdivide, though the process was far from complete by the time of the Religionero revolt.

The Bajío of Puruándiro and the ciénega of Zacapu witnessed significant political conflict during the nineteenth century. The region as a whole developed a strong insurgent pedigree, rallying to the Catholic republicanism of the early independence period. The parish priest of Huango, Manuel Ruiz de Chávez—a relative of Father Hidalgo and descendent of the conqueror Villaseñor—was an important player in José Mariano Michelena's Valladolid Conspiracy in 1809, and insurgents under Ignacio Rayón and José María Morelos used the region as a recruiting base in the early years of the insurgency. Another cura, Luciano Navarrete, led the independence movement in Zacapu and became a close associate of Morelos. For the Bajío of Puruándiro, especially, the insurgency exacted a heavy toll, since insurgent and royalist troops frequently disputed its towns. Puruándiro's colonial parish church was even burned to the ground during the fighting in 1810.[23]

The zone's insurgent heritage translated into early support for federalism, with the town of Coeneo, especially, producing key leaders. Until the rise of Epitacio Huerta, however, such figures were not anticlericals. Priests had led the insurgency in the area, and their political heirs proved little inclined to antagonize the Church. Onofre Calvo Pintado, one of Michoacán's first constitutional governors and a native of Penjamillo, for example, renounced his post rather than carry out the expulsion of Bishop Gómez de Portugal, as he was ordered to do by the Gómez Farías government in 1833.[24] In the wake of Santa Anna's 1836 proclamation of the centralist "Siete Leyes" government, central Michoacán rallied to the cause of federalism. In Zacapu, Nieves Huerta raised a federalist guerrilla movement, organizing popular assemblies to elect ayuntamientos in towns under rebel control. Such actions occasioned strong opposition from the clergy of La Piedad, whose parish priest, José María Cabadas, preached that federalism meant the destruction of the Catholic cult. The response of the state's federalist leaders, based in Aguililla and Coeneo, was to adopt the slogan "God, Liberty, and Federation."[25]

Coeneo produced further federalist mobilizations in the 1830s, solidifying a tradition of popular republican service and minting new leaders and martyrs. Among these were Eustaquio Arias and Francisco Ronda, natives of the greater Guanajuato/Michoacán Bajío who had acquired ranchos in the municipality of Coeneo during the early decades of the nineteenth century.[26] Arias and Ronda raised popular militias that operated across the Bajío and into the Meseta Purépecha, facing off against the forces of Morelia's José de Ugarte. Integral players in Michoacán's federalist movement, both fell victim to centralist assassination plots after receiving pardons for their revolutionary activities in 1839—Arias in the Purépecha village of Comanja and Ronda at his rancho near Coeneo.[27] Despite such a setback, however, Zacapu and Coeneo would go on to nurture liberal mobilizations and produce some of the principal leaders of Michoacán's Ayutla movement. In Zacapu, patriotic rebels disgusted with the centralist government's concessions to the US invaders launched a liberal rebellion in 1848, and Coeneo was the staging ground for the rebellion against Santa Anna in 1854. Here, Epitacio Huerta and his brother Antonio (nephews of the federalist Nieves Huerta) established their credentials as "soldiers of the pueblo," joining with Francisco Ronda's son Eugenio, Rafael Rangel, and Rafael Arias and seconding the Plan of Ayutla. Central Michoacán once again became a battlefield, with the taking of Puruándiro in April 1855 a crucial turning point in the liberals' march to power.[28]

The triumph of Ayutla heralded the first serious offensive against entailed property in Michoacán, a process that had significant impacts in the Puruándiro and Pátzcuaro districts. Church properties, especially those administered by the Franciscans and Augustinians, were the targets of adjudication processes during the governments of José Santos Degollado (1856–1858) and particularly Epitacio Huerta (1858–1861). Liberal caudillos benefited handsomely from disamortization. Huerta denounced and purchased land from the Augustinian hacienda of Chucándiro, for example, and, along with several other comrades, he also acquired property from the expansive Bellas Fuentes Hacienda.[29] Yet the assault on ecclesiastical properties, along with the Huerta government's punitive actions against the Michoacán Church, divided local elites. In La Piedad and Zamora, it stimulated conservative and monarchist movements. In the face of the French invasion of 1863, the liberal caudillos of central Michoacán once again rallied to the defense of the republic. Here, Eugenio Ronda and his Coeneo compatriots the "Three

Rafaels"—Rafael Garnica, Rafael Rangel, and Rafael Arias—played important roles in combatting imperialist troops from Zamora and La Piedad.[30] Huaniqueo, meanwhile, offered passive support to imperialist troops throughout the conflict. Despite a liberal pedigree, then, central Michoacán did not uniformly support Juárez's republican movement. The imperialist general Ramón Méndez disputed the plaza of Puruándiro with Eugenio Ronda in 1865, and the future Religionero Juan de Dios Rodríguez, at the head of some four hundred troops, scored a victory against republican soldiers near Coeneo in 1866. Even Antonio Huerta defected to the imperialist cause in 1864, fighting opposite his brother Epitacio until returning to the liberal fold in 1866.[31]

The restoration of the republic in 1867 did not bring lasting peace to the newly organized Puruándiro district. Petty banditry plagued the zone, as the ex-imperialist guerilla band Los Potrereños attacked mule trains and haciendas from their base in Guanajuato.[32] Nor was the triumphant liberal army any more united than the coalition it defeated. In the aftermath of the 1868 elections, in which Juárez bested Riva Palacio, Díaz, and Lerdo, Juan Cervín de la Mora and Epitacio Huerta pronounced against the government. The so-called Plan of Coeneo decried the creeping centralization and economic incompetence of the Juárez regime, but its most telling article called for just recompense and consideration for the patriots who had fought the French invaders. Simply put, Huerta and his compatriots had been passed over for important political positions by the juarista government, and they resorted to arms in order to right the wrong. The 1871 Noria rebellion provided Huerta and his comrades with yet another opportunity to seek local power.[33] However, as Chowning notes, Huerta's autocratic spirit and anticlericalism had engendered ill will among Michoacán's middle-class liberals during his gubernatorial tenure, and consequently he garnered little support.[34] In revenge, Huerta and his compatriots failed to come to the Carrillo government's defense during the Religionero rebellion, even when Coeneo suffered repeated attacks by Socorro Reyes and Pedro González.

In addition to sectarian politics, central Michoacán saw significant agrarian conflict during the Restored Republic. Third-wave liberal disentailment laws proved especially disruptive in the region, which was home to some of Michoacán's largest clerically owned haciendas and served as one of its last strongholds of indigenous communal holding.[35] Nonetheless, a survey of the reparto in the district demonstrates the complex and sometimes contradictory impacts of land division on Religionero mobilization. Purépecha communities in the ciénega of Zacapu had fought encroachment by neighboring haciendas since at least the late colonial period. By the time of the state government's 1869 reparto law, many had already lost significant territory to the haciendas of Bellas Fuentes, Zipimeo, Tecacho, and Cortijo. As noted, some of these rural properties had changed hands during the Reforma, when Eptiacio Huerta and others adjudicated large sections of the Bellas Fuentes Hacienda. Moreover, lands under dispute between Bellas Fuentes and the pueblos of Zacapu, Naranja, Tiríndaro, and Tarejero were simply parceled out to the new owners without taking Purépecha claims into account.[36] The community of Tarejero had lost nearly all of its property by the time of the reparto, its members reduced to the status of hacienda laborers. Zacapu, Naranja, and Tiríndaro, although they still possessed communal land bases, were engaged in long-standing boundary disputes among themselves and with Bellas Fuentes. Under such circumstances, many ciénega communities resisted carrying out the reparto, not so much on principle as for fear of losing lands under litigation, and others asserted that they had already subdivided on their own terms.[37] Purépecha leaders from Azajo and Comanja both claimed to have carried out their own repartos, and they further explained that Bellas Fuentes had usurped their only remaining communal patrimony. If the government could help them recover the lands, though, they would happily subdivide them. The process thus stalled for the next three decades.[38]

In response to such foot dragging, civil authorities sometimes used fiscal measures, especially the levying of taxes on parcels that had not been registered as private property, to pressure the communities to complete the process. In other cases, hacendados—with the backing of local authorities—resorted to more coercive means in order to push comuneros off disputed lands, and armed conflict sometimes ensued. The comuneros of Teremendo attempted to stop a Tecacho sharecropper from planting on disputed terrain in 1869. When *acordada* forces intervened on the latter's behalf, a tumult ensued, leaving six Indians dead.[39] In Tarejero, meanwhile, a simmering dispute between the community and hacendado Luis G. Obregón came to a head in 1869, when the latter attempted to prevent the community from taking water from a well on a disputed Bellas Fuentes plot. Tarejero communalists captured the small acordada force from Zacapu sent to repress them, and a major conflict was averted only after the municipal president of Zacapu called off a larger National Guard contingent and the *tarejereños* released their hostages. The underlying conflict between Bellas Fuentes and Tarejero did not subside, however, and in 1873 acordada forces from Coeneo were called to the hacienda to prevent comuneros from planting on disputed land. During the incident, Tarejero's apoderado was shot dead while being escorted back to Coeneo, allegedly by a drunken hacienda worker.[40]

Agrarian tension, then, ran high in many of the communities of the ciénega at the time of the Religionero rebellion, though the reparto process was far from over in 1873 and its outcome unpredictable in most places. In fact, like Azajo and Comanja, Zacapu and Naranja mostly avoided carrying out the reparto until the 1890s and 1900s, using various legal strategies to delay implementation while waiting for judicial rulings on land disputes with Bellas Fuentes.[41] Violent conflict during the initial reparto process, therefore, proved unique to Tarejero and Teremendo. If the reparto directly motivated local Purépechas to join the Religionero movement elsewhere, we lack conclusive evidence, since the ciénega communities did not produce well-known Religionero leaders. True, some comuneros in Zipiajo, Naranja, and Comanja seem to have offered material support to gavillas led by the mestizos from Huaniqueo and Huango, and others may have joined in an April 1875 attack on Zacapu.[42] In general, though, the ciénega served as little more than a passive transit point for Religionero armies, and local Purépecha leaders sometimes even aided the government.[43] In sum, the 1869 reparto law exacerbated long-standing agrarian tensions in the ciénega, but its relationship to local Religionero revolts remains tenuous.

Further north in the district, meanwhile, the reparto proved less destabilizing to communal land tenure but sometimes menaced village religious economies. Generally, the communities of the zone often avoided carrying out the division until much later in the Porfiriato or divided their lands on their own terms, but local elites responded to the stalling of the reparto by targeting religious properties using the Lerdo Law.[44] Delaying tactics were used successfully in Angamacutiro, where the local land commission attempted to bend the reparto to its own customs in 1870, carving out twenty-three parcels that would each be administered communally by several dozen families. Treasury officials nullified the division as contrary to state law, but a new reparto did not take place until the early 1880s.[45] Though Coeneo's indigenous community had already divided most of their communal lands by 1869, they likewise agreed to quickly subdivide these few "little plots."[46] In Huango, by contrast, Purépecha leaders carried out the reparto on their own terms, but in early 1873 district treasury officials claimed that since they had not approved the division, the community would still have to pay 134 pesos in back taxes. Community leaders then petitioned the government for a temporary reprieve from taxation, complaining that the ayuntamiento had seized its Augustinian hospital building as payment. The governor's office replied that it could not exempt the community from taxation, though it would give communal leaders three months' time to come up with the taxes. Unable to meet this obligation, however, the community lost its hospital building, which the local and district government wanted to convert into a school.[47] Even if violent conflict was avoided in the more mestizo-dominated towns of the Bajío, then, the reparto process did not bode well for the communal religious economy, since it made religious properties vulnerable to adjudication.

In Huaniqueo, cradle of the Socorro Reyes revolt, the stalled reparto process stimulated both an attack on communal religious property and an effort to curtail public worship by municipal authorities. In 1869–1870, Huaniqueo suffered a number of intracommunal disputes over leadership and management of funds, with a majority faction complaining that one Hilario Román usurped communal lands (including cofradía lands supporting the cult of Our Lord of Health) and failed to place the money in the communal coffers.[48] Because of such "obstacles" and the inability of the community to agree on who should head up the reparto committee, the process stalled in 1870. By 1873, however, other conflicts had surfaced between the community's new apoderado, Antonio Cilagua, and the ayuntamiento of Huaniqueo. In the words of Cilagua, the ayuntamiento had "violated the [community's] constitutional guarantee of property" by appropriating an urban plot in front of the old parish church, a space the Indians still used for their "customs of religious feasts and processions."[49] The ayuntamiento responded that if indeed the community had traditionally used the lot for processions, the Laws of Reform had rendered such an argument irrelevant. Further, the Indians also used the space to sell meat and vegetables in an "unhygienic" way, so the municipal corporation had sold off small sections of the plaza to "vecinos de razón" (Hispanicized residents) who were building "proper" market stalls. The ayuntamiento added darkly that the Indians had long considered themselves owners of virtually all municipal lands. If the government heeded their complaints, the municipality would find itself subjected to the "capricious whims of the Indians."[50] Governor Carrillo struck a neutral stance, informing Cilagua that he would have to take his claims against the ayuntamiento to the courts.[51] Given the animosity between Cilagua and the municipal government, though, it should perhaps not come as a surprise that the former figured among the leaders of the Religionero revolt of Huaniqueo in January 1875.[52]

Yet this was no simple agrarian revolt. For Cilagua and his constituency, the ayuntamiento was implicated in both the suppression of their religious customs and the attack on the material base of communal religious and political power. In Huaniqueo, then, the religious, material, and political factors driving the revolt remained deeply intertwined, though religious factors clearly came to the fore.

As the above discussion makes clear, communal disentailment processes proved highly conflictual in the ciénega of Zacapu and the Bajío of Puruándiro, though the outcomes of such processes varied widely from pueblo to pueblo. If agrarian pressure clearly contributed to a general atmosphere of polarization, its impact on Religionero mobilization was far from straightforward. Where haciendas edged onto village commons, as in the Purépecha communities around Zacapu, the reparto was experienced as a primarily agrarian process and Religionero mobilization was consequently weak. By contrast, religious grievances took center stage in Huaniqueo and Huango, where stalled repartos left communities intact but provoked municipal authorities to conduct targeted strikes on religious properties using the Lerdo Law. Such findings should caution historians against understanding disentailment as a purely agrarian process or measuring peasant discontent in hectares lost.[53] Indeed, as we will see below, the Purépecha communities facing intense agrarian pressure from Bellas Fuentes and other estates largely sat out the Religionero conflict, while Purépecha Catholics in Huango and especially Huaniqueo joined Guadalupe Raya and Socorro Reyes or even led local uprisings.

The Religionero Revolt in Central Michoacán

The Religionero movement in central Michoacán began—and in many ways ended—with Socorro Reyes. With a scant half-dozen rebels, Reyes took up arms against the government in Huaniqueo in January 1874. A known quantity to the district's liberal officials since his 1870 rebellion, Reyes prudently kept on the move and in the shadows during the first few months, escaping to Zacapu and Quiroga when the prefect of Puruándiro searched his home in Cañada de San Isidro in March.[54] District authorities quickly turned their attention to the incursion of gavillas from Guanajuato in the spring of 1874 and declared the Huaniqueo problem solved.[55] Not only had Reyes not disappeared, though, he was out recruiting soldiers and helping to form new gavillas in Quiroga. Together, the two gavillas attacked Coeneo in June and Quiroga in August.[56] During the latter event, Reyes's comrade Manuel Rangel was captured by Rafael Garnica and imprisoned in the local jail, a turn of events that prompted an audacious rescue attempt by Reyes and a small mob of "léperos" (paupers) in September.[57] The plan failed, but Reyes escaped and soon after issued a political plan in Teremendo—the first of the uprising. After decrying the effects of the Laws of Reform on the harmonious equilibrium between the "social and political" constitutions of society, the plan's four articles affirmed the principle of Catholic exclusivity, declared all Protestants traitors to the patria and subject to capital punishment, promised guarantees to merchants who collaborated with the rebellion, and restricted gavilla activity unauthorized by the movement's leaders.[58] Reyes's, then, was an especially severe and vindictive form of Catholic nationalism.

District officials, with the help of Rafael Garnica, managed to keep the Reyes rebellion mostly in check during its 1874 gestation, but at the turn of the new year things changed dramatically. Reyes and his new associate Pedro González invaded Huango with forty rebels in January 1875, sacking the municipal treasury office and stealing fourteen rifles and several horses.[59] Days later, Jesús Ortega, a Teremendo native educated in the seminary of Morelia, led an insurrection from his home rancho, where he posted a manifesto decrying the "aristocratic" and autocratic bent of the lerdista government and reminding the Mexican people that "the freedom of worship is not in your interest, because you are exclusively Catholic."[60] Meanwhile, the publication of the Ley Orgánica was met with a major rebellion in Huaniqueo, when communal leader Antonio Cilagua, 150 Indians, and an equal number of rancheros from Tendeparacua burned the municipal archives and briefly kidnapped the municipal president before several principal vecinos intervened to secure his release.[61] The revolt then spread to Coeneo, where rebels under locals Jesús Gil and Jesús Fuentes took the town and demanded twenty-five pesos from the alcalde before leaving town to join Socorro Reyes.[62]

By early spring, the district government was facing a crisis. Reyes, Ortega, González, and the new chief Juan Barajas carried out repeated attacks on Huaniqueo, Coeneo, and Huango in February, and the "Bajío gavillas" under Félix Dueñas and Guadalupe "El Gorrión" Raya invaded from their base of operations on the Guanajuato/Michoacán line.[63] These Bajío rebels killed the municipal president of Panindícuaro, and gavilla activity and a dearth of government troops also left Huaniqueo and Huango without authorities.⁶⁴ In an emergency session, the municipality of Quiroga voted to issue the state government an ultimatum: more weapons and a detachment of fifty soldiers or it would be forced to dissolve the ayuntamiento and leave the town to the rebels.⁶⁵ State officials promised that federal aid was on the way, but they could not spare troops from Morelia because they worried that Reyes might be brazen enough even to attack the capital.⁶⁶ The efforts of Colonel Félix Briseñas and General Garnica, who were placed at the head of the efforts against the central gavillas, proved insufficient, and by early March General Régules had come to the zone. As in the northwest, however, increased military pressure led the central Michoacán and Bajío gavillas to move south temporarily, where they collaborated with Reza in the burning of Taretan in April.⁶⁷ That same month, two hundred Religioneros coming from Naranja fell on Zacapu, burning the houses of several principal vecinos and killing the chief of the military garrison.⁶⁸ By May, Prefect Fuentes Acosta estimated the number of rebels in the district at over six hundred.⁶⁹

The federal army subsequently increased its involvement in the zone, sending Colonel Santiago Nieto at the head of 150 troops to aid Garnica and his equally matched force in suppressing rebel activities in the Religionero hotspots near the Tecacho (Huaniqueo) and Villachuato (Puruándiro) haciendas.⁷⁰ Despite the frequent "dispersal" of gavillas, however, the increased military presence bore little fruit. In May, several hundred Religioneros attacked Pátzcuaro, and in June Pedro González killed one of the Three Rafaels—Rafael Arias—at his home in Cortijo.⁷¹ Meanwhile, Socorro Reyes collaborated more frequently with both Pátzcuaro's Domingo Juárez and the Bajío gavillas, helping to drive out municipal authorities in Cuanajo and Chucándiro in June and July, respectively.⁷² Worse, it had become increasingly apparent to local officials that the Religioneros had friends among the region's landed elite, who voluntarily offered them loans or—as did the hacienda foreman at Bellas Fuentes—collected and held forced loans for Reyes.⁷³ For their part, liberal authorities at Puruándiro and Coeneo faced chronic shortages of cash and resources, a situation that endangered their ability to pay local troops and employees.⁷⁴ Such a problem likely had much to do with the jailbreak that took place in November, an event for which Prefect Fuentes Acosta was blamed and even sentenced to jail time.⁷⁵

The government's run of bad luck in central Michoacán finally began to abate in late 1875, however. In December, government troops killed Pedro González on the Zipimeo Hacienda, a victory that for local liberals doubled as retribution for the assassination of Arias.[76] Escobedo arrived in the zone shortly thereafter, where he reorganized the military garrisons and named new municipal officials in towns frequently overrun by the gavillas.[77] A military surge, which combined the forces of Escobedo, Nieto, and Garnica, prompted Socorro Reyes to move further into the Bajío, where he collaborated in an eight hundred–strong Religionero attack on Abasolo (Guanajuato) in January.[78] In their leader's absence, however, a smaller, poorly armed contingent of Reyes's army was routed in Zipiajo. Among the nine slain rebels, army officials discovered an assortment of "rosaries, scapulars, medals, and printed prayer books they call relics, to save the owners from dying without confession."[79] Meanwhile, Escobedo's indulto policy had begun to take its own effect. Sixteen rebels, mostly from Puruándiro and Villachuato, laid down their arms in late January, and Huango's Francisco Martínez Salazar and his twenty subordinates soon joined them.[80] By late March, two dozen Huaniqueo natives had followed suit.[81] Yet the most crushing blow to the movement came in April, when the government captured and executed Socorro Reyes. Indeed, although gavilla activity continued in the Michoacán/Guanajuato borderlands through 1876, the revolt in the Huaniqueo and Coeneo municipalities declined precipitously after Reyes's death.[82] Instead, it was Domingo Juárez and the Bajío chieftains Raya and Silvestre Llamas that would carry forth the Religionero/porfirista torch in the central districts after mid-1876. If these men were shrewd caciques who maneuvered the fluid political context of 1876–1877 with relative ease, they did not share Reyes's impeccable reputation or his organic popular following. For the denizens of Reyes's native Huaniqueo, the revolt was already over.

The Religionero movement in Puruándiro district was second only to that of Jiquilpan in its intensity and power to destabilize. Though it proved amenable to collaboration with gavillas from neighboring districts, it was more geographically focused than that of the northwest and tierra caliente, and it displayed a high level of ideological cohesion. Further, the revolt left important evidence of its religious content. The "relics" used by the rebels in Zipiajo, for instance, suggest both an attachment to sacred objects and an attempt to adjust sacramental observance to a battlefield setting where priests were not available to perform last rites. Meanwhile, near the Ururuta Hacienda a gavilla of ten rebels rallied to the leadership of one María Eugenia González, known as "La Virgen," and her father, Casimiro, in November 1875.[83] Unfortunately, details about María Eugenia are lacking, but she may well

Figure 7. El Padre Cobos's response to the news of a female Religionero chief operating with a small *gavilla* near Hacienda Ururuta. *El Padre Cobos*, 6 February 1876. Reprinted in *El Padre Cobos y La Carabina de Ambrosio* (Mexico City: Cámara de Senadores de la LVII Legislatura, 2000). The Spanish reads: "The latest scene from the war in Michoacán." Photo courtesy of Daniel Alonzo.

have figured as a popular mystic not unlike the rebel/folk saint Santa Teresa of Chihuahua.[84] Socorro Reyes, as we have seen, was an ardent antiprotestant, a Catholic nationalist, and a devotee of the Lord of Health whose dying wish was a pious bequest of wax for the Lord's candles. In sum, the central Michoacán revolt displayed a unique—and specifically baroque—religious character. To further substantiate the link between such baroque religiosity and Religionero mobilization, however, we need to comprehend both central Michoacán's longue durée religious history and its more recent engagement with Ultramontane reformism.

Baroque Religion and the Limits of Catholic Reformism

Catholicism put down deep roots in both the Zacapu marshlands and the Bajío of Puruándiro, though devotional styles varied widely between the poles of the old Purépecha heartland and the former Chichimeca frontier in the Bajío. The region once hosted both a Franciscan and an Augustinian convent, and even in the nineteenth century it bore the marks of the evangelizing religiosity of the mendicants. Central Michoacán retained a strong clerical—but specifically friarly—presence throughout the colonial period, and it seldom faced the kind of ecclesiastical neglect that plagued the southern sierra.[85] Such a clerical presence did not always translate into less vernacular religious styles, however. Indeed, despite their commitment to sacramental piety and preference for priest-led festivities, the Purépecha communities of the ciénega jealously guarded their religious and political autonomy and strove to uphold baroque traditions. If priests were a necessary part of Catholic life, Purépecha villagers often set the terms for the relationship between the cura and the community. The more ethnically integrated communities of the Bajío also shared such a mixed sacramental and baroque religiosity, as we will see, though the content of popular practice diverged widely between the mestizo/Augustinian town of Huango and the Purépecha/Franciscan town of Zacapu. By the coming of the Religionero rebellion, however, the first seeds of Ultramontane reformism had been planted in the region, as young priests attempted to reform popular practices in both populations. Even so, baroque religious traditions proved especially resilient, and the Morelia hierarchy declined to back a rigorous spiritual reform.

The ciénega region was an important center of Franciscan evangelization. The Friars Minor chose Zacapu—one of the earliest Purépecha settlements in Michoacán and the center of the gestational Purépecha Empire until the mid-fifteenth century—for the site of a missionary convent in 1530.[86] By the mid-sixteenth century, the marshland was firmly integrated into the pastoral project of Bishop Vasco de Quiroga and the Franciscans of the Province of San Pedro and San Pablo. Strictly ascetic and steeped in medieval mysticism, the Franciscans hoped to establish the millennial kingdom of God in Mexico, a place whose inhabitants they saw as mercifully free from the corruption of the Old World.[87] As such, the New World offered the last chance to establish a utopian Christian society before Armageddon. Such a millennial kingdom was to be built through communal effort and isolated from the influence of ordinary Spanish immigrants. Guided both by Franciscan apocalyptic mysticism and the utopian ideas of Thomas Moore, Quiroga and his followers congregated Indians into pueblos—centered on hospital-chapel structures—established native cofradías to finance the cult and help to order community life, and instructed the neophytes in the mysteries of the faith through religious pageantry and the translation of Christian concepts into the Purépecha language.[88]

Mendicant methods left plenty of room for indigenous cultural survival, and indeed the Catholic sodalities and fiestas introduced by the friars became primary vehicles for Purépecha identity in the colonial period.[89] Typically, Purépecha leaders and their constituents wedded Catholic festivities to indigenous agricultural rites and adopted Catholic rituals as a way to perform communal belonging and leadership. In particular, the feast of Corpus Christi—a celebration of the mystery of transubstantiation—became a pillar of Purépecha religiosity in both the lacustrine and *serrano* regions of Michoacán in the seventeenth century. Corpus Christi combined high Catholic orthodoxy with carnavalesque revelry and idiosyncratic local customs. At the center of the celebration stood the Eucharist, a symbol that belonged wholly to the institutional Church and that, with the exception of the viaticum, was at no other time carried through the streets in procession. Because of the solemnity of the rite, priestly involvement in the procession (as the bearer of the Eucharistic Host) and its attendant Mass was crucial.[90] Yet outside of Corpus Thursday's priestly core, the seven other days of the Corpus Christi octave were commonly given to alcohol-fueled revelry, Purépecha dances, mock battles, masquerades, frenzied market activity, and the procession of mojigangas. On these days, people also celebrated the social and economic roles of the various groups that made up the communal whole (artisans, farmers, cofradía members, etc.). For their part, the elders of the cabildo and the mayordomos of the various cofradías dramatized hierarchy through their organization of the events and through acts of economic redistribution, while the celebrating community paid the officiating priests in agricultural products and animals, in accordance with local pindecuarios. Moreover, the pindecuario also specified when the festivity would take place, since it ultimately corresponded to local agricultural cycles. Purépecha Corpus Christi festivals thus privileged local planting traditions over the Roman liturgical calendar, an idiosyncrasy tolerated by the friars and diocesan officials well into the nineteenth century. The staggering of Corpus Christi celebrations also helped facilitate ecclesiastical oversight, since it allowed one priest to preside over at least part of the eight-day festivities in several villages between May and June.[91]

Between the late colonial and early republican periods, Corpus Christi festivals also developed into a medium for intervillage solidarity in central Michoacán. During the early colonial period, the religious head town of a doctrina or parish traditionally hosted the festivity, inviting its satellite pueblos and their patron saints to attend as honored guests.[92] In the ciénega, however, Purépecha communities developed a rotational structure, with each of the six pueblos (Naranja, Zipiajo, Azajo, Tarejero, Tiríndaro, and Comanja) taking turns hosting the octave—the eighth and final day of the fiesta cycle. The other five pueblos sent delegations of local leaders to the host pueblo, perhaps accompanied by their respective patron saint's image. Thus, although each pueblo carried out their own Corpus Christi celebrations according to their own customs and calendar, the rotational structure of the octave tied the communities together and fostered a sense of Purépecha Catholic identity.[93]

Purépecha religiosity, then, was characterized by shared authority over religious matters between priests and indigenous leaders, the more-or-less regular celebration of sacraments, and a highly festive piety that satisfied the need for village social reproduction and economic redistribution. Built both on strong indigenous leadership and on communal land tenure, this devotional style continued to mark the communities of the ciénega long after the secularization of the Franciscan doctrinas in the eighteenth century.[94] Although perhaps averse to change, communal religious structures proved capable of adaptation in the face of more serious structural shifts. The encroachment of Bellas Fuentes and other haciendas in the late colonial period slowly eroded the resources of many of the region's cofradías, for instance, but festive traditions persisted often in the form of mayordomías (individual financing of fiestas by elected mayordomos).[95] Moreover, if cofradía lands were in decline, they had not been extinguished by the time of the 1869 repartos. Indeed, an anonymous nineteenth-century travelogue noted the survival of cofradías in most of the ciénega pueblos, despite the encroachment of Bellas Fuentes. Cofradías in Zacapu, Naranja, and Tiríndaro also maintained considerable herds of animals at this time, though they were forced to graze them on land rented from Bellas Fuentes. The communities continued to elect civic-religious leaders annually and mayordomos for each fiesta, and their priests could expect significant in-kind payments and sacramental fees. Indeed, each of the six pueblos of the ciénega paid the priest of Coeneo a fixed yearly salary of between 129 pesos (Tarejero) and 324 pesos (Azajo), in addition to individual clerical fees for sacramental services performed.⁹⁶ Although considerable variation existed between pueblos, Canon Romero in the 1850s found the ciénega communities generally to possess adequate religious architecture and ornamentation. He singled out the wealthier Azajo for special praise, calling its chapel "very good, and with decent ornaments."⁹⁷ Perhaps most important, Purépecha religiosity continued to revolve around very public and corporate celebrations of Corpus Christi.

If Purépecha/Franciscan religiosity defined the southern tier of central Michoacán, the northern tier of the region fostered a more complex mix of mendicant, indigenous, and Spanish religious styles. The Augustinian friars that Vasco de Quiroga invited to this part of Michoacán in the 1530s to shore up Spanish control on the Chichimeca frontier shared many of the Franciscans' evangelizing methods and goals, if not their utopian outlook. Yet, as Robert Jackson has demonstrated, the Augustinians incorporated native religious symbols and geography into larger narratives about the order's role in the development of early Christianity. Their tradition of asceticism and monasticism, they believed, made the Augustinians direct heirs of the early Church fathers, and they proposed to bring this ancient Christian faith to Mexico's natives.⁹⁸ Early episodes of persecution and martyrdom on the Chichimeca frontier helped consolidate narratives linking the friars to the "Desert Fathers" who developed the monastic and hermetic traditions in the third century. Like other Augustinian outposts, the Huango convent was subject to frequent and deadly Chichimeca raids. A particularly bad 1585 raid—in which several neophytes were taken captive—prompted the two resident friars to pursue the raiders, unarmed, into Chichimeca territory. According to their hagiographers, the friars' habits miraculously protected them from Chichimeca arrows, a miracle that so startled the raiders that they released their captives and fled.⁹⁹

In their evangelizing mission, the Augustinian fathers found a powerful ally in Juan de Villaseñor. A devout protector of the Augustinian order, the conqueror and his family also helped to shape religious culture in the region as patrons of the Church. Villaseñor and his heirs built local chapels, funded devotions through obras pías, and sent numerous sons and daughters into religious professions.¹⁰⁰ The family also helped to spread devotion to Huango's chief Christological saint, Nuestro Señor del Perdón (Our Lord of Mercy). The image came to Michoacán with the first Augustinian missionaries, who had reportedly received it from the hands of Tomás de Villanueva, the Augustinian archbishop of Valencia whose reputation for charity and healing had placed him on the road for sainthood by the time of his death in the mid-sixteenth century.[101] The Augustinian fathers of Michoacán then entrusted the image to Villaseñor while they finished work on the Huango convent. The monumental and "pompous" convent structure envisioned by the missionaries was never to fully take shape, however, and the finished sacristy became Huango's parish church. The image of the Lord of Mercy moved to an altar inside the temple, though it had to share space with the parish's patron, Saint Nicholas of Tolentino.[102] Shortly before secularization in the 1790s, the resident clergy and multiethnic *vecindario* pooled their resources to build a new parish church.[103] But the burgeoning devotion to the Lord of Mercy would soon require the construction of a separate chapel, as we will see.

The frontier quality of the Bajío of Puruándiro in the colonial period encouraged the development of multiethnic local religious cultures over the longue durée. On the one hand, the friars congregated Purépecha and Otomí communities around Huango and Puruándiro in the late sixteenth century, and the former retained an Indian hospital and its attendant cofradía into the nineteenth century.[104] On the other, the enslaved Africans brought to work the estates of Villachuato, Ururuta, La Estancia, and Buenavista, through processes of mestizaje and manumission, came to form a sizable free Afro-mestizo population, most of whom worked as cattle herders for the haciendas. Along with poor Spaniards and mestizos, the Afro-mestizos went on to form small rancherías on lands belonging to haciendas or cofradías.[105] By the mid-nineteenth century, the indigenous population in the Bajío of Puruándiro had dropped off sharply, constituting only one-eighth of the population in Huango while retaining a slim majority in the head town.[106] Nevertheless, surviving Indian communities in the Bajío retained cofradía structures and preserved festive traditions centered on their Augustinian hospitals. In contrast to the ciénega, though, indigenous religious life was more thoroughly integrated into the colonial whole. A primary account of the 1791 fiesta of Saint Joseph, during which the faithful crowned the image belonging to the cofradía of the Huango hospital, describes a thoroughly baroque scene of procession and coronation. The festivities were made possible by the participation of various ethnicized cofradías, from the indigenous brotherhood of the hospital and the Spanish cofradía of El Santísimo to the heavily Afro-mestizo cofradía of Saint Nicholas Tolentino, all of which performed their place in Huango's religious community and contributed financially to the celebration. The procession of Saint Joseph also included numerous, if outmoded, paraliturgical displays, including dances of *mecos* and matachines (costumed dancers derived from the Moors and Christians tradition), mounted "gypsies," and children dressed as "little Moors" playing oboes. The golden "imperial crown," replete with thirty-eight gemstones, was purchased by the owners of the Cerano Hacienda.[107] This, then, was a religious culture that brought together all of the various social groups and ethnoracial religious corporations of the greater Huango area, and it betrayed few signs of the enlightened currents (internal, individually focused piety, a distaste for excessive pomp) then circulating among elites in larger cities.[108]

In sum, religious cultures in the Bajío of Puruándiro and the ciénega of Zacapu retained a strong baroque imprint well into the national period. Such local religious cultures shared key features, despite divergences in content. In both areas, parishioners retained close relationships with the missionary orders well beyond their sixteenth-century heyday. Missionary religion—with its focus on pageantry, festivity, and the performance of social belonging—and the baroque syncretisms that resulted from evangelization thus planted deep roots throughout the region. Popular religious practice, whether centered on local Christologies (the Lord of Mercy) or liturgical rites (Corpus Christi), also required a cooperative—if seldom completely harmonious—relationship with the local clergy and a balance of power between lay religious leaders and parish priests. While often syncretic in content, local religion was not declericalized, though it relied on, and perhaps attracted, a distinctive segment of the clergy. Throughout their histories, the towns of the region were well attended by the clergy, which played a crucial role in mediating believers' access to the divine.[109]

Central Michoacán did not remain immune from Catholic revitalization efforts in the nineteenth century, but such campaigns proved notably weaker here than in the northwest and the southern sierra. In part, such weakness owed to structural factors. The economic and demographic changes that were reshaping rural life and devotional tastes in Zamora and Cotija simply had not yet overturned the colonial order in central Michoacán. Consequently, movements to strip baroque "excess" from devotional practices lacked adequate constituencies in Huango and Huaniqueo. Additionally, institutional attitudes in Morelia's archbishopric diverged sharply from the upstart Zamora diocese. As we saw in chapter 2, archdiocesan authorities in Morelia, though they shared the *labastidista* clique's enthusiasm for the revitalization of the faith, stopped short of endorsing Zamora's Europeanizing model of reform. As a result of its more inward-looking approach, the new devotional associations and lay social and educational projects that were making great strides in the Diocese of Zamora lagged behind in the Archdiocese of Michoacán. Further, local Ultramontane circles and their priests could not always count on the support of the hierarchy in their attempts to remake local religion. Indeed, the Árciga administration often privileged custom over newfangled Roman standards of practice, and it endeavored to honor the prerogatives of the ancient parishes. Guardians of a unique Quirogan heritage, Morelia's clergy pursued reform at its own pace and in accordance with its own spiritual outlook.[110]

Central Michoacán parishes, and especially the Purépecha parishes of the ciénega, were subject to periodic attempts at reform of popular practice since at least the mid-seventeenth century. Such attempts—aimed most often at fiesta practices—generally failed to affect major changes, however, since priests and parishioners often resisted implementing the reforms prescribed by the hierarchy and crown officials.[111] The social and institutional disruptions of the independence wars may well have helped to derail the most vigorous reform attempt of the colonial period, initiated by Bourbon officials in the late eighteenth century.[112] By the mid-nineteenth century, diocesan authorities in Michoacán had renewed their efforts to reform popular practice, especially as it related to the celebration of Corpus Christi, but they generally declined to suppress indigenous customs altogether. Archbishop Árciga, in particular, took a moderate stance toward baroque religious practice—sometimes mandating the "reform of customs" and other times allowing priests and parishioners ample autonomy in shaping local religious culture. For example, Árciga failed to discipline Purépecha leaders in Zacapu who, after an argument with Father Ramón Estrada over the ownership of the keys to the church building in 1868, chased the priest out of town and proceeded to "take out the images of the temple in a procession . . . without the permission or license of the priest," and indeed he promptly sent a new cleric to replace Estrada.[113] During his 1871 pastoral visit of the same town, however, Árciga identified a number of problems and irregularities in religious practice, which he ordered Father Leonides Dávalos to correct. Dávalos was to ensure that parishioners did not render devotion to the image of Fray Jacobo Daciano, the sixteenth-century Franciscan evangelizer and founder of the parish, and he should prevent the Indians from placing images of the friar inside the church. Purépecha parishioners were to refrain from carrying out "races" (*carreras*) between saints' images or loudly chanting the rosary through the streets "at very late hours" on Christmas Eve. They would also be expected to honor the terms of their colonial pindecuario or risk being subjected to the same clerical fee schedule as non-Indian parishes. Further, Dávalos should curtail the "irreverence" that often accompanied the celebration of Corpus Christi, ensuring that the procession did not include traditional dancers.[114]

Elsewhere, the archdiocese did not consistently impose the kind of strict oversight of popular festivals that it ordered in Zacapu. Indeed, it often issued warnings or prohibitions only when local priests asked for them. When the community of Zipiajo asked for permission to hold a procession with the Blessed Sacrament during Corpus Christi in 1864, archdiocesan authorities approved the request on the condition that the Indians refrain from selling alcohol and that they "avoid the abuses and disorders of past years." On the advice of Father Diego Navarro, they also prohibited the procession of the "vaqueros" (cowboys) and "the other guilds with the ridiculous costumes that they are accustomed to using."[115] However, ecclesiastical authorities approved Corpus Christi processions without imposing such conditions in Naranja in 1867 and Tiríndaro in 1870.[116] Zipiajo was denied a license for its Corpus Christi procession in 1872, after the reformist priest Hilario Castro sent a blistering critique of Purépecha heterodoxy in all of the pueblos of Coeneo's parish.[117] However, Árciga's government was unwilling to issue such a blanket prohibition, and in 1873 it conceded a Corpus Christi license to Zipiajo, satisfied that the parishioners had done their part to ensure the "decency" of their chapel.[118] Indeed, in 1873 the six pueblos broke from their custom of rotating the octave of Corpus in six-year cycles and instead all had a celebration concurrently. That June, the vicario Juan Menéndez informed his superiors that he could not come to Morelia for an interview with Árciga because he was busy celebrating the octave in each of the six pueblos of the jurisdiction. He could not find a substitute, since the priests of Zacapu and Coeneo had to preside over their own Corpus celebrations. If he left for Morelia, the pueblo of Naranja would be deprived of its service, something Menéndez worried would cause the *naranjeños* to "be displeased with me, as would the other pueblos of this jurisdiction [who need me to preside over] their octave; and other comments very unfavorable to my honor and reputation as a priest would be made."[119] The archdiocese acceded to the wishes of Menéndez and the Purépecha pueblos: He could come after the end of the Corpus cycle. This exchange is notable as much for the priest's solicitous attitude with the Indians as for the archbishop's reluctance to antagonize his flock.

Strikingly, Árciga's administration continued issuing licenses for Corpus Christi and other festivities—and even for public processions—in the midst of the Religionero crisis. The archdiocese granted licenses for Corpus processions in both Tiríndaro and Naranja (despite the resumption of the rotational scheme) in April 1874, adding that public processions could take place with a "written permission" from the civil authorities of the pueblos.[120] This was tantamount to asking the state to do the see's work for it by suppressing the processions, something that the archdiocese did not have the stomach to do. Corpus seems to have been suspended throughout the region in 1875, when its populations suffered the worst phase of the armed conflict. However, by the summer of 1876 the pueblos had resumed Corpus processions with the collusion of local civil authorities and the license of the archbishop.[121] Such arrangements continued in the summer of 1877, when Porfirian authorities also proved willing to allow processions in the Purépecha pueblos as well as between Coeneo and Puruándiro.[122] The parishioners of the region, then, were highly successful in overturning the prohibition on public worship, a primary goal of the Religionero movement. However, as we will see below, they did not have to take up arms to achieve such a goal, since both the archbishopric and village authorities generally supported the festive pretentions of the communities.

This is not to suggest that the region's towns were immune from Ultramontane revitalization or from intraflock conflict. The mania for Church restoration had caught on in many central Michoacán communities by the mid-nineteenth century, and the area was not impervious to the lay devotional activism of the Vela Perpetua, especially. Puruándiro, Coeneo, and Huaniqueo all had Vela chapters by 1860, and their members financed the purchase of various ornaments. The Vela wielded particular influence in Coeneo and, as in other places, it was the subject of occasional parish conflict, as we will see below. However, the other drivers of Catholic restorationism at this time—the Vincentian conferences, the lay educational and social projects, the French- and Italian-style devotions—remained notably absent in the region. Most important, strong festive traditions and tolerant ecclesiastical authorities often conspired against religious reform in central Michoacán, where Ultramontane Catholicism faced an uphill battle. What is more, the complex engagement between baroque religion, Ultramontane reformism, and lerdista anticlericalism led to widely divergent patterns of political mobilization in the region. In Coeneo, where Purépecha Catholics could both ward off Ultramontane challenges to their festive cultures and negotiate the return of public worship with liberal elites, rebellion proved unnecessary. In Huaniqueo and Huango, by contrast, baroque devotions served as lightning rods for spiritual resistance against Ultramontanism as well as armed resistance against the liberal authorities' attacks on public worship and corporate religious properties.

The Negotiation of Baroque Worship in the Ciénega

As we have seen, the Purépecha communities of the Zacapu marshland demonstrated little real commitment to the Religionero movement. Indeed, pueblos such as Zipiajo and Naranja served as little more than passive transit points for gavillas, and larger towns such as Zacapu and Coeneo were more often targets of Religionero attacks than scenes of rebel mobilization. Religionero fortunes in these towns owed something to the strength of local liberal factions, which had controlled local politics for decades. Yet the weakness of the local Religionero movement also had much to do with parishioners' ability to achieve Religionero goals and block Ultramontane reformism through negotiation with both ecclesiastical and liberal authorities. In Coeneo, for example, Purépecha Catholics failed to come to their priest's assistance when he ran afoul of municipal authorities and instead sided with local liberals in a successful bid to replace the reformist and divisive Father Castro with a priest more amenable to their religious customs. When some of Castro's local allies resorted to arms in his defense in 1873, then, Purépecha community members mostly remained on the sidelines, since they had already obtained the religious concessions they sought. The resulting Religionero mobilization in Coeneo was smaller and more mestizo than in Huaniqueo and Huango, and Religionero attacks on Coeneo generally came from without.[123]

Parish correspondence reveals that Castro's divisive style of religious leadership had engendered ill will among segments of Coeneo's population from early on in his tenure, which began in 1868. That year, Coeneo's Purépecha leaders attempted to have Castro disciplined when he failed to preside over traditional Holy Week festivities. In this instance, the archdiocese cleared Castro of responsibility, instead blaming the "inept and imprudent conduct" of his vicar.[124] Yet Castro soon faced further popular challenges. An earnest enemy of the religious customs of the Purépechas of Coeneo and its sujeto villages, Castro attempted to suppress their Corpus Christi traditions in 1872.[125] Citing the "complete demoralization" that reigned in the pueblos and the "grave significance of the abuses" that they committed during the festivities, Castro asked that the archdiocese not grant any Corpus Christi licenses to the pueblos of his jurisdiction for the foreseeable future. As we have seen, ecclesiastical authorities in Morelia proved more amenable to Purépecha customs than Castro, and they simply ordered the communities to clean and decorate their chapels properly or risk losing their licenses for the celebration.¹²⁶ Moreover, the tension between Castro and Purépecha leaders in Coeneo went beyond the conflict over Corpus Christi. Indigenous leaders of the head town accused Castro of bigotry when he began making alliances with a small contingent of mestizo parishioners in 1871 and attempted to sell the ancient parish cemetery without consulting the Indians. Castro had even refused to live in the *casa cural* provided to him by the indigenous community (a house the Indians considered one of the best in town), preferring to rent a private home from a mestizo family. This prompted pueblo leaders to question pointedly, "What does he mean by this conduct? That non-Indians are better in condition than those of us who are Indians?"¹²⁷ Answering these charges before the archdiocese, Castro painted the parish's history in apocalyptic colors, lamenting the historical strength of the "enemies of the clergy" in Coeneo and underlining the sacrifices he had made to subjugate a "multitude of dissidents" to Church authority. Further, the Purépechas of Coeneo operated under the "always bastard and foolish pretension that they are authorities over their priest."¹²⁸

Such a pretension helped solidify an alliance between the comuneros and liberal civil officials, who sought Purépecha support in their bid to subjugate the local Church. José Dolores Zavala and Francisco Ramos, personal enemies of the priest and members of the municipal corporation, led the effort. As alcalde, Zavala had fined Castro twenty pesos for convening the faithful for a set of spiritual exercises that brought a throng of parishioners into the church atrium back in 1871, allegedly inciting a riot against the priest replete with cries of "Death to the cura!"¹²⁹ Two years later, district officials threatened to imprison Castro after he issued permits for canonical burial at Bellas Fuentes, thereby bypassing the civil registry.¹³⁰ According to Castro, the civil officials hoped to use such persecution to cover their usurpation of 580 pesos belonging to the Church. In an insolent flourish, Castro declared that the archdiocese could not conceivably side with the dissidents. "It is not possible, Illustrious Sir, to combine truth and justice with the barbarity and stupidity that characterizes some of the pueblos of our archdiocese, with the idiotism and atrocities of the barbarous [Indians] who, without a God outside of that of their passions, do not even give consideration to the causes of God alongside those of their idols."¹³¹

Castro's acolytes, a group that included "principal vecino" Antonio Huerta and the women of the Vela Perpetua, quickly came to his defense.¹³² The male vecinos blamed the influence of "Satanic ideas" for the disorders of 1873.[133] For its part, the Vela declared that Castro's moralizing influence, and especially his disregard for differences in "condition or sex," had inflamed more impious and traditionalist segments of the population.[134] Archdiocesan officials ultimately sided with Castro, but their support proved insufficient to safeguard the priest's tenure. In February 1873, he renounced his post and fled to Morelia. From the capital, Castro explained his hasty departure to archdiocesan authorities, complaining that during his time in Coeneo he had suffered "uninterrupted slights, calumnies, and accusations from [his] enemies." By the time of his departure, the conflict had become acute, and Castro worried that outright violence could ensue if he returned to the town. His detractors were determined to keep him out, and his defenders had vowed to resort to arms in order to ensure his return. Castro feared that a violent clash would play directly into the hands of his local enemies, allowing them to paint him as a rebel.[135] Under such circumstances, the archdiocese decided it best to transfer Castro to the eastern Michoacán village of Tuxpan, near "liberal" Zitácuaro. Not long after, however, Castro found himself in trouble with the law again, when vecinos of Jungapeo accused him of conspiring with the Religioneros. District personnel searched Castro's person, found the "little pistol" that he carried for personal security, and threw him in Zitácuaro's municipal prison, where he languished for several weeks.[136] Such was the fate of one of the archdiocese's most ambitious Ultramontane reformers—exile to Michoacán's most stridently anticlerical zone, followed by incarceration.

In Castro's absence, meanwhile, Coeneo witnessed a small organic Religionero mobilization under Jesús Gil and Guadalupe Contreras. Notably, local Religioneros directed their ire especially at local liberals José Dolores Zavala and Rafael Arias.[137] While at least one of Castro's supporters, Perfecto Reyes, joined the small Religionero contingent from Coeneo, we lack evidence of a single Purépecha leader from the area participating in the movement.[138] Rather, as we saw above, the Purépecha communities of the ciénega mostly remained uncommitted to the struggle, occasionally providing the government with information about rebel movements and other times serving as a passive transit point for rebel gavillas.

Hilario Castro seems to fit the liberal stereotype of the rebellious, fanatical curate. He violated the Laws of Reform with impunity, he carried a gun and allegedly preferred the company of rebels, and where he went, violent conflict followed. However, our examination of the religious culture and politics of Coeneo complicates this picture. Castro lacked a constituency among the

Purépecha Catholics of Coeneo and its sujetos, and his presence in the parish proved divisive. While we lack definitive evidence that he colluded with Religioneros in Jungapeo in 1874, in Coeneo his conflict with the Purépecha communities and civil officials most certainly did help to shape Religionero bellicosity after 1874. Yet Castro did not serve as an avatar for the defense of baroque religious practices against the anticlerical government. Rather, his reformist zeal endeared him to Ultramontane, mestizo segments of the population and alienated the Purépecha comuneros, who ultimately joined a local liberal clique against their priest. If Castro's ouster was a victory for civil officials who had chafed at his "fanaticism," it was also a victory for the town's Purépecha Catholics. In fact, Castro's replacements, Juan Menéndez (1873), the vicario Antonio Hernández (1867–1877), and the aging Francisco de Paul Morrilón (1874–1877), proved significantly more respectful of local religious customs—including Corpus Christi traditions—and they consequently garnered more sympathy from the parishioners. As we saw, under Menéndez's administration Coeneo's sujeto pueblos resumed Corpus Christi celebrations that were prohibited under Castro. Morillón, for his part, showed himself especially sensitive to Purépecha tradition, consulting parish archives on numerous occasions to confirm the "immemorial" status of practices, reestablishing the rotational scheme of Corpus Christi, and intervening with civil officials on behalf of communities to secure processions.[139] He was successful in this latter task, since in 1876 and 1877 public Corpus Christi processions took place in Naranja, Tiríndaro, and Zipiajo. In part, such a success may have owed to the rapport that Morillón and Vicar Hernández established with Purépecha villagers. The pair confessed hundreds of Purépechas in Coeneo and its sujetos during Holy Week in 1875, even obtaining protesta retractions from the judicial authority and police chief of Zipiajo.[140] Antonio Hernández, who spoke Purépecha and "kn[ew] well how to cultivate the sympathies of the faithful," must have been instrumental to such an effort.[141] In sum, under the care of priests such as these, the threat to baroque religion represented by Hilario Castro and his reformist acolytes subsided. Yet Purépecha Catholics had not had to take up arms. They had achieved Religionero goals before the rebellion began.

Huaniqueo: Religioneros Rally behind Father Arroyo

Unlike in Coeneo, popular constituencies in Huaniqueo and Huango did not negotiate with local liberals and instead dove headlong into the Religionero revolt. In Huaniqueo, the relative cohesion of the flock and a weak Ultramontane challenge meant that baroque Catholics felt the full weight of the ban on public worship from the state, and they rallied to the defense of village traditions and religious properties. An ethnically mixed municipality with a Purépecha core surrounded by the Tecacho Hacienda and a number of mestizo rancherías, Huaniqueo was a conservative foil to nearby liberal Coeneo, supporting *santanista* centralism in the 1830s and serving as an imperialist garrison during the 1860s.[142] Its church in 1866 possessed an impressive inventory of gold and silver ornaments and two brand new confessionals, and its eleven saints' images boasted new vestments and linens, several silver crowns, and other accoutrements. The image of Our Lord of Health attracted special devotion, surrounded as it was by gilded silver *potencias* (rays of light) and a new floral arch and bedecked in a satin cloth and an "imperial crown of gilded silver."[143] It is unclear whether hacendados, comuneros, or pious rancheros were primarily responsible for subsidizing such objects of faith, but in any case, the parish's material wealth suggests a high level of parishioner investment. It bears repeating that with his dying breath, Socorro Reyes would later donate the entirety of his meager estate to the cult.

Huaniqueo seems to have suffered relatively few of the disruptions to its religious economy associated with the Reforma. Between 1865 and 1877, its priests and parishioners constructed a new parish church to replace the dilapidated Franciscan sanctuary.[144] Though account books are missing from the archive, other evidence suggests that Father Pedro Arroyo and his coadjutor, Ramón Moreno, were adept at eliciting small voluntary contributions from their flock. In 1877, for example, several dozen contributors to the new church—a simple cruciform edifice decorated with allegorical paintings on its interior walls and "exquisite" latticework on its doors and windows—wrote to the archbishop to express their pride in the building and praise their priests.[145] For his part, Arroyo had maintained significant parish income through clerical obventions in the 1860s and 1870s, collecting around 1,000 pesos a year in baptism, marriage, and burial fees despite the institution of the civil registry.[146]

Arroyo, especially, aroused great sympathy among his parishioners. He had served as parish priest since 1866, and during his tenure he had earned the love of the people of Huaniqueo, so vecinos stated, "because of the great spiritual and temporal benefits [they] received in the long epoch during which [they] were under his paternal care."[147] The parishioners experienced his departure in 1875—the result of persecution by civil authorities in

Puruándiro—as a "blow of death" and a divine punishment for their sins. Arroyo had also won the support of Huaniqueo's Purépechas, since he had promised their leaders that he would help them obtain ecclesiastical permission to sell cofradía lands belonging to the Franciscan hospital and divide the profits among community members.[148] Thus, Arroyo endorsed community control of cofradía property, and this was not his only old-fashioned trait. He was also known to be lax in his administrative style, according to Father Moreno, celebrating Mass in the new church before it was properly prepared, allowing pigs and donkeys to enter into the building, and failing to correct parishioners even when it was discovered that "persons of both sexes" were entering the building late at night.[149] Moreno, who substituted for Arroyo during a brief sick leave in 1875 and subsequently took over the parish administration after the latter's departure, also complained of Arroyo's poor bookkeeping habits. His failure to keep accurate accounts of tithes and obventions meant trouble for Moreno, who found that vecinos balked when he asked them for tithes that they claimed to have paid to Arroyo.[150] Likely, the priest kept track of tithes informally and only partially, and parishioners must have appreciated such laxity. This, then, was a priest who enjoyed close and informal relationships with his flock and generally tolerated its spiritual errors, in addition to enduring its hostility to the centralization of church taxes.

Moreno's complaints must be taken with a grain of salt. He had tangled with Arroyo two years earlier, when he was serving as coadjutor of Huango. In that instance, Arroyo had allegedly conspired with the "ancient" priest of Huango, Ramón Cipriano Torres, to remove Moreno from the casa cural.[151] Further conflict came soon after Moreno arrived in Huaniqueo, in February 1875, when Arroyo demanded that his substitute hand over one-third of the income he would receive in the priest's absence. Since he had come to Huaniqueo in the midst of the Religionero rebellion and an outbreak of fever, Moreno had spent most of his time traveling between ranchos to hear confessions, poorly fed and riding lame horses abandoned by the rebels. Why, after such tribulations, should he give Arroyo a third of his meager salary? Such complaints were ignored. Archbishop Árciga had already promised Arroyo that he would receive the money, and he would not intervene on Moreno's behalf.[152] Whether or not personal or financial issues motivated Moreno's complaints, then, his letters do suggest that Arroyo had little of the reforming spirit that animated younger clerics in Michoacán. Further, Arroyo's parishioners seemed to prefer it that way, and even the archbishopric declined to correct his supposed deficiencies.

Tellingly, the Religionero rebels of the region proved to be acolytes of the old-style cura Arroyo and not the younger, more Ultramontane Moreno. Religioneros Jesús López and Ramón de la Cruz, to give but two examples, were among the signatories of pro-Arroyo petitions.[153] Purépecha leader Antonio Cilagua, who joined the rebellion in early 1875, must have seen in Arroyo an ally in the fight against the usurpation of the hospital plaza by the ayuntamiento, since the priest had shown himself amenable to communal claims to religious property in the past, as we have seen. Liberal newspaper editors, meanwhile, considered Arroyo the true author of the Socorro Reyes revolt, and they even claimed that military authorities had found letters from the priest in the possession of captured rebels.[154] Arroyo's involvement in the rebellion cannot be verified, but he most certainly stood at the heart of the local conflict. In June 1874, a few months after the Socorro Reyes pronunciamiento, Arroyo traveled to Puruándiro in order to testify on behalf of two captured rebels. Upon hearing that their priest had been escorted to the district head town at the behest of the prefect, the community erupted into violence.[155] District forces quickly put down the riot, but Huaniqueo would for the remainder of the conflict serve as a Religionero bastion. During 1875, the town suffered the repeated desertion of civil authorities, sometimes remaining without leadership for months at a time.[156]

Huango: Baroque Catholics Nurture the Religioneros and Defeat an Ultramontane Cura

A similar pattern of popular mobilization can be observed in the more mesticized Huango, though here Ultramontane reformism constituted more of a threat, and it exacerbated lerdista pressures on village religion. Parish correspondence paints Huango as a devout but hardly orthodox religious community. Like Huaniqueo, it was home to a mixed population of indigenous comuneros and mestizo rancheros, artisans, and merchants. By the time of Canon Romero's visit in the 1850s, Indians constituted only one-eighth of the population, likely as a result of the growth of mestizo rancherías on the entailed lands surrounding the town.[157] Indeed, according to Ramón Cipriano Torres, parish priest of Huango from 1850 until his death in 1873, the rancho of Batuecas had been formed in the 1830s by tenants on a plot of ex-Augustinian land whose proceeds had traditionally been used to pay the priest's salary. Yet the rancheros of Batuecas had "insurrected" against the parish and used liberal legislation to adjudicate the plot in 1857.[158] The rebellious attitude of Batuecas was not Father Torres's only problem, either. In 1872 he complained that his young male parishioners continually abducted their fiancées from their parents' houses and eloped in order to dodge clerical fees.[159] In a report to the archdiocese the same year, he also lamented that parish revenues had fallen off considerably since the end of civil coercion in the collection of tithes.[160] Nevertheless, Torres's own accounts do not show a significant decline in parish obventions over the period of 1864 to 1872, suggesting that his parishioners were generally still willing to pay for the sacraments.[161] Further, one particular local devotion elicited strong popular piety and financial support from parishioners (and even pilgrims)— Our Lord of Mercy.

In 1873, a large group of petitioners requested archdiocesan support for the construction of a new chapel for the image, describing the cult of the Lord of Mercy as an antidote to modern religious indifference. Working with their priest, they had convened general meetings in the community to collect donations for the project, and they had received prior archdiocesan approval to sell the old cemetery plot in order to subsidize the chapel. Petitioners declared that the project had "exalted the religious zeal of the vecinos, and because of this [they were] willing to endure whatever sacrifices were necessary in order to obtain for the parish such an important improvement and the beautification and exaltation of the pueblo."[162] The image, it should be remembered, had come with the first Augustinian missionaries, but it had apparently been kept in a private house for an indefinite period of time until Father Torres rescued it and placed it in the parish church. In the hands of Torres, it took on new, miraculous qualities. In a separate petition, vecinos led by the Gaitán, Raya, and Bolaños families claimed that ever since Torres had "given" them the image, "all of the disgraces and calamities [of the pueblo] ceased."[163] In his letter of support, the ancient Torres confirmed the miraculous nature of the image, claiming that before he had brought it to the church, the vecinos were "immoral" and suffered poor harvests. The image changed all of that, though, reforming local customs and attracting widespread devotion. By 1873, groups of vecinos visited the image every night to pray, and it even attracted travelers on the Camino Real.[164] Devotion to the Lord of Mercy seems to have crossed ethnic boundaries, too. Genaro García, a member of the indigenous community of Huango, donated the urban plot that he received in the reparto to the parish in 1872, stipulating that it serve as the site for the new chapel.[165]

Torres and the image of the Lord of Mercy, then, stood at the center of a local religious revival, and the community rallied around them despite its tendencies for "spiritual error" in the Ultramontane sense. When the young and ambitious Ramón Moreno came to the parish as coadjutor in 1873, meanwhile, he failed to endear himself to Torres's constituency, and conflict soon ensued. Moreno was not impressed with the state of the parish when he arrived in Huango. He found the church lacking basic supplies such as wax and wine, and the dormant Vela chapter could not cover such expenses. Moreno described Torres as "very unhappy" about his arrival in the parish, and he was already busy "inflaming" the Indians against the new coadjutor. Further, Torres and his family did not wish to share the casa cural with Moreno and were purposely making life difficult for him.[166] By December 1873, Torres's constituency had begun drafting petitions against Moreno, allegedly with the help of Huaniqueo's Father Arroyo, and Moreno could no longer tolerate living in the casa cural. The archbishop demonstrated sympathy with Moreno's plight, but he ultimately instructed Moreno to treat Torres with "delicacy and prudence, in attention to his advanced age."[167] In another letter, Archdiocesan Secretary Luis Macouzet addressed Torres with uncommon affection, calling him "our good friend" and expressing the archbishop's concern for his health.[168] Meanwhile, a large faction of vecinos and Indians was seeking Moreno's removal, calling him "rigid, intemperate, and lacking in prudence." He insulted parishioners in his frequent "declamations" from the pulpit and fomented the Vela Perpetua in a "vulgar" fashion; his terrible treatment of the revered Father Torres had even affected the latter's health.[169]

A smaller faction of vecinos came to Moreno's defense in early 1874, assuring the archbishop that the Indians were simply upset with Moreno for trying to "remove certain bad customs" they enjoyed.[170] An investigation by the priest of Puruándiro shed further light on such "customs." During interviews with three "honorable" vecinos (all merchants), the investigator found that Moreno had tried to prevent the Indians from placing "an image" on the main altar of the church on December 8, because he was going to use the altar to exhibit the Blessed Host. The witnesses did not believe Moreno had offended parishioners from the pulpit, though one testified that the priest once used "some vulgar concepts" during an exhortation to revive the Vela. All three witnesses pointed to Father Torres as the principal author of the campaign against Moreno.[171]

The archdiocese cleared Moreno of the charges, but that did him little good. The majority of the community was against him, and when Torres died in early 1874 parishioners partially blamed Moreno for causing the ancient priest so much grief. Moreno left the parish soon after, bound for a short and problematic tenure as coadjutor of Huaniqueo, and archdiocesan authorities sent Leonides Dávalos to replace him.[172] Dávalos's own tenure was cut short by the instability of the Religionero rebellion, since he was accused of supporting the rebels and voluntarily left the parish in October 1876. Yet during his time in Huango, the new chapel of the Lord of Mercy enjoyed its debut Mass, and the intraflock conflict that had overtaken the parish during Moreno's tenure quickly subsided.[173] If the baroque Catholics of Huango had lost a champion with Torres's death, they had also won the battle against the reformist Moreno. Crucially for our purposes, and as in the previous case of Huaniqueo, parish correspondence reveals that it was these Catholics who joined or supported the Religionero rebellion. For example, don Rafael Raya and his brother, the Religionero chief Donaciano Raya, were primary supporters of Torres and devotees of the Lord of Mercy.[174] Described by civil authorities as a "principal vecino," don Rafael had not only failed to defend Huango from the Religionero attack of March 1875, he had actively sheltered the rebels. Indeed, military reports indicated that the majority of Huango's principal vecinos had "done absolutely nothing to cooperate in the defense" and that, more predictably, the town's "lower classes ha[d] been [the army's] primary enemy."[175] With few exceptions, then, Huango closed ranks with the Religioneros. Civil authorities fled the town in early 1875, leaving Religionero "El Licenciado" Ortega to "reestablish order" and name new officials.[176] The prefecture of Puruándiro repeatedly had to send armed forces to Huango in order to restore government control, and the municipal authorities it imposed reported frequent desertions by National Guard troops. During an attack by Religioneros under Félix Dueñas and Guadalupe Contreras in March 1875, dozens of vecinos joined the rebels, and the municipal authorities were again driven from town. By the summer of 1875, the town essentially served as a safe haven for Religioneros under Socorro Reyes, Pedro González, and Guadalupe Raya, whose forces numbered over three hundred.[177]

The Religioneros of Huango—both leaders and rank-and-file soldiers—were apparently immersed in baroque religion. The largest local uprising in the town occurred during Holy Week of 1875, which beyond its traditional liturgical significance also coincided with one of the Lord of Mercy's three traditional feasts.[178] Among the devotees who signed the petition for the new chapel for the latter image were Jesús Magaña and Rafael Villacaña, Religioneros who received indultos in 1876.[179] Another Religionero, Ignacio Gaitán, belonged to a prominent local Catholic family, many of whose members were supporters of the new chapel project and lay donation collectors. Relatives of Religionero chiefs Antonio Bolaños and Donaciano and Antonio Raya were also prominent devotees of the Lord of Mercy.[180] At least two local men known by the district prefect to be Religioneros—Juan Tinoco and Nabor Zavala—continued to make meager tithing payments in the midst of the conflict.[181] In sum, the baroque religious constituency in Huango cut across class and ethnic lines, uniting the community around the miraculous image of the Lord of Mercy, which served as an avatar for resistance to lerdismo. Most important, not only did Huango's baroque Catholics successfully defeat Father Moreno's reformist project and wage a war on the state, they also managed to emerge from the Religionero rebellion in positions of local power. Post-rebellion authorities in Huango included members of the Religionero-aligned Villacaña and Magaña families.[182] In essence, Huango's baroque Catholic faction had managed to tame both reforms—Catholic and liberal—through their involvement in the Religionero rebellion.

Conclusions

The cases of Coeneo, Huaniqueo, and Huango aptly demonstrate the impacts of baroque religion on local patterns of Religionero mobilization. However, the picture would not be complete without a more nuanced exploration of local material relations and political histories. That is, if each of these three communities rallied to popular, especially Christological devotions, those devotions did not uniformly lead them into the Religionero rebellion. Rather, a complex interplay of material, political, and religious factors determined patterns of partisanship in central Michoacán. Where parishioners united around baroque devotions and tolerant priests against the destabilizing effects of the reparto and the Laws of Reform, the Religionero rebellion retained a strong, organic constituency. In such places, the role of the lerdista state in attacking religious practice was thrown into sharp relief, and divisions within the flock minimized. In contrast, the historical strength of liberalism and the threatening character of Catholic reformism in Coeneo left its Purépecha parishioners stuck between a rock and a hard place. Rather than defending their Ultramontane priest from liberal attacks, then, they allied with local liberals while simultaneously petitioning the archdiocese for a new priest. It is unlikely that such a strategy would have borne fruit in the Diocese of Zamora, where the Ultramontane impulse generally worked against indigenous religious prerogatives. But the archdiocese was a different institution. Indeed, religious authorities in Morelia sympathized with the region's indigenous Catholics. Even though Árciga wanted to see the most questionable Purépecha practices muted or eliminated during traditional festivities, he proved less zealous in his reformism than priests such as Hilario Castro and Ramón Moreno. Archdiocesan tolerance helped persuade Purépechas not to join the rebellion. In short, they had achieved the religious concessions they had sought through archdiocesan channels and found local solutions to the protesta challenge. Under such circumstances, rebellion made little sense. For Socorro Reyes and his Huaniqueo followers, however, the restoration of local cults would require martyrdom.

CHAPTER 5

"Spiritual Orphans"

Religioneros and the Modernization of Southwest Michoacán

In January 1874, the pious Encarnación Farfán found himself in the Religioneros' sights. Farfán had served as municipal president and school director of the coastal sierra town of Coalcomán in 1872 and 1873, but he had refused to take the protesta without reservations, insisting that he would only enforce the laws "insofar as they d[id] not prejudice the rights and liberties of the Church." The district government promptly removed him from office for his failure to take the oath. Nevertheless, he told Bishop de la Peña, all of the people of the surrounding ranchos and many from Coalcomán considered him "*protestado*, in the heretical sense." Farfán even took to the pages of *El Pensamiento Católico* to clear the air, but he still worried that the rebels would come after him.[1] A vecino of Chinicuila, the mestizo ranchería belonging to Coalcomán, Farfán had long proved an active and ambitious ally of the Church. He regularly sent Bishop de la Peña long, detailed reports on Catholic restoration projects in the parish head town of Coalcomán, he backed local efforts to found a new Catholic school, and he was the principal author of a bid to create a new parish headquartered in Chinicuila.[2] What, then, did he have to fear from rebels who had taken up arms in defense of the Church?

Interestingly, Farfán was not the only devout Catholic targeted by Religioneros in Coalcomán. During their August 1875 attack on the head town, rebels burned the house of Ignacio Moreno, a lay tithe collector from nearby Aguililla who had recently purchased property in Coalcomán.[3] On their retreat, Religioneros then robbed the parish priest, José María Sandoval, of 200 pesos belonging to the local Vela Perpetua chapter.[4] The women of the

Vela had offered vocal support for the local clergy, contributed funds to the construction of a new parish church, and promoted Catholic educational projects.[5] Along with the local female chapter of the Sociedad Católica, they had also led Coalcomán's critique of the Lerdo regime and the Laws of Reform, publishing a carta de protesta in *La Idea Católica* and sending a letter of appreciation to the legislators who had opposed the Ley Orgánica in the national congress.[6] Certainly, the attack on Father Sandoval may have represented simple opportunism by rebels strapped for resources. Yet the larger pattern of clear Religionero animosity toward leaders of Coalcomán's Catholic restorationist movement complicates the question of motives and the easy conflation of political and religious identities. If the Coalcomán rebels had taken up arms out of disgust for the Lerdo regime, they were obviously not supporters of Catholic restorationism. The liberal state and national press routinely characterized the Religionero movement as the revolt of fanaticized, papist hordes directed by local priests. Yet such characterizations did not hold true in Coalcomán. Rather, the revolt there followed other, more convoluted logics.

This chapter analyzes the sociopolitical and religious origins of the Religionero movement in Michoacán's southwestern coastal sierra, focusing on the district of Coalcomán. Through a careful reconstruction of the region's political, economic, and spiritual history, it untangles the multiplicity of religious and extrareligious variables that shaped Religionero partisanship in the district. Agrarian pressure, demographic changes, and squabbles among rival political clans figure chiefly among such extrareligious variables, and they proved more tangled here than in Jiquilpan or Puruándiro, where more purely spiritual concerns guided political revolt. This is not to say that the Religioneros of the coastal sierra lacked religious motives, such as an abhorrence of "protestants" and an outrage at the liberal prohibition of public worship. Yet the coastal rebellion distinguished itself more for the overlapping and contradictory interests of its various internal factions. Furthermore, even religious concerns in Coalcomán retained a highly materialistic character. As we will see below, such a complex and explosive milieu was the result of a nineteenth-century "second conquest" of this long-peripheral region, enacted by several waves of mestizo settlers who used both liberal legislation and Catholic restorationism to wrest control of the earth, and the faith, from its Nahua owners and the mestizo caciques that had dominated political affairs and the pastoral economy there since the independence wars. The despoiled then reacted by making war against the intruders.

The chapter begins with a narrative recapitulation of the southern sierra's longue durée history and that of its triple Religionero constituency of Indian comuneros, liberal caciques, and pious mestizo rancheros. Special emphasis is paid to the geographic and historical factors that kept the coastal sierra an ecclesiastical and commercial backwater until after the Reforma. The chapter then describes the "second conquest" of the coastal sierra, a period that saw important demographic changes, increasing commercial interest in the zone related to its extractive resources and the projected creation of a commercial port, as well as the renewed attempt to transform the system of land tenure inherited from the colony. As we will see, the 1871 disentailment process opened a deep rift within the indigenous community of Coalcomán, when a small faction of former communal leaders conspired with mestizo newcomers in order to profit from the reparto. Indeed, after a sustained legal challenge to the reparto failed, a majority faction of Nahua coalcomenses under the Cándido family opted for armed rebellion, merging their agrarian movement with the Religionero mobilization led by mestizos from Aguililla, Tepalcatepec, and (to a lesser extent) Coalcomán itself in 1874. After the Nahua Religioneros suffered a crushing defeat in April 1875, however, the movement was mostly carried forward by a second Religionero constituency, mestizos such as Bonifacio Vaca, Jesús Valencia, and the Guzmán brothers. The belated participation of the Guzmáns warrants further exploration. Scions of the political clan that had helped win Mexican independence and fought on behalf of federalism and liberalism throughout the first half of the nineteenth century, the Guzmáns primarily took up with the Religioneros as a way to reassert their power in the region—threatened as it was by political trends in Morelia, the erosion of their Nahua client base, and the machinations of their local political rival, Julio García.

The final two sections of the chapter explore southwestern Michoacán's religious history in order to demonstrate the complex linkages among the religious, political, and agrarian factors behind the revolt. That agrarian and political grievances moved many of the rebels in the southern sierra does not negate the importance of religious factors. Devout ranchero Catholics from the mestizo-dominated towns of Aguililla and Tepalcatepec constituted the third major Religionero constituency in the region. However, a comparable but more politically involved demographic group rejected armed revolt in Coalcomán's head town, and indeed leading exponents of Ultramontane reform efforts in the cabecera defended the government against Religionero attacks. Ultimately, such contradictions stemmed from the particular characteristics of the "second conquest" of the southern sierra. Ambitious priests, devout laywomen, and enterprising ranchero immigrants were central players in the transformations that threatened to eclipse the indigenous community of Coalcomán, and they were the modern Church's leading backers. Conscious of their role as modernizers of the sierra, they sought to supplant the corporate model of Nahua religiosity with a piety based on voluntary, individual contributions and tithing from private property. If Catholic restorationism helped to unify the community against lerdista anticlericalism in mestizo towns such as Aguililla, in Coalcomán it fractured it, marginalizing the Indian community and making bitter enemies of the faction of comuneros led by Antonio Cándido. In short, Catholic restoration in the southern sierra was an integral part of the second conquest. Not only did it seek to remake the faith along Ultramontane lines, it actually depended on the triumph of a ranchero-style agrarian economy and the erasure of the Indian community and its religious culture.

Michoacán's Southwest Coastal Sierra to 1873

The region that would become known politically as the district of Coalcomán stretched across much of Michoacán's Pacific coastline and east to the Sierra Madre del Sur and the Tepalcatepec River. It encompassed several distinct climatic and geographic zones, varying from the stifling heat and humidity of the Tepalcatepec River basin in its northeastern extremity to the temperate sierra highlands of the southwestern coast. Heavily forested and mountainous, the coastal zone suffered from historically poor communications with the major settlements of central-western Mexico. This pattern extended back to preconquest times, when the indigenous groups in the area retained only weak ties to the Purépecha capital at Tzintzuntzan. Though nominally subjects of the Purépecha state, the Cuahcomeca-speaking people of the region nevertheless had ample contact with Nahuas from central Mexico. With the conquest of Mexico, more Nahuas came to the area seeking a safe harbor from Spanish domination, and by the late colonial period their cultural influence had virtually erased the Purépecha connection.[7] This demographic takeover was compounded by the fact that the region's climate and geographic isolation had already conspired to make the demographic collapse of the seventeenth century particularly devastating. The population did not begin to rebound until the second half of the nineteenth century, and then it did so

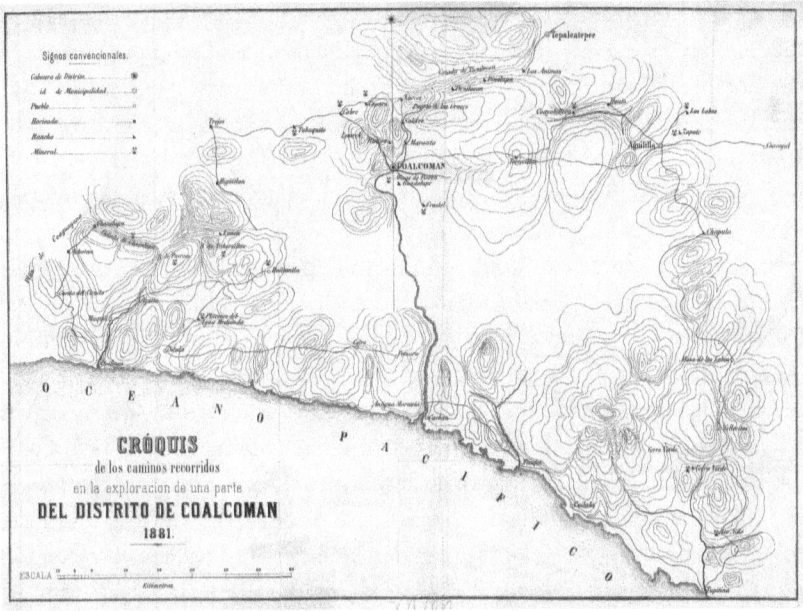

Map 6. The district of Coalcomán in the late nineteenth century. *Croquis de los caminos recorridos en la exploración de una parte del distrito de Coalcomán.* Courtesy of the Mapoteca "Manuel Orozco y Berra," del Servicio de Información Agroalimentaria y Pesquera, SAGARPA, Classification No. 2889-OYB-7234-A.

primarily through mestizo immigration.[8] By that time, the Nahua pueblos of the coast had developed unique, inward-looking communal cultures.

Catholic evangelization represented an early attempt to integrate coastal communities into the Spanish colonial project, but the results were decidedly mixed. Two of the original twelve Franciscan missionaries who came with Cortés—Fray Martín de Jesús and Fray Juan de Córdova—began the evangelization of the region in the decade after the fall of Tenochtitlán. Franciscans from the new convent at Tancítaro and the Augustinians of Tacámbaro carried out subsequent evangelization campaigns.[9] The missionaries congregated Nahua communities and established cofradías, but the influence of the friars here paled in comparison to northwestern and central Michoacán. Indeed, secular priests—brought by encomenderos to serve the spiritual needs of their laborers—entered the region as early as the 1530s, and they mostly supplanted the regulars by the late sixteenth century. The change of religious personnel did not herald significant shifts in administration, however, and a long-standing pattern of ecclesiastical understaffing and frequently shifting religious jurisdictions was established.[10]

Ecclesiastical neglect aside, the Spanish conquerors did not lack interest in the zone. The early discovery of precious metal deposits in the southern sierra led to a short-lived gold rush, as the Spanish conquerors used their encomienda grants to send Indians and enslaved Africans into the mines. Low mineral yields and a dearth of laborers conspired against the mining industry, however, and it collapsed in the late sixteenth century. By the early seventeenth century the few Spanish settlers in the region—often crown officials—had begun to refocus their energies on commercial cacao and cotton production.[11] Abuses by Spanish authorities and the slow growth of haciendas on surrounding indigenous lands led to conflict from early on in the colonial period. Notwithstanding such problems, Nahua leaders in the region proved adept at maneuvering the colonial legal system—mastering Spanish and petitioning crown authorities in defense of their cherished local autonomy. As a result of both Nahua efforts and the dearth of non-Indian inhabitants, communal lands still constituted the majority of the region's vast terrain at the beginning of the nineteenth century.[12]

Despite its isolation, the coastal sierra saw more than its fair share of political conflict between the Bourbon Reforms and the Reforma. Indian coast guard units were created by the Bourbon state in an attempt to discourage other European powers from encroaching on Spanish territory, and the zone became a recruiting hot spot for the insurgents under Gordiano Guzmán soon thereafter.[13] The sons of humble Afro-mestizo parents who worked on sugarcane plantations in southern Jalisco, Gordiano and his brother Francisco led a movement that mirrored the populist and localocentric militancy of Morelos's early revolt.[14] Although the Guzmán brothers controlled a large swath of western Mexico—from northwestern Michoacán through their native Tamazula (Jalisco) and down to the southern sierra—Gordiano himself established his headquarters on the hacienda of Aguililla, from which he would launch further federalist/liberal movements. In part, Gordiano's enduring interest in the zone came from its mineral resources—metal deposits found in Coalcomán were processed into insurgent weapons, and the Guzmán family itself dabbled in mining in the 1860s—but the cacique also began building a personal network of allegiances among the inhabitants of the sierra.[15] By the mid-nineteenth century, Gordiano had firmly established himself as a liberal strongman, one renowned for acts of populist generosity to his plebeian and indigenous clients.[16] As we will see, however, the Guzmáns' liberalism had its limits, and their support of Benito Juárez and his Michoacán-based followers did not translate into allegiance to the more radically anticlerical Lerdo.

The endemic warfare and economic instability of the early republic forbade any real commercial development in Coalcomán, though its metals and coasts continued to attract the attention of ambitious michoacanos. By midcentury, non-Indian settlers had made some inroads in the region, however. Mestizo towns such as the ranching hub of Aguililla and the cotton-intensive Coahuayana had sprouted from the seeds of colonial haciendas. A handful of private agricultural estates—including Terrenate, Trojes, and Ahuindo—bumped up against Indian commons, while mixed-race renters and squatters multiplied on both communal and estate land. These mestizo renters and squatters, whom one local historian characterized as largely criminals fleeing from justice in Colima and Jalisco, had begun arriving during the insurgency, and a few of them even rented urban plots in Coalcomán proper by 1850.[17] With few exceptions, though, these hacendados and early mestizo immigrants tended to respect Nahua communal holding, and modernization projects aimed at breaking corporate monopolies made little headway.[18] Several investors had attempted to exploit the mineral wealth of the sierra, but such projects repeatedly failed to get off the ground, primarily because the region lacked the necessary infrastructure.[19] In short, Coalcomán at midcentury remained a backwater to Michoacán's central settlements. Head town of the least populous district in the state, Coalcomán in the late 1850s boasted a mere 2,800 souls, several "miserable" churches, and no schools.[20] Its mining apparatus had been reduced to rubble during the independence wars. There were no reliable roads leading to the Indian communities of the coast or the abandoned Spanish port of Maruata. Indian comuneros controlled the vast majority of the land stretching westward from Coalcomán to the coast and south toward Guerrero. In many of these communities, Indians and non-Indians maintained a rigid separation. The Indian corporation was still renting lands to mestizo arrivals at midcentury, but there exists little evidence of intermarriage between the groups until the final decades of the nineteenth century. Indeed, in his 1863 report on the southern sierra, Canon Romero described the coastal Indian communities as being "extremely vigilant [to ensure] that foreigners are not allowed to enter, and even marriages between individuals from different pueblos are viewed by the Indians with horror."²¹ An 1875 report on the region penned by an unnamed Michoacán correspondent maintained that the Indians of the coastal sujetos "do not allow white people to settle among them, because as they say, 'those white-faced people are thieves. If they come, they kill Indians and take their land and gold. They speak beautifully, but do not believe them.'"²²

Thus, an overarching feature of the southern sierra was not so much its marginality—it was considered economically and strategically important—but its inaccessibility to modernizers and entrepreneurs radiating from Morelia or from nearby Colima. Indeed, the general trend in the relationship between this coastal zone and the cultural and economic core of Michoacán and the Bajío would look more like repeated, sporadic, and frustrated attempts at incorporation, set within a longue durée history of isolation. This pattern changed decisively after the Reforma, when a new generation of non-Indian settlers and government officials endeavored to integrate Coalcomán into the national fabric. Incorporation, they believed, necessitated the disentailment of the colonial Indian communities.

The Second Conquest of the Southern Sierra

Historian Marcello Carmagnani has aptly described liberal modernizing projects in Reforma-era Oaxaca as a "second conquest" of the region's indigenous people, since they undercut communal autonomy and centralized state authority through military and administrative reforms.²³ Such reforms, of course, were part of a larger liberal project aimed at abolishing the corporate structures of the colonial past and assimilating indigenous people into the fabric of the new nation-state. Yet the fate of liberal modernizing projects diverged widely from one region to another, and indigenous people engaged with them in a variety of ways.²⁴ Like Oaxaca, Michoacán's southern sierra also saw the beginnings of a "second conquest" in the Reforma and Restored Republic periods, though the "conquerors" and their means of conquest proved quite distinctive. Here, land-hungry immigrants from farther north encroached on Nahua communal lands, and mineral speculators, hacendados, and local officials endeavored to convert the region into an economic engine through land disentailment and the opening of a commercial port at Maruata. The latter project, like previous efforts dating back to the early colonial period, was destined to fail in the long run. However, commercial development projects and ranchero encroachment did create real pressures for Nahua communalists, whose continued existence modernizers saw as an obstacle to development.

Interestingly, the initial push to modernize the southern sierra came not from juarista republicans but from Michoacán clerics aligned with Maximilian's empire.[25] In 1863, Canon Romero published a long report aimed at stimulating imperial intervention in the zone in the journal of the Mexican Society of Geography and Statistics. Noting its abundance of mineral resources and potential for agricultural riches, Romero suggested that Maximilian's regime take a number of steps to "give life, population, and commerce" to the region. Such measures included colonizing the sierra with European Catholic families, making a cadastral survey, and parceling out vacant tracts to individual Indians or newcomers interested in developing commercial properties. Finally, Romero advocated establishing an imperial iron foundry in Coalcomán to produce rails for Mexico's projected railroad network, and he advised Maximilian to stimulate the formation of investment companies (agricultural, mineral, and pearl harvesting) and the development of a commercial port at Maruata.[26]

The instability of the imperial regime precluded any real movement along the lines Romero suggested, but the restoration of the republic in 1867 brought renewed interest in the natural resources and strategic location of the coastal sierra. In an 1869 piece of Michoacán boosterism, an anonymous Cotija-based correspondent for Mexico City's *El Siglo Diez y Nueve* declared that the coastal sierra could be rife with California-style alluvial gold deposits. The area was also rich in iron ore and hardwood timber, and its proximity to Maruata situated it ideally for the establishment of a new trade with the ports of California. Indeed, the author averred, Coalcomán lacked only "population and an entrepreneurial spirit" in order to wring astounding profits from the sierra and a major revenue boon for the state treasury.[27] New companies, with partners based in Morelia, Colima, and even California, had recently renewed mining and smelting operations in the greater southern sierra, and local correspondents prognosticated that if state and local authorities protected their activities, Coalcomán would enjoy a "new era of progress and mercantile movement."[28]

Such "mercantile movement" stimulated new attempts by state and local authorities to rehabilitate the port of Maruata, a near-ghost town on the Pacific Coast seventy-five miles from the district head town.[29] The idea was to cut a trade route westward from Apatzingán through the rugged sierra to the coast, thus opening new markets for the agricultural operations of the tierra caliente and Michoacán's interior as well as attracting new investors to the sierra's near-defunct mining industry. Among the various obstacles the project faced—inhospitable climate, impassable mountains, plagues of mosquitos—were the Indian communities of Ostula, Coire, and Pómaro, which controlled virtually the entire sierra between Coalcomán and the Pacific.[30] Fearing that Nahua resistance could derail the project, some principal vecinos of Coalcomán arranged for a diplomatic mission to the communities headed by local priest José María Sandoval in November 1872.[31] The vecinos trusted in the power of priestly influence to sway the Indians, and they were apparently not wrong. After a long conference, Sandoval "defeated the resistance of some [community members]" and obtained declarations of support for the project by leaders of the three pueblos.[32] Michoacán's legislature then approved a budget of 20,000 pesos for roads and infrastructure. Work on the port got off to a rough start, however, as political instability, disagreements over the planned route to Maruata, and the hardships of the coast plagued the project in its early years.[33] Although Maruata did function as a port in the early Porfirian era—doing a brisk trade with San Francisco in the 1880s—by the first decade of the twentieth century it had already fallen into disuse, facing competition from commercial ports at Manzanillo (Colima) and San Blas (Nayarit).[34]

Despite its rocky start and eventual failure, the Maruata project did portend major changes in the southern sierra, since it brought new immigrants and commercial interests into the zone. However, as Father Sandoval's diplomatic mission underlined, opportunities for non-Indian entrepreneurs in the sierra remained blocked legally by the persistence of the Nahua communities and the practice of communal land tenure. True, estate owners and their tenants at Trojes and Ahuindo could and did buy, rent, or usurp Indian lands, as they had since colonial times. In the end, however, it was not the hacendado but the humble squatter who overcame the obstacle of the commons. As Hubert Cochet demonstrates, mestizo settlers, often poor muleteers, rancheros, or artisans from Cotija or the Altos de Jalisco region, transformed the agrarian system in Coalcomán in the late nineteenth and early twentieth centuries. Pushed out of their home communities by the saturation of land and their insistence on the continual subdivision of property on family lines, these non-Indian immigrants moved south into Aguililla and Coalcomán, renting or squatting on Indian communal land.[35]

Despite its remoteness and rocky terrain, the area seemed ripe for

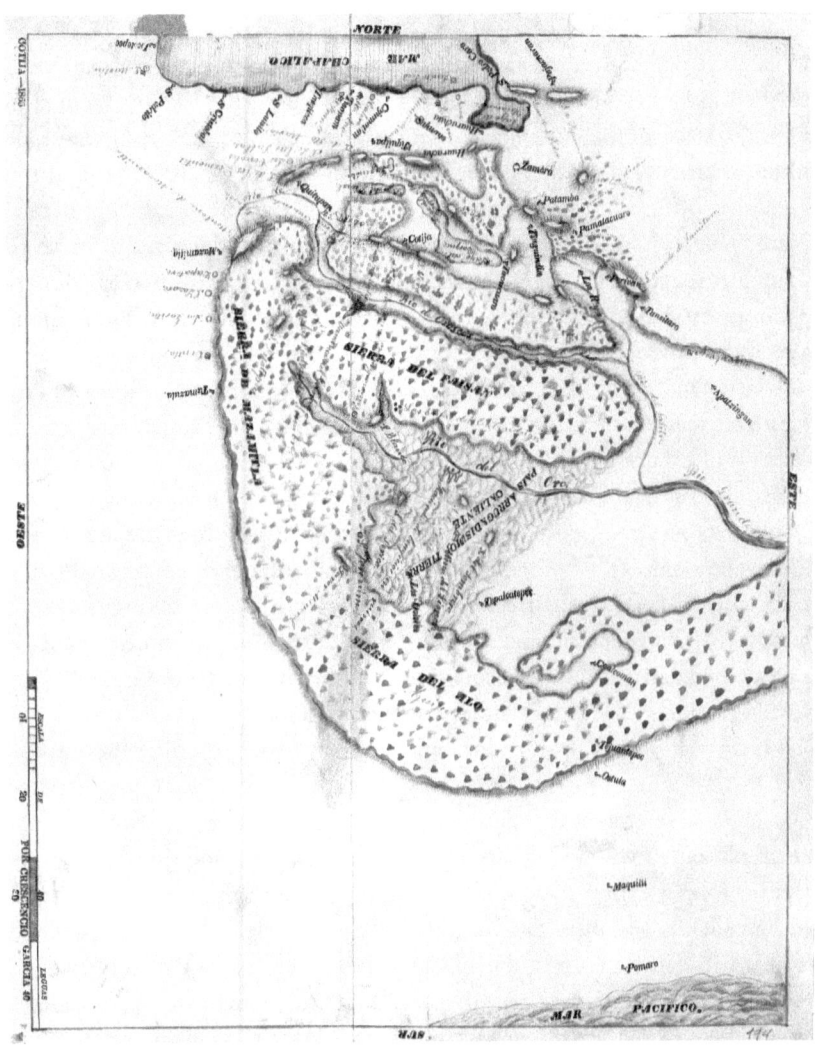

Map 7. Jiquilpan prefect Crescencio García's unique 1865 map of western Michoacán depicts the rugged terrain that characterized the Coalcomán district, but it also underlined its historic ties to the Chapala region in the northwest. Courtesy of the Mapoteca "Manuel Orozco y Berra," del Servicio de Información Agroalimentaria y Pesquera, SAGARPA, Classification No. 194-OYB-7234-A.

colonization. The sparsely populated Indian communities of Coalcomán and its satellite pueblos on the Pacific Coast controlled a vast territory enclosed by the Balsas and Tepalcatepec Rivers. To outsiders, the Indians seemed to make little use of their abundant resources. In reality, of course, the communities' rotational slash-and-burn agriculture, the raising of cattle, and the gathering of forest resources all necessitated a large communal land base.[36] Nevertheless, non-Indian immigrants found the area open and suitable to their needs, and they began to move in increasing numbers onto Coalcomán's community holdings.[37] There, they joined the relatively few non-Indians already in residence, whose connection to the area belonged to another era. The latter included the local priest, district and municipal officials, a few mestizo squatters from the insurgency era, and the owners (and, more often, renters) of estates such as Trojes, Terrenate, and Ahuindo. Some of these non-Indian actors, in alliance with Nahua factions in the surviving pueblos, would make a strong push for disentailment in the last three decades of the nineteenth century. The initial push for the alienation of communal lands coincided with Coalcomán's Religionero uprising. Before taking up arms, however, Indian communalists sought legal redress, and the process became a protracted and conflictual debate over the terms of land tenure and religious worship among various local and regional actors.

As district prefect, it was Gordiano Guzmán's son Antonio who oversaw the initial measurement and division of the communal property of Coalcomán—a process that allotted 329 parcels to an equal number of Indian heads of household—in January 1871.[38] Grave problems soon surfaced, however, as former comuneros rapidly began to sell off their parcels to ranchero renters such as Antonio Pallares, and a large faction of dissenters stepped forward to decry the irregularities and illegalities of the division process. Among such irregularities, the dissenters underlined the exclusion of widows and orphans from the list of pueblo beneficiaries, the allotting of pueblo lands to non-Indian outsiders such as the cotijense Father Sandoval, Morelia-based surveyor Vicente Gómez, as well as the prefect himself, and the exclusion of other legitimate pueblo members who "without reason were despoiled of their part [in the reparto] to which their character as Indians entitle[d] them."[39] The exclusion of orphans and widows could be explained by the patriarchal nature of the process as designed by Gómez and the Nahua qualifying committee, whereby individual plots were allotted only to male heads of household. But according to the petitioners, some Nahua men had also been excluded, "even though they had fulfilled their *cargos* [civic and religious duties] according to the ancient custom of the pueblo."[40] Such claims betrayed the dissidents' cultural and ethnicized understanding of communal membership—participation in the local cargo system and indigenous identity, and not simple residence on communal lands, made one a legitimate community member. Yet if such customs had been ignored and outsiders introduced into the process, Indians themselves were partially responsible. Indeed, the petitioners blamed the crooked reparto on a small clique of former Indian communal leaders, principally Marcelino Alcaraz and Nemecio Vázquez, who approved the division and allegedly profited handsomely from illegal sales of pueblo lands.[41] For its part, the Guzmán family had clearly benefitted from the illegal reparto but remained uncommitted to the wholesale displacement of the Nahua community, a long-term client, by immigrant upstarts such as Pallares. In fact, in November 1871 Antonio Guzmán asked Governor Mendoza for an executive order prohibiting indigenous coalcomenses from selling their plots, citing the "absolute misery" afflicting the community since the reparto. In January 1872, Antonio's son, Jesús Guzmán, admitted to the governor that Gómez's reparto suffered several defects, including its failure to resolve outstanding disputes with the Trojes hacienda, and he asked that Mendoza send the surveyor back to Coalcomán to rectify the problems. The governor acceded but could not locate Gómez.[42]

Meanwhile, Nahua dissidents under Antonio, Bernabé, and Hilario Cándido formulated their own legal strategy against the usurpers. Producing a flurry of petitions, gathering legal testimony from excluded community members, and employing a discourse that combined claims for Indian corporate privileges with the liberal language of equality, the dissidents waged a tenacious and initially successful legal campaign against the reparto between early 1871 and early 1874. Indeed, despite the attempts of local officials to discredit the antireparto faction as "rebels" who had already sold their legitimate plots and now sought to recover them without reimbursing the buyers, the state government under Justo Mendoza and Rafael Carrillo tended to side with the Cándido faction, acknowledging the overwhelming evidence of foul play in the execution of the reparto. Thus, in February 1874, Carrillo ordered the new district prefect to reconvene the Indian community and elect a new communal committee, which would carry out a new reparto. When queried by the district prefecture about the ramifications of such an order for the numerous land sales that had already taken place, Governor Carrillo flatly responded that since his office had never approved the 1871 reparto, property sales to non-Indians were to be considered null and void.[43] The governor's decision shocked local officials and ranchero buyers such as Antonio Pallares and Ignacio Manzo, the latter a judge of first appeal from Aguililla who had also served in the prefecture, and they protested bitterly that the governor's resolution would revive a colonial entity (the Indian community) that had no place in a modern, liberal republic.[44]

Emboldened by such apparent sympathy from the governor's office, the Cándido faction moved to recreate the old pueblo, seeking the eviction of ranchero buyers and attempting to reclaim the *casa de comunidad* (village hall), which had been sold to one Susana Gutiérrez. When local authorities and proreparto Indians such as Marcelino Alcaraz resisted such moves, the Cándidos opted for more violent means, likely aware that the Religionero conflict unfolding in early 1874 had debilitated the local government and its recently organized National Guard. In late March 1874, the Cándido faction kidnapped Ignacio Manzo, whose freedom they attempted to exchange for a favorable resolution of the reparto conflict.[45] The rebels released Manzo shortly thereafter, but their armed activities intensified through the end of 1874. According to their local ranchero enemies, the Cándidos expelled one doña María Quiñones from the house she had purchased from an Indian comunero, holding it through armed force until driven out by district forces. Then, the rebels moved out to the outlying ranchos, harassing travelers and allegedly even impressing local pacíficos into their antigovernment guerrilla force.[46] Led by Antonio Cándido, who had reportedly served Maximilian as a local "chief of forces," the Nahua rebels thus began to exert pressure on a district government already facing a significant security crisis. When the Religioneros appeared in the zone, the indigenous rebels quickly made common cause. Joining the Religioneros, however, meant an alliance with their erstwhile enemy, Jesús Guzmán, since he and his brother Juan Antonio came to figure as rebel leaders in the zone. To understand how such an alliance was possible, we must first analyze the role of the Guzmáns and other caciques in shaping the history of the southwestern sierra and assess their stake in the Religionero conflict.

Southern Sierra Political Clans and the Religionero Rebellion

The southern sierra was dominated throughout the nineteenth century by caciques who carved out semiautonomous spheres of influence through military service. This particular brand of leadership—centered on demands for local autonomy and solidified through patron-client relations—made the region a bastion for federalism and liberalism throughout the early nineteenth-century conflicts. As we have seen, Gordiano Guzmán adopted the southern sierra as his base of operations during the insurgency. By the 1840s, he had acquired land on the Ahuindo and Orilla Haciendas, and he rented other lands on the Terrenate Hacienda.[47] Members of his extended family (and perhaps even political clients) seem to have followed, since by the 1860s numerous Guzmáns and other Tamazula natives were to be found on Aguililla's sacramental rolls.[48] Guzmán's particular brand of caciquismo included a populist streak, as he was remembered locally for distributing corn and other basic necessities to Indians and hacienda peons and treating villagers respectfully.[49] Sometimes, the Church itself was the victim of such redistributionist acts. In the late 1830s, the cacique appropriated corn, rice, and chile from the tithe barns of Apatzingán and Tancítaro in order to feed his troops and their families.[50]

After Guzmán died in the midst of the Ayutla Revolution, his son Antonio carried on his legacy in Aguililla and Coalcomán, where he maintained an important presence. Antonio made a name for himself as a defender of Michoacán's territorial integrity in 1866, when he aided state forces in repelling an attempt by the liberal cacique Julio García to annex southwestern Michoacán to Colima. For his service, Governor Mendoza named Guzmán as district prefect, a role the latter filled until his death in 1872, when his son Jesús briefly took up the mantle.[51]

Julio García, an ex-governor of Colima who rented a large tract of land on the Trojes Hacienda northwest of Coalcomán, played his own role in the French Intervention. In 1866 García and a band of guerrillas from Coalcomán defeated the imperialist General Alfredo Berthelín, whom they reportedly decapitated.[52] Riding high on that victory, García had attempted to extend his dominion to Coahuayana and Coalcomán through the 1866 annexationist attempt.[53] Defeated by Guzmán, he accepted an amnesty offer and returned to Trojes, but he may have nurtured other irredentist movements in later years through his web of clientage. For example, in November 1871 the hacendado Antonio Ugarte, acting as apoderado general (general attorney) of the indigenous communities of the coast, threatened secession to Colima over the alleged meddling of Prefect Guzmán in local elections in Coahuayana and the imposition of new taxes.[54] Ugarte was backed by the pueblo leaders of Coahuayana, whose own petitions invoked the Indians' service in the republican guerrillas that defeated General Berthelín and declared that Guzmán's meddling in local affairs amounted to a betrayal of the principle of municipal autonomy for which they had fought. But García's involvement raises questions about claims of Guzmán's tyranny. After all, García was the principal republican leader in the zone, and it is thus likely that Ugarte and the indigenous leaders of Coahuayana were his clients.

Whether or not García was involved in the 1871 irredentist plot, his rivalry with the Guzmán clan only deepened in the succeeding years, and it affected patterns of partisanship in the era's conflicts in significant ways. García joined the Noria rebellion in 1871, once again facing off with Antonio Guzmán, who had stayed loyal to Juárez and Governor Mendoza. In July 1872, García killed Guzmán during an attack on Coalcomán.[55] The assassination of the son of the revered Gordiano Guzmán proved deeply unpopular among liberals in Michoacán and Mexico City, but García soon made peace with the Lerdo regime, under the terms of the general amnesty in August 1872.[56] The bad blood between García and the Guzmán clans lived on, however, next manifesting itself in the statewide split between juaristas and lerdistas. Antonio Guzmán's son, Jesús, succeeded to the prefecture of Coalcomán after his father's assassination, but his tenure was to be short-lived. Conflict surrounding the 1871 reparto had soured relations between the Guzmán clan and Governor Carrillo, since the elder Guzmán had clearly had something to do with the "irregularity" that marred the initial reparto. Other interpersonal dynamics may have been at work in the fallout, too. Carrillo, a lawyer who hailed from a family of Zinapécuaro merchants, had cut his political teeth in electoral campaigns against liberal caciques such as Epitacio Huerta, and he generally took a dim view of the kind of populist liberalism that Huerta and the Guzmáns espoused.[57] Tensions between such "soldiers of the pueblo" and more genteel, middle-class liberals ran high in Michoacán in the Reforma era.[58] Considering Carrillo's position as a leader of what Chowning aptly calls Michoacán's "lawyerly liberal" faction, he may well have been keen to see the Guzmán clan replaced with more credentialed and polished liberal functionaries. Factional politics likely also played a role in dividing the juarista Guzmán clan from the lerdista Carrillo.

The final straw came in late 1873, when Jesús Guzmán refused to take the protesta and was ousted from office by the Carrillo administration. Soon after, his brother Juan Antonio pronounced against the government. The circumstances surrounding the Guzmán rebellion remain murky. According to local authorities, the revolt resulted primarily from a quarrel between Guzmán and the local chief of the auxiliary forces. Drunk and hostile,

Guzmán had allegedly accosted and beaten the official, and when the prefect confronted him, Guzmán threatened him with a knife. The prefect ordered Guzmán's arrest, but when confronted by soldiers from the small army garrison in Coalcomán, the scion of the Guzmán clan opened fire, wounding several men before retreating to the family property at Terrenate.[59] Jesús joined his brother in the rebellion shortly thereafter. Unsurprisingly, Julio García soon offered to aid the lerdista district government in putting down the sierra rebellion.[60]

The Guzmáns soon took up with the Aguililla-based chief Bonifacio Vaca, who by this time had joined the Religionero fray, attempting to foment revolts against the "protestant" authorities of Coalcomán in the Nahua communities of Huizontla and Ostula.[61] Vaca's activities, which reportedly included plans to sack Coalcomán and the customs house at Maruata, elicited shrill cries for state support from local authorities, but such aid was not forthcoming. In January 1874, municipal desertions left Aguililla "without authorities of any kind." Further, the town's residents refused to pay taxes to the municipal treasury, convinced by their priest that supporting a "protestant" government would taint them with the "contagion" of heresy.[62] Acephalous and bankrupt, Aguililla and its surrounding ranchos became the scenes of nightly gatherings of vecinos, who chanted "Death to the Protestant authorities!" and threatened violent retribution against anyone who dared occupy a municipal post.[63] Worse, district efforts to create new National Guard battalions ran into resistance in Tepalcatepec and Coahuayana, whose vecinos refused to either join the small Coalcomán-based Guard or pay the mandatory exemption fees.[64] Facing a debilitating shortage of funds and a growing armed movement, the prefecture fell into chaos, changing hands three times in 1874.[65]

By the spring of 1875, the Religionero rebellion had also engulfed Michoacán's greater tierra caliente. Two hundred rebels from Peribán sacked Tancítaro, in the neighboring district of Apatzingán, in early February, and new gavillas of several dozen dissidents also appeared in Aguililla and Tepalcatepec.[66] Aguililla soon developed into a clear Religionero stronghold, with some three hundred rebels operating in its mountainous environs.[67] Meanwhile, Antonio Reza had pronounced against Lerdo in Taretan in January, and he would soon establish links to other southern rebellions. Coalcomán's Nahua communal leaders, Antonio Cándido and Cruz Meza, likewise declared for the cause of religion, amassing their troops in Huizontla, and on February 11 they attacked Coalcomán. Tellingly, the Nahua rebels first targeted their former leader and current ally of the ranchero usurpers, Marcelino Alcaraz, whom they kidnapped.[68]

Driven from town by National Guard troops, the Cándidos retreated to Aguililla, where they joined the Guzmán brothers and began to plan a coordinated attack on Coalcomán.[69] The Nahua rebels, many armed only with machetes, would serve as the infantry, while Guzmán and several of his allies, including Antonio Mendoza and Vicente Tejada, led the cavalry. Government officials would later estimate rebel forces at two hundred.[70] The Religioneros marched on Coalcomán on April 3, 1875, but the prefecture's interception of a rebel communication allowed the government to anticipate the attack and quickly gain the upper hand. On the outskirts of Coalcomán, General García met the rebels with sixty national guardsmen, and, after a brief firefight, Guzmán and his Religionero cavalry fled, abandoning the Nahua infantry to slaughter. When the smoke cleared, thirty rebel troops lay dead or injured. Antonio Cándido and Antonio Mendoza had both died in the fight, and García reported that the indigenous infantry had been "completely destroyed."[71] Indeed, over the course of the next month, Indian rebels began to appear at the prefecture, seeking indulto for their role in the rebellion. Governor Carrillo declined to grant the pardons.[72] The Nahua Religioneros had been crushed, and they largely abandoned armed rebellion as a strategy thereafter.[73]

Yet if the Cándidos disappeared from the coastal sierra's anti-Lerdo revolt in the spring of 1875, the Religionero movement itself carried on under Bonifacio Vaca, the Guzmán brothers, fellow coalcomense Jesús Valencia, Miguel Vega (a Guzmán ally from Aguililla), and Crespin Orozco, a rebel chief from Tancítaro with ties to Reza.[74] In fact, even as district forces neutralized the Cándidos, Aguililla and Tepalcatepec fell more firmly into Religionero hands. Meanwhile, the costs of funding his own operations had led Julio García to all but cease his aid to the prefecture of Coalcomán.[75] New prefect Narciso Garcilazo pursued the gavillas into the sierra repeatedly, but they always returned to Aguililla, from which they were planning another invasion of Coalcomán with the help of other southern chiefs. In July 1875 some two hundred rebels under the Guzmán brothers, Reza, and Miguel Vega attacked the fortified plaza. For several hours, Garcilazo, Antonio Pallares, and seventy soldiers held off the attack. However, the rebels succeeded in looting and burning a number of houses, including those of Pallares, Ignacio Moreno, and Judge José María Mata, before dispersing and retreating to their base at Aguililla.[76]

Still lacking a detachment of federal troops, Coalcomán's district government requested and received authorization to fund further repressive efforts led by Julio García.[77] Such a strategy quickly bore fruit, when García routed the rebels at Tepalcatepec in July and Aguililla in October.[78] Indeed, faced with García's more effective persecution, the sierra gavillas entered a stage of relative dormancy, even as the principal scene of the southern Religionero conflict shifted to Uruapan, which suffered an attack by the combined forces of Reza and the Jiquilpan chieftains in early November.[79] General Régules toured the tierra caliente soon after, and Escobedo finally assigned a federal detachment to Coalcomán.[80] Increased federal attention in southern Michoacán quickly produced favorable results for the government. By spring of 1876, the army had driven Reza into the desolate inferno of the southern Michoacán/Guerrero borderlands, and the Jiquilpan chieftains had returned north, where they would turn their attention toward a new alliance with porfirista emissaries.[81]

In the south, too, the rebels were changing flags. Reza had joined the ranks of Tuxtepec by May, and the sierra rebels received their own overtures from the porfirista agent Francisco Trejo, whom Díaz had sent to Aguililla from Colima.[82] Trejo and the Guzmáns were dislodged from their base at Aguililla in late October 1876, but the fall of the Lerdo government precluded further persecution.[83] Indeed, the Guzmáns transitioned back into local power in Coalcomán with the tacit approval of Porfirio Díaz and his agents. Yet Julio García remained opposed to such a move, and conflict between the two clans quickly resurfaced in February 1877.[84] After more than ten years, then, the struggle for local power between the clans of the southern sierra continued, with or without the backdrop of national political conflict.

It is difficult to gauge the Guzmáns' personal investment in the religious question that underpinned the larger Religionero movement. Gordiano Guzmán's clear federalist and liberal proclivities make his grandsons' involvement in the rebellion puzzling, though the family's *juarismo* and populist cacical style offer some important clues. As Jaime Olveda argues, Gordiano's liberalism was rooted in local autonomy and the popular struggle against the abuses and exploitations of creole authorities and hacendados.[85] Certainly, such a struggle could lead to conflict with the local clergy, as when Guzmán's troops targeted tithe barns.[86] Nevertheless, the Guzmáns were just as clearly a family of Catholics. Antonio Guzmán added his signature to several petitions to diocesan authorities in the 1860s, including one in favor of the reappointment of Father Juan Valdéz and another supporting a request by parishioners for additional priests to serve the extensive and understaffed parish.[87] In these cases, Antonio's support for Coalcomán's heavily Nahua parishioners may well have been a form of religious populism.[88] Regardless of their spiritual and ideological backgrounds, however, the Guzmáns' rivalry with García was clearly a key factor motivating their Religionero activity, and it helped shape political developments in the zone from at least 1866 until 1877. In this light, the younger Guzmáns' decision to ally with the Cándidos makes more sense—the Religionero rebellion offered them a chance to reassert their historic influence in the region.

What, then, of the religious component of the Religionero rebellion in the southern sierra? Were the Nahua rebels and the Guzmán brothers simply opportunists in search of a political banner to legitimate their aspirations? Did the religious question find no reverberation along the southern coast? Again, even if the ideological orientation of individual rebels remains out of reach, an analysis of the religious history of the region makes clear that spiritual concerns did help drive the revolt, though the link between religious revival and Religionero mobilization was complex. Simply put, the demographic and material changes that had overtaken the southern sierra in the 1860s and 1870s had a religious counterpart, a kind of "second acculturation" that saw a sustained effort by Catholic immigrants to wrest control of the faith from the Nahua parishioners who had long dominated the local Church.[89] Such a second acculturation did not just entail an attack on the cultural prerogatives of the Nahuas of Coalcomán and its sujetos; it also depended on a transformation in the parish's socioeconomic framework. From a corporately funded and communally oriented religiosity that celebrated Nahua identity, local Catholicism would move toward an individuated and voluntary piety of Ultramontane rigor underpinned by the ranchero economy. Such religious changes had important ramifications for the Religionero movement.

Ultramontane Catholicism and the Second Acculturation of the Sierra

The southern sierra did not remain aloof from the wave of Catholic restorationism animating the northwestern towns in the new Zamora diocese after 1862. In fact, the increasing migration of mestizo rancheros from northwestern Michoacán and northeastern Jalisco after midcentury ensured that the less clericalized religious cultures of the southern sierra would be exposed to new spiritual trends. As in the northwest, the primary exponents of religious reform in the zone were female-led lay associations, young secular priests, and mestizo artisans and rancheros. In accordance with their more Ultramontane piety, the newcomers worked to remedy what one priest termed the southern sierra's "spiritual orphanhood" (that is, ecclesiastical neglect and decadence).[90] The effects of such projects differed from place to place. In mestizo settlements such as Aguililla and the ranchería of Chinicuila, Catholic reformism tended to unify the flock around church-building projects and lay voluntarism. In Coalcomán proper (and in many of its satellite pueblos on the coast), restorationism was experienced as a profound disruption. Indeed, Coalcomán's religious reform was part and parcel of a mestizo second conquest, since the pious newcomers targeted communal spiritual property for privatization and undermined Nahua religious autonomy in their quest to remake local Catholicism.

As we saw above, the coastal sierra remained an ecclesiastical backwater from the early colonial period. The short-lived missionary projects of the sixteenth century, though they certainly left their mark on the region, resulted in a decidedly partial acculturation. As John Gledhill asserts, the Quirogan utopia remained especially distant from the spiritual reality of the southwestern sierra. Nahuas in Maquilí and Ostula called miserable Franciscan hermitages "hospitals" in the mid-seventeenth century, despite the fact that they did not function as such (principally for lack of funds). Each of the pueblos celebrated only the feast of their respective patron saint, Marian images of the Immaculate Conception (Ostula) and the Assumption (Maquilí) that were tied to nascent cofradías.[91] With little missionary oversight and few non-Indian neighbors, Nahua Catholicism developed along its own idiosyncratic path. Sixteenth-century friars reported difficulty eradicating Nahua "idolatry" in Ostula and Coalcomán, where communal leaders claimed to be descendants of Mexica nobles who had fled to the sierra during the conquest.[92] One legacy of this Mexica identity, which sierra communities continued performing into the mid-nineteenth century during religious festivities, was a strong tradition of local autonomy and religious leadership by pueblo authorities.[93] By the mid-eighteenth century, the communities had developed solid civil-religious structures of governance and festive traditions funded by considerable cofradía wealth. Nevertheless, the regional clergy complained incessantly about the difficulty of making ends meet in the sierra, where isolated Nahua communities made only small and infrequent payments for services.[94]

The early secularization of mendicant doctrinas in the seventeenth century did little to fortify ecclesiastical control. Indeed, jurisdictional instability—with frequently shifting boundaries and ecclesiastical status—characterized the secularized parishes of the region throughout their long colonial history, a product of demographic changes and a chronic shortage of priests.[95] The near total absence of non-Indians in the region throughout the colonial period must have helped solidify such patterns. A 1760 report on the southwestern sierra, when Maquilí and Coalcomán each constituted separate parish seats, lists one "interim" priest living among the fifty Nahua families of Coalcomán and one permanent priest living in Maquilí. The closest civil authority was based in Tancítaro, some ninety miles northeast of Coalcomán.[96] This ecclesiastical neglect and instability continued to mark the old colonial parishes of the coastal region into the mid-nineteenth century, when Canon Romero found most of the region's parishes "miserable" and underserved.[97] In the 1860s, parish priests stationed at Coahuayana complained of long treks through broken highlands and sweltering lowlands—from La Orilla, near present-day Lázaro Cárdenas, to the Colima border—in order to attend to the spiritual needs of the zone.[98] Although the pueblos of Maquilí and Pómaro nominally served as parish seats, only Coalcomán and Coahuayana could afford to benefice a priest, and the diocese of Michoacán lacked sufficient ecclesiastical personnel to heed the region's repeated requests for assistance. Church infrastructure also showed signs of neglect. Coalcomán had only a "miserable little chapel" hardly befitting a parish seat.[99] Father Daniel Rivera complained that Pómaro's parish church was not "decent" enough for the celebration of Mass in 1864, and Maquilí's parish church had collapsed in the early 1860s, though Rivera was helping parishioners to rebuild it. The latter, stationed in the pueblo of Achotán, had been "dispatched" by the parish priest of Coalcomán in 1864 to cover the entire coastal region, stretching from Coahuayana to Pómaro, without diocesan appointment or license. He hoped that the new Diocese of Zamora would regularize his status as *cura propio* (tenured priest) so that he could continue offering his services.[100] Rivera's letter underlines the ad hoc nature of ecclesiastical administration in the sierra. Even Coahuayana, long a mestizo-dominated parish serving a territory whose sugar- and cotton-growing estates could presumably fulfill their tithing obligations, possessed only a deteriorated "shack" for a parish church and endured several years without a priest in the 1860s and 1870s.[101]

Under such conditions of historic deterioration, the Nahua communities of the southern sierra developed declericalized, village-based religious cultures quite distinct from those of northern or central Michoacán. By the 1860s, the parish priest of either Coalcomán or Coahuayana made only one appearance in each satellite pueblo per year, during a visit of twenty days. For the rest of the year, Nahua *topiles* (native leaders) led religious services and cared for the church grounds.[102] Sacramental duties, then, took a back seat to locally directed religious festivities, many based on a fusion of indigenous agricultural rites and the cult of the saints. Nahua cofradías, especially active in the eighteenth century, still played an important role in financing and organizing festive religiosity in the coastal sujetos, whose large communal land base and temporary evasion of the reparto allowed for the survival of these colonial traditions.[103] Nonetheless, such organizations often became the object of conflict between priests and their parishioners. When Father Francisco de Paul Ochoa took over the parish of Coalcomán in 1847, he found that the church lacked even the most basic ornaments and accoutrements necessary for Mass. The three Nahua cofradías that had existed in the 1820s had dissolved, when the Indians unilaterally appropriated the animals and lands of the brotherhood. Accordingly, the priest enjoined the community and mestizo vecinos to contribute cattle, as a voluntary donation and not to a cofradía, in order to help finance parish expenses. After a few months, during which fifteen animals were collected, however, the parishioners had begun to insist that they had given the animals with the understanding that they were forming a new cofradía. Accordingly, they expected some control over the fate of the animals and the revenues they would bring. Further, in the words of one of the discontents, "All of the people who donated animals [were] very unhappy that they remain[ed] in the possession of Felipe Valencia," whom the priest had designated as mayordomo of the fund. In a traditional cofradía, of course, a mayordomo was elected by the members and not imposed by the priest. The complainants also demanded that the priest say Masses for the souls of deceased donors, since they expected such a spiritual return on their material investment. If Father Ochoa would not accede to their wishes, they would take the animals back.[104]

It remains unclear how the dispute was resolved (diocesan authorities at Morelia categorically denied that a cofradía had been formed, since they had never issued a license), but the episode underlines the stubborn autonomy of the sierra community in religious matters and the tendency of Coalcomán's parishioners to resist clerical authority when it conflicted with their aims. Moreover, if ecclesiastical personnel had a role to play in such communities, since they alone could celebrate sacraments and lead Mass, Nahua serranos often insisted on dictating the terms of the relationship, sometimes resisting remunerating the priest for his services. In 1852, for example, indigenous leaders demanded that Father Manuel de Paul Ochoa celebrate Corpus Christi, a feast that had fallen into abeyance in previous decades, initially offering to pay the customary eight pesos. Yet they then approached a local civil judge, who invoked state laws against "abusive" contributions for religious services and demanded that Ochoa not charge the eight pesos. The priest replied that the law could not qualify an act of piety as "abusive," but he also offered another, more revealing objection to the judge's demand. He maintained that the state law, decreed in October 1851, only exempted Indians from service in the civil-religious cargos that traditionally funded religious festivals. That is, the law considered the cargos, and not the religious service itself, as abusive. "And what are these abusive cargos?" Ochoa asked rhetorically: "the naming of mayordomo, captains, priors, church guardians, etc., all of whom are ruined by the costs of fandangos, fireworks, vats of wine, banquets at which all are invited to eat, and all of this for two or three consecutive days."[105] In short, the law sought to undermine the communal structures of religious celebration and replace them with a simple, voluntary fee for service, something that Father Ochoa clearly supported. For its part, the Nahua community wanted to retain the cargo system but do away with the clerical fee, a position that demonstrates their creative adaptation of liberal legislation in the service of local religious autonomy. They would decide which feasts to celebrate, and they would readily make use of liberal legislation to correct an "abusive" priest. Such an autonomous outlook in matters of religion dovetailed with Nahua forms of government, in which patriarchal communal leaders known as *ancianos* controlled the civil and judicial powers with minimal input from government officials at Coalcomán and Coahuayana.[106]

Conflicts over religious practice intensified in the early years of the new episcopate of Zamora, to which Coalcomán was transferred in 1862. In December 1868, for example, Father Pedro María Villalobos complained to diocesan authorities that the Indians of Coalcomán had stopped asking for most of his religious services. The number of feast days celebrated by the community had fallen to four in the past few decades, and since Villalobos had arrived in July 1867 communal leaders had canceled two more—the feast of All Saints and that of the patron saint, Santiago. Such cancellations would have left in force only Corpus Christi and another, unnamed celebration, perhaps that associated with the cofradía of the Immaculate Conception. But Villalobos even had trouble getting his parishioners to invest in these celebrations or their pastor's well-being in general. As per "immemorial" custom, the Indians paid eight pesos for each feast-day Mass, but tradition also mandated that they provide a house for the priest and two members of the community to serve as cantor and sacristan. Yet the community had allowed the dilapidated casa cural to collapse, and they only provided the required fees and volunteers for the remaining two celebrations after repeated prodding by Father Villalobos. How could he expect to survive in the vast, isolated wilderness of the coastal sierra under such circumstances?[107] Such apathy on the part of Coalcomán's parishioners may well have represented a reassertion of minimalist, Nahua Catholic values or a protest against the new, Ultramontane regime in Zamora. Whatever the case, Nahua religious autonomy clearly rankled the parish's new pastor, and such conflict would only deepen in later years. Meanwhile, Coahuayana's priest, whose jurisdiction at this time included the coastal pueblos, also reported trouble with Indian religiosity. The Nahuas of Maquilí believed that the Virgin of Guadalupe had appeared on a massive boulder near the village, and, according to the priest "the author or imposter of such a deception has named himself mayordomo of the supposed image and is collecting donations to build a chapel [on the boulder]." Bishop de la Peña informed the priest that he had already written to Prefect Guzmán asking him to cooperate "using peaceful means, to remedy such ills."[108] Strikingly, then, diocesan authorities trusted the liberal cacique to intervene with his Nahua base in order to suppress the autonomous cult developing at Maquilí.

By the late 1860s, however, village catholicisms were increasingly confronted not only with diocesan censure but with new styles of piety brought by mestizo immigrants. Indeed, everywhere the northern ranchero immigrants went, Catholic restorationism followed. The trends were most apparent in the new ecclesiastical units populated primarily by the immigrants, such as the parish of Aguililla (founded circa 1780) and the *vicaría* of Chinicuila (created circa 1830). The product of both mestizo immigration and the fracturing of colonial haciendas, these new congregations began to demand a level of religious service befitting their more clericalized and sacramental piety by the early 1860s. If Chinicuila and Aguililla had first begun to receive mestizo immigrants—especially those of the Tamazula-based Guzmán clan—during the insurgency, these were followed in the 1860s by a second major wave of immigrants from the north who differed in their religious style and economic ambitions. José María Chávez, who served various municipal posts in Coalcomán in the 1870s, reserved special praise for these more recent immigrants, drawing a stark contrast between the rancheros of Chinicuila and the Nahua community in the nearby barrio of Huizontla in his 1873 report on the Coalcomán district. While the latter were "semi-savages" who lived communally and did not know how to read or write, the former, he averred, were "so honorable and laborious, that within three or four years of arriving here they have, through force of perseverance, been able to fabricate eighty or a hundred adobe houses... properly aligned and well made, without forgetting to construct an elegant chapel, in which it is admirable to observe all of the necessary trappings of the Catholic cult. Vecinos such as those of Chinicuila well deserve the attention of the government."[109]

The poor but devout rancheros who began arriving in large numbers in Chinicuila in the 1860s had indeed pooled their meager resources to build a new chapel by 1867, a project the priest of Coalcomán called their "only object of enthusiasm."[110] Despite such enthusiasm, however, the lack of a permanent vicar in Chinicuila hindered sacramental observance, and the parishioners pressured the diocese to send them a permanent priest. In their pretensions, they received the support of municipal officers and Prefect Antonio Guzmán himself, who confirmed that "various vecinos" of Chinicuila had died unshriven.[111] By 1873, they had begun to petition the diocese to create a new parish in Chinicuila, noting the "considerable growth" of the population of the ranchería due to the immigration of "Catholic families" and the "mercantile movement" at Maruata.[112] The petitioners guaranteed a monthly pension of twenty-five pesos for the parish priest. Despite the offer, however, the Diocese of Zamora was simply in no position to send another full-time priest to the sierra.[113] In spite of such a setback, Chinicuila's ranchero inhabitants had already begun to establish an important presence in the municipal and parish politics of Coalcomán, as will become apparent below.

Aguililla offers an even clearer picture of the progress of Ultramontane Catholicism in the sierra. Carved from the colonial hacienda of the same name in 1833 (on land purchased by the priest don Antonio Méndez de Torres), the town experienced sustained growth through immigration from Zamora and Cotija between 1830 and 1860.[114] Facing chronic ecclesiastical instability in the late 1860s, its vecinos petitioned the diocese frequently for spiritual support. The parish lacked a resident priest between 1867 and 1870 and so had to rely on infrequent visits by the cura of Coalcomán, something its parishioners found intolerable.[115] In a telling petition, Benito Méndez (a trained priest, one-time municipal authority, and relative of the town's founder) informed the diocesan secretary that Aguililla was more populous and better prepared for the Catholic cult than Coalcomán and should thus take precedence in ecclesiastical staffing. Aguililla had a decent baptismal font and sacristy, new bells, and several new ornaments, things Coalcomán lacked. Further, since Coalcomán's chancel lacked the proper structural separation from the nave, by way of stairs or railings, during Mass the priest had to hang a piece of cloth between the two, "as if he were conducting a puppet show."[116] The reasons for such a structural deficiency in Coalcomán's colonial church remain unclear. Perhaps the chancel was originally separated from the nave by way of the often ornate and decorated "rood screens" described so colorfully by Eamon Duffy in pre-Reformation England.[117] If so, it would point to a very unreformed notion of the Mass indeed. Besides serving as a medium for local devotional tastes via carved or painted saints' images, medieval rood screens partially obscured the priests from parishioners' view, heightening the mystery of the Mass. Coalcomán's ancient church, then, might conceivably have conformed to such a late medieval style. However, the parish's poverty or the lack of attention to detail on the part of the original builders may have played a role. Whatever the case, the Aguililla petition clearly implied a critique of what its authors considered the old-fashioned and shabby devotional style of Coalcomán.

In short, the vecinos of Aguililla hoped to see Coalcomán's long spiritual domination of the region overturned and Aguililla's star rise. To do so, they worked to regularize tithe collection in the parish and began gathering donations for the building of a brand-new parish church in 1872. The same year, the parish priest also established the Vela Perpetua, which began to supply excess funds to the church project a year later.[118] Completed in the mid-1880s, the new church received not only tithing revenues and Vela funds but also a number of donations from the poor but pious vecinos of the community. Aguililla's Catholic cult, then, relied on funds of an individuated and voluntary nature, rather than the corporate and collectivized structure of the cofradía, as in Coalcomán. Individual donations ranged from forty-five centavos to twenty-five pesos, and the project employed dozens of locals as laborers and artisans. Indeed, among the names of church contract laborers we find that of Religionero chief Bonifacio Vaca, a local stonemason who was paid some thirty-six pesos for work on the church in 1873.[119] Restorationism in Aguililla tied poor farmers, female associations, and middling artisans to the economic and political elite.

Of course, Aguililla's pious immigrant society was not without its internal conflicts. Between 1870 and 1873, the town played host to a bitter fight over the fate of the old casa cural, when both Benito Méndez and the parish priest claimed ownership of the lot. Prefect Guzmán then intervened, ordering municipal authorities to instead build a school on the property, but the new school soon became a focal point of conflict.[120] Father Abundio Martínez wrote an alarmed letter to the diocese in December 1873 claiming that, in the face of his pulpit prohibitions, Prefect José María Chávez was attempting to force Catholic families to send their children to the school under the threat of fines.[121] Martínez was resolved to resist the pretensions of the prefecture, but the principal vecinos of Aguililla had a different, more effective idea. Recognizing the benefits of primary education, they worked with municipal officers to ensure that the school would be directed by don Ignacio Bello, a man "distinguished for his honor and religiosity." The new director had not taken the hated protesta (something municipal officials were willing to overlook), and the vecinos of Aguililla hoped that with the diocese's help they could get Father Martínez to collaborate with the project. The petitioners assured the bishop that the protesta requirement had "not had any effect on any of the people of this vecindario."[122] Diocesan authorities were ultimately convinced, and they informed the vecinos that Martínez would be apprised of the licit nature of the new school.[123]

Such a development betrayed a larger pattern of passive resistance of the Laws of Reform and, later, material and moral support for the Religioneros in Aguililla. Unlike in Jiquilpan and Coalcomán, Aguililla did not erupt into a local civil war during the conflict of 1873–1877. Instead, principal vecinos retained government posts without taking the protesta, and the town served as a base of operations for Religionero operations by Bonifacio Vaca, Vicente Tejeda, and the Guzmán brothers.[124] Vaca directed his ire not at Aguililla's functionaries but at the new prefect of Coalcomán, José María Chávez, who had replaced Jesús Guzmán when the latter failed to take the protesta. He recruited among the Indians of Huizontla and Ostula, "offering them under his own authority a general sacking of the population [of Coalcomán] and the extermination of its supposed Protestants," according to Prefect Chávez. Vaca and the Guzmáns also retained the sympathy of Aguililla's inhabitants throughout the conflict.[125] Though it is not clear how many of the town's ranchero inhabitants actually took up arms, the Guzmán family's deep historic connection to Aguililla explains why townspeople decided to take his side.[126] For their part, loyal government officials in the region suspected Aguililla's authorities of collusion with the rebels. For example, the prefect of

Apatzingán complained that the alcalde of Aguililla, Pedro Caballero (a signatory of the 1873 school petition), attempted to disguise a Religionero pronunciamiento in the rancho of Potreros as a simple domestic dispute in early 1875.[127] By May 1875, Aguililla lacked civil officials entirely, since all of the municipal officers fled or renounced their posts rather than fight the Religioneros.[128] In 1876, military authorities arrested Father Martínez during a public spiritual exercise for men who wished to gain the indulgences associated with Pius IX's Papal Jubilee. Explaining the situation to the diocese, Martínez declared that in Aguililla no laws had been promulgated banning public worship. Luckily for the priest, a number of vecinos intervened with military authorities to secure his freedom, paying half of the 200-peso fine demanded by the authorities.[129] When order was finally restored to the town, under the new governments of Porfirio Díaz and Bruno Patiño, a number of principal Catholic vecinos availed themselves of the Church-state détente and took positions in municipal government. Father Martínez, perhaps unaware of recent moves by the diocese to allow Catholics to serve in government posts, fretted in September 1877 that for the first time "even highly distinguished" vecinos of Aguililla were beginning to take the protesta.[130] Yet he need not have worried; among the new municipal officers of Aguililla were Felipe Bustos, Cándido Ponce, Zenon García, and Juan Manuel Carriedo, all signatories of the December 1873 petition for Catholic schooling and promoters of the new church project in Aguililla.[131] Throughout the conflict of 1873–1877, then, Aguililla was a bastion of Catholic resistance. Its support for the Religionero rebellion paid off in the end: It never implemented lerdista legislation, and lay supporters of Catholic restorationism managed to come out of the conflict in positions of local power. As we will see, Coalcomán's head town suffered a very different fate.

Religion and Partisanship in Coalcomán

Coalcomán saw its own pious revival in the 1860s and 1870s. The restoration of the parish church, especially, brought new splendor to the head town, and its diverse parishioners mostly united behind the effort. However, unlike in Aguililla and Chinicuila, other Catholic revivalist projects tended to exacerbate divisions within the community, often along ethnic, class, and gender lines. The widening breach between the indigenous community and the mestizo immigrants, as evident in the realm of parish politics as in material relations, led to strikingly different patterns of partisanship during the conflict of 1873–1877.

The demographic and religious changes associated with the arrival of mestizo rancheros in the southwestern sierra did not go unnoticed in Coalcomán. The parish priest Joaquín Valdéz and the indigenous community of Coalcomán called for a vicar to help administer the sacraments in 1867, for instance, noting that the rapidly increasing population had helped to spread diseases. Valdéz had served the extensive parish by himself for thirteen years, focusing his attentions on Coalcomán and the Nahua sujetos of the coast; but with increasing demands for sacramental services on the Trojes Hacienda and the ranchería of Chinicuila, he could no longer afford to travel the parish constantly without endangering the souls of his parishioners in Coalcomán.[132] Likely, Valdéz was simply getting too old, but it is also significant that several vecinos had petitioned the diocese to replace him, which it did in the summer of 1867. The identity of the petitioners remains unclear, but they likely did not belong to the Indian community. Indeed, in November 1868 pueblo authority Francisco Santa Anna petitioned the diocese on behalf of dozens of Nahua coalcomenses for Váldez's return. Santa Anna declared that Coalcomán's parishioners had "a thousand reasons for gratitude" to Valdéz, and he maintained that "only this señor, who is robust and so acclimated to this region, can administer this vast parish."[133]

In the end, the non-Indian vecinos got their way. In July 1867, the active and reformist priest Pedro María Villalobos took over the parish administration. He immediately established the Vela Perpetua and began working to regularize tithe collection.[134] By 1872, he had also established a women's chapter of the Sociedad Católica, which subsequently provided vocal support for Villalobos and his projects.[135] One such project was the construction of a new parish church, which got underway in 1871 and was finished in 1875, under Villalobos's successor. The project relied on donations from principal vecinos such as Antonio Pallares and José María Chávez, excess funds from the Vela Perpetua, and even the donation of an urban plot by the indigenous community. The Indians also provided a small, rotating volunteer labor force for the project.[136] Yet if such actions suggest that Nahuas were still underwriting parish life, other evidence points to the increasing prominence of new actors, especially individual donors and tithers and the women of the Vela Perpetua and the Sociedad Católica. Besides subsidizing the new church, the women of these associations (which shared several key members between them) authored several petitions asking for additional priests in Coalcomán and requesting that the diocese overturn its order to replace Villalobos with José María Sandoval in 1872.[137] Further, both associations spearheaded an effort to establish a parochial school and secondary Catholic school in Coalcomán, as well as a project to "put a stop" to the diffusion of the Protestant pamphlets that appeared in the parish in 1875.[138]

Despite his sickly nature, Villalobos also provided more prompt sacramental service to the vecinos of Chinicuila. Likely, Villalobos preferred Chinicuila's more Ultramontane style of piety to that of the Nahua community, which, as we have seen, had begun to cancel religious services and refuse to pay clerical fees during this time.[139] Through such service, Villalobos won the support of vecinos such as Encarnación Farfán, a principal vecino of Chinicuila who would serve as municipal president and school director in Coalcomán in 1873 before the protesta requirement drove him from office.[140] As the previous dispute over religious feasts suggested, though, Villalobos's relationship with the indigenous community (whose members tended to prefer their long-time priest Joaquín Valdéz) proved less harmonious. Further conflict with the Nahuas came in 1871, when their leaders attempted to sell the casa cural, which the priest used for storing seeds accruing from tithe payments. Father Valdéz had made some improvements to the building, but the indigenous community had compensated the priest for his expenses and therefore considered itself the owner of the property. The curia of Zamora, however, saw things differently, and it declared that the property belonged to the Church. The Indians would incur the penalty of excommunication if they went through with the sale.[141]

As we have seen, Coalcomán in the early 1870s was in the midst of a drastic and disorganized transformation resulting from the reparto of 1871. The land rush affected the parish in various ways. Bishop de la Peña's nephew, Manuel Navarro de la Peña, who was sent to take charge of tithing operations in early 1874, foresaw significant improvements in Church revenues with the division of communal land and the arrival of mestizo immigrants. Antonio Pallares, he noted, had already been especially cooperative in tithing on his newfound possessions.[142] Navarro projected that he would soon be able to "increase the decimal rent, since by good fortune I am establishing good relationships, and I can already count on Sr. Pallares, who is the best [of these relationships]." Not only was Pallares an ally of the Zamora hierarchy, then, but his willingness to sacralize alienated communal land through tithing was helping to lay the foundation for a new ranchero spiritual economy based on individual, voluntary funding of the faith. In the midst of the reparto, the signs of such changes were everywhere. Father Villalobos himself had received a parcel of communal land in the division, and in the center of Coalcomán vecinos such as Pallares and municipal president José María Chávez busied themselves buying up other plots and expanding their properties onto lands nominally belonging to the Church or to the defunct community.[143] Villalobos and his successor, José María Sandoval (a native of the Ultramontane Cotija), mostly turned this development into a boon for parish coffers, establishing friendly relations with Pallares and other newcomers and selling off unused ecclesiastical property (with diocesan approval) in order to subsidize church construction.[144] Chávez donated ten pesos from the sale of the ancient parish cemetery to the new church project in 1871, and Pallares made cash donations totaling twenty pesos the same year.[145] In 1874, Father Sandoval obtained diocesan approval to sell the very same casa cural that the Indians had attempted to sell three years earlier. In his letter to the diocese, he noted that if it were not sold, "sooner or later, the Indians or the enemies of the Church will seize [the property] and it will be lost."[146]

Thus, the new, Ultramontane clergy of Coalcomán in the late 1860s and early 1870s had aligned itself with the mestizo newcomers and their project to conquer the sierra. As we saw above, Sandoval's role in this project even extended to official efforts to develop Maruata, as a member of Coalcomán's Exploratory Commission on Ports.[147] Such an alliance was not without its internal contradictions. Sandoval's efforts to transform the parish earned him the admiration and affection of the principal vecinos and municipal authorities of Coalcomán and Chinicuila.[148] Yet he failed to win over the women's associations, which maintained a fierce loyalty to the equally reformist Father Villalobos. Indeed, in 1872 and 1873 the Vela and the Sociedad Católica petitioned repeatedly for the return of Villalobos, whom they credited with the spiritual rebirth of Coalcomán.[149] Not coincidentally, such spiritual rebirth had much to do with Villalobos's foundation and promotion of their associations, but the members of the Vela and the Sociedad also pointed to increased sacramental observance among the flock and improvements in morals under the priest's administration. Further, the women considered Sandoval cold, and they asserted that this defect nurtured "religious indifference" among the parishioners. Likely, Sandoval simply objected to the influence wielded by the women. When he left the parish to attend to his health, in the fall of 1875, the women requested that the diocese name a priest "who understands and wants to direct our religious societies."[150]

Regardless of such internal divisions, the major fault lines in Coalcomán during the Religionero conflict would not be between pious laywomen and the acolytes of Father Sandoval. Nor did the Catholics in either of those two camps support the Religioneros. Rather, the conflict in Coalcomán retained a decidedly ethnic flavor, with Nahua community members and the Guzmán brothers facing off against immigrant upstarts such as Antonio Pallares and José María Chávez and the Guzmáns' old enemy, Julio García.[151] Indeed, the rebels often targeted the exponents of Catholic restorationism in Coalcomán, as the letter from Encarnación Farfán that opened this chapter makes clear. In their attack on the head town in August 1875, moreover, Religionero troops specifically targeted the houses of Antonio Pallares and lay tithe collector Ignacio Moreno.[152] They even burned the casa cural in an attempt to breach the house of Pallares, and before they left town, they robbed Father Sandoval of some 200 pesos belonging to the Vela Perpetua.[153] Clearly, then, the rebels had a personal vendetta to avenge against Pallares, and they were no friends of Sandoval. Such animosity could have owed to many factors, from Sandoval's role in the transformation of the property regime in Coalcomán to his friendship with Julio García (he had acted as García's confessor and convinced him to formalize an illicit relationship via canonical marriage in 1873).[154] In any case, it is clear that the Religionero uprising in Coalcomán was the work of two very specific and disaffected sectors of the population and—in a marked contrast with Aguililla—did not attract widespread support among the pious mestizo immigrants. Rather, the rebellion in Coalcomán turned into a civil war that pitted the newly powerful mestizo immigrants and their Ultramontane proxies against the old guard of local power—the Nahua community and the heirs of the Guzmán cacicazgo.

Conclusions

The Religionero rebellion in the coastal sierra proved deeply destabilizing, though the reported number of combatants (three hundred) failed to match that of more populous districts.[155] Further, the rebellion was vindictive and intractable in line with its rather worldly causes. The rebels debilitated local governments in Aguililla and Tepalcatepec and repeatedly threatened to overrun the district head town between 1874 and 1876, and continuing hostilities between the Guzmán and García clans made the district one of the last pacified in 1877.[156] Partially, such destabilization owed to the tangled web of allegiances and rivalries that characterized the uprising in the southern sierra. As we have seen, the rebellion grew out of a set of distinct but intertwined pressures that linked Nahua communalists, old-style liberal caciques, and pious mestizos in a struggle against the new power players of the sierra—ambitious ranchero immigrants from the north who, for all that they took their religious cues from Ultramontane Zamora, were willing to serve the lerdista government. The most clearly defined "trigger" of the rebellion was the division of communal lands in 1871, a deeply flawed process that set a large faction of Nahua coalcomenses on the path of armed resistance. As we have seen, however, the reparto was just one part of a larger "second conquest" of the sierra—a set of transformations that threatened to eclipse the traditional power holders in the material, political, and religious spheres alike. Ranchero immigration, commercial development, and the more urbane politics favored by the Carrillo regime threatened to undermine the Guzmáns' cacicazgo. Finally, the religious changes heralded by the pious immigrants further divided the parish of Coalcomán, as mestizo Ultramontanes attempted to remake the declericalized Nahua religiosity that had long reigned in the sierra and sacralize the alienation of communal land. However, the impacts of such restorationism proved uneven and complex. In Aguililla and Chinicuila, where the communal regime and its indigenous cofradías had never existed, Catholic restorationism unified the mestizo populace against lerdista anticlericalism and provided novel solutions to the challenge of the protesta. In Coalcomán, meanwhile, Catholic restorationism aligned itself decisively with the project for capitalist development and the erasure of the Nahua community. Not surprisingly, then, the heavily indigenous Religioneros of Coalcomán were enemies of the reformist priest and his acolytes.

The case of southern sierra demonstrates the internal diversity of the Religionero movement in Michoacán. Simply stated, lerdismo and its state and local varieties alienated wide swaths of the population, and hatred of the regime sometimes made strange bedfellows. Catholic restorationism further complicated the picture, since it unified flocks in some places while dividing them in others. Such complexity helps explain both the widespread and destabilizing nature of the Religionero rebellion and its failure to cohere into a national political platform. The alliance between the Guzmáns and the Nahua communalists was unstable from the start, since the former had played a dubious role in the reparto of 1871. Further, pro-Guzmán allies in Aguililla, if indeed they sometimes recruited among Nahua populations, likely would not have fared well in Coalcomán, given the ethnic and religious tensions that reigned there. One measure of the internal fragmentation of the Religionero coalition is the decision of the mestizo cavalry under the Guzmáns to desert the Cándidos and their Nahua infantry during the attack on Coalcomán in April 1875.[157] If hatred of the local lerdista/Catholic reformist clique was enough to bring the two camps together in 1873, it was not enough to bridge Coalcomán's widening ethnic, class, and religious rifts for long.

CHAPTER 6

Lerdismo Derailed

The Religioneros, Porfirio Díaz, and the Twilight of the Reforma in Michoacán, 1876–1878

In the midst of his Tuxtepec Revolution, Porfirio Díaz came to represent the hope for an end to lerdista anticlericalism and authoritarianism in Michoacán, winning over the state's moderates and conservatives. This was no mean feat, since the young Oaxacan military officer had no real Michoacán constituency before 1876. Díaz failed to receive a single vote from the state's electoral college in the presidential election of 1871, in which Lerdo—widely perceived as the proclerical candidate—received twice as many votes as Juárez.[1] Díaz's Noria movement that year, meanwhile, faced an uphill battle in Michoacán from the start. The caudillo could count on support from a handful of liberal veterans in the state, including Coeneo's Epitacio Huerta and Juan Cervín de la Mora and Coalcomán's Julio Garcia, but he lacked an organic base of support among michoacanos and thus attempted to "make the revolution" from without. He sent a military agent, Agustín García, to the state for such purposes in early 1872, but the movement was cut down in its infancy, suffering major defeats to juarista troops in the Zinapécuaro district.[2] Huerta notwithstanding, don Porfirio's agents in the state simply failed to attract significant local constituencies. Indeed, a porfirista agent stationed in nearby Jalisco reported in late June 1872 that the revolution in Michoacán "has not progressed, due to the lack of a competent chief of character."[3]

Yet by late 1876, the Oaxacan caudillo had repaired his reputation in Michoacán, a state that proved to be a crucial battleground during the Tuxtepec movement that delivered Díaz the presidency. In fact, Díaz's defeat of Lerdo was received with accolades in many parts of the state, and in the elections of March 1877, Michoacán's electors unanimously awarded the interim presidency to the Hero of Puebla, who had received the official endorsement of the editors of both the liberal *El Progresista* and the intransigent *El Pensamiento Católico*.[4] Díaz had thus achieved the inconceivable, bringing liberals and conservatives together around his candidacy. What accounts for such a striking change of fortunes in Michoacán?

Put simply, the "religious question" proved to be the most important factor in Díaz's meteoric rise to popularity in Michoacán, and it was key to the state's adhesion to the Tuxtepec cause. If the widespread national discontent with the Lerdo government owed to several factors—including the president's betrayal of antireelectionism, his executive authoritarianism, and his failure to create economic and political stability—for michoacanos the movement against Lerdo was about the Laws of Reform, the protesta controversy, and the Religionero revolt. Nonetheless, if Díaz wanted to harness the power of Michoacán's mobilized Catholic rebels and influential proclerical activists, he would need to give them hope that lerdista anticlericalism would be reversed. And he did just this. Díaz rose to fame as a defender of the liberal republic against the French invaders and their conservative Mexican collaborators, yet in his long quest for power the Oaxacan caudillo shrewdly brokered alliances with ex-imperialist generals, moderate statesmen, radical liberals, and Catholic rebels. Such political flexibility helped to lend the Tuxtepec movement its peculiar character—a loose coalition of regional chieftains of diverse, sometimes starkly divergent, political affiliation and personal interests.[5] In short, Tuxtepec represented different things to different constituencies. For porfiristas on the Texas frontier, the movement stemmed from Lerdo's failure to protect borderlanders from the "predations" of the "barbarous" Indians of the north. Nahua national guardsmen in the Sierra of Puebla rallied to Díaz's side in order to protect a hard-won tradition of local autonomy. In Díaz's own native Ixtlán (Oaxaca), the Zapotec national guardsmen who carried the torch of Tuxtepec did so in an attempt to oust a lerdista governor who failed to respect their historic influence in the region.[6] In Michoacán, meanwhile, the Tuxtepec Revolution came to mean an end to lerdista anticlericalism and the restoration of some of the rights enjoyed by the Catholic Church before the Reforma. The fluid, labyrinthine quality of nineteenth-century politics allowed for these kinds of drastic political metamorphoses. Much as Lerdo could be pilloried as a Jesuit and a "son of a priest" in 1872 before presiding over the century's most anticlerical legislative period in 1873–1875, the liberal freemason Díaz could become the defeated Conservative Party's champion in Michoacán.[7]

The Religioneros had much to do with such a transformation. In fact, Díaz actively sought to merge his revolution with the Catholic insurrection of Michoacán and the greater Bajío. He courted Religionero chiefs, converted most of the state's rebel armies to his cause, and rewarded Religionero converts with official posts in his Army of Regeneration. Further, he went to great pains to placate more "respectable" (middle and upper class) conservative constituencies in the state after driving Lerdo from office. The historic strength of liberalism in parts of Michoacán ensured that such a strategy would soon become a precarious balancing act, however, with Díaz scrambling to nurture conservative hopes without alienating his liberal adherents. While not without its difficulties, the strategy ultimately worked. Don Porfirio sought Religionero and conservative support in his quest for national power, and then he quickly made concessions to liberals. Even as he moved to confirm his commitment to the Reforma, however, conservatives did not abandon Díaz altogether. Further, a revived Religionero rebellion against the Díaz regime in the Jiquilpan district and the Guanajuato borderlands achieved almost no traction after 1877. In large part, then, conservative michoacanos and former Religioneros made peace with the Díaz regime because of the latter's limited incorporation of Religionero militants into the federal army and also because of the development of an early and informal process of Church-state conciliation. If Díaz proclaimed the continuity of anticlerical reformism publicly in 1877, local porfirista authorities soon relaxed their enforcement of the Laws of Reform, and the Catholic hierarchy responded in kind by moderating its stance on the hated protesta. In short, the porfirista transition was brokered in Michoacán through a precarious détente among liberal officials, Religionero rebels, middle-class conservatives, and the regional Church.

If historians have long understood the Revolution of Tuxtepec as a marriage of convenience among diverse political constituencies, they have failed to take seriously the Religioneros' place within the early porfirista coalition.[8] Perhaps as a result, Mexicanist historiography sees the Porfirian Church-state modus vivendi as a solely late nineteenth-century phenomenon—the product of opportunistic alliances between Díaz and high clergymen such as Eulogio Gillow after 1885.[9] Clearly, Díaz did pursue rapprochement with influential clerics in the later Porfiriato, "modeling" Church-State détente rather than codifying it, as Edward Wright-Ríos argues.[10] Don Porfirio intervened personally with the Oaxaca clergy to secure Gillow's appointment to the archbishopric of Oaxaca, and Gillow used his diplomatic skills and his ties to Roman clerical circles to secure Pope Leo XIII's acquiescence for

Díaz's de facto assumption of the Patronato after 1887.[11] Further, as Riccardo Cannelli demonstrates, much of Díaz's high ecclesiastical policy hinged on a shrewd deployment of the politics of hope. With Gillow as a key mediator, he cultivated good relationships with papal emissaries, but he ultimately kept Rome waiting and hoping for full diplomatic recognition without giving away everything the Holy See wanted.[12]

If this was an artful strategy, it was not Díaz's first time negotiating with Catholics. Indeed, this chapter shows that Díaz's later religious politics had a Michoacán foundation. As Díaz's own correspondence clearly demonstrates, the Religionero conflict provided the Oaxacan caudillo with an important object lesson in how destructive and slippery religious questions could be, and it taught him to deploy the politics of hopeful dependency when dealing with Catholic would-be adepts.[13] Such a strategy was not without its pitfalls. An astute but by no means omnipotent leader, Díaz often found himself simply responding to events out of his control.[14] In fact, after his courting of Catholics led to a significant conservative resurgence in Michoacán and other states, he struggled to persuade his new tormentors to accept a kind of liberal modus vivendi that combined the formal continuity of the Laws of Reform with broad local power to enforce (or not enforce) them. The Porfirian regime's break with the Religioneros, following a chorus of liberal complaints in Michoacán, took the form of a low-profile anti-Religionero campaign carried out by General Abraham Plata. A swift but far from definitive purge of Religionero leaders from the Porfirian army, the Plata campaign quelled the last stirrings of the Religionero movement as an armed rebellion, but the Díaz regime would nevertheless employ more conciliatory measures in order to ensure long-term peace in Michoacán. In fact, an ad hoc, informal modus vivendi was taking shape between Catholics and the Porfirian government in the state as early as 1877. In a real sense, then, the Religioneros and their increasingly close conservative allies helped to shape the conciliatory national politics and lopsided secularization that developed under Díaz in the decades before the Mexican Revolution.

The Revolution of Tuxtepec: A Disparate Coalition

Porfirio Díaz had begun planning his revolution against Lerdo with a close circle of collaborators as early as summer of 1875. In December that year, he sailed from Veracruz to Brownsville with General Manuel González to put the

Figure 8. The satirical *El Padre Cobos*, edited by the porfirista Ireneo Paz, was a leading liberal critic of the Lerdo government's campaign in Michoacán. *El Padre Cobos*, January 27, 1876. Reprinted in *El Padre Cobos y La Carabina de Ambrosio* (Mexico City: Cámara de Senadores de la LVII Legislatura, 2000). Photo courtesy of Daniel Alonzo.

plan in motion. In his absence, Vicente Riva Palacio and Ireneo Paz continued to nurture antilerdista sentiment in the Mexico City press. As the intellectual wing of the porfirista movement, they would also author and edit the Plan of Tuxtepec in January 1876.[15] It is important to underline that Riva Palacio's and Paz's liberalism was a pragmatic one in regard to the religious question. Riva Palacio, in particular, had long led the moderate critique of Lerdo's religious policy in *El Ahuizote*, often invoking the old trope about the poor fit between radical anticlericalism and Mexican society.[16] In his "Dreamed Revolution" (the plan imputed to General Sóstenes Rocha in 1875), Riva Palacio specifically decried the "divisions" caused by lerdista policy, labeling the protesta "unnecessary" and suggesting that "tolerance" of religious belief was not incompatible with the republican system of government.[17] High-level porfiristas and Catholic dissidents, then, were not such strange bedfellows.

Nevertheless, in penning the Plan of Tuxtepec, Paz and Riva Palacio muted the religious question and instead focused on lerdista authoritarianism. Much like the plan of the "Dreamed Revolution," Tuxtepec denounced Lerdo's creeping political centralization, his military rule, and the personalist policies that favored a small group of the president's friends. Unlike the Rocha plan, however, Tuxtepec made no allusion to Lerdo's "division" of Mexican society, the protesta controversy, or religious "toleration." Indeed, the plan's first article affirmed the continuity of the Constitution of 1857 and the Laws of Reform. However, it also called for a constitutional guarantee of "municipal independence," a measure that could effectively prevent district prefects, state governors, or the federal government from imposing municipal authorities when popularly elected officials refused to take the protesta.[18] Tuxtepec's ethos, then, was a kind of locally managed, antiauthoritarian liberalism. Finally, the plan would remove Lerdo and his cabinet from power and elevate the doctrine of no-reelection to constitutional status.[19] After taking Matamoros in March, Díaz issued a reformed version of the Plan of Tuxtepec in Palo Blanco, Tamaulipas, which granted the interim presidency to the leader of the revolution in the event that the president of the Supreme Court, José María Iglesias, failed to join. An attempt both to capitalize on Iglesias's recent declaration against Lerdo and to lend legal weight to the Tuxtepec movement, the plan's provisions for the presidential succession would soon cause confusion and conflict within porfirista ranks when Iglesias rejected the banner of Tuxtepec in April and later made his own bid for national power in October, after the fall of the Lerdo government.[20]

The first porfirista pronunciamientos were led by Hermenegildo Carrillo and Fidencio Hernández, in the Sierra de Puebla and Oaxaca, respectively, in January 1876. The veteran liberal caciques of the Sierra de Puebla, Juan N. Méndez, Juan Francisco Lucas, and Juan C. Bonilla, soon followed suit.[21] In February, General Donato Guerra, a native of the Jalisco/Michoacán border town of Teocuitatlán and a veteran of the republican cause against the French, seconded the Plan of Tuxtepec in San Juan de los Lagos and marched toward Guadalajara with three hundred soldiers.[22] In his proclamation, Guerra signaled his support of the doctrine of no-reelection, but the jalisciense's rebellion was also a repudiation of federal intervention in his state. In early 1875, the porfirista Jesús Camarena had taken possession of the state government after elections rife with conflict and irregularities. Responding to the outrage of Jalisco's lerdistas, the Lerdo government unilaterally removed Camarena, declaring a state of emergency and sending General José Ceballos to take over as interim governor and military commander.[23] Against this backdrop, the Tuxtepec Revolution in Jalisco took the form of a struggle against prolerdista military intervention. Such antifederal feeling would provide a common ground between the porfiristas of Jalisco and the Religioneros of Michoacán.

Guerra's vaunted antilerdismo and knowledge of the central-western terrain made him an ideal candidate to broker such a porfirista/Religionero alliance. Back in December 1875, Díaz had considered placing Vicente Riva Palacio in charge of "extending [Tuxtepec's] operations to Michoacán," betting that the latter's extensive experience as the leader of the republican campaign in the state during the French Intervention would help him to secure allies in liberal towns such as Zitácuaro and Uruapan.[24] However, by early 1876, Díaz changed tack, instead entrusting Donato Guerra and other, lower-profile collaborators with the task of converting the Religioneros of Michoacán to his cause. Guerra may well have known some Religioneros personally. Indeed, the rebel army of Benito Meza, composed of some five hundred rebels who operated in the borderlands close to Guerra's native Teocuitatlán, received the first porfirista overture. In November 1875, a Zamora correspondent for Mexico City's *El Eco de Ambos Mundos* reported that Díaz had sent agents to Tingüindín to confer with Meza. The alliance failed to solidify at this point, due to insuperable political differences between the parties—the porfiristas wanted to maintain the Constitution of 1857 as the legal framework for the rebellion, while Meza demanded a return to the (Catholic federalist) Constitution of 1824.[25] In the wake of Meza's death in early 1876, however, the Jiquilpan rebels under Eulogio Cárdenas, Ignacio Ochoa, and Blas Torres reconsidered joining Díaz. Across the state, the Religioneros' fortunes were changing, as government forces cut down high profile leaders such as Meza (February) and Socorro Reyes (April) and Escobedo's indulto policy thinned rebel ranks. Though far from beaten, the movement found itself more amenable to pragmatic alliances by the time of Jalisco's Tuxtepec uprising. Donato Guerra met with the northwestern Religioneros in Mazamitla, Jalisco, in late February, their combined forces totaling some 615 rebels.[26] Government forces quickly dispersed the gavillas, and Guerra returned to Jalisco and later to Aguascalientes to continue the porfirista campaign there, but he had already consummated the alliance with the Religioneros. In fact, Eulogio Cárdenas graduated to the rank of general and began directing the Jiquilpan movement in Díaz's name soon after the conference with Guerra.[27] Subsequently, reports of Religionero leaders proclaiming in favor of Porfirio Díaz proliferated throughout the state.

Such changes in allegiance raise important questions. What were the terms of the negotiation between Religionero and porfirista agents? Did Díaz's agents make promises to temper lerdista anticlericalism after coming to power? Why did Religionero chiefs agree to fight for Tuxtepec despite its promise to uphold the Laws of Reform? If we lack detailed evidence about the manner in which porfiristas secured the allegiance of the Religioneros, personal correspondence between Díaz and his agents offers some suggestive clues. Firstly, the letters demonstrate conclusively that Díaz and his agents viewed collaboration with the Religioneros as the principal strategy for winning Michoacán. In a May 1876 letter, for example, one "José" in Mexico City offered to go to the state in order to organize the "many armed but disorganized elements" of Michoacán into a porfirista army.[28] Another letter from an agent in Morelia to Vicente Riva Palacio the same month reported that the "revolution of Michoacán remains disorganized, for lack of leadership," but he also indicated that once organized, the rebels would prove "invincible."[29] Antonio Reza had evidently joined Díaz's movement around this time, since a porfirista agent in Guerrero asked Vicente Riva Palacio in June to write to Reza asking him to help "moralize" an unruly Religionero movement that had developed around Coahuayutla.[30] Letters from other porfirista agents show that negotiations did indeed take place in order to solidify such alliances. Octaviano Fernández, a merchant from La Piedad, served as Díaz's principal agent in the Michoacán/Guanajuato borderlands.[31] In a November 1876 letter, Fernández reminded Díaz that the latter had authorized him back in late 1875 to organize the campaign in Michoacán. To these ends, Fernández had used 8,000 pesos of his personal funds in order to unite "900 men from the Religionero guerrilla bands in the state" under the banner of Tuxtepec.[32] Fernández had been defeated, captured, and pardoned after encounters with lerdista troops near La Piedad in June, but he had returned to Mexico City in order to offer further services to the revolution.[33] Luis Camacho, in an aggrieved letter from early 1877 lamenting Díaz's failure to repay him for his services with a "placement," also claimed to have been sent to Michoacán in order to "change the religious revolution into a progressive revolution."[34] In short, "progressive" and Catholic rebels could find common ground in their rejection of lerdista centralism. For their part, some Religionero leaders showed themselves amenable to such arrangements. Domingo Juárez agreed to work with another Díaz ally to "take the religious element out" of the rebellion and restrict Religionero abuses of civilian populations.[35] For his trouble, Juárez received the recommendation of other Díaz allies and ultimately a promotion to the rank of general in the Army of Regeneration.[36] In this case, Díaz's willingness to incorporate antilerdista rebels into his ranks soon paid off; Juárez and his Pátzcuaro-based Religioneros managed to capture General Régules and the small force that accompanied him near Pátzcuaro in December 1876.[37]

The increasingly fluid political situation in Mexico in the winter of 1876 proved the advantages of Díaz's strategy of courting the Religioneros. Lerdo fell from power in September 1876, fleeing southwest with a large entourage of cabinet members and a military escort through Jalisco and Michoacán in an attempt to escape the country by way of the Pacific Coast.[38] Meanwhile, José María Iglesias, invoking constitutional law, declared his intention to succeed Lerdo at the end of his constitutional term, in December. Supporters of this so-called *decembrista* movement mobilized against both lerdista holdouts and the Tuxtepec rebels in November, however, making significant gains with the adhesion of Guanajuato governor Florencio Antillón. In the scramble for power and the confusion of rumors and pronouncements, many of Díaz's allies—including those of Morelia—mistakenly backed Iglesias, on the basis of Tuxtepec's call for the president of the Supreme Court to succeed to the interim presidency. Exploiting such confusion, Antillón invaded Michoacán and briefly held Morelia, where he seized twenty pieces of artillery from the state's armory before moving north to take Zamora. Meanwhile, a number of other Michoacán towns, including Maravatío, Zitácuaro, and Pátzcuaro, adhered to the Plan of Tuxtepec and petitioned Díaz for aid against the decembristas.[39] Governor Carrillo, in a desperate attempt to defend Morelia, had called all district political and military personnel to the capital in November, leaving rural Michoacán without legitimate government authorities.[40] In the midst of such chaos, local political power was up for grabs, and various parties made overtures to Religionero rebels for their support. During his march into Michoacán, Antillón allied with the Bajío Religionero chiefs Silvestre Llamas and Anselmo Vega, for example.[41] Such an alliance may have represented more than simple opportunism. A porfirista agent in Mexico City warned Díaz in mid-November that "Iglesias is running the risk of leading us towards reaction," suggesting that the president of the Supreme Court even enjoyed the support of Archbishop Árciga.[42] For liberal porfiristas such as Morelia's Jesús Garibay, Iglesias and Antillón were offering the Religioneros a second lease on life, with disastrous consequences for Michoacán. "The traitorous and recalcitrant Conservative Party has reawakened," he warned, "and it is working constantly to impose an *ad hoc* governor on the state." Garibay pleaded with Díaz to come impose order in Michoacán, adding that he could never be an iglesista "or much less a *mocho*, whose mantle Antillón and his ilk have shamelessly adopted."[43] Having recently fought Religioneros, iglesistas, and lerdistas, Garibay found himself surrounded by enemies in Michoacán's capital, and he looked to Díaz to rescue him.

In the face of such chaos, Díaz relied on Religionero chiefs and other conservative allies both within and outside Michoacán to win the state for his cause. In particular, he harnessed the long-standing anti-Lerdo ferment in western Mexico State (born, as we saw, of the brutal repression of early Religionero riots in Tejupilco and Zinacantepec), and he empowered specific Religionero chiefs in Michoacán to take the fight to the iglesista interlopers. The rural hinterlands of Toluca had erupted into insurrection as early as May 1876, and Díaz's agents moved quickly to align themselves with the conservative chiefs at the movement's head. Mexico State porfiristas such as Ignacio Mañón y Valle took this early agitation in the Toluca district as evidence of widespread social dissolution caused by the lerdista fiscal and military policies that immiserated rural people without offering them security in return. How else could he explain such a "general uprising affected by people who in large part do not even understand if Mexico is ruled by a viceroy or president"?[44] Despite his refusal to consider the religious question or the political fallout of Tuñón Cañedo's actions in Tejupilco and Zinacantepec in 1873, the porfirista observer was right that western Mexico State was ripe for rebellion against Lerdo. Though porfiristas could capitalize on hatred of the Lerdo government among the region's indigenous communities, Mañón y Valle worried that the movement could move toward outright caste war without guidance from Díaz or his agents.

The conspirators found their agent in Felipe Chacón, an ex-imperialist general from Toluca.[45] Correspondence between Chacón and Vicente Riva Palacio demonstrates that the alliance between Díaz and the Mexico State conservatives came together in May, and by November Chacón's troops had driven lerdista forces out of Toluca. Tellingly, Chacón and his lesser chiefs recruited heavily from conservative towns such as Tejupilco, and they wasted little time in making enemies of liberal porfiristas.[46] Indeed, a porfirista agent in Tenango complained in late November of the "mysterious" and "suspicious" behavior of Chacón, who had unilaterally taken over the local government in Toluca and refused to allow porfirista forces from liberal Temascaltepec to enter the city.[47] Meanwhile, the Religionero colonel Ignacio

Buenrostro, who had pronounced for the cause of religion in Tulillo (Mexico State) in 1875, also joined the porfiristas in November.[48] Thus, old conservative and imperialist hotspots in Mexico State were being rekindled, and they would play a vital role in bringing Michoacán to Díaz's side. Indeed, conservative porfirista forces moved into eastern Michoacán as early as late November and helped to bring Maravatío to the cause of Tuxtepec.[49]

Even so, Díaz had bigger plans for the likes of Chacón, whom he would send to Michoacán as interim governor and military commander in early December. Responding to panicky letters from Michoacán liberals about the chaos in the state capital, don Porfirio assured them that Chacón would be coming to the state with "a column [of troops] and the necessary arms for the pueblos that wish to defend the popular cause that [Chacón] [was] advancing."[50] Such a development discouraged Chacón's supporters in Toluca, who asked Díaz to reverse the order. Chacón had managed to bring various towns, "including Tejupilco, Tenango, and Valle," to the revolution. If he were removed, the petitioners could not guarantee that the state would remain within porfirista ranks.[51] Nevertheless, Díaz needed Chacón's services in Michoacán, and he alerted his most important agents in Michoacán to put themselves under his command on December 6. Interestingly, this priority communication went out to the Morelia liberals Francisco Menocal and Bruno Patiño as well as to the Religionero Domingo Juárez in Pátzcuaro.[52] Further, though Díaz allies initially worried about possible hostilities between Chacón and Díaz's main military ally in Michoacán, Epitacio Huerta, the transition was affected in a curiously smooth fashion. Indeed, Huerta, a man who had presided over one of Michoacán's most radically anticlerical gubernatorial administrations to date, quickly announced his intention to hand over power to Chacón and to aid the ex-imperialist general in any way he could.[53]

Chacón found Michoacán in disarray. By the time of his arrival on December 23, porfirista troops under Epitacio Huerta had regained a tenuous hold on Morelia, though decembrista forces still controlled Zamora and La Piedad. The state had had nearly a dozen governors in the space of twenty days, and "complete anarchy" reigned in the capital. State government was "skeletal, without resources of any kind," including promised salary payments for loyal forces that remained active in the campaign against Iglesias. Yet with the war effort ongoing, Chacón had no time to remedy such ills. He appointed Dr. Francisco de Sales Menocal, an "honorable liberal with a very honorable background," to the state interior ministry and began preparing to march north with a thousand irregular troops to drive decembrista general Francisco Franco out of Zamora.[54]

Menocal, scion of a wealthy landed family from Pátzcuaro and brother of a liberal hero of the Reform Wars, had indeed weathered the tumultuous era of the French Intervention with his liberal credentials intact, refusing to sign the pledge of allegiance to Emperor Maximilian in 1864. However, like other Michoacán elites, he had also opposed the radical anticlericalism and autocratic style of both the Huerta and Lerdo governments.[55] Perhaps not surprisingly, then, the moderate Menocal welcomed Díaz's choice of Chacón over Huerta to head up the interim government. On December 26, he informed Díaz that "the arrival of Chacón ha[d] been met with incredible enthusiasm" in Morelia. However, Menocal worried that Huerta could continue to cause problems in the state. During the Religionero rebellion, Huerta had refused to participate and had offered his support to General Escobedo. Further, when Antillón arrived in Morelia, in December 1876, Huerta had allowed him to take control of the majority of the state's artillery and other war materiel. It was no wonder, then, that the moderate liberals of Morelia rejected Huerta and found common ground with antilerdista conservatives such as Chacón. Lastly, Menocal reminded Díaz:

> Michoacán is extremely difficult to govern, as much because of the ideas that dominate here, as you well know, as because of the profound misery and elements of discord we inherited from the past administration. As such, we need a highly prudent administration to guide us and perhaps even some extraordinary measures in these imperious circumstances.[56]

Díaz responded that he had chosen Chacón precisely because of his "prudence," and he hoped Menocal would continue lending his support to the interim government.[57] Such calls for "prudence" in the face of the "dominant ideas" of Morelia entailed a mandate for conciliation to conservative Catholics. Indeed, Chacón's appointment was widely and rightly understood as a triumph for the state's conservatives and Religioneros. By February 1876, the editors of Morelia's intransigent *El Pensamiento Católico* loudly proclaimed their support for the interim governor, using their pages to promote the new "Club Díaz y Chacón."[58] Meanwhile, General Eulogio Cárdenas received a hero's welcome in Cotija, where he would serve as Díaz's primary military and political commander, and Reza, Juárez, and Francisco Gutiérrez all reported to Morelia to receive orders from Chacón.[59] Reports such as these gave heart to Catholic editorialists, whose support for the more ideologically pure Religionero generals had increased significantly over the course of 1875 and 1876. Among civilian conservatives, the coming of Chacón and the promotion of the Religioneros also stimulated a flurry of political organizing under the auspices of several new clubs, including the "Club Conservador" and "Club Díaz y Chacón." Following the lead of the latter club, *El Pensamiento Católico* endorsed Díaz for interim president in the elections of February 1877 and urged José de Jesús Cuevas—whose refusal to swear the protesta in 1873 had helped touch off the Religionero rebellion—to run for state governor.[60]

For his part, Chacón offered himself to michoacanos as an icon of conservative revival. The governor signaled his commitment to uphold the "civil and religious liberties" of all michoacanos in a December decree. He had not come to the state as "an instrument of any party" and would work with all of Michoacán's political factions to undo the damage of the past administration. He would begin by abolishing the deeply unpopular extraordinary contributions (emergency war taxes) levied by the Carrillo administration.[61] The editors of Michoacán's new official paper, batting away criticism from the national press about the state's flirtation with conservatism, explained in February that the Revolution of Tuxtepec sought first and foremost to do away with the nepotism and exclusivism of the Lerdo government. If conservatives were unduly excluded from political power under Lerdo, Díaz would welcome all parties to participate in the project of national reconciliation.[62] Here, in broad outline, were the terms of the Michoacán/Díaz pact as local elites understood them: Conservatives could leave the shadows of political exile if they committed themselves to the task of repairing a social fabric torn by federal authoritarianism and partisan rancor. A known conservative but a neutral party to Michoacán's destructive Religionero conflict, Chacón was well positioned to play the role of broker. Díaz's decision to back Chacón thus represented a bid for the loyalty of the conservatives and moderates who dominated the state, and it was paying off handsomely, as demonstrated by the unanimous support he garnered in the elections. Menocal's appointment, meanwhile, would demonstrate to liberals that Díaz would not completely abandon them. However, this delicate balancing act became increasingly precarious as Michoacán's conservatives pushed forward their resurgence and liberal porfiristas grew disgusted with Chacón. Indeed, liberal discontent ultimately convinced porfirista leaders to replace Chacón with a more reliably liberal leader, Manuel González. Yet by the time González turned the state over to its first post-Lerdo elected governor, Michoacán's conservatives had already made significant political gains and begun to accommodate themselves to the new order.

Liberal Backlash and the Porfirian Balancing Act

Liberal porfiristas in Michoacán had objected to the appointment of Chacón from the outset. Lauro González, a porfirista from Maravatío, informed Díaz on December 24 that Chacón's presence in Morelia had dashed the hopes of Michoacán liberals who had supported Tuxtepec and portended the resurrection of the "retrograde and Pharisaical party." "Religious fanaticism" threatened to overtake the liberal tenets of the Tuxtepec movement in the state, and González urged Díaz to take decisive action to prove that he still stood by the principles of the revolution. Specifically, he prescribed a "swift change in personnel"—that is, the removal of Chacón and other conservatives from office.[63] Díaz's reply, which he limited to the words "patience and trust," suggests that don Porfirio already had plans to betray his conservative allies in Michoacán after using their energies to secure the state for his cause, but before then his liberal allies would have to suffer more indignities, as helpless witnesses to a conservative resurgence. On his march to Morelia, Chacón attempted to remove the forces of the liberal Prisciliano Ortega from their command at Acámbaro and replace them with "some traitors [ex-imperialists] that came with him from Toluca." Ortega stated flatly that he could not obey someone like Chacón, and he warned that the militants of the "Partido Porfirista" were indignant that a former imperialist had been allowed to "raise the standard of reaction" in Michoacán.[64] Ortega's comrade in arms, Joaquín Delgado y Camacho, painted the scene in even more apocalyptic tones. "Don Felipe Chacón has come from Toluca to reestablish the reaction. There is no pueblo big or small where he has passed and not placed traitors at the head of the municipal government. It is the insolent pleasure of this man to insult liberals loudly and in public."[65] Delgado claimed that Chacón had surrounded himself with a cabal of old traitors and Knights of the Order of Guadalupe. Meanwhile, the defeated Conservative Party had rebounded "overnight" in Morelia, where they set to work preparing boisterous demonstrations of support for Chacón as the "defender of religion." In a symbolic gesture not lost on Morelia liberals, Chacón had the gall to "come out on the balcony of the same house where Maximilian had stayed . . . in order to acclaim religion. From his lips not a word passed in favor of the Constitution, the Plan of Tuxtepec, or Porfirio Díaz."[66] Delgado warned that if Díaz failed to act decisively against Morelia and Toluca, "the vanguard of the reaction," the country would soon witness yet another "crusade."

Its hyperbole notwithstanding, Delgado's letter pointed to real gains by conservatives and former Religioneros and showed that these had become increasingly close allies under the protection of Chacón and Díaz. According to Epitacio Huerta, liberals lost all of the elections for interim authorities in Michoacán, with the exception of Díaz's own candidacy for president.[67] After a brief tenure as interior minister, Menocal also stepped down in February and was substituted by Benigno Ugarte, of the powerful Morelia-based conservative clan.[68] Meanwhile, Reza, Juárez, Cárdenas, and Gutiérrez, now generals in the Army of Regeneration, threatened to take revenge on liberal militants such as Arcadio Ruiz Zepeda, who had fought the Religioneros on behalf of the Carrillo regime before joining Tuxtepec.[69] Twenty-two other Michoacán liberals—all exiled in Guadalajara—petitioned Díaz for help that same month, saying that they fled the state in the face of threats from Chacón's Religionero allies.[70] Elsewhere, José María Chávez, a district judge and municipal authority under the Carrillo administration who later joined Díaz, was reduced to petitioning Domingo Juárez for help protecting his family from the Religionero chiefs that controlled Coalcomán in Díaz's name in late December.[71] Even in districts controlled by liberal porfiristas, the conservative resurgence took on threatening hues. In Tlalpujahua, rioters shouting vivas to Porfirio Díaz and religion attacked the houses of several prominent liberals in January 1877, gravely injuring several of the men, and rumors spread that Angangueo would soon second the movement.[72] Across the entire state, then, some michoacanos were looking to Díaz to complete the revolution initiated by the Religioneros.

Díaz mostly took such news of conservative resurgence in stride, aware of how much he needed, or was powerless to discipline, his Catholic allies. At the national level, in fact, his government continued to send conciliatory signals to conservative Catholics. Díaz's interior minister, Protasio Tagle, issued a circular on January 15, 1877, stating that although the new government intended to uphold the Constitution of 1857 and the Laws of Reform, the triumph of Tuxtepec would not usher in "an epoch of intolerance or persecution." It also promised that religious differences "would not serve as a pretext to destroy the equality and rights of citizens." Such statements were interpreted by conservatives in Michoacán as a promise to respect Catholic religious practices.⁷³ In response to complaints from liberal *michoacanos*, meanwhile, Díaz asked his interlocutors to send him more detailed reports about the actions and antecedents of Religioneros operating under the banner of Tuxtepec. Thus, because he was hesitant to act preemptively against his Catholic allies, Díaz placed the burden of proof of Religionero predations on liberal *tuxtepecanos*. He told Ruiz Zepeda, for example, that although he possessed the "best intentions" with regard to ameliorating the problems of Michoacán, he needed "thorough reports, free of passion," in order to determine how to proceed.⁷⁴ Other responses show a Díaz hesitant to take actions that might tarnish his reputation among conservatives in the state. In particular, he could not risk alienating Chacón, whose services against the decembristas in Zamora and La Piedad proved essential to the pacification of the region.⁷⁵ In a response to Lauro González in December, moreover, don Porfirio asked his liberal partisans in Michoacán not to lose faith, hoping that they would continue to support the state government "with sword and pen, which is the only way to avoid even the smallest conflict in the state, which at this moment would destroy all of my work. Whatever deformity [in public administration] is not straightened out right away can be remedied in circumstances other than those of the present."⁷⁶ Further, Díaz planned to pass through Morelia on his way from Guadalajara (where he had been fighting the decembristas) to Mexico City, and he could talk personally with his disgruntled Morelia allies then.

The promise that Díaz would come to Morelia to resolve their troubles seems to have satisfied the likes of Lauro González and Joaquín Delgado.⁷⁷ It did not, however, satisfy Díaz's national collaborators, who had begun to see Michoacán's conservative resurgence as part of a more troubling national trend. Díaz's partisans in Querétaro, Jalisco, and Guanajuato had also begun to send alarming reports and requests for action against conservative upstarts in their states, who were mobilizing for the elections of February.⁷⁸ Since Michoacán played host to the strongest of such conservative resurgences, it behooved the Tuxtepec government to set a firm precedent there and cleanse the state government of Catholic intransigents. Interim Minister of War Pedro Ogazón put the matter to Díaz most forthrightly, advising him in mid-January to "think seriously" about the creeping influence of the "clerical party" in Michoacán, Querétaro, Guanajuato, and Puebla and insisting that the time had come to remove the conservatives from government posts in Michoacán. A win for the clerical party in the February elections, he said, would imperil the gains of the revolution and tarnish the reputation of its leaders.⁷⁹ Díaz responded that he would take steps to correct the problem, though they might not be as "radical" as Ogazón wished.[80] Ultimately, though, the tuxtepecanos in the federal government proved little inclined to wait for Díaz's gradualist solutions, and on February 6 Interim President Juan N. Méndez (6 December 1876–17 February 1877) informed Díaz via telegram that "grave considerations have obligated the council of ministers to entrust the government of the state of Michoacán to General Manuel González."[81]

Díaz's correspondence offers no clue of his opinions on such a resolution. Nevertheless, the transition from Chacón to González went remarkably smoothly. Chacón offered no resistance to his replacement and even appeared with González in Morelia on February 16, where the two delivered speeches highlighting the state's progress toward peace. Chacón underlined his strategy of political inclusivity in staffing the state and district governments, secure in the notion that "there [was] room for all legitimate political aspirations under the banner of Tuxtepec." Chief among the accomplishments of his brief tenure, Chacón identified his government's work to procure "religious liberty" for the inhabitants of the state, who could now "freely profess their religion under the protection of the law."[82] For his part, González lauded Chacón's work in the state, hinting that if he had to rely on people formerly excluded from government, he had done so in the interests of building a lasting peace.

González's own complex political trajectory made him something of an unknown quantity in Michoacán. Born in Matamoros (Tamaulipas), he had militated in the conservative cause in the War of the Reform before the French invasion persuaded him to join Juárez's republican army. He later supported Díaz during the Noria Rebellion, and his substantial influence in the northern borderlands helped to win the region for Tuxtepec early on. Notwithstanding his mixed political record, by the time Díaz had risen to the presidency, González cultivated a reputation as a radical liberal.[83] In Michoacán, he wasted little time in removing some of Chacón's conservative appointees, and he signaled his intentions to enforce the protesta requirement for government employees. Such gestures quickly won the support of Morelia's Junta Liberal.[84]

Conservative michoacanos thus rightly viewed the arrival of González with trepidation. In early February groups of "respectable señores" from Zamora and Morelia organized petitions to Díaz asking for him to reconsider the removal of Chacón, and González's first days in power elicited even more shrill complaints.[85] One M. Degollado told Díaz that the campaign against

Chacón was the work of a small group who had been excluded from public posts because of their lerdista sympathies. Further, if Chacón had indeed appointed some conservatives, he had not excluded liberals altogether.[86] Ramón Romero went further, demanding that Díaz "uphold the tenets of Tuxtepec" and cleanse lerdistas from government posts. Apparently, the latter had gained several important appointments within a few days of Governor González's arrival. Romero specifically objected to the appointment of Eduardo Gil to the prefecture of Pátzcuaro, where he would have authority over his old Religionero enemy Domingo Juárez. "Is it possible," Romero asked, "that the dignified Juárez, who has suffered so much in the service of Tuxtepec, including the murder of several of his family members, will be subordinated to the same man who persecuted them with such cruelty?"[87]

Nevertheless, González declined to take decisive action against the conservatives, adopting a pragmatic approach to Michoacán's messy political milieu and keeping his attempts to tip the balance back toward liberals out of the spotlight. He would pursue détente with "respectable" conservatives through assurances of his moderation on ecclesiastical issues and work to separate the more malleable Religionero chiefs from those who represented a threat to public peace. In a pair of exhaustive reports to Díaz on the state of affairs in Michoacán in the spring of 1877, the new governor indicated that the conservatives of Michoacán had become "too powerful" under the protective shadow of Chacón. González thus met with some of their principal leaders face to face in order to "make them see that if they insisted on availing themselves of the state, liberals would arm themselves" and Michoacán would return to civil war. Instead, they should reconcile themselves to a liberal government, secure in the promise that the tuxtepecanos would not recreate the divisive anticlericalism of the Huerta government.[88] With regards to Chacón's political appointments, González "regretted" having to remove several of them for incompetence or because of their fame as "recalcitrant traitors." Meanwhile, the various Religionero captains who had been in Morelia with Chacón had retreated upon the arrival of González, requesting two-month licenses to return to their home territories but taking their troops and armaments with them.[89] Here, González had begun to lay the groundwork for the criminalization of the Religioneros, since he claimed some of them had returned to their old custom of robbing mule trains. Further, as part of his military strategy for the state, González favored creating a trustworthy liberal militia in Coeneo to counterbalance the influence of the "cristeros" that had controlled the zone, and he sent home the chaconista troops that had come from Mexico State.⁹⁰ He would also dispatch a large cavalry division to conflictual Coalcomán, where Lerdo's departure had precipitated an open struggle for power between the Guzmán and García clans. Meanwhile, González would send General Abraham Plata, a bandit pardoned and recruited by Díaz in the early days of the Tuxtepec Revolution, to northwestern Michoacán, where he could check the advances of the "clerical party."⁹¹ If such actions seemed to signal a hostile posture to the main Religionero chiefs, González nonetheless worked to court lesser ones, recruiting Guadalupe Raya to his military command and incorporating his gavilla into army ranks.⁹² Jesús Camarena, governor and military commander of Jalisco, adopted a similar strategy in own state, incorporating the forty-strong gavilla of Silvestre Llamas into federal columns in February.⁹³ Such a divide-and-conquer strategy would ultimately pay off, when former Religioneros betrayed Reza and Gutiérrez in October.

Aside from trying to bring the state back from the "hideous bankruptcy" that paralyzed its administration, González's main task in Michoacán was to ensure a peaceful and advantageous transfer of power from the interim to the constitutional government in the municipal and state elections that would respectively take place in April and May. On this front, Díaz had hoped that González would adopt some of the conciliatory style of his predecessor. In preparing the terrain for the gubernatorial elections of March 1877, for example, don Porfirio asked González to promote the candidacy of don José María Martínez Negrete, owner of the Buenavista Hacienda near Apatzingán, "without becoming alarmed about the friendships he maintain[ed] with conservatives."⁹⁴ Even after Chacón's tenure, then, Díaz continued to seek out allies with close ties to conservative groups. González offered no protest to such an order, but he soon found that the "notorious provincialism" of michoacanos worked against Martínez Negrete, who was not well-known in the state. Instead, he suggested backing the lawyer Bruno Patiño, who was known and respected despite having served Huerta as secretary of government in the late 1850s. The less provincial Patiño also boasted a "vast clientele" of both liberals and conservatives, a fact that González hoped would help him to unite Michoacán's divided liberal party.⁹⁵ Such disunity between former lerdistas and tuxtepecanos, along with a flurry of political organizing by conservatives in advance of the elections, threatened a disaster at the polls.

According to numerous reports appearing in Michoacán's Catholic newspapers, González's government averted the impending "disaster" of conservative electoral victories partially through fraud, intimidation, and vote suppression. March's municipal elections were accompanied by an avalanche of complaints by local conservatives, often concerning the subversion of the democratic process by military forces. In Morelia, state forces arrested Mariano de Jesús Torres, Catholic candidate for *síndico primero*, on suspicions of "conspiracy" hours before the election.[96] Electoral officers in Capula refused to receive the ballots of the indigenous community, which were presented at the voting tables by its apoderado, because they did not favor the Tuxtepec candidate.[97] In Quiroga, the municipal president illegally took charge of the voting table in an apparent attempt to control the elections, prompting mass vote abstention by the populace.[98] A state cavalry regiment nullified elections in Santa Ana Maya on a technicality, and conservative ballots remained uncounted or were "lost" in Tacámbaro.[99] Other elected officials, including the municipal treasurer of Tacámbaro, could not assume their posts because they attempted to take the protesta "as Catholics," something the Chacón government had allowed during its brief tenure.[100]

For his part, Governor González admitted to don Porfirio that conservatives proved better organized and more unified than liberals, leading to "several disasters" on election day. Military patrols had been able to "keep order" in the face of conservative "insolence," and in the end tuxtepecano candidates won most electoral posts. However, if Chacón had still been in charge, González warned, the conservatives would have perpetrated "a new Saint Bartholomew's Day [Massacre] and extinguished the liberals."[101]

González's remarks suggest that his government indeed employed illegal measures in order to squash conservative mobilization at the polls. Nonetheless, conservative candidates triumphed in a few municipalities, including Zamora and Maravatío. With few exceptions, however, these conservative candidates opted to forgo their traditional resistance to the protesta. In fact, González reported to Díaz in early April that public officials even in the clerical bastions of Zamora and Jiquilpan had taken the protesta.[102] Tuxtepec-approved candidates had triumphed in most municipalities as well as in the races for the federal congress, and Bruno Patiño won the gubernatorial election handily in April.[103] Notably, Zamora elected the conservative-friendly tuxtepecano José María Martínez Negrete to the federal congress.[104] In the presidential race, Porfirio Díaz won unanimously, even in places such as Maravatío, which had elected Jesús Herrera, another "recalcitrant conservative," to the post of congressional deputy in March.[105]

Despite sporadic episodes of conflict, then, Michoacán's conservatives had begun to reconcile themselves to the Porfirian order from an early date. The protesta-related outrage that had accompanied elections after 1873 was notably muted in April and May 1877, and González reported in mid-May that the government faced no real resistance from conservative michoacanos. He credited such a development to his government's rejection of lerdista "exclusivism" and particularly its attempt to reconcile with the conservatives of western Michoacán, who "for a long time had been excluded from public matters and were reduced to the category of pariahs."[106]

Yet the calming of Catholic ire in Michoacán also had much to do with Díaz's artful deployment of the tenet of local autonomy and his cultivation of conservative hopes. In the draft of a speech from February 1877 found in Díaz's archive, for example, the caudillo counseled his audience that a vote for tuxtepecano candidates was a vote to "declare the independence of the municipality and the independence and respect of the judicial power so that it can administer justice fully and so that the courts can judge public functionaries and enforce the Constitution of 1857 and the Laws of Reform."[107] The Chacón government and many of its local ancillaries, which had often declined to enforce the protesta requirement, provided an apt example of what such autonomy could mean for Catholic communities in Michoacán. Then, in May 1877, Díaz sent out circulars to a select group of allies across the country thanking them for their support and asking how they thought Mexicans "wished to be governed." These circulars were sent to Mexicans of various political stripes, but the impassioned responses he received from several michoacano moderates and conservatives suggest that they saw the circular as a genuine call for citizen input on the shape of the new government. Fermín Ortega, a moderate Morelia liberal who had supported the Second Empire, reminded Díaz that governments that intentionally excluded God from public administration could not count on His providential protection.[108] He suggested authoring a law that would overturn the Laws of Reform, and he counseled don Porfirio to use his authority to ensure that Mexican Catholics enjoyed "true freedom to exercise their religion, taking into account that they constitute the absolute majority" of citizens.[109] Another *moreliano*, Francisco de P. Infante, asked Díaz to restore to Catholics' right to "manifest our religious beliefs publicly and privately, guaranteeing the Church the tranquility that rightfully belongs to it and restoring its rights." Such, Infante averred, was the "great desire of the majority of Mexicans, and principally the vecinos of this state, who do not profess any other religion than Catholicism, the one true faith."[110] Manuel de Estrada, another moderate who had raised his voice against freedom of worship in 1856 and later supported Maximilian, opined that Mexico's chronic instability owed to the ill-advised attempts by liberal governments to change the centuries-old "customs and ideas" of the people and make Mexican society conform to a mold that did not fit its particular historical character. Díaz would be best advised not to fight against such "national customs," and he should invite qualified men of all political stripes to participate in his administration. He ended by informing Díaz frankly that he owed his triumph over Lerdo to the "force of public opinion," a force that could also unseat him if he chose to ignore the will of the people.[111] Díaz declined to respond to the letters solicited by his circular. However, the tone of the responses by Catholics in Michoacán make clear that don Porfirio's gambit had inspired hope among conservatives that his government might blunt the radicalism of the Reforma.

This, then, was a politics of hope, a tactic Díaz would later employ with the national high clergy and the Holy See in the 1880s and 1890s, and it ultimately paid off.[112] By the time Bruno Patiño took the reins of the state government in July 1877, the simmering conflict between the clans of Coalcomán and a pair of lerdista uprisings on the Pacific Coast and in Puruándiro proved more pressing issues than conservative mobilization.[113] González, who had stayed on in Michoacán as state military chief, undertook several military reforms in order to better insure the state against gavilla activity, reorganizing federal troops and giving new weight to the famed "rurales" in protecting rural highways from bandit attacks and suppressing rural pronunciamientos.[114] Even more pressing, though, was the economic reconstruction of the state, which constituted a dire emergency at the time of Tuxtepec's triumph. Facing a budgetary shortfall of 200,000 pesos, the state needed federal subsidies just to stay afloat well into Patiño's gubernatorial term.[115] Patiño's principal goal, then, was to raise revenues by stimulating commerce and investment. To such ends he planned to devote his energies to finishing construction on the causeway over Lake Cuitzeo, a continually delayed project that would facilitate trade with the Bajío.[116] If the state government increasingly turned its attentions to economic matters, however, the religious conflict did not disappear completely, as the Díaz government moved to sever its ties with the Religioneros. Subsequently, the government's betrayal and assassination of its former Religionero allies would occasion outrage from middle-class conservative sectors and stimulate new, more limited uprisings in the name of religion. However, such outrage ultimately failed to congeal into a more widespread conservative movement against the Porfirian government, in large part because Michoacán's Catholic conservatives had found new routes to political inclusion.

The End of the Porfirista-Religionero Honeymoon

The spring of 1877 marked the beginning of the end for the alliance between Michoacán's remaining Religionero chiefs and the Porfirian government. Consciously or not, Chacón had contributed to the forging of a new legal framework for attacking his old allies. In April, his government issued a decree aimed at curtailing banditry and the alleged collusion between gavillas of various stripes with rural property holders. The decree prohibited ranchos and haciendas from allowing people on their property who were not employees or family members, and it required hacienda administrators to remit lists of "legitimate inhabitants," to district authorities, register any firearms with the prefecture, and destroy any gavilla campsites found on the property. Any armed bands that were not part of a legitimate military unit would be destroyed.[117] As it turned out, it took little more than the suggestion by government officials that the Religioneros had returned to their "old customs" of banditry in order for them to be prosecuted. Manuel González's administration had then set the scene for the Religionero purge by sending loyal troops to Religionero zones and turning more opportunistic Religioneros such as Guadalupe Raya against their former allies. This was the beginning of a new strategy of criminalization, which would employ selective arrests and executions to purge the Religionero chiefs from the Tuxtepec coalition.

The government fired its first volley in April 1877, when Abraham Plata's troops captured Eulogio Cárdenas near Jiquilpan. González explained that while Cárdenas had not taken up arms against the government, he was found roaming the district with his gavilla, not "entirely subjected to the government's authority."[118] After questioning Cárdenas, the prefecture of Jiquilpan found that he possessed a piece of artillery, various armaments, and "other elements of war," some of which he had already turned in to the authorities. Cárdenas also offered to arrange the surrender of the cannon through an intermediary, Gerardo Reyes. However, when approached by government forces, Reyes fled to Cotija, where he reportedly attempted to instigate a riot. González instructed Plata to pursue Reyes, and Cárdenas was escorted from Jiquilpan to Zamora to await trial. En route, however, Cárdenas "tried to escape" and was killed by his escorts.[119]

Coming on the heels of a bloody proclerical riot that shook the city of León during Holy Week, the assassination of Cárdenas signaled deteriorating relations between conservatives and the Porfirian government.[120] The editors of *El Pensamiento Católico* decried the "criminal assassination" of

Cárdenas, whom they claimed had retired from politics and was living peacefully in Cotija at the time he was apprehended. Perhaps more disturbingly, Cárdenas's persecution appeared to be part of a larger campaign against Religioneros. The paper also reported the assassination of Religioneros Arcadio García and Francisco Monje by the prefecture of Ario—now controlled by the porfirista (and former lerdista) Jesús Garibay—and it told of an attempt on the life of Ramón Padilla by the prefect of Tacámbaro's henchmen. Domingo Juárez, too, had allegedly survived an assassination attempt by government forces.[121] Were Michoacán's sacrifices in the service of Tuxtepec all for naught?

This first wave of assassinations provoked shifts in allegiance among Religionero chiefs. Rumors circulated in September that Silvestre Llamas was mixed up in an anti-Díaz plot, and Guadalupe Raya—no doubt fearing that his government allies would turn on him next—also pronounced against the Díaz administration that month.[122] Such events offered further rationale for purging the Catholic militants from the porfirista coalition, but simple fiscal issues may also have played an important role. Several Religioneros, including Juárez, Reza, and Gutiérrez, continued to draw monthly pension payments of a hundred pesos each from a bankrupt state government, a fact that had prompted complaints from the new interior minister in August 1877.[123] A couple of months later, Reza, Gutiérrez and other Religioneros found themselves in the government's sights. On October 3, former Religionero troops incorporated by González and obeying Plata's orders arrested Antonio Reza in his home in Taretan. According to government sources, Reza had tried to kidnap a woman in town, and upon arrest government troops found documents pointing to an antigovernment conspiracy by Reza, Gutiérrez, and one Florencio Escalera. Correspondents for *El Pensamiento Católico*, meanwhile, averred that Plata's forces deceived Reza, who they found peacefully retired from political matters in his home, with an offer of promotion in the army. What remains above dispute, however, is that a small squadron of soldiers, accompanying Reza to Uruapan to stand trial, then applied the notorious *ley fuga* and killed him "as he tried to flee."[124] Plata's forces captured and imprisoned Gutiérrez shortly after.

News of the assassination of Reza echoed far beyond state boundaries and was met with a chorus of outrage in national newspapers of all political stripes. Editors from papers as politically divergent as *El Monitor Republicano* and *La Voz de México* expressed dismay at what they saw as the extrajudicial killing of a Tuxtepec ally, and they demanded an explanation of the Plata brigade's actions.[125] In response, the government of Michoacán released copies of the telegrams between Plata and his subordinates in Taretan, and it promised to investigate the circumstances of Reza's death. Yet the assassination of Reza proved only the beginning. In a series of articles on the Patiño government's creeping authoritarianism in October, *El Pensamiento Católico* claimed that government forces had also quietly assassinated Ignacio Ochoa, Mariano Guerra, Arcadio García, Francisco Monje, and others in the past month.[126] With the help of local correspondents, *La Voz de México* supplied more details about this rash of executions: Ochoa and Guerra were apprehended in Mazamitla and shot on the road to Jiquilpan, where they were to stand trial; Monje was arrested in his home near Ario by Garibay and subjected to the ley fuga; two Religioneros from Peribán, who had voluntarily turned in their weapons, were scooped up at a local feria and imprisoned. One was later ordered shot by the municipal president.[127] Clearly, Reza's death was part of a larger Religionero purge.

Despite popular outrage over the government's actions against its ex-allies, late 1877 did not see the rebirth of a widespread Religionero challenge to the Tuxtepec regime, though sporadic gavilla violence continued in the state into early 1878. The Atilano Montes gavilla resurfaced in Zamora in December 1877 but quickly disappeared again.[128] In Jiquilpan, Florencio "El Fepe" Escalera, whose fifteen-member gavilla allegedly sought to collude with that of Silvestre Llamas, launched a new pronunciamiento against the government but was quickly put down by General Plata, who killed Escalera in Los Reyes in February 1878.[129] Meanwhile, the Guanajuato/Michoacán borderlands did not cease to provide cover for a number of small bandit gangs.[130] Nevertheless, such movements achieved very little traction. Most of the more effective Religionero leaders were dead, and even rumors of lerdista conspiracies in the state caused Díaz little consternation.[131] The threat of widespread Religionero mobilization, it seemed, no longer gripped the state, which was well on its way to reconciling with the new Porfirian order.

Such Catholic accommodation also rested on measures taken by both the Díaz regime and the Catholic hierarchy. In ecclesiastical affairs, Díaz and his close collaborators showed little interest in antagonizing the Church hierarchy, even in the early days of Tuxtepec. When the governor of Colima fined Bishop Ignacio Montes de Oca 500 pesos for leading what he called a "strike of the Sociedad Católica" at Manzanillo in February 1877, Díaz quickly reversed the order, citing a lack of evidence that the bishop of Tamaulipas had actively infringed the Laws of Reform when thousands of Catholics came to greet him at the port of Manzanillo.¹³² The same month, Mexico City's central chapter of the Association of Our Lady of Lourdes named Díaz as "honorary president and protector."¹³³ In April, Archbishop Labastida felt comfortable enough with the Porfirian authorities to ask Mariano Riva Palacio, recently elected to the federal congress for Mexico State, for donations for the celebration of Pius IX's thirtieth anniversary in the pontificate.¹³⁴ Vicente Riva Palacio, meanwhile, maintained ties to the Ladies of Charity through his wife, who was elected president of the association in September 1877.¹³⁵

Civil enforcement of the Laws of Reform proved a mixed bag after 1876, too. As Karl Schmitt demonstrates, the Porfirian government showed little interest in prosecuting infractions of the Laws of Reform at the federal level, instead giving state and local officials—be they puros or ex-imperialists—ample leeway in implementing the laws.¹³⁶ State officials in Michoacán received an avalanche of petitions requesting permission to stage public processions in the months leading up to Holy Week in 1877, a fact that indicates widespread hope that Tuxtepec would bring back public worship. The state's official periodical stood firm, explaining that before 1874, local officials could permit processions "at their discretion," but such discretionary power had disappeared with the Ley Orgánica.¹³⁷ Nonetheless, public processions did resume in some parts of Michoacán, often with the collusion of civil authorities. Morelia's *El Pensamiento Católico* announced in January that solemn public processions had taken place all over the state, a development they took as evidence of a new era on the horizon.¹³⁸ Documentation from Michoacán's ecclesiastical archives confirms such claims, especially for the Purépecha heartland of the Puruándiro and Pátzcuaro districts, where public processions were held with the consent of local authorities in May and June.¹³⁹

For its part, the Catholic hierarchy also contributed to the Porfirian atmosphere of détente by quietly changing its stance on the protesta. Such a move officially removed the spiritual obstacles from the path of Catholics who wanted to participate in civil government, thereby legitimating Catholic political engagement and eliminating a major source of civil-religious unrest in the decades after 1857. The curia of Zamora, in a direct response to Minister Tagle's ambiguous circular of January 15, offered a simple solution to the protesta quandary, allowing oath-taking Catholics to respond simply, "Yes, I swear, under the guarantees of freedom of conscience granted to me by the Circular of January 13 [sic] 1877."¹⁴⁰ But while Zamora officials relied on the perceived good faith of the government with respect to individual religious conscience and the protesta requirement, the Archdiocese of Mexico sought a new ruling on the matter from Rome. The decision came in April 1877, when the Archdiocese of Mexico issued a circular with the news that papal officials had authorized the use of a new counterprotesta. Based on a model used by Italian Catholics since 1873, the counterprotesta asked elected functionaries to come before ecclesiastical authorities or their parish priest before taking the unmodified civil protesta. There, they would sign a written oath using the following format:

> I [full name] promise that in the exercise of my employment I will respect divine and ecclesiastical laws, and I promise to not offend in the smallest way my Catholic beliefs; in consequence I will avoid complying with civil laws wherever they contravene divine ecclesiastical laws, and I will use the legal means that are available to me to revoke the anti-Catholic provisions of those [civil] laws, declaring as I do that this oath is absolutely irrevocable.[141]

The signed document was to be kept in a secret archive. Unlike the public retractions of the previous years, then, the counterprotesta allowed Catholics to negate the protesta without jeopardizing their jobs.[142] Further, not only did it clear the path for the participation of Catholics in public administration, it also committed them to reversing anticlerical legislation from within. Though it could not yet endorse Catholic political parties (and would not until 1911), the high clergy's decision to soften its stance on the protesta signaled its desire to see individual lay Catholics in positions of power and to retain clerical influence over those Catholics.[143] The Church had essentially embraced liberal republicanism as a means to safeguard its preeminent place in Mexican society.

The Mexican episcopate's change of direction found immediate echo in communities of Michoacán. As Manuel González had reported, elected officials even in highly conservative communities began to take the protesta without reservations after the municipal elections of spring 1877.[144] Almost certainly, these functionaries used the "formula" prescribed by the episcopate of Zamora. Such was the case in Chilchota, whose police chief Ladislao Álvarez took the protesta "in the understanding that the government ha[d] declared its respect for religious beliefs and individual conscience."[145] In the Archdiocese of Michoacán, meanwhile, the new papacy-approved counterprotesta was put to use. Newly elected municipal authorities in the Religionero bastion of Huango reported having attempted to take the protesta "with reservations," under the 1873 formula, in October 1877. When the civil judge declined to admit such a modified oath, they wrote to the archdiocesan government requesting guidance. Secretary Macouzet, referring them to the diocesan circular of April 19, instructed them to perform the counterprotesta with their parish priest before returning to the judge.[146] Thus, the protesta controversy, a two-decade-long thorn in the side of Church and state alike, was finally abating, and committed Catholics could now enter the public arena without fear of spiritual censures. Thanks to such developments, Michoacán would serve as a fertile ground for the Catholic political resurgence of the late nineteenth century.[147]

Conclusions

As the foregoing narrative has demonstrated, Díaz's courting of Catholics began early and represented something more than personal alliances with clerical plutocrats. Díaz proved keen to harness the power of Michoacán's religious conflict in his own search for national power by making overtures both to Religionero leaders and their middle-class allies. His ability to convert Michoacán's Catholic rebels to his cause—through intermediaries such as Donato Guerra and Octaviano Fernández—proved critical to the overall success of his movement. Indeed, in an interesting inversion of traditional historiographical narratives about the rise of Porfirio Díaz, the editors of Mexico City's *La Bandera Nacional* (the reincarnation of *El Pájaro Verde*, edited by Ignacio Águilar y Marocho) described the Religionero rebellion as the "spark that ignited the Revolution of Tuxtepec."[148] Here, Águilar y Marocho foregrounded the role played by Michoacán's conservatives in resisting the authoritarian anticlericalism of the Lerdo regime. If historians continue to understand the Revolution of Tuxtepec primarily as a contest between two national strongmen over the issue of reelection, contemporary observers both within and outside of Michoacán tended to view it as an outgrowth of the sustained Catholic mobilization of 1873–1876. The Religioneros had demonstrated that a radically secularized Michoacán would be ungovernable, and Díaz took the appropriate lesson.

Beyond courting Religionero rebels, Díaz and his subordinates in Michoacán also abetted a significant political resurgence among well-heeled conservatives and signaled the beginning of a partial, ad hoc relaxing of state enforcement of the Laws of Reform.[149] Such gestures, in addition to the Tuxtepec movement's inclusivity and the muscle of the Religionero groups, convinced defeated conservatives that they could come out of the shadows and participate in national politics once again. In fact, January and February 1877 witnessed an explosion of political organizing by conservatives all across Mexico. As we have seen, such conservative political mobilization did not go unnoticed by liberal tuxtepecanos in Michoacán, who used political fraud and targeted military repression in order to limit such gains. Catholics loudly protested such measures, and in short order the Michoacán political scene became a minefield for the astute but far from omnipotent Díaz, who struggled to convince all of the parties involved that he remained in their corner. Yet by the time General Plata cut down Antonio Reza, it had already become clear to Michoacán's Catholics that further armed struggle was unnecessary, given the Church's maneuvers on the protesta and the Díaz regime's willingness to overlook infractions of the Laws of Reform in the name of municipal autonomy. Further, the precedent for Catholic political participation as Catholic citizens (rather than representatives of the Church or members of the defunct Conservative Party) had been established.[150]

The early Porfirian Church-state conciliation lacked the force of law, depending instead on the collusion of local civil authorities with the faithful and the continuing goodwill of Church leaders. However partial and informal, such developments represented a substantial win for the Catholics who had taken up arms against Lerdo in Michoacán. Gone were the spiritual censures for serving in public administration, and so gone, too, were the "protestants" whose heresy the Religioneros had attempted to punish. Public religious celebration, too, had returned to many communities, though the piecemeal enforcement of the Laws of Reform would continue to cause friction between Catholics and the Porfirian government for decades to come. Mexico did not achieve a concordat with the Holy See as demanded by the Plan of Nuevo Urecho, yet the precedents had been established for increasingly harmonious Church-state relations in the years after 1877, including Díaz's de facto use of the Patronato in the appointment of new bishops. Further, don Porfirio's government often declined to enforce provisions against religious education, communal residency by religious men and women, and the wearing of clerical garb in public.[151] By the early twentieth century Mexico's nascent Protestant community complained bitterly about Díaz's cozy relationship with the high clergy and its failure to enforce the Laws of Reform or protect Protestant converts from acts of violence and vandalism.[152] In short, the secularizing promises of the Reforma remained unfulfilled in Porfirio Díaz's Mexico, a fact that owed much to the Religioneros of Michoacán.

Conclusions

The Religionero rebellion exerted a significant influence over the course of Mexico's post-Reforma history. The wave of protest, resistance, and armed insurrection that followed the Lerdo regime's anticlerical turn in 1873 plunged Michoacán into crisis, and state security forces and local National Guard units soon proved to be unequal to the task of suffocating the revolt. By the time the Ley Orgánica took effect and the Hermanas de la Caridad left for exile in early 1875, the federal government had to intervene in Michoacán, imposing a kind of martial law in order to prevent the spread of the Religionero contagion. However, lerdista authoritarianism at the state and federal levels—which included the suppression of the partisan press, the assumption of "emergency powers" and suspension of constitutional guarantees, and the federal army's scorched-earth campaign in Religionero-friendly populations in northwestern Michoacán—carried serious political risks for the government. Indeed, Lerdo's draconian response to the crisis not only inflamed the increasingly Religionero-sympathetic Catholic press, it also provided plenty of partisan fodder for the porfirista opposition and even turned once-loyal lerdistas against their president. Mariano Escobedo's new strategy of offering indultos to Religionero fighters in late 1875 represented a clear attempt by the beleaguered Lerdo administration to regain liberals' trust and turn a corner in the campaign against the Religioneros. Yet by the time the indultos began to thin rebel ranks, it was too late, since the rebellion had proven politically attractive enough to warrant the attention of Porfirio Díaz himself.

As we have seen, Díaz and his agents actively recruited the Religionero leaders even before the publication of the Plan of Tuxtepec. Once the Tuxtepec revolution was underway, moreover, Díaz looked to Michoacán as a key stepping-stone on his path to national power. He sought the allegiance of the Religioneros and their Catholic supporters as a priority, entrusting the ex-imperialist general Felipe Chacón (rather than the more reliably liberal Vicente Riva Palacio or Epitacio Huerta) with the task of completing Michoacán's conversion to Tuxtepec and warding off the decembrista threat from Guanajuato. Discontent with lerdista authoritarianism provided the common ground upon which porfiristas, Religioneros, and conservative michoacanos could meet. Yet Díaz's courting of Catholics had unforeseen consequences, stimulating a conservative political resurgence in Michoacán and other states and provoking a significant backlash from liberal porfiristas. An astute but never omnipotent *político*, Díaz struggled to keep Michoacán's Tuxtepec coalition intact by reaffirming his commitment to Reforma liberalism even while his agents worked to reincorporate conservative Catholics into the fabric of state politics. Further, Díaz himself nurtured Catholic hopes that Tuxtepec's tenet of "municipal autonomy" would allow local officials to contravene the Laws of Reform. This artful but perilous strategy ultimately paid off, since Díaz's politics of hope convinced conservative Catholics that it was safe to leave the shadows of political exile, and the Catholic hierarchy moved to moderate its position on the protesta. Díaz had essentially piloted Church-state modus vivendi in Michoacán, whose Religionero crisis had provided him with valuable, and durable, lessons on how to govern a Catholic nation while forging an ostensibly secular state. Indeed, don Porfirio's later ecclesiastical policy—which included the courting of high clerics and the nurturing of Roman hopes for a concordat without making any formal move to reform the Constitution of 1857—relied on strikingly similar tactics.[1]

If the Religioneros were defeated or co-opted by mid-1877, then, they had played a significant role in shaping the porfirista transition and brokering Díaz's alliance with conservative Catholics and the Church. In fact, since the Porfirian "policy of conciliation" left many aspects of the Laws of Reform unenforced and abetted the Catholic renaissance and political resurgence of the late nineteenth century, the Religioneros' role in debilitating Mexico's most vigorous nineteenth-century secularization program cannot be understated.[2]

Partisan concerns and a durable liberal teleology have long worked against serious study of the Religioneros. However, structural factors have also contributed to the rebellion's relative obscurity. The diffuse, decentralized, and popular character of the revolt and the absence of nationally recognized conservative or clerical leaders in its ranks have confounded contemporary historians as much as they confused nineteenth-century observers. Indeed, the Religionero rebellion has evaded easy categorization, and scholars who have approached the phenomenon have faced considerable interpretive hurdles. Simply put, the uprising was internally heterogeneous and stubbornly provincialist: a cumulative protest of locally oriented rebels who displayed wide inconsistencies in military practice, self-identification, religious orientation, and ideology. Further, the fluid and unstable political context of the Restored Republic ensured that the Religionero flag would also serve to cover the actions of more petty and opportunistic rebels.

Fragmentary nineteenth-century archives at the national and state levels offer few clear clues about the identities, motivations, and worldviews of Religionero leaders and even fewer glimpses of their followers. No published or manuscript chronicles of the revolt written by people who lived it have surfaced. Nineteenth-century newspapers can at times appear rife with rumor, innuendo, and partisan bias, and military accounts are structured to reduce all antistate action to banditry. Municipal and parish archives in the rural areas most affected by the revolt may well reveal much about individual Religioneros, though security concerns related to Michoacán's ongoing narco wars present barriers to outside researchers. Armed with the sometimes-flawed "data" of military engagements, historians of the Religioneros thus have their interpretive work cut out for them, yet the task of understanding the Religioneros in a more systematic way is not insurmountable. Unique patterns of partisanship can be detected throughout the state; violent acts situated into longer histories of local rivalries; rural unrest traced to larger changes in culture, property, and power.

As this book has argued, neither the materialist nor the Church-state conflict approach that have thus far dominated the historiography offer a satisfactory interpretation of the movement. Simply put, the effects of land privatization in the early 1870s were multiple and complex, and a direct causal link between the reparto and the Religionero rebellion cannot be established. As we have seen, local revolts were either definitively not agrarian (not correlated with significant alienation of indigenous lands), only partially agrarian (triggered by an inseparable mix of agrarian and religious factors), or agrarian in a wholly different way than historians have asserted (related to agrarian decompression, not compression). Further, liberal disentailment laws tended to contribute more to Religionero bellicosity in places where indigenous communities paradoxically managed to retain communal land bases but lost specific religious properties to adjudication efforts (Chilchota, Huaniqueo, Huango). In these places, agrarian and religious factors cannot be neatly disentangled, since attempts by individuals or municipal actors to privatize church atriums, Indian hospitals, or cemeteries threatened the baroque structure of local religion even while leaving communal subsistence economies intact. Only in Coalcomán's head town did the reparto serve as a clear and immediate trigger for rebellion, and there land division constituted only one part of a larger sociocultural transformation that led indigenous comuneros to make common cause with Religioneros.

A Church-state conflict approach to the revolt brings its own problems. To be sure, military reports demonstrate that religion—both a general loyalty to the Church and more specific, often local, devotions—moved many rank-and-file Religioneros and their leaders. Religionero violence was often triggered by civil intervention in local religious acts or the perceived persecution of local priests by civil authorities, and the rebellion reached its apogee at the height of the ritual year in 1875. Ecclesiastical injunctions against the protesta certainly played an important role in the outbreak of hostilities in 1873 and 1874. Yet the near-total absence of clerics in the movement and the explicit condemnation of armed revolt by the Mexican hierarchy in their 1875 collective pastoral complicate the assumption that the revolt was a uniform, Church-based protest against the modernizing state. Further, confiscated Religionero paraphernalia, rebel invocations of divine aid, and the known devotional preferences of Religionero leaders suggest that the rebels were religiously diverse. Interpretations that highlight religion as a preeminent factor in the revolt must therefore take care to identify what kind of religion they mean. Like agrarian transformation, Catholicism was not a unitary and straightforward driver of revolt but a complex and multiple variable.

As such, an analysis of the Religioneros' religious context and an appreciation for the local manifestations of the revolt become paramount. The rebellion did not reflect the knee-jerk defense of a static and solidary "Catholicism" but rather emerged from a context of significant institutional flux and religious change and conflict. As we have seen, the Church hierarchy's Lerdo-era turn away from confessional politics was part of a larger shift within Mexican Catholicism, during which the locally oriented, external, and collective worship that had long dominated baroque religiosity fell out of favor with Catholic elites and reformers. Indeed, the 1875 collective pastoral came on the heels of over a decade of intense internal reform in Mexico's central-western Catholic heartland. The most vigorous revitalization since the Bourbon Reforms, the mid-nineteenth century restoration sought to remake the region's diverse local catholicisms along European, Ultramontane lines. The impetus for such a project had come primarily from the reorganization of the Mexican episcopate in 1862, an innovation meant to tighten clerical control over key Catholic constituencies and counter the pull of liberalism in the center-west. Crucially, the restructuring also freed the new dioceses of Zamora and León from the entrenched power of Morelia's cathedral chapter and seminary, whose leaders, if they imbibed the era's Ultramontanism, were also keen to preserve their Quirogan heritage and affect a more inward-looking pastoral and clerical reform. Archbishop Labastida intended Zamora, in particular, to serve as a laboratory for Ultramontane restoration, since he had run into similar resistance from the powerful cabildo and seminary of Mexico.[3] It was thus that the Mexican hierarchy, with the aid of Zamora's Bishop de la Peña and Labastida's nephew José Antonio Plancarte, shifted the axis of Catholic restorationism to Michoacán, a development that had important ramifications for the Religionero revolt.

At high ecclesiastical levels, Catholic restorationism involved the promotion of European devotions, the tightening of personal and institutional relationships between Mexican reformers and Pius IX's Rome, and various attempts at seminary reform. On the ground, however, it often meant direct clerical attacks on indigenous religious practices and communal control over local cults, the spread of modern, voluntary associations that threatened baroque sodalities with obsolescence, and attempts to modernize and individualize Church tax collection. Paradoxically, Ultramontane reformism often dovetailed with liberal reformism, since—for all that the Ultramontanes' deference to Rome diverged from the liberals' "enlightened" regalism—they both favored an interiorized, voluntary piety over the raucous, corporate religiosity of the countryside. In a word, Ultramontane reformism threatened baroque constituencies whose religious cultures were already under attack by lerdista legislation that undermined the material base of corporate religion and severed the ritually maintained bonds between Catholic communities on earth and their patrons in heaven. Such religious dynamics significantly affected patterns of Religionero bellicosity in Michoacán. In the solidly conservative northwest, reformist attacks on baroque religion were particularly ferocious (even subjecting indigenous saints' images to Ultramontane autos de fé, as in Cherán) and modern lay associations became particularly active and influential in shaping local religious culture. Baroque Catholics subsequently turned to armed rebellion as a way both to defend the universal Church and to reassert their traditional religious prerogatives. In central Michoacán, whose communities faced a more tolerant archdiocesan administration, baroque religion was both positively and negatively correlated with the revolt. Purépecha communities threatened by the Ultramontane reformism of their pastor turned to the entrenched liberal elite of Coeneo and the sympathetic Archdiocese of Michoacán in order to successfully negotiate a return of their baroque religious customs and subsequently declined to join the rebellion. Meanwhile, diverse constituencies rallied to baroque devotions in Huaniqueo and Huango in order to ward off Ultramontane challenges and punish liberal municipal authorities who had targeted religious properties using Reforma legislation. In the southwestern coastal sierra, meanwhile, Ultramontane reformism of the Zamora style was an integral part of the mestizo "second conquest" of a vast indigenous hinterland, since it threatened to displace the indigenous religious leaders and their cacical patrons and sacralize the privatization of communal lands through a new fiscal regime of individual, voluntary tithing. Such agrarian and religious conflict within the flock reached such extremes that baroque Catholics directly attacked their Ultramontane counterparts.

Thus, religious change and conflict shaped Religionero bellicosity, though it did so in complex, sometimes contradictory ways. Local revolts were driven by distinct constellations of religious and extrareligious factors, and even the spiritual stakes of the rebellion differed from place to place. Considering such internal diversity and the clear trend of conflict between Ultramontane and baroque Catholics in the Religionero context, the question of the Religioneros' relationship to conservatism deserves further exploration. Were the Religioneros, properly speaking, conservatives? Yes and no. The ideology elaborated by the movement's diverse leadership between 1874 and 1876 consisted of an eclectic mix of traditional conservative ideas (Catholicism as Mexico's only social glue; the demand for state protection of the Church), Maximilian-style patronage (the insistence on a concordat), and liberal discourse on popular sovereignty and individual rights. That conservative and ex-imperialist veterans such as Juan de Dios Rodríguez, Félix Venegas, Antonio Reza, and "El Ranchero" González played key roles in shaping Religionero ideology helps to explain its traditionally conservative elements. Meanwhile, the involvement of political shape-shifters such as Abraham

Castañeda and Domingo Juárez likely moderated the Religionero program in some aspects and ultimately helped to build bridges with Lerdo's enemies in other political camps. Yet the movement's appropriation of liberal tenets also faithfully reflected trends in lay Catholic and ecclesiastical thought of the time, which increasingly conceived of the Church as a countercultural silo in a laicized society and encouraged the faithful to avail themselves of liberal rights. Invocations of popular sovereignty, after all, even made their way into the pronouncements of more organic, village-level Religionero chiefs such as Jesús "El Licenciado" Ortega, who, during his 1875 Teremendo uprising, proclaimed that he did not want theocracy and reminded Mexicans that "freedom of worship is not in your interest, because you are exclusively Catholic."[4] In some ways, then, the Religioneros aligned themselves with the mainstream conservative Catholic ideology of the time, and their movement clearly attracted many ex-imperialists and militants of the defunct Conservative Party. As it became increasingly professional and ideologically coherent, moreover, the movement gained the sympathies of the conservative literati, who used the pages of *El Pensamiento Católico*, *La Voz de México*, and *El Pájaro Verde* to legitimate the rebellion as a political revolution and not a rash of Catholic rage and opportunistic banditry.

Yet we cannot assume that the Religionero rank and file (or even village-level chiefs) always shared the concerns of mainstream conservatives or the most famous rebel leaders—many of whom came relatively late to the movement. Indeed, rebels and more well-heeled conservatives only moved toward rapprochement—and then tentatively and partially—after the publication of the Plan of Nuevo Urecho and the pronunciamientos of more trusted and recognizable leaders such as Rodríguez, Domingo Olaciregui, and Francisco Ugarte. Further, attempts to professionalize the Religionero coalition and uniformize its ideology could only go so far, since the movement remained highly localist and internally heterogeneous and its leaders acted autonomously. Even if the conservative press lionized Socorro Reyes in the days following his 1876 execution, for instance, it bears emphasizing that a large gulf separated the crude and vengeful Catholic nationalism of Reyes's political plan (which was basically a four-point articulation of the Religionero battle cry, "Death to the Protestants! Long live religion!") from the more politically astute Plan of Nuevo Urecho. Further, despite Religionero appropriation of the discourse of popular sovereignty, and despite the increasingly close relationship between Religionero leaders and the conservative elite in Michoacán between late 1875 and late 1876, it should be remembered that armed rebellion in the defense of the Church went against the grain of elite contemporary Catholic thought. Further, it directly contravened the mandates of the hierarchy, whose 1875 collective pastoral letter so clearly traced the "circle" within which Catholic citizens should work toward the reconquest of civil society. What is more, divergent strategies for the defense of the Church—armed rebellion versus the re-Catholicization of civil society—often brought believers into direct, violent confrontation, especially when loyal Catholics retained government posts. If the Religionero movement was a conservative mobilization, then, it also represented a significant conflict within Catholic conservatism. Ultimately, the Religioneros refused to abide either liberal or Catholic reforms, since each threatened the material and spiritual integrity of their communities in different ways.

This book has argued that the rifts evident in the conservative Catholic coalition in 1873–1877 were often religious in nature, since baroque-minded Catholics more often rallied to the Religioneros' side while Ultramontanes confined their efforts to the archbishops' countercultural "circle." Clearly, some orthodox rancheros, old-line conservative caudillos, and the latter's supporters in the Catholic press opted to ignore the hierarchy's injunctions against rebellion once the Religionero movement had become a going concern in 1875, thus making one last bid for a conservative coup. As it became increasingly unlikely that they could take power on their own, moreover, they turned to Porfirio Díaz, who had showed himself amenable to the kinds of informal compromises that could further abet the Catholic hierarchy's projected reconquest of civil society. Yet our analysis of the local logics of the revolt suggests that the larger, more popular component of the Religionero movement ignored the archbishops' prohibition of armed rebellion for other reasons. Succinctly put, as acolytes of a more corporate and baroque religious style, rank-and-file Religioneros and their organic chiefs (Eulogio Cárdenas, Socorro Reyes, Antonio Cándido) rejected the Church hierarchy's accommodationist stance toward the state as well as the reformist religious outlook that underpinned it. If for Ultramontane Catholics the lerdista conflict was an unpleasant dispute over the jurisdictional boundaries of Church and state, the damages of lerdismo could be mediated through spiritual and charitable means and through the embrace of their rights as Catholic citizens. For baroque Catholics, however, the prohibition of public worship and the attack on corporate religious properties represented an existential crisis, since they undermined the very foundation of the relationship between communities and their divine patrons. Such a crisis could not be averted simply by interiorizing and individualizing piety and joining voluntary associations, as the Ultramontanes wished. Baroque Catholicism was an eminently collective and external endeavor—sustained by communal, public worship; organized by semiautonomous religious guilds, mayordomos, and indigenous cabildos; guided by tolerant, old-fashioned mendicants or secular priests who respected local traditions; and funded by entailed properties and collective labor. The laicization of the public sphere and the privatization of communal life disrupted the entire baroque religious system.

Religioneros from the baroque camp—who initiated the movement in late 1873 and made up its rank and file throughout the conflict—went to war to defend their feast-day processions from both liberal and Catholic reformers, and they sometimes died with the names of their local saints on their lips. These, then, were "small c" conservatives, since they defended a traditional religion from a reformed state and a reformed Church. Correspondingly, their relationships with the more formally conservative elements within and without the movement were complex and often fraught. Jiquilpan rebels such as Eulogio Cárdenas and the late-arriving Florencio "El Fepe" Escalera—who faced an especially strong local Ultramontane restoration—remained in the field long after the Ultramontane conservatives of northwestern Michoacán had begun to accommodate the new Porfirian regime through the use of diocesan-approved counterprotestas. Conversely, Socorro Reyes's peasant followers mostly returned to their fields and ranchos after the execution of their leader, and they quickly adjusted to the Porfirian regime through the use of counterprotestas and negotiations with civil officials that brought the partial resumption of baroque public worship. The Purépechas of the ciénega, meanwhile, provided only passive and partial support to more formally conservative rebels from Coeneo, because they had already warded off an Ultramontane challenge and negotiated the return of their processions through diocesan and liberal channels before the revolt began. Finally, Coalcomán's Religionero coalition of indigenous comuneros, juarista caciques, and pious rancheros from Aguililla and Tepalcatepec proved too internally fragmented to endure after its disastrous attack on the head town in 1875, after which scores of indigenous comuneros sought indulto and left the fighting to their old patrons, the Guzmán brothers.

Such internal contradictions—the stubborn provincialism of the movement, the complexity of factors driving local revolts, the divergent fortunes of Ultramontane reformism and baroque retrenchment across Michoacán, and the persistent divisions between the "small c" conservative rebels and the more formally conservative elements who attempted to ride the Religionero wave in 1875 and 1876—ultimately kept the rebellion from cohering into a broader movement capable of taking national power. Nonetheless, in destabilizing the Lerdo regime and contributing meaningfully to the rise of Porfirio Díaz and the establishment of a more conciliatory form of Church-state politics, the Religioneros had shaped the course of Mexican history and achieved many of their goals. Of course, such a victory was not uniformly shared across the Religionero-conservative spectrum. To be sure, Ultramontane conservatives had won the right to participate in politics as Catholic citizens, and they subsequently strengthened their resolve to create a Catholic counterculture (and, eventually, a confessional political party) within a laicized regime.[5] Meanwhile, baroque factions in central Michoacán successfully negotiated the return of their festive customs and the end of the protesta crisis in the medium term, though such gains would be partially reversed in the ciénega communities, particularly, in the late Porfiriato.[6] Local outcomes were more mixed in other places, however, and especially in the bishopric of Zamora. Baroque Catholics in the Levitical northwest, if they had helped to defeat the lerdista program, would continue to face pressures from Ultramontane reformers and their ranchero followers in subsequent decades.[7] In Coalcomán, the Guzmán clan weathered the Religionero storm and regained a measure of local power, and their Catholic allies in Aguililla managed both to halt the lerdista program and to conquer the local power structure. However, for the indigenous comunero faction in Coalcomán, military defeat at the hands of Julio García in 1875 would be followed by further legal defeats in the struggle to reverse the damages of the reparto and the "second acculturation" initiated by the mestizo immigrants. Indeed, by the early twentieth century, the Nahuas of Coalcomán had all but disappeared, and the local Cristero movement was subsequently directed by the sons of the Ultramontane rancheros who had conquered the southern sierra.[8] In short, despite the Religioneros' crucial role in bringing Porfirio Díaz to power and shaping the lopsided secularization of Mexico's prerevolutionary ancien régime, the conflict of the 1870s had ultimately left many questions—about the nature of Catholicism, the place of the Church in a laical society, the continuing validity of colonial corporations and baroque practices—unresolved. Indeed, even if the Pax Porfiriana successfully papered over the myriad religious, political, and ethnic divisions that had animated the Religionero conflict, it could not erase them. In the open contest for power heralded by the Mexican Revolution, Michoacán would once again fall into a series of complex local conflicts.[9]

Further research will be needed to fully assess the Religioneros' connection to the Revolution and the Cristero Wars of the early twentieth century. Yet events in Michoacán during our own disordered century offer striking parallels to the 1870s and suggest that more durable cultural structures are at work in the state's seemingly eternal cycles of conflict. True, the geopolitical and economic circumstances have changed radically since Eulogio Cárdenas's day; yet in present-day Michoacán's tragic saga of narco predation, government impotence (or collusion), and vigilante retrenchment, certain Religionero resonances appear. Michoacán, after all, is a place where the cartels take the name of medieval Catholic military orders, where drug lords distribute handmade "bibles" to their subordinates and erect altars to themselves in the terrorized countryside, fashioning an elaborate religious ethos for their murderous narco-capitalism. It is a place, too, where self-defense militias (*autodefensas*) rely on renegade priests like Padre Goyo (cura of Apatzingán) for sustenance and sanctuary; where townspeople create warning systems with parish church bells and saints-day fireworks; and vigilantes receive the Holy Sacrament after retaking towns from the narcos. The religious topography of Michoacán remains ever complex and combustible, and everyday life, even or perhaps especially in extraordinary times, retains ritual qualities. As autodefensa leader José Manuel Mireles makes clear in a recent memoir, the people of Tepalcatepec took up arms in 2013 primarily because they could not stand the increasingly grotesque and painful exactions of the narcos. But in armed self-defense, they also reclaimed their public festive life, which had been "suspended by the total and absolute dominion of organized crime" for twelve years. Thus it was that in February 2014, in commemoration of the anniversary of the creation of the autodefensa, Mireles's now narco-free hometown gave itself over to public, communal celebration. "With great pomp, according to our traditions and culture," Mireles says, Tepalcatepec's people unburdened themselves of their fear and anxiety, celebrating their liberty with processions, dances, poems, and a communal feast, in which "some supplied the meat, others the preparation, others the drinks, and others played music." The climax of the night, of course, was a "magnificent, emotive" Mass, led by local priest Padre Miguel, who had aided the autodefenses from the start.[10] Through collective struggle and divine aid, it seemed, the town's public festive culture had been restored once again, at least temporarily.

Appendix A
The Plan of Nuevo Urecho

Mexicans:
Considering that the constitution that currently governs us has been imposed on the nation by force of arms and without its express will; that the men that rule us have violated it to such an extent that we can no longer say that we are constitutionally governed; that, defrauding the popular vote and making a mockery of national sovereignty, they have empowered themselves of the [public] posts, usurping public power; that they have injured the religious sentiment of the Nation; regulating and systematizing the persecution of Catholicism, religion of the majority of Mexicans; that they have attacked the national and civil liberties of the citizens, establishing a tyranny that can in no way be acceptable to those who can proudly call themselves free men: we, making recourse to the right that our fathers used in their defense of the liberty of Mexico, have believed it to be our duty, as men, as Christians, and as citizens to proclaim the following Plan:

> Art. 1. The federal constitution of the United Mexican States, sanctioned on 5 February 1857, its reforms and additions of the regulating law, along with all laws that have emanated from that Charter, are hereby repealed.
>
> Art. 2. Sr. Lic. D. Sebastián Lerdo de Tejada and all of the functionaries of the legislative, political, and judicial order, who against the expressed will of the people form today the personnel of the government of the Mexican Republic, are hereby removed from the exercise of public power.
>
> Art. 3. After this plan has been adopted by the majority of the Nation, an interim president of the Republic will be named. The election will

Source: AGHPEM, Guerra y Ejército, caja 3, exp. 28, "El Plan de Nuevo Urecho," 3 March 1875. All translations in these appendices are mine.

be carried out by a council of representatives convoked by the General in Chief of the forces that sustain this plan, in the place judged most convenient by that same Chief.

Art. 4. The interim president will of course be invested with broad powers in all of the branches of Public Administration; but he will be strictly obligated to respect the Catholic religion and individual rights, to attend to the security and independence of the nation, and to promote by all means possible its prosperity and exaltation.

Art. 5. As soon as the interim president enters office, he will without delay name a plenipotentiary close to the Holy See, invested with the necessary powers to negotiate a concordat that, by soothing consciences, will repair the effects of the acquisitions of ecclesiastical properties by way of the so-called Laws of Reform.

Art. 6. Within two months of taking office, the interim president will convoke an extraordinary session of congress, which will dedicate itself exclusively to constituting the nation under the form of a representative, popular Republic, and to revising the accounts of the actual government and the provisional executive discussed in Art. 3.

Art. 7. The constitution will recognize, as religion of the State, the Apostolic Roman Catholic Church, bestowing upon it the rights and exercises of its high and lofty mission on the earth, as well as its spiritual and temporal powers, without sacrificing its respective independence.

Art. 8. The principal chief of the forces that sustain this plan in each state will each convoke a council formed of municipal representatives which will elect an interim Governor, and the latter will exercise the necessary functions to organize the public Administration of his respective territory.

Art. 9. The so-called laws of the Stamp [Duty], of the National Guard, of extraordinary taxes and personal contributions currently in force in some states, are hereby repealed. The General Government and the state governments, during their short interim periods, will be reduced to those offices and employees that are strictly necessary for good public service, and they will moderate the taxes and contributions, taking into account the very urgent attentions of the Administration and the state of misery in which the people have been left by the wasteful Government in power.

Art. 10. All those who oppose this plan will be treated as enemies of the people and of the national independence: the chiefs of the army that second this plan will be recognized with the same military rank that they had [in the federal army] on the date of their adhesion.

> God and Oder. Nuevo Urecho, 3 March 1875.
> Signed by Antonio Reza and Abraham Castañeda

Article Added to the Plan of Nuevo Urecho in Tzitzio*

Art. 11. This plan will be modified if it is judged necessary by the majority of the Nation: the principal chief of the force that sustains this plan is empowered to name an interim authority in each town, so that this authority can severely punish criminals.

---

* Source: AGHPEM, Guerra y Ejército, caja 3, exp. 51, Copy of the Plan Religionero de Tzitzio and Proclamation of Jesús "el Ranchero" González, Tzitztio, 14 April 1875.

Appendix B

The Manifesto of Tzitzio

Citizens and companions in arms:
You know well that this so-called *Ley Orgánica de Adiciones* has powerfully moved all of the classes of society. For this reason, we the undersigned, sons of the Holy Roman, Apostolic, Catholic Church, considering it our duty to raise our feeble voices against those who have made themselves enemies of Catholicism, that mob of 113 deputies of the 7th Congress, usurpers of power, who made themselves representatives of the Mexican nation against the will of the people; those allies of the other enemies of the Church that work without rest to take away our faith, our morality; and who therefore prohibit Christian education, persecute and slander our priests, and who, condoning any measure in order to obtain their ill-fated goals, do not heed or fear the anathemas of the Pastors of the Church, and who are not even moved by the tears and entreaties of so many pious souls, nor the protests of almost all of the states that ask for justice, that ask for the revocation of that iniquitous Law that, by force of arms and a capricious belief in their own power, they want to make us obey.

They mock everything and they remain blind, and their hearts are harder than bronze. And what can we do in this conflict? Will we remain indifferent and let them frighten us with impious cries? Will we idly watch as they persecute the Holy Church with a cold heart? No, this would be a crime. Just look at the abyss into which they want to submerge us. Just think of your families. What will become of our children if things remain in this state? Let us ask God for the remedy for such ills and [pray] for the souls in defense of the current cause. The Deputies are not content with what they have; they want to be absolute owners of everything; gold is their God; they are no

Source: AGHPEM, Guerra y Ejército, caja 3, exp. 51, Copy of the Plan Religionero de Tzitzio and Proclamation of Jesús "el Ranchero" González, Tzitztio, 14 April 1875.

longer the liberators of the sovereign people, they are no longer members of humanity; that was an illusion. Do you know who they are? They are enemies of God and his ministers, enemies of peace and order, enemies of the well-being of the Nation. It matters little to them that our brothers spill their blood, because they are men without faith, without religion, without piety. But we, firm in our beliefs, will combat their designs even at the cost of our blood, fulfilling in that way the most sacred duty that we have in life. With this thought, we put ourselves in the hands of Providence, inviting all pueblos to second our plan. To arms, defenders of the holy cause of God, of our religion and of our Fatherland!

War to all of the enemies of the good doctrines; of the institutions, rights, and liberties of the Catholic Church; war to the enemies of the prosperity and aggrandizement of Mexico, war without quarter to the universal lie. Death or victory.

God and Order. Tzitzio, 14 April 1875.
Signed by D. Jesús María González, D. Toribio Bucio,
D. Francisco de J. Jiménez, and D. Guadalupe Bucio

Appendix C

Proclamation of Colonel Juan de Dios Rodríguez

To the generals, official chiefs, and soldiers of the Republican Army:

The Nation is tyrannized, and in a most undignified manner: she is dressed as a sovereign, and she is greeted as a queen. Queen and sovereign of mockery! While she suffers deeply and laments in vain, they, the tyrant and his *satélicas* [sic], laugh at her pain and mock her lamentations.

You are the ones who give them the confidence for their laughter and the courage for their jeers.

If they did not have your support, they would not laugh or jeer at the Nation.

You have to withdraw your support if you do not want to be accomplices to such disgrace and abuse.

Do not let loyalty or obedience, the honor of a soldier or the vigor of discipline, stop you; you are not the servants of the oppressor of the Nation but rather [the servants] of the oppressed Nation.

The Nation and only the Nation is the owner of your obedience.

Toppling the tyrant, you would place Mexico, today covered in filth, on the throne. Removing that Caesar in a Phrygian cap, who tramples the [Nation], you would contribute to the aggrandizement and the glory of the fatherland.

This is the noble mission of the solider: this is the most honorific heraldry of the militia.

Cast your eyes upon our flag, and you will see that the insignia that adorns its tricolor bands is not the arms of the feudal lord, nor the axe, nor the torch of the great demagogue, but rather the glorious and triumphant Mexican eagle, with its everlasting memories of Dolores and Iguala, of Hidalgo and Iturbide!

Join us!

Come to the side of the Nation: You will be our brothers and we will

Source: Ceballos, *Aurora y ocaso*, 879–80.

triumph together; you will save the Nation and give it days of happiness, of true glory.

Although you see us naked and almost without arms, our triumph is sure. Be firm of will; the Nation sympathizes with us, and it covers us with the powerful shield of its sovereign opinion; and in this world, will and opinion are omnipotent.

Against will and opinion, as you know well, numerous armies and destructive weapons are nothing.

Observe what is happening in the State:

The forces that the Government has deployed to destroy us have given us triumph; in a thousand unequal confrontations, the violence and death with which they threaten us, and that have claimed already many victims in their attempt to divide us, have instead multiplied us; we were a mere hundred, now we are thousands; now, as then, we are resolved to fight for the religion that they persecute, for the liberty that they kill. Yet what will become of the existing [order]? It will not be what we say; it will not be what you want; it will be what the Nation wants; it will be the reconciliation of the good people of all parties, the forgiveness and repentance of the bad; it will be order and harmony; good will and concord; it will be prosperity and fortune; peace and justice; it will be light and activity in all parts, progress and civilization. Are you true patriots and men of heart? You cannot tolerate the reign of iniquity and tyranny; you cannot allow the fatherland to be dragged, much less pushed, into the abyss that is opening to engulf it.

On the contrary, you must proclaim with us, ENOUGH of that kingdom; we must restitute [the nation] it to its old well-being and primitive glory.

"The fatherland is in danger" one of the leaders of the politics you defend claimed falsely in order to destroy it.

"The fatherland is perishing," it says now to you so that you will save it, so that you will fight until you triumph or die with the Nation.

Republican soldiers!

Let the oppressor of the Nation be delivered to us by your forces; come fight with us, break your chains.

Cry with us LONG LIVE RELIGION! She is and has been your mother; we will cry with you LONG LIVE LIBERTY! She is and has been the treasure of our hearts and the enchantment of our lives . . .

> General Headquarters, Patámbaro, 15 June 1875.
> Juan de Dios Rodríguez

Notes

Introduction

1. Iñiguez Mendoza, "¡Viva la religión y mueran los *protestantes!*," the first full-length thesis on the Religioneros, tends to paint rebels as pawns of the Church, an institution whose near-totalizing sway over the populace and intransigent positions on the Laws of Reform led inexorably toward revolt.
2. On the ramifications of the Bourbon Reforms for Mexican Catholicism, see especially Brading, *Church and State in Bourbon Mexico*, and Taylor, *Magistrates of the Sacred*.
3. On the independence-era clergy, see especially Taylor, *Magistrates of the Sacred*, and Connaughton, *Clerical Ideology in a Revolutionary Age*. On the Patronato conflict, see Costeloe, *Church and State in Independent Mexico*. On clerical responses to the Reforma, see Mijangos y González, *Lawyer of the Church*.
4. The literature on the Reforma is vast. Key texts include Sinkin, *Mexican Reform*; Covo, *Las ideas de la reforma en México*; Hamnett, *Juárez*; and Mijangos y González, *Lawyer of the Church*. On responses to the oath of fidelity to the Constitution of 1857, see Mijangos y González, "La respuesta popular al juramento constitucional en 1857."
5. Knowlton, *Church Property and the Mexican Reform*, 72–75; and Staples, "El matrimonio civil y la epístola de Melchor Ocampo."
6. Hamnett, *Juárez*, 100–10; and García Ugarte, *Poder político y religioso*, 815–22.
7. Pani, *Para mexicanizar el segundo imperio*; and Galeana, *Las relaciones estado-iglesia durante el segundo imperio*.
8. Pi-Suñer Llorens, "Sebastián Lerdo de Tejada y su política hacia la iglesia católica"; Olimón Nolasco, "Proyecto de reforma de la iglesia en México"; and Knapp, *Life of Sebastián Lerdo de Tejada*, 122–24, 214–15.
9. Alazraki, "Liberalismo a prueba."
10. Riva Palacio, *Historia de la administración de D. Sebastián Lerdo de Tejada*, 305–6. For the text of both laws, see Pi-Suñer, *Sebastián Lerdo de Tejada, canciller/estadista*, 249–60.
11. As Elizabeth O'Brien argues, the Hermanas were probably targeted as much for their autonomy from Mexico's nascent medical establishment as for their

infringement of the Laws of Reform. See O'Brien, "If They Are Useful, Why Expel Them?."

12. "Reglamentación de las leyes de reforma," 14 December 1874, in Pi-Suñer, *Sebastián Lerdo de Tejada, canciller/estadista*, 253–60.

13. Bastian, *Los disidentes*, 50–65; and Pi-Suñer, "Sebastián Lerdo de Tejada y su política hacia la iglesia católica," 136–37. See also "Contestación de Sebastián Lerdo de Tejada a la delegación de sacerdotes protestantes que se presentaron a expresarle su gratitud por el modo en que eran respetadas sus creencias religiosas," in Pi-Suñer Llorens, *Sebastián Lerdo de Tejada, canciller/estadista*, 248.

14. Before Iñiguez Mendoza's 2015 dissertation ("¡Viva la religión y mueran los *protestantes*!"), the rebellion had attracted scant historiographical interest, the subject of only a handful of chapters and stand-alone articles in the 1980s and 1990s. See Ochoa Serrano, "La protocristeriada"; Ochoa Serrano, "Tres corridos cristeros del noroeste michoacano"; Ochoa Serrano, "Religioneros en Michoacán: Eulogio Cárdenas y otros"; Ochoa Serrano, "Macario Romero"; Soto Correa, "De bandidos sociales a religioneros," in *Movimientos campesinos de derecha*; and Pineda Soto, "El discurso del movimiento religionero en la prensa moreliana." Other authors discuss the Religioneros briefly within chapters or articles. See especially Meyer, *La cristiada*, 31–43; Bautista García, "La reorganización de la iglesia," 90–101; and Falcón, "El estado liberal ante las rebeliones populares," 994–95, 1021–24.

15. Cosmes, *Historia general de México*, 694–95; and Ceballos, *Aurora y ocaso*, 283.

16. Cosío Villegas, *Historia moderna de México*, esp. vol. 1, *La República Restaurada*; and Cosío Villegas, "Sebastián Lerdo de Tejada."

17. Cosío Villegas, *La República Restaurada*, 615–22. Cosío Villegas's characterization of the revolt as weak and nonideological seems to emerge directly from his reading of congressional papers, in which opposition statesmen accused the Lerdo regime of inflating the gravity of the conflict in order to suspend constitutional guarantees and stave off an electoral challenge. See *El diario de los debates*, 535–41, 581–86.

18. Meyer, *La cristiada*, 31–43. Zenaida Adriana Pineda Soto's brief 1999 article on the press's treatment of the rebellion is also instructive for what it reveals about the movement's gravity. See Pineda Soto, "El discurso del movimiento religionero en la prensa moreliana."

19. Luis González y González pioneered the field of Mexican microhistory with *Pueblo en vilo*. Since its publication, the state government of Michoacán has invested heavily in local history by publishing its "Municipal Monographs" series. For key local studies, see Ochoa Serrano, *Jiquilpan*; Martínez Álvarez, *La Piedad*; Ortíz Ibarra and González Méndez, *Puruándiro*; and González y González, *Zamora*. University presses in Zamora and Morelia, meanwhile, have published more analytical works in local and regional history since the 1980s. See, for example, Tapia Santamaría, *Campo religioso y evolución política*;

Sánchez Díaz, *El suroeste de Michoacán: estructura económica-social*; Sánchez Díaz, *El suroeste de Michoacán: economía y sociedad*; Cochet, *Alambradas en la sierra*; Moreno García, *Guaracha*; and Zárate Hernández, *La tierra caliente de Michoacán*. For a cogent analysis of Michoacán's modern historiography, see Oikión Solano, "Un nuevo pasado michoacano."
20. See Ochoa Serrano, "Tres corridos cristeros del noroeste michoacano"; "Religioneros en Michoacán"; and "Macario Romero."
21. Soto Correa, *Movimientos campesinos de derecha*, 11–17.
22. See Stauffer, "Community, Identity"; Böehm, "Las comunidades de indígenas de Ixtlán y Pajacuarán ante la reforma liberal en el siglo XIX"; Purnell, "With All Due Respect"; and Sánchez Díaz, *El suroeste de Michoacán: economía y sociedad*.
23. Soto Correa, *Movimientos campesinos de derecha*, 65–111. On "social banditry," see Hobsbawm, *Primitive Rebels*.
24. Jesús "El Ranchero" González, the Taximaroa-based rebel chief whose actions Soto Correa follows closely, was, after all, a "ranchero" and thus a member of a class that proved extremely dynamic in various parts of Michoacán, Jalisco, Guanajuato, and Hidalgo during the second half of the nineteenth century. See, for example, González y González, *Pueblo en vilo*; Schryer, "Ranchero Economy in Northwestern Hidalgo"; Brading, *Haciendas and Ranchos in the Mexican Bajío*, esp. chap. 7; Tutino, *From Insurrection to Revolution in Mexico*, 260, 342–45; Tutino, "Revolution in Mexican Independence"; Barragán López, *Mas allá de los caminos*, esp. chap. 3; Cochet, *Alambradas en la sierra*; and Stauffer, "Community, Identity." In the Cristero context, Matthew Butler shows how upwardly mobile rancheros could become involved in armed Catholic movements. See "'Liberal' Cristero."
25. Iñiguez Mendoza, "¡Viva la religión y mueran los *protestantes*!," 448–49.
26. See, for example, Thomson, "Popular Aspects of Liberalism in Mexico"; Thomson with LaFrance, *Patriotism, Politics, and Popular Liberalism in Nineteenth-Century Mexico*; Mallon, *Peasant and Nation*; Guardino, *Peasants, Politics, and the Formation of Mexico's National State*; Guardino, *Time of Liberty*; Ducey, *Nation of Villages*; McNamara, *Sons of the Sierra*; and Schaefer, *Liberalism as Utopia*.
27. Joseph and Nugent, *Everyday Forms of State Formation*, 3; Mallon, *Peasant and Nation*, 14–15; Knight, "El liberalismo mexicano desde la reforma hasta la revolución," 59.
28. Ducey, for instance, dismisses centralist/conservative politics as "neocolonial," and Mallon's description of "populist" forms of conservatism in the Puebla sierra serves largely as an underdeveloped foil set against a sophisticated peasant liberalism. See Ducey, *Nation of Villages*, 172; Mallon, *Peasant and Nation*, 93–96.
29. Smith, *Roots of Conservatism in Mexico*, 15–17.

30. Van Oosterhout, "Confraternities and Popular Conservatism on the Frontier"; and Van Oosterhout, "Popular Conservatism in Mexico." Other recent works on popular conservatism include Brittsan, *Popular Politics and Rebellion in Mexico*; Fowler, "Pronunciamientos and Popular Centralism in Mid-1830s Mexico"; Hamnett, "Mexican Conservatives, Clericals, and Soldiers"; and Thomson, "La contrarreforma de Puebla." These works build upon the insights of an earlier generation of intellectual historians, whose work disaggregated the category of "conservative" and denaturalized the liberal ascent. See, for example, Noriega, *El Pensamiento conservador y el conservadurismo mexicano*; and Pani, *Conservadurismos y derechas en la historia de México*.
31. The notion that 1867 spelled the end of organized conservatism in Mexico in the nineteenth century appears in general texts such as Meyer and Beezley, *Oxford History of Mexico*, 396; and MacLachlan and Beezley, *El Gran Pueblo*, 75–83; as well as in more specialized works such as Rugeley, *Of Wonders and Wise Men*, 60–61; and Cannelli, *Nación católica y estado laico*, 61.
32. Ceballos Ramírez, *El catolicismo social*; Wright-Ríos, *Revolutions in Mexican Catholicism*; Meyer, *La cristiada*; Butler, *Popular Piety and Political Identity*; O'Dogherty, *De urnas y sotanas*; Mireles Valverde, *Todos somos autodefensas*; and Lomnitz, "La religión de Los Caballeros Templarios."
33. Butler, "Religious Developments in Mexico," 705–6. See also Cannelli, *Nación católica y estado laico*, 151–206; Moreno Chávez, *Devociones políticas*, 63–75; Staples, "El Estado y la Iglesia durante la república restaurada"; Juárez, *Reclaiming Church Wealth*; and Bautista García, *Clérigos virtuosos e instruidos*.
34. Cannelli, *Nación católica y estado laico*, 31–32, 79–110; Wright-Ríos, *Revolutions in Mexican Catholicism*, 18; Adame Goddard, *El pensamiento político y social de los católicos mexicanos*, 103; Bastian, *Los disidentes*, 173–74; Meyer, *La cristiada*, 44–45; Iturribarría, "La política de conciliación del general Díaz y el arzobispo Gillow"; and Schmitt, "Díaz Conciliation Policy on State and Local Levels."
35. McNamara, *Sons of the Sierra*.
36. Important exceptions to such a rule of neglect include the studies of Church wealth and Church-state relations published in the 1960s and 1970s. See, for example, Costeloe, *Church Wealth in Mexico*; Bazant, *Alienation of Church Wealth in Mexico*; Knowlton, *Church Property and the Mexican Reform*; and Costeloe, *Church and State in Independent Mexico*.
37. For a cogent discussion of recent historiographical trends, see O'Hara, "Politics and Piety." Among the most important new histories of Catholic politics are Connaughton, *Clerical Ideology in a Revolutionary Age*; Voekel, *Alone before God*; Adame Goddard, *El pensamiento político y social de los católicos mexicanos*; Ceballos Ramírez, *El catolicismo social*; Bautista García, *Las disyuntivas*; Cannelli, *Nación católica y estado laico*; and Moreno Chávez,

Devociones políticas. Clerical biography and new institutional history have also proven fertile fields for study. See Brading, "Ultramontane Intransigence and the Mexican Reform"; García Ugarte, *Poder político y religioso*; Rosas Salas, *La iglesia mexicana en tiempos de la impiedad*; Camacho Mercado, *Frente al hambre y el óbus*; Mijangos y González, *Lawyer of the Church*; Díaz Patiño, *Católicos, liberales, y protestantes*; Bautista García, *Clérigos virtuosos e instruidos*; Ornelas Hernández, "A la sombra de la revolución liberal"; and Ibarra López, *La iglesia de Michoacán*.

38. See Bautista García, *Clérigos virtuosos e instruidos*, 27–67.
39. Butler, *Popular Piety and Political Identity*, 9–10.
40. Smith, *Roots of Conservatism in Mexico*, 12. Here, Smith is adapting Alan Knight's argument about the diversity of local political cultures in Mexico to the religious sphere.
41. Christian, *Local Religion in Sixteenth-Century Spain*; Davis, "Some Tasks and Themes in the Study of Popular Religion"; Davis, "From 'Popular Religion' to Religious Cultures"; Eire, "Concept of Popular Religion"; and Smith, *Roots of Conservatism in Mexico*, 12–13.
42. Christian, *Local Religion in Sixteenth-Century Spain*, esp. chap. 5. The same goes for Eamon Duffy's "traditional religion," which the author describes as spanning class divisions. See Duffy, *Stripping of the Altars*.
43. Voekel, *Alone before God*; Voekel, "Liberal Religion"; Brading, *Origins of Mexican Nationalism*, 31–38; and Covo, *Las ideas de la reforma en México*, 199–228.
44. Bautista García, *Clérigos virtuosos e instruidos*, 27–47; Moreno Chávez, *Devociones políticas*, 38–62; Harris, *Lourdes*; and Clark and Kaiser, *Culture Wars*.
45. Bautista García, "La afirmación del orden social en el estado"; and Chowning, "Catholic Church and the Ladies of the Vela Perpetua." The term *collective action* comes from an 1875 collective pastoral letter penned by Mexico's three archbishops that encouraged the faithful to work together in a voluntary fashion to counteract the deleterious effects of the Laws of Reform. See "Instrucción pastoral que los Ilmos. Sres. Arzobispos de México, Michoacán, y Guadalajara dirigen a su Venerable Clero y a sus fieles con ocasión de la Ley Orgánica expedida por el Soberano Congreso Nacional en 10 de diciembre del año próximo pasado y sancionada por el Supremo Gobierno en 14 del mismo mes" (hereafter, CPC 1875), 19 March 1875, reprinted in Alcalá and Olimón, *Episcopado y gobierno en México*, 293–338.
46. Larkin, *Very Nature of God*, 4–7; and Voekel, *Alone before God*, chap. 1.
47. On the importance of corporations to Habsburg rule, see Cañeque, *King's Living Image*. On the persistence of colonial corporate identities and baroque practices, see O'Hara, *Flock Divided*; and Larkin, *Very Nature of God*.
48. Echeverría, *La modernidad de lo barroco*, 9, 30–55. In more recent years, the historian Jorge Cañizares-Esguerra has also argued for the radically modern

character of the Spanish-American baroque—particularly with regard to its epistemological innovations—as against the cultural conservatism described by José Antonio Maravall in his classic work *La cultura del barroco*. See Cañizares-Esguerra, *How to Write a History of the New World*, 9.

49. Indeed, in Echeverría's apt formulation, the baroque ethos sought to replace "capital" with "Church" as the organizing force of modern society.

50. Echeverría, *La modernidad de lo barroco*, 157–58. Here, Echeverría is most concerned with the rise to global dominance of what he calls the "realist ethos," corresponding closely to Max Weber's "Protestant ethic," which essentially denies the contradictions inherent in capitalist modernity and subjects itself to the logic of the market.

51. O'Hara, *Flock Divided*, chap. 5 and 6. On liberal anticorporatism, see Hale, *Mexican Liberalism in the Age of Mora*, 133–40. On the effects of liberalism on local religious structures, see Traffano, "Para formar el corazón religioso de los jóvenes"; Larkin, *Very Nature of God*, esp. chap. 9; and Chance and Taylor, "Cofradías and Cargos."

52. Mijangos y González, *Lawyer of the Church*, chap. 2; and Bautista García, *Clérigos virtuosos e instruidos*, 69–122.

53. Chowning, "Catholic Church and the Ladies of the Vela Perpetua"; Bautista García, "La afirmación del orden social en el estado liberal"; Velasco Robledo, "Institución bendita por Dios"; Bautista García, *Las disyuntivas*, 278–82; and Arrom, *Volunteering for a Cause*.

54. Like Terry Rugeley, Edward Wright-Ríos, and Ben Smith, I see Catholicism as an arena for contestation and not as a datum. The Church was a hegemonic institution subject to continual negotiation among the hierarchy, the clergy, and the diverse faithful over the nature of the faith. The baroque religious cultures of Michoacán were not passive objects of reform, and hierarchy-led projects were accommodated, modified, and resisted by local Catholic constituencies. Unlike in Oaxaca, however, where Wright-Ríos and Smith found relatively more harmonious forms of negotiation over local religious cults and more solidarity among conservative elites and Mixtec peasants in religious and political matters, in Michoacán conflicts within Catholicism partially had to be worked out through violence. See Rugeley, *Of Wonders and Wise Men*; Wright-Ríos, *Revolutions in Mexican Catholicism*; and Smith, *Roots of Conservatism in Mexico*.

55. Brittsan, *Popular Politics and Rebellion in Mexico*; Van Oosterhout, "Popular Conservatism in Mexico"; Smith, *Roots of Conservatism in Mexico*; and Butler, *Popular Piety and Political Identity*. For the culturalist approach, see Van Young, "In the Gloomy Caverns of Paganism"; and Van Young, *Other Rebellion*. Another notably culturalist study of a nineteenth-century rebellion is Vanderwood, *Power of God against the Guns of Government*. For examples of materialist interpretations of popular revolt, see Tutino, *From Insurrection to*

Revolution in Mexico; Meyer, *Esperando a Lozada*; and Soto Correa, *Movimientos campesinos de derecha*. Even Tutino's rich and important work of economic and cultural history *Making a New World* tends to reduce the role of religion to that of justifier of patriarchal capitalism.

56. Nineteenth-century newspapers must be approached with care, since they often prove rife with rumor, exaggeration, and political bias. Where possible, I have endeavored to triangulate accounts of military action between periodical and archival sources and to consult both Catholic and liberal newspapers in order to mitigate the risks of distortion. On the role of rumor and exaggeration in nineteenth-century Mexican political culture, see Van Young, *Other Rebellion*; and Guardino, *Time of Liberty*.
57. Álvaro Ochoa Serrano has tracked down crucial, locally produced documentation about Religionero leader Eulogio Cárdenas, but the rank and file mostly remains out of reach.
58. Smith aptly characterizes such a moving snapshot as the "religious expression of changing local identities" (*Roots of Conservatism in Mexico*, 13–14). For further discussion of the rewards and drawbacks of using parish correspondence, see Butler, *Popular Piety and Political Identity*, 11–12.
59. Taylor, *Magistrates of the Sacred*.

Chapter 1

1. *El diario de los debates*, 536–37.
2. A native of Burgos, Spain, and a veteran of the First Carlist War (1833–1839), Nicolás de Régules Cano came to Mexico on the eve of the American invasion and was quickly incorporated into the Mexican army at the rank of cavalry captain. He served the liberals in the Revolution of Ayutla and in the civil wars of 1857–1860, almost exclusively in Michoacán, where he had made his permanent residence. By the time of the French Intervention, he was a divisional general, in which capacity he defended the city of Puebla from the French incursion in 1863 and, along with Vicente Riva Palacio, took a leading role in pushing the imperial troops out of Michoacán between 1865 and 1867. See Archivo Histórico de la Defensa Nacional (hereafter, AHDN), Cancelados, Nicolás de Régules, T. 1, ff. 1–6, 9, 53–54, 82; *Corona fúnebre que la redacción de "El Republicano"*; and Ruiz, *Historia de la Guerra de Intervención en Michoacán*, 39–40, 253–57, 323–24, 332–52, 390–95, 593–610, 679–86.
3. *El diario de los debates*, 4:537–39.
4. *El diario de los debates*, 4:539–41; and Cosío Villegas, *La República Restaurada*, 250–56.
5. *El diario de los debates*, 4:541.
6. *El diario de los debates*, 4:581–84, 586.

7. It is easy to sympathize with the confusion of more skeptical deputies such as Briseño, who confessed that he had "completely lost count of the endless men who had risen up in arms, of the places that they occupy, and of their strange names," immediately after Lerdo's minister had finished reading his report. See *El diario de los debates*, 4:539.
8. Both the *partes militares* (brief military reports) and the accounts of prominent newspapers suffer from inconsistencies regarding Religionero actions and encounters with government troops. In particular, discrepancies in the number of rebels reported at a given skirmish, the name(s) of the gavilla leader(s), and the location of the event can occasionally be noted across and within both of these source types. There are several possible reasons for such discrepancies. Local officials and military officers may have exaggerated the number of rebels in order to cultivate a favorable impression with their superiors or excuse a military defeat. Partisan divides also account for discrepancies, with liberal newspapers often downplaying Religionero strength and conservative outlets exaggerating it. Independently of political affiliation, nineteenth-century newspapers were rife with rumor, speculation, and exaggeration, and editors were not afraid to print a rumor today and issue a correction tomorrow. Honest mistakes—misidentification of the rebel leader or a poor estimate of rebel numbers—are another possibility.
9. Chowning, *Wealth and Power in Provincial Mexico*, 229.
10. Ochoa Serrano, *Jiquilpan*, 90–93.
11. Chowning, *Wealth and Power*, 246–47.
12. Tapia Santamaría, "Identidad social y religión," 55–58; Brading, "Ultramontane Intransigence and the Mexican Reform," 138–40; and García Ugarte, *Poder político y religioso*, 2:1042–46, 1148.
13. Ruiz, *Historia de la Guerra de intervención en Michoacán*, 3–4, 43, 70–81; Butler, *Popular Piety and Political Identity*, 29–49; and Soto Correa, *Movimientos campesinos de derecha*, 50–60.
14. Barbosa, *Apuntes para la historia de Michoacán*, 271, 298; Ruiz, *Historia de la Guerra de intervención en Michoacán*, 305, 674; Ochoa Serrano, *Afrodescendientes*, 116–24; Moreno García, *Guaracha*, 109; Moreno García, *Cotija*, 152–57; and Iñiguez Mendoza, "¡Viva la religión y mueran los *protestantes*!," 120, 297–98.
15. Ochoa Serrano, "Religioneros en Michoacán," 178.
16. Ochoa Serrano, *Afrodescendientes*, 116–17.
17. Soto Correa, *Movimientos campesinos de derecha*, 132–47. Several of González's properties, seventy fanegas of corn, and sixty pigs were expropriated by the federal government in 1868 as a result of his activity in the service of Maximilian. See Archivo General de la Nación (hereafter, AGN), BN 346, caja 107, exp. 74, Copia del expediente sobre la intervención de los bienes del traidor Jesús González (a) "El Ranchero."

18. Hobsbawm, *Primitive Rebels*; and Soto Correa, *Movimientos campesinos de derecha*, 132–47.
19. This according to the military file of his erstwhile enemy, Nicolás de Régules. See AHDN, Serie: Cancelados, XI-111/1–38, Nicolás de Régules, T. 1, f. 7; and Iñiguez Mendoza, "¡Viva la religión y mueran los *protestantes!*," 143.
20. Soto Correa, *Movimientos campesinos de derecha*, 138–207, 261–62; and Florescano, *Historia general de Michoacán*, 116–25.
21. *El Progresista*, 6 August 1871. The term used repeatedly to describe the Catholic rioters was *populacho*. Tavera Alvaro's *Morelia en la época de la república restaurada* also contains a brief description of the revolt (176–82).
22. Rivera Reynaldos, *Desamortización y nacionalización de bienes civiles y eclesiásticos en Morelia*, 131.
23. Archivo Histórico del Poder Judicial del Estado de Michoacán (hereafter, AHPJEM), Suprema Tribunal de Justicia/Penal/Juzgado Primero de Morelia, exp. 2, Testimony of José Dolores Vargas, 6 August 1871.
24. Cabero and his sacristan, Agustín Fermín Gutiérrez, later testified that Alvarado threatened to bring Cabero down from the pulpit with a bullet if he would not come down on his own. See AHPJEM, Suprema Tribunal de Justicia/Penal/Juzgado Primero de Morelia, exp. 2, Testimony of Hilario Cabero, 6 August 1871.
25. *El Progresista*, 6 August 1871.
26. *El Progresista*, 21 September 1871.
27. Archivo General e Histórico del Poder Ejecutivo del Estado de Michoacán (hereafter, AGHPEM)/Secretaria de Gobierno/Gobernación/Religión, caja 1, exp. 4, D. Mariano León, D. Luis Bonilla, D. Juan Berrospelli, D. Dionissio G. de Carrasquedo, Morelia, to Interior Minister, Morelia, 8 August 1871; and *El Progresista*, 14 August 1871, 21 September 1871.
28. AGHPEM, Secretaria de Gobierno/Gobernación/Religión, caja 1, exp. 4, M. León, Morelia, to Interior Minister, Morelia, 6 August 1871.
29. AGHPEM, Secretaria de Gobierno/Gobernación/Religión, caja 1, exp. 4, Interior Minister, Morelia, to Minister of War and Navy, Mexico City, 8 August 1871.
30. AGHPEM, Secretaria de Gobierno/Gobernación/Religión, caja 1, exp. 4, fojas 30–34, dated 17 August 1871.
31. AHPJEM, Suprema Tribunal de Justicia/Penal/Juzgado Primero de Morelia, exp. 2, Sentencing of José Dolores Vargas, 8 September 1871.
32. AGHPEM, Secretaria de Gobierno/Gobernación/Religión, caja 1, exp. 6, Police Chief of Chucándiro asks for the removal of Presbyter Felipe Castañón for subversive conduct, November 1872–August 1873.
33. Police Chief Luis Nuñez also complained about Castañón's behavior to the ecclesiastical authorities at the archbishopic of Michoacán, in November 1872. In this instance, Nuñez identified himself as a conservative concerned

about the damage Castañón was doing to the faith of the community, and his complaints against the priest included adultery, concubinage, and "paganism." Likely, then, we are dealing as much with personal antipathy as with civil-religious strife. See Archivo Histórico Casa de Morelos (hereafter, AHCM), Diocesano/Justicia/Procesos Legales/Denuncias, caja 715, exp. 249, Luis Nuñez, Coeneo, to Luis Macouzet, Morelia, 20 November 1872.

34. AGHPEM, Secretaria de Gobierno/Gobernación/Religión, caja 1, exp. 8, Juan Saucedo, Zitácuaro, to Interior Minister, Morelia, 6 June 1873; and Soto Correa, *Movimientos campesinos de derecha*, 247–48. Such an accusation was not entirely implausible, given Tuzantla's colonial history as a Jesuit fief. See Butler, *Popular Piety and Political Identity*, 19–20.
35. AGHPEM, Secretaria de Gobierno/Gobernación/Religión, caja 1, exp. 10, Prefect of Zitácuaro to Interior Minister, Morelia, 8 July 1873.
36. AGHPEM, Secretaria de Gobierno/Gobernación/Religión, caja 1, exp. 10, Interior Minister, Morelia, to Prefect of Zitácuaro, 15 July 1873.
37. AGHPEM, Secretaria de Gobierno/Gobernación/Religión, caja 1, exp. 9, Prefect of Zitácuaro to Interior Minister, Morelia, 24 June 1873.
38. Mijangos y González, "La respuesta popular al juramento constitucional en 1857."
39. *La Voz de México*, 17 July 1873, 30 August 1873, and 27 October 1873.
40. *El Monitor Republicano*, 9 September 1873, 28 September 1873; *El Radical*, 5 December 1873; *La Voz de México*, 15 October 1873, 5 September 1874; and Iñiguez Mendoza, "¡Viva la religión y mueran los *protestantes*!," 258.
41. *El Progresista*, 13 October 1873.
42. For a detailed discussion of the effects of such renunciations on local governments, see Iñiguez Mendoza, "¡Viva la religión y mueran los *protestantes*!," 167–70.
43. *El Progresista*, 30 October 1873, and 10 November 1873.
44. *El Progresista*, 27 November 1873.
45. The letter was paraphrased by the editors of Michoacán's official newspaper, *El Progresista*. See *El Progresista*, 13 November 1873.
46. AGN, 2nd Section, caja 5, exp. 1, Rafael Carrillo, Morelia, to Minister of Government, Mexico City, 22 December 1873.
47. *El Progresista*, 17 November 1873, and 24 November 1873.
48. Bastian, "Las sociedades protestantes y la oposición a Porfirio Díaz," 476–77; and Mijangos Díaz and Mendoza García, "Tolerancia de cultos en Michoacán." It should be noted that some contemporary observers considered the masons involved in the Morelia Riot of 1871 a religious sect. Leticia Mendoza suggests that they were "evangelicals," though I have found no evidence to support this assertion. Witnesses called to testify in the case against Hilario Cabero referred to the group as "the sect known as masons."
49. See chapter 2.

50. Powell, "Los liberales, el campesinado indígena, y los problemas agrarios durante la reforma," 671–72; Falcón, "El estado liberal ante las rebeliones populares," 994–95, 1021–24; *El Monitor Republicano*, 5 November 1873, 7 November 1873, 11 November 1873, 12 November 1873, 25 November 1873, 17 December 1873; and *La Revista Universal*, 29 November 1873.
51. Romana Falcón suggests that "hundreds" of indigenous community members might have been extrajudicially executed by Tuñón Cañedo in Zinacantepec in November. T. G. Powell, for his part, refers to newspaper reports from Toluca that list fifteen victims whose bodies were found piled in a ditch.
52. Powell, "Los liberales, el campesinado indígena, y los problemas agrarios durante la reforma," 671–73; Falcón, "El estado liberal ante las rebeliones populares," 1021–24; and *La Voz de México*, 29 November 1873, 14 December 1873, 16 December 1873, 14 January 1874, 10 March 1874, and 26 May 1874.
53. *La Voz de México*, 14 January 1874.
54. *La Voz de México*, 26 March 1873; and *El Monitor Republicano*, 16 January 1874, 25 February 1874, 29 April 1874, 12 May 1874, and 4 June 1874. Editors at *El Monitor Republicano* accused judge Ramón Ortigiosa, who released the priests, of "intimate ties" with the lay charitable organization the Sociedad Católica.
55. *La Voz de México*, 14 January 1874.
56. *El Monitor Republicano*, 12 November 1873. These words belong to Vicente G. Torres, editor and owner of *El Monitor Republicano*, who published under the pseudonym "Tancredo."
57. *La Colonia Española*, 6 November 1873; and *El Monitor Republicano*, 29 April 1874, 12 May 1874, and 4 June 1874.
58. AHCM, Policía y Guerra/Aprehensiones, caja 27, exp. 13, District Prefect, Coalcomán, to Interior Minister, Morelia, 11 November 1873. See chapter 5 for more details about the Coalcomán rebellion.
59. *El Progresista*, 25 December 1873; and *El Pájaro Verde*, 5 January 1874.
60. For more on the history of the *pronunciamiento* as an expression of popular politics in nineteenth-century Mexico, see Fowler, *Forceful Negotiations*.
61. *El Monitor Republicano*, 10 March 1874; and González y González, *Sahuayo*, 114. We have no evidence that the Jiquilpan district rebels actually authored textual pronunciamientos. However, contemporary observers referring to their actions as "pronunciamientos" suggests that the rebel leaders had at least verbally made known their intent to rebel against the liberal government.
62. *El Progresista*, 16 February 1874. Chapter 4 profiles the Socorro Reyes revolt in central Michoacán.
63. Soto Correa, *Movimientos campesinos de derecha*, 252; and *El Progresista*, 2 March 1874, and 5 March 1874.

64. AGHPEM, Secretaria de Gobierno/Gobernación/Religión, caja 1, exp. 11, Aurelio López de Nava, Zirizícuaro, to Interior Minister, Morelia, 21 January 1874; and Interior Minister, Morelia, to Aurelio López de Nava, Zirizícuaro, 21 January 1874.
65. *El Progresista*, 2 April 1874.
66. AGHPEM, Secretaria de Gobierno/Gobernación/Religión, caja 1, exp. 12, Santos González and Mariano Francisco, San Felipe de Alzati, to Interior Minister, Morelia, 23 February 1874. Zitácuaro's "heroic" designation, bestowed by the Juárez government in 1868, was born of repeated military sacrifices for the causes of independence and liberalism between 1810 and 1867. See Ruiz, *Historia de la Guerra de intervención en Michoacán*, 3–4, 43, 70–81.
67. AGHPEM, Secretaria de Gobierno/Gobernación/Religión, caja 1, exp. 12, Interior Minister, Morelia, to Santos González, San Felipe de Alzati, 2 March 1874.
68. AGHPEM, Secretaria de Gobierno/Gobernación/Religión, caja 1, exp. 13, Interior Minister, Morelia, to Prefect of Uruapan, Uruapan, 8 June 1874.
69. *El Progresista*, 2 March 1874. Complaints by local and Morelia liberals about government officials in Zamora and Pátzcuaro were common in the early months of 1874. As José Napoleón Guzmán Ávila argues, conservatives and ex-collaborators with Maximilian's empire found their way back into various positions of power all across Michoacán during the Restored Republic. To the chagrin of the state's liberals, governors Justo Mendoza and Rafael Carrillo did little to reverse this trend. See Guzmán Ávila, "La república restaurada."
70. *El Progresista*, 12 March 1874.
71. *El Progresista*, 23 July 1874. The quorum would require two regidores, or councilors, and one sindico, or municipal advocate.
72. *El Progresista*, 9 February 1847, 16 March 1874, 18 May 1874, and 25 June 1874.
73. Carlos Martínez García, "Los asesinatos y sucesos de Ahualulco," *Protestante Digital*, http://protestantedigital.com/magacin/13887/Los_asesinatos_y_sucesos_de_Ahualulco, 14 September 2013, retrieved 10 October 2014; *El Monitor Republicano*, 14 March 1874, 26 March 1874, and 28 March 1874; *El Siglo Diez y Nueve*, 7 March 1874, 14 March 1874, 10 April 1874, and 11 April 1874; *La Voz de México*, 17 March 1874, 19 April 1874, and 24 April 1874; and *El Pájaro Verde*, 23 April 1874.
74. AGN, Second Section, caja 6, exp. 3, ff. 1–28, Communications related to the assassination of Juan Stephens and Jesús Islas, March–April 1874; *La Revista Universal*, 21 April 1874; *El Siglo Diez y Nueve*, 28 April 1874; *El Foro*, 19 June 1874; *La Voz de México*, 25 August 1874; and *Second Section, Forty-Third Congress*, 734, 756–58, 763.
75. *El Progresista*, 11 May 1874.

76. AHPJEM, Suprema Tribunal de Justicia/Penal/Juzgado Primero de Jiquilpan, exp. 8, "Diligencias relativas a los abusos que se denunciaron por el Juez de Letras de Jiquilpan," July 1874, *La Democracia*, Supplement to Issue no. 20, 4 July 1874. Then as now, the pejorative term *mocho* denoted Catholic fanaticism.
77. *El Progresista*, 12 October 1874; *El Pensamiento Católico*, 25 September 1874, and 16 October 1874; and *La Bandera de Ocampo*, 29 November 1874.
78. The "Law of Highwaymen and Kidnappers," initially decreed by the federal congress in 1868, was extended in 1869, 1871, and 1872. See Coromina, *Recopilación de los leyes, decretos, reglamentos, y circulares expedidas*, 30–31; Cosío Villegas, *La República Restaurada*, 221–23; and Frazer, *Bandit Nation*, 52–58.
79. Pineda Soto, "El discurso del movimiento religionero en la prensa moreliana," 91–99.
80. *El Pensamiento Católico*, 29 January 1875. Also reproduced in Iñiguez Mendoza, "¡Viva la religión y mueran los *protestantes*!," 471. The cartas de protesta are further discussed in chapter 2.
81. "Protesta de las señoras de Maravatío," *La Voz de México*, 20 January 1875. Saint Felicitas was a wealthy Christian widow in Rome in the early centuries of the faith whose seven sons were martyred by the Roman state under Marcus Aurelius. See Kirsch, "St. Felicitas."
82. "Protesta de los vecinos de Zamora," *La Voz de México*, 9 January 1875.
83. Cosío Villegas, *La República Restaurada*, 610–15; *El Progresista*, 18 May 1874; and *El Federalista*, 14 May 1874.
84. *El Progresista*, 21 September 1874.
85. *El Progresista*, 5 October 1874.
86. *El Progresista*, 14 September 1874, 17 September 1874, 24 September 1874, 1 October 1874, and 29 October 1874; and *La Bandera de Ocampo*, 4 October 1874.
87. *El diario de los debates*, 4:538; *El Progresista*, 18 January 1875, and 21 January 1875; and *El Pensamiento Católico*, 19 February 1875.
88. AGHPEM, Guerra y Ejército, caja 3, exp. 46, Ignacio Jiménez, Jiquilpan, to Interior Minister, Morelia, 14 April 1875; caja 3, exp. 49, Albino Fuentes Acosta, Puruándiro, to Interior Minister, Morelia, 8 April 1875; and caja 3, exp. 50, Manuel Treviño, Apatzingán, to Interior Minister, Morelia, 10 April 1875.
89. AGHPEM, Guerra y Ejército, caja 2, exp. 20, Ignacio Jiménez, Jiquilpan, to Interior Minister, Morelia, 9 January 1875; caja 2, exp. 15, Albino Fuentes Acosta, Puruándiro, to Interior Minister, Morelia, 17 February 1875; and caja 3, exp. 33, Eduardo Gil y Villamil, Pátzcuaro, to Interior Minister, Morelia, 19 March 1875.
90. AGHPEM, Guerra y Ejército, caja 2, exp. 27, Jesús Corral, Zinapécuaro, to Interior Minister, Morelia, 26 February 1875. The shrine of Lord of Araró

was an important pilgrimage destination from the seventeenth century. See Butler, *Popular Piety and Political Identity*, 26, 46; and López Lara, *Zinapécuaro*, 119–25.

91. AGHPEM, Guerra y Ejército, caja 3, exp. 32, Juan Saucedo, Zitácuaro, to Interior Minister, Morelia, 26 February 1875; and Juan Saucedo, Zitácuaro, to Interior Minister, Morelia, 21 March 1875.
92. AGHPEM, Guerra y Ejército, caja 3, exp. 33, Eduardo Gil y Villamil, Pátzcuaro, to Interior Minister, Morelia, 25 February 1875.
93. AGHPEM, Guerra y Ejército, caja 4, exp. 57, Eduardo Gil y Villamil, Pátzcuaro, to Interior Minister, Morelia, 17 April 1875.
94. See, for example, AGHPEM, Guerra y Ejército, caja, 3, exp. 38, Cayetano Martínez, Huango, to Interior Minister, Morelia, 20 March 1875; caja 4, exp. 49, Jesús Rodríguez, Uruapan, to Interior Minister, Morelia, 3 April 1875; caja 3, exp. 32, Dionisio Catalán, La Piedad, to Interior Minister, Morelia, 19 March 1875; and caja 4, exp. 67, J. Prado, Apatzingán, to Interior Minister, Morelia, 24 May 1875.
95. AGHPEM, Guerra y Ejército, caja 3, exp. 33, Eduardo Gil y Villamil, Pátzcuaro, to Interior Minister, Morelia, 2 March 1875; *La Bandera de Ocampo*, 25 March 1875; and *El Monitor Republicano*, 10 April 1875. The municipal president of Taretan reported six to seven hundred "plebeians" in his letter describing the attack to the district prefect. Newspaper accounts put the number at five hundred.
96. AGHPEM, Guerra y Ejército, caja 3, exp. 33, J. Ocampo, Morelia, to Interior Minister, Morelia, 11 March 1875; and G. Velázquez, Uruapan, to Interior Minister, Morelia, 13 March 1875; *El Progresista*, 11 March 1875; *La Bandera de Ocampo*, 14 March 1875; and *El Pensamiento Católico*, 19 March 1875.
97. *El Siglo Diez y Nueve*, 1 February 1875.
98. *El Siglo Diez y Nueve*, 10 June 1875; and *El Correo del Comercio*, 19 November 1875. León's bishop attracted particular suspicion. A May 1875 editorial in Mexico City's *El Monitor Republicano* declared that "there remain[ed] no doubt that the clergy direct[ed] the rebellion" over which the bishop of León presided as a "herald" of Catholic revolution. See *El Monitor Republicano*, 1 May 1875.
99. See chapter 2; Iñiguez Mendoza, "¡Viva la religión y mueran los *protestantes!*," 348; and Bautista García, "La reorganización de la iglesia," 47–48.
100. *El Progresista*, 22 April 1875; *El Correo del Comercio*, 14 April 1875; *El Monitor Republicano*, 17 April 1875; and *El Eco de Ambos Mundos*, 22 April 1875. The collective pastoral of 1875 will be discussed at length in chapter 2.
101. For the Stamp Duty, see Dublán and Lozano, *Legislación mexicana*, 13–36.
102. AGHPEM, Guerra y Ejército, caja 3, exp. 28, "El Plan de Nuevo Urecho," 3 March 1875. See Appendix A for the full text of the plan.

103. This provision of the Laws of Reform would continue to be a stumbling block for attempts at a concordat well into the Porfiriato. See Cannelli, *Nación católica y estado laico*, 103–8.
104. AGHPEM, Guerra y Ejército, caja 3, exp. 28, "El Plan de Nuevo Urecho," 3 March 1875.
105. *El Diario Oficial*, 21 December 1874; *El Siglo Diez y Nueve*, 10 December 1874; *El Eco de Ambos Mundos*, 22 December 1874; and *El Pájaro Verde*, 22 December 1875.
106. Ceballos, *Aurora y ocaso*, 290; Cosío Villegas, *La República Restaurada*, 610–12; and González y González, *Zamora*, 121.
107. *El Pájaro Verde*, 9 June 1875; and Cosío Villegas, *La República Restaurada*, 611.
108. *La Voz de México*, 6 June 1875.
109. Juan de Dios Rodríguez had achieved the rank of colonel in the imperialist army, though he assumed the rank of general after joining the Religionero rebels in April 1875. The text of his proclamation is reprinted in Ceballos, *Aurora y ocaso*, 880–82. See Appendix C for the full text of the document.
110. Copy of the Proclamation of Juan de Dios Rodríguez, Patámbaro, 15 June 1875, reproduced in Ceballos, *Aurora y ocaso*, 880.
111. An editorial run by *El Correo del Comercio* on 29 May 1875, for example, claimed that all of the Religionero leaders had criminal pasts. See also Pineda Soto, "El discurso del movimiento religionero en la prensa michoacana," 96–98. It is true that the Religionero movement emerged in the context of widespread rural banditry, particularly in the Michoacán/Guanajuato borderlands. Likely, much of this criminal activity derived from the social dislocations of the liberal-conservative civil wars, economic paralysis, and uncertainty over liberal legislation that mandated the break-up of communal properties. Nevertheless, the Religionero mobilization cannot be reduced to simple "social banditry," even if some of its leaders and participants engaged in brigandage at various points in their careers. As Paul Vanderwood and Chris Frazer note, the lines between banditry, political mobilization, and rural policing remained blurred throughout most the nineteenth century. Furthermore, as Gilbert Joseph and Alan Wells remind us, the term *banditry* often functioned as a discursive tool of state actors attempting to control defiant subaltern behavior. On the "discourse of counterinsurgency" in modern Mexico, see Joseph and Wells, *Summer of Discontent, Seasons of Upheaval*, 12–15. As such, we cannot uncritically accept the charges of banditry leveled at Religioneros. The fluid and highly unstable political context of the 1860s and 1870s provided plenty of opportunity for both brigandage and armed political mobilization, and in Michoacán and Guanajuato the lines between these two activities often blurred.
112. This sampling of aliases, only a small fraction of the whole, is culled from newspaper accounts and the *partes militares* provided by state forces, in AGHPEM, Guerra y Ejército, cajas 2–6.

113. *El Pensamiento Católico*, 16 April 1875; *La Bandera de Ocampo*, 25 April 1875; *La Voz de México*, 30 April 1875; Ochoa Serrano, "Tres corridos cristeros," 159–65; Ceballos, *Aurora y ocaso*, 304; Ruiz, *Historia de la Guerra de intervención en Michoacán*, 440–41, 491; Barbosa, *Apuntes para la historia de Michoacán*, 297–98; and AGHPEM, Guerra y Ejército, caja 5, exp. 79, Andres Villegas Rendón, Zamora, to Interior Minister, Morelia, 13 May 1875.
114. Ruiz, *Historia de la Guerra de intervención en Michoacán*, 440–41, 491.
115. *La Voz de México*, 26 April 1876; *El Pensamiento Católico*, 27 June 1877, and 12 October 1877; *El Pájaro Verde*, 10 June 1875; and AGHPEM, Guerra y Ejército, caja 2, exp. 15, Copy of a note from Jesús Ortega to Jesús Ramos, Huango, 18 February 1875; caja 2, exp. 20, Copy of a letter from Eulogio Cárdenas, San Diego Hacienda, to municipal president of Cotija, 2 January 1875; and caja 5, exp. 75, Rafael Ahumada, Morelia, to Interior Minister, Morelia, 22 July 1875.
116. AGHPEM, Guerra y Ejército, caja 4, exp. 59, Ignacio Jiménez, Jiquilpan, to Interior Minister, Morelia, 28 April 1875.
117. *El Eco de Ambos Mundos*, 2 June 1875.
118. Meza died in Los Reyes, and since he appeared shortly after Cárdenas and Ochoa's first attack on that same town, it remains possible that he was a Los Reyes native who seconded the revolt during that January 1875 offensive. See *El Eco de Ambos Mundos*, 2 June 1875; AGHPEM, Guerra y Ejército, caja 4, exp. 70, Ignacio Jiménez, Jiquilpan, to Interior Minister, Morelia, 29 May 1875; *El Progresista*, 7 February 1876; *La Voz de México*, 18 February 1876, and 29 February 1876; *El Siglo Diez y Nueve*, 9 February 1876, and 22 February 1876; and *La Colonia Española*, 18 February 1876.
119. *El Progresista*, 20 May 1875, and 16 August 1875; *El Monitor Republicano*, 30 June 1875; *La Voz de México*, 28 April 1875; *El Siglo Diez y Nueve*, 9 September 1875; and Soto Correa, *Movimientos campesinos de derecha*, 274–75.
120. *La Bandera de Ocampo*, 24 January 1875.
121. *El Progresista*, 12 August 1875; *La Voz de México*, 14 August 1875; and Ceballos, *Aurora y Ocaso*, 306. The editor of *El Progresista* likely alluded to Lorenzo Olaciregui, a Morelia-based priest who later served as a canon in the Morelia Cathedral. Jesús Soravilla, who had ridden out from Morelia with Ugarte and Olaciregui, fared better in the revolution than his companions. He began working closely with "El Ranchero" González in the fall of 1875, served as a signatory of the Religionero Manifesto of December, and was finally captured and pardoned in June 1876. See *El Progresista*, 12 June 1876.
122. AGHPEM, Guerra y Ejército, caja 4, exp. 65, Copy of a letter from Pedro González, Comanja, to the Jefe Político de Comanja, 5 June 1875.
123. After Juárez joined Díaz's Tuxtepec movement, he changed the title to "El Ejército Salvador de la Religión y Buen Orden y Porfirista." See *El Progresista*, 30 June 1876.

124. AGHPEM, Guerra y Ejército, caja 5, exp. 78, Jesús Rodríguez, Uruapan, to Interior Minister, Morelia, 2 May 1875, and Nicolas de Régules, Morelia, to Interior Minister, Morelia, 6 May 1875; and *El Progresista*, 2 August 1875.
125. Ochoa Serrano and Sánchez Díaz, *Breve historia de Michoacán*, 148.
126. AGHPEM, Guerra y Ejército, caja 3, exp. 36, Miguel Solís, Tancítaro, to Interior Minister, Morelia, 28 February 1875; caja 5, exp. 80, Intercepted rebel communication, signed by Antonio Candido, Aguililla, 27 March 1875; caja 4, exp. 65, Copy of a letter from Pedro González, Comanja, to the Jefe Político de Comanja, 5 June 1875; and caja 2, exp. 15, Copy of a note from Jesús Ortega to Jesús Ramos, Huango, 18 February 1875.
127. Although the Plan of Nuevo Urecho was invoked by El Ranchero's allies at Tzitzio and Tichiqueo in April 1875 and again in Félix Venegas's pronunciamiento, no single Religionero document formally united the various rebel generals until the Manifesto of December 1875 (discussed below). For the pronunciamiento of Tzitzio and Tichiqueo, see AGHPEM, Guerra y Ejército, caja 5, exp. 90, M. Lombarda, Huetamo, to Interior Minister, Morelia, 16 July 1875; caja 3, exp. 51, Copy of the Plan Religionero de Tzitzio and Proclamation of Jesús "el Ranchero" González, Tztiztio, 14 April 1875; and Iñiguez Mendoza, "¡Viva la religión y mueran los *protestantes*!," 311–14. A full-text translation of the Manifesto of Tzitzio is provided in Appendix B. With few exceptions, such as the widely traveled Abraham Castañeda and Juan de Dios Rodríguez, Religionero rebels remained tied to specific local bases throughout the conflict, and they tended to be caught or killed very close to home—Socorro Reyes in Huaniqueo; Antonio Reza near Taretan; Benito Meza in Los Reyes; Eulogio Cárdenas in Jiquilpan; and Abraham Castañeda near Pátzcuaro. See, respectively, *La Voz de México*, 26 April 1876; *El Pensamiento Católico*, 27 July 1877, and 12 October 1877; *El Eco de Ambos Mundos*, 20 February 1876; *La Colonia Española*, 18 February 1876; *El Siglo Diez y Nueve*, 17 February 1876; and *El Correo del Comercio*, 13 October 1875.
128. For González's relationship with indigenous communities, see Soto Correa, *Movimientos campesinos de derecha*, 132–47. For indigenous Religionero militancy in Zamora, Puruándiro, and Coalcomán districts, see chapters 3, 4, and 5, respectively.
129. The ethnic and religious dimensions of Religionero mobilization in Jiquilpan are analyzed at length in chapter 3.
130. AGHPEM, Guerra y Ejército, caja 3, exp. 32, Juan Saucedo, Zitácuaro, to Interior Minister, Morelia, 21 March 1875.
131. AGHPEM, Guerra y Ejército, caja 4, exp. 72, Prudencio Casillas, Zamora, to Interior Minister, Morelia, 14 June 1875.
132. *El Pájaro Verde*, 22 December 1874. For Socorro Reyes's devotion to the Señor de la Salud, see chapter 4.

133. AGHPEM, Guerra y Ejército, caja 3, exp. 46, Andres Villegas Rendón, Zamora, to Interior Minister, Morelia, 29 March 1875.
134. *El Siglo Diez y Nueve*, 10 March 1875.
135. *El Siglo Diez y Nueve*, 10 March 1875; and *El Progresista*, 3 April 1876. For a sophisticated analysis of the use of the Sacred Heart as a symbol of Catholic resistance to liberalism, see James, *France and the Cult of the Sacred Heart*.
136. *El Progresista*, 24 January 1876.
137. For examples of military and government officials complaining of popular support for the rebels, see AGHPEM, Guerra y Ejército, caja 2, exp. 21, Ignacio Jiménez, Jiquilpan, to Interior Minister, Morelia, 17 February 1875; caja 5, exp. 79, Andrés Villegas Rendón, Zamora, to Interior Minister, 30 April 1875; caja 5, exp. 76, Jesús Ocampo, Maravatío, to Interior Minister, Morelia, 27 April 1875; caja 3, exp. 51, Jesús Corral, Zinapécuaro, to Interior Minister, Morelia, 9 April 1875; and caja 5, exp. 86, Albino Fuentes Acosta, Puruándiro, to Interior Minister, Morelia, 14 July 1875; and AHDN, Operaciones Militares, XI/481.4/9211, Ignacio Mejía, Mexico City, to José Ceballos, Guadalajara, 11 May 1875.
138. For some examples of (alleged) Religionero robberies, see AGHPEM, Guerra y Ejército, caja 2, exp. 20, Telegram, Andres Villegas Rendón, Zamora, to Interior Minister, Morelia, 13 January 1875; AGHPEM, Guerra y Ejército, caja 2, exp. 24, Prefecto R. Valdéz, Zamora, to Interior Minister, Morelia, 29 January 1875; AGHPEM, Guerra y Ejército, caja 5, exp. 79, Prudencio Casillas, Zamora, to Interior Minister, 28 May 1875; and AGHPEM, Guerra y Ejército, caja 5, exp. 86, Albino Fuentes Acosta, Puruándiro, to Interior Minister, 4 June 1875.
139. *El Pájaro Verde*, 29 April 1876; AGHPEM, Guerra y Ejército, caja 5, exp. 75, Rafael Ahumada, Morelia, to Interior Minister, Morelia, 22 July 1875; and AGHPEM, Guerra y Ejército, caja 2, exp. 15, Albino Fuentes Acosta, Puruándiro, to Interior Minister, Morelia, 18 February 1875.
140. See AGHPEM, Guerra y Ejército, caja 5, exp. 78, Jesús Rodríguez, Uruapan, to Interior Minister, Morelia, 13 May 1875.
141. AHDN, Operaciones Militares, XI/481.4/9211, Jesús Camarena, Guadalajara, to Secretary of Defense, Mexico City, 3 May 1875.
142. *Memoria leida por el c. gobernador de este libre y soberano estado de Guanajuato*, 50–52.
143. *La Bandera de Ocampo*, 18 April 1875, and 25 April 1875.
144. *El Pájaro Verde*, 8 June 1875, and 10 June 1875; and *El Pensamiento Católico*, 9 April 1875, 16 April 1875, and 2 May 1875.
145. *El Progresista*, 18 February 1875, and 1 March 1875.
146. *El Progresista*, 26 April 1875, 6 May 1875, 17 May 1875, and 14 June 1875. Owners of properties burned by the Religioneros would receive an exemption from the tax.

147. Cosío Villegas, *La República Restaurada*, 255–56; *El diario de los debates*, 4:586; *El Siglo Diez y Nueve*, 1 June 1875; and *La Voz de México*, 30 May 1875. The law, passed by the federal congress on 25 May 1875, temporarily revived the law of 2 December 1871, which Juárez had used in order to combat the Noria rebellion.
148. Pineda Soto, "El discurso religionero," 98–100. Conservative outlets such as *El Pájaro Verde* and *La Voz de México* frequently published editorials and reports from local correspondents in Michoacán with a sharply critical perspective on government efforts against the Religioneros. Many of the same pieces also praised Religionero leaders for ethical behavior in their military campaigns. See, for example, *El Pájaro Verde*, 8 June 1875, 10 June 1875, and 17 June 1875; and *La Voz de México*, 5 May 1875, 1 July 1875, and 11 July 1875.
149. AGHPEM, Guerra y Ejército, caja 5, exp. 77, Circular on the obligations of district prefects to combat gavillas, 7 May 1875.
150. *El Progresista*, 1 April 1875; AHDN, Operaciones Militares, XI/481.4/9211, Ignacio Mejía, Mexico City, to José Ceballos, Guadalajara, 11 May 1875; and AHDN, Operaciones Militares, XI/481.4/9211, Prisciliano Flores, La Piedad, to José Ceballos, Guadalajara, 12 May 1875.
151. AHDN, Operaciones Militares, XI/481.4/9211, Ignacio Mejía, Mexico City, to José Ceballos, Guadalajara, 11 May 1875.
152. *El Progresista*, 17 May 1875; and AGHPEM, Guerra y Ejército, caja 4, exp. 59, Nicolás de Régules, Morelia, to Ignacio Jiménez, Jiquilpan, 20 May 1875.
153. *El Progresista*, 7 June 1875, and 14 June 1875; *El Siglo Diez y Nueve*, 8 June 1875; *La Voz de México*, 15 June 1875; *El Correo del Comercio*, 23 June 1875; *El Eco de Ambos Mundos*, 26 June 1875; and AHDN Operaciones Militares, XI/481.4/9211, Prisciliano Flores, La Piedad, to José Ceballos, Guadalajara, 20 May 1875; Command of the plaza of Zamora to Prisciliano Flores, La Piedad, 30 May 1875; and José Ceballos, Guadalajara, to Minister of War and Marines, Mexico City, 3 June 1875; and AGHPEM, Guerra y Ejército, caja 4, exp. 72, Prudencio Casillas, Zamora, to Interior Minister, Morelia, 31 May 1875; and exp. 65, Albino Fuentes Acosta, Puruándrio, to Interior Minister, Morelia, 11 June 1875.
154. *El Progresista*, 31 May 1875, 9 August 1875, and 11 November 1875; AGHPEM, Guerra y Ejército, caja 4, exp. 68, Eduardo Gil y Villamil, Pátzcuaro, to Interior Minister, Morelia, 30 May 1875; and exp. 67, J. Prado, Apatzingán, to Interior Minister, Morelia, 24 May 1875.
155. *El Progresista*, 12 August 1875, 13 September 1875, and 4 October 1875; *El Correo del Comercio*, 13 October 1875; *El Siglo Diez y Nueve*, 9 September 1875; and *La Voz de México*, 16 September 1875.
156. *El Progresista*, 11 November 1875, 9 December 1875, and 17 January 1876; *La Voz de México*, 2 February 1876; and AGHPEM, Guerra y Ejército, caja 3, exp. 33, José María Vallejo, Tacámbaro, to Interior Minister, Morelia,

2 March 1875; and caja 5, exp. 78, Jesús Rodríguez, Uruapan, to Interior Minister, Morelia, 2 May 1875.
157. *El Progresista*, 31 May 1875, 25 November 1875, and 28 October 1875; *La Bandera de Ocampo*, 3 January 1875; *La Voz de México*, 12 November 1875; and *El Siglo Diez y Nueve*, 3 June 1875.
158. *El Progresista*, 13 September 1875, and 14 October 1875.
159. Soto Correa, *Movimientos campesinos de derecha*, 271–84.
160. *La Voz de México*, 3 June 1875, 5 June 1875, 8 June 1875, 27 June 1875, and 18 July 1875; *El Pájaro Verde*, 6 June 1875, and 8 June 1875. Both liberal and conservative observers agreed that government troops burned houses at San Juanico. However, the former argued that federal troops only targeted a rebel encampment and not neutral vecinos. See *El Eco de Ambos Mundos*, 8 June 1875; and *El Siglo Diez y Nueve*, 9 June 1875. *El Monitor Republicano* also accepted the fact that Garnica ordered the burning of Patámbaro. See *El Monitor Republicano*, 27 June 1875.
161. *La Voz de México*, 27 June 1875. Here, federal burning of villages foreshadowed the more extensive and organized policy of *reconcentración* (forced resettlement) during the Cristero Wars. See Meyer, *La cristiada*, 175.
162. *La Voz de México*, 5 June 1875.
163. AHDN, Operaciones Militares, XI/481.4/9211, José Ceballos, Guadalajara, to Minister of War, Mexico City, 21 October 1875.
164. *La Voz de México*, 9 November 1875; *El Progresista*, 11 November 1875; *El Siglo Diez y Nueve*, 13 November 1875; and *El Correo del Comercio*, 19 November 1875.
165. *El Progresista*, 25 November 1875, and 9 December 1875; and *La Voz de México*, 17 November 1875.
166. *El Siglo Diez y Nueve*, 13 October 1875.
167. Reprinted in *El Siglo Diez y Nueve*, 20 November 1875.
168. *El Progresista*, 25 November 1875; and *El Padre Cobos*, 12 December 1875.
169. *El diario de los debates*, 4:420.
170. Iñiguez Mendoza, "¡Viva la religión y mueran los *protestantes*!," 363, 373–74.
171. *El Ahuizote*, 3 November 1875, 12 November 1875, and 19 November 1875.
172. *El Padre Cobos*, 21 October 1875.
173. *El Padre Cobos*, 15 August 1875.
174. *El diario de los debates*, 4:535–58. López Portillo's quote is found on 549.
175. Piza, *Historia parlamentaria de la Cámara de Senadores*, 155–60; Pi-Suñer Llorens, "Prólogo"; Ceballos, *Aurora y ocaso*, 325–26; and Cosío Villegas, *La República Restaurada*, 613–24.
176. Lerdo had announced that he would send Rocha to the front lines in Michoacán in February but quickly and quietly changed courses, sending the general to Celaya and placing Riva Palacio under house arrest. An anonymous political plan soon surfaced in the press and was attributed to Rocha, though Cosío Villegas discovered evidence pointing to Riva Palacio as the author.

The plan, whose preamble focused principally on Lerdo's constitutional overreach, centralist tendencies, and political favoritism, offered no political innovations, limiting itself to the removal of Lerdo, the congress, and the Supreme Court president and the addition of a constitutional guarantee of municipal independence. See Ceballos, *Aurora y ocaso*, 870–77; and Cosío Villegas, *La República Restaurada*, 613–24.

177. *El Progresista*, 11 November 1875; *El Correo del Comercio*, 19 November 1875, and 29 February 1876; and *El Eco de Ambos Mundos*, 27 November 1875.
178. *El Progresista*, 23 December 1875; *La Voz de México*, 31 December 1875; Ceballos, *Aurora y Ocaso*, 292–93; and Ochoa Serrano, *Afrodescendientes*, 124–25.
179. *El Progresista*, 6 January 1876, 13 January 1876, 20 January 1876, and 31 January 1876.
180. *El Progresista*, 27 January 1876, and 3 February 1876. Organized by district of rendition and often listing the provenance of each pardoned rebel, these published indulto lists are an invaluable source of information about rank-and-file Religioneros. Though the government certainly could have inflated the number of "indultados," as a way to control the public narrative of the revolt, the use of full names and places of residence for each rebel listed makes such exaggeration less likely. Chapters 3, 4, and 5 utilize these lists in order to analyze the local logics of rebellion.
181. *El Pájaro Verde*, 9 February 1876, "Manifesto of the Leaders of the Revolutionary Forces of Michoacán to Their Subordinates and to All the Pueblos of the Republic."
182. *El Pájaro Verde*, 9 February 1876.
183. *El Progresista*, 31 January 1876, and 3 February 1876.
184. *El Progresista*, 10 January 1876, and 24 January 1876.
185. *El Progresista*, 7 February 1876; *La Voz de México*, 18 February 1876, and 29 February 1876; *El Siglo Diez y Nueve*, 9 February 1876, and 22 February 1876; and *La Colonia Española*, 18 February 1876.
186. *El Progresista*, 10 February 1876.
187. *La Voz de México*, 15 February 1876.
188. The Plan of Tuxtepec issued in Ojitlán (Oaxaca) on 10 January 1876 was signed by Hermenegildo Sarmiento and other Díaz allies but not by Díaz himself. As such, the Mexico City press was rife with speculation about whether Díaz was actually behind the uprising for several weeks. See *El Siglo Diez y Nueve*, 27 January 1876, 31 January 1876, 2 February 1876, and 14 February 1876; *The Two Republics*, 2 February 1876; and *El Progresista*, 3 February 1876.
189. *El Progresista*, 11 November 1875, 13 January 1876, and 3 February 1876; *La Bandera de Ocampo*, 6 February 1876, and 12 March 1876; and *El Eco de Ambos Mundos*, 27 November 1875.
190. *La Voz de México*, 5 March 1876.
191. *La Idea Católica*, 6 February 1876.

192. Eduardo Ruiz, "Temores," editorial, *El Progresista*, 13 January 1876.
193. Quoted in *La Voz de México*, 15 February 1876.
194. *The Two Republics*, 2 February 1876.
195. *El Eco de Ambos Mundos*, 17 February 1876.
196. *El Siglo Diez y Nueve*, 8 February 1876.
197. Tuxtepec named the president of the Supreme Court to the interim presidency after the fall of Lerdo, a provision that represented an attempt to attract Supreme Court President José María Iglesias to the movement. When Iglesias failed to sign on, however, Díaz issued a revised plan in Palo Blanco providing for the succession of the "chief of arms." See "El Plan de Tuxtepec, reformado en Palo Blanco," 21 March 1876, *The Pronunciamiento in Independent Mexico*, database compiled by Will Fowler and his research team, retrieved 28 May 2015 from http://arts.st-andrews.ac.uk/pronunciamientos/dates.php? f=y&pid=1610&m=3&y=1876.
198. For reports of Religioneros signing on with Tuxtepec, see *El Progresista*, 14 February 1876, 23 March 1876, 30 March 1876, and 10 April 1876; *La Bandera de Ocampo*, 19 March 1876, and 26 March 1876; *La Revista Universal*, 29 March 1876, and 19 April 1876; and *El Correo del Comercio*, 30 March 1876. For the rumor about El Ranchero, see *El Eco de Ambos Mundos*, 1 April 1876.

Chapter 2

1. Stauffer, "Routes of Intransigence."
2. Labastida y Dávalos, *Carta pastoral que el Ilmo. D. Pelagio Antonio Labastida y Dávalos*; and *Itinerario para una peregrinación espiritual que se practicará por los fieles católicos del Arzobispado de México en el próximo mes de octubre a algunos de los principales santuarios del país y del extranjero* (México: Tipografía Escalerillas, 1874). The term *decade* traditionally refers to the ten-prayer sets of the rosary, but here it connotes a ten-day period of pious prayer, organized as a spiritual itinerary.
3. De la Peña y Navarro, *Carta pastoral del Ilmo. Obispo de Zamora*, 7–11.
4. Labastida y Dávalos, *Carta pastoral que el Ilmo. D. Pelagio Antonio Labastida y Dávalos*, 11–12.
5. Moreno Chávez, *Devociones políticas*, 38–40; Bautista García, "Hacia la romanización de la Iglesia mexicana," 99–101; Wright-Ríos, *Revolutions in Mexican Catholicism*, 5, 31–32; and García Ugarte, *Poder político y religioso*, 1:20–21.
6. The reference is to Robert Ricard's classic work on Catholic evangelization after the conquest, which I adapt here to denote the attempt by new religious actors—principally diocesan authorities, reformist parish priests, and devout laypeople—to transform Mexico's religious culture in the second half of the

nineteenth century. My work shows Catholic restoration to be a highly contentious process, though, and the term *spiritual reconquest* should not be taken to mean complete or successful erasure of indigenous religiosity. See Ricard, *Spiritual Conquest of Mexico*.

7. On the proliferation of Catholic associations and congregations as both a response to and accommodation of the liberal order, see Bautista García, *Las disyuntivas*, 231–86; and Bautista García, "La afirmación del orden social en el estado liberal y las nuevas congregaciones religiosas." See also Chowning, "Catholic Church and the Ladies of the Vela Perpetua"; and Arrom, *Volunteering for a Cause*.

8. Bautista García, *Las disyuntivas*, 261–63.

9. See García Ugarte, *Poder político y religioso*, 1:37–38, and 2:1299–1301; Olveda, *Los obispados de México frente a la reforma liberal*; and Olimón Nolasco, "Proyecto de reforma de la iglesia en México."

10. I situate Michoacán within the greater center-west for two reasons. Firstly, the ancient bishopric of Michoacán (erected 1536) encompassed an expansive territory that included the present-day states of Michoacán, Guanajuato, Querétaro, San Luis Potosí, and parts of Jalisco (see map 2). The influence of Morelia's spiritual authorities was deep and long lasting, and only after two rounds of restructuring in the mid-nineteenth century did San Luis Potosí, León, Querétaro, and Chilapa emerge as independent (though suffragan) sees. Even then, however, Michoacán retained spiritual leadership of the region, since it was elevated to the status of archdiocese. Secondly, the Mexican Church's restoration project was highly regionalized—it prioritized the center-west in the allotment of new dioceses and seminaries and relied on ambitious clerical leaders in Zamora and León, especially, to blaze new paths toward religious reform. Occurring in the midst of Mexico's liberal-conservative crucible and the global Church's retrenchment against liberalism, such a regionalized renaissance imbued the central-western bishoprics with a set of common reformist characteristics, despite divergences in style, emphasis, and method among diocesan leaders.

11. On clerical involvement in the conflicts of the Reforma and French Intervention, see, among others, Hamnett, "Mexican Conservatives, Clericals, and Soldiers"; Mijangos y González, *Lawyer of the Church*; García Ugarte, *Poder político y religioso*; Thomson, "End of the Catholic Nation"; and Galeana, *Las relaciones estado-iglesia durante el segundo imperio*.

12. These letters, originally printed in Catholic newspapers, were later collected in a single volume by M. Villanueva y Francesconi entitled *El libro de protestas*. The content of the letters will be discussed further below.

13. On the "arreglos de consciencia," agreements between diocesan authorities and individual adjudicators by which the latter returned property or reimbursed the Church in exchange for a lifting of spiritual censures, see Juárez,

Reclaiming Church Wealth, esp. chap. 3; and García Ugarte, *Poder político y religioso*, 2:1448–62.

14. García Ugarte, *Poder político y religioso*, 2:1504–5; and Mijangos y González, "La respuesta popular al juramento constitucional en 1857." The penalty of excommunication extended to those who had taken part in the creation or passage of the Laws of Reform, those who executed them as public functionaries, and those who adjudicated Church property under the terms of the Laws of Reform.

15. Archbishop Labastida's office clarified in October 1873 that those who "could not avoid" performing the act could do so by adding "as a Catholic" when answering the protesta query in the affirmative or by publishing a note before the ceremony specifying that they would only take the oath "without prejudicing their beliefs." The circular also allowed employees whose work "had nothing to do with the Laws of Reform, such as simple notaries, guards, archivists, etc.," to take the protesta "within the bounds of their work." Of course, under the lerdista government's strict interpretation of the Laws of Reform, such a modified protesta would not be permitted. The official paperwork sent to state governments or federal superiors would betray the irregularity, and the candidate would lose their job, unless local officials conspired to conceal the reservation. For Labastida's instrucitons, see the circular, "Resoluciones dadas a los que han consultado sobre la protesta de guardar y hacer guardar la Constitución y leyes de Reforma," 18 October 1873, in Vera, *Colección de documentos eclesiásticos de México*, 3:221–22.

16. Diez de Sollano, *Décimatercia pastoral del Ilmo. Sr. Dr. y Maestro José María de Jesús Diez de Sollano y Dávalos*, 10–13.

17. Diez de Sollano, *Edicto del Obispo de León sobre el matrimonio sacramento*, 11–13.

18. Diez de Sollano, *Manifestación que hace el obispo de León*, 157–59.

19. See, for example, Labastida y Dávalos, *Carta pastoral que el Ilmo. Sr. Dr. D. Pelagio Antonio de Labastida y Dávalos*; Árciga, *Carta pastoral que el Ilmo. Dr. Don José Ignacio Árciga*; Árciga, *Segunda carta pastoral que el Ilmo. Sr. Don José Ignacio Árciga*; and de la Peña y Navarro, *Pastoral número cinco del Obispo de Zamora*.

20. Beirne, "Latin American Bishops of the First Vatican Council"; and García Ugarte, *Poder político y religioso*, 2:1375–1400.

21. Árciga, *Segunda carta pastoral que el Ilmo. Sr. Don José Ignacio Árciga*, 7–11. For Bishop Camacho of Querétaro, meanwhile, the crisis facing the Church was a form of divine punishment, and only acts of expiation by Catholics properly prepared via the sacrament of penitence could stay God's hand. See Camacho, *Carta pastoral del Ilmo. Sr. obispo de Querétaro*, 7–14.

22. Labastida y Dávalos, *Carta pastoral que el Ilmo. Sr. Dr. D. Pelagio Antonio de Labastida y Dávalos*, 8–9. The quoted section was part of Labastida's own commentary on Pius IX's Allocution.

23. Diez de Sollano, *Manifestación que hace el obispo de León*, 53–56.
24. Diez de Sollano, 102–3.
25. Árciga, *Segunda carta pastoral que el Ilmo. Sr. Don José Ignacio Árciga*, 10–11; and de la Peña y Navarro, *Pastoral número cinco del Obispo de Zamora*, 1–2.
26. De la Peña y Navarro, "Sr. Juez Ecco. de . . Circular número 26," 8–9.
27. Diez de Sollano, *Vigésima prima carta pastoral que el Ilmo. y Rmo. Sr. Obispo de León*, 16–21.
28. De la Peña y Navarro, *Sexta pastoral del Obispo de Zamora*, 15–16.
29. Camacho, "Advertencia a todos los fieles de la Diócesis," 13 November 1873, in *Colección de cartas, edictos, e instrucciones pastorales del ilustrísimo señor doctor D. Ramón Camacho y García*, 61–65.
30. Camacho, "Advertencia a todos los fieles de la Diócesis," 63–64.
31. CPC 1875, 298.
32. CPC 1875, 300.
33. See Diez de Sollano, *Décimatercia pastoral del Ilmo. Sr. Dr. y Maestro D. José María de Jesús Diez de Sollano y Dávalos*, 9–10.
34. CPC 1875, 335.
35. Villanueva y Francesconi, *El libro de protestas*, 143–76. As Iñiguez Mendoza shows, the cartas came principally from the central states, but Guanajuato and Michoacán far surpassed their closest rivals of Puebla, Mexico State, and Jalisco. As they had in 1856 during the debate over religious tolerance, women also played a leading role in the popular repudiation of lerdista anticlericalism—56 percent of the cartas studied by Iñiguez Mendoza were written by women. See "¡Viva la religión y mueran los *protestantes*!," 247, 248, table 3. For the 1856 precedent, see Sosenski, "Asomándose a la política."
36. Villanueva y Francesconi, *El libro de protestas*, 167–68.
37. Villanueva y Francesconi, 225–28. Emphasis added.
38. Villanueva y Francesconi, 249–51. Here, the women invoked the fourth-century Roman emperor Julian "the Apostate," who rejected Constantinian Christianity.
39. Villanueva y Francesconi, 321.
40. Villanueva y Francesconi, 328–32.
41. García Ugarte, *Poder político y religioso*, 2:1508–35.
42. CPC 1875, 336.
43. Bautista García, *Las disyuntivas*, 231–42.
44. *El Progresista*, 18 December 1873.
45. *El Progresista*, 25 April 1875.
46. On seminary reform in particular, see Bautista García, *Clérigos virtuosos e instruidos*.
47. "Europeanization" here denotes the deepening web of personal, institutional, and symbolic ties between Mexican and European (especially Italian and French) Catholicism in the second half of the nineteenth century. It can be

thought of as an earlier, more informal and cultural phase of the "Romanization" of Mexican Catholicism in the late nineteenth century, a trend Bautista García describes as a top-down process of reform and centralization affected by Pope Leo XIII and his diplomatic emissaries in Mexico in the 1890s. While Pius IX began a process of global devotional reordering around Rome, then, Leo's work primarily involved legal and bureaucratic centralization. See Bautista García, "Hacia la romanización de la iglesia mexicana a fines del siglo XIX." On the transnational bent of intransigent Catholicism, see also Clark and Kaiser, *Culture Wars*.

48. As Chowning demonstrates, center-western devotional ferment dates back at least to the 1830s and 1840s, when pious laywomen in Guanajuato and Michoacán innovated the Eucharistic association known as the Vela Perpetua. See Chowning, "Catholic Church and the Ladies of the Vela Perpetua," 197–203.

49. Guadalajara, another important seat of central-western Catholicism, also assumed the rank of archbishopric. Thus, Mexico's three archdiocesan hubs post-1862 would be concentrated in the center and central-western part of the country.

50. González y González, *Zamora*, 118–20; Rodríguez Zetina, *Zamora*, 203–5; and Buitrón, *Apuntes para servir a la historia del arzobispado de Morelia*, 228–30.

51. González y González, *Zamora*, 118–19. The parishes of the new diocese included the following: Zamora, Aguililla, Apatzingán, Coalcomán, Cotija, Coahuayana, Charapan, Chilchota, Capácuaro, Huacana, Ixtlán, Jacona, Jiquilpan, Maquilí, Nahuatzen, Peribán, Parangaricutiro, Pizándaro, Purépero, Paracho, Pichátaro, Patamban, Santa Ana Amatlán, Sahuayo, Tangancícuaro, Tarecuato, Taretan, Tancítaro, Tepalcatepec, Tingüindín, Tingambato, Tzirosto, Tlazazalca, Uruapan, and Urecho.

52. Rodríguez Zetina, *Zamora*, 211–12. According to Rodríguez Zetina, de la Peña was born in 1799 to a poor family and could only attend the seminary in Morelia with the financial support of a patron in whose shop he had worked as an accountant. Subsequently, de la Peña served as parish priest of Angamacutiro and Jacona before being named a canon in Morelia's cathedral chapter in 1843.

53. De la Peña y Navarro, *Primera pastoral del primer obispo de la nueva diócesis de Zamora*, 3–10, 23–30. Tapia Santamaría, *Campo religioso y evolución político*, 140–43. On the politics of the Immaculate Conception, see Harris, *Lourdes*, 14, 81.

54. La Virgen de la Luz, a miraculous image of Mary Immaculate that was revealed to a female servant of the Jesuit missionary Juan Antonio Genovesi in Sicily in the early eighteenth century, came to León in the 1730s with Genovesi, and she soon became the object of devotion among the provincial

Bajío city's largely mestizo population. Leon's Catholics credited the image with vanquishing an outbreak of cholera morbus in 1850 and protecting the city from the violence of the Reform Wars. See García y Moyeda, *Compendio histórico biográfico de la erección del obispado de esta ciudad*, 67–68; *Un retrato directo de la Madre de Dios*; and Veres Acevedo, *La maravillosa imagen de la Madre Santísima de la Luz*, 4–124.

55. García y Moyeda, *Compendio histórico biográfico de la erección del obispado de esta ciudad*, 47–49.

56. Diez de Sollano, *Primera carta pastoral que el Ilmo. Sr. Obispo de León*, 3–7; and Diez de Sollano, *Décima sexta carta pastoral que el Obispo de León dirige a su Ilmo. Cabildo*. On the devotion to the Sacred Heart in Europe and Mexico, see Correa Etchegaray, "El rescate de una devoción jesuítica."

57. Diez de Sollano, *Undécima pastoral que el Ilmo. y Rmo. Sr. Obispo de León*, 23; Diez de Sollano, *Tercera carta pastoral que el Ilmo. Sr. Obispo de León*, 10–11; Diez de Sollano, *Décimatercia pastoral del Ilmo. Sr. Dr. y Maestro José María de Jesús Diez de Sollano y Dávalos*, 12; and *Reglamento para la Congregación de la Buena Muerte*. A society with roots in seventeenth-century Rome, the Asociación de la Buena Muerte utilized collective prayer and a web of lay assistants to ensure that local Catholics died with the proper spiritual preparation. See Archivo Histórico del Arzobispado de México (hereafter, AHAM), Secretaría Arzobispal/Parroquias, caja 85, exp. 110, "El reverendo padre cura sobre que se le conceda establecer en su parroquia la Asociación de la Buena Muerte para hombres," 12 January 1874. The society was also established in the Levitical Zamora. See Archivo Diocesano de Zamora (hereafter, ADZ), DGP 1410 Zamora Sagrario, Sociedad Católica de Señoras, Zamora, to Juan R. Carranza, Zamora, 9 August 1873.

58. Tapia Méndez, *El siervo de dios*, 57–73; and *Descripción de la fiesta celebrada en Roma*. Felipe de Jesús was a Franciscan missionary born in Mexico and martyred in Nagasaki with twenty-five other Catholics while attempting to evangelize the Japanese. See Burroughs Conover V, "A Saint in the Empire," 1–10, 160–78; and Rubial García, *La santidad controvertida*, 128–60. Notably the 1863 canonization rekindled popular devotion to the Mexican martyr. See *Descripción de la fiesta celebrada en Roma*; and *Novena consagrada al culto y festividad del glorioso San Felipe de Jesús*.

59. García Ugarte, *Poder político y religioso*, 2:1374–1407; Saranyana, *Teología en América Latina*, 594–97; and Beirne, "Latin American Bishops of the First Vatican Council." Mexico's delegation of ten bishops was the largest from Latin America, though none of them dared to speak during the proceedings.

60. García Ugarte, *Poder político y religioso*, 2:1405. On Plancarte's effort to remake a local indigenous devotion in the image of Pius IX's Rome, see Cecilia Bautista Garcia's excellent article, "Dos momentos en la historia de un culto."

61. Plancarte is well known in Mexican historiography for his role in promoting several high-profile clerical projects in Mexico City, including the

reconstruction of the Basilica of Guadalupe (which he served as abbot from 1895 to 1898), the papal coronation of Virgin of Guadalupe in 1895, and the construction of the Expiatory Temple of San Felipe de Jesús (1885–1897).
62. Tapia Méndez, *El siervo de dios*, 62–77.
63. Ochoa Serrano, "El distrito de Zamora en 1877," 130–31.
64. The quote is from Tapia Méndez, *El siervo de dios*, 104.
65. Tapia Méndez, 111–12; Bautista García, "Clérigos virtuosos e instruidos," 156–57; and ADZ, DGP 444, Petition from the Vecindario of Jacona to the Diocesan Secretary, Zamora, 25 March 1871, and Petition from Rafael Hernández and indigenous women, Jacona, to Diocesan Secretary, Zamora, 28 March 1871. I offer more about these devotional reforms and the local conflicts they provoked in chapter 3.
66. Bautista García, "Dos momentos en la historia de un culto," 34–43; and Tapia Méndez, *El siervo de dios*, 133–34.
67. Plancarte allegedly changed the names of the two Jesuits, one Dutch and one Spanish, to cover up their identities as foreign religious.
68. Tapia Méndez, *El siervo de dios*, 109–22; and Bautista García, *Clérigos virtuosos e instruidos*, 172–73.
69. Bautista García, *Clérigos virtuosos e instruidos*, 162–98; O'Dogherty, "El ascenso de una jerarquía eclesial intransigente"; Aguirre Christiani, "Una jerarquía en tranción"; and García Ugarte, *Poder político y religioso*, 2:1388–95.
70. Bautista García, *Clérigos virtuosos e instruidos*, 183–85.
71. In a speech delivered to the girls of la Purísima Concepción in 1873, Plancarte declared that "the best remedy to cure the illnesses of our disgraced nation is the education of women." See José Antonio Plancarte y Labastida, "Discurso sobre la influencia de la mujer," reprinted in *La Voz de México*, 23 December 1873.
72. Tapia Méndez, *El siervo de dios*, 125–40; and Bautista García, "La afirmación del orden social."
73. The "feminization of piety" thesis posits the increasing demographic dominance of women in Christian congregations and religious orders as well as the increasingly "sentimental" and "feminine" character of religious culture—both Protestant and Catholic—in the nineteenth and early twentieth centuries. As men increasingly gravitated to the masculinized and secularized "public sphere" of the new nation-states, the thesis suggests, women sought opportunities for social leadership in their churches and developed a feminized "counterculture" in opposition to secularization. Developed by Barbara Welter and Ann Douglas for the North American context, the thesis has since been variously applied, modified, and rejected by scholars who work in a range of European and Latin American contexts. Patrick Pasture and Jan Art, in *Beyond the Feminization Thesis*, provide a useful summary of the historiographical debate. For Mexico, the case for a feminization of piety has been convincingly made by

Chowning, "Catholic Church and the Ladies of the Vela Perpetua"; Wright-Ríos, *Revolutions in Mexican Catholicism*; and Arrom, "Mexican Laywomen Spearhead a Catholic Revival," among others.

74. Bautista García, *Clérigos virtuosos e instruidos*, 131–50; and Verduzco, "Zamora en el porfiriato."
75. Biographers of Zamora's first bishop José Antonio de a Peña have remarked upon his reputation as "severe" and unbending. See Rodríguez Zetina, *Zamora*, 212.
76. Diez de Sollano, *Undécima pastoral que el Ilmo. y Rmo. Sr. Obispo de León*, 22–29. Little has been written about the devotion of the Most Powerful Hand, a popular theme of nineteenth-century retablos (devotional paintings) that retains a place in the culture of Mexican folk saints today. Then as now, the devotion seems to have been associated with *curanderismo*, and it was part of the spiritual repertoire of the noted early twentieth-century folk healer El Niño Fidencio. See Graziano, *Cultures of Devotion*, 199; and Quirate, "*Los Cinco Señores* and *La Mano Poderosa*." Details about the devotion of the Cuenta de Mil have not been located.
77. Diez de Sollano, *Undécima pastoral que el Ilmo. y Rmo. Sr. Obispo de León*, 28.
78. De la Peña y Navarro, "Sr. Cura Juez Ecco. de . . Circular número 26," 2–8, 15–16. Ecclesiastical conferences, an ancient institution reinvigorated by the Tridentine reforms, mandated that pairs of priests meet annually for a prescribed number of days (in the Mexican case, often two weeks), during which time they would discuss moral and theological matters. A kind of recurrent professionalization exercise, the ecclesiastical conferences aimed to discipline and educate the rural clergy on matters of doctrine and practice and clear up day-to-day problems in their parish administrations. See Fanning, "Ecclesiastical Conferences."
79. García Ugarte, *Poder político y religioso*, 1:24–25; Olimón Nolasco, "Proyecto de reforma de la Iglesia en México." Diez de Sollano demonstrated a particular zeal for imposing uniformity in religious practice and parish administration, often citing the Council of Trent and Third Mexican Provincial Council of 1585 as his inspiration. See, for example, his "Auto general de visita" from 1871, in Diez de Sollano, *Undécima pastoral que el Ilmo. y Rmo. Sr. Obispo de León*, 56–60; and Archivo Histórico del Arzobispado de León (hereafter, AHAL), Libro de Visitas, Libro 1, Edict of the Pastoral Visit, 14 April 1871, and Edict of the Pastoral Visit, 15 July 1876.
80. De la Peña y Navarro, "Sr. Cura Juez Ecco. de . . .Circular número 26," 8–10. Corpus Christi celebrations in the Purépecha pueblos of the highlands were traditionally staggered chronologically according to local agricultural rites and in order to facilitate clerical oversight in understaffed parishes. See chapter 4 for further details.
81. Extract of an 1874 circular of the Archbishop of Guadalajara, reprinted in *El Progresista*, 6 April 1874.

82. Diez de Sollano, *Undécima pastoral que el Ilmo. y Rmo. Sr. Obispo de León*, 31–32. This circular dates from 1868.
83. CPC 1875, 313–14.
84. Rubio Morales and Pérez Escutia, *Luz de ayer, luz de hoy*, 185–97; Bautista García, *Clérigos virtuosos e instruidos*, 27–67; Herrejón Peredo, "Don Ignacio Árciga y Ruiz de Chávez"; and Ibarra López, *La iglesia de Michoacán*.
85. Bautista García, *Clérigos virtuosos e instruidos*, chap. 2; and Rubio Morales and Pérez Escutia, *Luz de ayer, luz de hoy*, 186–208. Árciga and his cabildo appear to have recovered the Hermanas' building, as well as other private and former ecclesiastical properties, with the collusion of civil authorities.
86. Archivo Histórico de la Casa de Morelos (hereafter, AHCM), Diocesano/Gobierno/Mandatos/Instrucciones, caja 212, exp. 70, Edict of the Archbishop of Michoacán, 12 July 1869.
87. AHCM, Diocesano/Gobierno/Mandatos/Instrucciones, caja 212, exp. 67, Edict of the Bishop of Zamora about schismatic priests, 22 January 1866. For more about these "constitutional" priests and their relationship to the ecclesiastical hierarchy during the Reforma and Second Empire, see Voekel, "Liberal Religion," 78–105.
88. De la Peña y Navarro, *Sexta pastoral del Obispo de Zamora*, 14–15.
89. De la Peña y Navarro, "Sr. Cura Juez Ecco. de . . , Circular número 26," 5–7.
90. Bautista García, *Clérigos virtuosos e instruidos*, 176–90; and Tapia Méndez, *El siervo de dios*, 116–18.
91. Bautista García, *Clérigos virtuosos e instruidos*, 61–67; and García Ugarte, *Poder político y religioso*, 2:1388–95. Elsewhere, Bautista García argues persuasively that Labastida shifted the axis of his project for clerical reform from Mexico to Zamora after he encountered resistance from the seminary and cabildo of Mexico. See Bautista García, "Entre México y Roma."
92. Bautista García, *Clérigos virtuosos e instruidos*, 70–78; and Rubio Morales and Pérez Escutia, *Luz de ayer, luz de hoy*, 194–208.
93. Meehan, "Canonical Visitation."
94. Buitrón, *Apuntes para servir la historia del arzobispado de Morelia*, 153–66, 197–232; Bautista García, *Poder político y religioso*, 2:1331–33; and Romero, *Noticias para formar*, 22–25.
95. Mijangos y González, *Lawyer of the Church*, 193–95.
96. Clemente de Jesús Munguía had last performed a systematic pastoral visit in 1854. See Romero, *Noticias para formar*, 25.
97. See, for example, Árciga, *Segunda carta pastoral que el Ilmo. Sr. Don José Ignacio Árciga*, 5; and de la Peña y Navarro, *Sexta pastoral del Obispo de Zamora*.
98. AHAL, Libros de Visita, vol. 1, ff. 208–9, Edict of the Pastoral Visit, 25 June 1873.
99. Herrejón Peredo, "Don Ignacio Árciga y Ruiz de Chávez"; and Buitrón, *Apuntes para servir la historia del arzobispado de Morelia*, 241–44.

100. AHCM, Diocesano/Gobierno/Parroquias/Visitas, caja 286, exp. 35, "Instrucciones para la santa visita pastoral," 18 November 1868; and AHCM, Diocesano/Gobierno/Mandatos/Circulares, caja 189, exp. 271, "Auto de visita para la parroquia de Zacapu," 3 October 1871. The latter document is the only such report of the pastoral visit located from Árciga's administration. I offer more about the devotional customs of the Purépecha villagers of Zacapu and its surrounding towns in chapter 4.
101. AHCM, Diocesano/Gobierno/Parroquias/Visitas, caja 286, exp. 35, "Instrucciones para la santa visita pastoral," 18 November 1868, note 3.
102. Herrejón Peredo, "Don Ignacio Árciga y Ruiz de Chávez," 217; and Árciga, *Segunda carta pastoral que el Ilmo. Sr. Don José Ignacio Árciga*, 6–7.
103. Herrejón Peredo, "Don Ignacio Árciga y Ruiz de Chávez," 217; and Bautista García, *Clérigos virtuosos e instruidos*, 216–19. Bautista García sees the discursive appropriation of Vasco de Quiroga as originating among the Morelia clergy of the late eighteenth century. As such, Árciga's assumption of the mantle of Quiroga represented both the consolidation of longer-term trends in Morelia's clerical culture and a symbol of the archbishop's rejection of Labastida/Plancarte/de la Peña's Roman strategy for restoration.
104. Águilar, *Corona fúnebre*, 211–29.
105. Águilar, *Corona fúnebre*, section X.
106. In its missionary character, de la Peña's pastoral approach complemented that of Archbishop Labastida, who sent friars from the order of the Missionaries of Saint Vincent de Paul ahead of his own pastoral visits in order reacquaint the neo-"neophytes" in the fundamentals of the faith. See García Ugarte, *Poder político y religioso*, 2:1245–50.
107. See AHCM, Diocesano/Gobierno/Mandatos/Instrucciones, caja 212, exp. 67, Edict of the Bishop of Zamora about schismatic priests, 22 January 1866; de la Peña y Navarro, *Sexta pastoral del Obispo de Zamora*; de la Peña y Navarro, "Sr. Cura Juez Ecco. de . . .Circular número 26"; and Rosas Salas, "El proyecto pastoral de José Antonio de la Peña y Navarro."
108. De la Peña y Navarro, "Sr. Cura Juez Ecco. de . . . Circular número 26," 3–7.
109. De la Peña y Navarro, "Sr. Cura Juez Ecco. de . . . Circular número 26," 7–8. Ripalda's catechism was a sixteenth-century Spanish text used then as the standard catechistic primer in the Spanish-speaking world.
110. *Estadística de la Sociedad Católica de Señoras*, 47–49. Catholic schooling in the Archdiocese of Morelia boomed during the administration of Árciga's successor, Atenógenes Silva (1900–1911), for whom Catholic education formed a central plank of a larger project for "social and religious regeneration." See Díaz Patiño, "El catolicismo social en el Arquidiócesis de Morelia," 112–18. Díaz Patiño found 135 Catholic schools operating in the Archdiocese of Michoacán by 1905. The Sociedad Católica is discussed at length in the following section of this chapter.

111. Plancarte's girls' school educated some 170 girls between the ages of six and sixteen in its first decade (1867–1877), attracting students from nearby towns like Chavinda and La Piedad and from cities as far away as León and Uruapan. See Bautista García, *Clérigos virtuosos e instruidos*, 162–72.
112. Ochoa Serrano, "El distrito de Zamora en 1877." These included Plancarte's schools as well as a school run by the Sociedad Católica of Chavinda.
113. All the private schools not operated by Catholic organizations or parish priests are listed as schools "sustained by small payments by parents of the students." Such a description parallels with that offered by Bishop de la Peña, who referred to "private schools [run by] Catholics that are sustained by the parents of the students." We can reasonably assume that many of the schools listed in the report by the prefect of Zamora would have fit the bishop's description, though the extent of clerical influence over these institutions remains unclear.
114. *Estadística de la Sociedad Católica de Señoras*, 59.
115. These projects are discussed further in chapters 3 and 5.
116. Chowning, "Catholic Church and the Ladies of the Vela Perpetua," 210.
117. On Bourbon religiosity, see Voekel, *Alone before God*; and Bautista García, *Las disyuntivas*, 262–63. For the cabildo's deliberation over lay associations, see AHAM, Sección: Secretaria Arzobispal, Serie: Iglesias, caja 87, exp. 3, "El padre capellán sobre licencia para el establecimiento de la Asociación de Veladores de la Santa Casa de Loreto," October 1874.
118. Adame Goddard, *El pensamiento político y social de los católicos mexicanos*, 15–30; Ceballos Ramírez, *El catolicismo social*, 20–26; Traffano, "Para formar el corazón religioso de los jóvenes"; Wright-Ríos, *Revolutions in Mexican Catholicism*, 102–3; and Bautista García, *Las disyuntivas*, 261–63. Similarly, Bautista García identifies an explosion of pious associations—especially Marian organizations—in the Archbishopric of Mexico in the years between 1870 and 1890.
119. ADZ, DGP 1410 Zamora Sagrario, Sociedad Católica de Señoras, Zamora, to Juan R. Carranza, Zamora, 9 August 1873; and AHCM, Diocesano/Gobierno/Correspondencia/Secretaria, caja 118, exp. 564, Manuel García, Angangueo, to Luis Macouzet, Morelia, 15 April 1874, and Manuel García, Angangueo, to Luis Macouzet, Morelia, 15 April 1874.
120. ADZ, DGP 971, Sahuayo, Macario Saavedra, Sahuayo, to Diocesan Secretary, Zamora, 7 August 1875.
121. For Zamora, see ADZ, DGP 1111 Tangancícuaro, Accounts of the Vela Perpetua of Tangancícuaro, 1855–1904; DGPD 33 Coalcomán, Pedro M. Villalobos, Coalcomán, to Diocesan Secretary, Zamora, 15 July 1867; DGP 787 Peribán, José María Sandoval, Los Reyes, to Diocesan Secretary, Zamora, 23 November 1868; DGPD 2, Aguililla, Abundio Martínez, Aguililla, to Diocesan Secretary, Zamora, 2 June 1872; DGPD 22 Buenavista, Domingo Méndez,

Buenavista, to Diocesan Secretary, Zamora, 20 November 1873; DGP 643, Pajacuarán, Juan de Dios Porto, Pajacuarán, to Diocesan Secretary, Zamora, 12 May 1874; and DGP 643 Pajacuarán, Ramon Sánchez, Ixtlán, to Diocesan Secretary, Zamora, 10 June 1874. For Morelia, see AHCM, Diocesano/Gobierno/Parroquias/Solicitudes, caja 280, exp. 494, Luis G. García, Huango, to Diocesan Secretary, Morelia, 24 December 1873; and AHCM, Diocesano/Gobierno/Sacerdotes/Solicitudes, caja 523, exp. 557, Vicente F. Valdez, Puruándiro, to Diocesan Secretary, Morelia, 15 October 1875.

122. Chowning, "Catholic Church and the Ladies of the Vela Perpetua," 205–23; and Murillo, "Politics of the Miraculous," 33–34, 184–86. Though Michoacán had mixed-sex Velas in the nineteenth century, the association's constitution mandated that a female president and treasurer preside over each chapter, and women dominated membership even in the mixed-sex Velas from early in the organization's history.

123. Chowning, "Catholic Church and the Ladies of the Vela Perpetua," 216–17; and Murillo, "Politics of the Miraculous," 118–37, 185.

124. Never mere copies of their European counterparts, the Vincentians in Mexico also innovated by organizing visits to prisons, where they worked to reconcile the inmates with the Church and prepare them for the sacraments. Arrom, *Volunteering for a Cause*, 39–106; Arrom, "Filantropía católica y sociedad civil," 70–80; Arrom, "Las Señoras de la Caridad," 448–64; and Arrom, "Mexican Laywomen Spearhead a Catholic Revival," 65–71.

125. Arrom, "Las Señoras de la Caridad," 466. The 1860s saw the creation of regional councils of the Sociedad in both Morelia (1860) and Zamora (1864). Michoacán had more male conferences than all other states except Mexico City and Guanajuato in the 1870s, and it experienced prodigious growth in female conferences between 1878 and 1911. See Arrom, *Volunteering for a Cause*, 44, 85. The records of the Sociedad de San Vicente de Paul and the Señoras de la Caridad do not appear in the diocesan collections of Morelia or Zamora. Parish correspondence makes scant reference to the work of either association.

126. *Noticia sobre las Conferencias de la Sociedad de San Vicente de Paul*, 11. Chapters were also found in Atecucario, Purépero, Nahuatzen, Penjamillo, Zináparo, Churintzio, Los Reyes, Tanhuato, and Romero. While the organization likely maintained at least some presence in the Archdiocese of Michoacán, the Regional Council of Morelia failed to send data to the Central Council in 1869, and the records of the associations do not appear in the archive of the archbishopric.

127. Velasco Robledo, "Institución bendita por Dios"; and Bautista García, *Las disyuntivas*, 237–82.

128. Other periodicals created by the Sociedad include *El Seminario Católico* (1869), *La Sociedad Católica* (1869–1873), and *El Mensajero Católico* (1875–1876). Velasco Robledo, "Institución bendita por Dios," 157–65.

129. ADZ, DG 168, Diócesis de Zamora, Primera Acta de la Sociedad Católica de Zamora, 12 January 1870.
130. On the close relationship between the Catholic hierarchy and the emerging agrarian and commercial bourgeoisie in Zamora, see González y González, *Zamora*, 118–19; Tapia Santamaría, *Campo religioso y evolución política*; Verduzco, "Zamora en el Porfiriato," 57–62; Chowning, *Wealth and Power in Provincial Mexico*, 209–11; and Becker, *Setting the Virgin on Fire*, 13–19.
131. See ADZ, DG 84, Secretaria/Correspondencia y Datos, Juan R. Carranza, Zamora, to Diocesan Secretary, Zamora, 17 February 1872.
132. *Estadística de la Sociedad Católica de Señoras*, 57–58.
133. *Estadística de la Sociedad Católica de Señoras*, 46–49.

Chapter 3

1. ADZ, DGP 505, Jiquilpan, Prefect to Diocesan Secretary, Zamora, 20 March 1873.
2. ADZ, DGP 505, Jiquilpan, Various vecinos of Jiquilpan in association with the Indian community and various rancherías that compose this parish to Diocesan Secretary, Zamora, 5 June 1873.
3. ADZ, DGP 505, Jiquilpan, Narciso Martínez and the Indian Community of Jiquilpan to Diocesan Secretary, Zamora, 19 August 1872; Various Vecinos of Jiquilpan to Diocesan Secretary, Zamora, 30 December 1872; and Roberto Mendoza and the Indian Communities of Jiquilpan and Totolan to Diocesan Secretary, Zamora, 7 January 1873.
4. An 1875 report by the prefecture on religious buildings and denominations in Jiquilpan lists seven "temples" (parish churches or the smaller *vicarías*) and eleven chapels in the district, all of which were Catholic. AGHPEM, Secretaria de Gobierno, Gobernación, Religión, caja 1, exp. 18, District Prefect, Jiquilpan to Interior Minister, Morelia, 20 March 1875.
5. What little we do know about Religionero chieftains comes from brief periodical accounts and eulogies, the odd criminal file in regional judicial archives, and genealogical reconstructions from parish records performed by historians such as Álvaro Ochoa Serrano. See Ochoa Serrano, *Afrodescendientes* (91–129) for a brief biography of Eulogio Cárdenas.
6. Here, my study diverges sharply from Becker's *Setting the Virgin on Fire* (13–31), which tends to essentialize Michoacán's "peasant" religious cultures.
7. The term *Bajío Zamorano* denotes the westernmost section of central Mexico's fertile Bajío basin, a relatively low-lying region of plains, valleys, and foothills extending west from Querétaro through Guanajuato, northern Michoacán, and Jalisco.
8. Soto Correa, *Movimientos campesinos de derecha*, 11–17, 21, 65–111.

9. This book builds upon recent works on France and Mexico that have convincingly demonstrated the links between religious culture and patterns of political mobilization. See, for example, Tackett, *Religion, Revolution, and Regional Culture in Eighteenth-Century France*; Mijangos y González, "La respuesta popular al juramento constitucional en 1857"; Van Oosterhout, "Popular Conservatism in Mexico"; Butler, *Popular Piety and Political Identity*; and Van Young, *Other Rebellion*.
10. Heriberto Moreno García, *Cotija*, 34–56; Ochoa Serrano, *Jiquilpan*, 7–16; and Sánchez, *Bosquejo estadístico*, 71–96.
11. Warren, *Conquest of Michoacán*, 50–79; Ochoa Serrano, *Jiquilpan-Huanimba*, 44–59; González y González, *Sahuayo*, 50–78; Moreno García, *Guaracha*, 72–83.
12. González y González, *Zamora*, 33–88.
13. Moreno García, *Guaracha*, 75–77; and Gledhill, *Casi Nada*, 38–46. The encomienda system granted indigenous labor and tribute to the men who had participated in the conquest of Mexico.
14. Romero, *Noticias para formar*, 104; Moreno García, *Cotija*, 62–70; Romero Vargas, *Cotija*, 49–61; Tinajero Villaseñor, *Cotija*, 7–8; and González y González, *Zamora*, 34–52.
15. González y González, *Pueblo en vilo*, 31–47; González y González, *Sahuayo*, 60–63; Tapía Santamaría, *Campo religioso y evolución política*, 31–40; and Romero Vargas, *Cotija*, 32–48.
16. Buitrón, *Apuntes para servir a la historia del Arzobispado de Morelia*, 63–80; López Lara, "El Obispo"; Campos, "Métodos misionales y rasgos biográficos de Don Vasco de Quiroga"; Verástique, *Michoacán and Eden*, 92–109; Muriel, "Las cofradías hospitalarias"; Ochoa Serrano, *Jiquilpan*, 26–27; Ochoa Serrano, *Afrodescendientes*, 94–100; and González y González, *Sahuayo*, 50–68.
17. González y González, *Sahuayo*, 68; and Ochoa Serrano, *Afrodescendientes*, 99.
18. Bautista García, "Dos momentos en la historia de un culto," 21–30.
19. Moreno García, *Guaracha*, 89–91. In *Afrodescendientes*, Ochoa Serrano describes one specific cultural artifact of cultural hybridization in Jiquilpan, a variation of the *moros y cristianos* dance known as the "Danza de los Negros" (99–100).
20. Verástique, *Michoacán and Eden*, 136–40; Muriel, "Las cofradías hospitalarias"; Baltazar Chávez, "El Corpus Christi P'urhépecha," 153–86; González y González, *Sahuayo*, 60–68; Romero, *Noticias para formar*, 102; and Ochoa Serrano, *Afrodescendientes*, 114.
21. Ochoa Serrano, *Afrodescendientes*, 94; Ochoa Serrano, *Jiquilpan*, 64–65; Moreno García, *Guaracha*, 78–91; and González y González, *Sahuayo*, 59.
22. Ochoa Serrano, *Jiquilpan*, 89–90; Ochoa Serrano, *Jiquilpan-Huanimban*, 121–24; and González y González, *Sahuayo*, 100–1. The state congressional decree of 18 January 1827 confirmed indigenous communities' possession of colonial

properties (against claims by local governments) but mandated their division into individual lots. Another reparto law was issued in 1851 but had little effect because of the political instability facing the country. Santa Anna annulled the latter law in 1853. See Coromina, *Recopilación de leyes, decretos, reglamentos, y circulares expedidos*, 2:61, 3:29–39, 11:195–205, respectively. On the complex results of the 1827 reparto, see Cortés Máximo, "La desamortización de la propiedad indígena en una provincia mexicana." On the 1851 law, see Knowlton, "La división de las tierras de los pueblos durante el siglo XIX"; and Cortés Máximo, "La comunidad de Tarímbaro."

23. Tutino, *From Insurrection to Revolution in Mexico*, 215–16, 242–75; and Tutino, "Revolution in Mexican Independence." For complementary accounts of hacienda decline in the Bajío region in the postindependence period, see Brading, *Haciendas and Ranchos in the Mexican Bajío*, and González y González, *Pueblo en vilo*, 59–80. For discussions of the impact of liberal land reform on rural unrest, see Powell, *El liberalismo y el campesinado en el centro de México*; Katz, *Riot, Rebellion, and Revolution*; Reina, *Las rebeliones campesinas en México*; Kourí, *Pueblo Divided*; Purnell, "With All Due Respect"; and Stauffer, "Indianness, Community."

24. Soto Correa, *Movimientos campesinos de derecha*, 11–17.

25. AGHPEM, Hijuelas, Jiquilpan, vol. 4, District Prefect, Jiquilpan, to Interior Minister, Morelia, 15 February 1869.

26. AGHPEM, Hijuelas, Jiquilpan, esp. vols. 4 and 9.

27. AGHPEM, Hijuelas, Jiquilpan, vol. 7, [Acta] Civil Promovido por los Indígenas de este Pueblo sobre Reparto de sus Bienes, 14 September 1868.

28. AGHPEM, Hijuelas, Jiquilpan, vol. 4, Toribio Lucero and the Indian Community of Totolan, Jiquilpan, to Interior Minister, Morelia, 12 May 1869; District Prefect, Jiquilpan, to Interior Minister, Morelia, 7 May 1869; District Prefect, Jiquilpan, to Interior Minister, Morelia, 4 December 1869; and District Prefect, Jiquilpan, to Interior Minister, Morelia, 14 May 1870.

29. AGHPEM, Hijuelas, Jiquilpan, vol. 4, Land Division Committee, Tingüindín, to District Prefect, Jiquilpan, 26 November 1883, and vol. 7, Act of Land Division, Tacátzcuaro, 20 January 1869; and Herculano Nasario and the Indians of Tacátzcuaro to Interior Minister, Morelia, 13 February 1896.

30. AGHPEM, Hijuelas, Zamora, vol. 5, Act of Land Division, Pajacuarán, 18 September 1879.

31. The Plancarte family began as rancheros from Cotija who worked as sharecroppers on the Cojumatlán hacienda. Over the course of the eighteenth and nineteenth centuries, they established a network of kinship ties with the Dávalos and Labastida families, greatly expanded their landed holdings, and sent various sons into the clergy. See González y González, *Pueblo en vilo*, 30–33; and Tapia Santamaría, *Campo religioso y evolución política*, 55–58.

32. AGHPEM, Hijuelas, Zamora, vol. 12, Modesto Torres, Jacona, to Interior Minister, Morelia, 15 January 1869.

33. AGHPEM, Hijuelas, Zamora, vol. 12, Modesto Torres, Jacona, to Interior Minister, Morelia, 15 January 1869; and Tapia Méndez, *El siervo de dios*, 20.
34. AGHPEM, Hijuelas, Zamora, vol. 12, Modesto Torres, Jacona, to Interior Minister, Morelia, 15 January 1869. For discussions of indigenous engagement with liberal discourse in the context of the land division process, see Purnell, "With All Due Respect"; Kourí, *A Pueblo Divided*; Roseberry, "El estricto apego a la ley"; and Zárate Hernández, "Comunidad, reformas liberales, y emergencia del indígena moderno."
35. AGHPEM, Hijuelas, Zamora, vol. 10, Rafael Paz Romero, Zamora, to Interior Minister, Morelia, November 3 1871; and José María Reyes Constantino, Chilchota, to Interior Minister, 23 October 1872. Reyes Constantino himself, in a plea against the levying of taxes on the undivided portions of communal land, argued that Chilchota had long served as an "asylum for our brothers the liberals," and he went on to underline the services Chilchota's sons and daughters had offered to liberal political movements.
36. *La Idea Católica*, 25 April 1875, "Manifestación de las señoras de Chilchota en contra de la Ley Orgánica de Reforma," dated 20 January 1875; and AGHPEM, Guerra y Ejército, caja 5, exp. 85, Prudencio Casillas, Zamora, to Interior Minister, Morelia, 1 July 1875.
37. As other recent works have demonstrated, we can no longer speak of pueblo disamortization as a wholesale dispossession and victimization of indigenous communities. See, for example, Escobar Ohmstede and Schryer, "Las sociedades agrarias en el norte de Hidalgo"; Purnell, "With All Due Respect"; Kourí, "Interpreting the Expropriation of Indian Pueblo Lands in Porfirian Mexico"; Kourí, *A Pueblo Divided*; and Escobar Ohmstede and Butler, *Mexico in Transition*.
38. Tutino, "Revolution in Mexican Independence," shows that such agrarian trends dated from the independence period in the Bajío, where hacienda laborers and sharecroppers used the insurgency in order to break up large estates from within and renegotiate the terms of agricultural production.
39. González y González, *Pueblo en vilo*, 59–80; González y González, *Sahuayo*, 110–11; Ochoa Serrano, *Jiquilpan-Huanimban*, 148–49; and Moreno García, *Guaracha*, 109–11.
40. On the "JalMich" region, see Barragán López, "Identidad ranchera"; Barragán López, *Mas allá de los camino*; and Barragán López, *Con el pie en el estribo*. On hacienda decline and the rise of the ranchero in the culturally mixed northwest, see Moreno García, *Cotija*, 102–20; Ochoa Serrano, *Afrodescendientes*, 95–96; Ochoa Serrano, "Mitote, Fandango, y Mariachi en Jal-Mich"; González y González, *Sahuayo*, 60–68; and Chowning, *Wealth and Power in Provincial Mexico*, 261–73.
41. Cochet, *Alambradas en la sierra*, 21–32.
42. González y González, *Pueblo en vilo*, 71–80; and Barragán López, Hoffman, Linck, and Skerritt, *Rancheros y sociedades rancheras*, 13–16, 47–50, 57–78.

43. Archbishop Labastida hailed from Zamora, and his nephew, José Antonio Plancarte, pioneered the Romanization of rural Catholicism in nearby Jacona in the 1870s and 1880s. Zamora's first bishop, José Antonio de la Peña y Navarro, was a native of Tangamandapio. Cotija's local sons Juan Carranza, Benigno Tejeda, and Eligio Carranza all attained posts in the high clergy of Morelia and Zamora, as did Tingüindín's José María Cañedo and Presa de Herrera's José de Jesús Fernández Barragán, who served as assistant bishop of Zamora at the turn of the century. See Sánchez, *Bosquejo estadístico*, 182–91; González y González, *Zamora*, 91–92; and Barragán López, *Más allá de los caminos*, 102–6.
44. Tapia Santamaría, *Campo religioso y evolución política*, 51–67.
45. Ochoa Serrano, *Jiquilpan*, 90–93; González y González, *Zamora*, 91, 105; Chowning, *Wealth and Power in Provincial Mexico*, 227, 246; Moreno García, *Guaracha*; 103–8; Moreno García, *Cotija*, 136–40; and Sánchez, *Bosquejo estadístico*, 118–26.
46. Sánchez, *Bosquejo estadístico*, 164; Ochoa Serrano, *Jiquilpan*, 96; and Moreno García, *Cotija*, 151. AHCM, Gobierno, Parroquias, Visitas, caja 286, folio 30, Record of the Visit of Tingüindín and Cotija, 30 March 1854.
47. ADZ, DGP 442, Jacona, Alejandro Quezada, Morelia, to the Tithes Collector of Zamora, 4 June 1855; DGP 63, Charapan, José María Sandoval, Charapan, to Diocesan Secretary, Zamora, 6 January 1865; and José María Sandoval, Charapan, to Diocesan Secretary, Zamora, 13 July 1865.
48. Tapia Santamaría, "Identidad social y religión."
49. González y González, *Sahuayo*, 110; Moreno García, *Cotija*, 152–54; and González y González, *Zamora*, 103–4.
50. Tapia Santamaría, "Identidad social y religión," 55–58; Brading, "Ultramontane Intransigence and the Mexican Reform," 138–40; and García Ugarte, *Poder religioso y político*, 2:1042–46, 1148.
51. Bautista García, "Hacia la romanización"; Tapia Méndez, *El siervo de dios*, 225–34; and O'Dogherty, "El ascenso de una jerarquia eclesial intransigente."
52. Ochoa Serrano, *Afrodescendientes*, 116–24; Moreno García, *Guaracha*, 109; and Moreno García, *Cotija*, 152–57.
53. Ochoa Serrano, *Afrodescendientes*, 116.
54. Contemporary commentators remembered Gutiérrez as particularly bloodthirsty and avaricious. However, the murderous tendencies of "El Nopal" quickly proved intolerable to other regional leaders, and he was killed by the Religionero titan Ignacio Ochoa in late 1874. See Sánchez, *Bosquejo estadístico*, 131.
55. AGHPEM, Guerra y Ejército, caja 4, exp. 72, Prudencio Casillas, Zamora, to Interior Minister, Morelia, 14 June 1875; AGHPEM, Gobernadores, caja 1, exp. 5, Memoria de Gobierno, 30 July 1874, ff. 21–22; and *El diario de los debates*, 4:537–39.

56. *El Progresista*, 4 June 1874, and 11 June 1874; *La Voz de México*, 24 May 1874; and *El Pájaro Verde*, 26 May 1874. On the family relations among the Afromestizo rebels of Jiquilpan, see Ochoa Serrano, *Afrodescendientes*, 97.
57. *El Progresista*, 4 June 1874, and 11 June 1874; *La Voz de México*, 24 May 1874; and *El Pájaro Verde*, 26 May 1874. See *El Siglo Diez y Nueve*, 21 September 1874.
58. *El Siglo Diez y Nueve*, 7 September 1874; and *La Revista Universal*, 10 September 1874.
59. *El Siglo Diez y Nueve*, 21 September 1874; *La Voz de México*, 2 October 1874; *El Pensamiento Católico*, 25 September 1874, 16 October 1874, and 6 November 1874; and *La Bandera de Ocampo*, 29 November 1874.
60. *El Progresista*, 1 March 1875; AGHPEM, Guerra y Ejército, caja 2, exp. 21, Ignacio Jiménez, Jiquilpan, to Interior Minister, Morelia, 17 February 1875; and caja 4, exp. 59, District Prefect, Jiquilpan, to Interior Minister, Morelia, 28 April 1875.
61. González y González, *Sahuayo*, 114; *El Radical*, 10 January 1874; *El Pájaro Verde*, 9 March 1874; *La Voz de México*, 7 March 1874; and AHPJEM, Penal, Juzgado Primero de Jiquilpan, caja 1, exp. 8, Arcadio Villamar vs. Lic. José Dolores del Río, December 1874.
62. *La Bandera de Ocampo*, 31 January 1875; Sánchez, *Bosquejo estadístico*, 130–31; and González y González, *Sahuayo*, 116. Days later, a smaller contingent from Ochoa's gavilla returned and attempted to assassinate Osio's brother.
63. AHDN, Operaciones Militares, XI/481.4/9209, ff. 8–9; *La Iberia*, 20 May 1874; *El Correo del Comercio*, 20 May 1874; and AGHPEM, Guerra y Ejército, caja 2, exp. 21, District Prefect, Jiquilpan to Interior Minister, Morelia, 17 February 1875.
64. AGHPEM, Guerra y Ejército, caja 2, exp. 24, Telegram, Andrés Villegas Rendón, Zamora, to Interior Minister, Morelia, 29 January 1875; Rafael Valdéz, Zamora, to Interior Minister, Morelia, 29 January 1875; and Andrés Villegas Rendón, Zacapu, to Interior Minister, Morelia, 9 February 1875.
65. AGHPEM, Guerra y Ejército, caja 2, exp. 24, Andrés Villegas Rendón, Zamora, to Interior Minister, Morelia, 31 January 1875; and Andrés Villegas Rendón, Zamora, to Interior Minister, Morelia, 8 February 1875.
66. AGHPEM, Guerra y Ejército, caja 3, exp. 32, Jesús Ocampo, Morelia, to Interior Minister, Morelia, 11 March 1875; and Eduardo Gil y Villamil, Pátzcuaro, to Interior Minister, Morelia, 13 March 1875.
67. AGHPEM, Guerra y Ejército, caja 3, exp. 46, Andrés Villegas Rendón, Zamora, to Interior Minister, 29 March 1875.
68. AGHPEM, Guerra y Ejército, caja 5, exp. 79, Andrés Villegas Rendón, Zamora, to Interior Minister, Morelia, 30 April 1875; AHDN, Cancelados, Eulogio Zepeda, XI/III/4–6791, f. 154; and Iñiguez Mendoza, "¡Viva la religión y mueran los *protestantes*!," 283–84.

69. AGHPEM, Guerra y Ejército, caja 3, exp. 46, District Prefect, Zamora, to Interior Minister, Morelia, 16 April 1875.
70. AGHPEM, Guerra y Ejército, caja 4, exp. 72, Prudencio Casillas, Zamora, to Interior Minister, Morelia, 31 May 1875; and AHDN, Operaciones Militares, XI/481.4/9211, Prisciliano Flores, La Piedad, to José Ceballos, Guadalajara, 20 May 1875.
71. AGHPEM, Guerra y Ejército, caja 4, exp. 59, District Prefect, Jiquilpan, to Interior Minister, Morelia, 21 May 1875.
72. AGHPEM, Guerra y Ejército, caja 4, exp. 59, District Prefect, Jiquilpan, to Interior Minister, Morelia, 28 April 1875; caja 3, exp. 46, Andrés Villegas Rendón, Zamora, to Interior Minister, 18 April 1875; and caja 5, exp. 72, Prudencio Casillas, Zamora, to Interior Minister, 11 June 1875.
73. AGHPEM, Guerra y Ejército, caja 5, exp. 79, Interior Minister, Morelia, to Andrés Villegas Rendón, Zamora, 30 April 1875; and caja 5, exp. 77, Circular no. 37, issued 7 May 1875.
74. *El Siglo Diez y Nueve*, 9 September 1875; *La Voz de México*, 26 September 1875; and *El Progresista*, 24 June 1875, and 28 June 1875.
75. AHDN, Operaciones Militares, XI/481.4/9211, Prisciliano Flores, La Piedad, to Ignacio Mejía, Mexico City, 16 June 1875.
76. *El Progresista*, 1 July 1875, 8 July 1875, and 22 July 1875.
77. AGHPEM, Guerra y Ejército, caja 4, exp. 70, District Prefect, Jiquilpan to Interior Minister, Morelia, 17 June 1875; Interior Minister, Morelia, to District Prefect, Jiquilpan, 17 June 1875; District Prefect, Jiquilpan, to Interior Minister, Morelia, 13 July 1875; and AHDN, Operaciones Militares, XI/481.4/9211, Prisciliano Flores, La Piedad, to Commander and Chief of the Division, Guadalajara, 16 June 1875.
78. AHDN, Operaciones Militares, XI/481.4/9211, Prisciliano Flores, La Piedad, to Secretary of War, Mexico, 16 June 1875.
79. *El Monitor Republicano*, 18 August 1875, and 22 August 1875; and AHDN, Operaciones Militares, XI/481.4/9211, General Prisciliano Flores, La Piedad, to Secretary of War, Mexico, 14 August 1875.
80. AHDN, Operaciones Militares, XI/481.4/9211, Prisciliano Flores, La Piedad, to Secretary of War, Mexico, 18 October 1875; Sánchez, *Bosquejo estadístico*, 133; Ochoa Serrano, *Afrodescendientes*, 123; and Ochoa Serrano, "Tres corridos cristeros," 158. The ballad also acclaims Florencio Gálvez and Narciso "Valeriano" Mejía.
81. AHDN, Operaciones Militares, XI/481.4/9211, Prisciliano Flores, La Piedad, to Secretary of War, Mexico, 18 October 1875. The editors of *La Voz de México*, it should be noted, insisted that the girls followed the rebels voluntarily, as prostitutes. See *La Voz de México*, 5 November 1875.
82. *El Progresista*, 11 November 1875.
83. *El Progresista*, 6 February 1876; *El Siglo Diez y Nueve*, 9 February 1876; and *El Correo del Comercio*, 8 March 1876.

84. For Sandoval's indulto, see *El Progresista*, 31 January 1876. On Meza's capture and Ochoa's attack on Jiquilpan, see *El Progresista*, 19 June 1876, and 30 June 1876.
85. See AGHPEM, Guerra y Ejército, caja 2, exp. 21, District Prefect, Jiquilpan, to Interior Minister, Morelia, 3 February 1875; caja 3, exp. 33, District Prefect, Los Reyes, to Interior Minister, Morelia, 13 March 1875; and District Prefect, Jiquilpan, to Interior Minister, Morelia, 21 May 1875.
86. AGHPEM, Guerra y Ejército, caja 2, exp. 20, Prefect of Jiquilpan to Interior Minister, Morelia, 6 January 1875; and Prefect of Jiquilpan to Interior Minister, Morelia, 15 January 1875.
87. *El Monitor Republicano*, 25 September 1875.
88. AGHPEM, Guerra y Ejército, caja 5, exp. 79, Andrés Villegas Rendón, Zamora, to Interior Minister, Morelia, 30 April 1875.
89. *El Eco de Ambos Mundos*, 2 September 1875. In their raid, military authorities confiscated 114 pieces of clothing, "including pants, jackets, shirts, and two striped hats, [as well as] a sewing machine."
90. *La Bandera de Ocampo*, 10 January 1875; AHPJEM, Penal, Juzgado Primero de Jiquilpan, caja 1, exp. 8, Arcadio Villamar vs. Lic. José Dolores del Río, December 1874; ADZ, DGP 505, Jiquilpan, Pascual Bayllac, Jiquilpan, to Diocesan Secretary, Zamora, 20 October 1875; and Francisco Tejada de Leon, Jiquilpan, to Diocesan Secretary, Zamora, 12 June 1876.
91. Farías had previously shared doubts with friends about the tenet of papal infallibility, but he repented his errors and rejoined the fold in 1871. See ADZ, DGP 241, Cotija, Dr. Don Francisco Farías, Cotija, to Diocesan Secretary, Zamora, 28 October 1871.
92. *El Progresista*, 20 January 1876; and ADZ, DGP 444, Jacona, Juan N. González, Juan Tapia, and other vecinos of Jacona to Diocesan Secretary, Zamora, 25 March 1871.
93. It should be noted that indigenous populations were not uniform in their allegiance—large groups of Purépechas from San Pedro Caro, Charapan, Tarecuato, and Sahuayo joined Religionero attacks in 1875, but contingents of indigenous people in Cherán and Chilchota supported the government. See AGHPEM, Guerra y Ejército, caja 2, exp. 21, Ignacio Jiménez, Jiquilpan, to Interior Minister, Morelia, 12 February 1875; caja 5, exp. 78, Jesús Rodríguez, Uruapan, to Interior Minister, Morelia, 22 May 1875; caja 5, exp. 79, Prudencio Casillas, Zamora, to Interior Minister, Morelia, 28 May 1875; caja 5, exp. 85, Prudencio Casillas, Zamora, to Interior Minister, Morelia, 1 July 1875; *El Progresista*, 1 March 1875; El Progresista, 27 January 1876.
94. Tapia Santamaría, "Identidad social y religión," 43–52. It remains unclear why the image was dubbed "La Purísima." According to Rodríguez Zetina, the image belonged to the Dávalos family, and it was chosen by the community to confront the cholera epidemic by way of a raffle (*Zamora*, 470–71).
95. AHCM, Diocesano/Gobierno/Parroquias/Visitas, caja 286, exp. 32, Francisco Enríquez, Zamora, to Clemente de Jesús Munguía, Morelia, 15 April 1854.

96. Romero, *Noticias para formar*, 106–7. See also Rodríguez Zetina, *Zamora*, 115–16. One suspects that the conservative hacendados of the region contributed significant amounts of money to the project, though I have not located an account book.
97. Romero, *Noticias para formar*, 101–5; and Sánchez, *Bosquejo estadístico*, 151–62.
98. Romero, *Noticias para formar*, 118.
99. AHCM, Diocesano/Parroquias/Visitas, caja 286, exp. 32, Acta de Visita de Santiago Chilchota, 16 April 1854.
100. AHCM, Gobierno/Parroquias/Visitas, caja 286, exp. 30, Record of the Visit of Tingüindín and Cotija, 30 March 1854.
101. Mijangos y González, "Lawyer of the Church," x–xi, 197–200.
102. AHCM, Diocesano/Parroquias/Visitas, caja 286, Folio 32, Acta de Visita de San Juan Cotija, 30 March 1854.
103. Romero Vargas provides a list of Cotija natives who received priestly orders before 1872, and among the names we find Nicholás de Oceguera Cervantes, Francisco Antonio Oceguera, Eligio Carranza, Juan Rafael Carranza Valencia, and Alejo Carranza Valencia (*Cotija*, 293). The Oceguerra, Carranza, and Valencia families all owned capellanías in 1854.
104. Romero, *Noticias para formar*, 105; and Sánchez, *Bosquejo estadístico*, 162–63.
105. Chowning, "Catholic Church and the Ladies of the Vela Perpetua," 216–17.
106. ADZ, DGPD 22 Buenavista, Domingo Méndez, Buenavista, to Diocesan Secretary, Zamora, 20 November 1873; DGP 1111 Tangancícuaro, Accounts of the Vela Perpetua of Tangancícuaro, 1855–1904; DGP 643 Pajacuarán, Ramon Sánchez, Ixtlán, to Diocesan Secretary, Zamora, 10 June 1874; and Romero, *Noticias para formar*, 118.
107. ADZ, DGP 63, Charapan, José María Sandoval, Charapan, to Diocesan Secretary, Zamora, 22 September 1867; and Diocesan Secretary, Zamora, to José María Sandoval, Charapan, 24 September 1867.
108. ADZ, DGP 1111, Vela Perpetua Account Book for Tangancícuaro, Receipt for loan from the Vela Perpetua, signed by Pedro Arroyo, 19 November 1860; and account inscriptions for June 1873 and August 1874.
109. ADZ, DGP 972, Sahuayo, Ladies of the Vela Perpetua, Sahuayo, to the Diocesan Secretary, Zamora, 17 January 1869.
110. ADZ, DGP 505, Jiquilpan, Account Book of the Association of the Vela Perpetua, Jiquilpan, 29 December 1873. Like other Vela associations in Michoacán studied by Margaret Chowning, Jiquilpan's included male members and sometimes even officers, although it was dominated and directed by women. See Chowning, "Catholic Church and the Ladies of the Vela Perpetua," 217.
111. ADZ, DGP 643, Pajacuarán, Juan de Dios Porto, Pajacuarán to Diocesan Secretary, 12 May 1874; and Juan de Dios Porto, Pajacuarán, to Diocesan Secretary, 10 February 1876.
112. *Noticia sobre las Conferencias de la Sociedad de San Vicente de Paul*, 111.

113. As the *Manual para el uso de las Hijas de la Caridad* put it, "An Hermana is a mother, through grace, of the youth of the pueblo. She surrounds [the youth] with care, affection, and counsel, and with all of the devotion of maternity in order to ensure its salvation."
114. ADZ, DGP 505, Jiquilpan, Sociedad Feminina de Jiquilpan to Diocesan Secretary, Zamora, 17 August 1872.
115. ADZ, DGP 505, Jiquilpan, Various Vecinos of Jiquilpan to Diocesan Secretary, Zamora, 22 February 1876; Ochoa Serrano, *Jiquilpan*, 122; and *El Eco de Ambos Mundos*, 16 January 1875.
116. *Estadística de la Sociedad Católica de Señoras*, 58.
117. Tapia Santamaría, "Identidad social y religión," 51–66.
118. ADZ, DGP 972, Sahuayo, Miguel del Castillo, Sahuayo to Diocesan Secretary, Zamora, 10 January 1870.
119. Holweck, "Special Devotions for Months."
120. ADZ, DG 104, Registro de Circulares, Circular No. 20, dated 19 April 1870.
121. ADZ, DGP 817, Purépero, Vicente Gutiérrez, Purépero, to Diocesan Secretary, Zamora, 12 September 1874; and DGP 643, Pajacuarán, Juan de Dios Porto, Pajacuarán, to Diocesan Secretary, Zamora, 23 April 1874.
122. ADZ, DGP 63, Charapan, Juan Bautista Morales, Charapan, to Diocesan Secretary, Zamora, 25 May 1868.
123. ADZ, DGP 505, Jiquilpan, Cosme Santa Anna, Jiquilpan, to Diocesan Secretary, Zamora, 18 May 1870.
124. ADZ, DGP 972, Sahuayo, Macario Saavedra, Sahuayo, to Diocesan Secretary, Zamora, 7 August 1875.
125. For liberal praise of Plancarte, see *La Idea Católica*, 6 July 1873 (which cites an article from Michoacán's official periodical praising Plancarte's schools), and *El Siglo Diez y Nueve*, 17 July 1871. The editors of *El Siglo Diez y Nueve* were especially impressed with Plancarte's efforts to connect Zamora and Jacona via rail in 1877–1878, a project for which he received the support of the state government. See *El Siglo Diez y Nueve*, 20 October 1877; and Tapia Méndez, *El siervo de dios*, 137–38.
126. *El Siglo Diez y Nueve*, 17 July 1871.
127. ADZ, DGP 241, Cotija, Miguel García and the Indians of the Barrio of San Juan, Cotija, to Diocesan Secretary, Zamora, 31 January 1871.
128. ADZ, DGP 241, Cotija, Benigno Tejeda, Cotija, to Diocesan Secretary, 6 February 1871. Interestingly, local historians describe the Barrio of San Juan as primarily Afro-mestizo. See Romero Vargas, *Cotija*, 25–26; and Tinajero Villaseñor, *Cotija*, 133–35.
129. ADZ, DGP 505, Jiquilpan, José María Pulido and the Indians of Jiquilpan to Diocesan Secretary, Zamora, 2 February 1871.
130. AGHPEM, Secretaria de Gobierno, Gobernación, Religión, caja 1, exp. 15, District Prefect, Jiquilpan, to Interior Minister, Morelia, 6 June 1874. Here,

Osio contrasted the pure, primitive faith founded by Christ with the corrupt and "scandalous" fanaticism of contemporary Mexico. Rather than intransigent liberal secularism, then, Osio pined for a restoration of the primitive Church and the stripping of baroque excess from religious practice, desires that parish priests and diocesan authorities often shared to one extent or another.

131. ADZ, DGP 717, Patamban, Victoriano Rosas, Patamban, to Diocesan Secretary, Zamora, 8 June 1866; Gerónimo Laurel, Patamban, to Diocesan Secretary, Zamora, 18 June 1866; and Diocesan Secretary, Zamora, to Gerónimo Laurel, Patamban, 18 June 1866.

132. Iñiguez Mendoza, "¡Viva la religión y mueran los *protestantes!*," 191–92.

133. ADZ, DGP 972, Sahuayo, Diocesan Secretary, Zamora, to Macario Saavedra, Sahuayo, 19 July 1874. On Afro-mestizo cultural influences in Sahuayo religiosity, see Ochoa Serrano, *Afrodescendientes*, 91–111, 129–56.

134. Tapia Méndez, *El siervo de dios*, 111–12. The quote is from Bautista García, *Clérigos virtuosos e instruidos*, 186. Here, Plancarte compares his burning of the popular saints' images with the "inquisition" mounted by the priest and housekeeper of Don Quixote, who condemned and then burned his library of works of chivalry.

135. ADZ, DGP 444, Jacona, Rafaela Hernández and other indigenous women of Jacona to Diocesan Secretary, Zamora, 28 March 1871; and Vecindario of Jacona to Diocesan Secretary, Zamora, 25 March 1871.

136. ADZ, DGP 444, Jacona, Ramón Samano and other indigenous men of Jacona to Diocesan Secretary, Zamora, 27 March 1871. Unfortunately, the petition(s) of Plancarte's accusers are missing from the parish records. The three surviving petitions on the matter are from defenders of Plancarte—the first from a group of indigenous women, the second from "vecinos" of Jacona, including civil officials, and the third from a group of indigenous men—and it is from their defense that we can infer the accusations of the principales.

137. ADZ, DGP 444, Jacona, Vecindario of Jacona to Diocesan Secretary, Zamora, 25 March 1871.

138. ADZ, DGP 444, Jacona, Rafaela Hernández and other indigenous women of Jacona to Diocesan Secretary, Zamora, 28 March 1871.

139. ADZ, DGP 419, Ixtlán, Antonio Hernández, Porfirio Hernández, Braulio Hernández, and other indigenous men of the community of San Cristobal Pajacuarán to Diocesan Secretary, Zamora, 24 February 1871; Diocesan Secretary, Zamora, to José Antonio Plancarte y Labastida, Jacona, 2 March 1871; Diligences practiced by José Antonio Plancarte y Labastida in Pajacuarán, 6 March 1871; Father Plancarte's summation and results of the diligences, 8 March 1871; and Diocesan Declaration of Innocence of Macario Saavedra, Zamora, 9 March 1871.

140. ADZ, DGP 74, Chavinda, Copy of a diocesan order issued to the priest of Chavinda, 13 May 1873. On Purépecha appropriations of Corpus Christi, see Baltazar Chávez, "El Corpus Christi Purhépecha," 191–201.

141. ADZ, DGP 419, Ixtlán, Santiago Ochoa and Benito Méndez, Ixtlán, to Diocesan Secretary, Zamora, 11 June 1870; and Diocesan Secretary, Zamora, to Santiago Ochoa and Benito Méndez, Ixtlán, 11 June 1870; and DGP 643, Pajacuarán, Juan de Dios Porto, Pajacuarán, to Diocesan Secretary, Zamora, 30 May 1874.
142. ADZ, DG 84, Diocesano/Secretaria/Correspondencia y Datos, Decree of the Bishop of Zamora, 13 January 1871.
143. ADZ, DG 138, Circulares de la Peña, Diocesan Circular Number 24, dated 24 November 1871. For a brief discussion of the *parroquias de tasación* in colonial Michoacán, see *Anales del Museo Nacional de México*, 424–25.
144. ADZ, DG 84, Secretaria/Correspondencia y Datos, Manuel Bruno Gutiérrez, Zamora, to José Antonio de la Peña, 17 January 1873.
145. An example of a pindecuario, from the pueblo of San Francisco Pichátaro, is found in *Anales del Museo Nacional de México*, 425–26.
146. ADZ, DGP 63, Rafael Méndez, Charapan, to Diocesan Secretary, Zamora, 12 March 1875. Ironically, other indigenous comuneros from Charapan had participated in a Religionero attack on Paracho in May of the same year. It is possible that Méndez was indeed involved in the Religionero conflict in the area, but it is perhaps equally likely that a faction of indigenous *charapenses* leveled the accusation at the priest as a way to exact revenge.
147. ADZ, DGP 972, Sahuayo, Inventory of the Parish of Sahuayo, 4 March 1875; DGP 505, Jiquilpan, Pascual Bayllac, Zamora, to Diocesan Secretary, Zamora, 19 June 1871; and Julián Pulido and the Indian Community of Jiquilpan to Diocesan Secretary, Zamora, 2 February 1871; Romero, *Noticias para formar*, 102; and Sánchez, *Bosquejo estadístico*, 150–58.
148. Ochoa Serrano, *Afrodesendientes*, 114.
149. Bautista García, *Clérigos virtuosos e instruidos*, 198–219.
150. ADZ, DGP 419, Ixtlán, Antonio Hernández, Porfirio Hernández, Braulio Hernández, and other indigenous men of the community of San Cristobal Pajacuarán to Diocesan Secretary, Zamora, 24 February 1871; Diocesan Secretary, Zamora, to José Antonio Plancarte y Labastida, Jacona, 2 March 1871; Diligences practiced by José Antonio Plancarte y Labastida in Pajacuarán, 6 March 1871; and Father Plancarte's summation and results of the diligences, 8 March 1871.
151. ADZ, DGP 972, Sahuayo, Fray Miguel del Castillo, Sahuayo, to Diocesan Secretary, 23 March 1871. The Colegio Apostólico de Zapopan was founded in 1816 as a convent and college of propaganda fide (that is, a seminary tasked with producing regular priests who would serve as missionaries). The Franciscans were exclaustered in 1866 when liberal forces took Guadalajara, but many friars chose to seek posts as parish priests in Mexico over foreign exile. See Portillo, *Apuntes histórico-geográficos del departamento de Zapopan*, 79–166.
152. AHPJEM, Penal, Juzgado Primero de Jiquilpan, caja 1, exp. 8, Arcadio Villamar vs. Lic. José Dolores del Río, December 1874; *El Pájaro Verde*, 9 March 1874; and *La Voz de México*, 7 March 1874.

153. On the reformist projects of Benigno Tejeda, longtime parish priest of Cotija and later Canon of the Zamora Cathedral, see Romero Vargas, *Cotija*, 130–31; and Tinajero Villaseñor, *Cotija*, 60–62.
154. Religioneros established strongholds in friendly ranchero populations such as San Juanico and Chavinda, as well as heavily Afro-mestizo populations such as Guaracha. Indulto lists published by *El Progresista* in early 1876 suggest that many rank-and-file Religioneros came from Jiquilpan, Cotija, Sahuayo, Cojumatlán, and Chavinda. See *El Progresista*, 27 January 1876, 6 February 1876, 14 August 1876, 25 August 1876, and 6 September 1876.
155. See AGHPEM, Guerra y Ejército, caja 2, exp. 23, Telegram, Jesús Rodríguez, Uruapan, to Interior Minister, Morelia, 11 February 1875; caja 5, exp. 72, Prudencio Casillas, Zamora, to Interior Minister, Morelia, 28 May 1875; and caja 5, exp. 78, Jesús Rodríguez, Uruapan, to Interior Minister, Morelia, 22 May 1875; *El Progresista*, 1 March 1875, and 7 September 1876; and *El Progresista*, 10 January 1876, and 14 August 1876.
156. See AGHPEM, Guerra y Ejército, caja 2, exp. 21, Herculano Ortega, Sahuayo, to Interior Minister, Morelia, 12 February 1875; and Ignacio Jiménez, Jiquilpan, to Interior Minister, Morelia, 17 February 1875.
157. AGHPEM, Guerra y Ejército, caja 4, exp. 70, Ignacio Jiménez, Jiquilpan, to Interior Minister, Morelia, 29 May 1875; and *El Progresista*, 13 April 1876, and 24 April 1876.
158. A gavilla of twenty rebels under Guarachita native Manuel Sandoval requested indulto in March. See *El Progresista*, 9 March 1876. Tingüindín's Esteban Farías was pardoned in June 1876. See *El Progresista*, 30 June 1876.
159. *El Progresista*, 27 January 1876, 31 July 1876, 14 August 1876, and 25 August 1876.
160. Rodríguez Sánchez, *La parroquia de Jiquilpan*, 19–21.
161. ADZ, DGP 505, Jiquilpan, Cosme Santa Anna, Jiquilpan, to Diocesan Secretary, Zamora, 25 April 1870.
162. ADZ, DGP 505, Jiquilpan, Cosme Santa Anna, Jiquilpan, to Diocesan Secretary, Zamora, 25 April 1870.
163. ADZ, DGP 505, Jiquilpan, Cosme Santa Anna, Jiquilpan, to Diocesan Secretary, Zamora, 25 May 1870.
164. ADZ, DGP 505, Jiquilpan, Various Vecinos of Jiquilpan to Diocesan Secretary, Zamora, 17 August 1872.
165. According to local Church historian Leopoldo Rodríguez, Bayllac had come to northwestern Michoacán with the French invaders in 1864. After a liberal victory at the Cerro of Trasquila drove out the French generals, however, Bayllac stayed on in Jiquilpan, perhaps hoping for a permanent appointment as parish priest. See Rodríguez Sánchez, *La parroquia de Jiquilpan*, 21–22.
166. ADZ, DGP 505, Jiquilpan, Narciso Martínez and the Indian Communities of Jiquilpan and Totolan to Diocesan Secretary, Zamora, 19 October 1872.

167. ADZ, DGP 505, Jiquilpan, Sociedad Femenina de Jiquilpan to Diocesan Secretary, Zamora, 12 August 1872.
168. ADZ, DGP 505, Jiquilpan, Amadeo Betancourt, Toribio Cardenas, and other Vecinos of Jiquilpan to Diocesan Secretary, 5 December 1872.
169. ADZ, DGP 505, Jiquilpan, Cosme Santa Anna, Jiquilpan, to Diocesan Secretary, Zamora, 18 May 1870.
170. ADZ, DGP 505, Jiquilpan, Vecinos in Association with the Indian Community of Jiquilpan to Diocesan Secretary, Zamora, 5 June 1873. Teodoro Mejía and Manuel Macías were well known to district authorities as Religionero chiefs. See AGHPEM, Guerra y Ejército, caja 4, exp. 59, Ignacio Jiménez, Jiquilpan, to Interior Minister, Morelia, 28 April 1875; and caja 3, exp. 49, Manuel Arreola, Morelia, to Interior Minister, Morelia, 31 March 1875. Francisco Amezcua and Jesús Cárdenas laid down their arms and received a pardon in Jiquilpan in 1876. See *El Progresista*, 6 February 1876, and 25 August 1876.
171. ADZ, DGP 505, Jiquilpan, Vecinos in Association with the Indian Community of Jiquilpan to Diocesan Secretary, Zamora, 5 June 1873.
172. ADZ, DGP 505, Jiquilpan, Vecinos in Association with the Indian Community of Jiquilpan to Diocesan Secretary, Zamora, 5 June 1873.
173. *El Progresista*, 17 January 1876, "Proceso de la Revolución."
174. AGHPEM, Guerra y Ejército, caja 4, exp. 70, Report Prepared by the District Prefect on the Military Action at San Antonio Guaracha, 26 June 1875. Pulido was in fact injured during a Religionero attack on Guaracha.
175. ADZ, DGP 505, Jiquilpan, Pascual Bayllac, Jiquilpan, to Diocesan Secretary, Zamora, 20 October 1875.
176. ADZ, DGP 505, Jiquilpan, Francisco Tejada de Leon, Jiquilpan, to Diocesan Secretary, Zamora, 12 June 1876.

Chapter 4

1. AGHPEM, Guerra y Ejército, caja 6, exp. 92, Municipal President of Huaniqueo to Interior Minister, Morelia, 19 April 1876; *El Progresista*, 20; and *La Voz de México*, 26 April 1876. Ruiz's report placed the incident at Zirimicua, but a Puruándiro-based correspondent for *La Voz* maintained that it took place at Zirate Hill, near Huaniqueo.
2. *La Voz de México*, 26 April 1876.
3. *La Voz de México*, 26 April 1876, 28 April 1876, and 29 April 1876; and *La Iberia*, 30 April 1876. Reyes requested that his final real and one-half be given to an uncle who had come to see him in Puruándiro.
4. The other condemned rebels were Epitacio Vargas (18), Mauricio Medina (14), Francisco Góngora (21), and Teodosio Tovar (24). All were described as

"jornaleros." See "México, Michoacán, registros parroquiales y diocesanos, 1555–1996," database with images, *FamilySearch* (https://familysearch.org/ark:/61903/3:1:9392-5RS3-9J?cc=1883388&wc=3NYN-3TL%3A178865201%2C17 8154202%2C180065503 : 20 May 2014), Puruándiro > San Juan Bautista > Defunciones 1858–1885 > images 348 and 349 of 570; parroquias Católicas, Michoacan (Catholic Church parishes, Michoacan), burial certificates for Socorro Reyes, Epitacio Vargas, Mauricio Medina, Francisco Góngora, and Teodosio Tovar, 19 April 1876.

5. AHCM, Diocesano/Gobierno/Correspondencia/Secretario, caja 119, exp. 571, Vicente F. Valdéz, Puruándiro, to Luis Macouzet, Morelia, 26 April 1876.
6. *El Pájaro Verde*, 29 April 1876; *La Voz de México*, 10 May 1876; and Iñiguez Mendoza, "¡Viva la religión y mueran los *protestantes*!," 364–66.
7. *La Bandera de Ocampo*, 23 April 1876; *El Correo del Comercio*, 26 April 1876; and Iñiguez Mendoza, "¡Viva la religión y mueran los *protestantes*!," 364–66.
8. *La Bandera de Ocampo*, 21 February 1875, and 28 February 1875.
9. See especially Iñiguez Mendoza, "¡Viva la religión y mueran los *protestantes*!," 312–13, which suggests a close relationship between Reyes's ideology and that of the intransigent clergy and carta-de-protesta toting laity.
10. The region's liberal history has escaped sustained study. Even Epitacio Huerta, who hailed from Coeneo's Tunguitiro Hacienda, has failed to receive a serious biographical treatment, beyond Raul Arreola Cortés's hagiographic *Epitacio Huerta: soldado y estadista liberal*. Neither have other liberal titans from the area—Eugenio Ronda, Rafael Garnica, Rafael Arias, and Rafael Rangel—been profiled.
11. Ortíz Ibarra and González Méndez, *Puruándiro*, 24–27; Vázquez López et al., *Huaniqueo*, 32; and Friedrich, *Agrarian Revolt in a Mexican Village*, 5–6.
12. Verástique, *Michoacán and Eden*, 11–13. Zacapu was in fact one of the first Purépecha settlements in Michoacán, and its fourteenth-century rulers established the sociopolitical framework for the lacustrine Purépecha Empire of later years.
13. Warren, *Conquest of Michoacán*, 25–80; and Ortíz Ibarra and González Méndez, *Puruándiro*, 35–42.
14. Ortíz Ibarra and González Méndez, *Puruándiro*, 45–49; and Álvarez Lira, *Aportaciones históricas sobre Villa Morelos*, 16–43. Both Miguel Hidalgo y Costilla and Agustín de Iturbide were descendants of Villaseñor.
15. Ortíz Ibarra and González Méndez, *Puruándiro*, 50–58; Álvarez Lira, *Aportaciones históricas sobre Villa Morelos*, 30–37; and Jackson, *Conflict and Conversion*, 41–50.
16. Jackson, *Conflict and Conversion*, 48–50.
17. Verástique, *Michoacán and Eden*, 98–99; Buitrón, *Apuntes para servir a la historia del arzobispado de Morelia*, 98–102; and Friedrich, *Agrarian Revolt in a Mexican Village*, 6.

18. Mazín Gómez, *El Gran Michoacán*, 126–29; and Romero, *Noticias para formar*, 88.
19. Vázquez López et al., *Huaniqueo*, 32–35; Ortíz Ibarra and González Méndez, *Puruándiro*, 50–58; and Romero, *Noticias para formar*, 88–90.
20. In fact, a 1760 report qualified Puruándiro's adobe parish church as the "most deplorable in the bishopric." Mazín Gómez, *El Gran Michoacán*, 123–24. See also Ortíz Ibarra and González Méndez, *Puruándiro*, 58; and Romero, *Noticias para formar*, 190–91.
21. Ortíz Ibarra and González Méndez, *Puruándiro*, 60–62; Bravo Ugarte, *Inspección ocular de Michoacán*, 45; and Mazín Gómez, *El Gran Michoacán*, 129, 326–32.
22. Bravo Ugarte, *Inspección ocular de Michoacán*, 45–55; Romero, *Noticias para formar*, 88–89; Purnell, *Popular Movements and State Formation*, 116–17; and Friedrich, *Agrarian Revolt in a Mexican Village*, 6–9.
23. Álvarez Lira, *Aportaciones históricas sobre Villa Morelos*, 70–71; Ortíz Ibarra and González Méndez, *Puruándiro*, 39–76; Chowning, *Wealth and Power in Provincial Mexico*, 98; Ruiz, *Historia de la guerra de intervención in Michoacán*, 608; Romero, *Noticias para formar*, 121; and Martínez Álvarez, *La Piedad*, 33–36. Agustín de Iturbide, another descendent of Villaseñor, began his royalist career in southwestern Guanajuato.
24. Ortíz Ibarra and González Méndez, *Puruándiro*, 81.
25. Florescano, *Historia general de Michoacán*, 17–18; Martínez Álvarez, *La Piedad*, 38–39; and Arreola Cortés, *Epitacio Huerta*, 5.
26. As Tutino argues in "The Revolution in Mexican Independence," the insurgency and early republican decades witnessed a "revolution" in agrarian relations and rural production in the Bajío, as ranchero families took over agricultural production from hacendados and negotiated new terms in their relationships with the estates. The Arias and Ronda families fit this pattern of ranchero expansion.
27. Ruiz, *Historia de la guerra de intervención en Michoacán*, 608–9; Ortíz Ibarra and González Méndez, *Puruándiro*, 81–84; and Florescano, *Historia general de Michoacán*, 18.
28. Here, the heavy lifting was performed by Guanajuato-born José Santos Degollado. Zacapu's local liberal chief, Juan García, also joined the Ayutla movement. See Ochoa Serrano and Sánchez Díaz, *Breve historia de Michoacán*, 132–34; and Ortíz Ibarra and González Méndez, *Puruándiro*, 85–88.
29. Cedeño Peguero, *El general Epitacio Huerta y su hacienda de Chucándiro*, 103–16; Arreola Cortés, *Epitacio Huerta*, 14–20; Ochoa Serrano and Sánchez Díaz, *Breve historia de Michoacán*, 155; and Chowning, *Wealth and Power in Provincial Mexico*, 289–90.
30. Closer to home, the imperialists recruited Cristobal Orozco, a caudillo based on the Zipimeo hacienda. See Ochoa Serrano and Sánchez Díaz, *Breve*

historia de Michoacán, 139–45; Ortíz Ibarra and González Méndez, *Puruándiro*, 92–104; Martínez Álvarez, *La Piedad*, 40–42; and Arreola Cortés, *Epitacio Huerta*, 26–50.

31. Ruiz, *Historia de la guerra de intervención en Michoacán*, 153, 300–62, 500–635; and Ortíz Ibarra and González Méndez, *Puruándiro*, 96–103.
32. Ortíz Ibarra and González Méndez, *Puruándiro*, 106; Martínez Álvarez, *La Piedad*, 40–45; and Ruiz, *Historia de la guerra de intervención en Michoacán*, 440–41.
33. Cosío Villegas, *La República Restaurada*, 446–54; González y González, "El liberalismo triunfante"; Arreola Cortés, *Epitacio Huerta*, 52–57; and Florescano, *Historia general de Michoacán*, 125.
34. Chowning, *Wealth and Power in Provincial Mexico*, 294–98. The bad blood between Juárez and Huerta dated back to the War of the French Intervention, when Juárez deprived Huerta of a high military post and Huerta objected to Juárez's insistence on remaining in power after the defeat of Maximilian. See Arreola Cortés, *Epitacio Huerta*, 50–52.
35. Florescano, *Historia general de Michoacán*, 4–5. Pátzcuaro district had an especially strong communal tradition.
36. Bravo Ugarte, *Inspección ocular de Michoacán*, 46–52; and Purnell, *Popular Movements and State Formation*, 116–17.
37. Purnell, *Popular Movements and State Formation*, 117–19.
38. AGHPEM, Hijuelas, District of Puruándiro, vol. I, Acta de reparto de bienes indígenas de la comunidad de Comanja, 10 April 1869; and Juan Velasco, Puruándiro, to Interior Minister, Morelia, 21 April 1869. The reparto process began anew in 1896. See AGHPEM, Hijuelas, District of Puruándiro, vol. I, Esteban Saavedra and other vecinos of Comanja to Interior Minister, Morelia, 16 May 1896.
39. Florescano, *Historia general de Michoacán*, 116.
40. AHPJEM, Juzgado Primero de Puruándiro, Penal, Legajo 1, exp. s/n 235, "Causa instruida contra el jefe de acordada de Coeneo por asesinato en la persona de Damasano Telles, apoderado general de la comunidad de indígenas de Tarejero," 6 May–3 June 1873. The accused murderer later could not remember committing the act.
41. Purnell, *Popular Movements and State Formation*, 118–20; and Purnell, "With All Due Respect," 101–11. The delaying tactics of Zacapu and Naranja did not prevent the alienation of indigenous lands in the long run, since during the Porfiriato groups of mestizo outsiders insinuated themselves into the pueblos and worked to break up communal land through legal and extralegal means.
42. Accounts of the attack on Zacapu do not specifically mention the participation of Indians, but since Pedro González and Socorro Reyes often passed through the ciénega pueblos without resistance, it is reasonable to assume some communities offered passive support. See, for example, AGHPEM, Guerra y Ejército, caja 2, exp. 18, Telegram, Municipal President of Zacapu to Interior

Minister, Morelia, 19 February 1875; caja 4, exp. 57, Eduardo Gil, Pátzcuaro, to Interior Minister, Morelia, 17 April 1875; caja 4, exp. 65, Albino Fuentes Acosta, Puruándiro, to Interior Minister, Morelia, 11 June 1875; caja 5, exp. 78, Municipal President of Zacapu, to Interior Minister, 26 May 1875; and caja 5, exp. 88, Eduardo Gil, Pátzcuaro, to Interior Minister, Morelia, 7 June 1875.

43. Indigenous police officers in Zipiajo alerted the government to the movement of Socorro Reyes's gavilla in June 1875, for example. AGHPEM, Guerra y Ejército, caja 4, exp. 65, Albino Fuentes Acosta, Puruándiro, to Interior Minister, Morelia, 11 June 1875.

44. As Bazant shows in *The Alienation of Church Wealth in Mexico*, adjudications of ecclesiastical properties occurred more rapidly and with considerably fewer obstacles in Mexico than did the disentailment of indigenous communities.

45. AGHPEM, Hijuelas, District of Puruándiro, vol. 3, José María Herrera, Puruándiro, to Interior Minister, Morelia, 28 August 1870; Jesús Quirino, Morelia, to Albino Fuentes Acosta, Puruándiro, 13 July 1872; and Hesiquio Quiroz and other Indians of Angamacutiro to Interior Minister, Morelia, 25 August 1883.

46. AGHPEM, Hijuelas, District of Puruándiro, vol. I, Acta de reparto de bienes indígenas de la comunidad de Coeneo, 17 March 1869; and José María Barriga, Coeneo, to Interior Minister, Morelia, 10 April 1869.

47. AGHPEM, Hijuelas, District of Puruándiro, vol. 3, Antonio Vargas and the Indigenous Community of Huango to Interior Minister, Morelia, 11 June 1872; Interior Minister, Morelia, to Albino Fuentes Acosta, Puruándiro, 25 July 1872; Interior Minister, Morelia, to Albino Fuentes Acosta, Puruándiro, 23 February 1873; Albino Fuentes Acosta, Puruándiro, to Interior Minister, Morelia, 18 March 1873; and José María Real, Villa Morelos, to Interior Minister, 10 September 1902.

48. AGHPEM, Hijuelas, District of Puruándiro, vol. 2, Acta de Reparto, 25 January 1869; Comisión Repartidora of Huaniqueo, Puruándiro, to Interior Minister, Morelia, 6 April 1869; Juan Velasco, Puruándiro, to Interior Minister, Morelia, 7 April 1869; and Juan Velasco, Puruándiro, to Interior Minister, Morelia, 25 January 1870.

49. AGHPEM, Hijuelas, District of Puruándiro, vol. 2, Antonio Cilagua, Huaniqueo, to Interior Minister, Morelia, 28 January 1873.

50. AGHPEM, Hijuelas, District of Puruándiro, vol. 2, Albino Fuentes Acosta, Puruándiro, to Interior Minister, Morelia, 14 December 1873.

51. AGHPEM, Hijuelas, District of Puruándiro, vol. 2, Rafael Carrillo, Morelia, to Albino Fuentes Acosta, Puruándiro, 16 December 1873.

52. AGHPEM, Guerra y Ejército, caja 2, exp. 15, Albino Fuentes Acosta, Puruándiro, to Interior Minister, Morelia, 29 January 1875; and *El Eco de Ambos Mundos*, 20 February 1875.

53. Soto Correa, *Movimientos campesinos de derecha*; and Tutino, *From Insurrection to Revolution*.

54. *El Progresista*, 12 January 1874, 16 February 1874, and 16 March 1874.

55. *El Progresista*, 4 May 1874.
56. *El Progresista*, 25 June 1874, and 6 August 1874.
57. *El Progresista*, 17 September 1874. Rangel's death sentence was commuted to six years in prison on November. See *La Bandera de Ocampo*, 21 November 1874.
58. Excerpted in Bautista García, "La reorganización de la iglesia," 93.
59. AGHPEM, Guerra y Ejército, caja 2, exp. 13, Telegram, Albino Fuentes Acosta, Puruándiro, to Interior Minister, Morelia, 8 January 1875.
60. AGHPEM, Guerra y Ejército, caja 2, exp. 13, Albino Fuentes Acosta, Puruándiro, to Interior Minister, Morelia, 12 January 1875. The text of the manifesto reads: "People: long live fraternity, equality, liberty, and democracy, but death to monarchy and all of its despotic forces. Death to the cynical aristocracy that, draped in the democratic mantle, oppresses you and mocks your sovereignty; and instead of [sovereignty] you have the Deputies of the Congress, amongst them Sr. Lic. Don Justo Mendoza, who cynically confesses that in his office he has mocked Free Suffrage, and the confessions of this same person are the most useful. Mexican people: the freedom of worship is not in your interests, because you are exclusively Catholic. And it is not permissible for our Governors to authorize [it] even if this were an obvious truth. Because there are truths that when society does not ask for their explanation must be [considered] highly speculative. This is not to say I want to be a theocrat. Long live the Government where the public right follows logic and does not disturb the peace."
61. AGHPEM, Guerra y Ejército, caja 2, exp. 13, Rafael Salinas, Coeneo, to Interior Minister, Morelia, 26 January 1875; and exp. 15, Albino Fuentes Acosta, Puruándiro, to Interior Minister, Morelia, 29 January 1875; and *El Eco de Ambos Mundos*, 20 February 1875.
62. AGHPEM, Guerra y Ejército, caja 2, exp. 15, Albino Fuentes Acosta, Puruándiro, to Interior Minister, Morelia, 30 January 1875.
63. AGHPEM, Guerra y Ejército, caja 2, exp. 15, Albino Fuentes Acosta, Puruándiro, to Interior Minister, Morelia, 1 February 1875; Rafael Salinas, Coeneo, to Interior Minister, Morelia, 6 February 1875; Albino Fuentes Acosta, Puruándiro, to Interior Minister, Morelia, 13 February 1875; and exp. 38, Albino Fuentes Acosta, Puruándiro, to Interior Minister, Morelia, 20 March 1875.
64. AGHPEM, Guerra y Ejército, caja 2, exp. 15, Albino Fuentes Acosta, Puruándiro, to Interior Minister, Morelia, 17 February 1875; Albino Fuentes Acosta, Puruándiro, to Interior Minister, Morelia, 18 February 1875; Jesús Ladislao Ortega, 1st Section, Ejército Salvador de México, Central Operations, to Jesús Ramos, Huango, 18 February 1875; and Albino Fuentes Acosta, Puruándiro, to Interior Minister, Morelia, 21 February 1875.
65. AGHPEM, Guerra y Ejército, caja 3, exp. 55, Gerónimo Ponce, Quiroga, to Interior Minister, Morelia, 4 April 1875.

66. AGHPEM, Guerra y Ejército, caja 2, exp. 17, Interior Minister, Morelia, to Municipal President, Quiroga, 27 February 1875.
67. AGHPEM, Guerra y Ejército, caja 3, exp. 38, Interior Minister, Morelia, to Albino Fuentes Acosta, Puruándiro, 10 March 1875; caja 3, exp. 49, Jesús Rodríguez, Uruapan, to Interior Minister, Morelia, 3 April 1875; and Jesús Rodríguez, Uruapan, to Interior Minister, Morelia, 5 April 1875.
68. AGHPEM, Guerra y Ejército, caja 4, exp. 57, Eduardo Gil y Villamil, Pátzcuaro, to Interior Minister, Morelia, 17 April 1875; *El Progresista*, 22 April 1875; and *La Bandera de Ocampo*, 25 April 1875.
69. AGHPEM, Guerra y Ejército, caja 4, exp. 58, Albino Fuentes Acosta Puruándiro, to Interior Minister, Morelia, 9 May 1875.
70. AGHPEM, Guerra y Ejército, caja 4, exp. 58, Albino Fuentes Acosta, Puruándiro, to Interior Minister, Morelia, 7 May 1875; AHDN, Operaciones Militares, XI/481.4/9211, Prisciliano Flores, La Piedad, to José Ceballos, Guadalajara, 12 May 1875; and *El Progresista*, 24 May 1875.
71. AGHPEM, Guerra y Ejército, caja 4, exp. 65, Albino Fuentes Acosta, Puruándiro, to Interior Minister, Morelia, 11 June 1875.
72. AGHPEM, Guerra y Ejército, caja 4, exp. 65, Albino Fuentes Acosta, Puruándiro, to Interior Minister, Morelia, 6 June 1875; caja 4, exp. 68, Eduardo Gil y Villamil, Pátzcuaro, 22 June 1875; and caja 5, exp. 72, Rafael Ahumada, Morelia, to Interior Minister, Morelia, 10 July 1875.
73. *El Progresista*, 6 March 1875; AGHPEM, Guerra y Ejército, caja 3, exp. 53, Prisciliano Flores, La Piedad, to Interior Minister, Morelia, 3 April 1875; caja 5, exp. 78, Jesús Rodríguez, Uruapan, to Secretary of Government, Morelia, 13 May 1875; and caja 5, exp. 86, Albino Fuentes Acosta, Puruándiro, to Interior Minister, Morelia, 14 July 1875.
74. AGHPEM, Guerra y Ejército, caja 4, exp. 58, Rafael Salinas, Coeneo, to Interior Minister, Morelia, 30 May 1875.
75. *El Progresista*, 25 November 1875; and *La Voz de México*, 11 December 1875.
76. *El Progresista*, 2 December 1875; and *El Correo del Comercio*, 7 December 1875.
77. *El Progresista*, 13 January 1876.
78. *El Progresista*, 10 January 1876.
79. *El Progresista*, 24 January 1876.
80. *El Progresista*, 31 January 1876. Faced with a shortage of National Guard troops, local authorities placed Martínez Salazar and his former Religioneros in charge of defending Huango from further attacks. The plan backfired, since they quickly defected to the rebels' side when the Religioneros attacked Huango again in May. See *El Progresista*, 18 May 1876.
81. *El Progresista*, 9 March 1875, and 20 April 1875.
82. Raya sacked Huango again in May and attacked Angamacutiro in July. See *El Progresista*, 25 May 1875, and 6 July 1875.
83. *El Progresista*, 11 November 1875.

84. Vanderwood, *Power of God against the Guns of Government.*
85. See chapter 5; and Mijangos y González, "La respuesta popular al juramento constitucional en 1857."
86. Martínez Baracs, *Convivencia y utopia*, 96–97; Verástique, *Michoacán and Eden*, 98; and Domínguez, "Zacapu," 187–89.
87. Ricard, *Spiritual Conquest of Mexico*, 283–95; Leddy Phelan, *Millennial Kingdom of the Franciscans*, 59–68; and Verástique, *Michoacán and Eden*, 97–103.
88. Verástique, *Michoacán and Eden*, 97–107.
89. Muriel, "Las cofradías hospitalarias," 230–33; and Baltazar Chávez, "El Corpus Christi P'urhépecha," 191–201.
90. Rubin, *Corpus Christi*, chap. 3.
91. Baltazar Chávez, "El Corpus Christi P'urhépecha," 133–46.
92. Baltazar Chávez, "El Corpus Christi P'urhépecha," 133–46. See also Tanck de Estrada, "Las tres principales fiestas de los pueblos de indios."
93. Friedrich, *Agrarian Revolt in a Mexican Village*, 32–36. For references to the rotational structure in the 1870s, see AHCM, Diocesano/Gobierno/Parroquias/Solicitudes, caja 279, exp. 481, Luis Macouzet, Morelia, to Hilario Castro, Coeneo, 21 June 1872; and Diocesano/Gobierno/Correspondencia/Secretario, caja 118, exp. 565, Francisco de P. Morillón, Coeneo, to Luis Macouzet, Morelia, 13 April 1874.
94. Zacapu was secularized in 1782, Tzintzuntzan in 1762, and Quiroga in 1754. See Mazín Gómez, "Secularización de parroquias en el antiguo Michoacán," 33; and Mazín Gómez, *El Gran Michoacán*, 129–30.
95. Taylor and Chance, "Cofradías and Cargos," offers a now-classic account of how the collective fiesta sponsorship structure of the cofradía transformed during the eighteenth and nineteenth centuries into the modern cargo system, in which individual community members or families took turns financing fiestas. More recently, Daniela Traffano traces such a shift locally in her article "Para formar el corazón religioso de los jóvenes." In Michoacán, the evidence of both the persistence of cofradía lands and the use of mayordomías in extant documentation suggests that the two institutions coexisted for some time during the nineteenth century. The reparto process, especially, threatened the old fiesta system, since it mandated the break-up of cofradía lands. See Purnell, *Popular Movements and State Formation*, 112–24.
96. Bravo Ugarte, *Inspección ocular de Michoacán*, 43–53. Coeneo's cofradía possessed 100 head of cattle and 108 horses; Tarejero's, 15 cattle; Naranja's 50 cattle and 5 horses; Tiríndaro's 7 cattle, 20 sheep, and 20 horses.
97. Romero, *Noticias para formar*, 88–89. Romero singled out the more wealthy Azajo for special praise, calling its chapel "very good, and with decent *paramentos*."
98. Jackson, *Conflict and Conversion*, 40–58.
99. Jackson, 49–50; Basalenque, *Historia de la provincia de San Nicolás Tolentino de Michoacán*, 299–301; and Álvarez Lira, *Aportaciones históricas*, 5–6. Such

miracles had limits: The two friars died within several days, likely from their injuries.
100. Álvarez Lira, *Aportaciones históricas*, 30–37.
101. Álvarez Lira, 100–6. For a biographical sketch of Tomas de Villanueva, see Dohan, "St. Thomas of Villanova."
102. Saint Nicholas of Tolentino was a thirteenth-century Italian saint of the Augustinian order known for his preaching. See Garesché, "St. Nicholas of Toletino."
103. Álvarez Lira, *Aportaciones históricas sobre Villa Morelos*, 74–76; and Romero, *Noticias para formar*, 127.
104. Romero, *Noticias para formar*, 125–27.
105. Ortíz Ibarra and González Méndez, *Puruándiro*, 60–62; Bravo Ugarte, *Inspección ocular de Michoacán*, 45; Mazín Gómez, *El Gran Michoacán*, 129, 326–32; and Tutino, "Revolution in Mexican Independence."
106. Mazín Gómez, *El Gran Michoacán*, 123–24, 328; and Romero, *Noticias para formar*, 126.
107. Álvarez Lira, *Aportaciones históricas*, 77–80.
108. Voekel, *Alone before God*, 43–145; and Larkin, *Very Nature of God*, 168–87.
109. Mazín Gómez, *El Gran Michoacán*, 123–30; Bravo Ugarte, *Inspección ocular de Michoacán*, 40–55; and Romero, *Noticias para formar*, 87–89, 125–27. Canon Romero found that Coeneo, Teremendo, and Huaniqueo were each served by a priest and one vicar in the 1850s, while Huango and Zacapu both had a priest and two vicars.
110. Bautista García, *Clérigos virtuosos e instruidos*, 74–78.
111. Baltazar Chávez, "El Corpus Christi P'urhépecha," 186–89; Traslosheros Hernández, *La reforma de la iglesia del antiguo Michoacán*, 72–76; and Mazín Gómez, *Entre dos majestades*, 36–68.
112. On the instability of religious administration during the Insurgency, see Ibarra López, *La iglesia de Michoacán*. On Bourbon attitudes toward baroque festivals, see Linda Curcio Nagy, *Great Festivals of Colonial Mexico City*, 97–119; Voekel, *Alone before God*, 117–19; and Larkin, *Very Nature of God*, chaps. 8 and 9.
113. AHCM, Diocesno/Gobierno/Parroquias/Solicitudes, caja 278, exp. 463, Luis Ugarte and the indigenous community of Zacapu to Luis Macouzet, Morelia, 6 May 1868; and Luis Macouzet, Morelia, to Luis Ugarte and other principales of the indigenous community of Zacapu, 8 May 1868.
114. AHCM, Diocesano/Gobierno/Mandatos/Circulares, caja 189, exp. 271, Acta de Visita of the Villa of Zacapu, 3 October 1871. The chapels of San Juan and the hospital would also have to be properly cleaned and decorated before the priest could celebrate the Mass in them.
115. AHCM, Diocesano/Gobierno/Parroquias/Solicitudes, caja 278, exp. 449, Diego Navarro, Coeneo, to Archdiocesan Secretary, Morelia, 29 June 1864;

License for the procession of Corpus Christi in Zipiajo, 1 July 1864; and Juan Nepomuceno Malabehar, Coeneo, to Archdiocesan Secretary, Morelia, 30 June 1865.

116. AHCM, Diocesano/Gobierno/Parroquias/Solicitudes, caja 278, exp. 458, Luis Macouzet, Morelia, to Jacinto Juan and the cargo-holders of Tiríndaro, 2 April 1867; and AHCM, Diocesano/Gobierno/Parroquias/Solicitudes, caja 279, exp. 468, Luis Macouzet, Morelia, to Antonio Hernández, Coeneo, 28 May 1870.

117. AHCM, Diocesano/Gobierno/Parroquias/Solicitudes, caja 279, exp. 481, Cruz Silva and the authorities and community of Zipiajo to Luis Macouzet, Morelia, 15 June 1872; and Hilario Castro, Coeneo, to Luis Macouzet, Morelia, 1 July 1872. Castro's letter is discussed at greater length below.

118. AHCM, Diocesano/Gobierno/Parroquias/Solicitudes, caja 279, exp. 481, Luis Macouzet, Morelia, to Cruz Silva and the Indigenous Community of Zipiajo, 3 July 1872; Atanacio Rodríguez and the Indigenous Community of Zipiajo to Luis Macouzet, Morelia, 10 June 1873; and Luis Macouzet, Morelia, to Atanacio Rodríguez, Zipiajo, 1 July 1873.

119. AHCM, Diocesano/Gobierno/Correspondencia/Secretario, caja 117, exp. 559, Juan Menéndez, Naranja, to Luis Macouzet, Morelia, 13 June 1873.

120. AHCM, Diocesano/Gobierno/Correspondencia/Secretario, caja 118, exp. 565, Francisco de Paul Morillón, Coeneo, to Luis Macouzet, Morelia, 13 April 1874; and Luis Macouzet, Morelia, to Francisco de Paul Morillón, Coeneo, 13 April 1874.

121. AHCM, Diocesano/Gobierno/Correspondencia/Secretario, caja 119, exp. 573, Francisco de Paul Morillón, Coeneo, to Luis Macouzet, Morelia, 7 May 1876; Antonio Hernández, Zipiajo, to Luis Macouzet, Morelia, 28 June 1876; and Luis Macouzet, Morelia, to Antonio Hernandez, Zipiajo, 28 June 1876.

122. AHCM, Diocesano/Gobierno/Correspondencia/Secretario, caja 119, exp. 574, Francisco de Paul Morillón, Coeneo, to Luis Macouzet, Morelia, 22 March 1877; AHCM, Dioceano/Gobierno/Parroquias/Solicitudes, caja 280, exp. 511, Simón Medina and other vecinos of Puruándiro to Luis Macouzet, Morelia, 17 October 1877; and AHCM, Diocesano/Gobierno/Parroquias/Solicitudes, caja 280, exp. 507, Francisco de Paul Morillón, Coeneo, to Luis Macouzet, Morelia, 26 June 1877. In the latter petition, Morillón requests permission for Corpus processions in Tiríndaro and Naranja, adding that the tradition was "immemorial" in Tiríndaro and had taken place for at least ten years in Naranja.

123. An April 1875 report on the gavillas operating in the district of Puruándiro, for example, lists only nineteen Religioneros from Coeneo (compared to over fifty from Huaniqueo and nearly three dozen from Huango), none of whom were identified as indigenous. See AGHPEM, Guerra y Ejército, caja 3, exp. 49, Albino Fuentes Acosta, Puruándiro, to Interior Minister, Morelia, 18 April 1875.

124. AHCM, Diocesano/Gobierno/Parroquias/Solicitudes, caja 278, exp. 463, Santiago Marcial, Felipe Neri, and other members of the indigenous community of Coeneo to Luis Macouzet, Morelia, 12 April 1868; and Luis Macouzet, Morelia, to Santiago Marcial and Felipe Neri, Coeneo, 14 April 1868.
125. AHCM, Diocesano/Gobierno/Parroquias/Solicitudes, caja 279, exp. 476, Hilario Castro, Coeneo, to Luis Macouzet, Morelia, 1 July 1872.
126. AHCM, Diocesano/Gobierno/Parroquias/Solicitudes, caja 279, exp. 476, Luis Macouzet, Morelia, to the Principales of the Community of Zipiajo, 3 July 1872.
127. AHCM, Diocesano/Gobierno/Parroquias/Solicitudes, caja 279, exp. 476, Rosalio López and the Principales of Coeneo to Luis Macouzet, Morelia, 14 July 1871.
128. AHCM, Diocesano/Gobierno/Parroquias/Solicitudes, caja 279, exp. 476, Hilario Castro, Coeneo, to Luis Macouzet, 20 August 1871.
129. AHCM, Diocesano/Gobierno/Parroquias/Solicitudes, caja 279, exp. 476, Hilario Castro, Coeneo, to Luis Macouzet, 20 August 1871.
130. AHCM, Diocesano/Gobierno/Parroquias/Solicitudes, caja 279, exp. 476, José Dolores Zavala, Coeneo, to Hilario Castro, Coeneo, 30 April 1871; and Hilario Castro, Coeneo, to Luis Macouzet, Morelia, 18 February 1873.
131. AHCM, Diocesano/Gobierno/Parroquias/Solicitudes, caja 279, exp. 476, Hilario Castro, Coeneo, to Luis Macouzet, 20 August 1871.
132. It is unclear what role or position Epitacio Huerta took during the parish conflicts of 1871–1873. According to Castro, Epitacio and his brother Antonio attended the 1871 community meeting on the fate of the ancient cemetery plot, where they seem to have supported the effort to sell the land in order to finance the reconstruction of the parish temple. This fact, and the fact that Antonio Huerta would lend his signature to a petition in favor of Castro in 1873, suggests that the Huertas might have been supporters of the priest's reformist projects in general.
133. AHCM, Diocesano/Gobierno/Parroquias/Solicitudes, caja 279, exp. 487, Pedro Ponce and other vecinos of Coeneo to Luis Macouzet, Morelia, 15 February 1873.
134. AHCM, Diocesano/Gobierno/Parroquias/Solicitudes, caja 279, exp. 487, Women of the Vela Perpetua, Coeneo, to Luis Macouzet, Morelia, 13 February 1873.
135. AHCM, Diocesano/Gobierno/Parroquias/Solicitudes, caja 279, exp. 476, Hilario Castro, Coeneo, to Luis Macouzet, Morelia, 18 February 1873.
136. AHCM, Diocesano/Gobierno/Correspondencia/Secretario, caja 118, exp. 564, Hilario Castro, Zitácuaro, to Luis Macouzet, Morelia, 12 October 1874.
137. AGHPEM, Guerra y Ejército, caja 2, exp. 15, Albino Fuentes Acosta, Puruándiro, to Interior Minister, Morelia, 15 January 1875; AGHPEM,

Guerra y Ejército, caja 4, exp. 65, Albino Fuentes Acosta, Puruándiro, to Interior Minister, Morelia, 11 June 1875; *El Progresista*, 14 June 1875; and Iñiguez Mendoza, "¡Viva la religión y mueran los *protestantes*!," 286. Liberal observers claimed that Religioneros under Antonio Reza had attempted to recruit Arias earlier that year, and his assassination at the hands of Pedro González in June was thus punishment for declining to join the Religioneros. See *El Correo del Comercio*, 23 June 1875.

138. AHCM, Diocesano/Gobierno/Parroquias/Solicitudes, Domingo Herrera and other vecinos of Coeneo to Luis Macouzet, Morelia, 12 May 1877. Reyes is identified as a rebel in *El Progresista*, 16 March 1876.

139. AHCM, Diocesano/Gobierno/Correspondencia/Secretario, caja 118, exp. 565, Francisco de Paul Morillón, Coeneo, to Luis Macouzet, Morelia, 15 March 1874; Francisco de Paul Morillón, Coeneo, to Luis Macouzet, Morelia, 13 April 1874; Luis Macouzet, Morelia, to Francisco de Paul Morillón, 13 April 1874; and Francisco de Paul Morillón, Coeneo, to Luis Macouzet, Morelia, 14 June 1874; AHCM, Diocesano/Gobierno/Correspondencia/Secretario, caja 119, exp. 573, Francisco de Paul Morillón, Coeneo, to Luis Macouzet, Morelia, 7 May 1876 and 28 June 1876; and AHCM, Diocesano/Gobierno/Correspondencia/Secretario, caja 118, exp. 564, Francisco de Paul Morillón, Coeneo, to Luis Macouzet, Morelia, 22 March 1877.

140. AHCM, Diocesano/Gobierno/Correspondencia/Secretario, caja 119, exp. 569, Francisco de Paul Morillón, Coeneo, to Luis Macouzet, Morelia, 22 February 1875; and Antonio Hernández, Coeneo, to Luis Macouzet, Morelia, 9 March 1875.

141. AHCM, Diocesano/Gobierno/Correspondencia/Secretario, caja 119, exp. 574, Francisco de Paul Morillón, Coeneo, to Luis Macouzet, Morelia, 22 October 1877.

142. Chowning, *Wealth and Power in Provincial Mexico*, 139; and Ruiz, *Historia de la guerra de intervención en Michoacán*, 300, 360–62, 500.

143. AHCM, Diocesano/Gobierno/Parroquias/Inventarios, caja 252, exp. 86, Inventory of the Parish of Huaniqueo, 26 May 1866.

144. AHCM, Diocesano/Gobierno/Parroquias/Solicitudes, caja 279, exp. 485, Pedro Arroyo, Huaniqueo, to Luis Macouzet, Morelia, 25 May 1872; and Romero, *Noticias para formar*, 89.

145. AHCM, Diocesano/Gobierno/Parroquias/Solicitudes, caja 280, exp. 508, Manuel Díaz Barriga and other vecinos of Huaniqueo to Luis Macouzet, Morelia, 18 June 1877.

146. AHCM, Diocesano/Gobierno/Parroquias/Informes, caja 247, exp. 393, Pedro Arroyo, Huaniqueo, to Luis Macouzet, Morelia, 9 May 1872. While he declined to break down the numbers by month or year, Arroyo reported collecting 1,502 pesos in baptism fees, 1,452 in marriage fees, and 2,054 in burial

fees between April 1867 and April 1872, earning him an average of 1001 pesos per year in obventions.

147. AHCM, Diocesano/Gobierno/Parroquias/Solicitudes, caja 280, exp. 508, Wenseslao Pérez and other vecinos of Huaniqueo to Luis Macouzet, 20 June 1877.

148. AHCM, Diocesano/Gobierno/Parroquias/Solicitudes, caja 280, exp. 501, Trinidad Flores and Teofilo Villa, Huaniqueo, to Luis Macouzet, Morelia, 12 October 1875. The archbishop saw things differently, though, and he informed communal leaders that despite what Arroyo had told them, any profits resulting from the sale of cofradía lands properly belonged to the Church and not the community. See AHCM, Diocesano/Gobierno/Parroquias/Solicitudes, caja 280, exp. 501, Luis Macouzet, Morelia, to Trinidad Flores and Teofilo Villa, Huaniqueo, 12 October 1875.

149. AHCM, Diocesano/Gobierno/Correspondencia/Secretario, caja 119, exp. 567, Ramón Moreno, Huaniqueo, to Luis Macouzet, Morelia, 15 April 1875.

150. AHCM, Diocesano/Gobierno/Correspondencia/Secretario, caja 118, exp. 562, Ramón Moreno, Huaniqueo, to Luis Macouzet, Morelia, 8 June 1875.

151. AHCM, Diocesano/Gobierno/Correspondencia/Secretario, caja 117, exp. 559, Ramón Moreno, Huango, to Luis Macouzet, Morelia, 24 December 1873.

152. AHCM, Diocesano/Gobierno/Correspondencia/Secretario, caja 119, exp. 567, Ramón Moreno, Huaniqueo, to Luis Macouzet, Morelia, 15 April 1875; and Luis Macouzet, Morelia, to Ramon Moreno, Huaniqueo, 15 April 1875.

153. AHCM, Diocesano/Gobierno/Parroquias/Solicitudes, caja 280, exp. 508, Wenseslao Pérez and other vecinos of Huaniqueo to Luis Macouzet, Morelia, 20 June 1877; and AGHPEM, Guerra y Ejército, caja 3, exp. 49, Albino Fuentes Acosta, Puruándiro, to Interior Minister, Morelia, 18 April 1875 ("List of the individuals who have formed gavillas in this district").

154. *La Voz de México*, 1 April 1875; *La Bandera de Ocampo*, 6 February 1876, 23 April 1876; *El Correo del Comercio*, 28 April 1876; AGHPEM, Guerra y Ejército, caja 2, exp. 13, Albino Fuentes Acosta, Puruándiro, to Interior Minister, Morelia, 27 January 1875; and Iñiguez Mendoza, "Viva la religión y mueran los *protestantes!*," 264.

155. AHCM, Diocesano/Gobierno/Correspondencia/Secretario, caja 118, exp. 565, Pedro Arroyo, Huaniqueo, to Luis Macouzet, Morelia, 24 June 1874.

156. AGHPEM, Guerra y Ejército, caja 2, exp. 13, Rafael Salinas, Coeneo, to Interior Minister, Morelia, 26 January 1875; caja 2, exp. 15, Albino Fuentes Acosta, Puruándiro, to Interior Minister, Morelia, 16, 17, and 21 February 1875; caja 3, exp. 38, Albino Fuentes Acosta, Puruándiro, to Interior Minister, Morelia, 27 February 1875; caja 5, exp. 86, Albino Fuentes Acosta, Puruándiro, to Interior Minister, Morelia, 4 July 1875; and Albino Fuentes Acosta, Puruándiro, to Interior Minister, Morelia, 24 July 1875.

157. Romero, *Noticias para formar*, 126; and Tutino, "Revolution in Mexican Independence."
158. AHCM, Diocesano/Gobierno/Sacerdotes/Informes, caja 448, exp. 387, Ramon Cipriano Torres, Huango, to Luis Macouzet, Morelia, 3 April 1869.
159. AHCM, Diocesano/Gobierno/Correspondencia/Secretario, caja 117, exp. 553, Ramón Cipriano Torres, Huango, to Luis Macouzet, Morelia, 8 May 1872. For a discussion of the practice of ritual abduction and elopement, or "rapto," see Sloan, *Runaway Daughters*.
160. AHCM, Diocesano/Gobierno/Parroquias/Informes, caja 247, exp. 393, Ramón Cipriano Torres, Huango, to Luis Macouzet, Morelia, 13 February 1873.
161. AHCM, Diocesano/Gobierno/Parroquias/Informes, caja 247, exp. 393, Ramón Cipriano Torres, Huango, to Luis Macouzet, Morelia, 13 February 1873. For example, Torres collected 408 pesos in baptism fees in 1864, 385 in 1868, and 396 in 1871. Marriage fees, too, remained mostly flat, staring at 379 in 1864 and ending at 353 in 1871.
162. AHCM, Diocesano/Gobierno/Parroquias/Solicitudes, caja 279, exp. 487, Vecinos of Huango to Luis Macouzet, 5 June 1873.
163. AHCM, Diocesano/Gobierno/Parroquias/Solicitudes, caja 279, exp. 478, Antonio Gaitán, Ramón Bolaños, and other vecinos of Huango to Luis Macouzet, Morelia, 6 February 1873.
164. AHCM, Diocesano/Gobierno/Parroquias/Solicitudes, caja 279, exp. 478, Ramón Cipriano Torres, Huango, to Luis Macouzet, Morelia, 7 February 1873.
165. AHCM, Diocesano/Gobierno/Parroquias/Solicitudes, caja 279, exp. 478, Epigenio López and Antonio Gaitán, Huango, to Luis Macouzet, 20 February 1872. The image retained its popular appeal and miraculous qualities in subsequent years. According to an 1880 parish inventory, the Lord possessed eighty-one silver milagros (small stamped pieces of metal with human, animal, and anatomical shapes that serve as offerings to particular saints for miracles performed). See AHCM, Diocesano/Gobierno/Parroquias/Inventarios, caja 252, exp. 114, Inventory of the Parish of Huango, 22 December 1880.
166. AHCM, Diocesano/Gobierno/Correspondencia/Secretario, caja 117, exp. 559, Ramón Moreno, Huango, Luis Macouzet, Morelia, 24 December 1873.
167. AHCM, Diocesano/Gobierno/Correspondencia/Secretario, caja 117, exp. 559, Luis Macouzet, Morelia, to Ramón Moreno, Huango, 24 December 1873.
168. AHCM, Diocesano/Gobierno/Correspondencia/Secretario, caja 117, exp. 559, Luis Macouzet, Morelia, to Ramón Cipriano Torres, Huango, 13 December 1873.
169. AHCM, Diocesano/Gobierno/Parroquias/Solicitudes, caja 280, exp. 494, Luis G. García and other vecinos of Huango to Luis Macouzet, Morelia, 24

December 1873; and Pedro Ramón and the Indigenous Community of Huango to Luis Macouzet, Morelia, 20 December 1873.
170. AHCM, Diocesano/Gobierno/Parroquias/Solicitudes, caja 280, exp. 494, Various vecinos of Huango to Luis Macouzet, Morelia, 9 January 1874.
171. AHCM, Diocesano/Gobierno/Parroquias/Solicitudes, caja 280, exp. 494, Investigation carried out by Father Agustín Pallares of Puruándiro into the charges against Father Ramón Moreno, 5 January 1874.
172. AHCM, Diocesano/Gobierno/Correspondencia/Secretario, caja 118, exp. 563, Leonides Dávalos, Huango, to Luis Macouzet, Morelia, 25 March 1875. Dávalos, a native of Silao who studied in the seminaries of León and Morelia in the 1840s before serving a number of parishes in central Michoacán and eastern Guanajuato, was likely a member of the powerful Dávalos clan, whose extensive holdings in Michoacán originated in the conquest. See AHCM, Diocesano/Gobierno/Parroquias/Informes, caja 247, exp. 380, Career File of Presb. Leonides Dávalos [date unknown]; and Sánchez Rodríguez, "Los Dávalos."
173. AHCM, Diocesano/Gobierno/Correspondencia/Secretario, caja 119, exp. 573, Leonides Dávalos, Huango, to Luis Macouzet, Morelia, 13 May 1876; and Leonides Dávalos, Huango, to Luis Macouzet, Morelia, 17 October 1876.
174. AHCM, Diocesano/Gobierno/Parroquias/Solicitudes, caja 279, exp. 487, Vecinos of Huango to Luis Macouzet, 5 June 1873.
175. AGHPEM, Guerra y Ejército, caja 2, exp. 15, Albino Fuentes Acosta, Puruándiro, to Interior Minister, Morelia, 13 February 1875; and caja 3, exp. 38, Cayetano Martínez, Puruándiro, to Interior Minister, Morelia, 20 March 1875.
176. AGHPEM, Guerra y Ejército, caja 2, exp. 15, Jesús Ladislao Ortega, Huango, to Jesús Ramos, Huango, 18 February 1875.
177. AGHPEM, Guerra y Ejército, caja 2, exp. 15, Albino Fuentes Acosta, Puruándiro, to Interior Minister, Morelia, 1 February 1875, and 21 February 1875; caja 3, exp. 30, Nicolas de Régules, Morelia, to Interior Minister, Morelia, 22 March 1875; AGHPEM, Guerra y Ejército, caja 3, exp. 38, Albino Fuentes Acosta, Puruándiro, to Interior Minister, Morelia, 27 February 1875, 13 March 1875, 20 March 1875, and 21 March 1875; caja 3, exp. 49, Albino Fuentes Acosta, Puruándiro, to Interior Minister, Morelia, 18 April 1875; and caja 4, exp. 58, Albino Fuentes Acosta, Puruándiro, to Interior Minister, Morelia, 23 May 1875.
178. AGHPEM, Guerra y Ejército, caja 2, exp. 15, Albino Fuentes Acosta, Puruándiro, to Interior Minister, Morelia, 13 February 1875; and Álvarez Lira, *Aportaciones históricas sobre Villa de Morelos*, 105–7.
179. AHCM, Diocesano/Gobierno/Parroquias/Solicitudes, caja 279, exp. 487, Vecinos of Huango to Luis Macouzet, 5 June 1873. For Magaña and Villacaña's indultos, see *El Progresista*, 20 April 1876 and 16 October 1876, respectively.

180. Several Gaitáns signed the June 1873 petition for a new chapel. Antonio Gaitán served as the principal lay financial officer for the new chapel project between 1873 and 1876. See AHCM, Diocesano/Gobierno/Parroquias/Solicitudes, caja 279, exp. 487, Antonio Gaitán, Huango, to Luis Macouzet, Morelia, 4 February 1873; and AHCM, Diocesano/Gobierno/Correspondencia/Secretario, caja 119, exp. 573, Leonides Dávalos, Huango, to Luis Macouzet, Morelia, 13 May 1876. Ignacio Gaitán was identified as a Religionero rebel by the prefecture of Puruándiro in April 1875. See AGHPEM, Guerra y Ejército, caja 3, exp. 49, Albino Fuentes Acosta, Puruándiro, to Interior Minister, Morelia, 8 April 1875. Ramón and Nicolás Bolaños signed a February 1873 petition for the new chapel. See AHCM, Diocesano/Gobierno/Parroquias/Solicitudes, caja 279, exp. 487, Vecinos of Huango to Luis Macouzet, Morelia, 6 February 1873. Antonio Raya was the brother of Rafael and Donaciano.
181. AHCM, Diocesano/Gobierno/Diezmos/Puruándiro, caja 1446, exp. 29, Tithing Accounts for 1874, and exp. 30, Tithing Accounts for 1874. Tinoco and Zavala were identified as Religionero rebels by the prefect of Puruándiro in the spring of 1875. See AGHPEM, Guerra y Ejército, caja 3, exp. 49, Albino Fuentes Acosta, Puruándiro, to Interior Minister, Morelia, 8 April 1875.
182. AHCM, Diocesano/Gobierno/Parroquias/Solicitudes, caja 280, exp. 508, Juan N. Coria, Antonio Villacaña, Fernando Villacaña, and other vecinos of Huango to Luis Macouzet, Morelia, 10 October 1877.

Chapter 5

1. ADZ, DGPD 33, Coalcomán, Encarnación Farfán, Coalcomán, to Diocesan Secretary, Zamora, 18 January 1874.
2. ADZ, DGPD 33, Coalcomán, Vecinos of Coalcomán to Diocesan Secretary, Zamora, 24 October 1868; Encarnación Farfán and other vecinos of Coalcomán to Diocesan Secretary, 4 March 1869; and Encarnación Farfán, Coalcomán, to Diocesan Secretary, Zamora, 18 January 1874.
3. *El Progresista*, 9 August 1875; and AGHPEM, Guerra y Ejército, caja 3, exp. 54, Antonio Pallares, Coalcomán, to Interior Minister, Morelia, 13 April 1875.
4. ADZ, DGPD 33, Coalcomán, Celso González, Coalcomán, to Diocesan Secretary, Zamora, 10 July 1876; and Inquiry Practiced by Cura Celso González about the State of the Tithing Funds Administered by José María Sandoval, 17 July–4 August 1876.
5. ADZ, DGPD 33, Coalcomán, General Accounts of the Deposits and Expenses of the Fund Created for the Construction of the Temple of

Coalcomán, February–December 1871, and The Vela Perpetua and Sociedad Católica of Coalcomán to Diocesan Secretary, Zamora, 1 September 1875.
6. *La Idea Católica*, 25 April 1875; and *La Voz de México*, 9 April 1875.
7. Arreola Cortés, *Coalcomán*, 75–78. By the early nineteenth century, most of the indigenous inhabitants of Coalcomán and its environs spoke either Spanish or a distinct local version of Nahuatl.
8. Cochet, *Alambradas en la sierra*, 37–42.
9. Brand et al., *Coalcomán and Motines del Oro*, 132–34; and Gledhill, *Cultura y desafío en Ostula*, 173–77.
10. Brand et al., *Coalcomán and Motines del Oro*, 64–65, 132–37; Arreola Cortés, *Coalcomán*, 117–19; and Gledhill, *Cultura y desafío en Ostula*, 176.
11. Gledhill, *Cultura y desafío en Ostula*, 169–72; Brand et al., *Coalcomán and Motines del Oro*, 60–66; Arreola Cortés, *Coalcomán*, 102; and Sánchez Díaz, *El suroeste de Michoacán, estructura económica-social*, 77.
12. Gledhill, *Cultura y desafío en Ostula*, 185–200; and Cochet, *Alambradas en la sierra*, 40–41. In the neighboring Apatzingán district, meanwhile, the consolidation of several latifundios despoiled many indigenous communities of their land base as early as the seventeenth century—a process that accelerated in the nineteenth century. See Sánchez Díaz, *El suroeste de Michoacán, estructura economica-social*, 41–56.
13. Brand et al., *Coalcomán and Motines del Oro*, 83–88; Arreola Cortés, *Coalcomán*, 129–31; and Gledhill, *Cultura y desafío en Ostula*, 190.
14. Olveda, *Gordiano Guzmán*, 69–70, 82, 99–102; and Van Young, *Other Rebellion*, 498–505.
15. Arreola Cortés, *Coalcomán*, 102–5; and *El Siglo Diez y Nueve*, 12 October 1869.
16. Olveda, *Gordiano Guzmán*, 103–14, 156–57. In his populism, Gordiano cut a figure not unlike that of another coastal cacique—Manuel Lozada of Jalisco's Tepic canton. But unlike Lozada, who earned concessions of local autonomy and guaranteed corporate landholding through service to conservative and monarchist causes, Guzmán and his heirs threw in their lot with federalists and liberals. See Meyer, *Esperando a Lozada*; Brittsan, *Popular Politics and Rebellion in Mexico*; and Van Oosterhout, "Popular Conservatism in Mexico."
17. Vázquez Pallares, *Un nuevo regimen de propiedad y un pueblo*, 7–9. Such a pattern confirms Tutino's findings in "The Revolution in Mexican Inependence."
18. Sánchez Díaz and Arreola Cortés record few agrarian conflicts between Indians and non-Indians in or around Coalcomán between 1750 and 1850. The indigenous community of the cabecera rented parcels of land to outsiders in the 1810s and 1820s, but it suffered no legal modifications in the status of communal properties during this time, unlike in neighboring areas such as Apatzingán and Huacana. See Sánchez Díaz, *El suroeste de Michoacán, estructura económica-social*, 52–56; and Arreola Cortés, *Coalcomán*, 120–77.

19. Arreola Cortés, *Coalcomán*, 172–73; and Sánchez Díaz, *El suroeste de Michoacán, estructura económica-social*, 77–83.
20. Romero, *Noticias para formar*, 134–35. An 1869 state census published by *El Siglo Diez y Nueve* calculated the population of the Coalcomán district at 9,573, the least populous in the state. Neighboring Apatzingán district, with 13,995 souls, came second to last. See *El Siglo Diez y Nueve*, 10 May 1869.
21. Cochet, *Alambradas en la sierra*, 50–66; and Romero, "Noticias estadísticas sobre el partido de Coaclomán," 562.
22. *La Voz de México*, 1 August 1875.
23. Carmagnani, *El regreso de los dioses*, 229–32.
24. See, for example, Escobar Ohmstede, *Indio, nación, y comunidad en el México del siglo XIX*; Mallon, *Peasant and Nation*; Guardino, *Time of Liberty*; Thomson with LaFrance, *Patriotism, Politics and Popular Liberalism*; Ducey, *Nation of Villages*; and McNamara, *Sons of the Sierra*.
25. For many Mexican moderates and intellectuals of various political stripes, Maximilian's regime seemed to offer an "enlightened" form of governance without the baggage of partisan politics and thus an ideal milieu in which to carry out scientific and developmentalist projects aimed at bringing Mexico into the community of modern states. See Pani, *Para mexicanizar el segundo imperio*, esp. 193–209, 248–92.
26. Romero, "Noticias estadísticas del partido de Coalcomán," 555–64.
27. *El Siglo Diez y Nueve*, 12 October 1869.
28. *El Siglo Diez y Nueve*, 10 September 1869. The quote from the unnamed Coalcomán correspondent is found in *La Revista Universal*, 16 November 1869.
29. Romero placed the number of inhabitants of Maruata at 250 in 1860. See *Noticias para formar*, 132–33.
30. *El Siglo Diez y Nueve*, 5 April 1873 and 9 May 1873. Similar obstacles plagued the Port of San Blas, in Lozada's Nayarit. See Van Oosterhout, "Popular Conservatism in Mexico," 37, 184–86.
31. Arreola Cortés, *Coalcomán*, 201.
32. *El Progresista*, 20 August 1874.
33. Arreola Cortés, *Coalcomán*, 202–4.
34. Sánchez Díaz, *El suroeste de Michoacán: economía y sociedad*, 250–56; Gledhill, *Cultura y desafío en Ostula*, 218–19; and Van Oosterhout, "Popular Conservatism in Mexico," 184–88.
35. Cochet, *Alambradas en la sierra*, 42–67.
36. Kourí, *Pueblo Divided*, 34–79; and Cochet, *Alambradas en la sierra*, 75–96.
37. Cochet, *Alambradas en la sierra*, 50–66.
38. Sánchez Díaz, *El suroeste de Michoacán: economía y sociedad*, 67; Stauffer, "Indianness, Community," 26–29.
39. Stauffer, "Community, Identity"; and Stauffer, "Indianness, Community," 38–43.

40. Quoted in Stauffer, "Community, Identity," 161.
41. Stauffer, "Community, Identity," 162; and Sánchez Díaz, *El suroeste de Michoacán: economia y sociedad*, 74. Kourí notes similar intracommunal dynamics during the land division process in Papantla (*Pueblo Divided*, 107–86).
42. Stauffer, "Indianness, Community," 33–36.
43. Stauffer, "Community, Identity," 163–65; and Sánchez Díaz, *El suroeste de Michoacán: economia y sociedad*, 72–73.
44. Stauffer, "Community, Identity," 164–65; and Sánchez Díaz, *El suroeste de Michoacán: economia y sociedad*, 73.
45. Sánchez Díaz, *El suroeste de Michoacán: economia y sociedad*, 326; *El Progresista*, 13 April 1874; and *El Siglo Diez y Nueve*, 6 April 1874. *El Siglo* erroneously reported that the rebels had kidnapped Antonio Palleres, and not Ignacio Manzo, but it later issued a correction.
46. Stauffer, "Indianness, Community," 54–55; AGHPEM, Hijuelas, Coalcomán, Libro 4, f. 155, Antonio Pallares, Ignacio Manzo, and Other Possessors of Legitimate Titles to Properties that Belonged to the Extinguished Indian Community, Coalcomán, to Interior Minister, Morelia, 6 September 1874.
47. Sánchez Díaz, *El suroeste de Michoacán: estructura económica-social*, 49; Arreola Cortés, *Coalcomán*, 172; and Olveda, *Gordiano Guzmán*, 108–9.
48. ADZ, DGPD 2, Aguililla, Vicente Silva and other vecinos, Aguililla, to Diocesan Secretary, Zamora, 18 November 1867; and José María Merino and other vecinos, Aguililla, to Diocesan Secretary, Zamora, 7 November 1869; and "México, Michoacán, registros parroquiales y diocesanos, 1555–1996," database with images, *FamilySearch* (https://familysearch.org/ark:/61903/3:1:9392-5JVP-B?cc=1883388&wc=3NY4-C68%3A178153401%2C178153402%2C178825001 : 20 May 2014), Aguililla > Nuestra Señora de Guadalupe > Entierros 1871–1878, 1884–1893 > images 5 and 15 of 370, burial certificates for Ramón Guzmán, 13 February 1871, and María Paula Guzmán, 8 September 1871.
49. Arreola Cortés, *Coalcomán*, 172–73; Sánchez Díaz, *El suroeste de Michoacán: estructura económica-social*, 104–6; and Olveda, *Gordiano Guzmán*, 156–57.
50. Sánchez Díaz, *El suroeste de Michoacán: estructura económica-social*, 102.
51. Arreola Cortés, *Coalcomán*, 189–91; Sánchez Díaz, *El suroeste de Michoacán: economía y sociedad*, 303, 320–23; and Brand et al., *Coalcomán and Motines del Oro*, 98–101.
52. Ruiz, *Historia de la Guerra de intervención en Michoacán*, 665–67.
53. Ruiz, 665–67; and Arreola Cortés, *Coalcomán*, 190–91.
54. AGHPEM, Conflictos Políticos, exp. 1, ff. 1–31, esp. 27, Antonio Ugarte, General Representative of the Indians of Abaquité, Aquila, Ostula, Coire, y Pómaro to Interior Minister, Morelia, 31 November 1871. Coahuayana pueblo representatives Atanacio Jacinto and Francisco Moraña, in their petition to Governor Mendoza, declared that when the French invaded Mexico in 1863, they had "sought out a caudillo" to lead them into the fight against the

invaders. See AGHPEM, Conflictos Políticos, exp. 1, f. 3, Atanacio Jacinto and Francisco Moraña, Coahuayana, to Interior Minister, Morelia, 11 November 1871.
55. *El Monitor Republicano*, 28 July 1872; and *El Correo del Comercio*, 31 July 1872.
56. *La Iberia*, 31 August 1872.
57. Pérez, *Almanaque estadístico de las oficinas y guia de forasteros y del comercio de la república para 1875*, 433–37, includes a brief biography of Carrillo.
58. Chowning, *Wealth and Power in Provincial Mexico*, 294–98.
59. AHCM, Comunicados, caja 79, exp. 11, District Prefect, Coalcomán, to Interior Minister, Morelia, 15 August 1874.
60. AGHPEM, Guerra y Ejército, caja 3, exp. 50, District Prefect, Apatzingán, to Interior Minister, Morelia, 3 April 1875.
61. AHCM, Policía y Guerra, Aprehensiones, caja 27, exp. 13, Prefect of Coalcomán to Interior Minister, Morelia, 11 November 1873.
62. AHCM, Policía y Guerra, Comunicados, caja 79, exp. 18, State Treasurer, Morelia, to Interior Minister, Morelia, 8 January 1874.
63. AHCM, Policía y Guerra, Aprehensiones, caja 27, exp. 13, District Prefect, Coalcomán, to Interior Minister, Morelia, 24 December 1873.
64. AHCM, Policía y Guerra, Consultas, caja 156, exp. 29, District Prefect, Coalcomán, to Interior Minister, Morelia, 11 October 1873.
65. Clear reports on district administrative changes are not available, but military records suggest that José María Chávez, Antonio González, and Narciso Garcilazo all served as prefect during the year. See AHCM, Policía y Guerra, Comunicados, caja 29, exp. 17, Antonio González, Coalcomán, to Interior Minister, Morelia, 15 August 1874; and *El Progresista*, 24 November 1874, respectively.
66. AGHPEM, Guerra y Ejército, caja 3, exp. 36, Jefe Político, Tancitaro, to District Prefect, Apatzingán, 25 February 1875; Jefe Político, Tancitaro, to Interior Minister, Morelia, 28 February 1875; and District Prefect, Apatzingán, to Interior Minister, Morelia, 24 February 1875.
67. AGHPEM, Guerra y Ejército, caja 3, exp. 50, District Prefect, Apatzingán, to Interior Minister, Morelia, 10 April 1875.
68. AHCM, Policía y Guerra, Solicitudes, caja 393, exp. 4, Antonio Pallares, Coalcomán, to Interior Minister, Morelia, 15 February 1875.
69. AGHPEM, Guerra y Ejército, caja 5, exp. 80, Cruz Meza, Aguililla, to Antonio Cándido [no location given], (copy of rebel communication made by Luis C. Vargas), 27 March 1875.
70. AGHPEM, Guerra y Ejército, caja 3, exp. 54, Antonio Pallares, Coalcomán, to Interior Minister, Morelia, 13 April 1875.
71. AGHPEM, Guerra y Ejército, caja 3, exp. 54, Jefe Político, Coalcomán, to Interior Minister, Morelia, 13 April 1875; *El Siglo Diez y Nueve*, 12 April 1875; and *El Progresista*, 13 April 1875.

72. AGHPEM, Guerra y Ejército, caja 3, exp. 54, District Prefect, Coalcomán, to Interior Minister, Morelia, 12 May 1875; and Interior Minister, Morelia, to District Prefect, Coalcomán, 12 May 1875.
73. Nevertheless, their legal offensive against the 1871 reparto would continue on well into the Porfiriato. See Stauffer, "Community, Identity."
74. AGHPEM, Guerra y Ejército, caja 3, exp. 50, District Prefect, Apatzingán, to Interior Minister, Morelia, 10 April 1875.
75. AGHPEM, Guerra y Ejército, caja 4, exp. 63, District Prefect, Coalcomán, to Interior Minister, Morelia, 19 June 1875.
76. AHDN, Operaciones Militares, XI/481.4/9211, f. 48, Miguel Salcedo, Colima, to General José Ceballos, Guadalajara, 19 July 1875; and AHCM, Policía y Guerra, Movimientos de Fuerzas, caja 263, exp. 2, District Prefect, Coalcomán, to Interior Minister, Morelia, 15 July 1875.
77. *El Correo del Comercio*, 21 October 1875.
78. AHDN, Operaciones Militares, XI/481.4/9211, f. 48, Miguel Salcedo, Colima, to José Ceballos, Guadalajara, 19 July 1875; AHCM, Policía y Guerra, Movimientos de Fuerzas, caja 263, exp. 2, District Prefect, Coalcomán, to Secretary of Government, Morelia, 15 July 1875; and *El Correo del Comercio*, 21 October 1875.
79. *El Siglo Diez y Nueve*, 13 November 1875; and *La Voz de México*, 9 November 1875.
80. *El Eco de Ambos Mundos*, 17 March 1876; *La Revista Universal*, 19 April 1876; and *La Iberia*, 1 February 1876.
81. *La Bandera de Ocampo*, 19 March 1876 and 26 March 1876.
82. See Carreño, *El archivo del general Porfirio Díaz* (hereafter, APD), vol. XVI, 289–90, Francisco Trejo, Zamora, to Porfirio Díaz, Guadalajara, 19 January 1877.
83. *El Progresista*, 9 November 1876.
84. APD, vol. XVIII, 114–22, Manuel González, Morelia to Porfirio Díaz, Mexico City, 19 February 1877; and vol. XXIII, 148–49, Manuel González, Pátzcuaro, to Porfirio Díaz, Mexico City, 22 May 1877. Though we lack direct correspondence between Porfirio Díaz and the Guzmán brothers, letters from Díaz allies such as Manuel González demonstrate that the porfirista camp favored the Guzmáns overall. See APD, vol. XXIII, 211, Manuel González, Uruapan, to Porfirio Díaz, 26 May 1877.
85. Olveda, *Gordiano Guzmán*, 68–71.
86. Brand et al., *Coalcomán and Motines del Oro*, 86–87. The parish priest of Coalcomán complained in 1854 that Guzmán's guerillas robbed tithing funds to finance their rebellion and impressed pacíficos into their ranks. See AHCM, Diocesano/Justicia/Correspondencia/Provisor, caja 658, exp. 272, Manuel de P. Ochoa, Coalcomán, to Vicar-General of the diocese, Morelia, 5 June 1854.

87. ADZ, DGPD 33, Coalcomán, Antonio Guzmán and Other Vecinos of Coalcomán to Diocesan Secretary, Zamora, 10 November 1868; and Antonio Guzmán and Other Vecinos of Coalcomán to Diocesan Secretary, Zamora, 4 March 1869.
88. Another Guzmán, don Serefino, sought the assistance of the priest of Aguililla in 1876 in marrying María Patricia Flores, with whom he was cohabitating. ADZ, DGPD 2, Aguililla, Abundio Martínez, Aguililla, to Diocesan Secretary, Zamora, 21 July 1876. Serefino is described as a native of Tamazula, Jalisco, living on the Rancho of Ahuindo (a property tied to Gordiano).
89. Serge Gruzinski uses the term "segunda aculturación" to describe Bourbon assaults on Indian religious cultures that aimed to modernize indigenous communities and make them more economically rational. See Gruzisnki, "La 'segunda aculturación.'" The Bourbon "second acculturation" represents a clear precursor to liberal modernizing attempts in the nineteenth century, and I have thus adopted Gruzisnki's phrase to describe processes of religious change in the southwestern sierra.
90. The phrase comes from an 1872 letter from the priest Gregorio Trujillo to diocesan authorities. See ADZ, DGPD 33, Coalcomán, Gregorio Trujillo, Coalcomán, to Diocesan Secretary, Zamora, 15 February 1872.
91. Ostula's hermitage did possess a small garden plot, however, producing cacao to subsidize the activities of the priest. Gledhill, *Cultura y desafío en Ostula*, 177–87.
92. Gledhill, *Cultura y desafío en Ostula*, 173–76; and Romero, "Noticias estadísticas sobre el partido de Coalcomán," 561–62.
93. Romero, "Noticias estadísticas sobre el partido de Coalcomán," 562.
94. Cochet, *Alambradas en la sierra*, 40–41, 68n16; and Gledhill, *Cultura y desafío en Ostula*, 188–90. The cofradía of Ostula, richest of the coastal sujetos of Coalcomán, possessed 280 head of cattle at the end of the eighteenth century.
95. Brand et al., *Coalcomán and Motines del Oro*, 134–36.
96. Mazín, *El Gran Michoacán*, 155–63.
97. Romero, *Noticias para formar*, 129–35.
98. ADZ, DGPD 33, Coalcomán, Daniel Rivera, Achotán, to Diocesan Secretary, Zamora, 8 August 1864; and DGP 63, Charapan, Jesus Valverde, Achotán, to Diocesan Secretary, Zamora, 29 July 1867.
99. Romero, *Noticias para formar*, 134.
100. ADZ, DGPD 33, Coalcomán, Daniel Rivera, Achotan, to Diocesan Secretary, Zamora, 8 August 1864.
101. Romero, *Noticias para formar*, 132; and ADZ, DG 182, Estadísticas: Párrocos y Parroquias, f. 11.
102. Romero, "Noticias estadísticas del partido de Coalcomán," 562.

103. Gledhill, *Cultura y desafío en Ostula*, 61–110, 195–200. Francois Chevalier traveled to the coastal pueblo of Ostula in 1948 and was allowed a rare glimpse of a Corpus Christi celebration, replete with indigenous dances set to the rhythm of the Nahua teponaztli drum. More recently, Gledhill describes in minute detail the syncretic devotions of contemporary Ostula. Though we should not assume an easy identity between contemporary and nineteenth-century practices, the extant evidence suggests the pueblos had autonomous religious cultures, directed by local *topiles* in the absence of the priest, and likely combined Nahua and European Catholic elements.
104. AHCM, Diocesano/Gobierno/Sacerdotes/Consultas, caja 407, exp. 60, Francisco de P. Ochoa, Coalcomán, to Diocesan Secretary, Morelia, 25 October 1852; and Diocesan Secretary, Morelia, to Francisco de P. Ochoa, Coalcomán, 7 April 1853.
105. AHCM, Diocesano/Justicia/Correspondencia/Provisor, caja 658, exp. 269, Manuel P. de Ochoa, Coalcomán, to Provisor, Morelia, 17 May 1852.
106. Romero, "Noticias estadísticas del partido de Coalcomán," 562.
107. ADZ, DGPD 33, Coalcomán, Pedro María Villalobos, Coalcomán, to Diocesan Secretary, Zamora, 30 December 1868.
108. ADZ, DG 72, Libro de Despachos, f. 40, entry for 16 January 1869.
109. Chávez, *Noticias históricas, geográficas, y estadísticas del Distrito de Coalcomán*, 14–20, and quoted in Sánchez Díaz, *El suroeste de Michoacán: economía y sociedad*, 285.
110. ADZ, DGPD 33, Coalcomán, Pedro María Villalobos, Coalcomán, to Diocesan Secretary, Zamora, 25 November 1867.
111. ADZ, DGPD 33, Coalcomán, Pascual Ochoa, Coalcomán, to Diocesan Secretary, Zamora, 26 October 1868; and Antonio Guzmán, Coalcomán, to Diocesan Secretary, 19 November 1869.
112. ADZ, DGP 33, Coalcomán, Various Vecinos of Chinicuila to Diocesan Secretary, 15 September 1873.
113. ADZ, DGP 33, Coalcomán, Diocesan Secretary, Coalcomán, to Various Vecinos of Chinicuila, 22 September 1873.
114. Romero, *Noticias para formar*, 133; Sánchez Díaz, *El suroeste de Michoacán, estructura económica*-social, 43; and ADZ, DGPD 2, Aguililla, Bernabe de Jesús Torres, Aguililla, to Diocesan Secretary, 27 June 1871.
115. ADZ, DG 182, Estadísticas: Párrocos y Parroquias, f. 7.
116. ADZ, DGPD 2, Aguililla, Benito Méndez, Aguililla, to Diocesan Secretary, 7 January 1868.
117. Duffy, *Stripping of the Altars*, 40, 111–13.
118. ADZ, DGPD 2, Aguililla, Bernabé de Jesús Torres, Aguililla, to Diocesan Secretary, Zamora, 17 July 1870; and Abundio Martínez, Aguililla, to Diocesan Secretary, Zamora, 2 June 1872.

119. ADZ, DGPD 2, Aguililla, Cuenta de los donativos que se han reunido para la construcción de la parroquia de Aguililla y de los gastos que se han entregado en dicha fábrica, 1872–1885.
120. ADZ, DGPD 2, Aguililla, Bernabé de Jesús Torres, Aguililla, to Diocesan Secretary, 27 June 1871; and Bernabé de Jesús Torres, Aguililla, to Diocesan Secretary, 7 August 1871.
121. ADZ, DGPD 2, Aguililla, Abundio Martínez, Aguililla, to Diocesan Secretary, Zamora, 2 December 1873.
122. ADZ, DGPD 2, Aguililla, Ignacio Moreno, José María Merino, Ramón Palafox, and other Vecinos of Aguililla to Diocesan Secretary, Zamora, 3 December 1873.
123. ADZ, DGPD 2, Aguililla, Diocesan Secretary, Zamora, to Ignacio Moreno, José María Merino, Ramón Palafox, and other Vecinos of Aguililla, 4 December 1873. Other signatories of this petition include local alcalde Pedro Caballero and principal vecinos Cándido Ponce, Victor Bustos, and Juan Manuel Carriedo.
124. AGHPEM, Guerra y Ejército, caja 3, exp. 36, José María Verduzco, Apatzingán, to Interior Minister, 1 March 1875; and *El Progresista*, 2 August 1875.
125. AHCM, Gobierno del Estado de Michoacán, Secretaria de Gobierno, Policía y Guerra, Aprehensiones, caja 27, exp. 13, Prefect of Coalcomán to Interior Minister, Morelia, 11 November 1873; and *El Progresista*, 14 October 1875, and 9 November 1876.
126. As we have seen, Gordiano and members of his extended family constituted the first wave of mestizo immigration to Aguililla during the insurgency. The Guzmáns' political allies and clients may have followed soon after. Newspaper articles from the 1830s and 1840s suggest that among Guzmán's followers in the southern sierra were members of the Vega and Valencia families, as well as other "criminals" from Tamazula. Interestingly, both the Vega and Valencia families produced Religionero leaders (Miguel Vega from Aguililla and Jesus Valencia from Coalcomán). See *El Gladiador*, 25 April 1831, and 25 May 1831; and *El Siglo Diez y Nueve*, 10 June 1843.
127. AGHPEM, Guerra y Ejército, caja 3, exp. 36, José María Verduzco, Apatzingán, to Interior Minister, Morelia, 1 March 1875; and Pedro Caballero, Aguililla, to José María Verduzco, Apatzingán, 24 February 1875.
128. AGHPEM, Guerra y Ejército, caja 4, exp. 63, Narciso Garcilazo, Coalcomán, to Interior Minister, Morelia, 19 June 1875.
129. ADZ, DGPD 2, Aguililla, Abundio Martínez, Aguililla, to Diocesan Secretary, Zamora, 10 November 1876.
130. ADZ, DGPD 2, Aguililla, Abundio Martínez, Aguililla, to Diocesan Secretary, Zamora, 22 September 1877.
131. ADZ, DGPD 2, Aguililla, Ignacio Moreno, José María Merino, Ramón Palafox, and other Vecinos of Aguililla to Diocesan Secretary, Zamora,

3 December 1873; and Pedro Caballero, José María Merino, Cándido Ponce, and other Vecinos of Aguililla to Diocesan Secretary, Zamora, 8 January 1876.
132. ADZ, DGPD 33, Coalcomán, Joaquín Valdés and the Indian Community of Coalcomán to Diocesan Secretary, Zamora, 4 March 1869.
133. ADZ, DGPD 33, Coalcomán, Francisco Santa Ana and Virgen Baltazar, Coalcomán, to Diocesan Secretary, Zamora, 10 November 1868. The petition characterized Valdéz's detractors as "vecinos," a term often used to denote non-Indians and nonmembers of an indigenous community.
134. ADZ, DGPD 33, Coalcomán, Pedro María Villalobos, Coalcomán, to Diocesan Secretary, Zamora, 21 August 1867; and Luis G. Sierra, Zamora, to Pedro María Villalobos, Coalcomán, 26 October 1867.
135. ADZ, DGPD 33, Coalcomán, Sociedad Católica de Señoras of Coalcomán to Diocesan Secretary, Zamora, 31 January 1872.
136. ADZ, DGPD 33, Coalcomán, General Accounts of the Deposits and Expenses of the Fund Created for the Construction of the Temple of Coalcomán, February–December 1871.
137. ADZ, DGPD 33, Coalcomán, Sociedad Católica de Señoras of Coalcomán to Diocesan Secretary, Zamora, 31 January 1872; and Sociedad Católica de Señoras of Coalcomán to Diocesan Secretary, Zamora, 30 September 1872.
138. ADZ, DGPD 33, Coalcomán, The Vela Perpetua and Sociedad Católica of Coalcomán to Diocesan Secretary, Zamora, 1 September 1875.
139. ADZ, DGPD 33, Coalcomán, Pedro María Villalobos, Coalcomán, to Diocesan Secretary, Zamora, 30 December 1868.
140. ADZ, DGPD 33, Coalcomán, Various Vecinos of Coalcomán and Chinicuila to Diocesan Secretary, 24 October 1869; and Encarnación Farfán, Coalcomán, to Diocesan Secretary, Zamora, 18 January 1874.
141. ADZ, DGPD 33, Coalcomán, Pedro María Villalobos, Coalcomán, to Diocesan Secretary, Zamora, 7 July 1871.
142. ADZ, DGPD 33, Coalcomán, Manuel Navarro de la Péna, Coalcomán, to Diocesan Secretary, 20 January 1874.
143. AGHPEM, Hijuelas, Coalcomán, Libro 4, f. 320; and ADZ, DGPD 33, Coalcomán, Pedro María Villalobos, Coalcomán, to Diocesan Secretary, Zamora, 19 May 1870.
144. ADZ, DGPD 33, Coalcomán, Pedro María Villalobos, Coalcomán, to Diocesan Secretary, Zamora, 23 November 1871; Pedro María Villalobos, Coalcomán, to Diocesan Secretary, Zamora, 15 February 1872; and José María Sandoval, Coalcomán, to Diocesan Secretary, 23 December 1872.
145. ADZ, DGPD 33, Coalcomán, General Accounts of the Deposits and Expenses of the Fund Created for the Construction of the Temple of Coalcomán, February–December 1871. Doña Clemencia Gutiérrez also donated eight pesos "for indemnification of a Church plot."

146. ADZ, DGPD 33, Coalcomán, José María Sandoval, Coalcomán, to Diocesan Secretary, 23 December 1872.
147. ADZ, DGPD 33, Coalcomán, Encarnación Farfán and the members of the Exploratory Commission that Reconnoitered the Ports of Bucerías and Maruata, Coalcomán, to Diocesan Secretary, 26 March 1874.
148. ADZ, DGPD 33, Coalcomán, Ignacio Manzo, M. Villanueva, and other vecinos of Coalcomán to Diocesan Secretary, 26 March 1874; and José María Farías López and the municipal officers of Coalcomán to Diocesan Secretary, 27 March 1874.
149. ADZ, DGPD 33, Coalcomán, Sociedad Católica de Señoras of Coalcomán to Diocesan Secretary, Zamora, 31 January 1872; The Women of the Vela Perpetua and the Sociedad Católica of Coalcomán to Diocesan Secretary, Zamora, 30 September 1872; and Sociedad Católica de Señoras of Coalcomán to Diocesan Secretary, 16 October 1872.
150. ADZ, DGPD 33, Coalcomán, The Women of the Vela Perpetua and the Sociedad Católica of Coalcomán to Diocesan Secretary, Zamora, 1 September 1875.
151. The prefecture's account of the April attack on Coalcomán described the rebel infantry as Indians operating under Antonio Cándido. Indulto lists from May 1875 and September 1876 reveal more indigenous names.
152. *El Progresista*, 9 August 1875; and AGHPEM, Guerra y Ejército, caja 3, exp. 54, Antonio Pallares, Coalcomán, to Interior Minister, Morelia, 13 April 1875.
153. ADZ, DGPD 33, Coalcomán, Celso González, Coalcomán, to Diocesan Secretary, Zamora, 10 July 1876; and Inquiry Practiced by Cura Celso González about the State of the Tithing Funds Administered by José María Sandoval, 17 July–4 August 1876. Interestingly, the robbery triggered angry petitions by the women of the Vela, who wanted Father Sandoval to personally reimburse the association. The women considered Sandoval responsible for the loss because he had insisted on hiding the money in his home in order to protect it, perhaps thinking that Religionero troops would not attack the parish priest.
154. ADZ, DGPD 33, Coalcomán, José María Sandoval, Coalcomán, to Diocesan Secretary, Zamora, 14 September 1873.
155. This estimate comes from April 1875. See AGHPEM, Guerra y Ejército, caja 3, exp. 50, Manuel Trevino, Apatzingán, to Interior Minister, Morelia, 10 April 1875.
156. APD, vol. XVIII, 114–22, Manuel González, Morelia, to Porfirio Díaz, Mexico City, 19 February 1877; vol. XXIII, 148–49, Manuel González, Pátzcuaro, to Porfirio Díaz, Mexico City, 22 May 1877; and vol. XXV, 97–98, Manuel González, Morelia, to Porfirio Díaz, Mexico City, 26 June 1877.
157. AGHPEM, Guerra y Ejército, caja 3, exp. 54, Jefe Político, Coalcomán, to Interior Minister, Morelia, 13 April 1875; *El Siglo Diez y Nueve*, 12 April 1875; and *El Progresista*, 13 April 1875.

Chapter 6

1. APD, vol. IX, 251–55, Ezekiel Montes, Mexico, to Porfirio Díaz, Oaxaca, 20 August 1871. At the national level, meanwhile, Díaz edged out Lerdo for second place.
2. APD, vol. IX, 293, Miguel Negrete, Mexico City, to Agustín García, Morelia, n/d, August 1872; and vol. X, 75–76, Agustín García, Rancho del Durazno, to Porfirio Díaz, Wherever He May Be, 9 June 1872.
3. APD, vol. X, 90–91, Sebas Lomeli, Tototlán, to Porfirio Díaz, Wherever He May Be, 30 June 1872. In Laurens Ballard Perry's formulation, Díaz lacked a "political machine" in Michoacán, a fact that makes his Religionero strategy seem all the more daring and his success more surprising. See Ballard Perry, *Juárez and Díaz*, 174–76.
4. *El Progresista*, 6 February 1877; *El Pensamiento Católico*, 19 January 1877; and APD, vol. XXIII, 50–52, Manuel González, Morelia, to Porfirio Díaz, Mexico City, 16 May 1877.
5. As Daniel Cosío Villegas argues, the movement had no geographic center and instead consisted of a disparate patchwork of local rebellions united by the rebels' common distaste for lerdismo. See also Thomson, "Porfirio Díaz y el ocaso del partido de la montaña," 363; Cosío Villegas, *La República Restaurada*, 88–89, 644–45; Thomson with LaFrance, *Patriotism, Politics, and Popular Liberalism*, 217–23; Mallon, *Peasant and Nation*, 273–74; McNamara, *Sons of the Sierra*, 87–91; and Guerra, *México*.
6. The Plan of Tuxtepec's preamble blasted Lerdo's government for withdrawing the "paltry subsidy" for the defense of the borderland states from the "indios bárbaros." See also Alonso, *Thread of Blood*, 131–40. On the history of the Tuxtepec movement in Puebla and Oaxaca, see Thomson with LaFrance, *Patriotism, Politics, and Popular Liberalism*; Mallon, *Peasant and Nation*; and McNamara, *Sons of the Sierra*, 87–91.
7. Pi-Suñer, "Sebastián Lerdo de Tejada y su política hacia la iglesia católica," 130–31; and APD, vol. IX, 164–65, José María Díaz, Cuernavaca, to Porfirio Díaz, Oaxaca, 7 June 1871.
8. Cosío Villegas considers the Religionero movement an anachronism and its leaders ultimately pawns in a game of porfirista ambition. Jorge Adame Goddard, for all of his painstaking work in reconstructing the diverse political ideas and projects of Mexican Catholics in the late nineteenth century, states flatly that "conservative Catholics [did] not participate in the Tuxtepec movement [and could thus] not expect to benefit from it." Paul Garner and Laurens Ballard Perry scarcely mention Religionero-infested Michoacán at all. Alicia Hernández Chávez and Guy Thomson both underline the importance of the tenet of municipal autonomy to the Tuxtepec movement, but they decline to analyze the relationship between local autonomy and local

enforcement of the Laws of Reform. See Cosío Villegas, *La República Restaurada*, 609–31; Adame Goddard, *El Pensamiento político y social*, 95–96; Garner, *Porfirio Díaz*, 58–61; Ballard Perry, *Juárez and Díaz*; Hernández Chávez, *La tradición republicana del buen gobierno*, 60–81; and Thomson, "Porfirio Díaz y el ocaso del partido de la montaña," 363–64.

9. For José Fernando Iturribarria, for example, Díaz and other Porfirian officials cultivated friendships with high clergymen to defuse Catholic opposition without contravening the Laws of Reform. Iturribarría, "La política de conciliación del general Díaz y el arzobispo Gillow," 91–99. Jean Meyer concurs, characterizing the "policy of conciliation" as part of Díaz's larger strategy of governing above the partisan fray and maintaining social order. See Meyer, *La cristiada*, 44–45. Mark Overmeyer-Velázquez, meanwhile, sees the Church-state détente in Oaxaca as a pact between the porfirista state and the regional Church aimed at creating productive workers for the emerging capitalist order. See Overmeyer-Velázquez, *Visions of the Emerald City*, chap. 3.

10. Wright-Ríos, *Revolutions in Mexican Catholicism*, 18.

11. Medina Peña, *Invención del sistema político de México*, 317–18; and Traffano, "Indios, curas, y nación."

12. Cannelli, *Nación católica y estado laico*, esp. chaps. 2 and 3.

13. This chapter relies principally on correspondence between Díaz and a diverse array of friends, collaborators, and allies, a collection organized and published in twenty-nine volumes by the prominent Catholic intellectual Alberto María Carreño between 1947 and 1961 (APD). Carreño's volumes capture the majority of Díaz's personal and military correspondence between 1865 and 1880. However, I have also made limited use of the microfilmed correspondence of Díaz held at the Universidad Iberoamericana in Mexico City. Documents from the latter collection will be denoted Colección Porfirio Díaz (CPD).

14. For discussions of other kinds of cracks in the Porfirian façade, see also Falcón and Buve, *Don Porfirio, presidente*.

15. Cosío Villegas, *La República Restaurada*, 625–27.

16. *El Ahuizote*, 1 May 1874, and 5 May 1875; *El Padre Cobos*, 5 October 1873, and 22 October 1874; García Flores Chapa, "Vicente Riva Palacio y el periódico *El Ahuizote*," 79–80; Covo, *Las ideas de la reforma en México*, 145–86; and Pani, *Para mexicanizar el segundo imperio*, 148–49.

17. Reprinted in Ceballos, *Aurora y ocaso*, 876.

18. "Municipal autonomy," of course, had other proponents and other uses outside of Michoacán, as Hernández Chávez's, Thomson's, Mallon's, and McNamara's books make clear.

19. "El Plan de Tuxtepec, proclamado en la Villa de Ojitlán," 10 January 1876, *The Pronunciamiento in Independent Mexico*, database compiled by Will Fowler and his research team, retrieved 12 January 2015 from http://arts.st-andrews.ac.uk/pronunciamientos/dates.php? f=y&pid=1610&m=3&y=1876.

20. Cosío Villegas, *El porfiriato*, 39–58; and Barragán, *José María Iglesias y la justicia electoral*, 168–225.
21. Thomson with LaFrance, *Patriotism, Politics, and Popular Liberalism*, 212–17.
22. APD, vol. XI, 313, Unsigned Letter to Porfirio Díaz, 14 February 1876; and 321, Z. Martínez, Ciudad Victoria, to Porfirio Díaz, Brownsville, 24 February 1876.
23. Muría, *Breve historia de Jalisco*, parte III, "El liberalismo civil"; and APD, vol. XI, 309, Juan N. Méndez, San Luis Potosí, to Porfirio Díaz, [no location given], 10 February 1876; and vol. XI, 321, Z. Martínez, Ciudad Victoria, to Porfirio Díaz, Brownsville, 24 February 1876.
24. Vicente Riva Palacio Collection, 1790–1896, Benson Latin American Collection, General Libraries, University of Texas at Austin (hereafter, VRP), Porfirio Díaz, [location not specified], to Vicente Riva Palacio, Mexico City, 2 December 1875. Díaz suggests that if Riva Palacio can "empower himself [militarily] of Michoacán," his constituents in the state would likely call for Riva Palacio to take the reins of the state government and procure its "reorganization."
25. *El Eco de Ambos Mundos*, 27 November 1875. Interestingly, a Díaz confidant in Mexico City had recognized the potential of the Religionero crisis as early as 1874, suggesting that it would help advance the cause against Lerdo. See APD, vol. XI, 140–41, Jesús Alfaro, Mexico City, to Porfirio Díaz, Tlacotalpan, 10 June 1874.
26. *El Correo del Comercio*, 18 March 1876.
27. *El Correo del Comercio*, 29 February 1876; and APD, vol. XXIV, 134–36, Manuel González, Morelia, to Porfirio Díaz, Mexico City, 11 June 1877.
28. APD, vol. XI, 267, José [no surname given], Mexico City, to Porfirio Díaz, [no location given], 1 May 1876. The letter's salutation, "Dear Brother," suggests that writer may have been a relative, someone connected to Díaz through compadrazgo or even a fellow freemason. On Díaz's connection to the masons, see Garner, *Porfirio Díaz*, 28–29.
29. VRP, F. López, Morelia, to Vicente Riva Palacio, Mexico City, 24 May 1876.
30. VRP, M. Romero, Chilpancingo, to Vicente Riva Palacio, 1 May 1876.
31. Despite clear ties to Religionero gavillas, Fernández was destined for a long political career in Michoacán, where he even served as governor from 1879 to 1881.
32. APD, vol. XIV, 48, Octaviano Fernández, Mexico City, to Porfirio Díaz, Mexico City, 27 November 1876. The original Spanish reads: "Allí [en Michoacán] pude reunir cerca de 900 hombres de las guerrillas religioneras que había en el estado, pues a mi llegada logré que todas reconocieran el Plan de Tuxtepec."
33. APD, vol. XIV, 48, Octaviano Fernández, Mexico City, to Porfirio Díaz, Mexico City, 27 November 1876; *El Progresista*, 1 June 1876, and 15 June 1876,

"List of Rebels Pardoned by the Prefect of La Piedad"; Martínez Álvarez, *La Piedad*, 44; and Ochoa Serrano, *Afrodescendientes*, 183.
34. APD, vol. XVI, 81, Luis Camacho, San Juan de los Lagos, to Porfirio Díaz, Guadalajara, 6 January 1877.
35. APD, vol. XVI, 196–97, Eugenio Hacha, Guadalajara, to Porfirio Díaz, Guadalajara, 15 January 1877.
36. Nicolás de la Peña, who seconded the Plan of Tuxtepec in Guanajuato's capital city, asked Díaz in November 1876 to send a dispatch naming Juárez to the rank of general in the Army of Regeneration, which he apparently did. See APD, vol. XIII, Nicolás de la Peña, Guanajuato, to Porfirio Díaz, Mexico City, 15 November 1876.
37. APD, vol. XIV, 287, Telegram, Justo Benítez, Mexico City, to Porfirio Díaz, Tepeji del Río, 13 December 1876.
38. Cosío Villegas, *La República Restaurada*, 713; and APD, vol. XXVI, 298–99, Sebastián Lerdo de Tejada, New York, to José Ceballos, New Orleans, 30 March 1877.
39. APD, vol. XV, 67, Pedro Ogazón, Mexico City, to Porfirio Díaz, Querétaro, 20 December 1876; APD, vol. XIV, 108, Ángel Cancino, Toluca, to Lic. Luis G. Curiel, Mexico City, 30 November 1876; APD, vol. XIV, 209, Jesús Garibay, Morelia, to Porfirio Díaz, Mexico City, 6 December 1876; APD, vol. XIV, 110, Ladislao Paulino, Maravatío, to Porfirio Díaz, Mexico City, 30 November 1876; and APD, vol. XIV, 301, Telegram, Juan N. Méndez, Mexico City, to Porfirio Díaz, San Francisco Soyaniquilpan, 14 December 1876.
40. *Boletín Oficial del Gobierno del Estado de Michoacán*, 12 December 1876.
41. APD, vol. XII, 212–13, José O. Herrera, Silao, to Porfirio Díaz, [no location given], 13 November 1876.
42. APD, vol. XII, 199–200, Julio Falcón, Mexico City, to Porfirio Díaz, [no location given], 12 November 1876.
43. APD, vol. XIV, 209, Jesús Garibay, Morelia, to Porfirio Díaz, Mexico City, 6 December 1876.
44. Mariano Riva Palacio Collection, 1716–1880, Benson Latin American Collection, General Libraries, University of Texas at Austin (hereafter, MRP), Ignacio Mañón y Valle, Salitre Hacienda, to Mariano Riva Palacio, Mexico City, 3 May 1876.
45. For Chacón's military career, see AHDN, Cancelados, XI–111/1–62, General Felipe Chacón, "Hoja de Servicio Militar," 12 August 1889.
46. VRP, Luis G. Peniche, Temascaltepec, to Vicente Riva Palacio, Zacualpan, 26 May 1876; VRP, Prisciliano Coronel, Metepec, to Vicente Riva Palacio, Mexico City, 22 November 1876; and APD, vol. XIII, Felipe Chacón, Lerma, to Porfirio Díaz, Mexico City, 22 November 1876.
47. VRP, Antonio Vásquez, Sultepec, to Vicente Riva Palacio, Mexico City, 4 June 1876; and Juan Ayala, Tenango, to Donancio Hernández, Mexico City, 24 November 1876.

48. APD, vol. XII, 185–86, E. Arce, Tepetlixpa, to Porfirio Díaz, [no location given], 7 November 1876.
49. The Mexico State ex-imperialist colonel Joaquin Yañez took Maravatío in late November, capturing the lerdista congressman (and former governor) Justo Mendoza. See APD, vol. XIV, 110, Ladislao Paulina, Maravatío, to Porfirio Díaz, Mexico City, 30 November 1876.
50. APD, vol. XIV, 91–92, Jesús Echaiz, Hacienda de Apeo, to Porfirio Díaz, 30 November 1876; and Porfirio Díaz, Mexico City, to Jesús Echaiz, Hacienda de Apeo, 1 December 1876.
51. APD, vol. XIV, 97–98, Alejo González and various others, Toluca, to Porfirio Díaz, Mexico City, 30 November 1876. González also reported that the merchants of Toluca had spontaneously and voluntarily offered Chacón loans, which he had refused.
52. APD, vol. XIV, 209–10, Porfirio Díaz, [location not given], to Jesús Garibay, Morelia, 6 December 1876.
53. APD, vol. XIV, 275, Juan N. Méndez, Mexico City, to Porfirio Díaz, Querétaro, 12 December 1876; and Porfirio Díaz, Querétaro, to Juan N. Méndez, Mexico City, 12 December 1876. Here, Díaz explained to Méndez that his decision was meant "to avoid any kind of complication that might put Michoacán in a worse state than it already is." Huerta's declaration of support for Chacón is found in APD, vol. XVI, 214, Epitacio Huerta, Morelia, to Porfirio Díaz, Guadalajara, 15 January 1877.
54. APD, vol. XV, 23–24, Felipe Chacón, Morelia, to Porfirio Díaz, Querétaro, 12 December 1876.
55. Chowning, *Wealth and Power in Provincial Mexico*, 302–6; Florescano, *Historia general de Michoacán*, 56.
56. APD, vol. XV, Francisco de S. Menocal, Morelia, to Porfirio Díaz, Guadalajara, 26 December 1876.
57. APD, vol. XV, Porfirio Díaz, Guadalajara, to Francisco de S. Menocal, Morelia, 26 December 1876.
58. *El Pensamiento Católico*, 26 January 1877, and 9 February 1877.
59. *El Pensamiento Católico*, 26 January 1877, and 2 February 1877.
60. *El Pensamiento Católico*, 19 January 1877, and 19 February 1877. Such conservative political ferment was not limited to Michoacán. Conservatives in Guadalajara took advantage of Díaz's triumph to found a similar political club (la Junta Central Conservadora) and a conservative newspaper (*La Esperanza*), the first paper of its kind since 1861. As Robert Case shows, although the slate of conservative candidates fared poorly in federal elections of March, they nonetheless made important gains in local elections in states such as Michoacán and Puebla. See Case, "El resurgimiento de los conservadores en México," 219–20. Díaz also received numerous letters from alarmed liberal witnesses to the conservative political resurgence in other states. For complaints of conservative resurgence in the states of Querétaro, Jalisco, Guanajuato, Hidalgo, Colima,

and Puebla, see APD, vol. XVI, 230, Antonio Gayón, Querétaro, to Porfirio Díaz, Guadalajara, 17 January 1877; vol. XVII, 82, Ignacio Vallarta, Guadalajara, to Porfirio Díaz, Mexico City, 28 January 1877; vol. XVII, 125, Francisco Mena, Guanajuato, to Porfirio Díaz, Guadalajara, 1 February 1877; vol. XIX, 10, Dr. Jaime Llopis, San Miguel de Allende, to Porfirio Díaz, Mexico City, 28 February 1877; and vol. XIX, 295, J. O. Rubio y Mercado, Xochiacoaco, to Porfirio Díaz, Mexico City, 15 March 1877; vol. XXI, 21, Doroteo López, Colima, to Porfirio Díaz, Mexico City, 4 April 1877; and vol. XXI, 230–33, J. J. de Zamacona, Puebla, to Porfirio Díaz, Mexico City, 17 April 1877.

61. *El Regenerador*, Decree of General Felipe Chacón to the Inhabitants of Michoacán, 30 December 1877.
62. *El Regenerador*, 5 February 1877.
63. APD, vol. XV, 18, Lauro González, Morelia, to Porfirio Díaz, Guadalajara, 24 December 1876.
64. APD, vol. XV, 156, Prisciliano Ortega, Morelia, to Porfirio Díaz, Guadalajara, 24 December 1876.
65. APD, vol. XV, 175, Joaquín Delgado y Camacho, Morelia, to Porfirio Díaz, Guadalajara, 24 December 1876.
66. APD, vol. XV, 175, Joaquín Delgado y Camacho, Morelia, to Porfirio Díaz, Guadalajara, 24 December 1876.
67. APD, vol. XVI, 214, Epitacio Huerta, Morelia, to Porfirio Díaz, Guadalajara, 15 January 1877.
68. *El Progresista*, 6 February 1877.
69. APD, vol. XVI, 148–49, Arcadio Ruiz Zepeda, Guanajuato, to Porfirio Díaz, Mexico City, 11 January 1877.
70. APD, vol. XVI, 170–71, M. Salcedo, M. López, and Various Others, Guadalajara, to Porfirio Díaz, Guadalajara, 13 January 1877.
71. APD, vol. XV, 188–90, José María Chávez, Las Balsas, to Domingo Juárez, Pátzcuaro, 19 December 1876.
72. APD, vol. XVII, 57–58, Pedro Ogazón, Mexico City, to Porfirio Díaz, Guadalajara, 26 January 1877.
73. *Memoria que el Secretario del Estado*, 67–68; *El Regenerador*, 2 February 1877; and Case, *El resurgimiento de los conservadores*, 218. Cosío Villegas indicates that Tagle issued the circular without Díaz's knowledge or approval. See *El porfiriato*, 259.
74. APD, vol. XVI, 149, Porfirio Díaz, Mexico City, to Arcadio Ruiz Zepeda, Guanajuato, 11 January 1877. Díaz made a similar request to the twenty-two exiled petitioners in Guadalajara. See APD, vol. XVI, 171, Porfirio Díaz, Guadalajara, to M. Salcedo, M. López, and Various Others, Guadalajara, 13 January 1877.
75. Chacón secured Zamora for the cause of Tuxtepec in January, and one of his subordinates captured General Francisco Franco, one of Iglesias's most important military allies. See APD, vol. XVI, 186–87, Felipe Chacón, Zamora, to Porfirio Díaz, Guadalajara, 15 January 1875; and vol. XVI, 215,

Telegram, Pedro González, Irapuato, to Porfirio Díaz, Guadalajara, 15 January 1877.
76. APD, vol. XV, 261, Porfirio Díaz, Guadalajara, to Lauro González, Morelia, 29 December 1876.
77. APD, vol. XV, 261, Lauro González, Morelia, to Porfirio Díaz, Guadalajara, 29 December 1876.
78. See, for example, APD, vol. XVII, 82, Ignacio Vallarta, Guadalajara, to Porfirio Díaz, Guadalajara, 28 January 1877; and vol. XVII, 125, Francisco Mena, Guanajuato, to Porfirio Díaz, Guadalajara, 1 February 1877.
79. APD, vol. XVI, 278–79, Pedro Ogazón, Mexico City, to Porfirio Díaz, Guadalajara, 18 January 1877.
80. APD, vol. XVI, 279, Porfirio Díaz, Guadalajara, to Pedro Ogazón, Mexico City, 28 January 1877.
81. APD, vol. XVII, 178, Telegram, Juan N. Méndez, Mexico City, to Porfirio Díaz, San Juan, 6 February 1877.
82. *El Regenerador*, 20 February 1877, Speeches of Felipe Chacón and Manuel González.
83. Coerver, "From Confrontation to Conciliation," 73–74; Coerver, *Porfirian Interregnum*; and Almendaro Setién, "La carrera militar del General Manuel González en el Ejército Conservador"; and Garner, *Porfirio Díaz*, 57, 90.
84. *El Regenerador*, 27 February 1877, and 6 March 1877.
85. APD, vol. XVII, 210, Jesús Ochoa, Zamora, to José María Martínez Negrete, Buenavista, 9 February 1877; and vol. XVII, 246, Telegram, José María Herrera and others, Morelia, to Porfirio Díaz, Mexico City, 12 February 1877.
86. APD, vol. XVIII, 101–2, M. Degollado, Morelia, to Porfirio Díaz, Mexico City, 18 February 1877.
87. APD, vol. XVIII, 159–62, Ramón Romero, Morelia, to Porfirio Díaz, Mexico City, 21 February 1877.
88. APD, vol. XVII, 114–22, Manuel González, Morelia, to Porfirio Díaz, Mexico City, 19 February 1877.
89. APD, vol. XVII, 114–22, Manuel González, Morelia, to Porfirio Díaz, Mexico City, 19 February 1877.
90. APD, vol. XVIII, 210, Manuel González, Morelia, to Porfirio Díaz, Mexico City, 23 February 1877.
91. Plata went on to lead the 6th Company of the infamous rurales until well into Díaz's second presidential period. See Verján Vásquez, "Policías rurales y suspensión de garantías," 234; and Vanderwood, *Disorder and Progress*, 54.
92. APD, vol. XVIII, 210, Manuel González, Morelia, to Porfirio Díaz, Mexico City, 23 February 1877.
93. APD, vol. XVIII, 129–30, Jesús Camarena, Guadalajara, to Porfirio Díaz, Guadalajara, 19 February 1877.
94. APD, vol. XVII, 209, Porfirio Díaz, Guadalajara, to Manuel González, Mexico City, 8 February 1877.

95. APD, vol. XIX, 248, Manuel González, Morelia, to Porfirio Díaz, Mexico City, 12 March 1877. Son of a wealthy Morelia-based family, Patiño studied at Morelia's diocesan seminary and received a law degree from the Colegio de San Nicolás de Hidalgo. He became a close associate of Huerta in the 1860s, and although he collaborated with the imperialist regime in a limited fashion in 1866, he continued to offer his legal services to Huerta in the context of the subdivision of Huerta's Chucándiro hacienda during the Porfiriato. See Chowning, *Wealth and Power in Provincial Mexico*, 299–300; and Cedeño Peguero, *El General Epitacio Huerta y su hacienda de Chucándiro*, 125–29.
96. *El Pensamiento Católico*, 16 March 1877.
97. *El Pensamiento Católico*, 16 March 1877.
98. *El Pensamiento Católico*, 16 March 1877; and *El Regenerador*, 20 March 1877.
99. *El Pensamiento Católico*, 6 April 1877.
100. *El Pensamiento Católico*, 6 April 1877; and *El Regenerador*, 27 March 1877.
101. APD, vol. XIX, 248, Manuel González, Morelia, to Porfirio Díaz, Mexico City, 12 March 1877. Here, González referenced a sixteenth-century Catholic uprising and massacre in France directed against the Huguenots.
102. APD, vol. XXI, 148–50, Manuel González, Morelia, to Porfirio Díaz, Mexico City, 13 April 1877.
103. APD, vol. XXII, 212–15, Manuel González, Morelia, to Porfirio Díaz, Mexico City, 7 May 1877.
104. *El Regenerador*, 20 April 1877.
105. APD, vol. XXI, 148–50, Manuel González, Morelia, to Porfirio Díaz, Mexico City, 13 April 1877; and *El Regenerador*, 1 May 1877.
106. APD, vol. XXIII, 50–52, Manuel González, Morelia, to Porfirio Díaz, Mexico City, 16 May 1877.
107. APD, vol. XVII, 257–61, "Alocución," [no calendar day given] February 1877.
108. On Ortega's political trayectoria, see Chowning, *Wealth and Power*, 303.
109. APD, vol. XXIV, 16, Fermín Ortega, Morelia, to Porfirio Díaz, Mexico City, 4 June 1877.
110. APD, vol. XXIV, 53, Francisco de P. Infante, Morelia, to Porfirio Díaz, Mexico City, 6 June 1877. Francisco was likely a member of the powerful Morelia-based Infante clan, one of the first Spanish families to settle in Michoacán. See Yokoyama, "La familia Infante."
111. APD, vol. XXV, 93–95, Manuel de Estrada, Morelia, to Porfirio Díaz, Mexico City, 26 June 1877. Estrada was a signatory to an 1856 petition against the inclusion of an article guaranteeing the "toleration of cults" in the Constitution of 1857. See *Exposición que varios vecinos de Morelia elevan al soberano congreso constituyente*, 19. For Estrada's adhesion to the Second Empire, see Chowning, *Wealth and Power*, 301.
112. See Cannelli, *Nación católica y estado laico*.
113. APD, vol. XXV, 180–82, Bruno Patiño, Morelia, to Porfirio Díaz, Mexico City, 4 July 1877.

114. APD, XXIV, 134–36, Manuel González, Morelia, to Porfirio Díaz, Mexico City, 11 June 1877. The rurales were federal mounted police created by the Juárez government to suppress rural banditry. The definitive treatment of the subject is Vanderwood, *Disorder and Progress*.
115. APD, vol. XVII, 114–22, Manuel González, Morelia, to Porfirio Díaz, Mexico City, 19 February 1877; and APD, vol. XXV, 180–82, Bruno Patiño, Morelia to Porfirio Díaz, Mexico City, 4 July 1877. Patiño also planned and received government subsidy for an agricultural and artisanal exposition in Morelia in September.
116. APD, vol. XXV, 180–82, Bruno Patiño, Morelia, to Porfirio Díaz, Mexico City, 4 July 1877.
117. *El Regenerador*, 10 April 1877, Circular Number 44 of the State Government and Military Command of Michoacán, issued 9 April 1877.
118. APD, vol. XXII, 22–23, Manuel González, Morelia, to Porfirio Díaz, Mexico City, 25 April 1877.
119. APD, vol. XXIV, 134–36, Manuel González, Morelia, to Porfirio Díaz, Mexico City, 11 June 1877.
120. APD, vol. XXIII, 110–11, Mariano Camacho, León, to Porfirio Díaz, Mexico City, 20 May 1877; and Archivo Histórico Municipal de León (hereafter, AHML), Jefetura Política/Asuntos Eclesiásticos/Comunicaciones, caja 1, exp. 13, Máximoo Sánchez, León, to Jefe Político, León, 30 March 1877.
121. *El Pensamiento Católico*, 27 July 1877.
122. *El Pensamiento Católico*, 7 September 1877, and 14 September 1877.
123. APD, vol. XXVI, 118–19, Esteban Zenteno, Morelia, to Porfirio Díaz, Mexico City, 6 August 1877.
124. APD, vol. XXVII, 222–25, Manuel González, Tepic, to Porfirio Díaz, Mexico City, 9 October 1877; APD, vol. XXVII, 250–54, Bruno Patiño, Morelia, to Porfirio Díaz, Mexico City, 12 October 1877; and *El Pensamiento Católico*, 12 October 1877, 19 October 1877, and 26 October 1877.
125. *La Voz de México*, 16 October 1877; *El Siglo Diez y Nueve*, 16 October 1877; *El Foro*, 17 October 1877; *El Combate*, 21 October 1877; *El Monitor Republicano*, 27 October 1877; and *La Bandera Nacional*, 2 November 1877.
126. *El Pensamiento Católico*, 19 October 1877, 26 October 1877, and 2 November 1877. Monje had been killed at the behest of Prefect Garibay back in July. See *La Voz de México*, 14 July 1877.
127. *La Voz de México*, 14 July 1877, 10 October 1877, and 30 October 1877.
128. *El Pensamiento Católico*, 28 December 1877.
129. CPD, L2C3 1073–1075, Bruno Patiño, Morelia, to Porfirio Díaz, Mexico City, 5 November 1877; APD, vol. XXVII, 250–54, Bruno Patiño, Morelia, to Porfirio Díaz, Mexico City, 12 October 1877; APD, vol. XXVIII, 146, José J. Guido, Morelia, to Porfirio Díaz, Mexico City, 18 January 1878; and APD, vol. XXVIII, 241–42, Bruno Patiño, Morelia, to Porfirio Díaz, Mexico City, 27 February 1877.

130. APD, vol. XVII, 189, Abraham Plata, Morelia, to Porfirio Díaz, Mexico City, 3 October 1877; and APD, vol. XVII, 222–25, Manuel González, Tepic, to Porfirio Díaz, Mexico City, 9 October 1877.
131. APD, vol. XVIII, 237, Epitacio Huerta, Morelia, to Porfirio Díaz, Mexico City, 27 February 1877. Díaz rejected Patiño's proposition to suspend constitutional guarantees in the state in order to better persecute bandits and would-be revolutionaries. See APD, vol. XXVII, 250–54, Bruno Patiño, Morelia, to Porfirio Díaz, Mexico City, 12 October 1877.
132. APD, vol. XVIII, 167, Doroteo López, Colima, to Porfirio Díaz, Mexico City, 21 February 1877. In this case, the authorities of Colima settled for leveling the fine on the parish priest of Manzanillo, who, they claimed, had led a public procession to the port accompanied by ringing church bells. Ireneo Paz's new paper, *La Patria*, issued a sharp rebuke of the civil authorities of Manzanillo for their actions shortly after. See *La Patria*, 21 March 1877.
133. APD, vol. XVII, Amada C. de Furlong and Josefa del Castillo N. de Negrete, Mexico City, to Porfirio Díaz, Mexico City, 6 February 1877.
134. MRP, Pelagio Antonio Labastida y Dávalos, Mexico City, to Mariano Riva Palacio, Mexico City, 4 April 1877.
135. VRP, Victoriana Arriaga and María Lascuaraín, Mexico City, to Guadalupe Bros, Mexico City, 1 September 1877.
136. Schmitt, "Díaz Conciliation Policy on State and Local Levels," 513–32.
137. *El Regenerador*, 6 March 1877.
138. *El Pensamiento Católico*, 26 January 1877.
139. See chapter 4.
140. ADZ, DG 99, Fórmula de la protesta mandada observar por la circular de 13 de enero último, [no date recorded]. Diocesan authorities must have been referring to Tagle's circular of January 15, not 13.
141. AHCM, Diocesano/Gobierno/Mandatos/Circulares, caja 190, exp. 279, Circular Concerning Instructions for the Protesta, 19 April 1877.
142. The practice of dissimulation in order to avoid persecution had a long history in Western Christianity. See Zagorin, *Ways of Lying*.
143. García Ugarte, *Poder político y religioso*, 2:1520–25.
144. APD, vol. XIX, 70–72, Manuel González, Morelia, to Porfirio Díaz, Mexico City, 1 March 1877.
145. ADZ, DGP 125, Chilchota, Francisco García Ramos, Chilchota, to Diocesan Secretary, Zamora, 8 October 1877.
146. AHCM, Diocesano/Gobierno/Parroquias/Solicitudes, caja 280, exp. 508, Juan Coria, Pedro G. Camacho, Manuel Nieto, and others, Huango, to Luis Macouzet, Morelia, 10 October 1877.
147. Michoacán witnessed important mobilization in the name of social Catholicism and, subsequently, Catholic politics in the late nineteenth and early twentieth centuries. The state witnessed a surge in lay associations of a social

and even populist nature, and it hosted important Catholic congresses in the first years of the twentieth century, including the first Catholic meeting focused on labor issues, which was held in Zamora in 1906. The short-lived Partido Católico Nacional also enjoyed some of its strongest support in Michoacán. See Díaz Patiño, "El catolicismo social en la Arquidiócesis de Morelia," 116–21; Tapia Santamaría, *Campo religioso y evolución política*, 148–54; Solís Cruz, "De indianismo eclesiástico y otros," 18–20; and O'Dogherty, *De urnas y sótanas*, 17.
148. *La Bandera Nacional*, 13 October 1877.
149. Case, "El resurgimiento de los conservadores en México."
150. Pani, "Democracia y representación política"; and Adame Goddard, *El pensamiento político y social de los católicos mexicanos*, 96–100.
151. Schmitt, "Porfirian Conciliation Policy," 531–32.
152. Bastian, *Los disidentes*, 173–75.

Conclusions

1. Cannelli, *Nación católica y estado laico*, 79–110.
2. Adame Goddard, *El Pensamiento político y social de los católicos mexicanos*, 95–121; Ceballos Ramírez, *El catolisimo social*; Schmitt, "Díaz Conciliation Policy"; Bastian, *Los disidentes*, 173–75; and Cannelli, *Nación católico y estado laico*, 151–205.
3. Bautista García, "Entre México y Roma," 97–100.
4. AGHPEM, Guerra y Ejército, caja 2, exp. 13, Albino Fuentes Acosta, Puruándiro, to Interior Minister, Morelia, 12 January 1875.
5. Ceballos Ramírez, *El Catolicismo social*; Adame Goddard, *El pensamiento político y social de los católicos mexicanos*; Díaz Patiño, "El catolicismo social en el Arquidiocesis de Morelia"; Tapia Santamaría, *Campo religioso y evolución política*, 148–54; Solís Cruz, "De indianismo eclesiástico y otros," 18–20; and O'Dogherty, *De urnas y sótanas*, 17.
6. Purnell, *Popular Movements and State Formation*, chap. 5.
7. Tapia Santamaría, *Campo religioso y evolución política*, 81–148.
8. Stauffer, "Community, Identity"; Butler, "God's Caciques"; Cochet, *Alambradas en la sierra*, 136–45; and Gledhill, *Cultura y desafío en Ostula*, 276–78.
9. Butler, *Popular Piety and Political Identity*.
10. Lomnitz, "La religión de los Caballeros Templarios"; and Mireles Valverde, *Todos somos autodefensas*, 363–64.

Bibliography

Archives Consulted

Archivo Diocesano de Zamora, Zamora (ADZ)
Archivo General de la Nación, Mexico City (AGN)
Archivo General e Histórico del Poder Ejecutivo del Estado de Michoacán, Morelia (AGHPEM)
Archivo Histórico Casa de Morelos, Morelia (AHCM)
Archivo Histórico de la Defensa Nacional, Mexico City (AHDN)
Archivo Histórico del Arzobispado de León, León (AHAL)
Archivo Histórico del Arzobispado de México, Mexico City (AHAM)
Archivo Histórico del Poder Judicial del Estado de Michoacán, Morelia (AHPJEM)
Archivo Histórico Municipal de León, León (AHML)
Benson Latin American Collection, University of Texas at Austin (BL)
Colección Porfirio Díaz, Universidad Iberoamericana, Mexico City (CPD)

Newspapers

Boletín Oficial del Gobierno del Estado de Michoacán, Morelia
El Ahuizote, Mexico City
El Combate, Mexico City
El Correo del Comercio, Mexico City
El Diario Oficial, Mexico City
El Eco de Ambos Mundos, Mexico City
El Federalista, Mexico City
El Foro, Mexico City
El Gladiador, Mexico City
El Monitor Republicano, Mexico City
El Padre Cobos, Mexico City
El Pájaro Verde, Mexico City
El Pensamiento Católico, Morelia
El Progresista, Morelia
El Radical, Mexico City

El Regenerador, Morelia
El Siglo Diez y Nueve, Mexico City
La Bandera de Ocampo, Morelia
La Bandera Nacional, Mexico City
La Colonia Española, Mexico City
La Iberia, Mexico City
La Idea Católica, Mexico City
La Patria, Mexico City
La Revista Universal, Mexico City
La Voz de México, Mexico City
The Two Republics, Mexico City

Published Sources

Adame Goddard, Jorge. *El pensamiento politico y social de los católicos mexicanos, 1867–1914*. Mexico City: UNAM, 1981.

Águilar, Ignacio. *Corona fúnebre colocada sobre la tumba del Ilmo. Sr. Dr. D. José Antonio de la Peña y Navarro, primer obispo de Zamora*. Zamora, Mexico: Imprenta de J. M. T. Maldonado, 1877.

Aguirre Christiani, María Gabriela. "Una jerarquía en trancisión: el asalto de los 'piolatinos' al episcopado nacional, 1920–1924." *Interstitios Sociales* 4 (September 2012): 1–29.

Alazraki, Paola Chenillo. "Liberalismo a prueba. La expulsion de los 'extranjeros perniciosos' en México durante la República Restaurada (1867–1876)." *Revista de Indias* 72, no. 255 (2012): 377–406.

Alcalá, Alfonso, and Manuel Olimón, eds. *Episcopado y gobierno en México: cartas pastorales colectivas del episcopado mexicano, 1859–1875*. Mexico City: Ediciones Paulinas, 1989.

Almendaro Setién, Georgina Esperanza. "La carrera militar del General Manuel González en el Ejército Conservador (1846–1861)." Master's thesis, Universidad Iberoamericana, 2005.

Alonso, Ana María. *The Thread of Blood: Colonialism, Revolution, and Gender on Mexico's Northern Frontier*. Tucson: University of Arizona Press, 1997.

Álvarez Lira, Presb. Cirilo. *Aportaciones históricas sobre Villa Morelos, 1527–1982*. Self-published, 1982.

Anales del Museo Nacional de México, Segunda Época, vol. 3, no. 3. Mexico City: Imprenta del Museo Nacional, 1906.

Árciga, José Ignacio. *Carta pastoral que el Ilmo. Dr. Don José Ignacio Árciga, dignísimo Arzobispo de Michoacán, dirige a todos sus diocesanos con motivo de la publicación del Edicto de Jubileo extraordinario concedido por N. S. Padre el Sr. Pio IX, en 11 de abril de 1869*. Morelia, Mexico: Imprenta I. Arango, 1869.

———. *Segunda carta pastoral que el Ilmo. Sr. Don José Ignacio Árciga, dignísimo Arzobispo de Michoacán, dirige a todos sus diocesanos con motivo de las encyclicas expedidas por S. Santidad el Sr. Pio IX en 15 mayo y 4 de junio del presente año*. Morelia, Mexico: Tipografía I. Arango, 1871.

Arreola Cortés, Raul. *Epitacio Huerta: soldado y estadista liberal, Cuadernos de Lectura Popular*. Mexico City: SEP, Subsecretario de Asuntos Culturales, 1967.

Arrom, Silvia. "Filantropía católica y sociedad civil: los voluntarios mexicanos de San Vicente de Paul, 1845–1910." *Revista Sociedad y Economía* 10 (April 2006): 69–97.

———. "Las Señoras de la Caridad: pioneras olvidadas de asistencia social en México, 1863–1910." *Historia Mexicana* 57, no. 2 (October–December 2007): 445–90.

———. "Mexican Laywomen Spearhead a Catholic Revival: The Ladies of Charity, 1863–1910." In *Religious Culture in Modern Mexico*, edited by Martin Austin Nesvig, 50–77. Lanham, Md.: Rowman and Littlefield Publishers, 2007.

———. *Volunteering for a Cause: Gender, Faith, and Charity in Mexico from the Reform to the Revolution*. Albuquerque: University of New Mexico Press, 2016.

Ballard Perry, Laurens. *Juárez and Díaz: Machine Politics in Mexico*. Dekalb: Northern Illinois University, 1978.

Baltazar Chávez, Geraldo. "El Corpus Christi P'urhépecha: la apropiación indígena de una fiesta en la época colonial." Master's thesis, Universidad Michoacana de San Nicolás de Hidalgo, 2011.

Barbosa, Manuel. *Apuntes para la historia de Michoacán*. Morelia, Mexico: Talleres de la Escuela Industrial Militar Porfirio Díaz, 1905.

Barragán, Javier Moctezuma. *José María Iglesias y la justicia electoral*. Mexico City: UNAM/Instituto de Investigaciones Jurídicas, 1994.

Barragán López, Esteban. *Con el pie en el estribo: formación y deslizamientos de las sociedades rancheras en la construcción del México moderno*. Zamora, Mexico: El Colegio de Michoacán, 1997.

———. "Identidad ranchera: apreciaciones desde la sierra sur Jalmichiana, en el occidente de México." *Relaciones: Estudios de História y Sociedad* 11, no. 43 (1990): 75–106.

———. *Mas allá de los caminos: los rancheros del Potrero de Herrera*. Zamora, Mexico: El Colegio de Michoacán, 1990.

Barragán López, Esteban, Odile Hoffman, Thierry Linck, and David Skerritt, eds., *Rancheros y sociedades rancheras*. Zamora, Mexico: Colegio de Michoacán, 1994.

Basalenque, Fr. Diego. *Historia de la provincia de San Nicolás Tolentino de Michoacán*. Mexico City: Tipografía Barbedillo y Comp., 1886.

Bastian, Jean Pierre. "Las sociedades protestantes y la oposición a Porfirio Díaz, 1877–1911." *Historia Mexicana* 37, no. 3 (1988): 469–512.

———. *Los disidentes: sociedades protestantes y revolución en México, 1872–1911*. Mexico City: El Colegio de México, 1989.
Bautista García, Cecilia Adriana. *Clérigos virtuosos e instruidos: un proyecto de romanización clerical en un arzobispado mexicano. Michoacán, 1867–1887*. Morelia, Mexico: Universidad Michoacana de San Nicolás de Hidalgo, 2017.
———. "Dos momentos en la historia de un culto: el origen y la coronación pontificia de la Virgen de Jacona (siglos XVII-XIX)." *Tzintzun: Revista de Estudios Históricos* 43 (January–June 2006): 11–32.
———. "Entre México y Roma: la consolidación de un proyecto de educación clerical a fines del siglo XIX." In *Catolicismo y formación del estado nacional en la Península Ibérica, América Latina, e Italia, siglos XIX–XX*, edited by Yves Solís and Franco Savarino, 89–110. Mexico City: ENAH/INAH/Mil Libros Editorial, 2017.
———. "Hacia la romanización de la iglesia mexicana a fines del siglo XIX." *Historia Mexicana* 55, no. 1 (July–September 2005): 99–144.
———. "La afirmación del orden social en el estado liberal y las nuevas congregaciones religiosas." In *Formas de gobierno en México: poder político y actores sociales a través del tiempo*, vol. 2, edited by Victor Gayol, 447–84. Zamora, Mexico: El Colegio de Michoacán, 2012.
———. "La reorganización de la iglesia en el arzobispado de Michoacán, 1868–1897." Undergraduate thesis, Universidad Michoacana de San Nicolás de Hidalgo, 1997.
———. *Las disyuntivas del estado y de la iglesia en la consolidación del orden liberal: México, 1856–1910*. Mexico City: El Colegio de México, 2012.
Bazant, Jan. *The Alienation of Church Wealth in Mexico: Social and Economic Aspects of the Liberal Reform, 1856–1875*. Cambridge: Cambridge University Press, 1971.
Becker, Marjorie. *Setting the Virgin on Fire: Lázaro Cárdenas, Michoacán Peasants, and the Redemption of the Mexican Revolution*. Berkeley: University of California Press, 1995.
Beirne, Charles J. "Latin American Bishops of the First Vatican Council, 1869–1870." *Americas* 25, no. 3 (January 1969): 265–80.
Böehm, Brigette. "Las comunidades de indígenas de Ixtlán y Pajacuarán ante la reforma liberal en el siglo XIX." In *Estructuras y formas agrarias en México: del pasado y del presente*, edited by Antonio Escobar Ohmstede and Teresa Rojas Rabiela, 145–76. Mexico City: Registro Agrario Nacional/Archivo General Agrario/CIESAS, 2001.
Brading, David. *Church and State in Bourbon Mexico: The Diocese of Michoacán, 1749–1810*. Cambridge: Cambridge University Press, 1994.
———. *Haciendas and Ranchos in the Mexican Bajío: León, 1700–1860*. Cambridge: Cambridge University Press, 1979.

———. *The Origins of Mexican Nationalism*. Cambridge: Cambridge Centre of Latin American Studies, 1985.
———. "Ultramontane Intransigence and the Mexican Reform: Clemente de Jesús Munguía." In *The Politics of Religion in an Age of Revival*, edited by Austin Ivereigh, 115–42. London: Institute for Latin American Studies, 2000.
Brand, Donald D., et al. *Coalcomán and Motines del Oro: An "Ex-Distrito" of Michoacán Mexico*. Austin: University of Texas at Austin, 1960.
Bravo Ugarte, José, ed. *Inspección ocular de Michoacán, región centro y sudoeste*. Mexico City: Editorial Jus, 1960.
Brittsan, Zachary. *Popular Politics and Rebellion in Mexico: Manuel Lozada and La Reforma, 1855–1876*. Nashville: Vanderbilt University Press, 2015.
Buitrón, Juan B. *Apuntes para servir a la historia del arzobispado de Morelia*. Mexico City: Imprenta Aldina, 1948.
Burroughs Conover V, Cornelius. "A Saint in the Empire: Mexico City's San Felipe de Jesús, 1597–1820." PhD diss., University of Texas at Austin, 2009.
Butler, Matthew. "God's Caciques: Caciquismo and the Cristero Revolt in Coalcomán." In *Caciquismo in Twentieth-Century Mexico*, edited by Alan Knight and Wil Pansters, 94–112. London: Institute for the Study of the Americas, 2005.
———. "The 'Liberal' Cristero: Ladislao Molina and the Cristero Rebellion in Michoacán, 1927–9." *Journal of Latin American Studies* 31, no. 3 (October 1999): 645–71.
———. *Popular Piety and Political Identity in Mexico's Cristero Rebellion: Michoacán, 1927–29*. Oxford: Oxford University Press, 2004.
———. "Religious Developments in Mexico, 1865–1945." In *The Cambridge History of Religions in America*. Vol. 2, *1790–1945*, edited by Stephen J. Stein, 702–26. Cambridge: Cambridge University Press, 2012.
Camacho y García, Ramón. *Carta pastoral del Ilmo. Sr. obispo de Querétaro con motivo de la alocución de Ntro. Smo. Padre el Sr. Pio IX, en el consistorio de 25 de julio del presente año*. Querétaro, Mexico: Tipografía de M. Rodríguez Velázquez, 1873.
———. *Colección de cartas, edictos, e instrucciones pastorales del ilustrísimo señor doctor D. Ramón Camacho y García, dignísimo segundo obispo de la santa iglesia de Querétaro, precedida de apuntes biográficos sobre el mismo ilustrísimo señor*. Mexico City: Tipografía Berrueco Hnos., 1886.
Camacho Mercado, Eduardo. *Frente al hambre y el óbus: iglesia y feligresia en Totatiche y Cañon de Bolaños, 1876–1926*. Guadalajara, Mexico: Arquiodiocesis de Guadalajara/Universidad de Guadalajara, 2014.
Campos, Fr. Leopoldo, OFM. "Métodos misionales y rasgos biográficos de Don Vasco de Quiroga según Cristóbal Cabrera, Pbro." In *Don Vasco de Quiroga y Arzobispado de Morelia*, edited by Agustín Garón García, 107–55. Mexico City: Editorial Jus, 1965.

Cañeque, Alejandro. *The King's Living Image: The Culture and Politics of Viceregal Power in Colonial Mexico*. New York: Routledge, 2004.
Cañizares-Esguerra, Jorge. *How to Write a History of the New World: Histories, Epistemologies, and Identities in the Eighteenth-Century Atlantic World*. Stanford, Calif.: Stanford University Press, 2001.
Cannelli, Riccardo. *Nación católica y estado laico: el conflict político-religioso en México desde la Independencia hasta la Revolución (1821–1914)*. Mexico City: INEHRM, 2012.
Carmagnani, Marcello. *El regreso de los dioses: el proceso de reconstitución de la identidad étnica en Oaxaca, siglos XVII y XVIII*. Mexico City: Fondo de Cultura Económica, 1988.
Carreño, Alberto María, ed. *El archivo del general Porfirio Díaz, memorias y documentos*, 29 vols. Mexico City: Editorial "Elede," 1947–1961.
Case, Robert. "El resurgimiento de los conservadores en México, 1867–1877." *Historia Mexicana* 25, no. 2 (October–December 1975): 204–31.
Ceballos, Ciro B. *Aurora y ocaso, 1867–1906. Gobierno de Lerdo*. 2nd ed. Mexico City: Talleres Tipográficas 1a de López, 1912.
Ceballos Ramírez, Manuel. *El catolicismo social: un tercero en discordia: Rerum Novarum, la "cuestión social," y la movilización de los católicos mexicanos (1891–1911)*. Mexico City: El Colegio de México, 1991.
Cedeño Peguero, María Guadalupe. *El General Epitacio Huerta y su hacienda de Chucándiro, 1860–1892*. Morelia, Mexico: Instituto Michoacano de Cultura, 1990.
Chance, John, and William Taylor. "Cofradías and Cargos: An Historical Perspective on the Mesoamerican Civil-Religious Hierarchy." *American Ethnologist* 12, no. 1 (February 1985): 1–26.
Chávez, José María. *Noticias históricas, geográficas, y estadísticas del Distrito de Coalcomán*. Morelia, Mexico: Imprenta de Octaviano Ortiz, 1873.
Chowning, Margaret. "The Catholic Church and the Ladies of the Vela Perpetua: Gender and Devotional Change in Nineteenth-Century Mexico." *Past and Present* 221, no. 1 (November 2013): 197–237.
———. *Wealth and Power in Provincial Mexico: Michoacán from the Late Colony to the Revolution*. Stanford, Calif.: Stanford University Press, 1999.
Christian, William, Jr. *Local Religion in Sixteenth-Century Spain*. Princeton, N.J.: Princeton University Press, 1981.
Clark, Christopher, and Wolfram Kaiser, eds. *Culture Wars: Secular-Catholic Conflict in Nineteenth-Century Europe*. Cambridge: Cambridge University Press, 2003.
Cochet, Hubert. *Alambradas en la sierra: un sistema agrario en México: La sierra de Coalcomán*. Zamora, Mexico: El Colegio de Michoacán, 1991.
Coerver, Dan. "From Confrontation to Conciliation: Church-State Relations in Mexico, 1867–1884." *Journal of Church and State* 32, no. 1 (Winter 1990): 65–80.

―――. *The Porfirian Interregnum: The Presidency of Manuel González of Mexico, 1880–1884*. Fort Worth: Texas Christian University, 1979.
Connaughton, Brian. *Clerical Ideology in a Revolutionary Age: The Guadalajara Church and the Idea of the Mexican Nation, 1788–1853*. Translated by Mark Alan Healey. Calgary, Alberta: University of Calgary Press, 2003.
Coromina, Amador, ed. *Recopilación de los leyes, decretos, reglamentos, y circulares expedidas en el estado de Michoacán*, 28 vols. Morelia, Mexico: Imprenta de los Hijos de I. Arango, 1886–1923.
Corona fúnebre que la redacción de "El Republicano," con la cooperación de varios liberales, consagra a la memoria del esclarecido campeón de nuestras liberatades patrias, Ciudadano General Nicolás de Régules. Morelia, Mexico: Imprenta de la Escuela Industrial Militar Porfirio Díaz, 1895.
Correa Etchegaray, Leonor. "El rescate de una devoción jesuítica: el Sagrado Corazón de Jesús en la primera mitad del siglo XIX." In *Memoria del I Coloquio Historia de la Iglesia en el siglo XIX*, edited by Ramos Medina, 39–62. Mexico City: Condumex, 1998.
Cortés Máximo, Juan Carlos. "La comunidad de Tarímbaro: gobierno indígena, arrendameinto, y reparto de tierras, 1824–1884." In *Autoridad y gobierno indígena en Michoacán: ensayos a través de su historia*, edited by Carlos S. Paredes Martínez and Marta Terán, 441–68. Zamora, Mexico: El Colegio de Michoacán, 2003.
―――. "La desamortización de la propiedad indígena en una provincia mexicana. Los fines y efectos de la Ley de 1827 sobre reparto de tierras comunales en Michoacán." *Relaciones* 34, no. 134 (April 2013): 263–301.
Cosío Villegas, Daniel. *El porfiriato: vida política interior*, part 1. Mexico City: Editorial Hermes, 1970.
―――, ed. *Historia moderna de México*, 7 vols. Mexico City: Editorial Hermes, 1955–1965.
―――. *La República Restaurada, La vida política*. Vol. 1 of *Historia moderna de México*. Mexico City: Editorial Hermes, 1955.
―――. "Sebastián Lerdo de Tejada: mártir de la República Restaurada." *Historia Mexicana* 17, no. 2 (October–December 1967): 169–99.
Cosmes, Francisco. *Historia general de México. Continuación a la de don Niceto Zamacois; parte contemporánea; los últimos 33 años*. Vol. 24. Barcelona: Ramón de S. N. Araluce Editor, 1902.
Costeloe, Michael P. *Church and State in Independent Mexico: A Study of the Patronage Debate, 1821–1857*. London: Royal Historical Society, 1978.
―――. *Church Wealth in Mexico, 1800–1856*. Cambridge: Cambridge University Press, 1967.
Covo, Jacqueline. *Las ideas de la reforma en México (1855–1861)*. Translated by María Francisca Mourier-Martínez. Mexico City: UNAM, 1983.

Curcio Nagy, Linda. *The Great Festivals of Colonial Mexico City: Performing Power and Identity.* Albuquerque: University of New Mexico Press, 2004.

Davis, Natalie Zemon. "From 'Popular Religion' to Religious Cultures." In *Reformation Europe: A Guide to Research,* edited by Steven Ozmet, 321–42. St. Louis: Center for Reformation Research, 1982.

———. "Some Tasks and Themes in the Study of Popular Religion." In *The Pursuit of Holiness in Late Medieval and Renaissance Religion,* by Charles Trinkhaus and Heiko A. Oberman, 307–36. Leiden, Netherlands: E. J. Brill, 1974.

de la Peña y Navarro, José Antonio. *Carta pastoral del Ilmo. Obispo de Zamora, relativa a las peregrinaciones espirituales.* Publisher unknown, 1874.

———. *Pastoral número cinco del Obispo de Zamora, que con motivo del Vigésimo Quinto aniversario del pontificado de Nuestro Santísimo padre el Señor Pío IX, dirige a su Venerable Cabildo, a todo el clero y demás fieles de su diócesis.* Zamora, Mexico: Teodoro Silva Romero, 1871.

———. *Primera pastoral del primer obispo de la nueva diócesis de Zamora.* Zamora, Mexico: Imprenta Ignacio Arango, 1864.

———. *Sexta pastoral del Obispo de Zamora, que con objeto de combatir algunos errores del protestantismo dirige a su ilustre cabildo, venerable clero, y demás fieles de su Diócesis.* Guadalajara, Mexico: Tipografía Isaac Banda, 1872.

———. "Sr. Cura Juez Ecco. de . . . Circular número 26," 19 September 1873 (Publisher unknown).

Descripción de la fiesta celebrada en Roma con motivo a la canonización de San Felipe de Jesús y demás mártires del Japón, seguida de la alocución de los Sres. Obispos allí reunidos y un discurso en favor de la Iglesia del Oriente pronunciado por el monseñor Félix Dupanloup, obispo de Orleans. Guadalajara, Mexico: Imprenta de Rodriguez, 1862.

Díaz Patiño, Gabriela. *Católicos, liberales, y protestantes: El debate por las imágenes religiosas en la formación de una cultura nacional (1848–1908).* Mexico City: El Colegio de México, 2016.

———. "El catolicismo social en el Arquidiócesis de Morelia, Michoacán (1897–1913)." *Tzintzun: Revista de Estudios Históricos* 38 (July–December 2003): 97–134.

Diez de Sollano y Dávalos, José María de Jesús. *Décima sexta carta pastoral que el Obispo de León dirige a su Ilmo. Cabildo, V. clero, y fieles diocesanos sobre la doctrina de la Iglesia Católica acerca de los escritos perniciosos y su funesta lectura; y ademas sobre la consagración de la diócesis al Sagrado Corazón de Jesús, y establecimiento en ella del Apostolado de la Oración en honra del mismo Sacratísimo Corazón.* León, Mexico: Tipografía de Monzón, 1875.

———. *Décimatercia pastoral del Ilmo. Sr. Dr. y Maestro D. José María de Jesús Diez de Sollano y Dávalos para publicar la alocución de Su Santidad de 25 de julio, y la indulgencia plenaria concedida en la misma, formando parte de esta pastoral el cuaderno impreso con el título de exposición contra el proyecto de elevar a constitucionales las leyes de reforma*. León, Mexico: Imprenta de José María Monzón, 1873.

——. *Edicto del Obispo de León sobre el matrimonio sacramento*. León, Mexico: Tipografía de Monzón, 1874.

——. *Manifestación que hace el obispo de León a su venerable clero, fieles diocesanos, y todo el mundo católico contra el proyecto de ley orgánica que se discute en el congreso general*. León, Mexico: Tipografía José María Monzón, 1874.

——. *Primera carta pastoral que el Ilmo. Sr. Obispo de León, Dr. y Maestro D. José María de Jesús Diez de Sollano y Dávalos, dirige a sus diocesanos*. Querétaro, Mexico: Tipografía de Mariano Rodríguez Velázquez, 1864.

——. *Tercera carta pastoral que el Ilmo. Sr. Obispo de León dirige a su venerable clero y fieles diocesanos*. Guanajuato, Mexico: Tipografía a Cargo de Felix María Conejo, 1864.

——. *Undécima pastoral que el Illmo. y Rmo. Sr. Obispo de León, Dr. y Maestro D. José María de Jesús Diez de Sollano y Dávalos, dirige a su Illmo. y V. cabildo, señores curas y v. clero. La que contiene los estatutos disciplinares de la diocesis de León*. León, Mexico: Imprenta de J. M. Monzón, 1872.

——. *Vigésima prima carta pastoral que el Ilmo. y Rmo. Sr. Obispo de León, Dr. y Maestro. D. José María de Jesús Diez de Sollano y Dávalos dirige a su Ilmo. y v. cabildo, señores curas, y v. clero. Contiene la tercera parte de los estatutos diocesanos con el extracto alfabético de las circulares expedidas por la Sagrada Mitra de León, 10 enero de 1872 hasta 24 abril 1879*. León, Mexico: Imprenta de J. M. Monzón, 1879.

Dohan, Edward. "St. Thomas of Villanova." In *The Catholic Encyclopedia*, vol. 14. New York: Robert Appleton Company, 1912. Retrieved 10 March 2015 from http://www.newadvent.org/cathen/14696a.htm.

Domínguez, José Luis. "Zacapu: un pueblo que trabaja." *Estudios Michoacanos*, vol. 3. Zamora, Mexico: El Colegio de Michoacán, 1989.

Dublán, Manuel, and José María Lozano. *Legislación mexicana, o colección completa de las disposiciones legislativas expedidas desde la independencia de la república*, vol. 13. Mexico City: Imprenta de Eduardo Dublán y Compañía, 1886.

Ducey, Michael. *A Nation of Villages: Riot and Rebellion in the Mexican Huasteca, 1750–1850*. Tucson: University of Arizona Press, 2004.

Duffy, Eamon. *The Stripping of the Altars: Traditional Religion in England, 1400–1580*. New Haven, Conn.: Yale University Press, 1992.

Echeverría, Bolívar. *La modernidad de lo barroco*. Mexico City: Ediciones Era, 2013. Electronic edition.

Eire, Carlos M. N. "The Concept of Popular Religion." In *Local Religion in Colonial Mexico*, edited by Martin Austin Nesvig, 1–35. Albuquerque: University of New Mexico Press, 2006.

El diario de los debates. Séptimo Congreso Constitucional de la Unión, vol. 4. Mexico City: Imprenta de F. Díaz de León y Santiago White, 1875.

Escobar Ohmstede, Antonio, ed. *Indio, nación, y comunidad en el México del siglo XIX*. Mexico City: CIESAS, 1993.

Escobar Ohmstede, Antonio, and Matthew Butler, eds. *Mexico in Transition: New Perspectives on Mexican Agrarian History, Nineteenth and Twentieth Centuries/México y sus transiciones: reconsideraciones sobre la historia agraria mexicana, siglos XIX y XX*. Mexico City/Austin, Tex.: CIESAS/LLILAS, 2013.

Escobar Ohmstede, Antonio, and Franz J. Schryer. "Las sociedades agrarias en la Huasteca hidalguense, 1856–1900." *Estudios Mexicanos/Mexican Studies* 8, no. 1 (1992): 1–21.

Estadística de la Sociedad Católica de Señoras, hasta el día 2 de febrero de 1874. Mexico City: Imprenta José Mariano Fernández de Lara, 1874.

Exposición que varios vecinos de Morelia elevan al soberano congreso constituyente, pidiéndole se digne reprobar el artículo 15 del proyecto de constitución, sobre tolerancia de cultos. Morelia, Mexico: Imprenta de Ignacio Arango, 1856.

Falcón, Romana. "El estado liberal ante las rebeliones populares. México, 1867–1876." *Historia Mexicana* 54, no. 216 (April–June 2005): 973–1048.

Falcón, Romana, and Raymond Buve, eds. *Don Porfirio, presidente..., nunca omnipotente: hallazgos, reflexiones, y debates, 1867–1911*. Mexico City: Universidad Iberoamericana, 1998.

Fanning, William. "Ecclesiastical Conferences." In *The Catholic Encyclopedia*. New York: Robert Appleton Company, 1908. Retrieved 26 September 2014 from http://www.newadvent.org/cathen/04213b.htm.

Florescano, Enrique. *Historia general de Michoacán*, vol. 3, *El Siglo XIX*. Morelia, Mexico: El Gobierno de Michoacán, 1989.

Fowler, Will. "Pronunciamientos and Popular Centralism in Mid-1830s Mexico." Paper delivered at the XXXII International Congress of the Latin American Studies Association, Chicago, 23 May 2014.

Fowler, Will, ed. *Forceful Negotiations: The Origins of the Pronunciamiento in Nineteenth-Century Mexico*. Lincoln: University of Nebraska Press, 2011.

Frazer, Chris. *Bandit Nation: A History of Outlaws and Cultural Struggle in Mexico, 1810–1920*. Lincoln: University of Nebraska Press, 2006.

Friedrich, Paul. *Agrarian Revolt in a Mexican Village*. 2nd ed. Chicago: University of Chicago Press, 1977.

Galeana, Patricia. *Relaciones estado-iglesia durante el segundo imperio*. Mexico City: UNAM/Centro de Estudios Históricos, 1991.

García Flores Chapa, María. "Vicente Riva Palacio y el periódico El Ahuizote." *Secuencia* 35 (May–August 1996): 59–82.

García Ugarte, Marta Eugenia. *Poder político y religioso: México, siglo XIX*, 2 vols. Mexico City: Miguel Ángel Porrúa/UNAM, 2010.

García y Moyeda, Manuel, ed. *Compendio histórico biográfico de la erección del obispado de esta ciudad, vida y muerte del Ilmo. Sr. Sollano, sus funerales, etc*. León, Mexico: Imprenta de M. G. y M., 1881.

Garesché, Edward. "St. Nicholas of Toletino." In *The Catholic Encyclopedia*, vol. 11. New York: Robert Appleton Company, 1911. Retrieved 1 July 2015 from http://www.newadvent.org/cathen/11065a.htm.
Garner, Paul. *Porfirio Díaz*. Profiles in Power Series. Edinburgh and London: Pearson Publishing, 2001.
Gledhill, John. *Casi Nada: A Study of Agrarian Reform in the Homeland of Cardenismo*. Austin: University of Texas Press, 1991.
———. *Cultura y desafío en Ostula: cuatro siglos de autonomia indígena en la costa-sierra nahua de Michoacán*. Zamora, Mexico: El Colegio de Michoacán, 2004.
González y González, Luis. "El liberalismo triunfante." In *Historia general de México*, vol. 2, edited by Bernardo García Martínez, 635–704. Mexico City: El Colegio de México, 1976.
———. *Pueblo en vilo: microhistoria de San José de Gracia*. Mexico City: El Colegio de México, 1968.
———. *Sahuayo*. Monografías Municipales de Michoacán. Morelia, Mexico: Gobierno del Estado de Michoacán, 1979.
———. *Zamora*. Monografías Municipales de Michoacán. Morelia, Mexico: Gobierno del Estado de Michoacán, 1978.
Graziano, Frank. *Cultures of Devotion: Folk Saints of Spanish America*. Oxford: Oxford University Press, 2007.
Gruzinski, Serge. "La 'segunda aculturación': el estado ilustrado y la religiosidad indígena en Nueva España (1775–1800)." *Estudios de Historia Novohispana* 3 (1985): 175–202.
Guardino, Peter. *Peasants, Politics, and the Formation of Mexico's National State: Guerrero, 1800–1857*. Stanford, Calif.: Stanford University Press, 1996.
———. *The Time of Liberty: Popular Political Culture in Oaxaca, 1750–1850*. Durham, N.C.: Duke University Press, 2005.
Guerra, François-Xavier. *México: del antiguo régimen a la revolución*, 2 vols. Mexico City: Fondo de Cultura Económica, 1988.
Guzmán Ávila, José Napoleón. "La república restaurada: en busca de la consolidación de un proyecto liberal." In *Historia general de Michoacán*, vol. 3, *El Siglo XIX*, edited by Enrique Florescano, 101–36. Morelia, Mexico: El Gobierno de Michoacán, 1989.
Hale, Charles A. *Mexican Liberalism in the Age of Mora, 1821–1853*. New Haven, Conn.: Yale University Press, 1968.
Hamnett, Brian. *Juárez*. London: Longman Publishing Group, 1994.
———. "Mexican Conservatives, Clericals, and Soldiers: The 'Traitor' Tomás Mejía through Reform and Empire, 1855–1867." *Bulletin of Latin American Research* 20, no. 2 (April 2001): 187–209.
Harris, Ruth. *Lourdes: Body and Spirit in the Secular Age*. London and New York: Penguin Press, 1999.
Hernández Chávez, Alicia. *La tradición republicana del buen gobierno*. Mexico City: Fondo de Cultura Económica, 1993.

Herrejón Peredo, Carlos. "Don Ignacio Árciga y Ruiz de Chávez." In *Don Vasco de Quiroga y Arzobispado de Morelia*. Mexico City: Editorial Jus, 1965.

Hobsbawm, Eric. *Primitive Rebels: Studies in Archaic Forms of Social Movement in the 19th and 20th Centuries*. New York: W. W. Norton, 1965.

Holweck, Frederick. "Special Devotions for Months." In *The Catholic Encyclopedia*, vol. 10. New York: Robert Appleton Company, 1911. Retrieved 15 January 2015 from http://www.newadvent.org/cathen/10542a.htm.

Ibarra López, Daniela. *La iglesia de Michoacán, 1815–1821: guerra, independencia, y organización diocesana*. Morelia, Mexico: Universidad Michoacana de San Nicolás de Hidalgo, 2015.

Iñiguez Mendoza, Ulises. "¡Viva la religión y mueran los *protestantes*! Religioneros, catolicismo, y liberalismo, 1873–1876." PhD diss., El Colegio de Michoacán, 2015.

Itinerario para una peregrinación espiritual que se practicará por los fieles católicos del Arzobispado de México en el próximo mes de octubre a algunos de los principales santuarios del país y del extranjero. Mexico City: Tipografía Escalerillas, 1874.

Iturribarría, José Fernando. "La política de conciliación del general Díaz y el arzobispo Gillow." *Historia Mexicana* 14, no. 1 (July–September 1964): 81–101.

Jackson, Robert H. *Conflict and Conversion in Sixteenth-Century Central Mexico: The Augustinian War on and beyond the Chichimeca Frontier*. Leiden, Netherlands: Koninklijke Brill NV, 2013.

James, Raymond A. *France and the Cult of the Sacred Heart: An Epic Tale for Modern Times*. Berkeley: University of California Press, 2000.

Joseph, Gilbert, and Daniel Nugent, eds. *Everyday Forms of State Formation: Revolution and the Negotiation of Rule in Modern Mexico*. Durham, N.C.: Duke University Press, 1994.

Joseph, Gilbert, and Alan Wells. *Summer of Discontent, Seasons of Upheaval: Elite Politics and Rural Insurgency in Michoacán, 1876–1915*. Stanford, Calif.: Stanford University Press, 1996.

Juárez, José Roberto. *Reclaiming Church Wealth: The Recovery of Church Property after Expropriation in the Archdiocese of Guadalajara, 1860–1911*. Albuquerque: University of New Mexico Press, 2004.

Katz, Friedrich, ed. *Riot, Rebellion, and Revolution: Rural Social Conflict in Mexico*. Princeton, N.J.: Princeton University Press, 1988.

Kirsch, J. P. "St. Felicitas." In *The Catholic Encyclopedia*. New York: Robert Appleton Company, 1909. Retrieved 26 May 2015 from http://www.newadvent.org/cathen/06028a.htm.

Knapp, Frank, Jr. *The Life of Sebastián Lerdo de Tejada, 1823–1889: A Study of Influence and Obscurity*. Austin: University of Texas Press, 1951.

Knight, Alan. "El liberalismo mexicano desde la reforma hasta la revolución (una interpretación)." *Historia Mexicana* 35, no.1 (July–September 1985): 59–91.

Knowlton, Robert. *Church Property and the Mexican Reform, 1856–1910*. DeKalb: Northern Illinois University Press, 1976.

———. "La división de las tierras de los pueblos durante el siglo XIX: el caso de Michoacán." *Historia Mexicana* 40, no. 1 (1990): 3–25.

Kourí, Emilio. "Interpreting the Expropriation of Indian Pueblo Lands in Porfirian Mexico: The Unexamined Legacies of Andres Molina Enriquez." *Hispanic American Historical Review* 81, no. 2 (2002): 69–117.

———. *A Pueblo Divided: Business, Property, and Community in Papantla, Mexico*. Stanford, Calif.: Stanford University Press, 2004.

Labastida y Dávalos, Pelagio Antonio. *Carta pastoral que el Ilmo. D. Pelagio Antonio Labastida y Dávalos, Arzobispo de México, dirige a su venerable clero y fieles diocesanos con motivo del Breve Pontificio dado por nuestro Santísimo Padre Pio IX el 27 de marzo de este año*. Mexico City: Tipografía Escalerillas, 1874.

———. *Carta pastoral que el Ilmo. Sr. Dr. D. Pelagio Antonio de Labastida y Dávalos, Arzobispo de México, dirige al venerable clero y fieles diocesanos de este arzobispado con motivo de la alocución pronunciados en el Palacio Vaticano por Nuestro Santísimo Padre Pio Papa IX el 25 de julio 1873*. Mexico City: Imprenta de José Mariano Fernández de Lara, 1873.

Larkin, Brian. *The Very Nature of God: Baroque Catholicism and Religious Reform in Bourbon Mexico City*. Albuquerque: University of New Mexico Press, 2010.

Leddy Phelan, John. *The Millennial Kingdom of the Franciscans in the New World*. 2nd ed. Berkeley: University of California Press, 1970.

Lomnitz, Claudio. "La religión de Los Caballeros Templarios." Nexos online, July 16, 2016, https://www.nexos.com.mx/?%20p=28783, accessed June 12, 2018.

López Lara, Ramón. "El Obispo." In *Don Vasco de Quiroga y Arzobispado de Morelia*, edited by Sociedad de Historia y Estadística del Arzobispado de Morelia, 27–43. Mexico City: Editorial Jus, 1965.

———. *Zinapécuaro: tres épocas de una parroquia*. Zinapécuaro de Figueroa, Mexico: Fimax, 1970.

MacLachlan, Colin M., and William H. Beezley. *El Gran Pueblo: A History of Greater Mexico*. 3rd ed. Upper Saddle River, N.J.: Prentice Hall, 2004.

Mallon, Florencia. *Peasant and Nation: The Making of Postcolonial Mexico and Peru*. Berkeley: University of California Press, 1995.

Manual para el uso de las Hijas de la Caridad. Guadalajara, Mexico: Tipografía del Hospicio, 1874.

Maravall, José Antonio. *La cultura del barroco: analisis de una estructura histórica*. Barcelona, Spain: Editorial Ariel, 1975.

Martínez Álvarez, José Antonio, ed. *La Piedad*. Monografías Municipales de Michoacán. La Piedad, Mexico: H. Ayuntamiento de La Piedad, 2003.

Martínez Baracs, Rodrigo. *Convivencia y utopia: el gobierno indio y español de la "ciudad de Mechuacan," 1521–1580*. Mexico City: Fondo de Cultura Económica/INAH, 2005.

Mazín Gómez, Oscar. *El Gran Michoacán: cuatro informes del obispado de Michoacán, 1759–1769*. Zamora, Mexico: El Colegio de Michoacán, 1986.

———. *Entre dos majestades: el obispo y la iglesia del gran Michoacán ante las reformas Borbónicas, 1758–1772*. Zamora, Mexico: El Colegio de Zamora, 1987.

———. "Secularización de parroquias en el antiguo Michoacán." *Relaciones* 26, no. 7 (Spring 1986): 23–34.

McNamara, Patrick J. *Sons of the Sierra: Juárez, Díaz, and the People of Ixtlán, Oaxaca, 1855–1920*. Chapel Hill: University of North Carolina Press, 2007.

Medina Peña, Luis. *Invención del sistema político de México: forma de gobierno y gobernabilidad en México en el siglo XIX*. Mexico City: Fondo de Cultura Económica, 2004.

Meehan, Andrew. "Canonical Visitation." In *The Catholic Encyclopedia*. New York: Robert Appleton Company, 1912. Retrieved 20 September 2014 from http://www.newadvent.org/cathen/15479a.htm.

Memoria leida por el c. gobernador de este libre y soberano estado de Guanajuato, General Florencio Antillón, en la solemne instalación del sexto congreso constitucional verificada el 15 de septiembre de 1875. Mexico City: Imprenta de Ignacio Escalante, 1876.

Memoria que el Secretario del Estado y el despacho de gobernación presentó al Congreso de la Unión el día 14 diciembre 1877. Mexico City: Imprenta del Gobierno, 1877.

Meyer, Jean. *Esperando a Lozada*. Zamora, Mexico: El Colegio de Michoacán, 1984.

———. *La cristiada*, vol. 2, *El conflicto entre la iglesia y el estado, 1926–1929*. 19th ed. Mexico City: Siglo Ventiuno Editores, 2005.

Meyer, Michael C., and William H. Beezley. *The Oxford History of Mexico*. Oxford: Oxford University Press, 2000.

Mijangos Díaz, Eduardo N., and Leticia Mendoza García. "Tolerancia de cultos en Michoacán y la difusión de un protestantismo liberal en el oriente del estado, 1851–1911." In *Estado laico y derecho humanos en México: 1810–2010*, vol. 2, edited by Margarita Moreno Bonnett and Rosa María Álvarez de Lara, 109–40. Mexico City: UNAM, 2012.

Mijangos y González, Pablo. "La respuesta popular al juramento constitucional en 1857: un esbozo de geografía político-religioso del México de la reforma." In *México católico: proyectos y trayectorias eclesiales en México, siglos XIX y XX*, edited by Marta Eugenia García Ugarte, Pablo Serrano Álvarez, and Matthew Butler, 89–131. Mexico City: Universidad Intercultural del Estado de Hidalgo, El Colegio de Hidalgo, Consejo Estatal para la Cultura y las Artes de Hidalgo, 2016.

———. *The Lawyer of the Church: Bishop Clemente de Jesús Munguía and the Clerical Response to the Mexican Liberal Reforma*. Lincoln: University of Nebraska Press, 2015.

Mireles Valverde, José Manuel. *Todos somos autodefensas: el despertar de un pueblo dormido*. Mexico City: Grijalbo, 2017.

Moreno Chávez, José Alberto. *Devociones políticas: cultura católica y politización en la Arquiodiócesis de México, 1880–1920*. Mexico City: El Colegio de México, 2013.
Moreno García, Heriberto. *Cotija*. Monografías Municipales de Michoacán. Morelia, Mexico: Gobierno del Estado de Michoacán, 1980.
———. *Guaracha: Tiempos viejos, tiempos nuevos*. Zamora, Mexico: El Colegio de Michoacán, 1992.
Muría, José María. *Breve historia de Jalisco*. Mexico City: Fideicomiso Historia de las Américas/El Colegio de México/Fondo de Cultura Económica, 1994.
Muriel, Josefina. "Las cofradías hospitalarias en la formación de la consciencia comunitaria." In *La cultura Purhé: II Coloquio de Antropología e Historia Regionales. Fuentes e historia*, edited by Francisco Miranda, 225–36. Zamora, Mexico: El Colegio de Michoacán/FONAPAS, 1981.
Murillo, Luis. "The Politics of the Miraculous: Popular Religious Practice in Porfirian Mexico, 1876–1910." PhD diss., University of California at San Diego, 2002.
Noriega, Alfonso. *El Pensamiento conservador y el conservadurismo mexicano*, 2 vols. Mexico City: UNAM, 1972.
Noticia sobre las Conferencias de la Sociedad de San Vicente de Paul, dependientes del Consejo Superior de México, durante el año de 1869. Mexico City: Tipografía de la V. de Murguía e Hijos, 1870.
Novena consagrada al culto y festividad del glorioso San Felipe de Jesús, protomártir mexicano, que se reimprime a expensas de su Asociación fundada en Irapuato el día 5 de marzo del año de 1873, quien la dedica a su ilustrísimo prelado Dr. y Mtro. D. José M. de Jesús D. Zollano y Dávalos, por su felíz aprobación. Mexico City: Tip. Religiosa de M. Torner y Compañía, 1874.
O'Brien, Elizabeth. "If They Are Useful, Why Expel Them? Las Hermanas de la Caridad and Religious Medical Authority in Mexico City Hospitals, 1861–1874." *Mexican Studies/Estudios Mexianos* 33, no. 3 (Fall 2017): 417–42.
O'Dogherty, Laura. *De urnas y sotanas: el Partido Católico Nacional en Jalisco*. Mexico City: UNAM, 2001.
———. "El ascenso de una jerarquía eclesial intransigente, 1890–1914." In *Memoria del I Coloquio Historia de la Iglesia en el siglo XIX*, edited by Ramos Medina, 179–94. Mexico City: Condumex, 1998.
O'Hara, Matthew D. *A Flock Divided: Race, Religion, and Politics in Mexico, 1749–1857*. Durham, N.C.: Duke University Press, 2009.
———. "Politics and Piety: The Church in Colonial and Nineteenth-Century Mexico." *Mexican Studies/Estudios Mexicanos* 17, no. 1 (Winter 2001): 213–31.
Ochoa Serrano, Álvaro. *Afrodescendientes: sobre piel canela*. Zamora, Mexico: El Colegio de Michoacán, 1997.
———. "El distrito de Zamora en 1877." *Relaciones* 3, no. 12 (1982): 119–40.
———. *Jiquilpan*. Monografías Municipales de Michoacán. Morelia, Mexico: Gobierno del Estado de Michoacán, 1978.

———. *Jiquilpan-Huanimban: una historia confinada.* Jiquilpan, Mexico: Morevallado Editores, 1999.

———. "La protocristeriada: los religioneros michoacanos." In *La cultura Purhé: II Coloquio de Antropologia e Historia Regionales,* edited by Francisco Miranda, 238–43. Zamora, Mexico: El Colegio de Michoacán/FONAPAS, 1980.

———. "Macario Romero: apuntes, acompañamientos, y corrido (1852–1878)." *Estudios Michoacanos* 8 (1999): 25–47.

———. "Mitote, Fandango, y Mariachi en Jal-Mich." *Relaciones* 21, no. 6 (Winter 1985): 71–83.

———. "Tres corridos cristeros del noroeste michoacano." *Relaciones: Estudios de Historia y Sociedad* 54 (1993): 153–65.

Ochoa Serrano, Álvaro, and Gerardo Sánchez Díaz, eds. *Breve historia de Michoacán.* Mexico City: Fondo de Cultura Económica, 2003.

Oikión Solano, Verónika. "Un nuevo pasado michoacano. Una centuria historiográfica." *Relaciones: Estudios de Historia y Sociedad* 16, no. 60 (Fall 1994): 41–74.

Olimón Nolasco, Manuel. "Proyecto de reforma de la iglesia en México, 1867–1875." In *Estado, iglesia, y sociedad en México: siglo XIX,* edited by Álvaro Matute, Evelia Trejo, and Brian Connaughton, 267–91. Mexico City: Editorial Porrúa, 1995.

Olveda, Jaime, ed. *Gordiano Guzmán: un cacique del siglo XIX.* Mexico City: Centro Regional de Occidente/SEP-INAH, 1980.

———. *Los obispados de México frente a la reforma liberal.* Zapopan, Mexico: El Colegio de Jalisco, 2007.

Ornelas Hernández, Moisés. "A la sombra de la revolución liberal: iglesia, política, y sociedad en Michoacán, 1821–1870." PhD diss., El Colegio de México, 2011.

———. "La política liberal y las obvenciones parroquiales en el obispado de Michoacán, 1821–1860." *Hispania Sacra* 43, no. 128 (July–December 2011): 681–706.

Ortíz Ibarra, Hector, and Vicente González Méndez, *Puruándiro.* Monografías Municipales de Michoacán. Morelia, Mexico: Gobierno del Estado de Michoacán, 1980.

Overmeyer-Velázquez, Mark. *Visions of the Emerald City: Modernity, Tradition, and the Formation of Porfirian Oaxaca, Mexico.* Durham, N.C.: Duke University Press, 2006.

Pani, Erika, ed. *Conservadurismos y derechas en la historia de México,* 2 vols. Mexico City: Fondo de Cultura Económica, 2009.

———. "Democracia y representación política: la visión de dos periódicos católicos de fin de siglo, 1880–1910." In *Modernidad, tradición, y alteridad: la Ciudad de México en el cambio del siglo XIX y XX,* edited by Claudia Agostini and Elisa Speckman, 143–60. Mexico City: UNAM, 2001.

———. *Para mexicanizar el segundo imperio: el imaginario político de los imperialistas.* Mexico City: El Colegio de México/Instituto Mora, 2001.

Pasture, Patrick, and Jan Art, eds. *Beyond the Feminization Thesis: Gender and Christianity in Modern Europe*. Leuven, Belgium: Leuven University Press, 2012.

Pérez, Juan E. *Almanaque estadístico de las oficinas y guia de forasteros y del comercio de la república para 1875*. Mexico City: Imprenta del Gobierno, en Palacio, 1874.

Pineda Soto, Zenaida Adriana. "El discurso del movimiento religionero en la prensa moreliana." In *Movimientos sociales en Michoacán, siglos XIX y XX*, edited by Eduardo N. Mijangos Díaz, 91–102. Morelia, Mexico: Universidad Michoacana de San Nicolás de Hidalgo, 1999.

Pi-Suñer Llorens, Antonia. "Prólogo." In *El Padre Cobos y La Carabina de Ambrosio*, edited by Anotonia Pi-Suñer Llorens, 13–24. Mexico City: LVII Legislatura, 2000.

———. *Sebastián Lerdo de Tejada, canciller/estadista*. Mexico City: Archivo Histórico Diplomático Mexicano, 1989.

———. "Sebastián Lerdo de Tejada y su política hacia la iglesia Católica." In *Relaciones estado-iglesia. Encuentros y desencuentros*, edited by Roberto Blancarte and Patricia Galeana, 127–38. Mexico City: Archivo General de la Nación, 2001.

Piza, Agapito. *Historia parlamentaria de la Cámara de Senadores, Octavo Congreso Constitucional de la Unión*, vol. 1, *Sesiones ordinarias de 15 de septiembre a 15 de diciembre de 1875*. Mexico City: Imprenta del Gobierno Federal, en Palacio, 1882.

Portillo, Manuel. *Apuntes histórico-geográficos del departamento de Zapopan: historia del origen y culto de la imágen de Nuestra Señora de Zapopan e historia del Colegio Apostólico*. Guadalajara, Mexico: Tipografía M. Pérez Lete, 1889.

Powell, T. G. *El liberalismo y el campesinado del centro de México, 1850–1876*. Mexico City: SepSetentas, 1974.

———. "Los liberales, el campesinado indígena, y los problemas agrarios durante la reforma." *Historia Mexicana* 21, no. 4 (April–June 1972): 653–75.

Purnell, Jennie. *Popular Movements and State Formation in Revolutionary Mexico: The Agraristas and Cristeros of Michoacán*. Durham, N.C.: Duke University Press, 1999.

———. "With All Due Respect: Popular Resistance to the Privatization of Communal Lands in Nineteenth-Century Michoacán." *Latin American Research Review* 34, no. 1 (1999): 85–121.

Quirate, Jacinto. "*Los Cinco Señores* and *La Mano Poderosa*: An Iconographic Study." In *Art and Faith in Mexico: The Nineteenth-Century Retablo Tradition*, edited by Elizabeth Netto Calil Zarur and Charles Muir Lovell, 79–88. Albuquerque: University of New Mexico Press, 2001.

Reglamento para la Congregación de la Buena Muerte. León, Mexico: Imprenta de J. M. Monzón, 1872.

Reina, Leticia. *Las rebeliones campesinas en México, 1819–1906*. Mexico City: Siglo XXI Editores, 1980.

Ricard, Robert. *The Spiritual Conquest of Mexico: An Essay on the Apostolate and the Evangelizing of the Mendicant Orders in New Spain, 1523–1572*. Translated by Lesley Byrd Simpson. Berkeley: University of California Press, 1966.

Riva Palacio, Vicente. *Historia de la administración de D. Sebastián Lerdo de Tejada*. Mexico City: Biblioteca Mexicana de la Fundación Miguel Alemán, A. C., 1992.

Rivera Reynaldos, Lisette Griselda. *Desamortización y nacionalización de bienes civiles y eclesiásticos en Morelia, 1856–1876*. Morelia, Mexico: Universidad Michoacana de San Nicolás de Hidalgo, 1996.

Rodríguez Sánchez, Leopoldo. *La parroquia de Jiquilpan*. Jiquilpan, Mexico: Talleres Linotipográficos "Guía," 1964.

Rodríguez Zetina, Arturo. *Zamora: ensayo histórico y repertorio documental*. Mexico City: Editorial Jus, 1952.

Romero, José Guadalupe. "Noticias estadísticas sobre el partido de Coalcomán, y condiciones favorables del mismo para la colonización agrícola y extranjera." In *Boletín de la Sociedad Mexicana de Geografía y Estadística*, vol. 10. Mexico City: Imprenta de Vicente García Torres, 1863.

———. *Noticias para formar la historia y estadística del obispado de Michoacán*. Mexico City: Imprenta de Vicente Torres García, 1862.

Romero Vargas, Pbro. José. *Cotija: cuna de trotamundos, 1a parte*. Self-published, 1973.

Rosas Salas, Sergio. "El proyecto pastoral de José Antonio de la Peña y Navarro frente al protestantismo. Zamora, 1872–1875." Paper presented at the Coloquio Internacional: Historia, Protestantismo, e Identidad en el Continente Americano, Mexico City, October 6–8, 2011.

———. *La iglesia mexicana en tiempos de la impiedad: Francisco Pablo Vázquez, 1769–1847*. Puebla, Mexico/Zamora, Mexico: BUAP, Ediciones EyC, El Colegio de Michoacán, 2015.

Roseberry, William. "El estricto apego a la ley: ley liberal y derecho comunal en el Pátzcuaro porfiriano." In *Recursos contenciosos: ruralidad y reformas liberales en México*, edited by Andrew Roth Seneff, 43–84. Zamora, Mexico: El Colegio de Michoacán, 2004.

Rubial García, Antonio. *La santidad controvertida: hagiografía y consciencia criolla alrededor de los venerables no canonizados de Nueva España*. Mexico City: UNAM/FCE, 1999.

Rubin, Miri. *Corpus Christi: The Eucharist in Late Medieval Culture*. Cambridge: Cambridge University Press, 1991.

Rubio Morales, Pbro. Luis Daniel, and Ramón Alonso Pérez Escutia. *Luz de ayer, luz de hoy: historia del Seminario Diocesano de Morelia*. Morelia, Mexico: Parroquia del Señor de la Piedad/UMSNH/Editorial Morevalladolid, 2013.

Rugeley, Terry. *Of Wonders and Wise Men: Religion and Popular Cultures in Southeast Mexico, 1800–1876*. Austin: University of Texas Press, 2001.
Ruiz, Eduardo. *Historia de la Guerra de intervención en Michoacán*. Mexico City: Oficina Tipografía de la Secretaria de Fomento, 1896.
Sánchez, Ramón. *Bosquejo estadístico e histórico del distrito de Jiquilpan de Juárez*. Morelia, Mexico: Imprenta de E. I. M. Porfirio Díaz, 1896.
Sánchez Díaz, Gerardo. *El suroeste de Michoacán: economía y sociedad, 1852–1910*. Morelia, Mexico: Universidad Michoacana de San Nicolás de Hidalgo, 1988.
———. *El suroeste de Michoacán: estructura económica-social, 1821–1852*. Morelia, Mexico: Universidad Michoacana de San Nicolás de Hidalgo, 1979.
Sánchez Rodríguez, Martín. "Los Dávalos: una familia oligárquica del bajío zamorano." *Estudios Michoacanos 7*, no. 7 (1997): 93–128.
Saranyana, Josep Ignai, ed. *Teología en América Latina*, vol. 2. Madrid: Iberoamericana, 2008.
Schaefer, Timo. *Liberalism as Utopia: The Rise and Fall of Legal Rule in Post-colonial Mexico, 1820–1900*. Cambridge: Cambridge University Press, 2017.
Schmitt, Karl M. "The Díaz Conciliation Policy on State and Local Levels, 1876–1911." *Hispanic American Historical Review* 40 (November 1960): 513–32.
Schryer, Franz J. "A Ranchero Economy in Northwestern Hidalgo, 1880–1920." *Hispanic American Historical Review* 59, no. 3 (August 1979): 418–43.
Second Section, Forty-Third Congress: Executive Documents Printed by Order of the House of Representatives, 1874–1875. Washington, D.C.: Government Printing Office, 1875.
Sinkin, Richard. *The Mexican Reform, 1855–1876: A Study in Liberal Nation-Building*. Austin: University of Texas Press, 1979.
Sloan, Kathryn. *Runaway Daughters: Seduction, Elopement, and Honor in Nineteenth-Century Mexico*. Albuquerque: University of New Mexico Press, 2008.
Smith, Benjamin T. *The Roots of Conservatism in Mexico: Catholicism, Society, and Politics in the Mixteca Baja, 1750–1962*. Albuquerque: University of New Mexico Press, 2012.
Solís Cruz, José. "De indianismo eclesiástico y otros: catolicismo social, discursos y prácticas étnicas en Michoacán (1940–1950)." *Liminar: Estudios Sociales y Humanísticos* 3, no. 2 (December 2010): 15–28.
Sosenski, Susana. "Asomándose a la política: representaciones femeninas contra la tolerancia de cultos en México, 1856." *Tzintzun: Revista de Estudios Históricos* 40 (July–December 2004): 51–76.
Soto Correa, José Carmen. *Movimientos campesinos de derecha en el oriente michoacano: comuneros, campesinos, caudillos, y partidos (1867–1914)*. Mexico City: Hoja Casa Editorial, 1996.
Staples, Anne. "El Estado y la Iglesia durante la república restaurada." In *El dominio de las minorías: república restaurada y Porfiriato*, edited by Anne Staples, 15–54. Mexico City: El Colegio de Mexico, 1989.

———. "El matrimonio civil y la epístola de Melchor Ocampo, 1859." In *Familias iberoamericanas. Historia, identidad y conflictos*, edited by Pilar Gonzalbo, 217–29. Mexico City: El Colegio de México, 2001.

Stauffer, Brian A. "Community, Identity, and the Limits of Liberal State Formation in Michoacán's Coastal Sierra: Coalcomán, 1869–1940." In *Mexico in Transition: New Perspectives on Mexican Agrarian History, Nineteenth and Twentieth Centuries/México y sus transiciones: reconsideraciones sobre la historia agraria mexicana, siglos XIX y XX*, edited by Antonio Escobar Ohmstede and Matthew Butler, 149–80. Mexico City/Austin, Tex.: CIESAS/LLILAS, 2013.

———. "Indianness, Community, and the Limits of Liberal State Formation in Michoacán, 1869–1910." Master's thesis, University of New Mexico, 2009.

———. "The Routes of Intransigence: Mexico's 1874 'Spiritual Pilgrimage' and the Globalization of Ultramontane Catholicism." *Americas: A Quarterly Journal of Latin American History* 75, no. 7 (April 2018): 291–324.

Tackett, Timothy. *Religion, Revolution, and Regional Culture in Eighteenth-Century France: The Ecclesiastical Oath of 1791*. Princeton, N.J.: Princeton University Press, 2014.

Tanck de Estrada, Dorothy. "Las tres principales fiestas de los pueblos de indios, según los reglamentos de bienes de comunidad." In *La iglesia católica en México*, edited by Nelly Sigaut, 335–55. Zamora, Mexico: Colegio de Michoacán, 1997.

Tapia Méndez, Aurelio. *El siervo de dios José Antonio Plancarte y Labastida, profeta y mártir*. 2nd ed. Mexico City: Editorial Tradición, 1987.

Tapia Santamaría, Jesús. *Campo religioso y evolución política en el Bajío Zamorano*. Zamora, Mexico: El Colegio de Michoacán, 1986.

———. "Identidad social y religión en el Bajío Zamorano, 1850–1900. El culto a la Purísima, un mito de fundación." *Relaciones: Estudios de Historia y Sociedad* 7, no. 27 (1986): 43–71.

Tavera Alvaro, Xavier. *Morelia en la época de la república restaurada (1867–1876)*, 2 vols. Morelia, Mexico: Instituto Michoacano de Cultura, 1988.

Taylor, William. *Magistrates of the Sacred: Priests and Parishioners in Eighteenth-Century Mexico*. Stanford, Calif.: Stanford University Press, 1996.

Thomson, Guy P. C. "The End of the Catholic Nation: Reform and Reaction in Puebla, 1854–1856." In *Malcontents, Rebels, and Pronunciados: The Politics of Insurrection in Nineteenth-Century Mexico*, edited by Will Fowler, 148–70. Lincoln: University of Nebraska Press, 2012.

———. "La contrarreforma de Puebla, 1854–1886." In *El conservadurismo mexicano en el siglo XIX*, edited by Will Fowler and Humberto Morales, 239–64. Puebla, Mexico: Benemérito Universidad Autónoma de Puebla, 1999.

———. "Popular Aspects of Liberalism in Mexico, 1848–1888." *Bulletin of Latin American Research* 10, no. 3 (1991): 265–92.

———. "Porfirio Díaz y el ocaso del partido de la montaña (1879–1892): ¿Fin al liberalismo popular en la Sierra de Puebla?" In *Don Porfirio, presidente . . . , nunca omnipotente: hallazgos, reflexiones, y debates, 1867–1911*, edited by Romana Falcón and Raymond Buve, 361–85. Mexico City: Universidad Iberoamericana, 1998.

Thomson, Guy P. C., with David G. LaFrance. *Patriotism, Politics, and Popular Liberalism in Nineteenth-Century Mexico: Juan Francisco Lucas and the Puebla Sierra*. Wilmington, Del.: Scholarly Resources Press, 1999.

Tinajero Villaseñor, Leonel. *Cotija: un pueblo y una época*. Self-published, 1971.

Traffano, Daniela. "Indios, curas, y nación: la sociedad indígena frente un proceso de secularización: Oaxaca, siglo XIX." PhD diss., El Colegio de México, 2000.

———. "Para formar el corazón religioso de los jóvenes: Processes of Change in Collective Religiosity in Nineteenth-Century Oaxaca." In *Religious Culture in Modern Mexico Religious Culture in Modern Mexico*, edited by Martin Austin Nesvig, 35–49. Lanham, Md.: Rowman and Littlefield Publishers, 2007.

Traslosheros Hernández, Jorge E. *La reforma de la iglesia del antiguo Michoacán: la gestión episcopal de fray Marcos Ramírez del Prado, 1640–1666*. Morelia, Mexico: UMSNH, 1995.

Tutino, John. *From Insurrection to Revolution in Mexico: Social Bases of Agrarian Violence, 1750–1940*. Princeton, N.J.: Princeton University Press, 1986.

———. *Making a New World: Founding Capitalism in the Bajío and Spanish North America*. Durham, N.C.: Duke University Press, 2011.

———. "The Revolution in Mexican Independence: Insurgency and the Renegotiation of Property, Production, and Patriarchy in the Bajío, 1800–1855." *Hispanic American Historical Review* 78, no. 3 (1998): 367–418.

Un retrato directo de la Madre de Dios: o historia Madre Santísima de la Luz, tomado de "El Pueblo Católico" y aumentado por su autor. León, Mexico: Imprenta de Posada y Compañía, 1885.

Vanderwood, Paul. *Disorder and Progress: Bandits, Police, and Mexican Development*. Lincoln: University of Nebraska Press, 1981.

———. *The Power of God against the Guns of Government: Religious Upheaval in Mexico at the Turn of the Nineteenth Century*. Stanford, Calif.: Stanford University Press, 1998.

Van Oosterhout, Aaron. "Confraternities and Popular Conservatism on the Frontier: Mexico's Sierra del Nayarit in the Nineteenth Century." *Americas* 71, no. 1 (July 2014): 101–30.

———. "Popular Conservatism in Mexico: Religion, Land, and Popular Politics in Nayarit and Querétaro, 1750–1873." PhD diss., Michigan State University, 2014.

Van Young, Eric. "In the Gloomy Caverns of Paganism: Popular Culture, Insurgency, and Nation-Building in Mexico, 1800–1821." In *The Birth of Modern*

Mexico, 1740–1824, edited by Christon I. Archer, 41–65. Lanham, Md.: Rowman and Littlefield, 2003.

———. *The Other Rebellion: Popular Violence, Ideology, and the Mexican Struggle for Independence, 1810–1821*. Stanford, Calif.: Stanford University Press, 2002.

Vázquez Rosas, José Luis. *Huaniqueo*. Información Monográfica Municipal. Morelia, Mexico: Gobierno del Estado de Michoacán/H. Ayuntamiento de Huaniqueo, 1987.

Vázquez Pallares, Natalio. *Un nuevo regimen de propiedad y un pueblo: ensayo histórico sobre Coalcomán*. Morelia, Mexico: Sociedad Michoacana Morelos-Ocampo, Talleres Gráficas del Estado, 1944.

Velasco Robledo, Dinorah. "Institución bendita por Dios: la Sociedad Católica de México, 1868–1878." In *Política y religión en la Ciudad de México, siglos XIX y XX*, edited by Franco Savarino, Berenise Bravo Rubio, and Andrea Mutolo, 151–70. Mexico City: IMDOSOC, 2014.

Vera, Pbro. Br. Fortino H., ed. *Colección de documentos eclesiásticos de México*, vol. 3. Amecameca, Mexico: Imprenta del Colegio Católico, 1887.

Verástique, Bernadino. *Michoacán and Eden: Vasco de Quiroga and the Evangelization of Western Mexico*. Austin: University of Texas Press, 2000.

Verduzco, Gustavo. "Zamora en el porfiriato: una expresión liberal de los conservadores." In *El dominio de las minorías: república restaurada y porfiriato*, edited by Anne Staples, 55–70. Mexico City: El Colegio de México, 1989.

Veres Acevedo, Laureano. *La maravillosa imágen de la Madre Santísima de la Luz: su origen y su título, cultos que se le han venido tributando hasta la época de su solemne coronación y obsequios que podemos dedicarle*. Mexico City: Tip. Y Lit. "La Europea" de J. Águilar Vera y Compañía, 1901.

Verján Vásquez, Yanceli. "Policías rurales y suspensión de garantías: mecanismos de coacción y represión en el proceso de formación del estado mexicano, 1861–1896." Master's thesis, Universidad Autónoma Metropolitana, Unidad Iztapalapa, 2006.

Villanueva y Francesconi, M. *El libro de protestas: recopilación de las manifestaciones y protestas de los mexicanos católicos, contra la ley anticonstitucional orgánica de la Reforma, que ataca la libertad del culto y las inmunidades de la Iglesia de Jesucristo*. Mexico City: Imprenta Cinco de Mayo, 1875.

Voekel, Pamela. *Alone before God: The Religious Origins of Modernity in Mexico*. Durham, N.C.: Duke University Press, 2002.

———. "Liberal Religion: The Schism of 1861." In *Religious Culture in Modern Mexico*, edited by Martin Austin Nesvig, 78–105. Lanham, Md.: Rowman and Littlefield Publishers, 2007.

Warren, Benedict. *The Conquest of Michoacán: The Spanish Domination of the Tarascan Kingdom in Western Mexico, 1521–1530*. Norman: University of Oklahoma Press, 1985.

Wright-Ríos, Edward. *Revolutions in Mexican Catholicism: Revelation and Reform in Oaxaca, 1888–1935.* Durham, N.C.: Duke University Press, 2009.

Yokoyama, Wakako. "La familia Infante: los primeros colonizadores y la formación de la sociedad criolla novohispana." *Tzintzun: Revista de Estudios Históricos* 19 (January–June 1994): 43–62.

Zagorin, Perez. *Ways of Lying: Dissimulation, Persecution, and Conformity in Early Modern Europe.* Cambridge, Mass.: Harvard University Press, 1990.

Zárate Hernández, José Eduardo. "Comunidad, reformas liberales, y emergencia del indígena moderno: pueblos de la Meseta Purépecha (1869–1904)." *Relaciones* 32, no. 125 (2001): 17–52.

———, ed. *La tierra caliente de Michoacán.* Zamora, Mexico: El Colegio de Michoacán, 2001.

Index

adjudication of Church property. *See* Lerdo Law
Afro-mestizos, 13; and baroque Catholicism, 16, 19; and the Cárdenas family, 28–29, 46; in central Michoacán, 155; and the Religioneros of northwest Michoacán, 97–127 passim
Águilar, Canon Ignacio, 87, 93
Aguililla (Michoacán), 173–86 passim; and political partisanship, 141; religious culture in, 88, 90, 193, 197, 198–201; and Religionero violence, 187–91 passim, 205, 206
Ahualulco (Jalisco); 33, 37–38
Alonso, Casimiro, 28, 44
anticlericalism: Catholic responses to, 18, 19, 39, 61–95 passim, 98, 116, 127, 131, 176; and conservative revolts, 110, 135; of the Huerta government, 141, 142; and the Laws of Reform, 1; and secularization, 10; and the Tuxtepec Revolution, 209–26 passim
Antillón, Florencio, 48, 217–18, 220
Árciga y Ruiz de Chávez, Archbishop José Ignacio: alleged responsibility for revolt, 42, 45; attitude toward Purépecha religion, 157–58, 165, 171; pastoral letters of, 68; reformism of, 82–95 passim
Arias, Rafael: death of, 50, 148, 149; liberal militancy of, 28, 141, 142, 162

Army of Regeneration, 211, 217, 223. *See also* Revolution of Tuxtepec
arrangements of conscience, 66, 281n13
Arroyo, Father Pedro, 117, 164–66
Augustinian Order, 136–55 passim, 166, 167
autodefensas, 249

Bajío (region): and diocesan restructuring, 63, 75; and *gavilla* activity, 44, 48, 211; of Puruándiro, 135, 137–58 passim; Zamorano, 100–101, 292n7
Bajío *gavilla*, 28, 49, 147–49 passim. *See also* Potreros gavilla
Ballyac, Father Pascual, 97, 98, 129, 130, 131
banditry, 25–26, 44, 56, 142, 227–45 passim; social, 8, 30, 103
baptism, 116, 199
baroque religion, 14, 15–19, 22, 78, 84, 89, 99–100, 101, 103, 117–27 passim, 131, 135, 150–70 passim; and the Catholic hierarchy, 137, 157; and Socorro Reyes, 134
Betancourt, Amadeo, 114, 129, 131
Bolaños, Antonio, 167, 170
Bourbon Reforms, 15, 16, 89, 157, 178, 243
Buenrostro, Ignacio, 43, 219
Bustamante, Anastasio, 28, 108

Cabero, Father Hilario, 30–31

Camacho y García, Bishop Ramón, 34, 70, 73
Camarena, Jesús, 48, 214, 227
Cándido, Antonio, 28, 176, 186, 189, 190
Cándido family, 175, 185–92 passim
canonical burial, 1, 4, 92, 161, 164
capellanías. See *obras pías*
Cárdenas, Eulogio, 7, 19, 28–29, 41, 44–57 passim, 111–14 passim, 125, 130, 246, 247; and Afro-mestizo Religioneros, 46, 127, 128; assassination of, 231–32; pronunciamiento of, 35, 110; relationship with local hacendados, 46–47; relationship with Tuxtepec movement, 215, 220, 223; service in Maximilian's army, 109–10
Cárdenas, Lázaro, 28
cargo system, 16, 184–85, 196
Carnaval (festival), 78, 122
Carrillo, Rafael: and anticlerical legislation, 31–32; and middle-class liberals, 188, 206; and *reparto* in Michoacán, 145, 185; and response to Religionero revolt, 25, 36–40, 49–50 passim
cartas de protesta, 38, 41, 66, 71–72
Casillas, Prudencio, 51, 111
Castañeda, Abraham, 28, 41; death of, 50; ideology of, 30, 110, 244–45; and the Plan of Nuevo Urecho, 42, 253
Castro, Father Hilario, 158, 160–63, 171
catechism, 88, 91, 92
cathedral chapters, 84, 85, 89, 95, 243
Catholic Church. See Catholicism
Catholicism: European, 13, 63, 68, 73–80, 84; French, 63, 74, 159; intransigent, 47, 284n47; Italian, 75, 159, 235; local, 14, 192, 197; Nahua, 176, 177, 193–97; and pluralism, 3, 8, 66, 98, 120; popular, 13, 14, 15, 17, 66, 80–82, 95, 102, 122, 125, 135, 136, 150–51, 156, 167, 170; and Protestantism, 70; Purépecha, 78, 86, 124, 136–37, 151–59 passim, 161–63, 171; social, 10, 92, 340n147; and social cohesion, 56, 60, 229, 244. See also Ultramontane Catholicism
Catholic restorationism, 3, 13, 243; in the Archdiocese of Michoacán, 65, 95, 159; in the Diocese of Zamora, 65, 79–80, 94, 99, 120, 127; and Religionero violence, 17–19, 60, 65, 174, 205; and the Vela Perpetua, 90–91
Cervín de la Mora, Juan, 30, 105, 142, 209
Chacón, Felipe, 218–31 passim
charity, 17, 63, 65–75 passim, 79, 88–94 passim, 114, 117, 154
Chávez, José María, 197, 200, 202, 204, 205, 223
Chichimecas, 101, 137, 139, 151, 154
cholera, 54, 109, 115
Christology, 102, 133, 136, 154, 156, 170
Church properties: atriums, 19, 242; *casas curales*, 161, 165, 168, 197, 200, 203, 204, 205; cemeteries, 122, 129, 161, 167, 204; and liberalism, 18–19, 69, 103, 116, 141–46 passim; and Religionero mobilization, 135, 242–46, 252. See also *cofradías*; Lerdo Law
Cilagua, Antonio, 145–46, 147, 166
civil registry, 1, 4, 67, 161, 164
clergy: diversity of, 13; high, 41, 66–88 passim, 211, 230, 235, 237; reform of, 80–85; regular, 13, 99, 152; secular, 16, 85, 97, 126, 129, 139, 177, 193; Ultramontane, 18, 63, 80, 84, 204
clerical garb, 5, 6, 117, 164, 237
clerical obventions, 4, 124–25, 197, 203
Coalcomán (Michoacán), 28, 35, 46, 173–79 passim; attempts to develop,

180–84; and political clans, 186–92; and Religionero partisanship, 201–5; *reparto* in, 184–86
Coeneo (Michoacán): evangelization of, 139; political partisanship in, 28, 50, 140–42; Religionero militancy in, 136–37, 147–50 passim; religious customs of, 158–59, 160–63; *reparto* in 144–45
cofradías: and baroque religion, 15, 17, 40, 102–4 passim, 152–55 passim, 177, 193–96 passim; and Catholic restorationism, 89; and entailed lands, 105, 117, 123
Colegio Apostólico de Zapopan, 126, 128
Colegio Pío Latinoamericano, 79, 84, 85
Communion, 87, 93, 94
concordats, 42–43, 60, 237, 240, 244, 252
confession, 47, 87, 149, 165
confirmation (Catholic sacrament), 35, 85, 94
Congregation of Saint Vincent de Paul, 17, 91, 94; Ladies of Charity, 91–92, 117, 234 (*see also* Las Hermanas de la Caridad)
conservatism: and political movements in Michoacán, 27, 105–8 passim; popular, 10; and the Religioneros, 244–46
Conservative Party, 58, 92, 210, 217
Constituent Congress (1857), 4, 109
Constitution of 1824, 54, 215
Constitution of 1857, 1, 42, 54, 58, 214, 215, 251
Contreras, Guadalupe, 162, 169
Corpus Christi (Catholic feast): and Purépecha religion, 81, 122–24, 139, 152–63 passim; and the Vela Perpetua, 91
Cotija (Michoacán): Catholic restorationism in, 92, 93, 116–20 passim; migration to southern sierra from, 182, 198; Religionero militancy in, 40–57 passim, 111–15, 126
Council of Trent, 15, 85, 120
Cristeros, 6, 10, 18, 226, 248, 249
Cuevas, José de Jesús, 32, 67, 221
cult of the saints; 80, 81–82, 86; and baroque religion, 14, 15, 86, 102, 153, 195–99 passim

decembrista movement, 217–24 passim
de la Peña y Navarro, Bishop José Antonio, 42; pastoral projects of, 69–88 passim, 117–34 passim
del Castillo, Fray Miguel, 111, 118, 125–26
del Río, José Dolores, 38, 114
Díaz, Porfirio: alliance with Religioneros, 11–12, 22, 54, 57–59, 113, 191, 210–18; and breakdown of alliance with Religioneros, 231–33; conservative support for, 220–29, 335n60; and policy of conciliation, 11, 212, 233–37
Diez de Sollano y Dávalos, Bishop José María de Jesús, 67–70 passim, 75–77, 80–86 passim
disamortization, 4; historiographical treatments of, 7–8, 18–19, 103–4; and liberal strongmen, 141–46 passim, 180, 184; and Religionero violence, 21, 175. *See also* Lerdo Law
"Dreamed Revolution" (1875), 213–14, 278n176

ecclesiastical conferences, 80–81, 82, 84, 287n78
Echeverría, Bolívar, 15
elections: fraud in, 24, 187, 214, 228; conservative participation in, 35, 221, 223–27
emergency powers, 23–25, 49, 51, 54, 239
encomiendas, 101, 102, 138, 139, 178

Escalera, Florencio "El Fepe," 232, 233, 247
Escobedo, Mariano, 54, 55–56, 59, 113, 149, 191
Eucharist, 5, 81, 82, 90, 117, 151, 152, 158, 168
Europeanization, 65, 74–85 passim, 95, 99, 123, 125, 132, 136, 156
excommunication, 34, 67, 84, 123, 203
expiation, 15, 66, 89, 119
extraordinary powers. *See* emergency powers

Farfán, Encarnación, 173, 203, 205
feminization, 80, 99, 286n73
Fernández, Octaviano, 216, 236
First Vatican Council, 68, 77, 86
Flores, Prisciliano, 49, 112
folk saints, 150, 287n76
Franciscan Order, 19, 30, 97, 98, 102, 111, 125
Franco, Francisco (*decembrista* general), 220, 336n75
freedom of worship, 5, 6, 147, 229
freemasonry, 30, 210
French Intervention, 1, 5, 28, 43, 109, 129, 187, 215, 225
Fuentes Acosta, Albino, 51, 133, 148

Gálvez, Florencio, 35, 38, 40, 45, 110, 126
García, Julio, 175, 187–92 passim, 205, 209, 227
Garnica, Rafael, 28, 51, 133, 142, 147–49 passim
gender: and baroque religion, 130, 184–85; and Catholic restorationism, 17, 79, 84, 99, 201; and liberalism, 73, 80. *See also* feminization
Gil, Jesús, 147, 162
Gillow, Eulogio, 211, 212
Gómez de Portugal, Juan Cayetano, 85, 86, 140

González, Jesús "El Ranchero," 28, 29, 33, 41–49 passim, 51, 56, 59, 253
González, Manuel, 212, 221–31 passim
González, María Eugenia "La Virgen," 149–50
González, Pedro, 50, 135, 142, 147, 148–49, 169
Guadalajara (Archdiocese of), 10, 63, 68, 77, 81
Guanajuato (state of); and *decembrista* movement, 217, 240; conservative resurgence in, 224; Religionero violence in, 2, 24, 48, 56
Guaracha Hacienda, 28, 46, 47, 50, 102–13 passim
Guerra, Donato, 127, 214–15, 236
Gutiérrez, Francisco "El Nopal," 28, 109, 111, 220, 223, 227, 232
Guzmán, Antonio, 184, 191–98 passim
Guzmán, Gordiano, 28, 107, 178–91 passim
Guzmán, Jesús, 185–88 passim
Guzmán, Juan Antonio, 186, 188
Guzmán Clan, 192, 197–207 passim, 227

haciendas: Ahuindo, 179, 182, 184, 187; Bellas Fuentes, 47, 139, 140–48 passim, 153, 161; Buenavista, 108, 227; Cerano, 156; Janamuato, 139; La Estancia, 155; Platanal, 107; San Simón, 104, 107; Tamándaro, 105; Tecacho, 143, 148, 164; Terrenate, 179, 184, 187, 189; Trojes, 182–87 passim, 202; Ururuta, 149, 150, 155; Villachuato, 139–55 passim; Zipimeo, 139, 143, 149
heresy, 1, 34, 67, 70, 84, 173
Hidalgo y Costilla, Father Miguel, 44, 140, 257
Holy Week, 36, 41, 111, 160, 163, 169, 231, 234
hospitals: Augustinian, 145, 155; Franciscan, 19, 102, 104, 116, 121–22,

125, 133, 139, 152, 165, 193; secularization of, 166, 242
Huango (Michoacán): evangelization of, 151–54 passim; indultos in, 56–57, 149; parish politics in, 154–56, 166–69; partisanship in, 140; Religionero movement in, 134–37 passim, 147–48, 169–70; *reparto* in, 144–45; Villaseñor family's influence in, 138–39
Huaniqueo (Michoacán): evangelization of, 138–39; parish politics in, 134, 159, 163–66; partisanship in, 142; Religionero movement in, 19, 36, 40, 133–37, 146–49, 166; *reparto* in, 136, 140, 145–46
Huerta, Epitacio, 28, 181, 223, 227; and anticlerical policy, 140, 219, 220, 226; and disentailment of corporate properties, 136–43 passim; and dissident liberal movements, 30, 142, 209; as a "soldier of the pueblo," 141, 188

Iglesias, José María, 214, 217, 219
Iglesias Law (1857), 4, 124
Immaculate Conception of Mary: and local religion in Zamora, 75, 93, 115; and Ultramontane religion, 14, 95, 118. *See also* La Purísima Concepción
independence movement, 3, 107, 157, 175, 178–79, 197
individual guarantees: Catholic appropriation of, 66, 69, 72–73, 92, 234; suspension of, 23, 39, 49, 55
indulgences, 61, 72, 77, 118, 119, 123, 201
indultos, 56–59, 113, 127, 149, 169, 190, 215, 279n180
Iturbide, Augstín de, 44, 257

Jalisco (state of): migration to southern sierra from, 179, 182, 192; Religionero violence in, 2, 24, 56; Tuxtepec movement in, 214–15
JalMich region, 106–7
Jesuits. *See* Society of Jesus
Jiquilpan (Michoacán), 97–132 passim; and Afro-mestizo rebels, 46, 127; conquest and evangelization of, 102; parish politics in, 97–98, 121–37 passim; Religionero revolt in, 28, 35–39, 45, 49–50, 101, 110–14, 149, 200, 211, 215, 231; religious culture in, 115–18, 119; *reparto* in, 104, 106
Juárez, Benito, 4–5; and amnesty for imperialist fighters, 29; and banditry, 103; and enforcement of Laws of Reform, 5, 6, 32, 36, 66; liberal revolts against, 30, 105, 109, 110, 142
Juárez, Domingo, 45, 51, 56; and the Tuxtepec Revolution, 149, 216–26 passim
juramento, 4, 5, 32, 84

Labastida y Dávalos, Archbishop Pelagio Antonio: 4; and Catholic restorationism, 13, 61–62, 68, 69, 74–75, 79, 84, 90; role in French Intervention, 109
Ladies of Charity. *See* Congregation of Saint Vincent de Paul
laity: and Catholic restorationism, 13, 14, 61–95 passim; and religious conflict in northern Michoacán, 115–20 passim; and religious conflict in the southern sierra, 176, 193; and religious culture in central Michoacán, 156, 159
Lake Chapala, 28, 78, 101, 102–8 passim, 183
Lake Cuitzeo, 139, 230

La Purísima Concepción, 93, 115. See also Immaculate Conception of Mary

La Reforma, 25, 43, 63–91 passim; and corporate property, 21, 103, 117, 143, 164; and Porfirio Díaz, 210–11, 230, 237

Las Hermanas de la Caridad, 5, 91; and the *cartas de protesta*, 71–72; dissolution of, 6, 38, 40; in Jiquilpan, 117–18, 125, 125–30 passim

La Sociedad Católica, 17; and Catholic restorationism, 88–95 passim, 118, 119; Coalcomán chapter, 174, 202, 204; Jiquilpan chapter, 129

La Vela Perpetua, 90–91, 117, 159; and Catholic restorationism, 17, 89–95 passim; and parish politics in Coalcomán, 173–74, 199, 202, 204; and parish politics in Coeneo, 161–62; and parish politics in Jiquilpan, 129

Laws of Reform, 1–7 passim; clerical responses to, 30–33 passim, 61–71, 81–82, 90, 126, 162, 282n15; enforcement of, 36, 111, 114, 145, 200, 211–29 passim, 234–36; Plan of Nuevo Urecho and, 42–43, 252; Porfirio Díaz and, 58–59, 223, 233, 237

León (Guanajuato): diocese of, 63, 67, 74–75, 80, 81; Holy Week riot in, 231

Lerdo de Tejada, Sebastián, 1–6; and assumption of emergency powers, 23–25, 49, 239; clerical criticism of, 69, 70, 242; and expulsion of the Jesuits, 79; liberal criticism of, 25–27, 52–55, 213–14, 220, 245; overthrow of, 12, 59, 211–30, 248

Lerdo Law (1856), 4; and agrarian conflict, 105–6, 144; and Religionero revolt, 103, 125, 146. See also *reparto de tierras indígenas*

ley de salteadores y plagiarios (1868), 38, 39, 112

ley fuga, 231, 232, 233

Ley Orgánica de las Adiciones y Reformas a la Constitución, 5–6, 32–40 passim, 147, 174, 234, 255

liberalism: and anticorporatism, 16, 21, 116; clerical engagement with, 13, 62, 68–73, 118, 119; and enlightened piety, 14, 302n130; and local partisanship, 27, 32, 109, 115, 131, 136, 170, 175, 187, 211; popular, 9–10, 105, 188, 191

libertad de cultos. See freedom of worship

liturgical calendar, 40, 81, 103, 152, 153, 169

Llamas, Silvestre, 44, 149, 217, 227, 232

Los Reyes (Michoacán), 113, 233; burning of, 2, 41, 46, 111

Manifesto of Tzitztio, 253, 255–56

Marianism, 78, 93, 99, 102, 118–19, 132, 193

marriage (canonical), 1, 4, 5, 67, 164

Martínez Salazar, Francisco, 57, 149, 311n80

Maruata (Michoacán), 179, 180–89 passim, 198, 204

Mass (Catholic sacrament), 35, 199; and devotional associations, 89, 90, 91, 94

Maximilian of Habsburg: capture and execution of, 10, 55; and Laws of Reform, 5; and Religionero fighters, 23, 29, 43, 44, 186; support for, 12, 108, 229

mayordomías, 16, 36, 116, 120–21, 152, 153, 195, 196, 197

Mejía, Narciso "Valeriano," 110
Mejía, Teodoro "Quino," 110, 130
Méndez, Juan N., 214, 225
Mendoza, Justo, 25, 31, 185–88 passim
Meseta Tarasca. *See* Purépecha Highlands
mestizaje, 15, 102–3, 106, 139, 155
Mexican Revolution, 212, 248–49
Mexico (state of): and Religionero movement, 34, 35, 43; and Tuxtepec movement, 218, 219, 227, 234
Meza, Benito, 48, 50, 51, 56, 112, 113; background of, 44–45, 274n118; capture of, 57; relations with hacendados, 46, 47; relations with Porfirio Díaz, 54, 215
Michoacán, Archdiocese of: Catholic restorationism in, 73–95 passim, 134, 161–70 passim; creation of, 63; tolerance of baroque religion in, 19, 135–36, 157–60
Michoacán, Diocese of, 13, 64, 86
mining industry, 26, 32, 90, 101, 178–82
mojigangas, 102, 123, 152
monastacism, 5, 69, 128, 154
Month of Mary, 93, 94, 118–19, 129, 130
Moors and Christians dances, 13–14, 122, 156
Morelia (Michoacán): Catholic hierarchy of, 9, 13, 17, 42, 65, 74, 80, 85, 137, 151, 156, 161, 171, 195; and conservative movements, 28, 45, 50, 220, 223, 228; riot in (1871), 30–31, 33, 36; seminary of, 83, 85, 95, 147
Moreno, Father Ramón, 164, 165–66, 168–69, 171
Moreno Jaso, Diego, 28, 47, 108, 109
Munguía, Archbishop Clemente de Jesús, 4, 74, 77, 85, 108, 115, 116
municipal autonomy, 59, 187–88, 214, 237

Nahuas, 35, 101, 174–82 passim, 193, 194–97, 198, 202, 203, 205; and communal land tenure, 184–86, 206; and Religionero rebellion, 189–90, 192, 207
Najar, Fray José María, 97–98, 101, 122, 125, 126, 128–31
National Guard, 28, 32, 42, 51, 186, 189, 252
nationalism, 9, 68; Catholic, 43, 44, 147, 245
Noria Rebellion, 30, 110, 142, 188, 209, 225

oaths of fidelity to the constitution. *See juramento*; *protesta*
obras pías, 116, 117, 154
obventions. *See* clerical obventions
Ocampo Melchor, 28
Ochoa, Ignacio, 19, 35, 41, 45, 47, 110–15 passim, 127–28, 215, 233
Olaciregui, Domingo, 45, 50
Orgeta, Jesús "El Licenciado," 135, 147, 169, 245
Osio, Sabas, 111, 119, 122, 129, 302n130
Otomís, 137, 155
Our Lady of Guadalupe, 43, 46, 61, 79, 197
Our Lady of Health (of Pátzcuaro), 61, 86
Our Lady of Hope. *See* Our Lady of the Root
Our Lady of Light (of León), 75, 284n54
Our Lady of Lourdes, 14, 61, 75, 234
Our Lady of Remedies (of Totolan), 46, 119, 129–30
Our Lady of Sorrows, 90, 119
Our Lady of the Root (of Jacona), 77, 78, 102
Our Lord of Esquipulas (of Jiquilpan), 103, 125
Our Lord of Health (of Huaniqueo), 47, 133, 145, 150, 164
Our Lord of Mercy (of Huango), 136, 154–55, 156, 167–70 passim

Pallares, Antonio, 184, 185, 186, 190, 202, 203–4, 205
papacy, 14, 43, 63, 75, 134, 235
papal infallibility, 14, 54, 68, 77
Papal States, 61, 68
papism, 134, 174
pastoral letters, 65, 67–70, 75, 95; collective, 17, 42, 72, 73, 242–43, 246
pastoral visitation, 63, 85–87, 95, 108, 116, 122, 157
Patiño, Bruno, 201, 219, 227, 228, 230, 233
Patronato Regio, 3–4, 212, 237
Pátzcuaro (Michoacán), 137, 226; Religionero attack on, 50, 148
Paz, Ireneo, 52, 54, 213–14
periodical press: conservative, 48, 51, 58, 92, 134, 221, 239; and historical methodology, 20; liberal, 52, 58, 73, 120, 166, 174, 213; suppression of, 38, 49, 239
pilgrimage, 15, 36; "spiritual," 61–62, 77
pindecuarios, 124, 152, 157
pious associations, 3, 63–85 passim, 119, 234; Association of the Good Death, 75, 89, 90, 93; devotional, 89–91; social, 91–94. *See also* La Vela Perpetua
Pius IX: and global liberalism, 61, 62, 68–69; relationship with Mexican clergy, 13, 74–80 passim
Plancarte family, 105, 294n31
Plancarte y Labastida, José Antonio, 77–79, 84, 122–23; liberal support for, 119–20, 121
Plan of Nuevo Urecho, 27, 42, 43–44, 48, 49, 58, 237; text of, 251–53
Plan of Palo Blanco, 59, 214
Plata, Abraham, 212, 227–33 passim
policy of conciliation, 211, 237, 240
popular sovereignty, 42, 60, 66, 71, 72, 73
Porfiriato, 2, 10, 11, 144, 211

Potreros gavilla, 44–49 passim, 142, 147–48, 149, 217
processions, 5, 15, 32, 36, 40, 81–82, 111, 122–29 passim, 145, 152, 155–59 passim, 163, 234, 247, 249
pronunciamientos, 31, 43, 214, 230, 233
protesta, 6, 32–38 passim, 69, 70, 201, 203, 225, 234–36; and counterprotesta, 235–36
Protestantism, 1, 2, 5, 6, 16, 30–37 passim, 63, 70, 73, 80–94 passim, 114, 147, 189, 200, 203, 237
public worship, 14, 35, 80–82, 247; prohibition of, 1, 5, 17, 32–40 passim, 61–69 passim, 118, 119, 145, 164, 174, 201; restoration of, 159–60, 234
Purépecha Highlands, 75, 81, 102, 122, 124, 135, 137, 141
Purépechas, 13, 16, 19, 87, 100–125 passim, 137–70 passim; and Religionero militancy, 35, 136, 160, 166; and *repartos*, 140, 143–46; evangelization of, 151–52, 155
Puruándiro, 33, 39, 94, 95, 146–68 passim; conquest of, 137–39; political partisanship in, 140–41

Querétaro; Diocese of, 63, 74; state of, 55, 224
Quiroga, Bishop Vasco de, 85, 86–87, 95, 102, 139, 151–57 passim

rancheros, 13, 19, 20, 36, 106–7, 175–206 passim
Rangel, Rafael, 28, 141, 142
rationalism, 14, 68, 83
Raya, Guadalupe "El Gorrión," 146–49 passim, 169, 227, 231, 232
regalism, 4, 5, 69, 243
Régules, Nicolás de, 24, 50, 112, 148, 191, 217, 265n2

Religionero movement, 23–27, 41–60; agrarian factors in, 18–20, 103–6, 142–46, 184–86, 241–42; aliases of *cabecillas* in, 44–45; bandits in, 44–45; in central Michoacán, 146–50, 160–70; and clerical hierarchy, 41–42, 66–73; flags used by, 45–46; historical treatments of, 6–9, 103; involvement of priests in, 8, 88, 125, 162, 166, 169; localist character of, 9, 27, 46–48, 60, 245, 275n127; in northwestern Michoacán, 110–15, 127–31; relationship with Catholic elite, 44–49 passim, 56–57, 95, 98–99, 114, 221, 231–33; relationship with *pacíficos*, 47, 186; relationship with Tuxtepec Movement, 11–12, 54, 57–59, 209–37; in southwestern Michoacán, 186–92, 201–5
reparto de tierras indígenas: and Religionero violence, 18–19; in central Michoacán, 136, 140, 142–46, 167, 170; in northwest Michoacán, 103–6, 121–22; in the southern sierra, 175, 184–86, 188, 195, 203, 206
republicanism, 9, 14, 105, 136, 140, 213, 235
Revolution of Ayutla, 4, 56, 108–9, 141, 187
Revolution of Tuxtepec, 2, 11, 12, 57–59, 60, 191, 209–37
Reyes, Socorro, 19, 133–69 passim, 245, 247; and baroque Catholicism, 47, 134–35, 150, 164, 171, 246; execution of, 133–34, 149, 215; and involvement in French Intervention, 29; pronunciamiento of, 35–36, 147; reputation of, 44
Reza, Antonio, 29, 40–57 passim, 113, 148, 190, 244, 253; alliance with Porfirio Díaz, 191, 216, 220, 223; assassination of, 227, 232–33, 237; pronunciamiento of, 189
Risorgimento, 68–69
Riva Palacio, Vicente, 52–53, 54, 142, 213–18 passim, 234, 278n176
Rocha, Sóstenes, 7, 54, 213, 214
Rodríguez, Juan de Dios, 43–44, 50, 51, 142, 257–58
Romanization, 85, 99, 284n47
Romero, Canon José Guadalupe, 116, 154, 179, 181, 194
rosary, 80, 111, 119, 130, 157
royalism, 28, 108, 140, 141
rurales, 39, 230, 234, 338n114

Saavedra, Father Macario, 119, 123, 125, 126
Sacred Heart of Jesus, 14, 47, 75, 89, 95, 119
Sahuayo (Michoacán): Catholic restorationism in, 90, 92, 117–25 passim; conquest and evangelization of, 102, 103; Religionero activity in, 35, 40, 111–12, 126, 127
Sales Menocal, Dr. Francisco de, 219–20, 223
Sandoval, Father José María, 124, 173–74, 182, 184, 203, 204–5
San Felipe de Jesús, 77
San Juanico (Michoacán), 51, 56, 110, 111, 112, 113
Santa Anna, Antonio López de, 10, 24, 28, 108, 141
Santa Anna, Father Cosme, 119, 126, 128, 129
Santiago (James the Great), 122, 196
Saucedo, Juan, 32, 51
schismatics, 13, 84
schools, 41, 120, 145, 173, 200–201; Catholic, 69–94 passim, 115, 118, 130, 203; Colegio de la Purísima Concepción, 79, 88; Colegio de San Luis Gonzaga, 79, 88

Second Empire, 5, 62, 66, 229. *See also* French Intervention; Maximilian of Habsburg
secularization, 1, 10–11, 212; and Catholic counterculture, 62, 87, 114; and conservative revolts 101; of *doctrinas*, 128, 153, 155, 194
seminaries, 63, 74, 84, 95; reform of, 11, 65, 74, 82–85
sermons, 3, 6, 30, 31, 33
shrines, 36, 86
Sierra Madre del Sur, 112, 176
slavery, 101, 102, 139, 155, 178
Society of Jesus, 54, 75, 79, 84–85, 95, 118, 210; expulsion of, 5, 32, 79
spiritual exercises, 15, 87, 92, 94, 119, 161
Stephens, John, 37
strongman politics, 141–42, 174–75, 179, 187–92, 197, 206
Syllabus of Errors, 68

Tagle, Protasio, 223, 234
tierra caliente: development of, 182–91 passim ; and liberal movements, 27–28; and Religionero revolt, 48, 49, 50
tithes: end of civil coaction in collection of, 6, 91, 117, 167; and indigenous Catholics, 124; and Ultramontane piety, 72, 176, 199
Torres, Father Ramón Cipriano, 165–69
Tuñon Cañedo, Telésforo, 34–35, 218

Ugarte, Francisco, 45, 245
Ugarte, José de, 28, 45, 141
Ultramontane Catholicism, 14–15, 21, 17, 61–95 passim, 131; and central Michoacán, 134–35, 159; and northwestern Michoacán, 107, 119; and partisan politics, 95; and the southern sierra, 192–93, 198

Vaca, Bonifacio, 35, 46, 175, 189, 190, 199, 200
Venegas, Félix, 43, 46, 112, 244
viaticum, 5, 81, 111, 118, 134, 152
Villalobos, Father Pedro María, 196–97, 202–3, 204
Villa Morelos (Michoacán). *See* Huango
Villaseñor, Juan de, 136, 138–39, 140, 154–55
Villegas Rendón, Andrés, 50, 111, 114
Vincentians. *See* Congregation of Saint Vincent de Paul
Virgin Mary, 46, 80. *See also* Marianism; Our Lady of Guadalupe; Our Lady of Health; Our Lady of Light; Our Lady of Lourdes; Our Lady of Remedies; Our Lady of Sorrows; Our Lady of the Root

Zacapu (Michoacán): agrarian conflict in, 142–46; burning of, 2, 41, 50, 148; conquest and evangelization of, 137–39, 151–52; political partisanship in, 140–41; religious culture in, 86, 153, 156–58
Zamora (Michoacán): clerical hierarchy of, 9, 13, 17, 19, 65, 84, 93, 98, 123, 125, 127, 137, 197, 203; and the *decembrista* movement, 217, 219, 220, 224; political partisanship in, 28, 38, 48, 108–9, 114–15, 141–42, 228
Zamora, Diocese of, 13, 41, 42, 62–95 passim, 97–130 passim, 192–98 passim, 234, 235
Zitácuaro (Michoacán): liberal heritage of, 28, 36, 215, 217; National Guard of, 51

www.ingramcontent.com/pod-product-compliance
Lightning Source LLC
Chambersburg PA
CBHW030517230426
43665CB00010B/654